The Country Life Book of the

Natural History of the British Isles

The Country Life Book of the

Natural History of the British Isles

Consultant Editor: Pat Morris

Country Life Books

Created by Midsummer Books Limited
179 Dalling Road, Hammersmith,
London W6 0ES, England

Published by Country Life Books
an imprint of
The Hamlyn Publishing Group Limited
Bridge House, 69 London Road
Twickenham, Middlesex TW1 3SB, England

CREATED BY
Stan Morse,
Midsummer Books Limited

EDITORIAL ASSISTANT:
Penny Holmes

**ADDITIONAL EDITORIAL
CONTRIBUTIONS:**
Nancy Duin
Jeffrey Grimes
John Holmes
Trisha Palmer
Keith Walker
Tom Wellsted
Mèbe Windham

DESIGNER:
Chris Steer

STUDIO:
Robyn Fairweather
Del Tolton

CONSULTANT EDITOR:
Pat Morris

AUTHORS:
Michael Chinery
Barry Giles
Jeffrey Grimes
Hannah Grimes
Philip Horton
John Mason
Pat Morris
Peter Schofield
Tony South

ARTISTS:
Graham Allen: *Linden Artists*
Ann Baum: *Linda Rogers Associates*
Olivia Beasley
Wendy Bramall
Jim Channell: *Linden Artists*
Rosemary Chanter
Jill Coombs
Patricia Dale
Reginald B. Davis
Judy Derrick

ACKNOWLEDGEMENTS

The compilation of this complex volume has proved a major logistical
undertaking, and at many times it seemed that without the extra help provided
by the contributors the book would never have seen publication! The full
list of contributors is found elsewhere, but I would like particularly to thank a
few whose efficiency and enthusiasm not only made publication possible
but a pleasure.

Firstly, I would like to thank Pat Morris most sincerely for his dogged
dedication and his invaluable help in every conceivable area; 'Consultant
Editor' completely understates his manifold contribution. Some thirty-five
photographers contributed to the book but I would especially like to thank
Heather Angel, whose superb photographs make up the vast majority of those
used. In addition, she and her team spent many days cheerfully researching
our ever-changing requirements. Linden Artists Ltd introduced us to many
of the artists, and I would like to thank Bernard Thornton for the control he
exercised over this aspect of the book's production. Ian Garrard, who drew
the trees, water plants and grasses, also provided invaluable help over the
entire plant area. Gordon Riley spent many, many weeks painstakingly
drawing the butterflies, moths and snails, as did Richard Lewington with the
insects and the spiders. I would also like to thank Graham Allen for drawing
the mammals and Keith Linsell for drawing the fish.

Stan Morse

Pamela Dowson
Judy Fenton
Ian Garrard: *Linden Artists*
Pamela Haddon
Pat Harby: *Linden Artists*
Tim Hayward: *Linden Artists*
Kristin Jakob
Deborah King
Richard Lewington: *Garden Studio*
Stuart Lafford: *Linden Artists*
Keith Linsell
Kate Lloyd-Jones: *Linden Artists*
Suzanne Lucas
Alan Male: *Linden Artists*
Lura Mason
Caroline McDonald
James Nicholls
Dave Richardson
Gordon Riley
Nina Roberts
Diane Rosher
Varlerie Sangster: *Linden Artists*
Helen Senior
Mair Swan
Heather Wood

PHOTOGRAPHERS:
Aerofilms Limited
Heather Angel
Ardea
J. A. Bailey: *Ardea*
Ian Beames
S. C. Bisserot: *Bruce Coleman Ltd*
R. J. C. Blewitt: *Ardea*
British Tourist Authority
Jane Burton: *Bruce Coleman Ltd*
Michael Chinery
Bruce Coleman Ltd
J. A. L. Cooke: *Oxford Scientific Films Ltd*
Werner Curth: *Ardea*
Stephen Dalton: *Bruce Coleman Ltd*
Ernest Duscher: *Bruce Coleman Ltd*
André Fatras: *Ardea*
Kenneth Fink: *Ardea*
Peter Hinchcliffe: *Bruce Coleman Ltd*
Udo Hirsch: *Bruce Coleman Ltd*
Geoffrey Kinns: *Natural Science Photos*
John Mason
D. Middleton: *Bruce Coleman Ltd*

Pat Morris
Natural Science Photos
Charlie Ott: *Bruce Coleman Ltd*
Oxford Scientific Films Ltd
Hans Reinhard: *Bruce Coleman Ltd*
Richard Revels
Michael W. Richards: *(RSPB)*
Royal Society for the Protection of Birds
David Sewell
Robert T. Smith: *Ardea*
Bill Vaughan
P. H. Ward: *Natural Science Photos*
Gordon Williamson: *Bruce Coleman Ltd*
Tom Willock: *Ardea*

TYPESETTING
SX Composing Ltd and
Randall Typographic Ltd

COLOUR REPRODUCTION:
Process Colour Scanning Ltd and
Fleet Litho Ltd

The publishers are grateful to the
following individuals and organisations
for their assistance:

Paul Smart at the Saruman Museum
for providing specimens of butterflies
and moths; Dr M. Kerney for
providing specimens of snails; Brian
Baker and Hugh Carter at Reading
Museum for providing specimens of
insects; Jeffrey Wood and Philip Cribb
in the Orchid Herbarium at Kew
Gardens for assistance with the orchids;
Tom Cope at Kew for assistance with
the grasses; Bill Ward at Harrow
College of Art; The Royal Society for
the Protection of Birds for providing
the bird drawings. The outline map of
the British Isles is based on a map
provided by the Biological Records
Centre, Institute of Terrestrial
Ecology, Monks Wood Experimental
Station. The table which appears on
page 83 is based on statistical
information found in the *Journal of
Animal Ecology*, 30, 1961.

CONTENTS

INTRODUCTION

The British Isles, over 400 of them in all, face an ocean on one side and a continent on the other. From the ocean they receive a flow of warm water (in the form of the Gulf Stream) which serves to ameliorate climatic extremes, especially in the west. Winds tend also to come from the ocean more often than from elsewhere, having become moisture-laden, so the country is generally wet, especially in Ireland and western counties.

The continental influences are most obvious in the eastern regions, where winters can be bitterly cold due to the proximity of a large land mass (which cools much more in winter than does the sea) and to the winds that blow from it. Such winds bear little moisture, and prevailing westerlies have lost much of their rain before reaching eastern counties. The eastern regions are thus characterised by a drier climate with colder winters and warmer summers than are found in the equable west, where extremes are buffered by the effects of the ocean.

Climatic diversity is enhanced because Britain is long and thin. It spans 9° of latitude; a tenth of the distance separating the North Pole from the Equator. So Scotland has a generally cooler climate than the south, but also has longer days in summer (and thus more growing and feeding time per day).

Altitude, which is in turn governed by geological factors, also influences the climate and wildlife of an area. Temperatures and sunshine decrease markedly with increased altitude, so that the growing season at 600 metres is perhaps half as long as that at sea level. Moreover, moist air rising to cross high ground gets cooler and deposits its water as rain. Uplands are thus wet, leaving drier areas in the "rain shadow" beyond the high ground.

Geology

The formation of Britain's fabric has taken over 2,600 million years to fashion. The oldest rocks are found in the north west of Scotland; the youngest in the south east of England. In between lies a diversity of rock and soil types, greater than anywhere else of comparable area in the world. The geological background is important because older rocks tend to be harder and thus resist erosion and remain protruding as mountains and high ground. High ground traps moisture, is cooler, and less grows there. Younger rocks are smoothed by erosive forces and provide flatter landscapes and low rolling hills. Softer rocks erode more rapidly and contribute more of their chemical constituents to the soils derived from the rocks. Thus lowland soils are usually richer in nutrients. Certain rock types (particularly chalk and limestone) have a profound effect on soil acidity and calcium content; major factors in determining the distribution of many plants and animals.

Hard, old rocks provide jagged scenery and coastlines, steep rushing rivers and a generally more austere and open landscape. Younger rocks and the rich soils generated from them support a much greater diversity of species and a more varied landscape. They also are more fertile for agricultural use and provide flat land for towns, roads, airports and other major human modifications to the countryside. Today, man's is the greatest single influence in shaping the land and what lives on it, but in the past it was ice.

Britain's Ice Ages

During the last two million years there have been at least four major "Ice Ages" when masses of solid ice spread over Britain. In places it may have been several kilometres thick at times, and its tremendous weight gouged away rock, moulding and scraping the land, pushing soil and boulders to form new hills, and digging out valleys and basins which today contain major lakes and rivers.

In between the glacial epochs were long periods when the climate was often warmer than it is today. This alternation, over thousands of years, between a cold and warm environment, together with the direct effects of the ice, played a profound part in determining the flora and fauna of Britain today.

The effect of the Ice Ages on the British flora and fauna

At its maximum, the ice must have virtually covered Ireland, Wales and Scotland, and reached as far south as London. The last glaciation was less severe, but the ice did reach south Wales and the Wash, only about 20,000 years ago. South of the ice, open tundra vegetation covered the country, just as it does in northern Scandinavia today, and reindeer, lemmings and mammoths roamed the Home Counties. Very few of our present animals could have lived and bred here then—mountain hare, stoat and perhaps pigmy shrew among the mammals; ptarmigan and dunlin among the birds. Otherwise the ice wiped the slate clean, so to speak. With so much water locked up in the ice, the sea level was about 100 metres lower than it is now, so that these animals would have been able to wander across the floor of what is now the English Channel and the North Sea.

About 12,000 years ago, the climate started to improve, and plants and animals spread north in the wake of the retreating ice. First birch, then pine, and then deciduous trees such as oak and alder spread back into England, and with them came associated animals: black grouse with the pine, wild boar with the oak.

Excavations at Star Carr, an archaeological site in Yorkshire, show us that by 9,600 years ago badger, red fox, pine marten, wild boar, red deer, roe deer, elk and beaver had spread back and were living in pine-birch woodland. Unfortunately for the returning animals, as the ice melted away so the sea level rose, filling low lying areas with water. The channel between Scotland and Ireland, for example, is only about 60 metres deep and the sea level had soon risen sufficiently to isolate Ireland. The animals found at Star Carr all got across the land link to Ireland before it became flooded, as did those (e.g. pigmy shrew, stoat, mountain hare) which could tolerate a colder climate and so got across even earlier. But a large number of animals which either needed a warmer climate, or relied upon plants which did, failed to get across—the mole, common shrew, weasel, dormouse, the voles and the snakes were all apparently too late to get to Ireland and none (except the bank vole) are found in Ireland to this day.

The English Channel is much shallower, only 20 metres deep, and was flooded much later. The present sea level was reached about 5,500 years ago, by which time oak-dominated deciduous woodland was well established in England and woodland animals like the dormouse, red squirrel, woodmouse and bank vole must also have been present by then. These animals which made their own way into Britain are referred to as "native" species. They constitute less than two-thirds of the present terrestrial mammal fauna, and an even smaller proportion in more remote islands.

Many species (e.g. the garden dormouse, two species of white toothed shrew and also the midwife toad) failed to reach England in time and are now kept out by the sea barrier, though they are common in France and the Low Countries.

A similar history applies to the offshore islands of Britain. The Shetlands and St. Kilda, for example, are separated from Scotland by sea channels over 150 metres deep. These islands are never likely to have been joined by land bridges to Scotland and retain an impoverished fauna, their only mammals being species taken there (often accidentally) by man.

Obviously these arguments only apply to land animals; birds and bats could have flown to any part of the British Isles at any time since the ice retreated, so their presence or absence from any particular island is unlikely to be explained by reference to Ice Age climates and rising sea levels. Equally, any animal which is prepared to swim across stretches of sea, including most obviously the otter, but also the red deer, could have reached at least some of the islands of its own accord.

Man adds to the land

Whilst he has destroyed some habitats, man has also created others, some of which are discussed towards the end of this book. Similarly, having exterminated some species, he has introduced new ones. The pheasant, for example, must have been introduced, perhaps by the Romans or the Normans, and the fallow deer was probably introduced very early on.

The rabbit was also introduced; it was far too valuable as a source of food to be turned loose, and the Normans used to keep them carefully tended in enclosures termed warrens. The right to have a warren was a considerable privilege, a contrast to the modern attitude of farmers. The carp is another animal which was introduced in Norman times as a source of food; monasteries frequently had "stew ponds", used for rearing the carp needed for Friday's meat.

More recently, a number of animals have been imported for fur farms. The coypu, a large rodent from South America, and the American mink, have escaped and established themselves in the wild.

Many more foreign species have been imported simply for their aesthetic appeal. The muntjac and Chinese water deer were brought to Britain by the Duke of Bedford, but escaped and are now widespread. The edible dormouse and little owl were also introduced from southern Europe. The vogue for managing large estates in the nineteenth century resulted in the introduction of Sika deer from the Far East, and the red-legged partridge from the Mediterranean; both are now well established here. Canada geese, mandarin duck and, of course, the grey squirrel, also owe their original introduction to various park owners who thought they would look attractive in the grounds. This activity continues and many other exotic animals are locally established in the wild and may become more widespread (e.g. the golden pheasant, Egyptian goose, ruddy shelduck and even the ring-necked parakeet).

A number of animals have also been spread around by man quite unintentionally. The house mouse was probably the first of these, brought to western Europe from the Middle East in Stone Age times along with the wheat on which it often feeds. More recently, the black rat arrived, probably with the returning crusaders, and brought with it bubonic plague (Black Death); but the brown rat reached Britain (from Scandinavia) only in the middle of the eighteenth century.

The small mammal faunas of many small islands are largely the result of stowaways. St. Kilda seems to have received both wood mouse and house mouse from Norway, courtesy of the Vikings, while the Isles of Scilly have white-toothed shrews perhaps brought from Spain by the Phoenicians.

Within the last quarter century someone seems to have carried bank voles to Ireland where they were formerly unknown.

Habitat changes, particularly drainage and deforestation, caused many species to die out but others have become commoner. For example, starlings depend on open grassland for feeding, and it is difficult now to imagine that only 200 years ago the starling was scarce or absent from western Britain, including Wales and Scotland. It is typically a bird of open ground and has only been able to spread in the wake of forest clearance for farming. The jackdaw, rook and skylark are birds which were probably similarly affected and either rare or absent 4,000 years ago.

We have also seen within this century a change in attitudes, so that instead of persecuting animals, attempts are made to protect them. Many birds have now returned as breeding species (osprey, ruff, avocet, for example) and rare species have been helped to survive (red kite, marsh harrier, bearded tit, Dartford warbler, pine marten).

Thus the fauna of modern Britain comprises a legacy from the Ice Age, substantially modified by more recent human additions and deletions.

Animals lost from the British fauna

Though the retreat of the ice and the rising sea level determined what entered the British Isles, not all the animal immigrants are still present today. It is possible that early man played a part in the extinction of the mammoth, giant deer and horse, though changes of climate and vegetation are more likely to have been responsible.

In other cases direct attacks have certainly caused extinction, especially of potentially dangerous species. The wolf was once common, but the last was exterminated in Scotland about 1745 (the last in Ireland about 1775). The brown bear was once numerous and even exported to the Roman circuses, but was exterminated during Saxon times. Large herbivores were also wiped out, perhaps because they too were dangerous or because they were over-hunted; they might have interfered with domestic stock or perhaps they raided crops. The reindeer and the aurochs (wild ox) died out in the north of Scotland in the tenth century, and the wild boar in the seventeenth century.

More recently, the vogue for keeping estates stocked with game birds resulted in intense persecution of predators. The buzzard and the polecat, for example, were common throughout the British Isles in 1800, breeding in almost every county. By 1900, both were restricted to the western fringe, and the polecat became extinct in England and Scotland by about 1920; but both species are now staging a comeback in the wake of more enlightened attitudes.

The beaver must once have been quite common (the name Beverley, meaning "beaver meadow" is widespread) but the animal has a fine fur and old documents refer to a flourishing trade in pelts; the last record of the beaver in Britain refers to them in Wales in the twelfth century. Collecting of a different sort, for museum specimens, seems to have caused the final extinction of the great auk in the 1840s, though their breeding rookeries had been over-exploited as a source of food for centuries.

Not all losses have resulted from persecution. Habitat changes, particularly as a result of agricultural activity, have caused far greater modification of the fauna. In pre-Roman times, pelicans and cranes used to breed in the marshes of the south west; but draining of the marshes ensured their disappearance long before birdwatchers ever looked for them, and their presence is known today only from bones dug out of the peat. Drained marshland is very fine farmland and it is not surprising other wetland birds have been lost, as breeding species, including spoonbills, and species like the marsh harrier and bearded tit have also become scarce. Fortunately, these "lost" species remained common in the Low Countries and several of them (e.g. avocets, ruffs and godwits) have since managed to return.

Undoubtedly the major change caused by man has been deforestation. Eight thousand years ago, Britain was covered in deciduous forest, mostly oak; though some of the higher ground, especially of the Downs, had been cleared for pasture by Stone Age farmers. Forest animals, especially those dependent on oak, must have been abundant—jays, wood pigeons, (red) squirrels, badgers, deer and woodmice would have been widespread, but grassland species like larks, rooks and field voles much less numerous than now. By the end of the seventeenth century, woodland had been completely removed from large areas of the country, partly for farming but also by the need for charcoal used in smelting iron. The roe deer became extinct in England outside the Lake District, and was re-introduced to southern England in 1800. The red squirrel and the capercailie died out completely in Scotland, and had to be reintroduced. In many cases, animals became rare or locally extinct from a combination of habitat destruction and direct persecution, and it is now impossible to decide which was the most important cause. The absence of the fox and badger from the Isle of Man, for example, or the loss of red deer from Wales, are probably due to both factors.

Habitats of Britain

Britain possesses a wide variety of habitat types, containing an astonishing diversity of plants and animals, but these are not randomly distributed. Generally the wildlife is found in "sets" of associated plants and animals; the same (or similar) species occur wherever the same physical conditions exist, to form a distinctive living community in each habitat. This book attempts to describe the major types of habitat and the plants and animals specially associated with each.

The major habitat types found in Britain have been divided into seven categories: coastal, marine, woodland, upland, freshwater, grassland and man-made habitats. Obviously such a division has to be somewhat arbitrary. In a small, crowded country like Britain, few areas escape modification by man; so practically all our landscape and wildlife could be considered "man-made". This even applies to some of the most interesting species-rich habitats we have, like hedgerows and downland turf; neither would retain the same form or wildlife diversity unaided by cutting machines or man's grazing animals. Even our woodlands which are not managed or manipulated at the present time owe their current structure and diversity to particular types of economic exploitation in past centuries.

However, leaving aside man's role as a major modifying influence, it is clear that all woodland communities have certain common characteristics which are different from the factors that govern the ecology and inter-relationships of seashore communities or montane plants and animals. The habitat types considered here are thus intended as guides rather than rigidly defined categories. Using this approach it is perhaps easier to understand how plants, animals, soil, climate and the effects of man are all interdependent. Also, the visitor to a woodland, for example, can find in one book a selection of both plants and animals that may be found. Specialist field guides might contain more details of individual insects and birds, but nothing on plants or ecological inter-relationships.

There are drawbacks to this approach. Habitats are rarely precisely delineated: muddy shores grade into sandy ones; hedgerows, copses and woodland are a continuum, not discretely separate entities. Moreover, there is a tendency for things to change with time; scrub grows into woodland, ponds are invaded by marsh plants which create a wetland habitat which in time again becomes woodland. An artificial classification of habitats cannot adequately define the diverse and constantly changing patterns of nature.

Equally, when it comes to deciding which habitat an animal "belongs to", an artificial rigidity is being imposed upon a flexible system. The wood-mouse, for example, occurs in potting sheds, on the rocky summit of Snowdon and on sand dunes, quite apart from more obvious places. Also, many birds use their mobility to exploit one habitat for breeding and another for feeding, or they change habitats seasonally. Some of our commonest creatures are so abundant and familiar precisely because they are not associated with any one habitat and freely inhabit many different places. Assigning such animals to one or another part of this book must again be somewhat arbitrary.

The other area of compromise concerns numbers of species. We can easily illustrate all the British reptiles, for there are only six of them. We can adequately cover the mammals, though certain species of bats are impossible to tell apart unless much more detail is available than we have room for here. We can include all the common and resident birds, but not the many that have been recorded in Britain only on very rare occasions. But other groups must receive more superficial treatment. For example, there are two dozen British species of earthworm, 600 species of spider and some 3,700 different beetles! Obviously a single volume covering all of Britain's natural history cannot be exhaustive.

This book therefore aims to simplify diversity and complexity to the point where they become more easily comprehensible, to provide an understanding of the basic mechanisms by which our countryside "works". And since Britain is an island, it seems appropriate to begin with a consideration of the sea and the marine ecosystem.

The Sea

The sea has always held a great fascination for many people. This is perhaps due in part to the fact that most of its inhabitants are out of sight and at no time is it ever possible to catch more than a brief glimpse of the diversity and abundance of life that exists in the sea. Life is thought to have arisen in the sea and the stable chemical composition of sea water, which resembles the body fluids of many animals, means that its inhabitants are protected from the problems of maintaining the salt and water contents of their bodies within a narrow range in the face of environmental fluctuations. For this reason and because the unique properties of this vast volume of water mean that marine animals are protected from extremes of climate, the open sea is an ideal medium in which to live. However, where the sea meets the land, and especially on rocky shores, the inhabitants of the shore are exposed to widely fluctuating conditions as a result of tidal changes. This instability poses a major challenge to survival and yet the sea shore is rich in animal and plant life, all showing a range of adaptations to this unstable environment. Members of almost all of the invertebrate groups of animals are found there, together with shore fishes, while flocks of sea birds feed on the shore exposed by the ebbing tide. Occasionally marine mammals such as seals and even stranded whales are found on the shore. The open sea provides an important migration route for many fish, such as salmon and eels, for marine turtles, for whales and for many birds. This account, which examines the sea and seashore below the high water mark of mean tides, seeks to show something of the range of habitats represented there and of the living organisms they support.

The sea provides a home for many soft-bodied animals which gain support from the water and could not live on dry land. Many of these soft-bodied creatures, like the sea-slug shown here, need to live among rocks for protection, but others (like jellyfish) live out in the open sea and are protected by the presence of stinging cells.

The Continental Shelf and Coastal Waters

The seas and oceans cover about 70 per cent of the earth's surface. In the deepest oceans the bottom lies more than 10,000m from the surface. Life is found at all depths, even in the deepest trench known. Close to land the sea is mostly shallow, the bottom shelving gradually from the shore to a depth of between 200 and 300m. This ledge is the continental shelf and forms about eight per cent of the total sea area. It is bounded at its seaward edge by the continental slope, which extends steeply down to the ocean floor several thousands of metres below the surface. The extent of the continental shelf varies but it completely surrounds the British Isles. It is covered by the English Channel, Irish Sea and most of the North Sea, and its nearest edges are some 50km west of Ireland and 130km north of the mainland of Scotland. Open ocean is therefore rather remote from land and this account is therefore limited to the shallow coastal waters over the continental shelf and to the sea shore.

Several processes have contributed to the formation of the continental shelf, including the deposition of material eroded from the coast line by wave action and the deposition of silt carried out into the sea from estuaries. This silt is an important factor: it has been estimated that the rivers of the world transport eight thousand million tonnes of finely-ground rock down to the sea each year. Some areas of the continental shelf were originally part of the land. For example, much of the southern North Sea, including the Dogger Bank, has been formed as a result of either a rise in sea-level as the ice melted after the last Ice Age, or local sinking and inundation of the land.

The waters lying over the shelf around the British Isles are influenced by ocean currents, which are caused by the combined action of wind at the surface, density differences between different parts of the oceans, and forces due to the earth's rotation (Corioli's forces). In the North Atlantic, these result in surface water flowing in a clockwise direction around an area of relatively little movement, the Sargasso Sea, situated towards the western side of the Atlantic. As a result, warm water flows from the Gulf of Mexico northwards into the North Atlantic as the Gulf Stream, greatly influencing not just our marine life, but the whole of the British climate. As this surface water flows eastwards across the Atlantic part of the water is deflected towards the north east by the prevailing winds, the Westerlies, and forms the North Atlantic Drift. This flows along the west and north of the British Isles; some water eventually enters the northern North Sea, passing round to the east of the Shetlands and flowing due south. The water divides into three branches just before reaching the Dogger Bank. One flows east towards the Baltic and the other two branches flow south east and south west to form large swirls in the southern North Sea where they meet the stream of water flowing north up the Channel. Water leaves the North Sea mainly through a deep trough running northwards along the west coast of Norway. The extent of this inflow from the North Atlantic Drift varies from year to year.

Sea temperature

The major factor controlling the distribution of marine animals is temperature. The surface temperature of the sea around the British coast varies from a maximum of about 16°C and a minimum of 8°C in the south west to 13°C and 4°C respectively off the north east of Scotland. Because ocean currents bring warm water from the west, winter temperatures along west coasts are several degrees higher than those at corresponding latitudes on the east coast, and those of the north west of Scotland tend to be several degrees higher than the southern North Sea. The lowest winter sea temperatures are in the

Heavy waves breaking on the shore tend to dislodge and damage all but the most firmly attached and protected plants and animals.

south east and the eastern Irish Sea. For this reason, species which reach the limit of their geographical range in the British Isles extend their range further north on the west than on the east coast, and a break in distribution often occurs around south east England. During the summer months the surface water becomes warm and floats on deeper, cooler water. This leads to the formation of a temporary thermocline or transition zone (see section on freshwater habitats for explanation) at depths of between 15 and 30 metres. In winter, when the surface layers cool, this disappears. Permanent thermoclines occur only in the deeper oceans.

The coastline of England and Wales along the high water mark, including the larger islands, extends for about 4,400km. About 37 per cent of this comprises cliffs over eight metres, 10 per cent is salt marsh, 8 per cent sand dunes and 19 per cent shingle. The remainder includes other types such as sand and mud flats. The coast is bordered by a narrow strip of land lying between the extreme high and extreme low spring tides, known as the intertidal or littoral zone. Although the sea shore is relatively small in area when compared with the land mass of the British Isles, it contains a greater variety of animals and plants than other habitats in Britain. The sea shore offers a wide range of habitats, from hard rock to soft muds and sand, each being alternately exposed and covered by the tides. There is greater diversity here than in the open sea, but also greater challenge. Animals and plants on the sea shore must cope with a wider range of conditions, including the dangers of drying out, the destructive forces of the breaking waves, the wider variation in temperatures due to the greater effect of air temperatures changes in salinity due to rain or evaporation and the problems of finding food.

A guide to some interesting marine sites

1 Rona's Voe (Shetland). Site of a whaling station at the beginning of the century. From here the Atlantic right whale, rorquals and other whales were hunted by Norwegian ships. HU 28 83.

2 North Ronaldsay. A local breed of small short-tailed sheep found on North Ronaldsay (Orkney) feeds largely on seaweed. Its meat is dark and rich in iodine. HY 76 55.

3 Outer Hebrides. Much of the western shores of the Outer Hebrides consists of immense stretches of shell-sand which is used to improve the local soil. Incl. several NNRs.

4 Loch Sligachan, Skye. An example of the many long narrow sea lochs with little wave action found along the west coast. Sheltered shores develop dense growths of long-fronded brown seaweeds, especially *Ascophyllum*, and rich faunas. NG 52 33.

5 Soay, Skye. Site of a former experimental shark fishing station. Basking sharks harpooned from the waters of the Minch east of the Outer Hebrides were processed for liver oil and other by-products. NG 45 14.

6 Rockall. Isolated conical granite rock 250 km west of St. Kilda. 21 m high, it was annexed by Britain in 1955 thus considerably extending British territorial limits. Algae typical of very exposed shores with no brown seaweeds.

6

7 Barra, W. Isles. Collections of South American and West Indian seeds have been made from the shores of Barra and other parts of the Outer Hebrides, carried there by the North Atlantic Drift. NF 66 00.

8 Loch Ailort, Skye and Lochalsh. The clean waters of Loch Ailort provide a site for marine fish farming on a commercial basis. Sea cages floating offshore are used to rear salmon and rainbow trout under marine conditions. NM 73 79.

22

9 Loch Moidart, Skye and Lochalsh. Location for the intensive culture of plaice in cages floating in the sheltered basin of Loch Moidart. NM 65 73.

10 Ardtoe, Skye and Lochalsh. Site of the White Fish Authority station for experimental marine fish farming using flatfish cultured in cages suspended in the water. NM 64 70.

11 Kentra Bay, Skye and Lochalsh. The beaches include patches of "Coral sand" formed from fragments of the branches of a calcareous alga, *Lithothamnion calcareum*, which grows in sheltered shallow water offshore. NM 63 68.

12 Port Ellen (Islay), Argyll & Bute. Centre of the smallest tidal range. Spring range is about 60 cm and neap tides range less than 1 m, and the sea level remaining virtually constant for several days. NR 37 46.

13 Solway Firth. A third possible barrage site in the north-west. The sand flats of the upper Solway Firth are the roosting place of large numbers of pink-footed and barnacle geese.

14 Morecambe Bay, Cumbria/Lancs. A vast system of sand and mud flats has developed in this bay which contains four large estuaries. Largest overwintering population of waders in Britain and site for a possible barrage. SD 40 70.

15 Dee estuary, Merseyside. Site for a possible barrage. Estuary of international importance for wading birds with up to 125,000 present in winter together with large numbers of pintail, shelduck and other wildfowl. SJ 20 83.

16 Menai Straits, Gwynedd. A combination of sheltered rocky shores with strong tidal rapids, which prevent the accumulation of silt, has resulted in the development of a rich fauna and flora. SH 53 70.

17 Cardigan Bay, Dyfed. Legend tells of a lost land submerged beneath Cardigan Bay. Submerged forests and other evidence suggests this was a low lying boulder clay plain until submergence in Neolithic times.

18 Borth, Dyfed. A peat deposit exposed on the beach at low tide shows traces of a submerged forest from immediately after the Ice Age. Stumps exposed include those of alder, birch, oak and pine. SN 61 92.

19 Llanrhidian Sands, W. Glamorgan. Lime-rich sand flats grading to silt at higher levels support an important cockle fishery which is now threatened by the advance of cord grass planted elsewhere in the Burry estuary. SS 50 95.

20 Severn Bore. Tidal water entering the Severn estuary is confined to a relatively narrow channel. Consequently a surge of water (the bore) moves swiftly upstream, headed by a wave up to 1.8 m high.

21 Severn Estuary. Site for a possible barrage. Extensive sand and silt flats on both sides of the estuary with large overwintering goose and wader populations.

22 Celtic Sea. The main spawning ground of mackerel off the west coast during April. The Celtic Sea lies west of the Isles of Scilly at the edge of the continental shelf.

23 Cornish coast. The rocky coast of Cornwall is the location for commercial fisheries for prawns, crawfish, crabs and lobsters. Crawfish are caught mainly in pots, by tangle nets and by divers.

24 Seven Stones reef (nr. Scilly Isles). The supertanker 'Torrey Canyon' was wrecked on this reef 24 km west of Land's End in 1967, releasing 117,000 tonnes of crude oil and causing extensive damage to wildlife, especially sea birds. SW 05 24.

25 Newlyn, Cornwall. This port is the centre of the British drift net mackerel fishery with about half the English catch, caught off the south and west coasts, landed there. SW 46 28.

26 Falmouth Bay, Cornwall. A good example of drowned valleys with extensive invasion by the sea. Marine conditions are carried well into the mouths of the rivers, offering sheltered conditions to marine animals. SW 83 34.

27 Looe, Cornwall. Looe harbour is the centre for rod and line shark fishing off the south-west of England from May to October. SX 26 53.

47

28 Lulworth Cove, Dorset. An example of differential marine erosion. Outer harder cliffs (limestone) when broken through exposed relatively soft clays which were then eroded by the sea into a circular bay bounded on the inside by relatively harder chalk. SY 83 79.

29 Poole Harbour, Dorset. Large area of clay and silt flats with minimal tide-range of about 2 m and with a distinctive double tide. SZ 00 88.

30 Bembridge, Isle of Wight. The introduced Japanese sea weed (*Sargassum muticum*) was first recorded from this shore in 1973 and has since spread west along the coast as far as Plymouth. SZ 63 88.

31 Beachy Head, Sussex. The large scallop (*Pecten maximum*) occurs in sufficient abundance to be fished commercially off Beachy Head. They are caught in wide dredges. TV 58 95.

32 Thames barrier. Due for completion in 1982, the barrier at Woolwich is designed to prevent the flooding of London by storm surges. Unlike other barriers would only be closed at times of flood danger.

33 Thames estuary. In 1957 the inner Thames estuary was heavily polluted, with no fish. Twenty years later pollution was reduced to the extent that over ninety species of fish had been recorded there.

34 Maplin Sands, Essex. Over 10,000 ha. of flats with a large population of dwarf eel-grass. Largest area of continuous intertidal flats in Britain. Internationally famous for wintering bird populations. TR 05 90.

35 Flemish Bight. One of the main spawning areas of plaice in mid-winter, the Flemish Bight is situated midway between the Thames estuary and the coast of Holland. Warmer, more saline water enters the North Sea from the Channel at this point.

36 River Crouch, Essex. The creeks and shallow tidal estuaries of the Crouch (TR 03 96), Colne (TM 07 15), Blackwater (TM 00 10) and Roach (TQ 98 94) form the largest and best known native (natural) oyster beds.

37 Brightlingsea, Essex. The American oyster drill (*Urosalpinx cinerea*) was first accidentally introduced into this area with oysters at the end of the nineteenth century. This snail feeds by drilling through the shell of bivalves. TM 09 17.

38 Leman Bank. Site of one of the first natural gas fields. Pipeline brought to the Leman Bank to Bacton (Norfolk) in 1967. Several other natural gas fields are located to the north of this site.

39 The Wash, Lincs/Norfolk. One of the largest estuarine areas in Britain (over 20,000 ha.). Important for wintering wildfowl and waders and for breeding common seal. Site for a possible barrage. TF 55 39.

40 Yorkshire coast. With the Firth of Forth, the site of most frequent strandings of large squids, average length 1½ m. Brought into the North Sea by North Atlantic Drift.

41 Dogger Bank. Extensive sand bank in North Sea covered by shallow water. Fishing ground for plaice and nursery area for herring. Peat dredged from Bank shows that it was land at end of Ice Age.

42 Ekofisk Oil Field. Site of first major blow-out from North Sea oil rig in 1977 when over 22,000 tonnes of oil were released into the North Sea.

43 Great Fisher Bank. The Great Fisher and Ling Banks and the Long Forties to the east of Scotland form the main spawning ground for cod in British waters between February and April.

43
42

44 Lindisfarne, Northumberland. Extensive sand and mud flats between Lindisfarne and the mainland form an important wintering ground for wildfowl, especially wigeon, pale-bellied brent geese and whooper swans. NNR 3278 ha.

45 Coast from Forth to North Northumberland. Inshore fisheries located along this coast include crabs, lobsters, mussels, scallops and periwinkles. The Dublin Bay prawn is also taken offshore in this region.

38

46 St. Abbs Head, Berwickshire. Series of sea cliffs and wave-cut platforms formed from Silurian and Old Red Sandstone, supporting a very rich littoral and sublittoral fauna and flora owing to the diversity of habitats and lack of pollution. NT 85 70 to NT 91 67.

35

47 Forties. Site of a large oil field in the North Sea. Oil is pumped ashore through a pipeline to Cruden Bay on the coast north of Aberdeen.

48 Cromarty Firth, Ross-shire. Sand flats in the sheltered Firth are the most important wildfowl and wader haunt in north-east Scotland. Now threatened by industrial development associated with North Sea oil fields. NH 75 68.

49 Dornoch Firth, Sutherland/Ross-shire. Site of a large stranding (about 150) of the uncommon false killer whale. This whale lives in large schools and strandings therefore tend to involve large numbers. There have been several strandings on the east coast. NH 80 86.

Abbreviations:

NCC	Nature Conservancy Council
FC	Forestry Commission
RSPB	Royal Society for the Protection of Birds
NT	National Trust
NNR	National Nature Reserve
FNR	Forest Nature Reserve
NP	National Park
FNR (I)	Forest Nature Reserve (in Ireland)

The Marine Environment

The sea is a three-dimensional environment in which fish and other animals must either be buoyant or swim continuously in order to live in the upper regions and exploit their resources.

The range of tidal movement varies considerably, and it is likely that in the open sea the range is no more than about a metre. However, as the speed of the tidal surges is checked at the coast, their height rises: the average height of tides round British coasts is 4.5m at spring tides and 3.5m at neap tides. This varies widely from place to place and the tidal range in funnel-shaped inlets may be much greater. For example, the range at Chepstow in the Bristol Channel is about 12.7m at springs and 6.4m at neaps. Wind may modify tidal levels. For example strong onshore winds can pile water up along the coast to produce storm surges, when the high tide may be several metres above the predicted level, and flooding may result.

Tides round the coast of the British Isles are the result of the rise and fall of the Atlantic waters caused by gravitational pull from the moon. Two tidal surges move along the coast each day from the south west. Each wave is divided by the mass of Ireland and then again as it flows past the peninsula of Cornwall, one branch passing into the English Channel and the other up into the Irish Sea. The outer branch, after sending a minor wave down through the north Channel into the Irish Sea, travels north round Scotland and down into the North Sea. It then takes a further twelve hours to reach the southern end where it merges with the succeeding wave which has travelled up the English Channel. Thus the times of tides vary at different points round the coast, and some places get tidal surges from two directions causing four tides daily.

Animals and plants living in the sea may be broadly divided into two groups: those that float or swim in the water (the pelagic group) and those that live on, near or within the sea bed (the benthic group). Pelagic animals can be further divided into plankton, which are floating organisms entirely dependent on water currents, and nekton, which are swimming organisms living in the open water and able to resist the movements of water currents. The nekton include pelagic fish, such as the herring, and some invertebrates such as the squids.

British marine animals may be further divided into three distributional groups. The majority are boreal species because this country lies within the boreal or north temperate zone. The second group consists of a number of animals of Mediterranean or "lusitanian" origin which occur along the shores of north west Britain. The common Mediterranean sea-urchin, *Paracentrotus lividus,* may for example be found on western shores of Ireland and in the Hebrides.

This distribution is the result of the upwelling of water of Mediterranean origin along the north west coast. These animals reach the northern limit of their distribution in Britain and are rarely found on the east or south east coasts. The barnacle *Chthamalus stellatus,* which is abundant on the upper rocky shore in the south and west, is a lusitanian species and does not generally occur further eastwards than the Isle of Wight and is less frequent further north on western coasts. The third group are the arctic-boreal species whose distribution is influenced by the upwelling of colder Arctic water and are found mainly along northern and eastern coasts. An example is the eelpout or viviparous blenny

(Zoarces viviparus), which does not occur in the south west.

The most important producers of plant food (primary producers) in the sea are the small plants or phytoplankton. The shallow waters over the continental shelf are well illuminated and rich in plant nutrients such as phosphates and nitrates, ensuring a rich growth of phytoplankton. The turbulence of the water currents ensures a complete mixing of the shallow waters over the continental shelf and this, together with upwellings from nutrient-rich deeper water at the edge of the continental shelf, ensures that nutrients are replaced. Plant nutrients are also added to coastal waters from the rivers. The production of both phytoplankton (and hence the zooplankton which feed on it) varies with the seasons, and both are at a minimum during the winter when the surface layers of the sea are cold and poorly illuminated. The spring is a time of rapid growth for phytoplankton, especially diatoms, as the surface water temperature rises and the concentration of nutrients is high. This increased production is followed by a rise in numbers of zooplankton, augmented by numbers of eggs and larvae. With the increase of herbivorous zooplankton, the quantity of phytoplankton declines rapidly by early summer. The surface waters are warm and well illuminated during the summer but the concentration of nutrients is low as they have been taken up earlier by the phytoplankton, and cannot be replaced from deeper water because mixing is prevented by a thermocline. For this reason, and also because of grazing by zooplankton, production of phytoplankton is low, although dinoflagellates reach their greatest numbers at this time. However zooplankton reach a peak in summer. The thermocline is broken during the autumn as the surface water cools and the supply of nutrients is replenished by mixing. There is a consequent increase in phytoplankton production followed by a small increase in numbers of zooplankton, but numbers of both fall again with the coming of winter.

The sea bed below the low water mark slopes very gradually down to the edge of the conti-

Tides

Tidal movement is brought about by the combined gravitational forces of the moon and sun upon the oceans. The effect of the moon's gravitational pull is such that this distorts the water layer to produce two tidal bulges, representing high tides, one immediately below the moon and one in the same line on the opposite side of the earth. Low tide lies half-way between these bulges. During the earth's rotation the tidal bulges remain stationary relative to the moon so that at any point on the earth's surface there are two complete tidal cycles with a lunar day (24 hours 50 minutes) with the result that on successive days high tide appears about 50 minutes later than on the previous day.

The effect of the sun is weaker that that of the moon but is still significant. When the moon is new or full, the pull of the sun on the water is in nearly the same line as that of the moon. The combined pull of sun and moon causes very high and low tides known as spring tides. During the moon's first and last quarters the sun pulls at right-angles to the moon, reducing the height of the tidal bulges and causing tides of reduced range known as neap tides. Thus there is a 28-day rhythm of spring and neap tides which is especially marked at the equinoxes (March and September) when there is an exceptionally large tidal range at the spring tides.

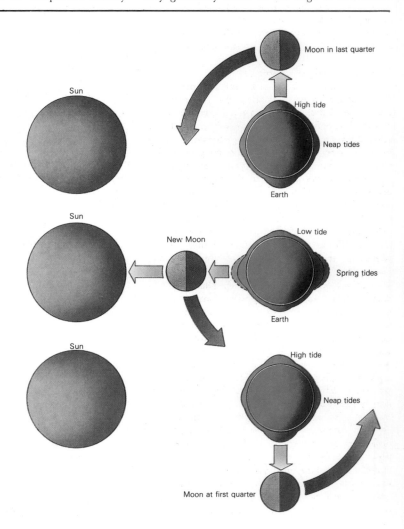

The marine ecosystem

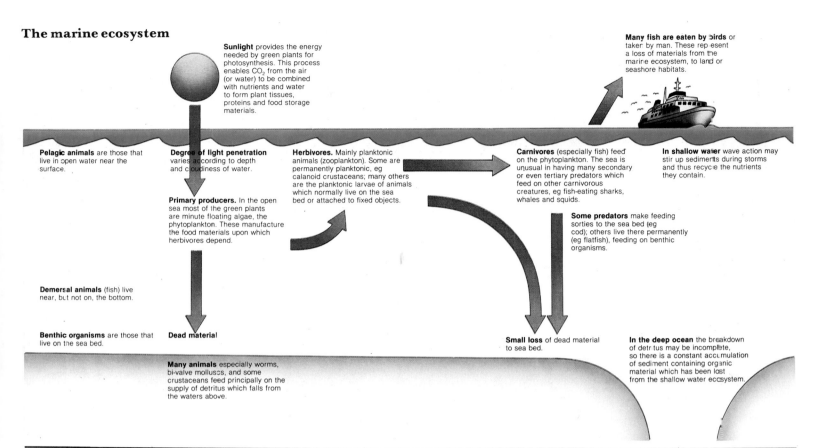

Sunlight provides the energy needed by green plants for photosynthesis. This process enables CO_2 from the air (or water) to be combined with nutrients and water to form plant tissues, proteins and food storage materials.

Many fish are eaten by birds or taken by man. These represent a loss of materials from the marine ecosystem, to land or seashore habitats.

Pelagic animals are those that live in open water near the surface.

Degree of light penetration varies according to depth and cloudiness of water.

Herbivores. Mainly planktonic animals (zooplankton). Some are permanently planktonic, eg calanoid crustaceans; many others are the planktonic larvae of animals which normally live on the sea bed or attached to fixed objects.

Carnivores (especially fish) feed on the phytoplankton. The sea is unusual in having many secondary or even tertiary predators which feed on other carnivorous creatures, eg fish-eating sharks, whales and squids.

In shallow water wave action may stir up sediments during storms and thus recycle the nutrients they contain.

Primary producers. In the open sea most of the green plants are minute floating algae, the phytoplankton. These manufacture the food materials upon which herbivores depend.

Some predators make feeding sorties to the sea bed (eg cod); others live there permanently (eg flatfish), feeding on benthic organisms.

Demersal animals (fish) live near, but not on, the bottom.

Benthic organisms are those that live on the sea bed.

Dead material

Small loss of dead material to sea bed.

In the deep ocean the breakdown of detritus may be incomplete, so there is a constant accumulation of sediment containing organic material which has been lost from the shallow water ecosystem.

Many animals especially worms, bi-valve molluscs, and some crustaceans feed principally on the supply of detritus which falls from the waters above.

nental shelf. This shallow sea provides a more constant environment than the sea shore. The temperature, salinity, and illumination are much less variable and wave action is imperceptible at depth. Although seaweeds do not grow deeper than 30m (considerably less in silt-laden waters), there is ample food available in the form of the remains of pelagic organisms and other organic detritus sinking from the surface water. These shallow coastal waters contain many animals which are unable to tolerate the more unstable conditions on the exposed shore, including many species of fragile plant-like hydroids and other colonial coelenterates. This offshore fauna is unlikely to be seen by those of us who are not skin-diving enthusiasts, but some of the plants and animals that normally live out of sight below low water mark can often be found washed up on the beach after a storm.

Barrages and pollution

Several estuaries in Britain are potential sites for barrages, including the Dee, Morecambe Bay, the Solway Firth, the Severn and the Wash. The object of the barrage is to catch and store fresh water by damming an estuary at or near its mouth. It is difficult to predict the effect of a barrage on an estuary but these five proposed barrages pose a threat to extensive areas of intertidal sand and mudflats which have rich invertebrate faunas and which provide food for very large numbers of overwintering waders and wildfowl and also act as feeding grounds for flatfish. These feeding grounds would be replaced by initially brackish and then non-tidal freshwater bodies. While the evidence suggests that new sand banks and mud flats might be laid down on the seaward side of any barrage, it seems likely that for various reasons, including the lack of silt and increased salinity and exposure, these new banks could not provide substitute feeding grounds for birds, as they would probably lack a rich invertebrate fauna.

Marine wild life is threatened by many other pressures. Populations of invertebrates and fish are depleted by bait digging and over-collecting by amateur and commercial skin divers. Increased urban development along the coast results in the destruction of whole stretches of shore. For centuries the sea has provided a convenient dumping ground for industrial wastes and untreated sewage, much of it carried into the sea from estuaries. Some of the industrial wastes include heavy metals such as lead, copper and mercury, poisonous chemicals such as cyanides and phenols, radioactive substances and a group of compounds known as P.C.B.'s, which have many industrial uses in paints, lubricants and plastics. While most of these substances are diluted in the open sea, many pollutants become concentrated several thousand times in the bodies of fish and other animals, especially the filter-feeding mussels and oysters, and are then transferred to predatory birds. The harmful effect of these compounds may not be immediately apparent and may be indirect, for example by hindering the breeding success of birds.

Industries such as paper mills and food processing plants discharge large quantities of organic wastes which are broken down by bacteria, thus rapidly using up the available oxygen in the water. Untreated sewage has a similar effect when discharged into an estuary. While this de-oxygenating effect is not important in the open sea, in sheltered waters and estuaries the lack of oxygen and the presence of poisonous substances like hydrogen sulphide, liberated by bacteria, may destroy most of the living organisms, often with serious consequences for fisheries developed in these waters. Nevertheless the effect of pollution is often reversible; a recent success story is the recovery of fish populations in the Thames within the last twenty years.

Many rivers carry industrial waste to the coast where extensive pollution of the beach and shallow waters may result. Even the deposition of silt may be harmful, let alone toxic wastes such as residues from mining activities.

Shallow coastal waters are the most seriously affected and these are the very regions that are of greatest economic importance for the production of human food from the sea.

The Rocky Shore

Rock pool fish are generally small and have adaptations to prevent them being washed away. Many live among stones like this sea scorpion *Cottus bubalis* which is also protected by sharp spines.

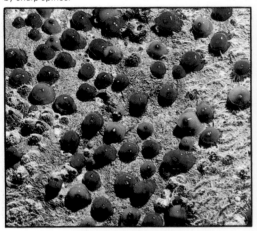

Sea anemones feed using their tentacles but when the tide goes out these are withdrawn and the anemone appears as a blob of jelly. The beadlet anemone *(Actinia equina)* occurs in both red and green forms.

Low tide on a rocky shore reveals numerous rock pools each with its own community of permanent and visiting residents. Brown seaweeds are particularly characteristic inhabitants.

R ocky shores exist where the effect of waves on the coastline is mainly erosive but there is sufficient exposure to prevent materials being deposited on the wave cut platform. The rocky substrate is stable and presents a secure attachment for a variety of organisms like large seaweeds and barnacles. The nature of the shore depends largely on the type of rock exposed. Hard igneous rocks such as granite are less hospitable but where sedimentary rocks of varying hardness are present, dipping towards or away from the sea, the wave cut platform consists of a succession of ridges of harder rock, with intervening rock pools where the softer rock has eroded away leaving a hollow filled by the receding tide.

The intensity of wave action has a profound influence on the composition of the community which develops on any particular shore, but the zonation of animals and plants, often clearly visible from a distance, is probably the rocky shore's most striking feature. The extent to which different plants and animals are adapted to life on the shore varies considerably. The intense competition for space on the lower shore creates a need to move up the shore, and the more highly adapted it is the higher up the organism can live. However adaptation can involve loss as well as gain since as organisms move up the shore, they necessarily cease living on the favourable conditions of lower shore. Many animals have successfully invaded the upper shore as they have become progressively better adapted to life in air instead of water.

Attached forms

The brown seaweeds show a well-marked zonation which is basically controlled by two factors, their capacity to withstand drying out and the speed at which they grow. The most resistant to desiccation are channelled wrack *(Pelvetia)* and spiral wrack *(Fucus spiralis)*, both of which make slow and short growth, thus limiting water loss when the tide is out. *Pelvetia* retains some water in channels along the underside of the fronds (hence its vernacular name) formed by inrolling of the margins, and its high oil content helps prevent it from shrivelling. The

Many creatures may burrow into the rock itself. These bivalves gain protection from their rocky surroundings and feed by drawing in water and filtering food particles from it.

remaining brown seaweeds are less able to withstand drying out but grow more rapidly and are able to outstrip their competitors on the middle and lower shores. The effect of wave action modifies the vertical distribution of seaweeds on the shore. For example, knotted wrack *(Ascophyllum nodosum)* is the most abundant alga in the middle zone on sheltered shores, where its long, elastic fronds are well suited to life in the up and down swell and surge of sheltered waters, while it is replaced on more exposed shores by bladder wrack *(Fucus vesiculosus)* which has shorter fronds but greater tensile strength to resist the pounding of the waves. Neither can withstand the action of the waves on very exposed shores. The large brown weeds at the bottom of the lower shore, such as the kelps *(Laminaria)*, have pliable stems which

The most conspicuous animals are the coiled shelled molluscs (gastropods) which browse the encrusting algae and, as in this case, sea squirts. Shown here is the painted topshell *Calliostoma*.

enable them to withstand violent wave action.

On all except the most exposed rocky shores, the dense growth of seaweeds hides the zoning of the animals. The most obvious are the barnacles, which are permanently fixed to the rock, and often completely cover large areas of the middle shore, forming a broad white band on exposed rocky coasts. The two most abundant are acorn barnacles *(Balanus balanoides)* and star barnacles *(Chthamalus stellatus)*, which show a clear zonation, with the former restricted to the middle shore and the latter mainly occupying the upper shore, since it cannot compete with *B. balanoides* but can withstand longer periods of exposure. The common limpet is also well adapted to life on the rocky shore. It has the same wave resistant broad base and conical form as the barnacle but is much larger and is

Filter feeders like these barnacles can only feed when the tide is in. At low tide they withdraw their filter feeding apparatus using their conical shape to withstand wave action.

Some fan worms like these *Spirorbis* live in hard calcareous tubes forming small white coils about a centimeter in diameter on rocks and seaweed fronds. Their tentacles are withdrawn at low tide.

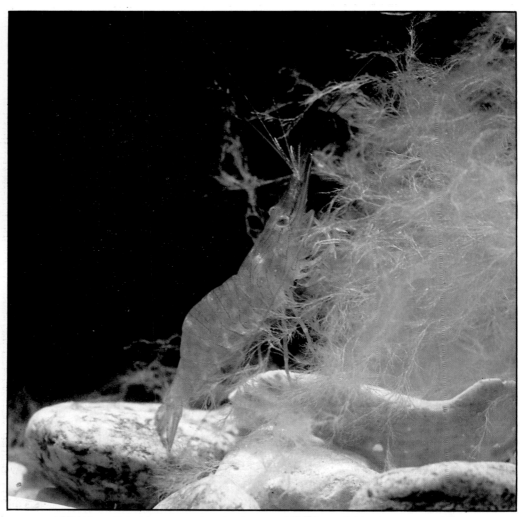

Prawns are often found among rockpool seaweeds, where they use their delicate pincers to pick up morsels of food. Their sensitive antennae are longer than the body and their prominent eyes are stalked like those of crabs. The abdomen ends in a broad tail fan which can be flicked under the body, causing the animals to dart backwards when threatened from the front. In life, shrimps and prawns are greenish and transparent; they go pink when cooked.

Often very complex interrelationships develop among seashore animals. Here a hermit crab inhabits a disused winkle shell which is covered by growths of sea fir which in turn forms the food for two sea slugs.

Animals which stick onto rocks for protection cannot easily move but the starfish achieves mobility by using hundreds of tiny sucking feet. This is the cushion starlet *Asterina gibbosa*.

able to move about, browsing on algae on the rocks. The conical shell allows for the broadest of attachment with the minimum of resistance to the waves and the harder the waves pound on the rock the harder the limpet clings, using its flat disc-shaped foot for attachment. Desiccation is overcome by retaining some water within the shell, and the rock and shell are ground away by the animal to ensure a tight fit between them. This site represents its "home" and it returns there after feeding. It has been shown that if limpets are removed from an area of rock which has been previously browsed, then seaweeds soon establish themselves. It is therefore clear that limpets impose significant control on algal growth. Two bivalves, the saddle oyster and edible mussel, are firmly fixed to the rock from the middle shore downwards by short byssal threads. Several other bivalves, such as the piddocks, are able to bore into softer rocks to resist the action of the waves. Fixed animals such as barnacles and bivalves must obtain food by filter feeding, removing plankton and detritus from the water at high tide.

The periwinkles do not rely on close adhesion to protect them from wave action but rather either retreat inside their thick shells and allow themselves to be rolled about by the waves or, like *Littorina neritoides* and *L. saxatilis,* shelter in crevices or empty barnacle shells. *L. littoralis* lives mainly under cover of seaweed, which protects it from waves and from drying out at low tide. Other gastropods on the middle and lower shore include the topshells and the predatory dogwhelk which feeds on barnacles and mussels. Many other animals adopt an encrusting form, like the sponges, or clinging habit, like the chitons and scale-worms, or anchor themselves to the rock, using an adhesive basal disc, like the sea anemones.

Rock pools form natural aquaria with a balanced population of plants and animals, but conditions in pools, especially those high up on the shore, may vary widely. The water is quickly warmed by the sun, but in cold weather loses heat quickly. Hot sun evaporates water and increases salinity, while rainwater dilutes the salt water. In hot weather, lack of oxygen can be a problem, as warm water dissolves less of this vital gas. Thus the higher pools, which tend to be brackish, contain only the *Enteromorpha* and other green seaweeds. Further down the shore, pools provide shelter which is otherwise absent from the exposed shore, and harbour a diverse community of plants and animals. These include many types of anemones, hydroids, algae, crustaceans and small fish described under later headings.

The Sandy and Muddy Shore

The appearance of a sandy beach as it is uncovered by the falling tide contrasts sharply with that of the rocky shore. The unstable nature of sand under the influence of wind and water, together with the lack of shelter, makes it unsuitable for most animals which live on the surface. Unlike rocky shores, there are no surfaces for attachment and this means that seaweeds, with their rich associated fauna, together with attached animals such as barnacles and sponges, are absent. The majority of animals of sandy and muddy shores must burrow in order to survive and these habitats harbour a surprisingly rich community of worms, small crustaceans and bivalves.

Beaches consist of a layer of material covering a platform of underlying rock which has often been cut from the land by wave erosion. It must be emphasised that beaches are not permanent and that the whole of a particular beach may be removed by a storm. The sands, gravels and other materials forming the beach are derived from various sources, such as the erosion of neighbouring cliffs, or material carried along the coast from other places by currents or even debris from the cutting of the platform itself. The material may persist as boulders or, when the waves are powerful or the rocks are soft, be quickly ground down to pebbles and shingle and so to sand or finer mud particles. Sand generally consists of particles of quartz of various sizes, often augmented by fragments of limestone, shale and other rocks. Locally, entire beaches may be formed of complete shells, fragments of coal or even the skeletons of calcareous algae. In sheltered regions, finely-divided mud carried in suspension in the water may be deposited and sand is gradually replaced by mud. In estuaries these deposits form extensive mud flats which are rich in animal life.

Wave action

The action of waves breaking obliquely on the shore carries sand up the beach at an angle while the backwash runs directly down the beach. Consequently some beach material is carried a short distance sideways along the shore by this beach drifting. The waves also have a sorting action on the sand so that different grades may be concentrated into regions, with coarser material accumulating higher up on the beach. There are many beaches around the British Isles with steeply sloping shingle at the top and flatter sand and mud on the middle and lower shore. The function of the wooden and concrete groynes on many beaches is to restrict beach drifting by trapping the sand between them. This preserves the beach and protects the land against erosion.

The size of particle is important in determining which animals live on a beach. Pebbles roll over each other and would crush any animals or plants that attempted to live among

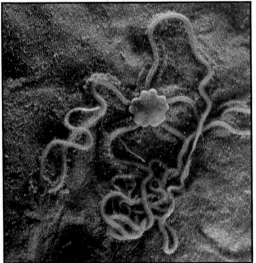

Some burrowers live in the top few centimetres of sand and are sometimes exposed at low tide. They are, like these brittle stars *Acronida brachiata*, often sandy coloured to reduce conspicuousness.

them. As a result, pebble beaches, perhaps the most lifeless habitat in Britain, are generally barren. Sand grains are irregular in form and, as they do not compact together, have spaces (interstices) between them. These interstices are filled with water at high tide but as the tide ebbs, the water table sinks and the sand dries out. Finer sands and muds have a higher water retaining capacity, because of their greater capillarity, and this is advantageous to burrowing animals during periods of exposure. Coarser, drier sands, on the other hand, tend to compact firmly, making it difficult for burrowing animals to penetrate. Where the interstices remain filled with water in finer sands, especially nearer the water's edge, the sand becomes thixotropic (semi-liquid) and is easier for burrowing. This is because the sand grains are able to glide over one another when subjected to pressure. Wading birds feed at the water's edge where their beaks can penetrate the thixotropic mud more easily. The effects of differing amounts of water in sand can be seen when walking across a sandy shore, the feet make wet sand softer, while drier sand whitens and becomes firmer when trodden on.

The interstitial spaces between sand grains are occupied by near-microscopic animals, including worms and crustaceans, which tend to be elongated and circular in cross section as an adaptation to moving through these restricted spaces. These minute animals are, in turn, preyed upon by larger burrowing animals such as ragworms. The interstitial fauna is reduced in muds where the spaces are smaller, but the greater surface area of the smaller mud particles supports a richer growth of bacteria, which multiplies rapidly at higher temperatures, as for example, when the mud is exposed to the sun at low tide, and when organic detritus accumulates

When the tide goes out animals on sandy shores are left totally exposed and the majority of the fauna adopts burrowing habits. There are few plants in this habitat because soft sand provides little anchorage.

The masked crab *Corystes cassivelaunus* is a typical crab of sandy shores. It burrows in the sand using its long antennae as a breathing tube to bring in fresh supplies of water from the surface.

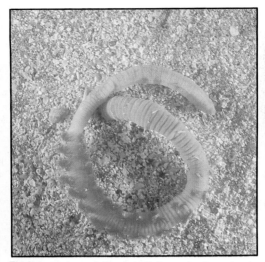

The lugworm spends its whole life burrowing in sand and mud. It maintains a constant current of water through the burrow from which it extracts oxygen using feathery gills along the sides of its body.

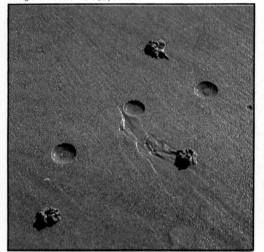

Lugworms live in a U-shaped burrow. At low tide the burrow entrance is marked by a shallow depression and the exit by a small pile of rejected sand.

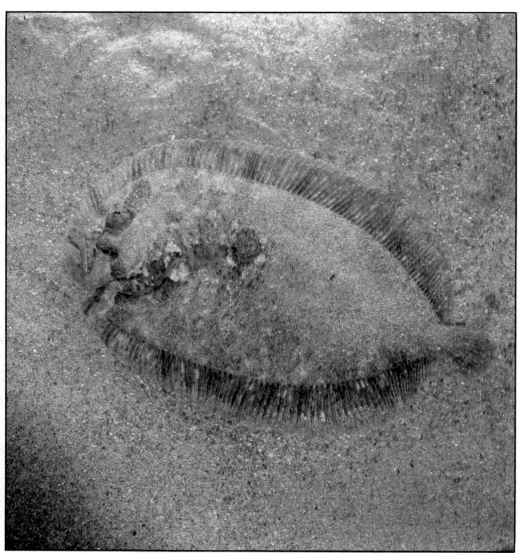

Those fish which live on sandy shores need to be well camouflaged. Flat fish like this topknot *Zeugopterus punctatus* also burrow into the surface layers of the sand.

in sheltered areas. The net result is that dissolved oxygen in the interstitial water of mud may be completely used up as the bacteria decompose the detritus and the mud becomes anaerobic. Anaerobic muds have a characteristic black colour due to the presence of iron sulphide, and give off an unpleasant smell. These conditions are generally harmful to animals, which are therefore usually restricted to the zone of brown oxygenated mud which lies between the black layer and the surface. Several animals have however become adapted to life in the black layer, including the red *Tubifex* worm, the lugworm and the peppery furrow shell.

Although plants cannot grow on the exposed sandy shore except where rocks offer a fixture, some algae become established on mud flats where there is sufficient shelter from strong tidal currents. The bladder wrack will grow on pieces of firm mud although it is more successful where stones, wood or other pieces of debris are present. The green seaweeds *Enteromorpha* and *Ulva* and filamentous green algae may be so abundant in summer on sheltered shores that they appear like fields of grass from a distance. Some microscopic algae such as diatoms live in the surface layers of the mud, coming up to the surface during the daytime when the mud is uncovered by the tide. Their numbers may exceed many thousands per square centimetre and their vertical movements produce changes

in the colour of the mud from brown to green as the tide retreats. In some localities, sandy and muddy shores are colonised from the low tide mark downwards by eel-grass *(Zostera)* which is one of the few flowering plants capable of surviving prolonged submersion in sea water. This plant has creeping rhizomes and fibrous roots which serve to anchor the plant and stabilise mud and sand. The scarcity of plants on sand and mud means that the animals present must feed either by filtering plankton and plant debris from the sea water at high tide (suspension feeders), or on detritus and micro-organisms living on the sand (deposit feeders).

Feeding methods of sandy and muddy shore animals

The diagram shows the relationships between some of the animals of the shore and the way in which they feed. Deeper burrowing animals such as the deposit feeding lugworm (*Arenicola*) and the peppery furrow shell (*Scrobicularia*) can survive anaerobic conditions in the mud as they draw oxygenated water from above the surface through burrows or siphons. The siphon is also used by *Scrobicularia* and the related Baltic tellin (*Macoma*) to collect food in the form of detritus which accumulates on the surface. *Macoma* is smaller and does not burrow deeply, in common with the spiny cockle (*Cerastoderma*) which lives just below the surface, extending its short siphons to draw in water containing suspended debris, which can be filtered for food. The small snail *Hydrobia* shelters in the top layer of the mud at low tide, becoming active at the surface and feeding on detritus as the tide rises. *Nereis* is a predatory ragworm, hunting its prey at the surface but retiring to a

burrow in the sand. Where stones are present, they afford shelter to crabs, such as the shore crab (*Carcinus*) and provide attachment for the common mussel (*Mytilus*).

The diagram also shows how competition is avoided amongst the many birds which feed on the sandy and muddy shore. Waders, such as the oystercatcher, redshank, knot and curlew have beaks of different lengths so that they feed at different levels in the sand on different animals. For example, only the curlew and a few other waders like the whimbrel can feed on the deeper burrowing invertebrates. Ducks, such as the shelduck, can filter large quantities of surface mud to extract numbers of *Hydrobia*. The turnstone searches for crabs and other invertebrates by turning over small stones, while gulls remove mussels at the surface and break them open by dropping them from a height.

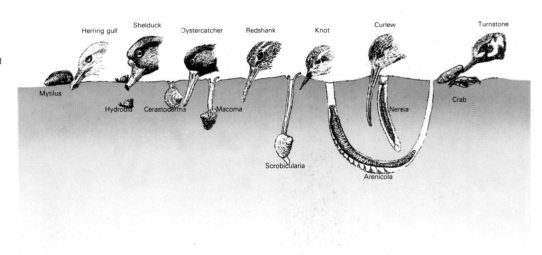

Seaweeds and Marine Plants

The seaweeds are simple organisms, yet highly adapted to their habitat; they need to be strongly attached and very pliant to withstand wave action and, although growing in water, need to withstand periods of drying out at low tide. Seaweeds are actually large algae; few higher plants grow on the shore, the eel-grass (*Zostera*) being almost the only one and characteristic of tidal mudflats.

Green seaweeds

Green algae are widely distributed on all types of shore and do not show any clear zonation. *Enteromorpha* and the sea lettuce *Ulva* may be so abundant in summer on sheltered estuarine mud flats that they appear like meadows; as they decay the mud becomes completely deoxygenated. *Enteromorpha intestinalis* is especially common in pools on the upper shore where there may be considerable dilution of the salt water by streams or rain water. Where these dry out during hot summers, the dried weed forms large white patches. *Enteromorpha* also grows in pools on the middle and lower shore and is common in estuaries and even in ditches on salt marshes where the water is practically fresh. The sea lettuce *Ulva* is also tolerant of fresh water and occurs at all levels on the shore even extending into the sub-littoral zone. Both these green algae continue to grow if they break free from the substrate and they often accumulate in masses in sheltered bays.

Brown seaweeds

The brown algae form large plants which are normally attached to the substrate. They are important members of the shore community. The wracks (*Ascophyllum, Fucus* and *Pelvetia*) show a well-marked zonation which has already been described. Their structural adaptations to life on the shore have also been described. The kelps (*Laminaria, Saccorhiza* and *Alaria*) replace the wracks on the lower shore and beyond to depths of up to 30m, although this is considerably reduced where the light intensity is diminished by water turbidity. The first to be exposed is *Laminaria digitata* which lies prostrate when the tide is low to reduce the effects of desiccation. *L. hyperborea* grows just below *L. digitata* but remains semi-erect at low tide. It has a rougher stem, providing anchorage for other seaweeds and encrusting animals like hydroids. *Laminaria saccharina* occurs even further down the shore and is rarely exposed except by the lowest tides, although it also grows in deep pools on the lower shore. The dry fronds of this alga are coated with a whitish deposit which is sweet to the taste and which gives it its name. It is also known as "Poor Man's Weather Glass" as it can be hung up and used as a rough indicator of atmospheric humidity. The fronds become soft and limp with the approach of rain, and brittle and rigid during dry spells. *Saccorhiza polyschides* grows among the *Laminaria* and is the

largest British seaweed, reaching a length of up to 4.5m with a span of 3m across the blade. *Alaria* replaces *Laminaria digitata* on exposed shores; it is a northern species which can withstand a good deal of battering. The sea thong *Himanthalia* is commonly found in deep pools and also on the lower shore.

Red seaweeds

The red algae are smaller and more delicate than the brown fucoids. Like the green algae, they do not show a clear zonation but are especially common in pools. There are more species of red seaweeds than brown algae and they show a greater diversity of form. A few examples are selected here to illustrate this. The edible Irish moss (*Chondrus*) may form a carpet on the lower shore, but several red algae depend on other seaweeds for attachment, including *Polysiphonia lanosa*, attached to *Ascophyllum*, and *Rhodymenia palmata*, which grows attached to laminarian stalks. Thus their distribution on the shore is determined by that of the host species. The laver (*Porphyra umbilicalis*) is widely distributed and grows on stones and rocks, particularly where sand is present. The sides of rock pools are often covered by encrusting calcareous algae, such as *Lithophyllum incrustans*, which are hard and rough to the touch. Such pools usually contain the common pink *Corallina officinalis*, an alga which has branches impregnated with calcareous deposits.

Seaweeds have been used for centuries as a source of food for man and as animal fodder. In the British Isles their direct use tends to be mainly restricted to those living on the coast. The laver (*Porphyra*) has a long history as a food and is still used in South Wales, where it is made into "laver bread", and in Ireland. When used directly, seaweeds are a relatively poor source of food, but their high mineral salt and vitamin content make a valuable addition to the diet of both man and animals. When processed, seaweeds produce a range of compounds which have many applications in the food and other industries. These include gelatinous substances such as agar and carrageen from the red algae and alginates from the brown algae, used in a

Toothed wrack *Fucus serratus* in a rock pool at low tide. The brown seaweeds are very soft and flexible so that they are not broken by the twisting and tearing action of the incoming tide.

variety of products from paint to ice cream. Seaweeds are also used as manures, especially calcareous algae, while at one time kelp was burned as a source of soda for the glass industry and for iodine.

Few flowering plants survive prolonged submersion in sea water. The eel-grasses (*Zostera*) are the only British examples which are truly marine. They are perennials with long grass-like leaves and creeping stems running along the surface and rooting at intervals. Eel-grass grows in the inter-tidal zone on sandy and muddy shores in sheltered areas, particularly in estuaries. *Zostera marina* extends below the low-tide mark into shallow water. The small inconspicuous green flowers are pollinated under water, the pollen being carried by water currents. Eel-grass often forms dense swards over estuarine flats, especially along the south and east coast, for example on Maplin Sands. Such swards help to stabilise the mud. The eel-grass also forms an important source of food for wildfowl, particularly the brent goose.

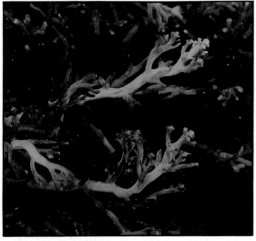

A brown seaweed *Cystoseira* which has a blue-green iridescence under water. The swollen tips of the fronds contain the reproductive structures.

Eel-grass *Zostera* underwater. Though superficially resembling a seaweed this is in fact a flowering plant, the only one found on the shore.

A guide to seaweeds

Sea Lettuce Ulvaceae *Ulva lactuca*. **Distribution:** Around all British Isles coasts. **Notes:** Variable; intertidal zone and to a depth of 20 metres; on all except the most exposed rocky shores; green when young, but becoming brown then black with age; somewhat pollution tolerant.

Channelled Wrack Fucaceae *Pelvetia canaliculata*. **Distribution:** Around all British Isles Coasts. **Notes:** Common; often abundant on rocks of the upper shore; forms a distinctive zone; can be above high-tide level when spray washed.

Spiral Wrack Fucaceae *Fucus spiralis*. **Distribution:** Around all British Isles coasts. **Notes:** Abundant on rocks of the upper shore, except where very exposed; not always spirally twisted; never has air bladders.

Enteromorpha intestinalis Ulvaceae. **Distribution:** Around all British Isles coasts. **Other habitats:** Estuaries and ditches where water is almost fresh. **Notes:** Very common, especially in upper shore rock pools.

Bladder Wrack Fucaceae *Fucus vesiculosus*. **Distribution:** Around all British Isles coasts. **Notes:** On rocks; forming a distinct zone of the middle shore; very variable; bladders usually in groups of two or three.

Oar-weed, Tangle Laminariaceae *Laminaria digitata*. **Distribution:** Around all British Isles coasts. **Notes:** On rocks at low-water level and to depths of 30 metres; common; stalk oval in cross-section and usually without epiphytic species.

Cuvie Laminariaceae *Laminaria hyperborea*. **Distribution:** Around all British Isles coasts. **Notes:** Attached to rocks and stones; in pools and forming a brown belt at low-tide level; stalk round in cross section, rough and usually covered with zoophytes.

Polysiphonia lanosa Rhodomelaceae. **Distribution:** Around all British Isles coasts. **Notes:** Usually parasitic, growing on *Ascophyllum nodosum*.

Furbelows Phyllariaceae *Saccorhiza polyschides*. **Distribution:** Around all British Isles coasts. **Notes:** On rocks at low-tide level and to a depth of 30 metres; common; up to 5 metres long and 3 metres wide; isolated plants.

Toothed Wrack Fucaceae *Fucus serratus*. **Distribution:** Around all British Isles coasts. **Notes:** Common; on all except the most exposed rocky shores; often forms a distinct zone low on the middle shore; frequently covered with zoophytes.

Sea Belt Laminariaceae *Laminaria saccharina*. **Distribution:** Around all British Isles coasts. **Notes:** From low-tide level to a depth of 20 metres; up to 2.5 metres long, ribbon-like; holdfast appears two-tiered; easily distinguished by wrinkled surface.

Irish Moss or **Carrageen** Gigartinaceae *Chondrus crispus*. **Distribution:** Around all British Isles coasts. **Notes:** On all kinds of shore except mud, but always growing on stones or rocks; abundant on lower and middle shore and in pools; turns green in strong light.

Knotted Wrack Fucaceae *Ascophyllum nodosum*. **Distribution:** Around all British Isles coasts. **Notes:** Rocky shores from high-tide to mid-tide zones; under sheltered conditions can blanket entire beach and plants can be very large; has no midrib.

Dulse Rhodymeniaceae *Rhodymenia palmata*. **Distribution:** Around all British Isles coasts. **Notes:** On rocks of the middle and lower shore; also on *Laminaria* and *Fucus* and in shallow water; very variable.

Dilsea carnosa Dumontiaceae. **Distribution:** Around all British Isles coasts, but more abundant in the south. **Notes:** Middle and lower shore, shallow and deep water; common; on rocks, or small stones on sand flats in shallow water.

Gigartina stellata Gigartinaceae. **Distribution:** Around all British Isles coasts. **Notes:** Common; fronds channelled; on rock near the low-tide level; variable; older plants covered with fleshy excrescences.

Sea Thong Himanthaliaceae *Himanthalia elongata*. **Distribution:** Around all British Isles coasts. **Notes:** Lower shore, pools and shallow water; common; often forming dense colonies; the basal "button" often exists without the rest of the frond; up to 2.5 metres long.

Dabberlocks Alariaceae *Alaria esculenta*. **Distribution:** Around all British Isles coasts; abundant in the north and rare in the south. **Notes:** On rocks near the low-tide level; always submerged; locally common; has a distinct midrib; grows best on exposed shores.

Laver Bangiaceae *Porphyra umbicalis*. **Distribution:** Around all British Isles coasts. **Notes:** Rocky areas, especially when covered by sand; on most levels of the shore; shape irregular and very variable; margin wavy, entire or unevenly dentate.

Codium tomentosum Codiaceae. **Distribution:** Around all British Isles coasts. **Notes:** Fairly common; mainly on middle shore and deep pools and down to a depth of 20 metres; on mud, sand or rock; has the texture of felt.

Lithophyllum incrustans Corallinaceae. **Distribution:** Around all British Isles coasts. **Notes:** Common in pools, especially on exposed beaches; forms a thick irregular crust up to 4cm thick; adheres strongly to substrate

Corallina officinalis Corallinaceae. **Distribution:** Around all British Isles coasts. **Notes:** Common throughout the intertidal zone, especially in rock pools of the middle shore; colour varies from purple to red to pink to yellow to white.

Gigartina stellata Gigartinaceae. **Distribution:** Around all British Isles coasts. **Notes:** Common; fronds channelled; on rock near the low-tide level; variable; older plants covered with fleshy excrescences.

Soft-bodied Marine Animals

Examination of the underside of rocks on a sheltered shore often reveals a wide variety of sessile and encrusting animals, of which a few examples are described below.

The sponges are a group of primitive colonial animals which are mainly marine. They are unlike any other animals and probably represent an evolutionary dead-end. Basically a sponge consists of a hollow mass of cells which draw water in through small pores between them and filter food particles from this water. The water then passes out through a large pore at the top of the sponge called the osculum. The walls of sponges are strengthened by a skeleton of hard spicules or soft fibres, as in the bath sponge. There are many species of encrusting sponges, many being brightly coloured; the breadcrumb sponge *(Halichondria panicea)* is one of the most common from the middle shore downwards, forming patches 1cm thick and 20cm or more across. The colour varies from white to green and the oscula are set on conical projections giving the appearance of tiny volcanoes. *Grantia compressa* is a simple sponge growing in groups, often on overhanging rocks. The other sponges illustrated have unusual habitats. *Suberites domuncula* is an orange-yellow sponge which occurs in the sub-littoral zone, often around whelk shells occupied by hermit crabs. It may dissolve away the shell and end up enwrapping the crab, providing it with direct shelter. *Cliona celata* is a sponge which may occur on the surface of soft rocks and shells as well as boring into them. Pieces of shell with empty holes in them made by the boring sponge are often found on the shore.

Coelenterates have a relatively simple structure, with bag-like bodies consisting of an inner layer of cells separated from an outer layer by a jelly-like material. The bag serves as a stomach and opens by a mouth which is surrounded by

tentacles. These are armed with stinging cells which hold tiny prey and immobilise it before pushing it into the mouth. This basic individual is called a polyp.

The coelenterates can be divided into three groups. The hydroids consist of colonies of polyps which grow close together and are interconnected. Colonies are often enclosed in a protective horny case with a cup for each polyp. Hydroids often have complicated life cycles with reproductive polyps which grow on the colonies to produce free-swimming medusae, which look like miniature jellyfish. These medusae are

Jellyfish are very simple animals but some of them can still be quite large. They swim by a pulsating movement of the bell and feed on tiny planktonic animal prey. Their tentacles bear stinging cells.

planktonic and produce fertile eggs which give rise to planktonic larvae; these eventually settle in the seabed to form a new colony. The sea fir *(Obelia geniculata)* is a typical colonial hydroid which grows up to 50cm in height attached to seaweeds, and is just about visible to the naked eye. The white weed *(Sertularia pumila)* is a larger and more plant-like hydroid, growing to 45cm in length. The eggs develop in the colony

The beadlet anemone *(Actinia equina)* with its tentacles extended in the water. Each tentacle bears tiny sticky and stinging cells which trap prey animals as they pass by. When the tide goes out, the tentacles are withdrawn and the animal retracts to form a jelly-like blob stuck to a rock. The species is variable in colour; some being red, others are brown or even green.

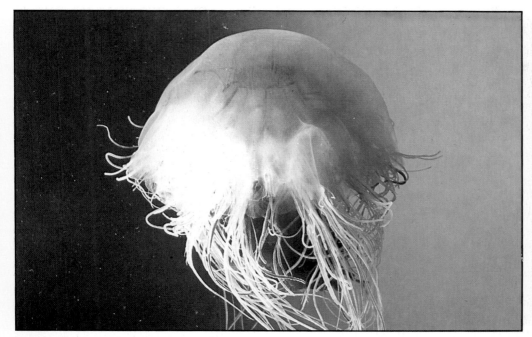

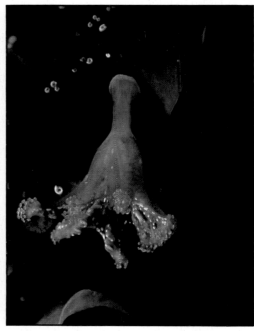

Lions mane jellyfish *Cyanea capillata* which can deliver a painful sting from its tentacles to kill fish and other prey but is not dangerous to larger creatures, like humans. Although jellyfish can propel themselves through the water, they are generally at the mercy of winds and currents and are frequently cast up on shore after severe gales. They cannot survive long on land and rapidly dry out in air.

The bell-shaped swimming jellyfish are only the pelagic stage of the life cycle. There is also a stalked phase which lives attached to rocks. In some species, this sedentary body form is retained by the adult.

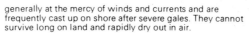

as the medusa stage is suppressed. White weed is sometimes commercially gathered for decoration. *Tubularia indivisa* has large pink polyps and a reduced horny case. Each polyp has two sets of tentacles and the medusae remain attached to the parent colony. *Tubularia* is common in pools from the lower shore downwards. The siphono-phores are free-floating hydroids (often mistaken for jellyfish) with polyps modified for various functions including feeding, defence, reproduc-tion and providing a float. The Portuguese man-o'-war *(Physalia)* floats above the water like a 30cm long inflated mauve plastic bag. The polyps and tentacles hang down and sometimes extend for several metres below the animal. The sting can cause major discomfort but *Physalia* normally feeds on fish. The by-the-wind sailor *(Velella)* is much smaller (6cm) and often occurs in shoals which are driven along by the wind on their flat transparent sails.

In the true jellyfish the medusa stage is predominant although there is often a small polyp phase during the life cycle. The common jellyfish *(Aurelia aurita)* has a world-wide distri-bution and even occurs in the brackish waters of estuaries. In external appearance it resembles a giant version of the tiny medusa of the hydroid *Obelia*. It seems likely that the common jellyfish is a plankton feeder, trapping zooplankton all over the bell in mucus and carrying them by tracts of cilia to the four arms hanging down round the central mouth. Jellyfish maintain their position in the water by rhythmic con-tractions of the bell which lift them in the water. If the contractions cease, the bell slowly sinks. Two other large jellyfish, *Chrysaora* and *Cyanea*, have much larger arms and long trailing tentacles round the margin of the bell. They are well equipped with stinging cells and feed on small fish and other animals. *Cyanea* can inflict stings and is best left alone. Most other common jellyfish are more or less harmless to humans.

The third group of coelenterates is the sea-anemones. These lack a medusa stage in their life cycle and the polyps, which are large and conspicuous, are more complex than those of hydroids. In some polyps a calcareous skeleton is developed to form corals, although only one of these occurs in British waters. The beadlet anemone *(Actinia)* is the most common anemone and is widespread, occurring high on the shore and even in fairly exposed positions. When the tide recedes, the tentacles are retracted and it resembles a small blob of reddish-brown jelly. Underwater the tentacles seize and close over small animals, even fish, that come within reach. The opelet *(Anemonia)* is a southern

species with similar habits, although restricted to the lower shore. Its tentacles cannot be fully retracted. One of the largest anemones is *Tealia felina* with a body extending up to 15cm tall. *Tealia* is fairly common, especially in shady places; large specimens are often camouflaged by pieces of shell and stone adhering to them. The plumose anemone *(Metridium)* is a sub-littoral species only exposed by the lowest tides. It has numerous crowded tentacles, giving it a feathery appearance in the water. It feeds mainly on small planktonic animals. *Sagartia* is a small but attractive anemone found from the lower shore downwards. It has up to 200 tent-acles with a variable colour pattern. Several anemones live in association with hermit crabs; an example is *Calliactis*, which occurs on empty whelk shells. Both crab and anemone can live

A hermit crab *Pagurus bernhardus* inhabiting a whelk shell on which is growing a cluster of sea anemones *Calliactis parasitica.*

separately, but when together the anemone gains food from the crab's feeding activities and the crab is protected from predators by the anemone. *Edwardsia* is an example of a group of anemones which burrow in sand and mud or in crevices in rock until only the tentacles are exposed. It occurs on muddy sands and gravels from the lower shore downwards. The ghoulishly named dead man's fingers *(Alcyonium)* is a colonial relative of the anemones having polyps embedded in a body mass which is strengthened by many calcareous fragments. These leave the body soft and flexible. Colonies are usually attached to the underside of rocks on the lower shore and in shallow water.

Marine Worms

The segmented worms are divided into three main groups: bristle worms (Polychaeta), earthworms and related species (Oligochaeta) and leeches (Hirudinea). In Britain, the polychaetes are almost entirely confined to marine habitats, while the other groups have few marine representatives, being mainly freshwater and land animals. One family of oligochaete worms has successfully invaded salt water, the Tubificidae or blood worms. These small reddish worms are particularly abundant in fine muds, with densities exceeding one hundred thousand per square metre. They can survive anaerobic conditions by living head down in the de-oxygenated mud with body extended, movements of the tail driving a current of water towards the head, thus circulating oxygenated water through the mud. *Peloscolex benedeni* is a common tubificid worm in estuarine muds, where it forms an important source of food for many fish and birds, particularly ducks.

Unlike other worms, typical polychaetes have a well-developed head with eyes, sensory palps, tentacles and jaws. The rest of the body consists of a large number of similar segments, each with a pair of lateral paddle-like flaps (parapodia) bearing numerous bristles (chaetae). The parapodia are used for locomotion and respiration. This basic pattern is modified according to the way in which the worm lives and polychaetes can be divided into three groups, based on their ecology. The first group, free-living polychaetes, are the least modified; typical examples are the ragworms, *Nereis diversicolor* and *N. virens*. These burrow into mud and sand from the middle shore downwards and are equipped with strong jaws. They are active swimmers and take a range of prey including tubificid worms. *N. diversicolor* can tolerate estuarine conditions and even survives for short periods in freshwater. *N. virens* is larger and may exceed 45cm in length. These large individuals can give a vicious bite if handled carelessly. *N. fucata* is one of the animals associated with hermit crabs and lives inside whelk shells occupied by these crabs.

Several free-living species develop a special pelagic sexual form (heteronereis) with enlarged parapodia forming paddles for swimming. These heteronereids swarm at the surface of the sea for spawning at times determined by the moon's cycle. The fertilised eggs develop into tiny planktonic larvae (trochophores) which gradually develop adult segments and sink to the sea bed. Other free-living worms include *Nephtys* and *Eulalia*, whose gelatinous green egg cases can be found on the lower shore attached to seaweeds or pebbles. *Tomopteris* is a specialised

planktonic polychaete and has been described in the section on plankton. Scale-worms have plate-like extensions (elytra) of the body wall, covering the dorsal surface like tiles. *Harmothoë* is a scale-worm commonly found under rocks and seaweed on the lower shore while the larger sea-mouse (*Aphrodite aculeata*), which has a mat of brownish hairs covering the scales (and also beautiful iridescent green bristles along its flanks), lives in the sand with its hind end exposed and draws water for respiration under the scales by muscular movements of the body wall. This worm normally lives below the low water mark but large numbers are often stranded on sandy shores after a storm.

The second group of polychaetes are sedentary and live either in burrows (eg *Amphitrite*) or in permanent tubes (eg *Pectinaria*). The material used in the construction of the tubes gives a clue to the identity of the worm. The sedentary polychaetes have no jaws and the head is

The peacock worm *Sabella pavonina* extends its delicate fan of tentacles to trap passing planktonic prey. Fan worms like these typically live in rubbery tubes.

modified for the collection of food particles consisting of plant and other debris from the water. The food collecting apparatus is varied, usually consisting of numerous tentacles with ciliated grooves for transferring food particles to the mouth. Various collars and other structures also help to direct food to the mouth and to plug the burrow when the animal has retracted. The body of most of these worms is divided into two regions, a thorax and an abdomen. The thorax is broad and has well-developed parapodia for moving up and down inside the burrow; it also may have pairs of gills. The abdomen is often narrower and has fewer appendages. Several species such as *Amphitrite* and *Cirratulus* have simple burrows in sand and mud lined with mucus. *Cirratulus* can tolerate anaerobic conditions by extending its long gills above the surface of the mud. *Chaetopterus* builds a U-shaped burrow which is continually irrigated by a flow of water caused by paddle-like parapodia in the middle region of its body. In place of tentacles this worm uses a mucus net for filtering food particles from the water. These burrowing worms are unlikely to be seen by the casual visitor to the seashore, but are fairly easy to dig up with a sturdy spade.

Tubed worms

Several sedentary worms produce a soft cementing substance which is used to bind sand grains and other material into tubes which project out of the sand and may be readily seen at low tide. The tubes of the sandmason worm (*Lanice*) are formed from a variety of materials and have ragged ends. They often occur in large numbers at the bottom of sandy shores, giving the beach a bristly appearance. The tubes of the peacock fan worms (*Sabella* and *Pectinaria*) are neater; the tube of the latter worm is cone-shaped and formed from sand grains of carefully selected sizes. The tube of *Pectinaria*, unlike other tube-worms, is inverted in the sand with the head directed downwards. The chaetae near the head form a comb-like structure which is used to dig a cavity in which

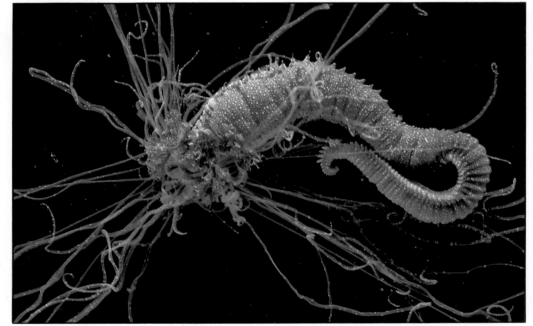

A terebellid worm (*Polymnia nebulosa*) which lives in a burrow or tube on the sea bed and is not normally seen exposed like this. Terebellids differ from other worms in having a swollen anterior end with a reduced head bearing many long, thin tentacles; these are used to trap food particles, though some species produce a mucus net for this purpose. A similar species, the sand mason worm, lives in such large numbers that its tubes form dense masses.

the feeding tentacles work. Excavated sand is passed through the tube and pushed out of the projecting end. *Pectinaria* is often abundant on offshore sand where it plays an important part in the diet of the plaice. *Sabellaria* is gregarious, building tubes of sand and shell fragments on the surface of rocks. Numbers of these worms form a reef which may be several inches thick over the rock. Several worms build tubes of white chalky material. They have characteristic shapes, such as the small coiled tubes on brown seaweeds which are constructed by *Spirorbis*. These worms have a tentacle modified to form a stopper to close the tube when the animal has retreated into it.

The third group is small and contains species of worms like the lugworm (*Arenicola marina*), which burrow but do not have feeding append-ages on the head, although they have a body which is divided into regions like the sedentary polychaetes. Lugworms feed in a similar way to earthworms, by taking sand into the gut and digesting the organic material present. The unwanted sand is passed out of the body and squirted from the rear end of the burrow to form the characteristic worm casts which are found all over the surface of sandy shores at low tide.

A guide to marine worms

Segmented worms are common seashore animals, but usually live in burrows or under stones. Most have prominent 'paddles' (parapodia) along the sides of the body which bear tufts of bristles (chaetae). Parapodia are lacking in oligochaetes (like the earthworm), few of which occur on the shore; marine worms are mostly polychaetes.

Free-living polychaetes are often found under stones or swimming in pools. They have short appendages on the parapodia head, well-developed paripodia and no division of the body into different regions. The scale worms have a characteristic form. Other free-living worms are difficult to distinguish from one another and require specialist keys.

Some have characteristic habitats such as *Nereis diversicolor* (brackish water) and *N. fucata* (inside mollusc shells occupied by hermit crabs). Many sedentary polychaetes burrow in sand, such as *Amphitrite* and *Cirratulus*, and are unlikely to be seen without a special effort to dig them up. The sedentary worms which build sand tubes generally produce distinctive structures like the ragged tubes of the sand mason worm (*Lanice*) and the neat cone-shaped tubes of *Pectinaria*. The colonial tubes of the reef building worm *Sabellaria* are also characteristic. The calcareous tube builders include *Pomatoceros*, with a tube which is triangular in section and cemented to some solid object, *Serpula*, with a rounded tube.

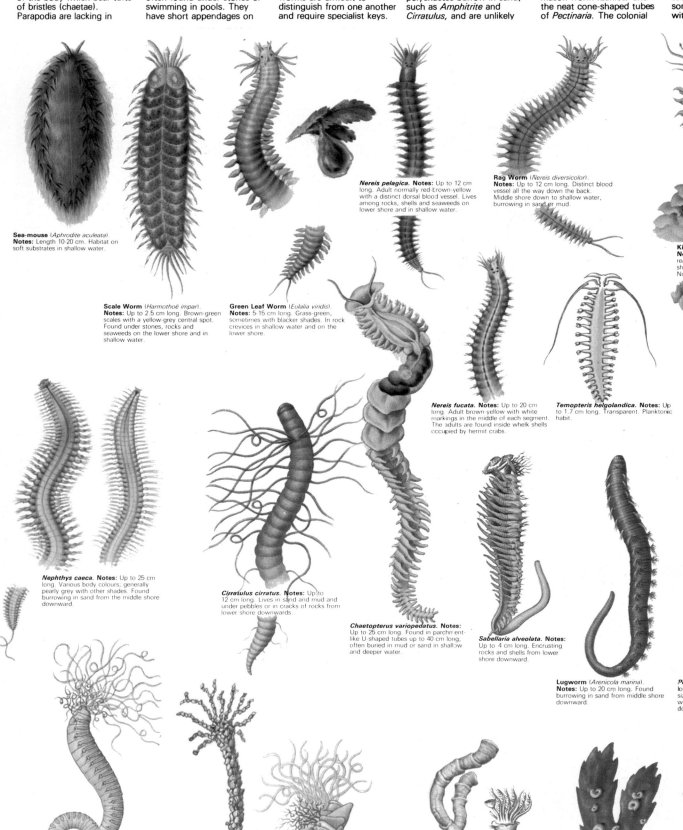

Sea-mouse (*Aphrodite aculeata*). **Notes:** Length 10-20 cm. Habitat on soft substrates in shallow water.

***Nereis pelagica*. Notes:** Up to 12 cm long. Adult normally red-brown-yellow with a distinct dorsal blood vessel. Lives among rocks, shells and seaweeds on lower shore and in shallow water.

Rag Worm (*Nereis diversicolor*). **Notes:** Up to 12 cm long. Distinct blood vessel all the way down the back. Middle shore down to shallow water, burrowing in sand or mud.

King Rag Worm (*Nereis virens*). **Notes:** Up to 20 cm long, occasionally reaching 40 cm. Lower shore and in shallow water, often burrowing in sand. Not found on southern coast.

Scale Worm (*Harmothoë impar*). **Notes:** Up to 2.5 cm long. Brown-green scales with a yellow-grey central spot. Found under stones, rocks and seaweeds on the lower shore and in shallow water.

Green Leaf Worm (*Eulalia viridis*). **Notes:** 5-15 cm long. Grass-green, sometimes with blacker shades. In rock crevices in shallow water and on the lower shore.

***Nereis fucata*. Notes:** Up to 20 cm long. Adult brown-yellow with white markings in the middle of each segment. The adults are found inside whelk shells occupied by hermit crabs.

***Temopteris helgolandica*. Notes:** Up to 1.7 cm long. Transparent. Planktonic habit.

Nephthys caeca. Notes: Up to 25 cm long. Various body colours; generally pearly grey with other shades. Found burrowing in sand from the middle shore downward.

***Cirratulus cirratus*. Notes:** Up to 12 cm long. Lives in sand and mud and under pebbles or in cracks of rocks from lower shore downwards.

***Chaetopterus variopedatus*. Notes:** Up to 25 cm long. Found in parchment-like U-shaped tubes up to 40 cm long; often buried in mud or sand in shallow and deeper water.

Sabellaria alveolata. Notes: Up to 4 cm long. Encrusting rocks and shells from lower shore downward.

Lugworm (*Arenicola marina*). **Notes:** Up to 20 cm long. Found burrowing in sand from middle shore downward.

***Pectinaria koreni*. Notes:** Up to 5 cm long. Lives in tubes made of medium-sized sand grains, laying in sand with worm upside down. Lower shore downward.

Amphitrite johnstoni Notes: Up to 25 cm. Body has 90-100 segments; 3 pairs gills. Lives in twisted burrows from lower shore downward.

Sand Mason (*Lanice conchilega*) **Notes:** Up to 30 cm long. Tube of moderate to large sand grains with frayed appearance at the top. From middle shore downward.

***Serpula vermicularis*. Notes:** Up to 7 cm long. Habitat free-standing tubes fixed to stones, rocks and old shells on lower shore and in shallow water.

Spirorbis borealis. Notes: Up to 0.35 cm long. Middle and lower shore, and in shallow water.

Pomatoceros triqueter. Notes: Up to 2.5 cm long. Common on the lower shore and in shallow water.

Starfish and Sea Urchins

The echinoderms (spiny-skinned animals) are distinct from other animal groups and have a unique five-rayed symmetry, with the mouth in the centre of the body. The skin contains calcareous plates which in the sea-urchins forms a rigid case or test. Echinoderms are an entirely marine group and include starfish, sea-urchins, brittle-stars, feather-stars and sea-cucumbers. The last two groups are rarely found on the shore although they are common offshore, small burrowing worm-like sea-cucumbers being frequently taken in trawls from shallow water over mud and sand. All echinoderms have rows of tube-feet containing fluid under pressure. These can be extended and retracted by the combined action of muscles and varying hydrostatic pressure within the foot. The tube-feet of sea-urchins and starfish have suckers at their ends for walking and adhering to hard surfaces; echinoderms are generally rather sedentary animals.

Starfish

The common starfish (*Asterias rubens*) is frequently encountered on rocky shores and under boulders. It is a fairly large orange-pink starfish and may reach up to 45cm in diameter, although it is usually much smaller. It normally has five arms but starfish are often found with one or more of these shorter than the others, usually through the regeneration of mutilated arms. The body is covered with irregularly arranged blunt spines and flexible arms near well-developed rows of tube-feet on the underside, which help in locomotion. The starfish is carnivorous and feeds mainly on bivalves. When it finds a mussel, it envelops the shell with its arms, gripping the two shell valves with the tube-feet. By a continuous steady pull it gradually succeeds in overcoming the pull of the muscles which keep the bivalve shell closed and, as the shell gapes open, protrudes its stomach through the gap and digests the bivalve inside its own shell. Thus the common starfish is a potentially serious pest of oyster beds and other shell-fisheries. The smaller scarlet starfish (*Henricia*) is widely distributed, extending to considerable depths. The attractive sunstar (*Crossaster*) reaches 25cm in diameter and is found on coarse sand and gravel in shallow waters. Besides feeding on molluscs it also attacks other echinoderms. In contrast to other starfish described here, *Astropecten irregularis* burrows in sand offshore; the tube-feet which in other starfish are used for creeping, have lost their suckers, taper to a point and are adapted for digging. Like other starfish, *Astropecten* is a carnivore feeding on molluscs, crustaceans and other animals which it swallows whole, later disgorging the empty shells.

The brittle-stars have a clearly demarcated central disc and five thin, jointed arms with

Starfish typically have five arms but the sun star *Solaster papposus* is the only British species which has many more. Starfish are radially symmetrical and can travel in any direction using the many tube feet on the underside of each arm. Movements are well coordinated despite the absence of eyes, brain and central nervous system.

Sea cucumbers are soft and rubbery to the touch unlike starfish and sea urchins, which have a hard calcareous skin. However, they do possess the typical tube feet and five sets of feathery tentacles of all echinoderms. Some members of the family eject white threads as a defence mechanism.

Brittle stars, like *Ophiothrix fragilis* differ from true starfish in having a small central disc and very long spindly arms. The arms are usually clothed in thin calcareous spines. They are delicate and readily break off, but can be easily regenerated.

prominent spines and sucker-less tube-feet. They move by snake-like writhing movements of their arms and by pushing and pulling on surrounding objects. The arms are very brittle but regenerate very quickly. Brittle-stars are often enormously abundant in shallow coastal waters but restricted in the littoral zone to the lower shore and rock pools, where they can be found tightly twined among the seaweeds. Both the common brittle-star *Ophiothrix* and the larger

A sea urchin is covered by long spines between which project the even longer tube feet seen here. In the centre of the underside of the animal lies the mouth and a complex system of levers and jaws. Sea urchin shells (called 'tests')

are often sold in souvenir-shops and over-collecting has made the larger species quite rare in places. They are also collected for use as food, the gonads being considered a delicacy.

The underside of a starfish bears large numbers of tube feet at the end of which are little suckers. Echinoderms are the only animals to possess these structures and the typical five-rayed symmetry.

The worm cucumber *Leptosynapta inhaerens* is unusual among echinoderms in having no tube feet on the body; instead they form a small cluster around the mouth.

The starfish *Henricia sanguinolenta* has roughly circular arms. As it crawls over the seabed some tube feet will grip the substrate tightly while others take up a fresh position.

Ophiocomina are found on rocks and sand, and in seaweeds to which they cling with their arms. In contrast, *Ophiura* is a burrowing animal living in sand, emerging to feed when the tide is in. None of these brittle-stars is large, the central disc rarely exceeding 2cm. Brittle-stars are scavengers, feeding in a variety of ways and passing food to their mouth by means of their flexible arms.

Sea-urchins

The sea-urchins differ from other echinoderms in possessing a rigid test with mobile spines mounted externally on small knobs. When the animal dies and the spines fall off these rows of knobs are clearly revealed, together with the holes from which the tube-feet protrude in life and the individual plates which form the test. The regular spherical sea-urchin *Psammechinus* clings tightly to rocks on the lower shore, where it browses on encrusting algae and animals, often camouflaging itself with pieces of gravel, algae and shell which it holds with its tube-feet. The larger *Echinus* is found more commonly on rocks in shallow water and its dried test is a common sight in seaside souvenir shops, often made into a small lampshade. The lusitanian species *Paracentrotus lividus* replaces *Psammechinus* on the west coasts of Ireland and Scotland.

The "irregular" urchins have modified their radial symmetry and become heart-shaped. They are burrowers and live at depths of 15–20cm in sand, using numerous flattened spines for digging. These spines are so dense that the urchin looks almost furry. Tube-feet are largely restricted to the upper surface where their holes form a star-shaped pattern on the fragile dried tests which are often found along the strand line. In living urchins, these rows of feet lie in clearly defined grooves between the dense coat of spines and have a variety of functions, including food collection and respiration. The heart-urchin *Echinocardium cordatum*, commonly called the sea-potato from its shape, is often abundant in sand near the low tide mark. Its presence can be detected by a small irregular hole which marks the top of the burrow through which it draws a current of water for respiration. This funnel is maintained by special elongated tube-feet. Heart-urchins are deposit feeders, taking sand into the mouth and scraping off the thin covering of organic material. The purple heart-urchin (*Spatangus purpureus*) is an offshore species with similar habits to *Echinocardium*, but may be dug up at very low tides.

A guide to echinoderms

The starfish can be separated from the brittle-stars by the small distinct rounded central disc and jointed arms. The sunstar is distinguished from the other starfish by its large central disc and large number (up to 13) of small arms which may be lighter in colour than the reddish disc. The common starfish is flattened, with prominent blunt spines on the dorsal surface. It is usually brownish-yellow above and lighter underneath. The red-purple *Henricia* has arms which are rounded in section, and less prominent spines, while *Astropecten* can be distinguished by the rows of marginal plates along the arms and the suckerless tube feet.

The burrowing brittle star *Ophiura* has less prominent arm spines than the other two species and the arms have a scaly appearance. There are two plates above the origin of each arm. *Ophiothrix* and *Ophiocomina* both have prominent arm spines and are often found together. *Ophiocomina* has a more prominent darker central disc than the other species.

Echinus has a more conical test than the other spherical regular urchins, and a reddish dried test. *Psammechinus* and *Paracentrotus* are flatter and smaller.

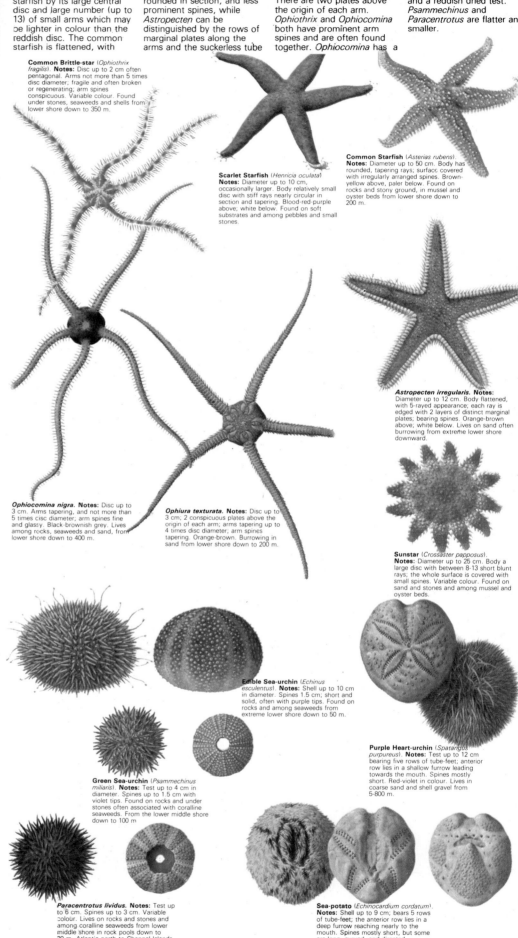

Common Brittle-star (*Ophiothrix fragilis*). **Notes:** Disc up to 2 cm often pentagonal. Arms not more than 5 times disc diameter; fragile and often broken or regenerating; arm spines conspicuous. Variable colour. Found under stones, seaweeds and shells from lower shore down to 350 m.

Scarlet Starfish (*Henricia oculata*). **Notes:** Diameter up to 10 cm, occasionally larger. Body relatively small disc with stiff rays nearly circular in section and tapering. Blood-red-purple above; white below. Found on soft substrates and among pebbles and small stones.

Common Starfish (*Asterias rubens*). **Notes:** Diameter up to 50 cm. Body has rounded, tapering rays; surface covered with irregularly arranged spines. Brown-yellow above, paler below. Found on rocks and stony ground, in mussel and oyster beds from lower shore down to 200 m.

Astropecten irregularis. **Notes:** Diameter up to 12 cm. Body flattened, with 5-rayed appearance; each ray is edged with 2 layers of distinct marginal plates; bearing spines. Orange-brown above; white below. Lives on sand often burrowing from extreme lower shore downward.

Ophiocomina nigra. **Notes:** Disc up to 3 cm. Arms tapering, and not more than 5 times disc diameter; arm spines fine and glassy. Black-brownish grey. Lives among rocks, seaweeds and sand, from lower shore down to 400 m.

Ophiura texturata. **Notes:** Disc up to 3 cm; 2 conspicuous plates above the origin of each arm; arms tapering up to 4 times disc diameter; arm spines tapering. Orange-brown. Burrowing in sand from lower shore down to 200 m.

Sunstar (*Crossaster papposus*). **Notes:** Diameter up to 25 cm. Body a large disc with between 8-13 short blunt rays; the whole surface is covered with small spines. Variable colour. Found on sand and stones and among mussel and oyster beds.

Edible Sea-urchin (*Echinus esculentus*). **Notes:** Shell up to 10 cm in diameter. Spines 1.5 cm; short and solid, often with purple tips. Found on rocks and among seaweeds from extreme lower shore down to 50 m.

Green Sea-urchin (*Psammechinus miliaris*). **Notes:** Test up to 4 cm in diameter. Spines up to 1.5 cm with violet tips. Found on rocks and under stones often associated with coralline seaweeds. From the lower middle shore down to 100 m.

Purple Heart-urchin (*Spatangus purpureus*). **Notes:** Test up to 12 cm bearing five rows of tube-feet; anterior row lies in a shallow furrow leading towards the mouth. Spines mostly short. Red-violet in colour. Lives in coarse sand and shell gravel from 5-800 m.

Paracentrotus lividus. **Notes:** Test up to 6 cm. Spines up to 3 cm. Variable colour. Lives on rocks and stones and among coralline seaweeds from lower middle shore in rock pools down to 30 m. Atlantic north to Channel Islands and the west coast of Ireland; rarely in the western English Channel.

Sea-potato (*Echinocardium cordatum*). **Notes:** Shell up to 9 cm; bears 5 rows of tube-feet; the anterior row lies in a deep furrow reaching nearly to the mouth. Spines mostly short, but some are long, curved, and directed backwards. Yellow-brown. Lives in sand from the lower shore to 200 m.

Partners

The echinoderms provide several good illustrations of commensalism (an association of one species with another). While the commensal benefits from the association, the host gains no advantage. Commensals usually form quite specific associations. For example, a common commensal in the burrows of the sea-potato is *Montacuta*, a small white bivalve, while a related bivalve, *Mysella*, is a commensal in the burrows of *Acrocnida*, a burrowing brittle-star. These burrows also harbour a species of the scale-worm *Harmothoë*. Other scale-worms are common commensals with various echinoderms.

Marine Crustacea

The arthropods, with their tough outer skeleton (exoskeleton) and jointed limbs superimposed on a segmental body plan, form by far the largest division of the animal kingdom. Insects, myriapods and arachnids are essentially terrestrial while the Crustacea are the dominant group in marine habitats, both in the zooplankton and on the sea bed. The crustacean exoskeleton is often thickened by deposits of calcium salts and the jointed limbs are modified in various parts of the body for different functions, including walking, swimming, breathing and feeding. A hardened skin fold (carapace), which grows back from the head, overhangs the anterior part of the body, protecting it and the gills and allowing currents to be set up by the limbs for respiration and feeding. All these developments allow some modification of the basic crustacean pattern and the group shows a wide diversity of body forms and ways of life. Three groups of crustaceans have already been described with the plankton. These were the copepods, and the shrimp-like mysids and euphausids.

Barnacles

The greatest modification of the basic crustacean form is shown by the barnacles (Cirripedia). Their planktonic larvae resemble those of other Crustacea but when they settle on a rock they metamorphose and develop a shell composed of four or six plates of calcium carbonate. The adult barnacle is completely unlike any other crustacean. Barnacles are attached to rocks at the head and their thoracic limbs have become modified to form a feathery net which is swept backwards and forwards through the water to collect particles of food, being extended through small plates at the apex of the shell and withdrawn into the shell when the tide is out. The zonation of common barnacles has already been described. Barnacles settle wherever there is a firm substrate, even living on the skin of whales. Goose barnacles are stalked animals which attach themselves to floating debris, boats and driftwood. Their name refers to the myth that they develop into barnacle geese. A parasitic barnacle, *Sacculina*, looks quite unlike typical forms and appears on the shore as a conspicuous smooth yellowish lump attached under the abdomen of crabs.

Isopods and sandhoppers

Many isopods are found on the shore; like their close relatives the woodlice, they are broad and flat. Most are generally scavengers, although they may also feed on seaweeds. Unlike terrestrial

The small spider crab *(Macropodia rostrata)* deliberately covers its body with fragments of seaweed and other debris in order to make itself inconspicuous to predators. Some sea urchins and anemones camouflage themselves in the same way.

The hermit crab *Pagurus prideauxi* lives in association with a sea anemone *Adamsia palliata*. The crab is wrapped around by the leathery body of the sea anemone whose tentacles are positioned close to the crab's mouth to trap stray food particles.

woodlice, however, they have swimming appendages and are good swimmers.

Crustaceans in general are less able to resist water loss than their terrestrial counterparts, the insects. They tend to frequent cool, shaded, damp places and the isopods are no exception. They live either amongst seaweeds, like *Idotea granulosa*, under stones, or burrow in mud and sand. *Sphaeroma* burrows but may roll itself into a ball to avoid desiccation before the next high tide. Many of these isopods can tolerate low salinities and are common on estuarine muds and in salt marsh pools. The sea-slater *(Ligia oceanica)* is a true woodlouse and is common among rocks in the splash zone.

The amphipods are another diverse group of small crustaceans, which are flattened laterally. Like the isopods, many species are found in estuaries and in some groups, like the genus *Gammarus*, there is a series of species occupying different salinities ranging from sea water to freshwater. Amphipods include the familiar sandhoppers which occur in large numbers under driftwood and dead seaweed along the drift line on sandy shores. Amphipods generally have similar habits to isopods but the curiously shaped *Corophium*, which burrows in fine sand and mud, is a filter feeder. Skeleton or ghost shrimps *(Caprella)* are common on colonial hydroids such as *Tubularia* growing at the bottom of the shore and in the sub-littoral zone. *Caprella* is a predator of small planktonic animals such as copepods.

Crabs and lobsters

The largest and probably the most well known crustaceans are the decapods which include many commercially fished species such as the lobster, shrimps, the Dublin Bay prawn (scampi) and the edible crab, which is described separately (box). The head and thorax of decapods are joined into one and the rear five pairs of thoracic limbs are adapted for locomotion, usually walking but sometimes swimming. In

Goose barnacles *(Lepas anatifera)* do not normally grow on rocks and fixed objects but attach themselves to floating debris. They are thus found in clusters on driftwood, logs and even discarded aerosol cans. The body is flattened and enclosed by greyish plates. Unlike other barnacles it is supported on a long flexible stalk, but it feeds by extending its feathery appendages to scoop planktonic food from the surrounding water.

Velvet Crab (*Macropipus puber*).
Notes: 8 cm or less; first pair walking legs bears strong pincers; last joint of back legs flat and rounded for swimming paddle. Lives among stones on lower shore.

Acorn barnacles *(Balanus balanoides)* exposed at low water or a rock face. When the adults die, their outer plates remain attached to the rock and may provide a small shelter for other tiny animals. Meanwhile planktonic larvae settle to grow into a new generation.

A guide to marine Crustacea

There are dozens of species of British crustaceans, but the largest and best-known are the crabs and lobsters. Although these two groups look very different, they are closely related. A crab is just like a flattened lobster with its abdomen shortened and folded up between the legs. We have about fifty species of crabs around the coasts of Britain, but most of them are unlikely to be found very often. The commonest are the shore crabs and porcelain crabs which live under stones in the inter-tidal zone. The edible crab and lobster are more likely to be found offshore or at very low tide on rocky shores. Live lobsters are blue and only go pink when cooked. The masked crab is a speciality of sandy and muddy shores where it burrows into soft wet sand. Hermit crabs live in old mollusc shells; young crabs prefer those of winkles but as they grow up they move into a larger home like a whelk shell.

many decapods, such as lobsters and crabs, the first pair of these legs bears a nipper or claw-like joint; lobsters have pincers on other legs too. Prawns and shrimps swim by using their abdominal appendages, the last pair of which is flattened and forms a tail fan. The common shrimp lives in shallow waters, moving into estuaries during the summer, and is common on sandy and muddy shores. It is nocturnal, burying itself during the day and leaving just a part of the dorsal surface exposed. Its first pair of legs is equipped with pincers so that in addition to acting as general scavengers, shrimps are capable of preying on small worms and other invertebrates. Prawns show similar seasonal movements but are found more frequently in rock pools where they scavenge using the fine pincers on the first two pairs of legs.

Lobsters and squat lobsters retain the tail fan and use this as a paddle to dart swiftly backwards in an emergency. Lobsters grow to a length of 30–50cm and weigh about 1 kg, although larger individuals are sometimes caught. Their normal habitat is rocky areas, where they live at similar depths to the edible crab; they are not normally found on the shore. They require fairly warm water and a high salinity for breeding and the eggs take nearly a year to hatch into planktonic shrimp-like larvae. Nocturnal feeders, they normally take bivalves, worms and dead animal material. The Dublin Bay prawn *(Nephrops)* is smaller, rarely exceeding 20cm in length, and lives in deeper water on soft bottoms. Like the lobster, these are predators feeding on worms and crustaceans.

Squat lobsters and porcelain crabs are found under stones on the lower shore, the flattened body of the latter, which is a filter feeder, enabling it to cling tightly to the surface of rocks. Small hermit crabs, living in dog whelk shells, are also common on the lower shore although larger individuals, in the shells of whelks, tend to move into deeper waters. A number of other animals may be associated with the shells of hermit crabs, including hydroids, anemones and polychaete worms. Examples of the many kinds of crab are given in the field guide. Most of these live on rocky coasts sheltering under stones and among the seaweed, although the masked crab lives buried in sand and uses its joined antennae as a pipe to allow water to reach its gills. Most crabs are scavengers but also feed on small invertebrates. The life history of the edible crab is typical of most crabs, and involves a larval stage called the zoea, which lives in the plankton and in no way resembles an adult crab. Many decapods, including crabs, are frequently in danger of having a leg trapped or held by a predator. Under these circumstances, they can sacrifice the limb in order to escape by a process known as autotomy where the limb breaks off at a pre-determined location and may be regrown later.

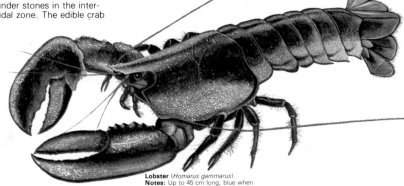

Lobster (*Homarus gammarus*).
Notes: Up to 45 cm long; blue when alive, massive pincers. Lives among rocks on lower shore and offshore.

Masked Crab (*Corystes cassivelaunus*)
Notes: Body 4 cm, longer than broad. Nippers longer than body, (esp. in male) and very long antennae joined throughout their length. On lower shore, usually buried in sand, most coasts.

Edible Crab (*Cancer pagurus*).
Notes: Up to 14 cm long, but usually much smaller. Body 1½ times wider than it is long; crinkled margin to carapace reminiscent of pie crust. Pincers heavy and tipped with black. Lower shore among rocks, most coasts.

Common Shore Crab (*Carcinus maenas*). **Notes:** Body up to 4 cm long, sharp serrations along leading edge of carapace which has a rather angular appearance. Common on all shores under stones, weeds and on mud.

Spiny spider Crab (*Maia squinado*).
Notes: Body 18 cm long with spikes and spines all over upper surface of carapace, often covered with lots of weed. Among sand and rocks, lower shore on southern coasts only.

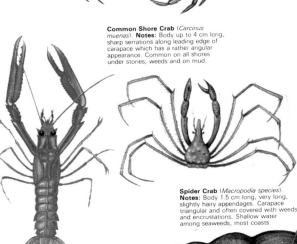

Spider Crab (*Macropodia species*).
Notes: Body 1.5 cm long, very long, slightly hairy appendages. Carapace triangular and often covered with weeds and encrustations. Shallow water among seaweeds, most coasts.

Dublin Bay Prawn or Scampi (*Nethrops norvegicus*). **Notes:** 15cm. Appears like a slender, pinkish lobster. Nippers have sharp spikes along ridges, second and third pair thoracic legs also bear pincers. Lives in mud and sand offshore round Atlantic and North Sea coasts.

Hermit Crab (*Eupagurus bernhardus*)
Notes: 10 cm long, including nippers which are unequal in size. Lives in old mollusc shells on lower shore, most coasts.

Porcelain Crab (*Porcellana platycheles*).
Notes: Body 12 mm long, round, shorter than antennae, and has hairy appearance. Lives under stones in mud and gravel on middle shore on most coasts.

Squat Lobster (*Galathea squamifera*).
Notes: Up to 4.5 cm long, with very long pincer arms and abdomen folded under thorax, giving squat appearance. Under stones on lower shore, most coasts.

Marine Molluscs

All five main groups of molluscs are represented in the sea, including chitons (Polyplacophora), slugs and snails (Gastropoda), bivalves (Bivalvia), squids and octopuses (Cephalopoda) and tusk shells (Scaphopoda). The last group is small and, although there are British representatives, they usually occur offshore.

Chitons, or coat-of-mail shells, are small and inconspicuous, rarely more than a centimetre long, but are common on rocky shores, where they stick to boulders and are well adapted to withstand the buffeting of the waves. The shell is made up of eight overlapping plates which are articulated so that the body can be bent readily. These plates are embedded in the tough skin or mantle which covers the body and hangs down at the side to make a perfect contact with the rock, like that of the limpet. If chitons are dislodged, they curl up like woodlice and so are less damaged by the waves. They feed by browsing on encrusting algae, using their long tongue or radula.

Gastropods

Gastropods are among the most successful and diverse of molluscs and show a wide range of form. Although the coiled shell is characteristic of gastropods, many have lost it, like the sea-slugs, the sea-hare and the planktonic sea butterflies, such as *Euclio* and even *Cymbulia*, which is almost indistinguishable from a jellyfish.

The limpet form has been described under the section on the rocky shore; several kinds may occur on the same shore at different levels. The common limpet *(Patella vulgata)* is usually the most abundant and is found on the middle and upper shore. The shape of its shell varies; animals that have grown on the exposed rock have a higher shell with a relatively narrow base while those which inhabit pools or live lower on the shore have a low broad shell. The two other species of *Patella* found on the lower shore are *P. aspera* and *P. intermedia*. The three species are not easily separated although *P. intermedia* is restricted to southern and south western shores. The smaller blue-rayed limpet *(Patina pellucida)* is an attractive creature that occurs on the lower shore attached to the hold-fasts and stems of kelps and other large seaweeds. It usually lies in hollows which it has eaten out of the stem. Two other limpets found attached to rocks on the lower shore are the tortoiseshell limpet *(Acmaea tessulata)* and the keyhole limpet *(Diodora apertura)*, the former being restricted to northern coasts. Limpets are browsers of algae and, in the case of *Diodora*, also sponges.

Other unrelated gastropods have adopted limpet-like habits, including the slipper limpet *(Crepidula fornicata)*. This animal was introduced accidentally with oyster stocks from America during the last century and is now common on the south and east coasts, where it is a serious pest. It does not attack oysters but smothers them and competes with them for food, since it is a filter feeder, using its enlarged gill to collect food particles. The slipper limpet is a static animal, each settling on the back of a

The razor shell *Ensis* is one of the most active of the burrowing bivalves. Using a pulsating action with its foot it can dig through wet sand as fast as a man uses a spade.

A guide to some sea shore shells

British chitons are tiny and unmistakeable, with a row of eight shell plates along the dorsal side.

The three limpet species (*Patella*) are not easily distinguished but the interior of the shell and the position on the shore are useful guides. The blue rays of *Patina* are characteristic but may fade with age. The shell of *Acmaea* can be identified by its tortoiseshell markings while *Diodora* has a characteristic hole at the apex. Topshells are spiral and conical in shape although not as pointed as winkles. Most topshells have purple or reddish markings. *Littorina neritoides* and *L. saxatilis* are smaller than the other periwinkles; the latter has a rough ridged surface while *neritoides* is smooth. *L. littoralis* has a flat top and the shells are often brightly coloured. *L. littorea*, the edible winkle, is the largest, reaching over 2cm in length. The shapes and colour patterns of most of the other marine snails illustrated are distinctive. The hinge between the two valves of the bivalve shell and the shapes of the muscle scars (marked by mother-of-pearl) on the inner surface of the shell, are useful pointers when identifying bivalves. Scallops can be distinguished by the shapes of their "ears". The elongated razor shells are distinct and the spoon shaped process on the left valve of *Mya* is characteristic of this genus. The gaping shells of the piddocks with the rough end enable these to be distinguished from other bivalves.

The flat-topped winkle *(Littorina littoralis)* is one of the commonest seashore gastropods. It is also one of the most variable in colour, the shells ranging from white through shades of yellow and orange to almost black.

Coat-of-mail Chiton (*Lepidopleurus asellus*). **Notes:** Up to 2 cm long. Found on shells and rocks on lower shore and in shallow water. Atlantic and English Channel.

Acanthochitona crinatus. **Notes:** Length up to 1.25 cm Lives among rocks on lower shore.

Keyhole Limpet (*Diodora apertura*). **Notes:** Shell up to 4 cm long. Found on rocks on lower shore and down to 20 m.

Tortoiseshell Limpet (*Acmaea tessulata*). **Notes:** Shell up to 2.5 cm. Found on rocks, on lower shore and in shallow water.

Blue-rayed Limpet (*Patina pellucida*). **Notes:** Shell about 1.5 cm long. Generally attached to the fronds and holdfasts of *Laminaria* on the lower shore and in shallow water.

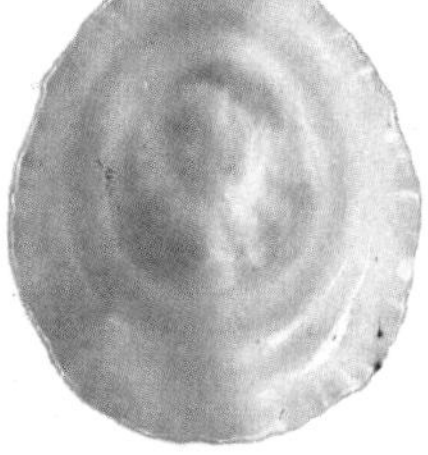

Common limpet (*Patella vulgata*). **Notes:** Conical rough ribbed shell up to 7 cm long. Lives on rocks on upper and middle shore; often found in exposed places.

Patella aspera. **Notes:** Up to 7 cm long. On rocks from about centre middle shore down to bottom lower shore, generally in exposed places.

Patella intermedia. **Notes:** Up to 4 cm long. On rocks on middle shore, often in exposed places.

Gibbula magus. **Notes:** Bumpy coiled shallow cone shell about 2 cm wide. Found buried in sand down to about 10 m. Not found on east coast.

Purple Topshell (*Gibbula umbilicalis*). **Notes:** Shell about 1.25 cm high. Lives on rocks on the middle shore and the upper part of the lower shore. Atlantic and English Channel only.

Grey Topshell (*Gibbula cineraria*). **Notes:** Shell about 1.25 cm high and of similar width. Found under stones and on seaweeds on the lower shore and down to about 20 m.

Toothed Topshell (*Monodonta lineata*). **Notes:** Found on rocks on the middle shore. Atlantic north to Anglesey and west English Channel.

Common or Painted Topshell (*Calliostoma zizyphinum*). **Notes:** 2.5 cm high. Found on rocks and under stones on lower shore and down to 100 m.

Rough Periwinkle (*Littorina saxatilis*). **Notes:** Lives in cracks and crevices and on stones on the upper shore.

Edible Periwinkle (*Littorina littorea*). **Notes:** 2.5 cm shell. Lives on rocks, stones and seaweeds on the middle and lower shores.

Small Periwinkle (*Littorina neritoides*). **Notes:** Shell about 0.5 cm high. On extreme upper shore, usually in crevices.

Laver Spire Shell (*Hydrobia ulvae*). **Notes:** Shell 0.6 cm. Found on mud in estuaries, on the middle shore in brackish water.

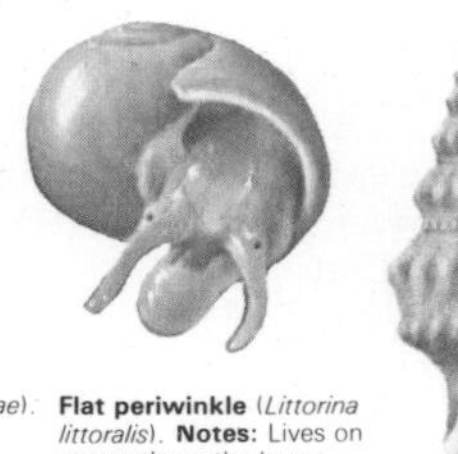

Flat periwinkle (*Littorina littoralis*). **Notes:** Lives on seaweeds on the lower middle and upper parts of lower shores.

Pelican's Foot Shell (*Aporrhais pespelecani*). **Notes:** Burrows in mud, sand or gravel down to about 80 m.

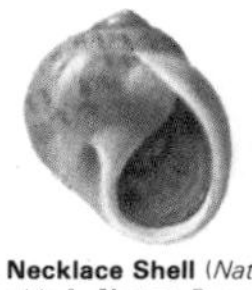

Necklace Shell (*Natica alderi*). **Notes:** Burrowing in sand on lower shore and down to about 70 m.

Violet Sea Snail (*Lanthina exigua*). **Notes:** Delicate violet shell about 1.5 cm high.

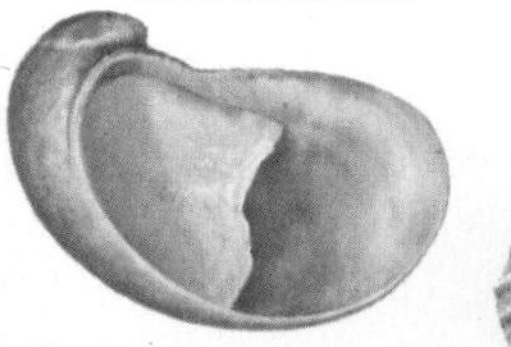

Slipper Limpet (*Crepidula fornicata*). **Notes:** Usually attached to others of the same species and to bivalves in shallow water.

Dogwhelk (*Nucella lapillus*). **Notes:** Shell 3 cm. Lives on rocky shores, except those which are very exposed, in crevices and among barnacles (on which it preys), middle shore.

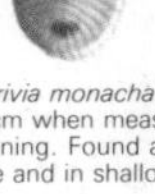

Cowrie (*Trivia monacha*). **Notes:** Shell about 1.2 cm when measured along the slit-like opening. Found among rocks on lower shore and in shallow water.

Sting Winkle or **Oyster Drill** (*Ocenebra erinacea*). **Notes:** Shell 6 cm. Found on muddy gravel, sand and rocks; lower shore.

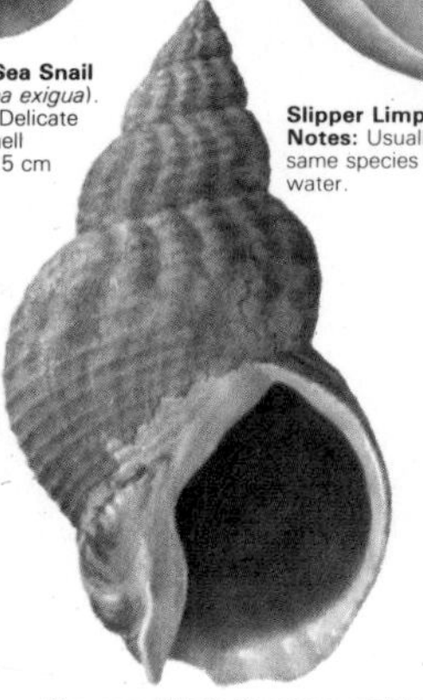

Common Whelk (*Buccinum undatum*); **Notes:** Shell 8 cm. Found on sand and mud and in shallow water. NB empty shells often inhabited by hermit crabs. The large, spongy egg masses often washed up on the shore.

Netted Dogwhelk (*Nassarius reticulatus*). **Notes:** Shell 3 cm. Lives under stones and in crevices, often muddy areas on lower shore.

Leucophytia bidentata. **Notes:** Shell 9 mm high. Lives in crevices and among debris on upper shore and salt marshes. Atlantic and English Channel coasts.

Common Nut-shell (*Nucula nucleus*).
Notes: Shell 1.25 cm long. Found in clay, gravel and sand, shallow water. NB animal lacks siphons.

Dog Cockle (*Glycymeris glycymeris*).
Notes: Shell 6.5 cm long. Burrowing in surface of mud, sand or gravel, shallow water. Mainly south and west coasts.

Saddle Oyster (*Anomia ephippium*).
Notes: Shell 6 cm long. Attached to rocks and other shells (to whose shapes it often conforms), middle shore downward.

Common Mussel (*Mytilus edulis*).
Notes: Lives on stones and rocks in estuaries and in extensive beds, from middle shore downward

Horse Mussel (*Modiolus modiolus*).
Notes: Shell may reach 20 cm. Found extreme lower shore down to about 150 m.

Queen Scallop (*Chlamys opercularis*).
Notes: Attached to substrate by byssal threads when young, usually on gravel and sand, occasionally or extreme lower shore and down to about 200 m.

Variegated Scallop (*Chlamys varia*).
Notes: Living free or attached by byssal threads, extreme lower shore down to 80 m.

Great Scallop (*Pecten maximus*).
Notes: Shell up to 15 cm long. Found on sand and gravel, usually in quite deep water.

Common Oyster (*Ostrea edulis*).
Notes: From shallow water down to about 80 m attached to rocks and stones.

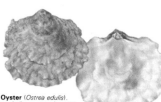

Portuguese Oyster (*Crassostrea angulata*). **Notes:** Shell up to 15 cm wide and about half as long. In shallow water on rocks and stones.

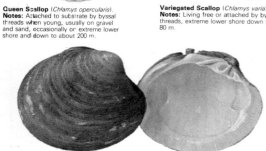

Arctica islandica. Notes: Burrowing in sand and mud from extreme lower shore downward.

Spiny Cockle (*Acanthocardia aculeata*).
Notes: Lives in sand, from about 10 m downward.

Common Cockle (*Cerastoderma edule*). **Notes:** Shell up to 5 cm. Found in estuaries and lower shore downward burrowing in mud, sand or gravel.

Warty Venus (*Venus verrucosa*).
Notes: Burrowing in sand or gravel from extreme lower shore down to about 100 m. Absent from East Coast.

Banded Venus (*Venus fasciata*).
Notes: Found just burrowing in sand or gravel from 3-100 m.

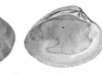

Striped Venus (*Venus striatula*).
Notes: Found burrowing in sand from lower shore down to about 55 m.

Pullet Carpet Shell (*Venerupis pullastra*). **Notes:** Oval shell 5 cm long. Found extreme lower shore.

Rayed Trough Shell (*Mactra corallina*).
Notes: Burrowing in sand and gravel from extreme lower shore down to about 100 m.

Common Otter Shell (*Lutraria lutraria*).
Notes: Up to 12.5 cm long. Surface layer brown and flaky. Burrows in mud, sand and gravel from extreme lower shore down to about 100m.

Thin Tellin (*Tellina tenuis*).
Notes: Burrowing in sand from the middle shore down to shallow water.

Baltic Tellin (*Macoma balthica*).
Notes: Burrowing in mud and sand in shallow brackish water.

Peppery Furrow Shell (*Scrobicularia plana*). **Notes:** Burrowing in mud and sand between the tidemarks.

Large Sunset Shell (*Gari depressa*).
Notes: Burrowing in sand from extreme lower shore down to about 50 m.

Razor Shell (*Ensis ensis*). **Notes:** Shell up to 12.5 cm. Burrowing in sand on extreme lower shore and in shallow water.

Pod Razor Shell (*Ensis siliqua*).
Notes: Shell up to 20 cm long. Burrowing in sand on extreme lower shore and down to about 35 m.

Blunt Gaper (*Mya truncata*).
Notes: Shell up to 7.5 cm long. Burrowing in mud and sand from middle shore down to 70 m.

Grooved Razor Shell (*Solen marginatus*). **Notes:** Shell up to 12.5 cm long. Burrowing in sand on the lower shore and shallow water.

Sand Gaper (*Mya arenaria*).
Notes: Shell up to 15 cm long. Burrowing in mud and sand from the lower shore down to 70 m and in estuaries.

Common Piddock (*Pholas dactylus*).
Notes: Shell up to 15 cm. Boring into soft rock, wood, firm sand or peat on lower shore. South and south west coast only.

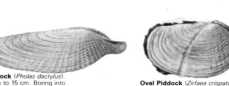

Oval Piddock (*Zirfaea crispata*).
Notes: Found boring in clay and soft rock on lower shore and in shallow water.

Ship Worm (*Teredo navalis*).
Notes: Found boring in submerged wooden structures.

slightly older individual until a chain of eight or more individuals is formed. The oldest in the chain are females, and the youngest males; the males gradually change to females as they grow bigger.

The periwinkles are probably the most familiar gastropods and have the characteristic coiled shell of the snail. They are abundant on rocky shores but are also found on softer substrates wherever there is a firm surface such as driftwood, stones or seaweeds. The four species illustrated provide a good example of the zonation described earlier. The smallest species, *Littorina neritoides*, lives in the splash zone where it is rarely submerged. It is partly air breathing and is more resistant to desiccation than other periwinkles. It is virtually a snail, but still liberates its eggs into the sea; the planktonic larvae settle out on the shore, gradually changing into the adult form as they move up the shore into the lichen zone. The young of the rough periwinkle (*L. saxatilis*) develop within the body of the female so that the small shelled young which emerge resemble the adult in all but size. This species thus avoids the hazards of planktonic life but at the same time sacrifices the advantages of dispersal by water currents.

Topshells are characteristic of the middle and lower shores although, unlike the periwinkles, they do not extend to softer substrates as their more elaborate gills become easily clogged by mud. However *Gibbula magus*, which occurs on rocks at the bottom of the shore, extends to muddy sand and gravel in the sub-littoral zone. This species and *Monodonta lineata* are largely confined to south and west coasts. Since the latter is found on the middle shore, its numbers are markedly affected by exposure in very cold winters. The attractive painted topshell (*Calliostoma zizyphinum*) occurs fairly frequently below the low tide level. The most common topshells, however, are the smaller grey topshell (*Gibbula cineraria*) and purple topshell (*G. umbilicalis*).

The small cowrie *Trivia monacha* and the related *T. arctica*, both occurring in pools and on the lower shore, are the only British representatives of the large and conspicuous tropical cowries. *Trivia* is a carnivore feeding on encrusting sea squirts. Other predators include the dogwhelk (*Nucella lapillus*), which is common on the middle shore and occurs in several colour varieties. It feeds mainly on barnacles and mussels but will attack other molluscs, boring a

The octopus

The octopods have lost all trace of the shell and have a bag-like body without fins and with eight tentacular arms arranged in a circlet linked by a web round the mouth. Two kinds of octopus are found on British coasts. The most widespread is the lesser octopus *Eledone cirrhosa*. This is about 50 cms long and measures about 84 cms across the widest span of tentacles, and occurs all round the coast of Britain. The large common octopus *Octopus vulgaris* is a warm water species which reaches the northern limit of its distribution in the English Channel. It probably does not breed on the English coast and is not common, numbers being maintained each year by an influx of planktonic larvae transported from the French coast. Occasionally a particular combination of temperature and water movements causes a plague, when they may be a nuisance to crab fisherman, especially in Devon and Cornwall. The inshore octopods live among rocks and stones in the sublittoral zone but are occasionally found in pools at low water. Although they can move quickly in an emergency by jetting water through the funnel, octopods spend much of their time on the bottom, and the prey, which consists of crabs and other crustaceans, is caught by a swift pounce from above which envelops the victim in the tentacles and web. It is then torn to pieces by strong beak-like jaws. The eggs, in capsules, are laid in large bunches like grapes in rock crevices. After hatching, the larvae spend some time in the plankton before settling down on the bottom.

The lesser octopus *(Eledone cirrhosa)* is more widespread than the common octopus *(Octopus vulgaris)*. It has a single row of suckers along its arms; the latter species has two rows and is only found on southern coasts.

A guide to marine molluscs with reduced shells or without shells

Two of the opisthobranchs illustrated have well developed shells but only *Actaeon tornatilis* can withdraw into its shell. *Scaphander lignarius* has a thinner shell which cannot contain the broad flaps of the mantle. The large sea hare (*Aplysia*) has no obvious shell and two flaps of skin (parapodia), one each side of the body. It can also eject a purple dye when irritated. *Elysia viridis* is like a miniature sea hare, rarely exceeding an inch in length, and is usually green in colour. *Pleurobranchus* has a characteristic shape, with a dorsal shield which nearly hides the large gill on the right side. The dorid sea slugs may be distinguished by the ring of feathery gills on the dorsal surface. The largest, the sea lemon, may reach five inches in length and has fewer gills than the smaller darker *Jorunna*. *Limacia*, which is less than an inch in length has both gills and processes along the back. The appendages of *Dendronotus* are many branched. The eolid sea slugs like *Facelina* and *Aeolidia* have no dorsal ring of gills but two rows of brightly coloured cerata along the back.

Netted dog whelks *(Nassarius reticulatus)* feeding on the carcass of a dead crab. Other dog whelks take live prey.

Egg cases of the dog whelk *Nucella lapillus* are attached to rocks to stop them being washed away. Most rocky shore animals attach their eggs but not all have tough egg cases; some produce masses of jelly.

Actaeon tornatilis. **Notes:** Shell about 2 cm long and barrel-like with up to 7 whorls. Pink-grey-yellow colour. Burrowing in sand or mud, generally on the lower shore and in shallow water.

Pleurobranchus membranaceus. **Notes:** Up to 12 cm, dorsal shield from under which protrudes broad red foot, 2 head tentacles and a gill on the right side. Orange-yellow-white colour. Lives on mud and gravel in shallow water. Not found on the east coasts.

Scaphander lignarius. **Notes:** Body may reach 14 cm and is unable to withdraw into the shell. Shell about half as long as body, aperture tapers towards the apex. Shell yellow-white. Found on sandy and muddy substrates. English Channel only.

Elysia viridis. **Notes:** Body about 3 cm; flattened and soft; 2 head tentacles; no gills. Green colour. Found on green seaweeds from the middle shore downward.

Sea-hare *(Aplysia punctata).* **Notes:** Body up to 14 cm; almost enclosing shell; 4 head tentacles. Younger individuals reddish colour; older ones brown-green. Found among seaweeds in shallow water and occasionally swimming. May eject purple dye when disturbed.

Facelina auriculata. **Notes:** Body up to 2.5 cm; thin; 2 dissimilar pairs of unbranched head tentacles and 6 groups of appendages on the back. Pale colour; appendages dark red with white tips. Lives among rocks on the lower shore and in shallow water. Not found on the east coasts.

Sea-lemon *(Archidoris pseudoargus).* **Notes:** Body up to 7 cm; 2 unbranched head tentacles; back covered with warts; 9 branching gills in a ring on the back. Yellowish with brown-green-pink markings. Moves up to the lower shore in summer to spawn, otherwise in deeper water.

Jorunna tomentosa. **Notes:** Body up to 4 cm; warts on the back; 2 brownish unbranched head tentacles and 15 whitish gills in a ring on back. Yellowish colour with brown markings.

Limacia clavigera. **Notes:** Body about 2 cm; flat with over 20 appendages of varying sizes; 3 branched gills around the anus. Body white, appendages usually have orange-red tips. Usually found in shallow water.

Dendronotus frondosus. **Notes:** Body about 5 cm; head tentacles are branched. There are many branched appendages arranged in pairs along the back. Yellow-pink-white with darker markings on back. Found among rocks and on sand in shallow water and down to 100 m.

Common Grey Sea-slug *(Aeolidia papillosa).* **Notes:** Body up to 8 cm; 2 pairs of unbranched head tentacles; many appendages carried on the back 'parted' in the middle. Grey-brown. Found on stony and rocky shores, between high and low water marks.

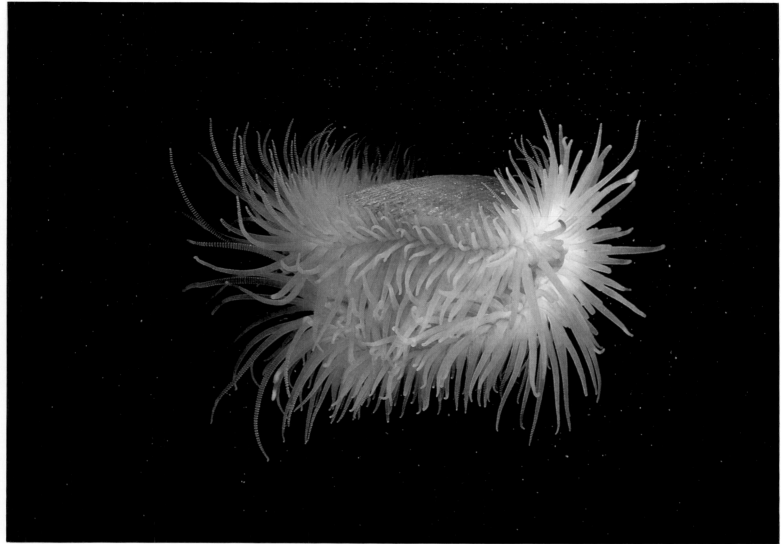

hole in the shell of its prey with its proboscis and rasping out the contents. The related rough tingle (*Ocenebra erinacea*) has similar habits but also occurs where rocks are mingled with mud and sand. The burrowing necklace shell (*Natica alderi*), which lives near the low water mark on sandy shores, also feeds in a similar way, especially on the small bivalves *Tellina* and *Donax*. The netted dogwhelk (*Nassarius reticulatus*) and common whelk (*Buccinum undatum*) are essentially carrion feeders, gaining access to dead molluscs by pushing the proboscis between the shell valves of dead bivalves. Empty pelican's foot shells (*Aporrhais pespelecani*) and tower shells (*Turritella communis*) are sometimes cast up on sandy beaches although the animals live partly buried in offshore sand and mud.

The opisthobranchs are exclusively marine snails which show a loss of shell to varying degrees. This, coupled with other structural changes, has enabled them to adopt a variety of forms and habits, including swimming, which are not available to the typical gastropods, encumbered as they are by a heavy shell. The best swimmers are the planktonic sea butterflies which have been described in the section on plankton. In place of the shell, opisthobranchs rely on camouflage and distasteful substances in the skin to deter predators. The bubble-shells *Actaeon tornatilis* and *Scaphander lignarius* are fully shelled and burrow into sublittoral sand assisted by flaps of skin which partly cover the shell. They occur all round the British coast and feed on small worms and bivalves. The sea-hare (*Aplysia punctata*) grows up to 15cm in length and has a small flat shell which is covered by skin. It occurs offshore among seaweeds on which it feeds but may also be found in pools on the lower shore in spring and summer.

The nudibranchs, or sea-slugs, are a large group in which the shell has been completely lost. Most of them live in deeper water offshore, coming inshore to spawn in the summer. The dorids, including the sea-lemon (*Archidoris pseudoargus*) are broad, slug-like forms with a ring of feathery gills on their back. Some browse on encrusting sponges while *Limacia* feeds on polyzoans encrusting the fronds of larger weeds such as *Laminaria*. The eolids, which include the purple sea-slug (*Facelina auriculata*) and grey sea-slug (*Aeolidia papillosa*), are more slender and highly coloured with hair-like processes called cerata along their back. These processes contain branches of the gut and store poison cells (nematocysts) derived from the hydroids, including anemones, on which the eolids feed. These can be discharged through pores in the cerata to repulse predators.

Bivalves

Bivalves share a basic pattern but, despite this restriction, show a wide range of forms and habits. In most bivalves the mantle covers the body and is itself protected on the outside by a

Sea-slugs are gastropods which lack a shell. Instead they develop finger-like projections in which they store the stinging cells of the sea firs on which they feed.

The file shell (*Lima hians*) is a bivalve which has long orange tentacles projecting beyond the margins of its shell. Normally it lives on the sea bed where it builds a nest of sand grains and shell debris.

The sea-lemon (*Archidoris pseudoargus*) is a sea-slug usually found under rocks. The feathery structures at one end of the body are a cluster of gills around the anus; at the other end are two sensory tentacles.

Sea-lemons (*Archidoris pseudoargus*) pairing. They are common among rocks on the lower shore in summer when they lay their eggs.

The common whelk (*Buccinum undatum*) is a carnivorous gastropod. Here it is crawling over the seabed with its siphon tube extended to sample the water ahead.

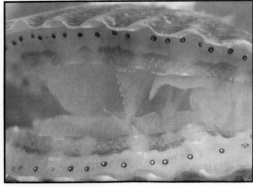

Bivalves have no head and their sense organs have been transferred to the margins of the body. Here, a scallop shows a series of eyes around the edge of the mantle.

shell consisting of two parts misleadingly called valves. There is no head and the animals are filter-feeders, collecting detritus from the water (suspension feeders) or from the surface of sand or mud (deposit feeders) using tube-like extensions of the mantle (siphons). Food is filtered from the water by the gills and is then transferred to the mouth by mucus moving along tracts of cilia. The most convenient way of describing the varied ways of life of different bivalves is to divide them into three groups: the normal group, which are free moving animals living on the surface or burrowing in the sand; the sessile group, which are attached by anchoring byssal threads; and the deep-burrowing group, which are less active with long tubular siphons and a gaping shell.

The normal group contains many common bivalves. Most have a well-developed foot and can burrow into the sand fairly rapidly. Some, such as the cockles (*Cerastoderma*) and the venus shells (*Venus*), are shallow burrowers, with short siphons, and are suspension feeders. Others, like the thin and narrow tellins (*Tellina*), have long siphons and are adapted for burrowing deeper in the sand and for deposit feeding. Razor-shells (*Ensis*) burrow deeply but are suspension feeders with short siphons. The body is extended to the surface to expose the siphons but the foot remains anchored at the base of the

The cuttlefish (*Sepia officinalis*) is a kind of squid. The familar "cuttle bone" found washed up on the shore is in fact a chambered shell within the animal's body.

burrow and the animal can withdraw rapidly if threatened, as the elongated shell slides easily through the sand.

The sessile group ranges from the slightly modified mussel (*Mytilus*), which is simply fixed to a rock or some other solid object by byssal threads, through to oysters (*Ostrea*), where the lower (left) valve is cemented to rock and becomes distorted as it grows to fit the surface to which it is attached. The shell of the saddle oyster (*Anomia*) has an aperture in the lower valve where byssal threads run to the rock. Scallops (eg *Chlamys opercularis*) are attached during early life but later become free and can actively swim by clapping their valves together.

The deep-burrowing group of bivalves includes the gapers or soft clams (*Mya*) which live in mud and sand at depths of up to 45cm below the surface. The two siphons are fused into a single mass and cannot be retracted within the shell if the animal is dug out of the mud. As the gaper becomes older the foot is gradually reduced so that, although the young gaper is mobile, the adult animal is unable to burrow if removed from the sand. The habit of deep and permanent burrowing is shared with the piddocks, which bore into soft rocks, and the ship worms, which are wood borers. In the latter the animals consist largely of siphon, with the viscera at one end and the shell reduced to a small abrading tool for boring.

Squids

The cephalopods are active predatory molluscs with a very reduced internal shell. Active pelagic squids, such as *Loligo forbesi*, are taken in trawl nets together with the benthic cuttlefish (*Sepia officinalis*), which comes close inshore to lay its eggs. The internal shell of the cuttlefish (cuttlebone), which is often washed ashore, has many gas-filled chambers and acts as a float enabling the animals to hover just above the bottom while looking for crustacean prey. The tiny lesser cuttlefish (*Sepiola atlantica*) is often very abundant on sandy shores and can be taken in hand nets. The octopus is described elsewhere.

Octopuses and squids

The cuttlefish, squid and octopus are Cephalopod molluscs. Their most distinctive feature is the set of eight sucker-bearing arms surrounding the mouth. Squid and cuttle have an additional, longer pair of tentacles which can be extended to seize prey but is normally retracted among the short arms. The mouths of Cephalopods have a horny beak (rather like that of a parrot) unique among molluscs. The body is very soft, easily damaged and unprotected against water loss. These animals are therefore rarely encountered in the intertidal zone, but may be caught in trawls or washed up on the shore. The octopus body is so soft that it can "flow" into tiny spaces among rocks on the sea bed. Squids have a thin stiffening rod acting like a "backbone" to keep the body more rigid. This allows them to swim constantly and they are normally only found in open waters. The cuttle's body contains a large "bone", giving the animal a more solid form; this is the "cuttlebone" found cast up on the shore. It consists of many flat chambers in which air is retained to maintain buoyancy, enabling the animal to hover motionless.

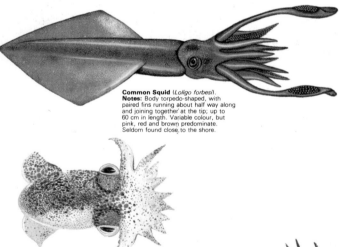

Common Squid (*Loligo forbesi*).
Notes: Body torpedo-shaped, with paired fins running about half way along and joining together at the tip; up to 60 cm in length. Variable colour, but pink, red and brown predominate. Seldom found close to the shore.

Common Cuttlefish (*Sepia officinalis*).
Notes: The mouth is surrounded by 10 tentacles. Body broad and flattened, paired fins run from behind the head to the tip of the body. Found over sand and in bays and estuaries.

Sepiola atlantica. **Notes:** Length up to 5 cm. Body short and cup-shaped with short flap-like fins. Very variable colour; black-brown to pale. Found swimming over or burrowing in sand in shallow water. Atlantic and English Channel.

Lesser Octopus (*Eledone cirrhosa*).
Notes: Arms bear 1 row of suckers; may be smooth or warty. Predominantly red-brown and white below. Found among rocks and stones, occasionally at extreme lower shore. Atlantic, English Channel and northern North Sea.

Common Octopus (*Octopus vulgaris*).
Notes: Bag-like body with 8 arms bearing 2 rows of suckers. Variable colour. Lives among rocks and often in a lair where stones have been arranged for camouflage and protection. Atlantic north to English Channel.

Marine Fish

More than fifty varieties of fish are landed by commercial fisheries in Britain and this number will probably increase as new species, such as the redfish and grenadier, are added by trawling in deeper water off the continental slope. The commercially important fish, however, represent only a part of the wide range of fish which occur in British waters. Many of these are northern species and include arctic and boreal fish such as cod, herring and plaice. A number of Mediterranean and other temperate water fish move northwards during the summer and are found mainly off the west and south coasts of Britain and around the north coast of Scotland. Examples include the pilchard, tunny and several sharks. Most of these fish lay eggs which float to the surface of the water and form part of the temporary plankton. Many of these eggs and the newly hatched larvae are eaten by plankton feeders. The fish larvae, which at first feed on the remains of the yolk from the egg, subsequently eat phytoplankton and zooplankton. They drift with the currents as they are initially poor swimmers. After some weeks of larval life, the young of demersal fish move down to the sea bottom, often in shallow water, to complete their development.

Herring are widely distributed across the northern North Atlantic from Newfoundland across to the British Isles and up into the Arctic. They are (or were) common round most of our east, north and west coasts, but become scarce towards the western part of the Channel and in the Bristol Channel. There are several distinct races of herring, spawning at different times and in different places. Herring fisheries are seasonal, with the boats following the movements of the fish. The relatively high fat content of the flesh of the herring makes it especially

suitable for smoking; kippers are made by smoking herring.

When the herring prepare to spawn they come together into large shoals which are often several kilometres in length and may contain over 500 million fish. Since each spawning female lays 40,000–60,000 eggs a year, herring populations, like those of most other fish, have an enormous capacity for increase. Since populations do not grow at this rate it is clear that an enormous loss takes place at the egg stage and during the early life of the larval fish in the plankton. Herring are the only sea fish of commercial importance to lay demersal eggs. These eggs, which are usually laid over gravel, sink and stick to whatever they touch. After hatching in about two to three weeks, the larval fish swims to the surface where it depends at first on the food reserves in the yolk sac. It then begins to feed on small planktonic organisms such as diatoms and crustacean larvae, until, as an adult, it feeds on larger zooplankton such as euphausids and the copepod *Calanus*. During the very young stages the fish are carried by the drift of the water (larval drift), but as they become able to swim more strongly, move into inshore waters, especially estuaries. From here they often move out as they grow older into nursery areas in deeper water, where they remain until they become mature and join the adult shoals. The majority of coastal North Sea herring become mature in their fifth or sixth years, although the Norwegian race matures later.

A close relative of the herring is the sprat, which rarely reaches more than 15cm in length. Sprats tend to live mainly in shallow coastal waters and have in the past supported small coastal fisheries. They feed on zooplankton and form an important part of the diet of predatory

The tompot blenny *(Blennius gattorugine)* is a small fish up to 25 centimetres long. It lives among stones and kelps on the lower shore around the Atlantic and English Channel coasts. Blennies and other rockpool fish do not need to be buoyant like open sea fish so they lack the airfilled swim bladder found in most bony fish.

fish. The sprat and herring belong to the northern groups of fish, unlike the pilchard, which is a southern species, reaching the northern limit of its range round the coasts of Cornwall and southern Ireland. The eastern limit of the pilchard in the English Channel varies each year according to the amount of warm water entering it. Prior to 1930, there was a decline in numbers, but from 1930 until 1966 pilchards in the Channel increased and even extended into the North Sea, while herring shoals declined. From 1967 onwards, however there was a return to the pre-1930 conditions with more herring and fewer pilchards in the Channel. Pilchards spawn off the south coast of Cornwall, laying floating eggs, like the sprat. The Cornish pilchard fishery was an important one for many years, with the pilchards being canned in oil. Young pilchards taken off Portugal and Spain are canned as sardines. The pilchard is a plankton feeder but takes finer organisms including diatoms.

The mackerel

Another southern pelagic species which is commercially important is the mackerel. Its range extends from the south coast of Norway and northern North Sea along the west coasts of Britain and into the English Channel. Until recently the mackerel was important to the small-boat fisheries of south west England but it is now in danger of being over-fished by larger vessels from further afield. Mackerel show marked seasonal changes in distribution. In late

The lumpsucker *(Cyclopterus lumpus)* has its pelvic fins modified to form a sucker. This enables the male to attach itself to rocks when it is guarding the egg-mass from crabs and other predators.

A male rock goby guards a mass of eggs stuck to a rock by its female mate. Many rockpool fish attach their eggs in this way to prevent them being washed off by wave action.

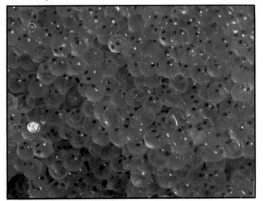

Part of the egg-mass of a lumpsucker. The eggs have reached the stage of development where the eyes of the embryos are visible.

October and early November they move down to the sea bed, where they remain until January in dense concentrations, often in depressions on the bottom. Many of the fish cannot find food at this time although when benthic invertebrates such as shrimps and polychaete worms are available they feed on these. Towards the end of January, the mackerel begin to make vertical movements and form surface shoals, which gradually move towards the spawning grounds. Spawning takes place over a prolonged period from April to June, the main spawning ground for British mackerel being located in the Celtic Sea, south of Ireland towards the edge of the Continental Shelf. Fish which have spawned move back again to coastal waters where they feed voraciously on zooplankton, especially copepods. It is at this time, during the pelagic phase, that the mackerel are fished by drift netting. From June until October, their behaviour changes and they disperse into smaller groups and feed actively inshore, mainly on small fish such as young herring, sprats and sandeels. In October they move down again to the sea bed. The garfish is another pelagic shoaling fish which is sometimes taken with mackerel in drift-nets and has similar migratory patterns to mackerel. The adult feeds mainly on small herring and other fish. The tunny is a southern species which may migrate northwards in the summer into British waters, where it feeds on pelagic fish such as herring, mackerel and garfish.

The grey mullet is also a southern surface-living fish which migrates north in summer and enters estuaries, where it feeds by straining debris and small organisms from the mud, making loud sucking noises as it does so. This shy fish can tolerate low salinities, and shoals of grey mullet may sometimes be seen feeding in salt marsh creeks. Many other sea fish move into estuaries to feed on the abundant invertebrates. In the Thames estuary, for example, well over eighty different species have been collected from power station intake screens in recent years. Most of these fish are only temporary residents at certain seasons and do not penetrate far into the estuary. Examples include the cod, bib and other members of the cod family, and also some flatfish such as the plaice and sole. The young of some fish spend part of their life in estuaries. Young herring and sprats, for example, are known as whitebait and were formerly the subject of important fisheries in some estuaries. The flounder, which is a common flatfish in estuaries, is exceptionally tolerant of changes in salinity and can even survive in fresh water. It feeds on crustaceans, especially mysids and *Corophium*. Like most other resident fish in the estuary, the flounder needs to return to the sea to spawn.

Another group of small fish, the elongated pipefish, relatives of the seahorse, are common in estuaries and other shallow coastal waters, especially among seaweeds and eel-grass, they feed on small planktonic crustaceans and fish larvae. Their grotesque, dried bodies may occasionally be found among debris along the strand line.

The bass is a southern species which migrates into rocky coastal waters and into estuaries during the summer months as far north as Wales in the west and East Anglia in the east. It is a voracious predator, feeding on small pelagic fish. The John Dory is a fish with similar habits and distribution. The lesser weever is a coastal species living in sandy areas, where it buries itself in the sand with only eyes and mouth showing above the surface, ready to catch shrimps and other small prey. The spines on the prominent dorsal fin and the operculum are grooved and discharge a venom which can cause painful wounds.

In British coastal waters there are more kinds of demersal than pelagic fish. The largest groups, and the most important commercially, are the cod family (Gadidae) and the flatfish. The flatfish are well adapted for life on the sea-bed, although their larvae are normal and live in the plankton, swimming upright in the water.

The plaice and the dab have similar habits. Although the latter often lives in shallower water, it probably competes with plaice for food. Dabs are not important commercial fish although taken in trawls as an incidental catch. The common or Dover sole, which is very valuable as a commercial fish, has similar habits to the other flatfish. All feed mainly at night, resting during the day partly buried in the sand.

The cod *(Gadus morhua)* is one of the most important British food fishes. It does not come into the tidal zone but is found in deeper water down to 600 metres living in large shoals. The small "whisker" or barbel projecting from the lower lip is typical of the cod family and is covered with sensitive cells. With the barbel the fish can taste food lying on the sea bed before it is taken into the mouth.

The turbot differs from the other flatfish described here in that it rests on its right side with its eyes on the left (uppermost) side. It is also a valuable edible fish which feeds mainly on other bottom-living fish such as sand eels and gobies.

The cod family has about twenty representatives in British waters, including several important commercial fish such as cod, haddock and whiting. The cod itself is the most important British food fish (worth over £50 million per year) and is a northern species extending throughout the Arctic and North Atlantic and as far south as the Bay of Biscay. In the North Sea the peak spawning period is between March and April, when the cod collect in shoals near the sea bed in fairly deep water. The main spawning grounds in the North Sea are to the east of Scotland over the Great Fisher and Ling Banks, the Long Forties and, to a lesser extent, further south off Flamborough Head. The eggs and fry are planktonic, the latter feeding on copepods. After about ten weeks the young cod go down to the sea-bed and their diet changes to benthic Crustacea including small crabs. The adult fish feeds both at the bottom and in mid-water where it includes pelagic fish, such as herring, and squid in its diet. The North Sea race of cod do not appear to undergo large scale migrations. Cod liver oil is produced from the liver and the roe may be marketed fresh or salted. It has been estimated that the annual catch in the North Atlantic is about two and a half million tonnes.

The haddock has a similar distribution to the cod but spawns in the northern parts of the North Sea at a greater depth. Although both are found together on the feeding ground they have different foods, with the haddock preferring invertebrates such as brittle-stars, worms and molluscs. Haddock are an important commercial fish, being more highly priced than cod,

Flat fish like this flounder *Platichthys flesus* spend most of their time on the sea bed. They lack a swim bladder so that swimming in mid water requires more effort than in buoyant pelagic fish. Flat fish lie on one side (left in this case) and both eyes are found on the other side. The upper surface is pigmented to match the sea bed.

and are often sold smoked in Britain. The whiting, pollack and bib have similar habits to the cod, although they are found closer inshore.

Two unrelated demersal fish taken incidentally in trawls and marketed are the red gurnard and angler fish. The gurnards have a characteristic form with a broad head, well protected by bony plates and two or three rays of the pectoral fin separated into long, finger-like processes on which they appear to walk as they explore the bottom for their food, which includes crustaceans and small fish. Several species of gurnard

The plaice

Plaice are bottom-living fish and are found in shallow waters from the Arctic to the eastern Mediterranean. They are common on sandy grounds but also occur on mud and gravel. Although occurring at depths of over 100m, most plaice are found in shallower water. Plaice feed mainly on molluscs but large numbers of crabs and larger worms such as *Pectinaria* are also taken.

They are important commercial fish, taken mainly by trawling, the most important fishing ground being the southern North Sea. The annual British catch is about 30,000 to 40,000 tonnes. There are several important spawning grounds where the mature fish congregate in the early months of the year, having migrated considerable distances. Some of the most

important grounds are in the southern North Sea at depths of about 30-40m. The eggs and newly hatched larvae are planktonic and the young larvae, which are the normal symmetrical fish shape, feed at first on diatoms and later on copepods. After one or two months the larvae become transformed: the left eye moves slowly across the upper edge of the head on

to the right side of the "face" and the young fish turns over and starts to swim with the left side downwards. The young plaice moves to the bottom in shallow inshore waters and metamorphosis is completed with the development of the dark pigmentation on the upper surface.

Thus the plaice is a fish which lies on its side,

whereas the skates and rays (which are also flat and live on the sea bed) lie on their belly and are, as it were, flattened from above. The skate's back is pigmented to match the sea bed, and its belly is white, whereas in plaice it is the (former) right side of the body which is coloured and the left side (on which it now lies) which is not pigmented. Other flatfish of the plaice family

(Pleuronectidae) also lie on their left side, (eg sole, flounder, halibut and dab) whereas those of the family Bothidae (eg turbot and brill) lie on their right side.

Newly hatched larvae of flat fish live among the plankton like other fish, but undergo a transformation in which one eye migrates to the other side of the head. The fish then turns onto one side, sinks to the sea bed and develops into the adult form.

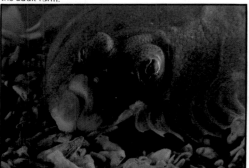

Flat fish of the family Pleuronectidae lie on their left side whilst those of the family Bothidae lie on their right side.

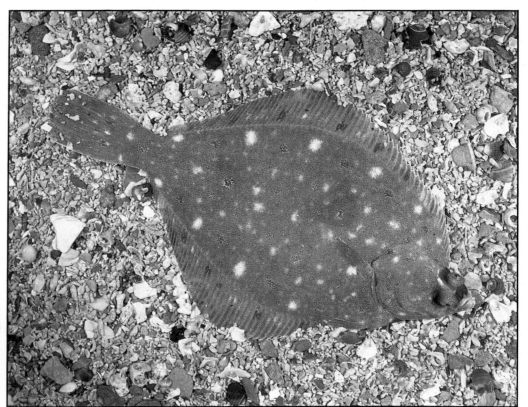

The plaice *Pleuronectes platessa* is an important food fish. It lives on sandy bottoms down to about 350 metres and large numbers congregate off the Thames estuary to spawn each year.

are taken in trawls and all are eaten. The grotesque angler fish occurs from coastal waters to depths of 1,000m and is related to the large group of deep-water angler fish. It is well adapted as a bottom-living fish; the first moveable dorsal fin ray is modified as a lure which attracts inquisitive prey into its enormous crescent-shaped mouth.

Sand eels are essentially fish of shallow water living on sandy bottoms down to depths of about 30m. They usually spend the day buried in sand but are active in small shoals at night feeding on zooplankton. They form an important part of the diet of many commercial fish and of many sea birds such as puffins and terns.

Rocky shores, especially rock pools, harbour many small fish. The long fifteen-spined stickleback is found in pools and shallow water where there are seaweeds for shelter. They make a nest in the branches of a fucoid seaweed and the male guards the eggs. The habit of guarding the eggs is found in many shore-living fish, unlike the fish of open waters which have planktonic eggs and fry. This is particularly shown by the lumpsucker, where the clumps of spawn are laid in shallow water and, in northern Britain, in pools in the lower intertidal zone. The male, which may be over 30cm long, remains to guard the eggs, stuck to the rock by a sucker formed from his pelvic fins. He is particularly vulnerable at low tide to attack by sea birds. Blennies and butterfish are among the most common and best adapted shore fish. Their elongate bodies enable them to hide in rock pools under stones or in crevices. The viviparous blenny is a larger

A guide to inshore fish

Gobies differ from blennies: their pelvic fins form a suction disc and they have scales, unlike the blennies. The first dorsal fin is clearly separated from the second in gobies.

Rocklings are elongated members of the cod family and it is the young fish which are found in pools. They have a barbel on the lower jaw and four barbels on the snout. Sticklebacks have spines in front of the dorsal fin. The lumpsucker is large, has a ventral suction disc formed from the pelvic fins and rows of bony lumps along the sides. Sea-scorpions have prominent flattened heads bordered by projecting spines. The head can be broadened further by raising the spiny gill covers. Wrasses are brightly-coloured fish with a long dorsal fin which has a spiny part at the front.

Straight-nosed Pipefish Sygnathidae *Nerophis ophidium*. **Distribution**: Locally common around Britain except north. **Other habitats**: Shallow water, 0–15 metres algal zone. **Notes**: Extremely elongate. No pectoral or tail fins. Outer bony skeleton often green. Straight snout. (Max. 30cm).

Great Pipefish Sygnathidae *Syngnathus acus*. **Distribution**: All around British Isles, commonest west Scotland. **Other habitats**: Algal zone in shallow water. **Notes**: (or Mediterranean Pipefish). Extremely elongate with long snout, bony outer skeleton. 18–19 bony rings between head and dorsal. (Max. 45cm).

Lumpsucker Cyclopteridae *Cyclopterus lumpus*. **Distribution**: All around British Isles. **Other habitats**: On, near bottom; intertidal zone; large specimens to 200 metres. **Notes**: Ventral fins modified into suction disc. Scaleless skin. Dorsal fin near tail, behind high ridge. Flanks with rows of thorns. (Max. 60cm).

Butterfish Pholidae *Pholis gunnellus*. **Distribution**: All around British Isles, very common. **Other habitats**: Algal zone; 0–30cm; rocky shores. **Notes**: (or Gunnel) 9–13 dark spots along base of long dorsal fin. Very elongate (15–25cm).

Clingfish Gobiesocidae *Lepadogaster* species. **Distribution**: Common around western Britain. **Other habitats**: Rocky shores; algal zone. **Notes**: Pelvics specialised to form suction disc supported by girdle. Dorsal fin longer than anal, both well back and may join tail. (Max. 8cm).

Corkwing Labridae *Crenilabrus melps*. **Distribution**: All around British Isles, commonest in south and west. **Other habitats**: Algal zone, rocky coasts. **Notes**: Large dorsal, spiny and jointed ray portions continuous. Dark spot behind eye, base of tail. ♂ base colour greeny, browny (15–20cm).

Sand Eel Ammodytidae *Ammodytes tobianus*. **Distribution**: All around British Isles. **Other habitats**: Shoals, open water at night – buried in sand daytime 0–30 metres. **Notes**: Small, elongate. Hind tips of pectorals reach behind front of dorsal fin. Protrusible mouth. (Max. 20cm).

Seahorses Sygnathidae *Hippocampus* species. **Habitat**: Algal zone, shallow water. **Notes**: Bony external, ridged skeleton. No tail fin, abdomen coiled to grasp seaweed. Head 90° to body. Fan-like dorsal fin.

Ballan Wrasse Labridae *Labrus bergylta*. **Distribution**: All around British Isles, commonest in west. **Other habitats**: Algal zone, rocky coasts. **Notes**: Large dorsal, spiny and jointed ray portions continuous 40–50 large scales along lateral line.

Rock Goby Gobiidae *Gobius paganellus*. **Distribution**: South-west England to western Scotland. **Other habitats**: Algal zone of rocky shores. **Notes**: Pelvics fused forming suckers; stocky with short tail base. Large head, eyes dorsal. Dorsal fins distinctly edged with white. (Max. 12cm).

Leopardspot Goby Gobiidae *Thorogobius ephippiatus*. **Distribution**: Dorset coast to north-west England; around most of Ireland. **Other habitats**: Crevices; rocky substrates; shore – 30 metres. **Notes**: Shy and wary, eyes dorsal, close together. Orange spotted. Pelvics form suction disc. (13cm).

Montagu's Sea Snail Liparidae *Liparis montagui*. **Distribution**: All around British Isles except south-east. **Other habitats**: Algal zone, rocky shores. **Notes**: Small, tadpole shaped, scaleless, soft and slimy. Rounded pectorals extend under neck. Ventral sucker for adherence. (Max. 6cm).

5-Bearded Rockling Gadidae *Ciliata mustela*. **Distribution**: All around British Isles. **Other habitats**: Shallow water algal zone, sandy or rocky substrates. **Notes**: Elongate with long dorsal, anal fins. Possess 1 barbel on lower jaw and 4 on snout. (3 and 4 bearded species exist.) (Max. 25–30cm).

Montagu's Blenny Blenniidae *Coryphoblennius galerita*. **Distribution**: South-western England, Ireland. **Other habitats**: Rocky shores, rock pools, amongst seaweed. **Notes**: Small. Dorsal fin long, strongly indented forming 2 portions. Fringed tentacles on top of head. Numerous blue spots. (Max. 7–8cm).

Eelpout Zoarcidae *Zoarces viviparus*. **Distribution**: Mainly east coast, occasionally Scottish west coast (northern species at southern limit). **Other habitats**: Rocky shores, coastal algal zones – 40 metres. **Notes**: (or Viviparous Blenny). Elongate; long, soft rayed dorsal with section of weak spines at rear. Reduced scales, very slimy. (Max. 50cm).

Shanny Blenniidae *Blennius pholis*. **Distribution**: All around British Isles, very common. **Other habitats**: Rocky shores; pools, amongst seaweed. **Notes**: Spiny dorsal fin with dip in middle. No tentacles on the head.

Tompot Blenny Blenniidae *Blennius gattorugine*. **Distribution**: All around British Isles, but rare. **Other habitats**: Rocky shores, amongst rock pools and seaweed. **Notes**: Small, dorsal fin long and only slightly indented. Fringed tentacles on top of head. Flanks weakly barred. (Max. 30cm).

fish and may be more common offshore. Wrasses are also common around the margin of rocky shores and in deep pools, and feed largely on molluscs and crustaceans which are crushed by powerful teeth and swallowed, together with the shell fragments.

The cartilaginous fishes include sharks, dogfish, rays and skates. These include the second largest fish in the world, the basking shark (a British species). Unlike this plankton-feeder, the majority of sharks are predators, feeding mainly on fish. Four other pelagic sharks are caught in British waters. The most common is the porbeagle, while the blue shark, thresher and macko are summer visitors from warmer waters and are caught by anglers off the south west coast. The thresher feeds on shoaling fish like herring and mackerel, and swims in circles round a shoal, threshing the water with its large tail fin to concentrate its victims. The remaining cartilaginous fish are demersal fish. The monkfish is a bottom-living shark which lies partly buried in sand and gravel. It is an active swimmer and its food consists of other benthic fish, crustaceans (mainly crabs), and molluscs. The tope and various species of dogfish are essentially

small bottom-living sharks which feed on benthic fish, molluscs and Crustacea, especially crabs. The spur dogfish is caught by trawling and on hooks and is often sold as rock salmon or "huss". Most sharks are unusual among fish in that they give birth to living young rather than eggs. The spiny dogfish has a gestation period of two years, longer than any other vertebrate, even the elephant.

Skates and rays are among the most common bottom-living fish and have some economic importance, only the elongated pectoral fins

(wings) being eaten. They swim by a wave-like flapping of the pectoral fins, the free edges of which undulate continuously while swimming, and normally locate their food by scent. Although the food is mainly benthic invertebrates and fish, rays and skates also feed on mid-water fish. The empty egg capsules of some rays and skates are common on the strandline, where they are known as mermaids' purses. Electric rays have part of their pectoral fins modified to produce electricity (up to 220 volts) but they are a southern species, uncommon off British coasts.

Cartilaginous fish like some dogfish, shark and rays produce large yolky eggs which take up to six months to hatch into a miniature version of the adult.

A guide to sharks

Sharks have a long, tapering body with a triangular cross-section. Unlike bony fish they have five external gill-slits and no operculum. The basking shark can be distinguished from the other pelagic sharks by its large size and elongated gill-slits. The thresher has a very long upper lobe to the tail fin, often half the length of the body. The pectoral fins of the blue shark are elongated and the upper parts are clearly blue. Bottom-living sharks include the tope, smooth hound, spur dog and the dogfishes. The tope and smooth hound are relatively small sharks, reaching a maximum of two metres in length. The tope has well-developed teeth while the smooth hound has flat, unpointed teeth for crushing the molluscs and crustaceans on which it feeds. The smaller spur dog (spiny dogfish) has no anal fin and has strong spines in front of each dorsal fin with associated poison glands.

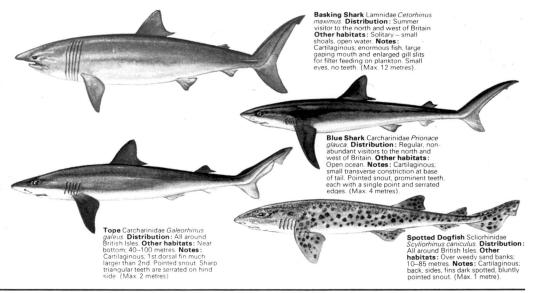

Basking Shark Lamnidae *Cetorhinus maximus*. **Distribution**: Summer visitor to the north and west of Britain. **Other habitats**: Solitary – small shoals, open water. **Notes**: Cartilaginous; enormous fish, large gaping mouth and enlarged gill slits for filter feeding on plankton. Small eyes, no teeth. (Max. 12 metres).

Blue Shark Carcharinidae *Prionace glauca*. **Distribution**: Regular, non-abundant visitors to the north and west of Britain. **Other habitats**: Open ocean. **Notes**: Cartilaginous; small transverse constriction at base of tail. Pointed snout, prominent teeth, each with a single point and serrated edges. (Max. 4 metres).

Tope Carcharinidae *Galeorhinus galeus*. **Distribution**: All around British Isles. **Other habitats**: Near bottom; 40–100 metres. **Notes**: Cartilaginous; 1st dorsal fin much larger than 2nd. Pointed snout. Sharp triangular teeth are serrated on hind side. (Max. 2 metres)

Spotted Dogfish Scliorhinidae *Scyliorhinus caniculus*. **Distribution**: All around British Isles. **Other habitats**: Over weedy sand banks; 10–85 metres. **Notes**: Cartilaginous; back, sides, fins dark spotted, bluntly pointed snout. (Max. 1 metre).

A guide to rays

The shape of the monkfish appears to be half-way between a shark and a ray, with an average length of about 120–150cm. The rounded banjo-shaped body of the electric rays is also distinctive, the marbled ray having a marbled appearance on the upper surface. The rays and skates are flattened, with the pectoral fins enormously developed and fused with the sides of the head. The three species illustrated reach an average length of 90–120cm. Unlike the other two, the stingray has a whip-like tail with a barbed poison spine about half way along it. The common skate and thornback ray have small dorsal fins on the tail, and the upper side of the body of the thornback ray is covered by numerous large sharp spines.

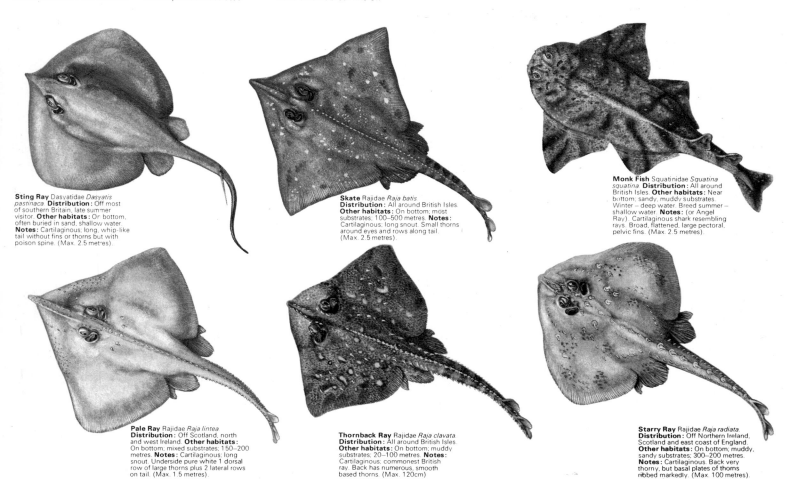

Sting Ray Dasyatidae *Dasyatis pastinaca*. **Distribution**: Off most of southern Britain, late summer visitor. **Other habitats**: On bottom, often buried in sand, shallow water. **Notes**: Cartilaginous; long, whip-like tail without fins or thorns but with poison spine. (Max. 2.5 metres).

Skate Rajidae *Raja batis*. **Distribution**: All around British Isles. **Other habitats**: On bottom; most substrates; 100–500 metres. **Notes**: Cartilaginous; long snout. Small thorns around eyes and rows along tail. (Max. 2.5 metres).

Monk Fish Squatinidae *Squatina squatina*. **Distribution**: All around British Isles. **Other habitats**: Near bottom; sandy, muddy substrates. Winter – deep water. Breed summer – shallow water. **Notes**: (or Angel Ray). Cartilaginous shark resembling rays. Broad, flattened, large pectoral, pelvic fins. (Max. 2.5 metres).

Pale Ray Rajidae *Raja lintea*. **Distribution**: Off Scotland, north and west Ireland. **Other habitats**: On bottom; mixed substrates; 150–200 metres. **Notes**: Cartilaginous; long snout. Underside pure white 1 dorsal row of large thorns plus 2 lateral rows on tail. (Max. 1.5 metres).

Thornback Ray Rajidae *Raja clavata*. **Distribution**: All around British Isles. **Other habitats**: On bottom; muddy substrates; 20–100 metres. **Notes**: Cartilaginous; commonest British ray. Back has numerous, smooth based thorns. (Max. 120cm).

Starry Ray Rajidae *Raja radiata*. **Distribution**: Off Northern Ireland, Scotland and east coast of England. **Other habitats**: On bottom; muddy, sandy substrates; 300–200 metres. **Notes**: Cartilaginous. Back very thorny, but basal plates of thorns ribbed markedly. (Max. 100 metres).

Whales

Whales are the largest animals which have ever existed. They evolved from land mammals and are the most thoroughly aquatic of the mammals, spending their entire lives in the water. The buoyancy offered by the water is important in allowing the large size (the blue whale may reach 30m in length and weigh over 100 tonnes) and the reduction of skeleton, which is characteristic of whales. The rapid death of the larger whales when stranded is often due to the collapse of the rib cage under their unsupported weight when out of water. Not all whales are large, however, and the common porpoise is smaller than a man. Whales have a fish-like body with no hind limbs, fore limbs in the shape of flippers and transverse tail-flukes which have no supporting bones. There is practically no hair on the body; its role in insulation is taken over by a layer of fat (blubber) just beneath the skin. This layer may be 30cm thick in large whales. The nostrils are on top of the head and the rapid emptying of the lungs when the whale "blows" causes the familiar spout, which is not due to the expulsion of water, but to the condensation of water vapour in the breath, together with a fatty emulsion expelled from the lungs.

Whales are able to submerge for long periods of time, in the case of sperm whales for up to an hour. They are adapted to resist the effects of compression when they dive deeply, especially the "bends" caused by nitrogen in the blood. The sperm whale, a warm-water species rarely seen in British waters, has been found entangled in submarine cables at a depth of 900 metres and it seems possible that they visit the sea-floor in search of food.

As a result of the changes in the nostrils, the need to support greatly elongated jaws, and other changes such as the development of the inner ear, the skull has become greatly modified. It seems likely that whales navigate by a similar method to that of bats, emitting clicks and squeaks underwater and interpreting the echoes produced by these sounds. They are even able to communicate with each other using this system.

There are two main groups of whales, the toothed whales and the whalebone whales. The whalebone whales (Mysticetes) are generally large whales with no teeth. Instead, their mouths are equipped with a series of horny plates, the whalebone or baleen, which project downwards along the inner margins of the upper jaw. These plates are frayed into a fringe of fibres which form a filtering system to remove large plankton, especially the euphausids or "krill", from the water which is pumped through the filters by the tongue. Of the six whalebone whales recorded from British waters, only one, the lesser rorqual or piked whale is a regular visitor, although it seems likely that the common rorqual or fin whale is also a fairly frequent visitor. Together with the blue whale and other whalebone whales, these two probably move northwards along the western coasts of the British Isles in the spring, returning south in the autumn to the warmer waters of lower latitudes, where the young are born. The lesser rorqual, the smallest of these mysticete whales, only grows to about 10 metres in length. It is probably more widely distributed than the common rorqual

Whales are air-breathing mammals and come to the surface to breathe. These pilot whales *Globicephala melaena* are among the larger species seen regularly in British waters, particularly off northern and western coasts.

in British waters, especially in late summer when it enters the North Sea around Scotland.

The toothed whales (Odontocetes), distinguished by the presence of simple teeth (and lack of baleen), are more frequently encountered in coastal waters. Eight of the seventeen species recorded from British waters are regular visitors, most of these being porpoises or dolphins which rarely exceed three or four metres in length, with the exception of the killer whale which may reach 10 metres. The smallest is the porpoise, only 180cm long and probably the commonest British whale. Porpoises are most common in British waters in late summer and early autumn although it is not clear where they migrate from. The greatest number of reported strandings occurs in the southern North Sea and English Channel. The porpoise often swims

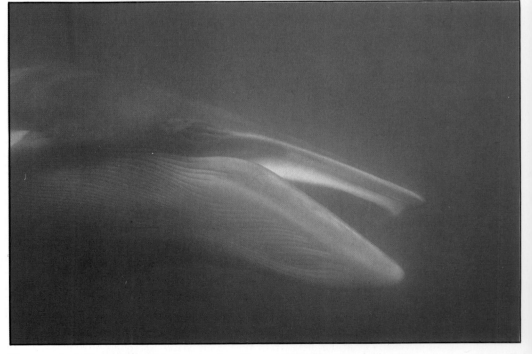

The rorqual whales are filter feeders; swimming with the mouth open, they take in a huge volume of plankton and then close the mouth, expelling water and straining off the plankton on a series of horny plates.

up larger rivers. It occurs mostly in small schools but occasionally larger groups of up to 100 are seen. It feeds on fish, especially herring and whiting.

The common dolphin belongs to temperate and sub-tropical regions, especially the Mediterranean, and the British Isles are at the northern edge of its range. It seems likely that schools of dolphin approach the west and south coasts in late summer and autumn and leave during the spring to move to deeper waters where the young are born. This dolphin is uncommon on the east coast. Four larger dolphins found in British waters are the white-sided, white-beaked, Risso's and bottle-nosed dolphins, the last two being the largest, reaching nearly four metres in length.

The white-sided dolphin mainly occurs in the northern North Sea and around Orkney and Shetland, while the white-beaked dolphin is especially common in the North Sea, migrating northwards in summer and returning in autumn and winter. Both live in very large schools of up to 1,000 or more individuals. The bottle-nosed and Risso's dolphin have similar distributions to the common dolphin and are mainly summer visitors.

Another northern visitor, the pilot whale or blackfish, is a larger dolphin and reaches six metres or more in length. It occurs especially round Orkney and Shetland. Schools of this whale entering bays and sea lochs used to be cut off by local fishermen using a line of boats and driven ashore, where they were killed for their oil. Two larger beaked whales, the bottle-nosed and Sowerby's whales, are occasionally stranded on British coasts. The bottle-nosed is the larger of the two, exceeding nine metres in length. Both are Atlantic whales which stray into British waters while migrating.

Until recently whales, like sturgeon, were "fish royal" and if taken in territorial waters or stranded became the property of the Crown. As a result, much of the information about whale strandings has come from the system begun in 1913 by the British Museum (Natural History), under which anyone finding a whale was required to report this to the coastguard or Receiver of Wrecks, who in turn reported it to the Museum. Although no longer "fish royal",

The porpoise *Phocaena phocaena* is the smallest British whale, only about one and half metres long. Schools of this species frequently come close inshore and many are stranded by the receding tide. All stranded whales and dolphins should be reported to the coastguard or Receiver of Wrecks.

stranded whales should be reported since this provides valuable information about their distribution. The total number of identifications up to 1966 was 1,549. Strandings reflect the decline of the large whalebone whales in recent years and also show that common dolphins have been less frequent since 1947, while strandings of pilot and Sowerby's whales have increased.

A guide to whales

The ten whales illustrated here are the species most frequently stranded on British shores. The only whalebone whale included here is the lesser rorqual or piked whale. Although no longer than many male killer whales, it has a distinctive shape, with no teeth and baleen plates along each side of the upper jaw. The remaining species are toothed whales with teeth in at least the lower jaw. The vagrant bottle-nosed and Sowerby's whales are medium-sized and belong to the group which have a well developed snout ("beak"),

and teeth in the lower jaw only. They feed largely on oceanic squids. The bottle-nosed whale has a characteristic high-arched forehead. The common porpoise, rarely exceeding 180cm long, can be distinguished from other small whales by its blunt snout and lack of beak. The pilot whale, or blackfish, reaches nearly 10m in length and has a very protuberant forehead. The remaining four whales are all dolphins and their characteristic features include a dorsal fin situated about halfway along the back, teeth in both jaws and

a more or less distinct beak on the head. The common dolphin is the smallest at about 240cm. It is variable in colour with stripes along the flanks. The white-beaked dolphin is another small species with a more or less white snout. Risso's dolphin is larger (up to 4m in length) and has a blunt head without protruding beak.

The bottle-nosed dolphin, which is about the same length, has a more obvious beak and has a darker upper side.

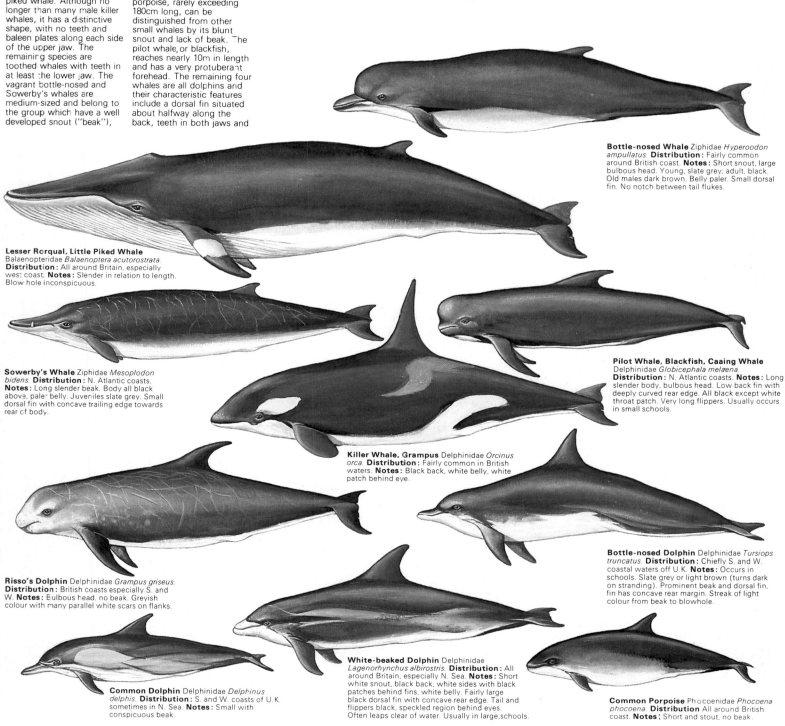

Bottle-nosed Whale Ziphidae *Hyperoodon ampullatus*. **Distribution:** Fairly common around British coast. **Notes:** Short snout, large bulbous head. Young, slate grey; adult, black. Old males dark brown. Belly paler. Small dorsal fin. No notch between tail flukes.

Lesser Rorqual, Little Piked Whale Balaenopteridae *Balaenoptera acutorostrata*. **Distribution:** All around Britain, especially west coast. **Notes:** Slender in relation to length. Blow hole inconspicuous.

Sowerby's Whale Ziphidae *Mesoplodon bidens*. **Distribution:** N. Atlantic coasts. **Notes:** Long slender beak. Body all black above, paler belly. Juveniles slate grey. Small dorsal fin with concave trailing edge towards rear of body.

Pilot Whale, Blackfish, Caaing Whale Delphinidae *Globicephala melaena*. **Distribution:** N. Atlantic coasts. **Notes:** Long slender body, bulbous head. Low back fin with deeply curved rear edge. All black except white throat patch. Very long flippers. Usually occurs in small schools.

Killer Whale, Grampus Delphinidae *Orcinus orca*. **Distribution:** Fairly common in British waters. **Notes:** Black back, white belly, white patch behind eye.

Bottle-nosed Dolphin Delphinidae *Tursiops truncatus*. **Distribution:** Chiefly S. and W. coastal waters off U.K. **Notes:** Occurs in schools. Slate grey or light brown (turns dark on stranding). Prominent beak and dorsal fin, fin has concave rear margin. Streak of light colour from beak to blowhole.

Risso's Dolphin Delphinidae *Grampus griseus*. **Distribution:** British coasts especially S. and W. **Notes:** Bulbous head, no beak. Greyish colour with many parallel white scars on flanks.

White-beaked Dolphin Delphinidae *Lagenorhynchus albirostris*. **Distribution:** All around Britain, especially N. Sea. **Notes:** Short white snout, black back, white sides with black patches behind fins, white belly. Fairly large black dorsal fin with concave rear edge. Tail and flippers black, speckled region behind eyes. Often leaps clear of water. Usually in large schools.

Common Dolphin Delphinidae *Delphinus delphis*. **Distribution:** S. and W. coasts of U.K. sometimes in N. Sea. **Notes:** Small with conspicuous beak.

Common Porpoise Phocoenidae *Phocoena phocoena*. **Distribution:** All around British coast. **Notes:** Short and stout, no beak.

The Coast

Few parts of the British Isles are more than 150 kilometres from the nearest coastline and most people live within 80 kilometres of the nearest tidal water. It is rare to find someone who has never visited the coast. Britain, for its size, possesses one of the most varied and attractive coastlines in the world. The coastal habitats range from towering cliffs, rising up to 300 metres from the sea, to flat estuarine salt marshes and mud flats a kilometre or more wide at low tide; from moving sand dunes and shingle beaches to offshore islands of varying sizes and shapes. This diversity is matched by a corresponding diversity of wildlife. It is difficult to remain unimpressed by the teeming bird populations of many offshore islands but even the salt marshes, which to the casual observer appear dull windswept stretches of coastline with soft mud underfoot, reveal many interesting features on closer examination. Yet behind this diversity is a unity, as the plants which grow in these habitats are linked by their tolerance to salt spray. Many of them do not grow naturally away from the influence of the sea.

Many elements have combined to produce the various types of coastline in Britain but the chief agents in its sculpture and formation are sea currents and erosion caused by the ceaseless pounding of the waves. The coast is continually changing under these pressures, sometimes rapidly, sometimes not. For example, sand dunes may form within a few decades while granite headlands show little change over several centuries. This account, which examines coastal habitats above the high water mark of mean tides, seeks to show why and how this varied coastline has been formed and how, because of its instability, it is susceptible to damage from the increasing pressure of human activity.

Coastal habitats, ranging from precipitous cliffs to flat salt marshes, are exposed to the ceaseless action of the waves. Many animals and plants have become adapted to life under these difficult and varied conditions.

The Physical Geography of the Coast

The shape of the British Isles was essentially determined before the Pleistocene Ice Ages. Examination of a geological map shows a gradual change in the type of rocks running across the country, from the older, harder granitic and volcanic rocks in the north west to the softer chalk and clays in the south east. The softer rocks have given rise to lowlands, particularly on the east coast between the Thames and the Humber, where there are long sections of coastline devoid of cliffs. The harder, more resistant rocks form the uplands of the north and west: some of the highest sea cliffs in Britain, over 300 metres in height, can be found on the islands off the north coast of Scotland.

This basic structure was modified during the Ice Ages by erosion and deposition. Glaciers gouged out valley floors to depths below sea level as they moved down to the sea. When the ice melted, the sea flooded these hollows to form the firths of the east coast and sea-lochs of the west coast of Scotland. The sloping cliffs of parts of East Anglia are formed from boulder clays and other materials deposited by the glaciers as they retreated. Material of this type is liable to rapid erosion both by the sea and, as a result of water percolating down from the land, by landslips. The material from these landslips often forms a barrier which protects the cliffs from further erosion until it is swept away by the waves.

Since the last Ice Age, the coastline has been further changed by two processes—the change in sea level through land and sea movement and the effect of further erosion and deposition. The sea level during the maximum development of the ice sheets was at least 600 metres lower than at present because much of the water was locked up in ice. As the ice melted, the water returned and the sea level rose, drowning much of the land, particularly the river valleys. Since the pre-existing land surface had been exposed to weathering, the coastline which was thus formed tended to be irregular, since the sea followed the contours of the land. The drowning of river valleys produced many of the land-locked harbours in the south such as Poole, Plymouth Sound and Milford Haven. During this period, whole areas of land were lost, for example in the southern North Sea and Cardigan Bay. Ample evidence of this remains in the form of submerged forests and in the legends of lost lands.

During the Ice Ages, the weight of the ice cap caused the earth's crust to sink. This pressure was transmitted laterally so that land at the edge of the ice cap rose. When the ice melted, land levels began to be restored and this process is still continuing. Land in the north west is rising while in the south east, for example in the Thames estuary, it is still sinking at a rate of several millimetres per year. There is ample evidence for these changes in land level. For example, there are numerous beaches which are now several metres above the level of the highest tides, especially in Scotland where the ice was thicker. These "raised beaches" indicate that the land has risen since the ice melted. Submerged forests, consisting of the remains of tree stumps in peat and soil, can also be seen on some coasts at very low tides. The depth at which these occur often indicates that a rapid and significant change in sea level has taken place in the past. When the land mass has risen in relation to the sea floor, the coast outline is initially smooth owing to the lack of weathering although, as a result of differences in hardness of rocks, an irregular coastline may eventually develop under the influence of wave action and weathering. On the other hand, where the land mass has sunk in relation to the sea level, it has already

The rugged cliffs of Rumps Point contrast with their associated farm land and the flat estuary of the River Camel, illustrating the diversity of British coastal habitats.

been subjected to weathering and an irregular coastline is formed as the sea finds its way into every hollow and around every rise.

The coastline as we see it today has emerged over the several thousand years since the sea reached its present level but it is important to realise that it is still evolving under the processes of coastal erosion and deposition. Where rocks are soft, especially on the clays in the south east, the cliffs are subject to rapid erosion by wave action. The London clay cliffs at Warden Point (Isle of Sheppey), for example, are unstable and liable to slip and collapse. It has been estimated that the coast recedes there by about 1.3 metres per year. Chalk cliffs, such as those at Beachy Head and the Seven Sisters in Sussex, are more resistant to collapse, and although they are rapidly eroded at the base by the waves, nevertheless maintain their vertical elevation. Erosion of older rocks is slower and there may be little change over a thousand years. However, since these older rocks are often geologically diverse, the jointing and bedding in the rocks may give rise to local erosion, resulting in the formation of ledges, caves and even stacks of rock isolated from the main body of rock by the sea, such as the well known Old Man of Hoy in Orkney. Many of the small islands and stacks off the coast have been formed in this way, by the sea working along a line of weakness and cutting off a block of cliff.

Material eroded from the cliffs is transported along the coasts and often forms the beaches, spits and marshes which are a significant part of the coastline. These low-lying areas of deposition are subject to rapid change. Examples include Dungeness and Orfordness.

A guide to some interesting coastal sites

1 Westray, Orkney. The Westray group of islands has 19 out of the 24 regularly breeding British seabirds, a greater diversity than anywhere else. Part RSPB. HY 45 45.

2 North Hoy, Orkney. West coast of Hoy has cliff walls reaching to 330 m at St. John's Head. A stack, The Old Man (137 m), is a famous geomorphological feature. HY 18 03.

3 North Rona and Sula Sgeir. Two isolated islands 70 km from Cape Wrath. Large breeding colony of grey seals on North Rona and young gannets from Sula are still harvested. NNRs. HW 81 32 & HW 62 30.

4 Machair on South Uist, Western Isles. Dunes along the low-lying west coast give rise to machair, a calcareous grassland which is often grazed. Easily damaged if sand is exposed. NF 76 59.

5 Waterstein Head, Inverness-shire. A precipitous cliff on the west coast of Skye reaching over 300 m in height. Formed from basalt this headland shows minor cliffing near sea level. NG 14 47.

6 South Ardnamurchan Coast, Argyll. A narrow rocky shore of low boulders and bedrock, bordered by grassy cliff terraces and wooded slopes. Most westerly point on mainland. Mild climate allows rich flora. NM 46 64 to NM 78 61.

7 Staffa, Argyll. The middle zone of the cliffs on the west side of this privately owned island shows a columnar structure formed by the contraction of basalt on cooling. Includes Fingal's Cave. NM 32 35.

8 Jura, Argyll. The west coast of the island of Jura shows a series of raised beaches at the 8 m and 32 m levels.

9 South-west coast of Ireland. The rugged coast of Kerry and west Cork has a mild climate and harbours several 'lusitanian' species of animals and plants characteristic of Mediterranean regions which are rarely found elsewhere in the British Isles. They include the striking spotted Kerry slug.

10 Giant's Causeway, Antrim. Well known promontory formed of closely packed basaltic columns, up to 40,000 in number. Most are five or six sided and are formed by the contraction of the molten rock on cooling.

11 Rathlin Island, Antrim. Large sparsely inhabited island covered largely by heath and rough grassland. North and west coasts consist of tall cliffs providing nesting sites for several thousands of seabirds. Part RSPB reserve. Access by boat from Ballycastle.

12 Mull of Galloway, Dumfries. High rugged cliffs supporting a varied seabird population and a range of plants. From the cliff top, England, Ireland and the Isle of Man can be seen. RSPB. NX 15 30.

13 Caerlaverock, Dumfries. Salt marsh and sandy foreshore showing development of marsh. Managed as wildfowl refuge and shelters in winter barnacle, pink-footed and greylag geese. NNR 5469 ha. NY 04 67.

14 St. Bees Head, Cumbria. Steep sandstone cliffs up to 100 m high supporting a large colony of cliff-nesting sea birds, including black guillemot. Ledges also with maritime plants. RSPB. NX 94 14.

15 Ainsdale Sand Dunes, Merseyside. These show a full range of dunes from the foreshore through to pinewoods. They support a range of wildlife including the rare sand lizard and natterjack toad. NNR 492 ha. SD 28 10.

16 Menai Straits. The Straits are formed from three separate drowned valleys. They have exposed a range of igneous and sedimentary rocks including well marked dykes. SH 53 70.

17 South Stack, Anglesey. High cliffs with breeding colonies of sea birds including choughs. The cliffs can be observed from steps which descend 50 m to the lighthouse. RSPB. SH 20 83.

18 Newborough Warren, Anglesey. Covering an area of over 600 ha, this is one of the largest dune systems in western Britain. Habitats range from bare sand to grassland. NNR 633 ha. SH 40 68.

19 Morfa Harlech, Gwynedd. Much of this area is salt marsh together with a system of young sand dunes which are actively growing. This diverse area supports a wide range of plants. NNR 491 ha. SH 56 25.

20 Ro Wen, Gwynedd. Just south of Barmouth this shingle and sand spit nearly blocks the estuary of the Mawddach. This bar has been formed by northward-directed beach-drifting. SH 62 14.

21 St. David's Head, Dyfed. Steeply sloping cliffs of mainly acid rocks with heathland giving way to species rich grassland in spray zone. Choughs, ravens and buzzards breed here. SM 72 27 to SM 74 29.

22 Skomer Island, Dyfed. Home of large numbers of breeding birds including Manx shearwaters, puffins, guillemots and razorbills. Mammals include a breeding colony of the grey seal and a distinct race of the bank vole. West Wales NT. Restricted access. SM 73 09.

23 Tenby Peninsula, Dyfed. Fine example of Carboniferous Limestone cliffs cut in a level plateau. Stacks, arches and caves common. Rich plant communities especially near Stackpole Head. SR 99 94.

24 Whiteford, Dyfed. Calcareous sand dunes, salt marshes and mud flats on the south side of the Burry estuary provide an important over-wintering area for wildfowl. NNR 782 ha. SS 44 95.

25 Slimbridge, Gloucester. Expanse of salt marsh attracting many wildfowl in winter. National Wildfowl Refuge managed by the Wildfowl Trust together with a collection of captive wildfowl. SO 72 05.

26 Lundy Island. This inhabited, privately owned island, formed from granite, has an area of over 250 ha and is largely covered by pasture with rocky headlands. Seabird colonies. Limited access. SS 14 45.

27 Braunton Burrows, Devon. Large sand dune system lying at the mouth of an estuary. Many of the dune ridges rise to 30 m or more. Rich flora and fauna. NNR 604 ha. SS 46 32.

28 The Lizard. Cornwall. Formed from serpentine, an uncommon rock in Britain. Supports a diverse plant community including some species found nowhere else in Britain. The Cornish heath grows here. Part NNR 42 ha. SW 66 17 to SW 79 19.

29 Isles of Scilly, Cornwall. A group of about 50 islands composed of granite continuous with that of the mainland. The climate is exceptionally mild and they provide a home for uncommon plants and animals. SV 90 12.

30 Slapton Ley, Devon. A large freshwater lagoon formed in post-glacial times by the damming of a marine bay by a shingle bar. The Ley contains a rich community of freshwater organisms. Part FSC reserve, limited access. SX 82 44.

31 Dawlish Warren, Devon. A double sand spit across the mouth of the Exe. The inner ridge is stable but the outer, longer ridge is gradually being eroded away by the sea. SX 98 79.

32 Chesil Beach, Dorset. One of the largest shingle beaches in Britain, enclosing a large tidal lagoon (The Fleet) which harbours many duck in winter. There is a characteristic shingle flora. SSSI. SY 56 84 to SY 67 75.

33 Poole Harbour, Dorset. This land locked harbour is a drowned valley which has become enclosed by the growth of sand and shingle beaches on either side of the entrance. Part NNR. SZ 00 89.

34 The Needles, Isle of Wight. Chalk stacks continuing the main chalk spine of the Isle of Wight. This chalk is highly folded and compressed which renders it unusually resistant to erosion. SZ 29 84.

35 Seven Sisters, E. Sussex. The sea eroding the soft Upper Chalk has produced the present outline of vertical cliffs from the valleys of former streams which drained seawards. TV 51 97 to TV 59 95.

36 Dungeness, Kent. The most extensive development of shingle in the British Isles. An important staging point for migrating birds, and flooded gravel pits provide nesting sites for terns. Part RSPB, limited access. TR 07 18.

37 Warden Point, Sheppey, Kent. Fossil sharks' teeth, pieces of fossil wood bored by *Teredo* and other plant remains are deposited on the beach by rapid erosion of the London Clay cliffs. TR 03 73.

38 North Kent Marshes. The low-lying mud flats, salt marshes and rough grazing marsh of the Medway (TQ 88 72) and Swale part NNR (TR 00 66) estuaries support a large overwintering population of wildfowl and waders.

39 Orfordness, Suffolk. One of the largest shingle spits in the country which diverts the mouth of the river Alde eleven miles southwards. Supports a well developed shingle flora. Part NNR, part RSPB, limited access. TM 40 46.

40 Dunwich, Suffolk. A thriving mediaeval port and city has disappeared here through cliff erosion, after the harbour was closed by drifting shingle, leaving a small hamlet. TM 48 71.

41 Winterton Dunes, Norfolk. Wide sand dune system has developed in front of an old cliff line marking the original shore. A wide range of dune habitats are present. NNR 105 ha. restricted access. TG 46 24.

42 Sheringham Cliffs, Norfolk. Formed from glacial deposits of sand, gravel and clay, these cliffs are subject to severe erosion and show evidence of land slips. TG 17 43.

43 North Norfolk Coast. The coast between Hunstanton and Weybourne demonstrates well the constructive action of the sea. All stages in the formation of dunes, marshes and spits are visible. TF 99 46.

44 Gibraltar Point, Lincolnshire. Extensive area of sand dunes and salt marshes showing succession of plant communities. Important shelter for migrant and wintering waders and wildfowl. LNR. Lincolnshire Trust for Nature Conservation. TF 56 58.

45 Flamborough Head and Bempton Cliffs, Humberside. Impressive chalk cliffs rising over 100 m sheer from the sea. Nesting colonies of thousands of seabirds including guillemots, kittiwakes, razorbills, puffins, fulmars and gannets. RSPB part access. TA 14 75.

46 Teesmouth, Cleveland. Estuary polluted by urban-industrial complex yet important staging post for migrating wildfowl and waders. Mud-flats and saltings support resident wader population of national importance. Includes several SSSIs. NZ 54 27.

47 Farne Islands, Northumberland. Group of small islands formed by outcrop of deeply fissured igneous rock. Large breeding colonies of sea birds including terns and auks, and grey seals. NT limited access, SSSI. NU 23 37.

48 Bass Rock, E. Lothian. Conical rocky island, flanked by sheer cliffs rising to 100 m. Site of a large gannet colony which was harvested for food until 1885. NT 60 87.

49 Tentsmuir Point, Fife. Area showing coastal sand accretion and subsequent colonisation by plants to form sand dunes. Dune succession leads to heathland much of which has been afforested. NNR 505 ha. limited public access. NO 50 27.

50 Sands of Forvie, Aberdeenshire. At mouth of Ythan estuary. Sand dunes, said to cover houses, with slacks and dune heath. Good series of dune plant communities and breeding colonies of birds. NNR 718 ha. limited public access. NK 02 27.

51 Loch of Strathbeg, Aberdeenshire. Fresh water lagoon formed by a shingle and sand bar. Tidal until the eighteenth century. Important area for migrating wildfowl including whooper swans and geese. RSPB limited public access. NK 08 59.

52 Culbin Sands, Morayshire. Area of shingle formations and extensive sand dunes, the older ridges reaching 30 m in height. Afforested sand dunes — FC. Flats and salt marsh enclosed by bars provides feeding ground for many birds. NJ 92 60.

53 Caithness Coast. Long stretches of impressive Old Red Sandstone cliffs. Weathering slowly but producing some fine stacks, especially near Duncansby Head. Large colonies of breeding seabirds. ND 40 73.

Abbreviations:

NCC	Nature Conservancy Council
FC	Forestry Commission
RSPB	Royal Society for the Protection of Birds
NT	National Trust
NNR	National Nature Reserve
FNR	Forest Nature Reserve
NP	National Park
FNR (I)	Forest Nature Reserve (in Ireland)

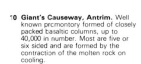

Estuaries, Flats and Salt Marshes

The estuary is that region at the mouth of a river where sea water is diluted by the inflow of fresh water derived from land drainage, forming a zone of variable salinity. Most British estuaries have been formed by the drowning of river valleys by a long-term rise in sea level or, more rarely, by land subsidence. Typically they have a funnel-like topography, the lower estuary being flanked by wide intertidal mudflats and extensive salt marshes, and dissected by tortuous drainage channels. This pattern may be modified by sea walls, where marshes have been reclaimed for grazing. The intertidal zone becomes gradually narrower and steeper in the upper reaches of the estuary.

The animals and plants which live in the estuary must adapt to cope with some of the most variable conditions on earth. Environments such as deserts may be more extreme but only an estuary presents conditions which are continually changing. For example, tiny laver spire snails living at the surface of the mud may be exposed at low tide to the full heat of the sun during the day and to frosts at night. They also face the dangers of drying out between tides. Worse still is the problem of changing salinities, since animals and plants need to maintain the water and salt contents of their bodies within narrow limits. If a marine animal, with blood as salty as sea water, is placed in fresh water, it will absorb water, swell up uncontrollably and die.

Salinity problems

The zone where sea and fresh water mix varies with the state of the tide and the quantity of fresh water flowing into the estuary. Thus the salinity at any particular point may vary widely during the course of a single tide. Where the outflow of fresh water is large, it tends to flow over the denser incoming sea water causing a vertical salinity gradient. In most British estuaries, however, the waves and tidal currents are sufficiently strong to ensure complete mixing of the two water bodies, and there is a gradual change from sea water to fresh water.

In sheltered locations, where the surface of the mud flats is relatively stable and tidal currents are not too strong, salt marshes develop above the level of neap high tides, with a pronounced zoning of plants as the marsh slopes up very gradually inland. Plants in the upper zone may be submerged for only a few hours each month during the highest tides, while plants at the bottom of the marsh are submerged for several hours each day. Glassworts are common primary colonisers of bare mud, but they cannot withstand strong currents as their roots are shallow and their place is often taken by the more robust rice-grass, particularly on soft muds. The effect of tidal currents is reduced as rooted plants become established and plant debris becomes tangled among the stems, trapping more mud. The level of the marsh thus gradually rises and it becomes flooded less

Field example: The River Great Ouse estuary

The River Great Ouse Estuary is situated in the south east corner of the Wash just north of King's Lynn in Norfolk. The river is canalised up to the point of entry into the Wash, and is tidal for several kilometres upstream. The Wash, into which it flows, is a tidal embayment on the Norfolk-Lincolnshire border. Beyond the estuary the river channel meanders across the mud and sand flats. On either side of the estuary there are areas of salt marsh, which have been partially reclaimed for agriculture by a series of parallel sea walls at different times in the past. Reclamation has been carried out since Saxon times by the piecemeal enclosure of sections of the salt marsh. The land to the east of the estuary was mostly reclaimed during the twentieth century, while some of that to the west was reclaimed in the eighteenth century to provide prime agricultural land as soon as the soil salinity declined. This usually happens a few years after initial reclamation and it will then support a wide variety of crops. Some of the marsh land behind the sea wall and the upper parts of the salt marshes are grazed marsh grassland, but further inland the fine soil is used for arable farming.

The older sea walls are rich in plant species, including rarities such as the small red goosefoot. The dykes and remnants of old creeks also contain rare species like the coiled pondweed. Outside the sea wall, salt marsh forms a fringe at the upper tidal levels, divided by the river channel. This fringe is narrow because the older portions have been reclaimed.

Species characteristic of the brackish estuarine transition are found only on the river banks, while the mud flats are colonised by several algae. In the winter the sand and mud flats are very important feeding grounds for waders and wildfowl. They are also an important source of cockles, mussels and brown shrimps.

The tidal sand flats of the Wash form the principal British nursery grounds for the common seal *(Phoca vitulina)*. Several hundred pups are born there each summer.

frequently. Plants which are less tolerant of salt become established, more mud accumulates and eventually the marsh is submerged only by the very highest tides.

Sea Manna grass forms a zone immediately above the glasswort. This narrow-leaved grass spreads to form a continuous turf which acts as an effective filter. Sea aster and herbaceous seablite are also common in this zone. A general salt marsh community develops as the level of the marsh continues to rise, and sea lavender may be so abundant that it forms a purple carpet, contrasting with the pink flowers of the thrift which is often dominant in drier areas. The winding courses of creeks cut by the scouring tides are marked by grey-green ribbons of sea purslane growing along their banks. Grasses, especially the ubiquitous red fescue, are often

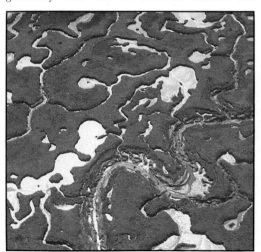

In sheltered estuaries, salt marshes develop at the edge of mud flats as halophytic plants become established. Small creeks cut through the marsh to form intricate patterns.

Salt marsh at low tide showing green algae growing on the mud in creeks and raised banks covered by shrubby sea purslane which stabilises the marsh by trapping more mud and debris.

The flowers of sea lavender, one of the most attractive of halophytic plants, form a purple carpet over the middle levels of the salt marsh as the accumulating mud becomes more stable.

Estuarine mud flats, rich in nutrients, harbour numerous invertebrates. The picture shows a mass of the detritus-feeding snail *Hydrobia* together with the scavenging shore crab *Carcinus*.

The rich invertebrate life of estuarine mud flats attracts dense flocks of wading birds such as the thousands of knot, seen here in flight in the Cheshire Dee estuary during winter.

found at the top of the marsh, particularly if it is grazed. The landward edge of the marsh may be marked by a zone of tall salt-mud and sea rushes.

Salt marsh animals come from two sources: terrestrial animals which can adapt to increasingly saline conditions, plus a few muddy shore animals which can cope with the increasingly drier conditions of the salt marsh. Sandhoppers, feeding on decaying vegetation, may be found in large numbers under driftwood, together with several species of small snail, including the laver spire shell. Terrestrial animals include insects, spiders and other arthropods which can tolerate brief periods of immersion. The wolf spider, which hunts by sight, chasing its prey and leaping on it, has a hairy body which traps a supply of air when immersed. Among the more common insects are brightly coloured plant bugs, caterpillars feeding on plants of the salt marsh community, and predatory ground beetles, which hunt over the surface of the mud.

Although conditions in an estuary are so variable and difficult, it is nevertheless a very productive area in terms of both plants and animals. The main site of plant production is the salt marsh. It has been estimated that the quantity of material which can be harvested from rice-grass may be three or four times greater than that from an equivalent area of agricultural grassland. Fresh supplies of plant nutrients are continually brought by the river and sea into the estuary. Most of the plant material produced by the salt marshes is eventually carried by the tides into the estuary as detritus, and, together with debris carried down by the river, supplies abundant food for the many invertebrates living in the mud flats. The lack of diversity of species is compensated for by the large numbers of individuals living in the estuary. It has been estimated that a single square metre of estuarine mud might contain up to sixty thousand laver spire snails, a similar number of the small crustacean *Corophium,* several thousand ragworms or over a hundred thousand *Tubifex* worms, although obviously not all at the same time. These huge populations of invertebrates provide food for the large number of fishes and birds which feed in estuaries.

The estuary and salt marsh ecosystem

The estuary is not a closed system like a lake or wood. Material is regularly added by the river and incoming tide. It is also regularly removed by the outgoing tide. Water movement is nevertheless very slow, allowing the deposition of fine mud which would normally be washed away. This forms extensive flat areas; if they were sloping more, water would run off faster and wash the mud away. Mudflats are therefore permanently wet and usually poorly aerated.

Energy from the sun is needed by green plants for photosynthesis, the process by which CO$_2$ (from the air or water) is used to build up plant tissues.

Land-based carnivores. At low tide, estuaries are used as feeding grounds (especially in winter) by large numbers of waders and other birds. The food they take away represents a loss from the estuarine ecosystem.

Light penetration is usually negligible in the muddy waters of estuaries, so phytoplankton production is relatively low.

Nutrients and detritus carried in by rivers. Agricultural fertilisers and urban wastes such as sewage and refuse enrich the water.

Herbivores. Animals which feed on the saltmarsh include residents (mainly invertebrates) and birds such as brent geese, which fly in to feed at low tide.

Primary producers. Most of the plant production in the estuary is by the saltmarsh and mud flat species when they are not covered by high tides.

Salt marsh plants

Bare, tidal mud flats

High tide level

Low tide level

Big input of detritus and nutrients with every tide.

Some organic material accumulates in estuarine mud where lack of oxygen hinders many animals which might have consumed it. Anaerobic worms and also many bacteria can use this material, but their special type of oxygen-free respiration causes hydrogen sulphide to be formed, imparting a nasty smell to the mud.

Detritus feeders in the mud. Most of the animals in estuaries feed on detritus swept in from terrestrial and marine ecosystems, rather than on plant material produced within the estuary itself. Many are filter feeders (notably bivalve molluscs which can reach astronomical numbers) which trap food particles from the water. Others are deposit feeders (mostly worms) which take in mud and digest from it what little nutrient material it may contain. Larger scavengers like crabs and fish actively seek out edible items on the mud surface, usually when the tide is in, but some, like gulls, may do so at low tide.

Sea-based predators. When the tide is in, marine creatures may come into the estuary to feed on bottom living worms, molluscs and crabs. Flatfish and mullet regularly feed in this way. The food they take away represents a loss from the ecosystem.

Sand Dune Systems

A thin belt of scattered plants often grows among the drifted seaweed left at the high spring tide mark. This foreshore community consists mainly of annual plants, the most characteristic being sea rocket, saltwort and one or more species of orache. These plants have more or less succulent stems and leaves, which conserve the little water that is available. The community is a temporary one, because sooner or later a storm or exceptionally high tide will destroy the habitat and the drift-line plants must then re-establish themselves.

Landward of this foreshore community, sand dunes begin to form. They differ from salt marshes in that they develop beyond the range of the highest spring tides. In order for dunes to develop, there must be a plentiful supply of sand from either a wide sandy shore or offshore shoals which are exposed at low tide. Dry grains of sand are blown towards the land in great quantities by the wind. Where the sand is stopped by any fixed object, such as a large stone or mass of stranded seaweed, piles accumulate round it, especially on the lee side. The embryo dune so formed can grow no higher than the top of the obstruction and it depends on growing plants for further development. In Britain, one plant, the marram grass, is largely responsible for the building of the main dune ranges. The exceptional powers of this plant for surviving inundation by sand and growing upwards are described later. Marram traps loose sand and grows up through it to trap more, thus the embryo dunes continue to grow until stopped by other causes. A second grass, the sea couch grass, may be important as a pioneer dune former but its capacity to grow up through the sand is restricted to about 1.5 metres. Unlike marram grass, however, it can withstand short immersion in sea water and may begin the formation of embryo dunes along the drift line among the foreshore community where its deep rhizomes are not easily shifted by storms. Another creeping plant of this habitat, the perennial sea sandwort, also helps to stabilise the sand and form low temporary fore-dunes.

Although marram grass plays a large part in the formation of dunes, it does not consolidate the surface of the sand since the marram plants grow in isolated tussocks separated by bare sand liable to be eroded by wind. Where there is some protection from marram tufts, several characteristic species occur, including the conspicuous sea holly, the sea spurge and the sea bindweed. The creeping rhizomes of the latter help to stabilise the sand by reducing its movement by wind. This type of dune, which has ridges up to 30 metres high and deep valleys, is known as yellow or mobile dune to distinguish it from the flatter, more stable dunes further inland, known as grey or fixed dunes. Their name is derived largely from the grey colour of the lichens which

frequently cover the sand of fixed dunes with an almost continuous grey carpet. The major role in stabilisation of yellow dunes is played by a variety of the red fescue grass and the sand sedge. Both have extensive creeping shoots which send up tufts of leaves at short intervals. They stabilise the bare sand and other plants, especially mosses and lichens, become established, while marram gradually dies out.

Wind and instability

A particularly strong wind, especially from an unusual direction, may blow away the entire side of a partly-fixed dune leaving a large depression in the sand. This "blow-out" may persist for a long time before it is eventually re-colonised and may even form the site for further erosion. One of the most common re-colonisers of these "blow-outs" is the sand sedge, which sends out straight rows of tufts from its long shoots. Even fixed dunes are liable to "blow-outs", especially where the sand is disturbed by rabbits or, more frequently, by the trampling of holiday-makers. Sea buckthorn, a very thorny shrub, is frequently planted to protect fixed dunes.

Fixed dunes are eventually colonised by a variety of flowering plants. The nature of this further development depends on the nature of the sand. Where this contains numerous shell

Where sand rather than mud accumulates, colonisation by plants results in the formation of sand dunes. This important habitat is especially vulnerable to erosion.

fragments and other calcareous material, the fixed dune will develop a flora similar to that of limestone grassland, especially if it is grazed. On the other hand, if the sand consists mainly of quartz grains, the shell fragments present on the fore-dunes are leached out by rain, and heathland develops. Damp hollows, extending down to the water table in the fixed dunes, are known as "slacks" and are especially well developed in the larger dune systems of the west coast. They contain a rich variety of plants, many of which are characteristic of wetland habitats, for example, rushes. Some of these plants are scarce at other wetland sites.

Yellow dunes present a difficult habitat for soil animals as sand is unstable and tends to dry out rapidly because it contains little organic material. The surface temperature on a hot, sunny day may rise above 60°C, which is lethal to many animals, although a few centimetres above the surface it may be considerably cooler. This is exploited by the sandhill snail, which is common on fore-dunes in the south west. It remains attached to marram stems in the cooler air in hot weather. Because dry sand is a poor conductor, the zone just below the surface also

Marram grass

Marram grass (*Ammophila arenaria*) is the most important species with regard to the development and stabilising of sand dunes. Plants become established on the upper parts of sandy shores above the drift line. Their deep rooting characteristic holds them firm in the unstable substrate, and wind blown sand collects around the base of the foliage in the region sheltered by the leaves. As the amount of sand builds up, the plant grows upwards and laterally by forking of the underground stem. More leaves grow through the surface of the sand so that the whole dune is clothed in foliage. As the build up of sand continues the plant grows to keep pace with the enlarging dune. It is the complex underground system that binds the sand and stablises the dune.

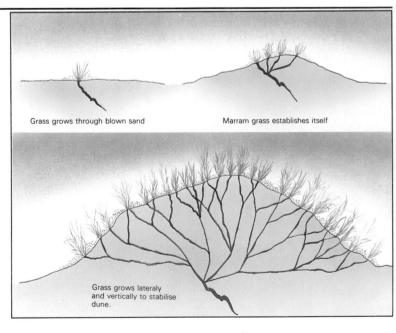

Grass grows through blown sand

Marram grass establishes itself

Grass grows laterally and vertically to stabilise dune.

The main grass concerned in dune formation is the marram *(Ammophila arenaria)* which consolidates the drifting sand.

remains cooler, while at night dew is deposited as moist air comes into contact with the cooler sand grains. This dew is an important source of water for plant roots.

The sand of yellow dunes is initially rich in shell debris, an important source of lime to the many larger thick-shelled snails, which become more common as the surface becomes more stable. The *Helicella* genus of snails is particularly prominent on dunes, together with the garden snail *Helix*, the banded snail *Cepaea* and the pointed snail *Cochlicella*. These snails are characteristic of dry places and, with the exception of the pointed snail, also occur on downland, pastures and walls. Flies are a common nuisance on dunes. They probably originate from other localities like the drift line where there is plenty of decaying material for their larvae. They provide food for many spiders. Although there are few web spinners, the yellow dunes provide a home for numerous species which actively hunt for their prey, lying in wait camouflaged among the marram stems. Swarms of the small hairy fly *Thereva*, whose predatory larvae live in the sand, provide food for wolf spiders, which in turn fall prey to spider-hunting wasps.

Ground and rove beetles are also common on the surface of the dunes, where they actively hunt for prey.

Many herbivorous insects appear as the dunes become stable and a variety of plants become established, and the fauna becomes more like that of grassland or heath.

Field example: Sand dune system: Studland Heath

Studland Heath National Nature Reserve lies at the south east corner of Poole Harbour in Dorset. The area is one of the sunniest in Britain and all six species of British reptiles may be found basking on the warm sandy soils.

Together with adjacent areas of heathland it supports a rich variety of animals typical of this habitat. Nightjars and Dartford warblers have bred in the area as well as a great diversity of heathland insects, especially dragonflies. Further richness is added by the presence of a freshwater lagoon and extensive marshes and bogs.

Perhaps the most instructive single feature of Studland Heath is its clear demonstration of how heathland may develop from coastal sand dunes. At the seaward side of the Reserve, extensive sand dunes have been built up by the wind. These have a typical dune flora, but a little further inland (behind the first dune ridge) the dunes have become stabilised and the rain has washed out the sea salt and numerous mollusc shells, leaving a nutrient-deficient sand. Still further from the sea, this leaching process is complete. The dry, sun warmed, impoverished sandy soil thus

developed from dunes originally formed some 300 years ago, now supports a typical heathland community dominated by heathers. Where heath has been established longest, a thin layer of peaty soil forms a crust over the sand and permits invasion by trees, mostly birch and pine. A heath community does not develop on dunes until their

sand has been leached of calcium and salts, leaving it slightly acid; nor does it form in the valleys between the dunes as these are too wet.

The fore dunes nearest the sea retain a maritime flora including beach plants like sea holly and marram grass. Shore birds like terns and ringed plovers used to nest here, but have been driven

away by the numbers of visitors attracted by the combination of sun, sea and sand. Most visitors to the Reserve are unaware of its unique biological interest. Moreover, despite a National Nature Reserve, Studland Heath is not national property and, like many other NNRs, is merely leased by the Nature Conservancy Council.

Mobile dunes are gradually succeeded by fixed dunes as the plant cover becomes more dense. Heather shows that heathland is developing as lime is leached from the sand.

Fixed dunes showing the development of scrub, including the sea buckthorn in the foreground, and dune slacks with patches of open water in the background.

The small greenish flowers of sea buckthorn are replaced in autumn by attractive orange berries which are eaten by birds.

The sand dune ecosystem

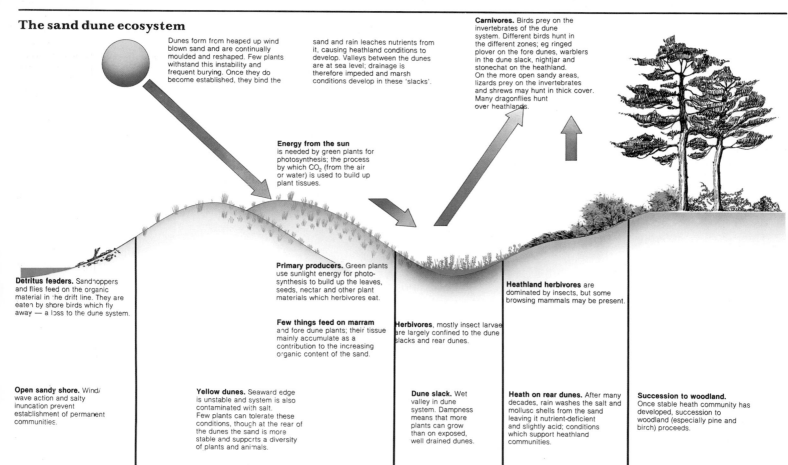

Dunes form from heaped up wind blown sand and are continually moulded and reshaped. Few plants withstand this instability and frequent burying. Once they do become established, they bind the sand and rain leaches nutrients from it, causing heathland conditions to develop. Valleys between the dunes are at sea level; drainage is therefore impeded and marsh conditions develop in these 'slacks'.

Energy from the sun is needed by green plants for photosynthesis; the process by which CO_2 (from the air or water) is used to build up plant tissues.

Carnivores. Birds prey on the invertebrates of the dune system. Different birds hunt in the different zones; eg ringed plover on the fore dunes, warblers in the dune slack, nightjar and stonechat on the heathland. On the more open sandy areas, lizards prey on the invertebrates and shrews may hunt in thick cover. Many dragonflies hunt over heathlands.

Detritus feeders. Sandhoppers and flies feed on the organic material in the drift line. They are eaten by shore birds which fly away — a loss to the dune system.

Primary producers. Green plants use sunlight energy for photosynthesis to build up the leaves, seeds, nectar and other plant materials which herbivores eat.

Few things feed on marram and fore dune plants; their tissue mainly accumulate as a contribution to the increasing organic content of the sand.

Herbivores, mostly insect larvae are largely confined to the dune slacks and rear dunes.

Heathland herbivores are dominated by insects, but some browsing mammals may be present.

Open sandy shore. Wind/wave action and salty inundation prevent establishment of permanent communities.

Yellow dunes. Seaward edge is unstable and system is also contaminated with salt. Few plants can tolerate these conditions, though at the rear of the dunes the sand is more stable and supports a diversity of plants and animals.

Dune slack. Wet valley in dune system. Dampness means that more plants can grow than on exposed, well drained dunes.

Heath on rear dunes. After many decades, rain washes the salt and mollusc shells from the sand leaving it nutrient-deficient and slightly acid; conditions which support heathland communities.

Succession to woodland. Once stable heath community has developed, succession to woodland (especially pine and birch) proceeds.

Vegetated Shingle Beaches and Coastal Lagoons

Shingle beaches are composed of water-worn pebbles of various sizes and material derived from coastal erosion. The simplest type of shingle beach, the fringing beach, is formed when the sorting action of the waves deposits the coarser shingle in a bank at the top of the shore, leaving the finer mud and sand on the middle and lower shore. Fringing shingle beaches are common along the shores of the Sussex coastal plain. A second type of shingle beach, the shingle spit, is formed as the result of beach drifting. This movement carries pebbles along the beach away from the direction of the prevailing winds. On the south coast, this movement is from west to east, but on the coast of Norfolk and Suffolk spits have been formed by drift from north to south, for example at Orfordness. The coast of north Norfolk, running along to the Wash, acts as a groyne, intercepting material moving down the east coast from north to south and causing it to be deposited from east to west. Where the line of the coast falls away landwards, for example at the mouth of an estuary, shingle deposition is often carried on in a direct line with the beach and a shingle spit is formed which projects into the sea across the estuary. Some spits formed in this way may be very long and the mouth of the river diverted for several kilometres, as for example by the great shingle spit at Orfordness. Some of these spits may be quite complex and show successive stages of growth between periods of storms. In cross section, definite regions are recognisable on the surface of a shingle spit, including successive steps corresponding to the levels reached by tides of different heights.

Extended spits and bars

Shingle spits sometimes extend across a bay to join the shore on the opposite side forming a shingle bar, the best known example being Chesil Beach in Dorset, which extends a distance of about 30 kilometres from Bridport to the Isle of Portland. Apposition beaches form when new shingle is deposited on the flank of an earlier beach, where it accumulates until lifted to form a ridge above tidal limits by an exceptionally high tide caused by a gale. A new beach then begins to form in front of this ridge. If this process is repeated, a succession of more or less parallel ridges is formed close together giving an extensive area of shingle. One of the best examples is the great triangular mass of shingle which juts out into the English Channel at Dungeness.

Although shingle spits differ from yellow dunes in that they are not liable to damage by strong winds, the shingle is still susceptible to disturbance by wave action when the highest spring tides are backed by strong winds. If the shingle

Field example: A vegetated shingle beach: Orfordness

Orfordness, on the coast of Suffolk, forms one of the largest vegetated shingle areas in the country. It begins as a narrow neck of shingle, only fifty metres wide at high water, which prevents the River Alde from reaching the sea just south of Aldeburgh. It continues due south as a wide high bank formed from shingle and then, following the coastline, turns south west, causing an 18 km deflection of the River Alde and also diverting the River Butley. In several places groups of older shingle ridges run landwards, providing information about the way that Orfordness has developed from a series of apposition beaches. The beach has good examples of shingle plant communities including sea kale, the yellow horned poppy and the sea pea, with its bright purple flowers, which is common and is said to have been eaten by the people of nearby Orford during a famine. The ness also provides nesting sites for colonies of lesser black-backed and herring gulls. The shingle spit encloses a stretch of water, the River Ore, bordered by mud flats and salt marshes dominated in places by sea lavender and sea purslane. This area provides important roosting and feeding sites for wildfowl and waders and the bare, muddy lagoons on Havergate Island are well known for the largest breeding colony of avocets in Britain. The island also has colonies of Sandwich and common terns among its breeding birds. Several rare insects and spiders have been recorded.

Sea kale *(Crambe maritima)* an uncommon shingle plant, is plentiful at Orfordness.

bank is high (as at Chesil Beach, where it reaches 8 metres above high water in places) the slope approaches the maximum steepness possible for loose pebbles, and sea water percolating through the bank causes local collapse of the shingle. Unlike the yellow dune, the water content of the shingle is high, partly from rainfall and partly from internal dew formation on the surface of the pebbles. Shingle plants rarely suffer from drought, and become established wherever sufficient humus accumulates to form a rudimentary soil for their roots.

Plants rarely grow in the steep exposed face of a shingle bank as the pebbles are moved to and fro freely by the tides, but beyond this a number of species typical of coastal habitats become established. There is no dominant plant of shingle beaches, unlike the sand dunes with their marram grass. One plant almost restricted to shingle habitats is the shrubby seablite. This has the capacity to grow up through the shingle and maintain its leafy shoots above the surface.

Shingle and sandy beaches are unstable coastal features. Rough seas churning up the shingle during storms may radically change the shape of the beach and may even remove it altogether.

The lower woody parts of the plant die when buried deep in shingle and the younger shoots send out fresh roots between the stones at the surface. In this respect, shrubby seablite resembles the marram grass of the yellow dunes, although it plays no significant part in stabilising shingle. Sea sandwort, common on the fore-dunes, is also common on shingle, especially where some sand is present. Another plant often abundant is the sea campion, which also grows on cliffs and partly-fixed dunes. Both the sand-wort and campion will survive covering by stones and form extensive carpets which help to bind the shingle. Other typical plants include the yellow horned-poppy, with long curved pods, and a fleshy variety of the curled dock, which forms a miniature forest with its dense, brown fruiting spikes. Patches of the bright purple flowers of the sea pea and the sea-shore form of the herb-robert can be found on a few beaches. Sea kale, a white-flowered perennial with broad cabbage-like fleshy leaves, likes shingle but has become less common since it became popular as a vegetable. There is generally little succession of plants on shingle ridges, as they usually

Lagoon formation

Waves tend to strike a beach obliquely breaking on one end of a bay before the other. The shore is thus subjected to a scouring action, loose pebbles and sand being swept along the coast ("the long-shore drift"). These are then deposited in places where the wave action is less powerful. Continued deposition leads to the development of a sand or shingle spit which may ultimately form a complete barrier across the mouth of the bay separating still water above it as a lagoon cut off from the sea.

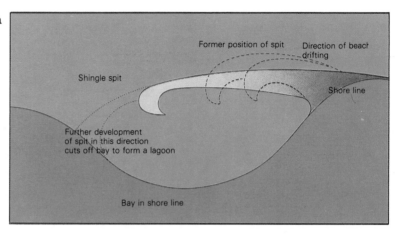

abut on to sand dunes or salt marshes, but where large expanses of shingle occur, for example at Dungeness, the shingle community gives way to grass and then scrub of gorse, broom, bramble, blackthorn, hawthorn and elder. The few animals of shingle beaches have been little studied and consequently little is known about food webs on vegetated shingle beaches.

Areas of shallow water are sometimes impounded behind sand and shingle deposits. These lagoons may remain tidal by maintaining a connection with the sea (eg the Fleet behind Chesil Beach in Dorset) or, if cut off from the sea, gradually become fresh water bodies (eg the Slapton Ley in south Devon). Large lagoons are, however, an uncommon feature of the coast.

Field example: A coastal lagoon: Chesil Beach and the Fleet

The Fleet has been formed by the development of a shingle bar, Chesil Beach, which extends from Bridport to the Isle of Portland leaving a small connection with the open sea at the extreme eastern end of the lagoon. This is the largest regularly tidal lagoon in Britain and contains a unique collection of all three British species of eel-grass together with the uncommon and related beaked tassel pondweed. Some of the invertebrates found in the lagoon associated with eel-grass are uncommon elsewhere as a result of the decline of this plant in many parts of Europe through disease in the 1930s. Many waders and wildfowl winter on the lagoon including wigeon, mallard, teal, pintail, shoveler, pochard and goldeneye and it supports the largest mute swan population in Britain. Since the level of the sea at high tide is well above the water level in the lagoon, over two metres in some instances, sea water percolates through the shingle beach into the lagoon. As Chesil Beach is unusually high, rising some ten metres above the lagoon in places, this water displaces shingle from the steep sides of the beach on the lee side. This percolation is localised, and the displacement results in a series of deeply cut ravines or "cans" separated by conspicuous buttresses developing along the southern edge of the Fleet. The displaced shingle fans out on the edge of the lagoon to form a terrace, which is covered by a continuous belt of shrubby seablite and by many lichens.

Some lichens, such as these crustose lichens, grow on shingle but are mainly confined to stable areas on the landward edge of the beach.

Slapton Ley, a large eutrophic freshwater shingle bar lagoon rich in plant and animal life. Beyond the reedswamp the open water of the Ley extends for over a mile.

In spring hundreds of mute swans nest at the Abbotsbury swannery on the north-west edge of the Fleet. In former times this swannery provided fat cygnets to the monks of the abbey.

Cliffs and Landslips

Except in areas such as dunes, marshes and certain shingle spits, where land has been built up by accretion, wave action gradually cuts a notch into the land surface which then widens to produce a beach platform and cliff. If the land slopes gently, the cliffs do not normally rise to a great height, but the platform may widen considerably. The subsequent development of the cliffs will depend on the nature of the underlying rocks, on weathering and on the action of waves, although the latter will lose much of their power as they cross a wide platform. The form of the resulting cliffs will also depend on the topography of the original land surface, which may have been flat and low-lying or rugged and mountainous. It also depends, in the case of sedimentary rocks, on the bedding of the strata composing the cliffs. When waves attack rocks with horizontal bedding, vertical cliffs are developed. Examples include the chalk cliffs of the Sussex and Yorkshire coasts and the colourful Old Red Sandstone cliffs of Caithness. The latter are well jointed at right angles to the bedding and the sea penetrates along these lines of weakness, producing caves and buttresses. This does not occur so frequently in the softer chalk, which breaks up too easily. Another factor in the case of limestone cliffs is their solubility. For example, the vertical Carboniferous limestone cliffs on the south side of the Pembrokeshire peninsula have many caves, arches, blowholes and stacks which have developed as a result of the sea cutting back into cave systems formed previously by the

The vertical chalk cliffs at Beachy Head. Cliffs are cut from a variety of rocks ranging from the precipitous cliffs of igneous rock to the gently sloping cliffs of London clay.

solvent action of surface water from above ground.

Cliff instability

Cliffs formed from soft rocks, such as the boulder clay of Norfolk and London clay of the Isle of Sheppey, are especially liable to serious erosion where the sea wears away the base and, together with the effect of the percolation of land water, causes landslips. The natural angle of slope of these materials will not allow the formation of vertical cliffs and they are seldom

Cliffs provide unique habitats for wildlife. The rare white rockrose *(Helianthemum apenninum)* grows in abundance on the limestone headland of Berry Head (Torbay).

Cliff formation

Wave action erodes the base of a cliff causing rock to fall from above. Fallen material leaves an exposure, often quite sheer, of rock, which we call the cliff face. Where softer rocks occur erosion leads to a general slumping or sliding instead of a vertical cliff.

Rocks at the foot of the cliff provide anchorage, pools and shelter for shore life. They also break the force of the waves thus protecting the cliff, slowing the rate of erosion, and leading to a relatively stable coastline.

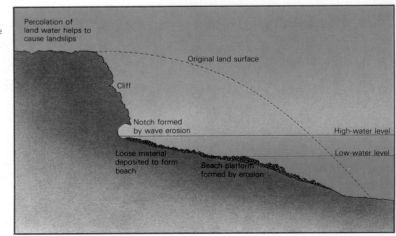

Cliff nesting birds spend most of their lives at sea but congregate in enormous numbers to breed on inaccessible cliffs. The picture shows kittiwakes nesting in close packed colonies on narrow ledges.

steep. Much of the harder material from these cliffs accumulates on the beach. On Sheppey, fossil shark teeth and plant remains which have come from the London clay are common on the shore.

Coasts formed mainly from igneous rocks show a very wide range of form, corresponding to the range of materials involved, such as granite, basalt and volcanic lavas. In the southern part of the Isle of Arran the sedimentary sandstone rock has been pierced by vertical dykes of igneous rock. Where these run out across the beach they stand out from the sandstone as a series of low ridges, where the softer sandstone has been eroded away. Similar structures can be seen at other sites on the coast of western Scotland. The precipitous cliffs of Skye are largely formed of volcanic lavas and basalts. Some of these, such as Waterstein Head, reach a height of nearly 300 metres, although there is a very low undercliff, formed by recent erosion, at the base of the major cliff, which was formed at some time in the distant past. Columnar lavas give rise to striking cliffs of polygonal blocks, such as the Giant's Causeway in County Antrim and those surrounding Fingal's Cave on the island of Staffa.

Sea cliffs have two important characteristics

as plant habitats. Their steepness gives refuge firstly to plants which are sensitive to competition from other plants, and secondly to plants which cannot tolerate grazing by rabbits and sheep. The vegetation of sea cliffs grades away from that of the splash zone of the rocky shore, with its characteristic lichens, into communities normally found in lowland grassland, heath or scrub.

The lower part of cliffs above the lichen-

The landslip of Cairn's Folly. Softer rocks such as shales and clays tend to slump when eroded at the seaward side to form steep slopes. These then develop permanent vegetation.

dominated zone is inhabited by plants which grow along ledges and in crevices and which are tolerant of exposure to sea spray. Many of these halophytic plants are also characteristic of salt marshes. They include thrift, sea plantain, buck's-horn plantain, sea lavender and sea campion. In southern Britain, the cushions of samphire are common. This plant was once considered a great delicacy. The related Scottish lovage is most abundant on cliffs in Scotland, where it has been eaten as a pot-herb. Other plants growing in this zone include the golden samphire, rock sea spurrey and common scurvy grass, which was often eaten in the past by sailors as a protection against scurvy. A fern characteristic of crevices in this zone is the sea spleenwort. Large bird colonies on cliffs cause mechanical damage to plants but also enrich the local cliff soils, particularly in nitrogen and phosphorus. This is detrimental to the growth of many plant species unaccustomed to chemical largesse, but favours the growth of a few vigorous species such as the tree mallow, a spectacular plant found especially on cliffs in the south west which grows to 1.5 metres in height. The sea beet, a close relative of the vegetable, is common on cliffs as well as along the drift line. Two other ancestors of well-known vegetables, the sea cabbage and the sea carrot, grow on sea cliffs but are restricted to the south and west coasts.

All these plants tend to cling to the exposed cliff face. Higher up, where the effect of sea spray is reduced, shallow dry pockets of soil develop which support additional plants such as the English stonecrop. On the exposed cliff top a short turf of red and sheep's fescues may be found and on western coasts this turf is covered by the vernal squill in spring. On non-calcareous rocks, a submaritime heath is found over deeper soils, with heather, heath and a wide range of flowering plants growing, including some species usually associated with limestone habitats. These depend on extra nutrients from the sea spray and become scarcer away from the cliff top.

Waves breaking on the Cornish coast show the continuing interplay of fundamental forces which are gradually shaping and re-shaping the earth's surface. The harder rocks of north and west Britain resist the force of

waves better than the softer rock elsewhere. They remain as vertical cliffs or as jagged pinnacles providing valuable ledges for nesting birds and cliff dwelling plants. The sea around cliffs is clearer than that around other shore areas.

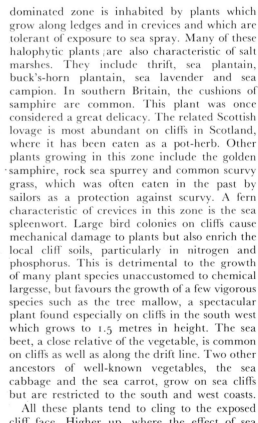

Coastal Flora

The plants of the coast consist of a mixture of species which fall into three groups. The largest group are widely distributed species which include the coast in their range of habitats. A good example is the red or creeping fescue, a grass which occurs throughout the British Isles, from sea level to over 1,000 metres, and on both dry and wet soils. At the coast it is found on sand dunes, salt marshes and on sea cliffs. Most British plants can in fact be found at the coast, since a variety of non-maritime habitats such as woodland, grassland and heathland are represented at the coast, where they show a gradual transition into the truly maritime habitats which are influenced by salt spray. A good example of this paramaritime type of community is the heathland which develops at the top of the cliffs formed from acidic rocks. Away from the influence of salt spray, heathland of the familiar heather-heath or heather-dwarf gorse type is found, but nearer the spray-washed cliff top, where nutrients are more readily available, many more species appear, including some more characteristic of calcareous habitats. It is perhaps surprising that a group of mountain plants is found in coastal habitats, such as on the sea cliffs in the north west of Scotland, but the cool oceanic climate allows summer temperatures

Sea campion *(Silene maritima)* and wild cabbage *(Brassica oleracea)* in flower. Coastal plants must adapt to the "physiological drought" caused by exposure to salt spray and to pressure from birds.

A guide to some muddy shore and salt marsh plants

Muddy shores are normally found only where there are sheltered waters such as creeks and estuaries. Such places where the mud flats are flooded at high tide are usually colonised by eel-grass (*Zostera*), the only true marine flowering plant, which needs a stable muddy substrate in which its long roots can ramify. Other common species are glasswort (*Salicornia*) and rice grass (*Spartina*). Many of the eel-grass beds were destroyed by disease in the 1930s and are still in the process of re-establishment.

As more mud and silt is deposited the substrate level rises and salt marsh develops.

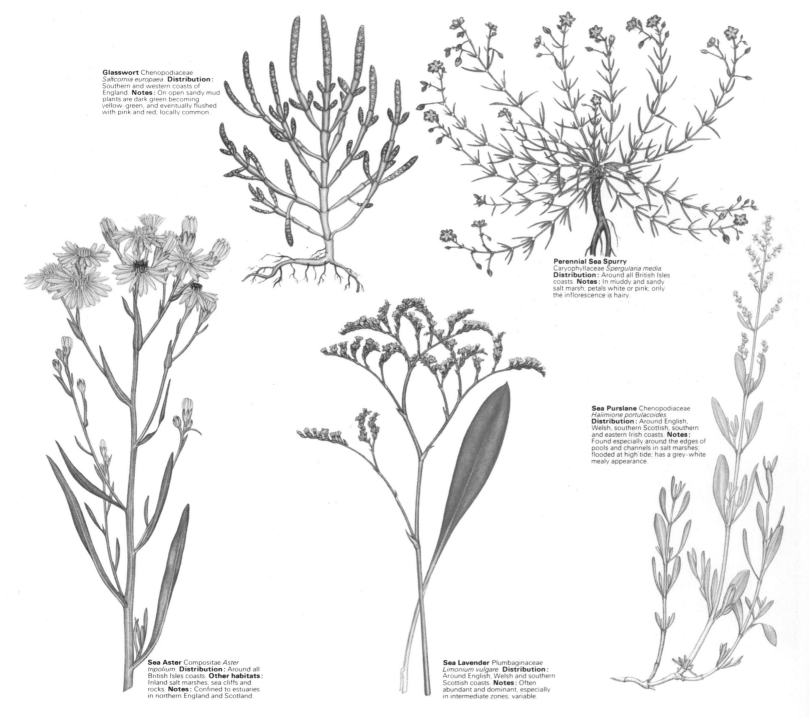

Glasswort Chenopodiaceae *Salicornia europaea.* **Distribution:** Southern and western coasts of England. **Notes:** On open sandy mud plants are dark green becoming yellow-green, and eventually flushed with pink and red; locally common.

Perennial Sea Spurry Caryophyllaceae *Spergularia media.* **Distribution:** Around all British Isles coasts. **Notes:** In muddy and sandy salt marsh; petals white or pink; only the inflorescence is hairy.

Sea Purslane Chenopodiaceae *Halimione portulacoides.* **Distribution:** Around English, Welsh, southern Scottish, southern and eastern Irish coasts. **Notes:** Found especially around the edges of pools and channels in salt marshes; flooded at high tide; has a grey-white mealy appearance.

Sea Aster Compositae *Aster tripolium.* **Distribution:** Around all British Isles coasts. **Other habitats:** Inland salt marshes; sea cliffs and rocks. **Notes:** Confined to estuaries in northern England and Scotland.

Sea Lavender Plumbaginaceae *Limonium vulgare.* **Distribution:** Around English, Welsh and southern Scottish coasts. **Notes:** Often abundant and dominant, especially in intermediate zones; variable.

which are not too high for these plants, while extreme exposure to wind helps to maintain bare, tree-less habitats and so reduce competition. These plants include several saxifrages, moss campion and the mountain avens. Again, typical marsh plants grow in the wet slacks which develop in dune valleys, including rushes, water mint and marsh forget-me-not.

The second group of coastal plants includes those species with a preference for coastal conditions because these give them an advantage. Many plants which are sensitive to disturbance by grazing flourish on steep slopes and cliffs by the sea, out of the range of sheep and rabbits. Some smaller fen plants such as the creeping willow and the rare fen orchid, which lead a precarious existence in inland marshes and fens because of competition from tall-growing reeds and other plants, also grow successfully in sand dune slacks where tall dominants are excluded by exposure to wind and sea spray and by soil instability. Other plants which are rarely found more than a few kilometres from the sea and yet are not specifically coastal plants include the slender thistle and two plants formerly grown as pot herbs, alexanders and fennel, both of which probably originated from the Mediterranean region.

The remaining group of flowering plants and ferns, probably less than ten per cent of the total British flora, is more or less confined to the coast and often shows special adaptations. The main problem for these plants is to obtain an adequate supply of water, particularly in the early stages of their growth. This applies equally to those growing in the saline mud of salt marshes or exposed to salt-laden spray on sea cliffs and to those growing in dry habitats such as sand dunes and shingle beaches, although the reasons for the difficulty are different. In dry habitats the soil is formed from coarse particles (sand and shingle) which cannot retain water after rain. Yellow dunes and shingle beaches also contain very little dead plant material or humus, which plays an important role in water retention. The plants of salt marshes have a different kind of problem. They suffer from a "physiological drought" because although water is abundant they cannot make use of it owing to its high concentration of salt. The problem of water supply is further aggravated for both kinds of plants by exposure to the drying action of the strong winds which are characteristic of coastal habitats, especially on exposed cliffs. This increases the rate of evaporation of water from the leaves (transpiration), which takes place through minute pores or stomata and is an essential process in the life of plants.

In order to reduce the water loss through transpiration many adaptations are found in coastal plants. Some develop a thick outer skin or cuticle over the leaves, which gives them a leathery feel. In the sea holly this is supplemented by a covering of wax on the leaf surface. These protective layers restrict evaporation to

The pink flowers of thrift *(Armeria maritima)* are a familiar sight at the coast, being common on salt-marshes, cliffs and on shingle beaches, often forming dense cushions.

A guide to some coastal grasses

In many coastal situations grasses play a major colonising role as well as being an important part of established habitats. On sandy shores *Agropyron*, *Elymus* and *Ammophila* often become established, their lateral and vertical growth stabilising the sand and causing dune formation. When dunes are established grasses dominate much of the succession. On rocky cliffs grass species are infrequent, except where pockets of soil occur. Salt marsh is usually established by the pioneering *Spartina* that stablises the substrate; other grasses rarely grow here until the soil is stable and the turf is covered only by the highest tides.

Sea Couch Grass Gramineae (Poaceae) *Agropyron junceiforme.* **Distribution:** Around all of the British Isles. **Notes:** Very salt tolerant and grows nearer to the sea than other grasses; forms small dunes at the top of the beach.

Sea Manna Grass Gramineae (Poaceae) *Puccinellia mantima* **Distribution:** Around all of the British Isles but most abundant in the south and east. **Other habitats:** Inland salt marshes. **Notes:** The main constituent of grassy salt marsh often covering large areas of mud flats; rarely among rocks or on sand or shingle; stoloniferous; forms a continuous turf broken only by drainage gullies.

Salt Mud Rush Juncaceae *Juncus gerardii.* **Distribution:** All British Isles coasts. **Other habitats:** Inland salt marshes. **Notes:** Salt marshes from the highest point of the highest tide and above; often abundant and locally dominant.

Sand Sedge Cyperaceae *Carex arenaria.* **Distribution:** Around all of the British Isles. **Other habitats:** A few inland localities. **Notes:** The dominant species of fixed dunes and areas of wind-blown low lime content sand.

Rice-Grass Gramineae (Poaceae) *Spartina X townsendii.* **Distribution:** Common around the coasts of north-west, central and southern England and Wales, with a restricted distribution around the rest of the British Isles. **Notes:** Tidal mud flats; often planted to stabilise mud; common near ports.

Marram Grass Gramineae (Poaceae) *Ammophila arenaria.* **Distribution:** Around all of the British Isles. **Notes:** The common grass of sand dunes; often abundant, usually dominant; planted to bind and consolidate drifting sand.

| Sea Manna Grass | Sand Sedge | Rice Grass | Marram Grass |

Sea Couch Grass   Salt Mud Rush

Sea holly *(Eryngium maritimum)*, with spiny leaves and heads of bluish flowers, is usually found on mobile sand dunes and is capable of growing up through loose sand.

the region of the stomata. In the marram grass, the stomata are mainly confined to the bottom and sides of deep grooves in the leaves. These leaves curl during dry weather into an elongated cylinder, maintaining a layer of moist air between the stomata and the outside air and so reducing evaporation. Many coastal plants are protected from excessive evaporation by hairs on the leaves. These include the buck's-horn plantain, yellow horned poppy and the silvery sea-purslane. Several cliff or shingle plants, such as thrift, grow in dense rosettes to reduce water loss, although if water is abundant this plant will develop in a more open way. Leaves are reduced in several plants to scales (glassworts) or spines (saltwort) to reduce the surface area of the leaf.

Plants especially adapted to saline conditions are known as halophytes. Many of them have succulent leaves or stems, owing to the presence of abundant water-holding tissue, swollen with sap which often contains large quantities of salt. The ash of some, like the saltworts, was formerly used to provide soda for glassmaking. Succulence, which is also a common feature in plants of dry habitats, is especially characteristic of coastal members of the plant family Chenopodiaceae, which includes the glassworts, saltwort and several other halophytes. The reason for this

succulence is not fully understood. Most plants of salt marshes and the spray-washed zone of cliffs are halophytes and can survive in soils where the water contains between twenty and fifty per cent seawater. In comparison, most dune plants are not halophytes and their growth

is reduced if the soil contains more than three per cent seawater. The fine mud of the salt marsh is badly aerated and salt marsh plants may have air-filled tissues in their roots to compensate for the shortage of oxygen in the anaerobic mud.

Long creeping stems of sea bindweed *(Calystegia soldanella)* make it an effective stabiliser of mobile sand dunes where it occurs. The flowers are frequently eaten by rabbits.

A guide to some plants of the sand and shingle shore

Most shingle beaches are unstable with their constituent stones so mobile that vegetation is unable to become established; it is only the stabilised portions that bear vegetation, albeit a very limited number of species. Shrubby sea blite which often becomes established as a drift line plant is probably the most commonly encountered species, though others such as yellow horned poppy and curled dock are frequent. Sandy shores have a much more complex system of vegetation which gradually changes with the dune succession. Many of the species that grow on shingle also grow on the sandy shore, though saltwort, sea buckthorn and sea bindweed are usually found only on sand.

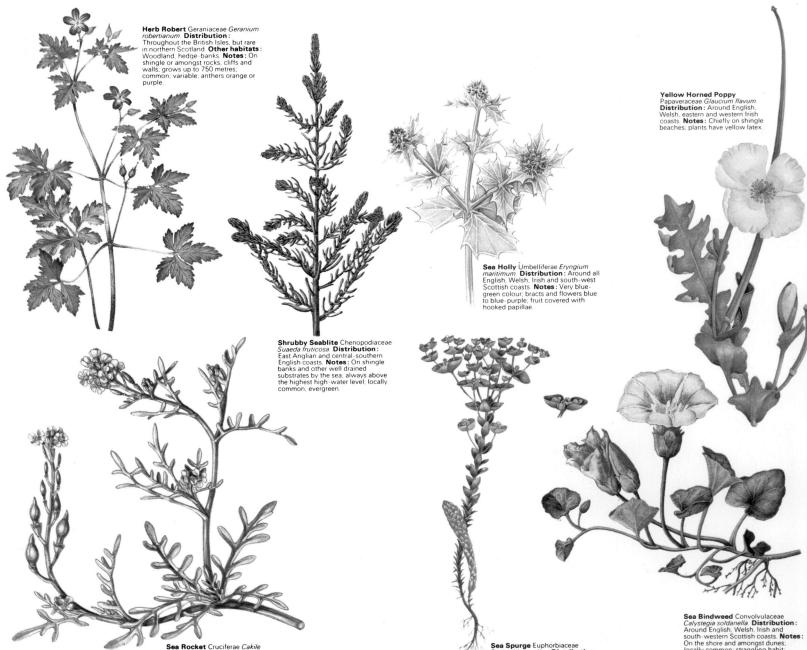

Herb Robert Geraniaceae *Geranium robertianum.* **Distribution:** Throughout the British Isles, but rare in northern Scotland. **Other habitats:** Woodland, hedge-banks. **Notes:** On shingle or amongst rocks, cliffs and walls; grows up to 750 metres; common; variable; anthers orange or purple.

Yellow Horned Poppy Papaveraceae *Glaucium flavum.* **Distribution:** Around English, Welsh, eastern and western Irish coasts. **Notes:** Chiefly on shingle beaches; plants have yellow latex.

Sea Holly Umbelliferae *Eryngium maritimum.* **Distribution:** Around all English, Welsh, Irish and south-west Scottish coasts. **Notes:** Very blue-green colour; bracts and flowers blue to blue-purple; fruit covered with hooked papillae.

Shrubby Seablite Chenopodiaceae *Suaeda fruticosa.* **Distribution:** East Anglian and central-southern English coasts. **Notes:** On shingle banks and other well drained substrates by the sea; always above the highest high-water level; locally common; evergreen.

Sea Rocket Cruciferae *Cakile maritima.* **Distribution:** Around all British Isles coasts. **Notes:** A drift-line plant; common; seeds dispersed by the sea; variable, especially the leaves which can be simple or deeply lobed.

Sea Spurge Euphorbiaceae *Euphorbia paralias.* **Distribution:** Around western, southern and south-eastern English, Welsh and Irish, except for the west, coasts. **Notes:** On sand and mobile dunes; locally common; milky latex.

Sea Bindweed Convolvulaceae *Calystegia soldanella.* **Distribution:** Around English, Welsh, Irish and south-western Scottish coasts. **Notes:** On the shore and amongst dunes; locally common; straggling habit; flowers pink or pale purple.

The marram grass *(Ammophila arenaria)* is one of the most important and characteristic plants of our coasts. Its value as a binder and consolidator of drifting sand lies in its exceptional power to push its underground shoots through the loose sand. These branch and continually form fresh roots in the moist sand where dew forms, just below the air-dried surface layer. Thus the size of the obstacle presented to the blown sand is continually increased and the dunes grow in height. Marram grass is able to grow through several metres of sand provided the latter is not deposited too quickly and the dunes thus formed can reach a height of 30 metres. Where a dune has been eroded by wind, the extensive skeleton of marram shoots and roots, forming a network which penetrates throughout the dune, is revealed. The marram grass is not a halophyte and cannot withstand immersion in sea water.

Another important coastal grass is the cord or rice-grass *(Spartina × townsendii)*. The part played by this grass in the stabilisation of muddy shores has already been noted. It is an erect type of grass which may grow up to a metre or more in height, and its importance lies in a combination of deep, anchoring roots and horizontal feeding roots, which effectively bond

Coastal ferns

Of the fern species found in the British Isles very few can survive the unfavourable conditions encountered on the coast. Sea-spleenwort is the only widespread coastal fern and is recognised as a characteristic sea cliff species. It cannot tolerate grazing and is most frequent in inaccessible places and caves. However, other species such as the lady fern and the broad buckler-fern (both woodland species) are occasionally found. They may survive due to reduced competition or they may be a relict of former woodland. Where grazing is heavy, bracken (another non-maritime fern) can take over fixed dune systems and exclude most other species.

Sea-spleenwort Aspleniaceae *Asplenium marinum* **Distribution:** Around the British Isles coasts except east and south-east England. **Notes:** Clefts of sea cliffs; less common on walls near the coast; requires salt spray; absent from sheltered shores and those without rocky substrates.

Maidenhair-fern Adiantaceae *Adiantum capillus-veneris* **Distribution:** South-west England. South Wales, Westmorland, Isle of Man. west Ireland. **Notes:** Walls and sheltered places on sea cliffs; especially on calcareous tufa; very local.

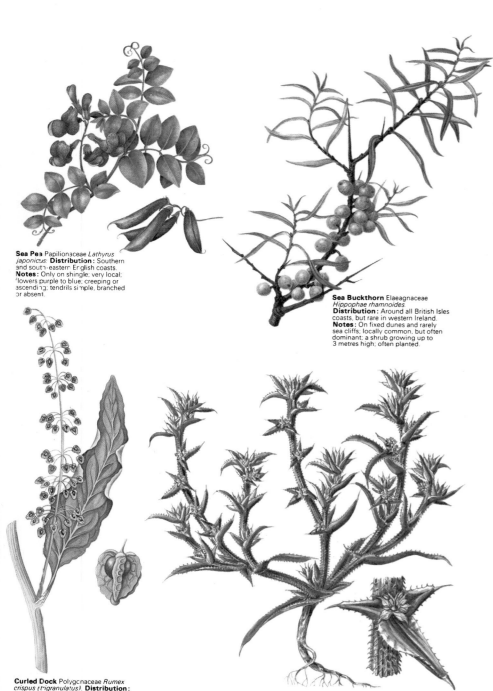

Sea Pea Papilionaceae *Lathyrus japonicus*. **Distribution:** Southern and south-eastern English coasts. **Notes:** Only on shingle; very local; flowers purple to blue; creeping or ascending; tendrils simple, branched or absent.

Sea Buckthorn Elaeagnaceae *Hippophae rhamnoides*. **Distribution:** Around all British Isles coasts, but rare in western Ireland. **Notes:** On fixed dunes and rarely sea cliffs; locally common, but often dominant; a shrub growing up to 3 metres high; often planted.

Curled Dock Polygonaceae *Rumex crispus (trigranulatus)*. **Distribution:** Throughout the British Isles, but rarer in the north. **Other habitats:** Grassy places; waste ground; cultivated land. **Notes:** Dune slacks and shingle beaches; common.

Saltwort Chenopodiaceae *Salsola kali*. **Distribution:** Around all British Isles coasts. **Notes:** On sandy shores; prickly; straggling habit.

Sea Kale Cruciferae *Crambe maritima*. **Distribution:** Scattered around the coasts of the British Isles, but most common along the south of England. **Notes:** Sand, shingle, rocks or cliffs; often a plant of the drift-line; sprouts readily after being buried under shingle; fruit dispersed in sea-water where it remains viable for several days.

Sea Sandwort Caryophyllaceae *Honkenya peploides*. **Distribution:** Around all British Isles coasts. **Notes:** Common on mobile sand and sandy shingle; forms miniature dunes, often with *Agropyron junceiforme*; tolerates short periods of immersion in salt water.

soft muds. The stems are very effective in slowing water currents and the rate of accumulation of new sediment is greatest where mud flats are covered by rice-grass. The foreshore level of a length of coastline in Somerset, for example, was raised by 1.5 metres in 35 years after rice-grass had been planted. Rice-grass has an interesting history, having been first noticed on the shores of Southampton Water in 1870. It probably arose there as a hybrid between the uncommon cord-grass *Spartina maritima* and another species, the smooth cord-grass *(Spartina alterniflora)*, which was probably introduced accidentally into the Southampton area from North America and which has subsequently been crowded out by the more vigorous hybrid species. *Spartina × townsendii* spread rapidly along the south coast and by 1915 was established in every estuary from Chichester to Poole. Because of its vigour and ability to stabilise soft muds, it has been planted extensively in land reclamation schemes and now covers more than 1,200 hectares of tidal flats around Britain. It has also spread to France, Holland and other parts of the Continent. The development of rice-grass thus provides an interesting example of the evolution of a new species within recent times. However, in spite of its value in land reclamation, the

Coastal lichens

At the extreme high water mark and above this in the splash zone, the lichens are the dominant plants on the rocky shore. Since they are land plants unlike the marine algae, their distribution down the shore is mainly limited by the amount of submersion which they can tolerate. Most lichens are restricted to the splash zone although one species *Lichina pygmaea* which resembles a small tufted seaweed, is common on the middle shore. Most shore lichens are encrusting species and some, like the extensive thin black crusts of *Verrucaria*, are hardly recognisable and may be mistaken for an oil stain. Others, including the yellow *Xanthoria parietina*, have a leafy form and are obviously plants. This lichen and several other species such as *Lecanora atra* are also found inland on rocks and walls wherever conditions are suitable. *Caloplaca marina*, on the other hand, is restricted to the rocky shore. Lichens growing on the shore are especially susceptible to the effects of oil spillages and the emulsifiers used to disperse the oil.

Lichens growing in the splash zone of the rocky shore, including the leafy orange *Xanthoria parietina* and the tufted *Ramalina siliquosa*.

Irregular patches of the lichen *Verrucaria mucosa* are common on rocks on the middle shore where they resemble patches of tar.

A guide to some cliff plants

Cliffs, unlike other habitats such as salt marsh, dune and shingle beach, have no clearly defined communities. Transitions from halophytes to non-halophytes and mixtures of the two are common. Even with such loose parameters certain species are regarded as being characteristic of, though not necessarily limited to, cliff habitats; these include samphire, thrift, sea campion, sea beet, wild cabbage and sea kale.

On ledges a short grassy turf develops which also has characteristic species. Most common (in the west of Britain), though found only locally, is the vernal squill which covers the turf with a mass of blue flowers in the spring. This species, like the wild cabbage, has an "Atlantic" distribution: southern and western Britain, France and Spain (the Mediterranean and areas warmed by the Gulf Stream).

Because of the relative inaccessibility of most cliff faces few ecological studies have been undertaken and information on the species present and their relative abundance is poor.

Maritime cliffs are often frequented by birds, and where populations are large the amount of droppings can considerably affect the flora.

Trees are absent from British cliffs due to grazing, especially by rabbits, and the susceptibility of our trees to salt spray. In other parts of the world wooded sea cliffs are common.

English Stonecrop Crassulaceae *Sedum anglicum.* **Distribution:** Around all British Isles coasts; very common in the west of England and Ireland. **Other habitats:** Rocks and grassland. **Notes:** On dunes and shingle; not on strongly basic soil; inland grows up to 1100 metres.

Tree Mallow Malvaceae *Lavatera arborea.* **Distribution:** Around the coasts of southern, south-eastern, south-western and western England, Wales and Ireland. **Notes:** On rocks or on waste ground; grows up to 160 metres; seeds are hairy or not; up to 3 metres tall.

Rock Sea-spurry Caryophyllaceae *Spergularia rupicola.* **Distribution:** Around the coasts of Wales, south and west England, south Scotland and Ireland. **Notes:** On cliffs, rocks and walls; locally common.

Sea Campion Caryophyllaceae *Silene maritima.* **Distribution:** Around most of the British Isles coast, but less common in the east; a few inland localities, especially in the north. **Other habitats:** Cliff ledges; gravelly lake shores; alpine streams. **Notes:** Sea cliffs, shingle and stony ground; locally abundant.

Wild Cabbage Cruciferae *Brassica oleracea.* **Distribution:** Southern English, northern and southern Welsh coasts. **Notes:** A cliff plant; may occur as an escape from cultivation.

Buck's Horn Plantain Plantaginaceae *Plantago coronopus.* **Distribution:** Around all British Isles coasts; scattered inland in England. **Notes:** Dry, more or less open habitats; sandy or gravelly soils; also in cracks in rocks.

Sea Beet Chenopodiaceae *Beta vulgaris* ssp. *maritima.* **Distribution:** Around English, Welsh, Irish and southern Scottish coasts. **Notes:** Only on sea shores; root is not conspicuously-swollen; plant a reddish colour.

advent of rice-grass is a mixed blessing. The very rapidity with which it spreads can be a cause of trouble. It may choke minor channels and also invade holiday beaches from nearby mud flats. Moreover, it may eliminate other salt marsh plants by competition and ruin the feeding grounds of over-wintering wildfowl.

The sea purslane, which grows along the borders of the creeks cut through salt marshes, has a similar effect. This low grey-green shrub is characteristic of well-drained habitats and examination of the edges of creeks shows that the mud there is raised slightly above the general level of the surrounding marsh. This is because material brought in by the tide is trapped as the tide flows slowly out again over the edges of the creeks. Silt and mud trapped in this way gradually builds up the creek borders. Once sea purslane is established, its tough stems assist further deposition of material so that the edges become further raised. When this shrub has become established, the cover is so dense that few other plants can survive in competition with it. Older, well-drained marshes may become colonised by sea purslane to the exclusion of other salt marsh plants.

The bird colonies of sea cliffs often have a marked effect on the vegetation by burrowing,

Sea pea *(Lathyrus japonicus)* is an uncommon plant of exposed shingle beaches. It is well adapted to this habitat with a long woody perennial rootstock.

trampling and manuring. The effect of trampling may be locally severe, as on the margins of cliff tops where puffins congregate and shuffle about, or on the points chosen by gulls for preening. Parts of the cliff edge made bare by

large colonies of puffins may become colonised in the summer, after the birds have departed, by annuals such as meadow grass. Burrowing by puffins and shearwaters may also destroy the turf by making it too dry, although thrift, which frequently possesses roots over a metre long, will often survive under these conditions. The effect of manuring varies. Extensive deposits of cormorant guano, together with the remains of semi-digested fish kill all plants, and several plants such as the samphire, which is widespread on sea cliffs, soon die out when exposed to bird excreta. On the other hand, enrichment by a moderate amount of bird manure encourages the development of grass swards and a number of algae, lichens and mosses are also generally associated with bird colonies for the same reason.

It is interesting that the forerunners of many cultivated food plants originated on the coast. Cultivated races of the wild cabbage include the various types of cabbage, kale, cauliflower and brussels sprout Sugar-beet, beetroot, mangolds and other vegetables have been developed from the sea beet. Other coastal plants such as the related sea kale and the samphire are also edible. It is important to conserve these plants to act as a reserve stock to improve the cultivated varieties if required.

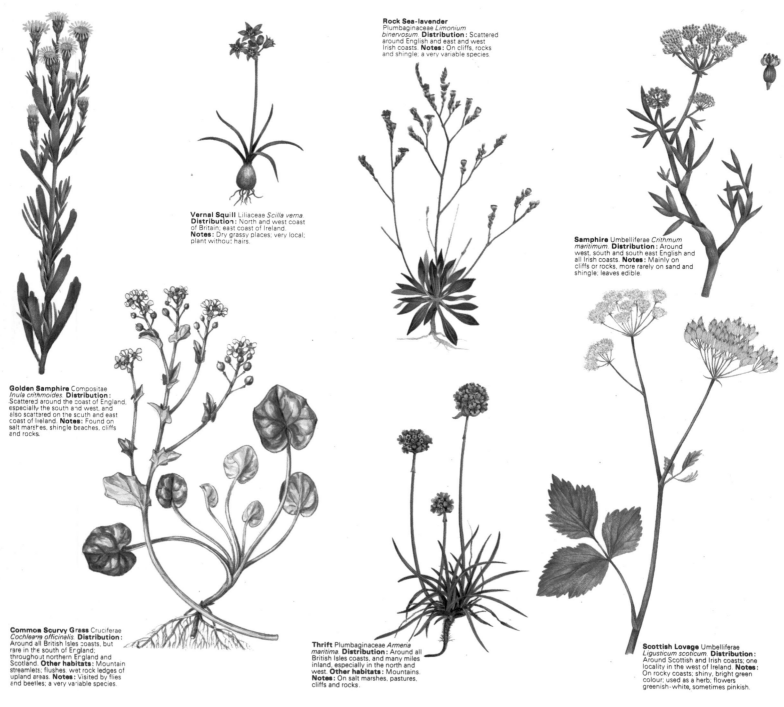

Rock Sea-lavender Plumbaginaceae *Limonium binervosum*. **Distribution:** Scattered around English and east and west Irish coasts. **Notes:** On cliffs, rocks and shingle; a very variable species.

Vernal Squill Liliaceae *Scilla verna*. **Distribution:** North and west coast of Britain; east coast of Ireland. **Notes:** Dry grassy places; very local; plant without hairs.

Samphire Umbelliferae *Crithmum maritimum*. **Distribution:** Around west, south and south east English and all Irish coasts. **Notes:** Mainly on cliffs or rocks, more rarely on sand and shingle; leaves edible.

Golden Samphire Compositae *Inula crithmoides*. **Distribution:** Scattered around the coast of England, especially the south and west, and also scattered on the south and east coast of Ireland. **Notes:** Found on salt marshes, shingle beaches, cliffs and rocks.

Common Scurvy Grass Cruciferae *Cochlearia officinalis*. **Distribution:** Around all British Isles coasts, but rare in the south of England; throughout northern England and Scotland. **Other habitats:** Mountain streamlets, flushes, wet rock ledges of upland areas. **Notes:** Visited by flies and beetles; a very variable species.

Thrift Plumbaginaceae *Armeria maritima*. **Distribution:** Around all British Isles coasts, and many miles inland, especially in the north and west. **Other habitats:** Mountains. **Notes:** On salt marshes, pastures, cliffs and rocks.

Scottish Lovage Umbelliferae *Ligusticum scoticum*. **Distribution:** Around Scottish and Irish coasts; one locality in the west of Ireland. **Notes:** On rocky coasts; shiny, bright green colour; used as a herb; flowers greenish-white, sometimes pinkish.

Coastal Invertebrates

The coastal habitats of Britain show some affinity with those of arable farmland as they tend to be unstable. As with coastal plants, some animals will continue to live on sand dunes and sea cliffs which cannot survive competition in more stable inland habitats. Two species of amber snails which were formerly widespread are now restricted to coastal sand dunes, while another snail, *Monacha cartusiana*, the numbers of which are declining, is now restricted to calcareous grasslands near the coast, although it formerly occurred inland. Some snails which have been introduced are also restricted to coastal habitats in the south and west. It is possible that they require the milder climate at the coast in order to survive.

Although it is possible to identify some invertebrates which are specifically coastal in their distribution, they are found in association with many others with a much wider distribution. For example, many sand dune species also occur inland where there are sufficiently extensive areas of sandy habitats. Examples include the sand dune spiders *Zelotes electus*, a nocturnal hunting spider, and *Arctosa perita*, a wolf spider, both of which occur on coastal sand dunes and also on inland southern heaths. However, at least twenty-eight species of spider are found exclusively on the coast, together with at least one false scorpion. In addition, sand dunes have a characteristic fauna of snails which are adapted to dry conditions. These include several species of the white banded snails *Helicella*, the yellow banded snails *Cepaea* and the garden snail *Helix*. None of these are restricted to dunes, however; they are also found in dry places inland. The species of *Helicella* are especially common on dry calcareous grassland. Two species of snail, the sandhill snail *Theba pisana* and pointed snail *Cochlicella acuta*, are restricted to coastal dunes.

Grasshoppers and bush crickets are particularly common in some coastal habitats in England. Their presence is often advertised more by their voice than by their appearance. At least twelve species of grasshopper are common on warm south-facing grassy slopes at the tops of cliffs along the south coast. These are all strictly vegetarian, feeding mainly on grass. They include the meadow grasshopper, common field grasshopper and stripe-winged grasshopper. Where scrub and bramble thickets occur along the tops of cliffs and on waste land, the more nocturnal bush crickets may be found, walking rather than hopping, among the bushes. Bush crickets also differ from grasshoppers in their diet, which consists of both vegetable and animal food, including small insects. One of the most striking is the great green bush cricket, which is about 5 centimetres long. Its loud song may be particularly frequently heard along the south coast from Dorset to Cornwall. The grey bush cricket and the long-winged conehead are seldom found away from the sea and are fairly common visitors along the cliffs of the south coast among rough vegetation. The short-winged conehead and lesser marsh grasshopper are found on moist low-lying grassland and especially

The painted lady *Vanessa cardui* is a migratory butterfly. Adults fly north from the continent to arrive in Britain each summer and may be seen crossing the English Channel on warm summer days.

The great green bush cricket *Tettigonia viridissima* is the largest British species of cricket and a frequent resident of coastal habitats. The female here is feeding and shows the long ovipositor which distinguishes her sex.

on salt marshes. The male conehead produces a quiet, high-pitched, reeling song which may continue without a break for up to two minutes. The scaly cricket occurs only on the seashore, where it lives in crevices among large stones. It may be found below the high tide mark, although it is not known whether it can survive immersion in sea water. Like several snails (for example the sandhill snail), this cricket has a restricted distribution in Britain, being found only on Chesil Beach.

Relatively few groups of terrestrial coastal invertebrates have been studied in depth, but the Lepidoptera (butterflies and moths) are among

The migratory humming-bird hawk-moth *Macroglossum stellatorum* feeds on nectar obtained through its long tongue whilst hovering in front of flowers.

A guide to some coastal butterflies

Although most species of butterfly may be found in coastal habitats, two groups may be regarded as pre-eminently coastal species. The first group are species which are generally restricted in their distribution to a few localities. These include the Glanville fritillary (Isle of Wight), Lulworth skipper (Dorset and south Devon), large blue (north Cornwall and Devon) and the Essex skipper (coasts of the Thames estuary). It seems likely that these uncommon butterflies are on the edge of their geographical range and the reasons for their restricted distribution have already been described.

The second group of coastal butterflies are the migrant species. Some, such as the painted lady and red admiral, arrive regularly each year and may be found throughout England and Wales. Others occur infrequently although sometimes in large numbers and these include the clouded yellow and pale clouded yellow. These species, together with other rarer immigrants such as the Queen of Spain fritillary, Bath white and some blue butterflies, are generally found on the south coast of England where they arrive from the Continent. Occasional monarch butterflies also arrive along the south west and south coasts of England and Wales.

The Glanville Fritillary Nymphalidae *Melitaea cinxia*. **Flight time:** May, June. Overwinters as larva. **Foodplant:** Sea plantain. **Distribution:** Coastal grasslands and undercliffs. Isle of Wight.

The Queen of Spain Fritillary Nymphalidae-*Argynnis lathonia*. **Flight time:** May to October. Does not overwinter in Britain. **Foodplant:** Violets. **Distribution:** A rare immigrant occurring occasionally in south and south-east England.

The Lulworth Skipper Hesperiidae-*Thymelicus acteon*. **Flight time:** July, August. Overwinters as larva. **Foodplant:** Tor-grass. **Distribution:** Confined to the coastal cliffs of Dorset and east Devon.

The Painted Lady Nymphalidae-*Vanessa cardui* **Flight time:** May to October. Probably never overwinters in Britain. **Foodplant:** Thistles. **Distribution:** Regular immigrant; numbers vary greatly year to year; early arrivals produce an autumn generation.

The Bath White Pieridae-*Pontia daplidice* **Flight time:** May to September. Spring immigrants produce late summer generation. Rarely overwinters in Britain. **Foodplant:** Mignonette, hedge mustard. **Distribution:** A rare immigrant. South coast of England. **Note:** Female with black spots on hindwing

The Red Admiral Nymphalidae-*Vanessa atalanta*. **Flight time:** March to November. Rarely overwinters as imago in Britain. **Foodplant:** Nettle. **Distribution:** A common immigrant occurring throughout the British Isles. Descendants of spring immigrants fly south in autumn.

The Clouded Yellow Pieridae *Colias croceus*. **Flight time:** Late summer (Aug-Sept). Overwinters as larva. **Foodplant:** Clovers, Melilots, Lucerne Etc. **Distribution:** Lucerne fields and waysides throughout Britain, but especially in the south.

The Berger's Clouded Yellow Pieridae *Colias australis*. **Flight time:** Late summer. Overwinters as larva. **Foodplant:** Horseshoe vetch. **Distribution:** Calcareous grassland in southern England.

The Pale Clouded Yellow Pieridae-*Colias hyale*. **Flight time:** May, June; August, September in two broods. Does not overwinter in Britain. **Foodplant:** Lucerne, clover. **Distribution:** An uncommon immigrant usually occurring in lucerne and clover fields in south-east England. **Note:** Male pale yellow. Female almost white.

The Monarch Danaiidae-*Danaus plexippus*. **Flight time:** August to November. Does not overwinter in Britain. **Foodplant:** Milkweeds (do not occur in Britain). **Distribution:** A rare vagrant from North America which most frequently occurs in south-west England.

The Camberwell Beauty Nymphalidae-*Nymphalis antiopa*. **Flight time:** August onwards. Overwinters as imago but only rarely in Britain. **Foodplant:** Sallows and willow. **Distribution:** A rare immigrant from Fennoscandia. South-east England occasionally more widespread.

the better known groups. Many species of butterfly may be found in coastal habitats, especially where the downs meet the sea. Several species are pre-eminently coastal, including the Glanville fritillary and the Lulworth skipper. The Glanville fritillary is restricted to the southern coasts of the Isle of Wight, where it is fairly common, particularly where the clay has slipped to form a series of small cliffs with grassy slopes. The larvae feed on sea and ribwort plantains which grow on these landslips. The Lulworth skipper is restricted to the Lulworth Cove area in Dorset and one or two localities in south Devon and is never found more than a few kilometres inland. The distribution of these two butterflies is unusual since they are not characteristically coastal species on the Continent. It seems likely that they are on the edge of their geographical range and that these localities suit their particular needs. Another very localised species is the rare ground lackey moth, which is restricted to the Thames estuary, where its larvae spin silken tents among the salt marsh plants on which they feed. Several widespread butterflies are commonly found in coastal habitats. The grayling, which does not like damp locations, is especially common on sand dunes, in company with the common blue, which ranges over the whole of Britain, as far as the north coast of Scotland and the Hebrides and Orkneys. Several species of moth are also associated with coastal habitats and in many cases the larvae feed on coastal plants. Examples include the scarce pug moth, whose larvae feed on the sea wormwood and which is restricted to salt marshes in Norfolk, and a small pyralid moth whose larvae feed on saltwort.

The most conspicuous butterflies and moths of the coast are the migrant species. Since these usually arrive from the Continent, they are most frequent along the south coast, especially in areas such as Dungeness, which juts out into the Channel and act as a landfall for migrants. Because of its geographical location it is perhaps not surprising that Dungeness has a number of rare and local species of moth. Many of the immigrants arrive regularly in the spring and breed during the summer, producing adults by early autumn. These include the red admiral, painted lady butterflies and silver Y moth and there is evidence of a return migration south-

A guide to some coastal moths

The silver Y moth provides an example of the many smaller moths which migrate to the British Isles each year. This moth is widely distributed and may be found from early spring to late autumn both along the coast and inland. A number of large hawk-moths arrive along the British coast each year, originating mainly from southern Europe and the Mediterranean region, and several examples are shown here. Immigrant hawk-moths, such as the convolvulus hawk and the death's-head hawk, are found mainly along the south and east coasts but occasional individuals have been found as far north as the Shetlands. The humming-bird hawk moth was common throughout Britain but has become less so in recent years.

The spurge hawk is a sporadic immigrant which occasionally breeds in coastal localities laying its eggs on sea spurge and portland spurge on shingle and sand beaches. Yellow tail and brown tail moths both produce urticating hairs that cause severe skin irritation when handled. The hairs are used to coat the eggs so that they are protected from predators.

Brown tail moths often become established on hawthorn and other shrubs in coastal areas and the larvae are also protected by irritating hairs. The colourful tiger moths are established in southern England where their larvae feed on a variety of flowering plants. The Jersey tiger is particularly a feature of the south Devon coast.

The Silver Y Noctuidae-*Autographa gamma*. **Flight time**: Early spring to late autumn as immigrants and progeny. Probably does not overwinter in Britain. **Foodplant**: Many herbaceous plants. **Distribution**: Throughout the British Isles, frequently abundant everywhere.

The Convolvulus Hawk-moth Sphingidae-*Agrius convolvuli*. **Flight time**: July to November. Probably never overwinters in Britain. **Foodplant**: Field bindweed. **Distribution**: A regular immigrant. Occurs throughout Britain in years of plenty.

The Brown-tail Lymantriidae-*Euproctis chrysorrhoea*. **Flight time**: July, August. Overwinters as larva. **Foodplant**: Blackthorn, hawthorn. **Distribution**: South and south-east coast of England, apparently spreading into the Midlands.

The White Satin Moth Lymantriidae-*Leucoma salicis* **Flight time**: July, August. Overwinters as larva. **Foodplant**: Poplar, sallow **Distribution**: Coastal in eastern and southern counties. Lancashire; inland in eastern England.

The Death's-head Hawk-moth Sphingidae-*Acherontia atropos*. **Flight time**: May to September. Probably never overwinters in Britain. **Foodplant**: Potato. **Distribution**: A regular immigrant recorded in most years.

The Humming-bird Hawk-moth Sphingidae-*Macroglossum stellatarum*. **Flight time**: Throughout the year except winter. Occasionally overwinters as imago in extreme south-west England. **Foodplant**: Bedstraw, wild madder. **Distribution**: Immigrant. Numbers vary greatly; in some years occurs throughout much of Britain.

The Jersey Tiger Arctiidae-*Euplagia quadripunctaria*. **Flight time**: End July to early September. Overwinters as larva. **Foodplant**: Dandelion, plantain, dead-nettle, ground ivy. **Distribution**: South coast of Devon from Seaton to Torquay; elsewhere as an immigrant.

The Spurge Hawk-moth Sphingidae-*Hyles euphorbiae*. **Flight time**: June. Overwinters as pupa; probably never in Britain. **Foodplant**: Spurge. **Distribution**: A very rare immigrant occasionally occurring in southern England. Absent in many years.

The Grass Eggar Lasiocampidae-*Lasiocampa trifolii*. **Flight time**: August, September. Overwinters as ovum. **Foodplant**: Grasses, trefoils and other herbaceous plants. **Distribution**: Very local; almost entirely confined to coastal sandhills in England—Lancashire, Cornwall, Devon, Dorset, Hampshire, Sussex, Kent, Suffolk and Norfolk. **Note**: Male chocolate brown, female lighter.

The Thrift Clearwing Sesiidae-*Bembecia muscaeformis*. **Flight time**: End June, July. Overwinters as larva. **Foodplant**: Internally in the roots of thrift. **Distribution**: Coasts of Devon, Cornwall, Wales, Cumbria, north-east Scotland.

The Scarlet Tiger Arctiidae-*Callimorpha dominula*. **Flight time**: June, July. Overwinters as larva. **Foodplant**: Nettle, dock, comfrey etc. **Distribution**: Very local, in south and south west England and south Wales.

The Ground Lackey Lasiocampidae-*Malacosoma castrensis*. **Flight time**: July, August. Overwinters as ovum. **Foodplant**: Sea wormwood, sea plantain, wild carrot. **Distribution**: Confined to the salt-marshes of Suffolk, Essex and Kent. **Note**: Male yellowish. Female dark brown.

The larva of the death's-head hawk-moth *Acherontia atropos* feeds on the potato plant; the species has not become established because our winter climate is unsuitable.

wards, in the autumn, of the newly emerged adults. Those adults which remain usually die in the winter, although a few red admirals may survive. Several other species arrive from abroad in large numbers at irregular intervals. They may breed, but do not overwinter successfully. Examples include the clouded yellow and pale clouded yellow. Small numbers of the Camberwell beauty occur from time to time but, unlike the other butterflies, they are found in eastern England, and appear to originate from Scandinavia. Since this species is a late summer migrant it does not breed in Britain, although one or two individuals may overwinter. Other rare migrants which never appear in large numbers include the Queen of Spain fritillary and the long-tailed and short-tailed blues. The Bath white is also scarce but a few large immigrations have occurred in past years. A small number of monarch butterflies have been found mainly in the south west and along the south coasts. This is a North American butterfly which migrates from the southern USA to southern Canada in spring, with a return movement in autumn of newly-emerged butterflies. While it seems likely that some of the monarchs reaching British shores have crossed the Atlantic on ships there are indications that some insects flying south in the autumn have crossed the Atlantic aided by westerly winds.

The populations of several resident British butterflies are reinforced by immigration. Perhaps the most important of these is the large white butterfly, which is an important pest species. Its main immigration period is at the end of July and early August and it comes chiefly from the east across the North Sea. The migrating butterflies seem to originate mainly in southern Scandinavia and move south and west across Europe. It has been suggested that without these reinforcements the large white might not survive in Britain, since large numbers of British-reared pupae are killed by parasites. The total number of British moths which have been shown to migrate is considerable, probably in excess of one hundred species. It includes at least nine of the large hawk-moths. The two most frequent hawk-moth migrants are the humming-bird hawk and the convolvulus hawk, both of which are widely distributed abroad. The humming-bird hawk is a small-sized moth which hovers in the sunshine in front of a flower, with wings beating rapidly and long tongue extended. It migrates to the British Isles from southern Europe in the spring and returns in the autumn. The convolvulus hawk-moth, a large, powerful, fast-flying moth, has a similar migration pattern, but is found mainly along the south and east coasts of England. The death's-head hawk-moth is the largest British moth and has the frightening habit of forcing air through

The **ruby-tailed wasp** *Chrysis ingita* is commonly found around sandy coastal areas. It is a parasitic cuckoo-wasp laying its eggs in the nest of bees and other wasps. Its young feeds on the host's grubs or stored prey.

its short tongue when alarmed to make a squeaking noise. It is less common than the other species and occurs most frequently in the south east.

Many other kinds of insect arrive along the British coasts as the result of migration. These have even included occasional migratory and

desert locusts; for example 32 migratory locusts were captured in 1947, nearly all on the south coast from Kent to Devon. These visits, which take place in late summer and autumn, depend on unusual weather conditions over north Africa and western Europe and many years may pass between one batch of immigrants and the next. It is unlikely that these locusts could survive for very long in Britain. At least a quarter of the British dragonflies are also migrants. The migrations of dragonflies resemble those of butterflies in that there is evidence of a return flight south in the autumn. Among other migratory insects the ladybirds and hoverflies are especially noticeable, as they appear suddenly in enormous numbers, particularly near the south and east coasts in years when their prey, the aphis or green-fly, is particularly numerous. At such times they are a considerable nuisance to holidaymakers on beaches. On one occasion at Bournemouth, the bodies of hoverflies were so numerous along the drift line that they could be collected with shovels.

Several animals from marine groups have established themselves at or just above the high tide mark. These include the sandhopper, *Orchestia gammarella*, which feeds on decaying seaweed. It is often abundant under drift cast up on the shore and on salt marshes. The closely-related sandhopper *Talitrus saltator* lives on sandy shores and burrows in well-drained sand just above the high tide mark. When they are disturbed, the jumping hoppers form a cloud above the surface of the sand.

Invertebrates of the drift line

A thin belt of drift-wood, dead seaweeds and other plant material accumulates at the level of the highest spring tides on the turf of salt marsh and at the seaward edge of sand dunes. This drift is often accompanied by early colonising plants such as saltwort and sea rocket on sandy shores. The drift line represents an ecotone between the truly marine and truly terrestrial habitats, and has a rich fauna of invertebrates feeding on the decaying plant material together with their associated predators. Animals living in the drift are exposed to unstable conditions since the salinity varies widely from sea water to rain water, and considerable mechanical disturbance may result from wave action at very high tides. Among the most obvious animals are the sandhoppers, which, when disturbed, jump for distances of several feet and, since their numbers are so large, often form a cloud above the surface of the drift. Large numbers of small snails such as the two-toothed white snail and the mouse-ear-shelled snail also shelter under drift on salt marshes. Many fly larvae feed on the decaying seaweed including the kelp-fly, which in mild autumns may be present in such large numbers that it causes a problem. Common predators in the drift include ground beetles and surprisingly large numbers of spiders. The moist atmosphere under the drift attracts large numbers of springtails and mites, some of the latter being predatory on the springtails. Woodlice are often common including one species, *Armadillidium album*, which is confined to the drift line on the west coast.

Springtails *Lipura maritima* feeding on the underside of a dead limpet. Their presence on the seashore is unusual in that insects as a group are relatively rare; their place being usually taken by species of crustacean.

The Essex skipper is a butterfly which inhabits old saltings along the Essex coast. The red spot on its eye is a mite and a regular predator of butterflies and other insects.

Two sandhoppers *Talitrus saltator* crawl among sand and rotting seaweed on the strand line. These crustaceans are vulnerable to drying by the wind and sun and rarely venture far from the damp strand line.

Two bristletails *Petrobius maritimus* crawling over a rock. These primitive insects, relatives of the household "silverfish", are particularly characteristic of the splash zone at the top of the shore.

Coastal Birds

Most species of British birds can be seen near the coast because of the range of habitats found there. But there are about three dozen birds which are truly characteristic of the coast and which form a well-defined group made up of a limited number of families. Although many species are flexible in their requirements and occur over a wide range of coastal habitats, other birds have much more specific needs in terms of feeding grounds, nesting sites and climatic conditions and their distribution is correspondingly limited. Two factors help to determine this distribution: firstly the wide range of form and structure of the coastline, and secondly the special position of the British Isles, situated between a continent and the open Atlantic. The British coast is thus exposed to a wide range of climatic conditions, depending partly on whether a particular stretch of coast faces towards or away from the much larger continental land mass. In general, there is a difference of three or four degrees centigrade between the average temperature of the colder and warmer areas in the British Isles at any one time. In addition the composition of the coastal bird fauna shows seasonal changes, with a winter fauna markedly different from that in summer. Between these seasons, in autumn and spring, there are two periods when migrating birds move along the British coast because it forms part of their migration route. In addition to this complex of factors the distribution of coastal birds is also modified locally by the activities of man.

Colonial cliff nesters

Seabirds as a group are the most colonial of birds, often returning year after year to certain favoured stretches of coast which offer safe nesting sites on cliffs and islands. These colonies are often enormous; the colony of fulmars on St. Kilda, for example, contains over 22,000 pairs, while the colony of gannets on the same islands, the largest in Europe, numbers about 52,000 pairs. The colony of Manx shearwaters on Skomer Island (Pembrokeshire) numbers about 50,000 pairs, while there are an estimated 6,000 pairs of storm petrels on nearby Skokholm. Between 13,000 and 16,000 pairs of black-headed gulls nest on the sand dunes at Ravenglass in Cumberland, and about 1,000 pairs of great black-backed gulls nest on the grassland of North Rona.

The most crowded colonies are those of gannets and guillemots. There may be less than a metre between one nest and the next in many gannetries and since guillemots have no true nest, they crowd even closer together on cliff ledges, standing shoulder to shoulder. The reason for the formation of colonies is not entirely clear. Colonial seabirds feed on fish which, though locally abundant in shoals, are widely scattered. It is possible that by living in colonies the birds are able to exploit each shoal more efficiently. The colony may also afford additional

Birds nesting on narrow cliff ledges show adaptations for this habitat. Kittiwakes have longer, sharper claws for a more secure hold on narrow ledges and their nests often jut out over the edge.

Wading birds, such as the dunlin seen here, are well adapted to life on open mud flats with their relatively long legs and beaks adapted for probing sand for food.

protection to the nests, as the continuing existence of a colony indicates that the location is inaccessible to predators. One bird may alert the others to possible danger and often the birds will join in a communal attack on an intruder, which can be very effective, as any visitor to a ternery will confirm. A less likely reason is the lack of suitable ledges and other nesting sites in more inaccessible and therefore safer places. Evidence for this is that some species require particular kinds of sites. The young of guillemots and razorbills, for example, jump into the sea before

Part of a breeding colony of gannets. Gannets only nest in large colonies where they space themselves out so as to be just beyond pecking distance from their neighbours.

they are fully fledged and require cliffs which fall straight into the water, at least at high tide. Sheer cliffs are therefore necessary and those with undercliffs are unsuitable for these birds.

On high cliffs, especially on islands, guillemots and razorbills tend to nest on open ledges, laying their eggs on bare rock. They are incubated clutched between the legs of the birds, which stand in rows along the ledges. Kittiwakes also nest on cliff ledges, but they build a true nest of seaweed and other debris, even on narrow ledges where the nest has to jut out beyond the ledge. Large colonies of kittiwakes are found on vertical or even overhanging cliffs.

Several hole-nesting birds form colonies on the earthy slopes which develop at cliff tops. Puffins excavate burrows up to 3 metres in length using their bills and feet. Since colonies may contain several hundreds of nests, the ground becomes so honeycombed that it may even collapse in places. The Manx shearwater, storm petrel and Leach's petrel nest in a similar way, although they may also use ready-made holes such as rabbit burrows, or nest in crevices among boulders. These three species are restricted to the west coast, where they usually nest on islands. During the breeding season, they are active mainly at night. The related fulmar prefers ledges with some soil, where the egg can be laid in a depression scraped in the earth. The cormorant and shag also build their large untidy nests on cliff ledges but are not restricted to these sites, the shag also nesting in deep crevices and in cavities among boulders, and the cormorant choosing flat exposed rocky sites, grassy headlands and even occasionally trees inland. Gannets build nests of flotsam and seaweed in compact colonies on steep rocky slopes. There are 13 gannetries in the British Isles, all of them, with only one or two exceptions, on isolated offshore islands. One of the most famous gannetries is that on Bass Rock in the Firth of

The Arctic tern

The Arctic tern may be regarded as the champion traveller of the bird world, since the northern limit of its breeding range is high inside the Arctic Circle and in the autumn it travels southwards along the coast of Europe and Africa, to winter off the coast of South Africa and in the Antarctic Ocean, a journey of up to 16,000 kilometres which is repeated the following spring. The Arctic tern is very similar to the common tern and both have similar nesting habits but the Arctic tern has a more northerly distribution, rarely breeding south of a line from Anglesey to the Wash. The common tern's breeding range extends over the whole country and it may even nest inland.

The Arctic tern is intensely aggressive in its breeding colonies, dive-bombing intruders, and has been known to draw blood from a man's head. The colonies often number several thousands of pairs and the nest is simply a scrape in the sand or shingle lined with grass or other materials. Three eggs are usually laid in May or June. These hatch in about three weeks and the young, which are fully active and leave the nest after a few days, fly after three or four weeks. The ground colour of the eggs varies considerably and often eggs of different colours, laid by the same bird, can be found in a single nest. In common with other terns, numbers have probably declined owing to the loss of nesting sites and disturbance by holiday makers. Terns are also taken for food as they pass along the coast of Africa during migration.

The Arctic tern in flight, showing the slender body, long narrow wings and forked tail, characteristic features of most British terns. Annually the Arctic tern migrates to and from the Antarctic.

The fulmar, a bird of the open sea, has long, narrow wings adapted for effortless gliding flight. They follow trawlers and other ships in search of food.

Forth. The young birds in many of these colonies were formerly harvested for food by islanders and this practice is continued in a few places such as Sula Sgeir.

On the increase

These days, when so many species seem to be declining, especially certain seabirds, it is pleasing to note that one—the fulmar—is certainly increasing in numbers and range. For many centuries, St. Kilda was the only home for this species in Britain. Then, in 1878, they were found nesting in Shetland and over the past 100 years the species has colonised most of the cliffs of our coasts. With a breeding population of over 300,000 pairs, the fulmar is now one of our most numerous seabirds. Many colonies are still growing by 5 per cent per year.

Gulls have also become more abundant, though this is perhaps a less welcome trend. Large colonies of the ubiquitous herring gull breed on many cliffs and also amongst the vegetation on the tops of many offshore islands. Non-breeding colonies consisting of many hundreds of individuals can also be found in the spring and summer on cliffs. The herring gull has extended its choice of breeding sites in recent years to include the chimneys and roof tops of houses in coastal towns, where it has become a considerable nuisance. This bird is essentially a scavenger and the recent increase in its numbers may be due to the increasing amount of domestic refuse on rubbish tips, where large flocks of herring gulls can be seen feeding. These recent changes in feeding behaviour and nesting sites give some cause for concern, as the gulls present a potential health hazard and may transmit harmful micro-organisms to man. The lesser black-backed gull has similar nesting and feeding habits. Both birds may cause damage to nesting colonies of other sea birds by eating eggs and young birds, but the principal problem they cause in coastal nature reserves is the displacement of rarer and more interesting species. The large, aggressive gulls nest early and occupy all the best sites. They then prevent other birds, particularly terns, from nesting in the same area. The increase in gull populations has thus caused many difficulties and the gulls have had to be drastically reduced in numbers; many thousands have been removed from the Isle of May, for example.

The Arctic and great skuas rob nests in sea bird colonies and also feed by chasing gulls, terns and other birds until they disgorge their meal. These skuas breed mainly on moorland and grassy hills by the sea in a few remote islands in the far north and west of Scotland, although they may be seen while migrating off other coasts in autumn.

Perhaps the most important predator of sea bird colonies is the great black-backed gull, the largest of Britain's gulls. It breeds on cliffs but in much smaller numbers than the other gulls and mainly in the west and north. Like other large gulls it is increasing in numbers and poses a threat to rarer birds which nest in the same

areas, such as the Manx shearwater.

Other birds of the coast

Several non-maritime crows and birds of prey breed on coastal cliffs, including the raven, carrion crow, jackdaw, peregrine, common buzzard and kestrel. One notable coastal crow species is the chough, which formerly occurred all along the west coast but is now restricted to north Wales, the Isle of Man and a few localities on the west coast of Scotland. It forms part of the Cornish coat of arms, but has not bred there since the 1950s. These birds are particularly spectacular in flight, soaring on the updraught at the edge of cliffs and swooping down from ledge to ledge. They also perform acrobatics, diving with the wings almost closed and turning

over on their backs in the air. The rock pipit is a common bird on most rocky shores, breeding in holes or crevices in cliffs and feeding on insects and other invertebrates, particularly amongst rotting seaweed. In winter it moves on to muddy shores and salt marshes. The rock dove, from which domestic pigeons are descended, nests in holes or on ledges, often in sea caves. It is now restricted in the British Isles to a few colonies in Scotland and Ireland, mainly on the north and west coasts. However, on many rocky coasts there are plenty of multicoloured feral pigeons to be seen, descendants of the original rock doves.

Terns breed in closely-packed colonies of varying size and two or more species may be found nesting together. Dense colonies provide protection in numbers. Moreover, in such colonies, egg laying is synchronised so that thousands of eggs may all be laid in the space of a couple of weeks. The sheer numbers ensure that predators like foxes and crows are saturated with food. They cannot possibly eat more than a few at one time, leaving the rest to survive. The five British coastal terns are found mainly on sand dunes and shingle beaches where they make a scrape in the sand or shingle, which may be unlined in the case of the roseate tern, lined with small stones by the little tern or lined with pieces of grass and other plant material by the common, arctic and sandwich terns. The eggs and the newly-hatched chicks are well camouflaged against their background of stones and pebbles. The little tern tends to be restricted to shingle beaches and is very vulnerable both to human disturbance and to storm waves. The other species also nest on grassy slopes and beaches of rocky islands. On the Farne Islands, for example, all four species, including the rare roseate tern, occur together.

The brent goose

The brent goose, like other geese, is a winter visitor. However, it is more maritime than other geese and feeds in large flocks along the water's edge, or even on the water by up-ending like a duck to find food. It roosts on the sea at night. This goose relies mainly on eel-grass for its food and when a disease severely reduced the eel-grass beds in the 1930s, numbers of the goose also declined considerably. The numbers have since recovered, partly due to protection from

shooting. When eel-grass is scarce, the brent goose will also feed on adjacent agricultural land. Two races of this goose visit the British Isles. The pale-breasted form comes from Greenland and winters mainly in Ireland, and the dark-breasted from Arctic Russia and Siberia, winters mainly on the east coast of England. Since about twenty per cent of the European population of dark-breasted, brent geese overwinter on the Maplin Sands and on the adjoining coasts, overwintering

populations of this race of the goose would have been threatened by the building of a new airport on the sands. Experiments with marked birds have shown that about half the birds returned to the sites where they had been marked, in the following year, although as the winter progresses, some birds from the Maplin Sands disperse further to other estuaries along the south coast and even into France.
A number of other localities on the eastern and southern coasts of Britain support

significant numbers of brent geese during the winter months, notably the mud flats of the Wash, on the coast of Lincolnshire and Norfolk and in the estuaries of the Essex coast at sites like Fingringhoe. The harbours on the south coast of Hampshire and Sussex are also important sites, especially Langstone harbour.

Dark-bellied brent geese feeding along the edge of salt marsh. This sea goose lives in large flocks and feeds in winter mainly on eel-grass, one of the few flowering plants to grow in sea water.

A guide to gulls, terns and skuas

Gulls are long, moderately broad winged, medium to fairly large birds. Most adult gulls are white with grey or black backs and wings, usually with dark wing tips. The head of the black-headed gull is entirely chocolate-brown in summer, changing to white in winter. Immature gulls are usually mottled with dark brown. Beaks are stout, wedge-shaped, slightly hooked; the feet are webbed, with the colour of bill and legs important characters in identification. Flight is powerful and buoyant, with wing beats slow and regular; the bird often soars and glides. Wings are held angled in flight. The tail is square or rounded. Gulls can be seen all round the coast throughout the year, and frequently roost on the sea.

Terns are slender, small to medium sized gull-like birds with long, narrower wings. Most terns are whitish, with black caps. The slender, sharply pointed beak is held downwards in flight; the colour is important for recognition. The feet are webbed but the bird rarely alights on water, although it frequently rests on rocks and posts along the shore. Flight is graceful and swallowlike. The bird feeds by hovering within a few feet of the water and then plunging for fish. The tail is forked. Terns are summer visitors and occur on beaches, salt marshes and rocky islands.

Skuas are moderately large birds with stout, hooked beaks and long well-developed wings. Colour is variable, but generally brownish with a flash of white on the wing. The feet are webbed; skuas often rest on water. Flight is powerful; the bird remains in the air for long periods, manoeuvring well when chasing other seabirds and robbing them of their food. It will also take food from the surface of the sea. There are elongated central tail feathers, although these are not well developed in the great skua. Skuas are essentially marine birds but breed on moorland on Scottish islands off the north coast.

Great Skua Stercorariidae *Stercorarius skua.* **Distribution:** Breeds in northern Scotland. Passage migrant elsewhere. **Other habitats:** Maritime, breeds on moorland and rough pasture on islands. **Notes:** Size: 58cm. Distinguished from Arctic Skua by blunt tail, conspicuous white wing-patches and broad, rounded wings. Dashing, hawk-like flight. Voice is a loud "hah-hah-hah-hah".

Arctic Skua dark phase

Arctic Skua light phase

Arctic Skua Stercorariidae *Stercorarius parasiticus.* **Distribution:** Breeds in northern Scotland. Passage migrant elsewhere. **Other habitats:** Maritime, breeds on moorland and rough pastures on islands. **Notes:** Size: 45cm. Flight is graceful and hawk-like. Pursues other sea-birds. Wings pointed with white flash at tip. Long, pointed tail projection. Voice is a wailing "ki-aow".

Great Black-backed Gull Laridae *Larus marinus.* **Distribution:** Breeds in Ireland and Great Britain, except east coast. **Other habitats:** Breeds on rocky coasts and islands. Estuaries, lakes and rivers in winter. **Notes:** Size: 65cm. Distinguished from Lesser Black-backed by black back, pink legs, larger size and deeper voice. Behaviour fiercely predatory. Voice is a barking "aouk".

Lesser Black-backed Gull Laridae *Larus fuscus.* **Distribution:** Breeds on north and west coasts. Passage migrant and winter visitor. **Other habitats:** Breeds on islands and inland moors. **Notes:** Size: 53cm. Grey back, yellow legs. Flight is powerful, usually with much gliding. Voice is a loud "kiaow-kiaow".

Herring Gull winter

Herring Gull summer

Herring Gull Laridae *Larus argentatus.* **Distribution:** Resident. **Other habitats:** Coast, estuaries and fields inland. Breeds on cliffs. **Notes:** Size: 56cm. Distinguished from Common Gull by heavier yellow bill, with red spot and flesh-pink legs. Voice is a loud "kyow-kyow", also varied mewing and barking notes.

Herring Gull juvenile

Common Gull Laridae *Larus canus.* **Distribution:** Breeds in Scotland and Ireland. Winter visitor elsewhere. **Other habitats:** Breeds on moorlands and around lochs. Winters on coasts. **Notes:** Size: 41cm. Has black band on white tail. Greenish yellow bill and legs. No red spot on bill. Voice is a shrill, mewing "kee-ya".

Black-headed Gull winter

Black-headed Gull summer

Black-headed Gull Laridae *Larus ridibundus.* **Distribution:** Resident in Great Britain and Ireland. **Other habitats:** Breeds on coasts, gravel pits, sewage farms and pools. **Notes:** Size: 36cm. Adults have chocolate brown hood in summer. Wings are pointed with pure white leading edge. Flight is buoyant and often follows ploughs. Voice is a harsh "kwarr".

Kittiwake adult

Kittiwake juvenile

Kittiwake Laridae *Rissa tridactyla.* **Distribution:** Resident in Great Britain and Ireland. **Other habitats:** Breeds on sea cliffs. **Notes:** Size: 41cm. Distinguished from Common Gull by black wing tips, dark diagonal band across wing and dark neck bar. Voice is a screaming "kitt-ee-wake".

Black Tern summer

Black Tern winter

Black Tern Laridae *Chlidonias niger.* **Distribution:** Breeds in Cambridgeshire. Passage migrant north to central Scotland. **Other habitats:** Breeds on wet marshes and fens. Coast and inland waters on passage. **Notes:** Size: 24cm. Plumage all black in summer except white under tail-coverts. Bill completely black. Dips erratically to pick insects off water. Voice is a squeaky "kik-kik".

Common Tern summer

Common Tern winter

Common Tern Laridae *Sterna hirundo.* **Distribution:** Summer visitor. **Other habitats:** Breeds on shingle banks, coastal lagoons, rivers, lakes and gravel pits. **Notes:** Size: 35cm. In summer bill is orange-red with black tip, in winter blackish with red base. Tail does not extend beyond wing tips when sitting. Voice is a high-pitched "kee-yah".

Arctic Tern Laridae *Sterna paradisaea.* **Distribution:** Breeds in northern England, Scotland and Ireland. Elsewhere a passage migrant. **Other habitats:** Coastal. **Notes:** Size: 35cm. In summer bill is wholly blood-red, in winter wholly blackish. Tail slightly extends beyond wings when sitting. Voice is a whistling "kee-kee".

Roseate Tern Laridae *Sterna dougallii.* **Distribution:** Breeds around Irish Sea, north-east England and eastern Scotland. **Other habitats:** Coastal. **Notes:** Size: 38cm. In summer bill is mainly black, in winter wholly blackish. Voice is a gutteral "aaak".

Sandwich Tern Laridae *Sterna sandvicensis.* **Distribution:** Summer visitor in Great Britain and Ireland. **Other habitats:** Breeds on sand-dunes, saltings and shingle. **Notes:** Size: 40cm. In summer and winter bill is black with yellow tip. Heavier built than other terns. Flight is more gull-like than other terns. Voice is a grating "kirrick".

Little Tern Laridae *Sterna albifrons.* **Distribution:** Summer visitor in Great Britain and Ireland. **Other habitats:** Coastal. **Notes:** Size: 24cm. In summer and winter bill is yellow with black tip. Yellow legs. Tail is short. Rapid wing-beats and long hovers before diving. Voice is a rasping "kik-kik".

A guide to some coastal waders

The term wader is applied to a number of small to medium-sized walking and running terrestrial birds that are generally associated with marshes, estuaries, the sea shore and similar habitats bordering fresh or sea water. In many cases the plumage is largely brown or greyish, uneven or finely mottled with dark colour on a light ground above, and paler or whitish beneath. Most species have distinct summer, winter and juvenile plumage. Many of these birds breed individually on moors and other inland habitats, but outside the breeding season are gregarious and generally occur in mixed flocks. Flight is rapid and direct with quick, regular wing beats and markedly angled wings. Identification characteristics in flight include bill length and presence of bars on the wings. The waders can be divided into two groups.

Charadriidae (plovers) are compact waders with thicker necks and more distinct patterns than the Scolopacidae. The bills are shorter and stouter and eyes larger. This family includes the grey plover, turnstone and ringed plover. In winter large numbers of another plover, the lapwing, join the flocks of waders along the coast. Scolopacidae (snipe, curlews, godwits and sandpipers) are a much larger and more varied group of wading birds. The legs are long or very long. The wings are markedly pointed and angular in flight, and the bills slender and often (e.g. in the curlew and the whimbrel) relatively long.

Three remaining waders, oystercatcher, avocet and spoonbill, belong to different families but their colour patterns are sufficiently distinct to make them unmistakable.

Curlew Scolopacidae *Numenius arquata.* **Distribution:** Resident in Great Britain and Ireland. **Other habitats:** Breeds in upland areas though also wet meadows, heaths and dunes. **Notes:** Size: 55cm. Flies at any hint of danger. Has regular, gull-like wing-beats. Voice is varied but loud "coorwee-coorwee" is familiar.

Whimbrel Scolopacidae *Numenius phaeopus.* **Distribution:** Summer visitor in Orkney and Shetland. Elsewhere occurs on passage. **Other habitats:** Breeds on moorlands. Passage birds on estuaries and rocky shores. **Notes:** Size: 40cm. Distinguished from Curlew by relatively shorter bill, boldly striped crown and faster wing-beat. Voice is a tittering "titti-titti-titti".

Bar-tailed Godwit Scolopacidae *Limosa lapponica.* **Distribution:** Passage migrant and winter visitor. **Other habitats:** Sandy shores and estuaries. **Notes:** Size: 36cm. In summer the whole of the underparts chestnut-red. No white wing-bars. Closely barred tail. Voice is a "kirruc-kirruc".

Oystercatcher Haematopodidae *Haematopus ostralegus.* **Distribution:** Resident, breeding on all coasts and inland from the Pennines north. **Other habitats:** Coast, estuaries and in the north; lakes, rivers and moorland. **Notes:** Size: 43cm. White rump with black and white tail conspicuous in flight. Flattened orange-red bill. Flies with shallow wing-beats. Voice is a noisy "kleep-kleep".

Turnstone Charadriidae *Arenaria interpres.* **Distribution:** Winter visitor, but non-breeders summer in many areas. **Other habitats:** Rocky or pebbly shores. **Notes:** Size: 23cm. "Tortoiseshell" plumage replaced by dusky brown in winter. Flies reluctantly and only for short distances. Turns stones when seeking food. Voice is a twittering "kitititit".

winter   summer

Purple Sandpiper Scolopacidae *Calidris maritima.* **Distribution:** Passage migrant and winter visitor. **Other habitats:** Rocky shores, weed covered piers and groynes. **Notes:** Size: 21cm. Short, yellow legs give portly appearance. Narrow appearance. Narrow white wing-bars. Flight is swift, direct and of short duration. Voice is a piping "wee-it".

Ringed Plover Charadriidae *Charadrius hiaticula.* **Distribution:** Resident. Breeds on all coasts. **Other habitats:** Shore-line and inland in the north. **Notes:** Size: 19cm. Active, running with brief pauses. Tilts to pick up food. Flight is rapid and low. White wing-bar conspicuous in flight. Voice is a liquid "too-li".

Little Ringed Plover Charadriidae *Charadrius dubius.* **Distribution:** Summer visitor in south and central England. **Other habitats:** Gravel pits, rivers and lakes. **Notes:** Size: 15cm. Distinguished from Ringed Plover by lack of white wing-bar, flesh-coloured legs and white line above black forehead band. Voice is a "pee-u".

Knot summer

Knot winter

Knot Scolopacidae *Calidris canutus.* **Distribution:** Passage migrant and winter visitor. **Other habitats:** Estuaries. **Notes:** Size: 25cm. Distinguished from Dunlin and Sanderling by pale wing-bars, pale rump and tail. Often in large, compact flocks. Voice is a mellow "twit-twit".

Ruff ♂ summer

Ruff ♀

winter

summer

Ruff Scolopacidae *Philomachus pugnax.* **Distribution:** Breeds in Cambridgeshire. Winter visitor in south. **Other habitats:** Water meadows. In winter: lakes, gravel pits and sewage farms. **Notes:** Size: 28cm. In winter distinguished from Redshank by dark tail with oval white patch on each side. Leg colours vary. Voice is a low "tu-whit".

Little Stint Scolopacidae *Calidris minuta.* **Distribution:** Passage migrant. **Other habitats:** Estuaries, inland reservoirs, sewage farms and lakes. **Notes:** Size: 13cm. In winter has cold grey upperparts. Flight is rapid. Narrow wing-bars and grey sides to tail. Voice is a sharp "chik".

Dunlin Scolopacidae *Calidris alpina.* **Distribution:** Breeds in Scotland and northern England. Elsewhere a passage and winter visitor. **Other habitats:** Breeds on moorlands. Estuaries in winter. **Notes:** Size: 18cm. Wheel and twist in flocks, alternately showing white undersides then darker upperparts. Feeding attitude is "hunched up". Voice is a weak "treap".

winter

Grey Phalarope Phalaropodidae *Phalaropus fulicarius.* **Distribution:** Passage migrant. **Other habitats:** Sea, occasionally on inland waters. **Notes:** Size: 20cm. Regularly swim which they do buoyantly, looking like miniature gulls. When feeding they "spin". Reluctant to take off and fly only short distances. Voice is a soft "twit".

Avocet Recurvirostridae *Recurvirostra avosetta.* **Distribution:** Summer visitor in Suffolk. Winters in south-west England. **Other habitats:** Breeds in shallow, brackish lagoons. Winters on estuaries. **Notes:** Size: 43cm. Black and white pattern conspicuous in flight, legs projecting beyond tail. Gait: a graceful, fairly quick walk. Noisy. Voice is a clear "klooit".

Sanderling Scolopacidae *Calidris alba.* **Distribution:** Passage migrant. **Other habitats:** Sandy shores. **Notes:** Size: 20cm. A very active bird almost ceaseless in its movements. Virtually white in winter plumage. Reluctant to take off. Has bright white wing-bars. Voice is a liquid "quit-quit".

winter

The ringed plover, like the little tern, nests mainly on shingle at the tops of beaches and has lost many of its nesting sites through seaside development. Numbers have been maintained, however, in reserves and the ringed plover is still a widespread species. The oystercatcher breeds on shingle, sand dunes and cliff tops and has recently begun nesting inland on moorland and arable fields. This bird has shown a marked increase in numbers over the past thirty years and is even considered a pest to shellfisheries in some localities. The shelduck, the largest British duck, nests on sand dunes and other rough ground near the sea using burrows which offer some protection against predators. Where the level of salt marshes is high enough to escape immersion except by the highest of spring tides, small colonies of black-headed gulls and common terns may be found where suitable nesting sites occur. Small islands cut off from the rest of the marsh are especially favoured because of the additional protection offered, particularly against rats. Shelduck also breed in estuaries if there are old rabbit burrows or similar holes in the sea wall suitable for nesting sites. Lapwing and occasionally redshank nest on reclaimed salt marshes, together with some inland birds such as the skylark.

The black tern, which nests in large colonies in freshwater marshes and lagoons in parts of Europe, occurs fairly frequently as a passage migrant along the coast of Kent and East Anglia. It formerly bred in south east England and has bred on one or two occasions recently in East Anglia. The avocet and spoonbill provide other examples of breeding birds which were lost to Britain during the eighteenth and nineteenth centuries, partly because of hunting and partly as the result of fen and marsh drainage. The return of the avocet as a breeding bird is one of the success stories of bird protection; it now breeds successfully on the Suffolk coast, although its rather specialised habitat of brackish shallow lagoons with sparsely vegetated mud flats must be maintained artificially by sea walls.

Seasonal changes

The distribution of breeding birds around the coast depends on the available habitats and climatic conditions. On the other hand, the distribution of passage migrants, winter visitors and, particularly, the vagrant or irregular visitors is largely determined by the position of the British Isles in relation to the Continent. A large proportion of migratory birds moving south in the autumn reach the Shetlands and Orkneys from Iceland and Greenland or from the northern coast of Norway and Spitzbergen.

The Puffin

Puffins are easily distinguished in summer by their huge, brightly coloured bills which serve as a weapon, a digging tool and to attract the female during courtship. In winter the bill loses its horny sheath and is less colourful. It is used to dig into the soil of the breeding sites to make nesting-burrows, loose earth being shovelled away with the bird's webbed feet. The single egg is laid in May in the burrow, which may be lined with grass and feathers. The nestling is fed for about six weeks and then deserted and left hungry. It eventually crawls out of the burrow and flutters down into the sea. Studies on puffin colonies off the Pembrokeshire coast showed that the most important foods brought to the chicks were sand-eels and sprats in loads averaging between seven and fourteen at a time. The adults fed quite close to the colony with a maximum feeding range of about thirty-two kilometres. Puffins carrying fish have been attacked on several occasions by lesser black-backed and herring gulls and jackdaws, which have attempted to steal their food.

The puffin has shown a marked decline in many breeding sites over the past few years especially on St. Kilda where it was the most numerous bird with a population estimated at two to three million pairs. The latest estimate is now about 160,000 pairs. The reasons for this decline are not fully understood although oil pollution and other forms of chemical pollution have undoubtedly contributed to this.

In Britain as a whole, the puffin has declined in numbers quite sharply in the past few decades. Many colonies on the marshland have been decimated by predators, disturbance or coastal development. The puffin's main strongholds today are the islands off the north and west coasts, most of which are relatively undisturbed and are still free of rats, foxes and other predators. Despite the declines, the puffin is still one of Britain's most abundant sea birds, totalling over half a million breeding pairs. However, its irregular behaviour and its habit of staying out of sight in inaccessible nest burrows make census taking a highly unreliable exercise.

A puffin arriving at its nesting burrow with food for chicks. Between seven and fourteen sand-eels or sprats are brought at a time.

Puffins breed in burrows in large colonies and this small group, with their prominent brightly coloured bills, seen sitting on rocks at the cliff edge probably represent only a small proportion of the total number of birds in the colony.

The avocet was once extinct in Britain as a breeding bird. However during the 1950's it was able to re-establish a colony on the Suffolk coast, protected by the RSPB. Avocets now breed in several coastal areas.

These groups divide into two streams, the greater number moving on down the east coast of Britain and away down the Channel. This stream is augmented by birds from the Baltic and southern Scandinavia coming across the North Sea. The western route runs south via the Hebrides to the north coast of Ireland, where it divides, joining again near the Isles of Scilly to continue along the west coast of France. In general, migrants tend to be less numerous along the north west coast of Scotland than along the east coast, although species like the Manx shearwater and the white-fronted and barnacle geese appear to prefer this route. Most migrant birds return in the spring by the same routes, but in some cases numbers appear to be less, probably because alternative routes are taken. Many of these migrants remain around the British coast during the winter months. It can be seen from the migration routes that some offshore islands such as Fair Isle (between Orkney and Shetland) and the Isles of Scilly are ideally situated as resting places for the maximum number of migrating birds, in addition to providing the first landfall for stray birds which have been driven by winds and storms over the Atlantic from North America, and oceanic birds such as albatrosses and petrels from the southern oceans and Atlantic islands. These islands and promontories (like Dungeness, Portland Bill, and Cape Clear) which jut out into the sea provide excellent places for viewing the passage of seabirds and are the sites of some of Britain's most important bird observatories.

During the spring and summer, the greater proportion of the coastal bird fauna consists of breeding birds, their distribution being determined by the availability of nesting sites. It has already been shown that these occur mainly on steep cliffs, offshore islands, and shingle shores and sand dunes. Relatively few birds nest in sheltered estuaries or on muddy shores, although non-breeding individuals such as immature gulls continue to feed in those localities which are used by the remainder of the population during the winter months. Marked changes in coastal bird populations take place in autumn. Most of the breeding seabirds are summer visitors and many species disperse over the open sea. These include the storm and Leach's petrels, kittiwake, fulmar, shearwaters, gannet, skuas and the auks. Some of these travel great distances; for example, some Manx shearwaters travel across the Atlantic in winter to the coasts of eastern South America. Others, like the razorbill and guillemot, travel less far from land and may be driven on to the coast during severe storms. Terns migrate south to the coasts of Africa or even further. Some lesser and great black-backed gulls may migrate but many remain and numbers of the latter species are reinforced by others coming from northern Europe.

Over-wintering in estuaries

During winter the open expanses of estuarine mud flats, with their rich supply of invertebrates and green algae and with little or no cover for the approach of predators, make ideal feeding grounds for geese, ducks and waders, particularly as these sheltered waters remain ice-free. The most obvious birds in winter are geese, often seen in flocks of several thousand, grazing on reclaimed salt marsh and crops such as winter wheat, or feeding on algae on the mud flats. Many of these birds are winter visitors from the Arctic tundra where they breed. The brent goose has a strong preference for eel-grass and tends to roost on water at night. It is characteristically found in winter on the mud flats and eel-grass beds of the estuaries of the south and east, whereas barnacle geese tend to prefer the northern coasts.

The **guillemot** is a very social bird on land, gathering during the breeding season in large numbers along cliff ledges and on the tops of stacks until packed almost shoulder to shoulder.

Large flocks of duck overwinter in estuaries, many roosting on salt marshes, particularly where extensive islands have been formed by the action of tides. The wigeon, however, is a shy duck, resting in large flocks on water by day or feeding on eel-grass and algae on the mud flats and then moving at dusk to graze on reclaimed salt marshes. Other common duck in estuaries include two visitors from freshwater habitats: teal, feeding on seeds of salt marsh plants and small molluscs and crustaceans, and mallard, feeding mainly on seeds and other plant food. The shelduck feeds on the snail *Hydrobia* and some algae, and is characteristically a coastal duck.

Wading birds are probably the commonest birds on mud flats and sandy shores during the winter. The most numerous are the tiny dunlin and the related knot, forming flocks many thousands strong. These flocks have been likened to wisps of smoke blown along the shore. The knot makes vast journeys each year from its

Common tern on its nest, which is simply a scrape in sand or shingle lined with pieces of plant material. The black tip on the beak distinguishes it from the Arctic tern.

Kittiwake with young in the cup-shaped nest made from seaweed and other plant material.

A guide to sea ducks and geese

Ducks and geese are essentially aquatic birds with robust bodies and usually short tails and webbed feet. They stand with the body parallel to the ground and head well up, and fly with neck extended. Wing beats are powerful and regular, seldom gliding for any distance.

Geese are large, heavily built birds with longer necks than ducks; the wings are long, fairly broad, and the tails short and rounded. On long flights the birds are usually arranged in a V-shaped formation on a regularly spaced line. Unlike ducks, the sexes have similar plumage. Wild geese are winter visitors, usually seen in flocks feeding on grasses and other vegetable foods in estuaries and on farm land near the coast.

Ducks are smaller than geese, with shorter necks and narrower wings. They are more aquatic in habit. Flight is less powerful than that of the goose, with more rapid wing beats. The sexes are usually different in appearance. For identification, the ducks fall into four groups: the shelduck, the largest duck, resembles the geese in many ways, being more terrestrial than other ducks; surface-feeding ducks feed by up-ending rather than diving and are essentially freshwater birds and include the mallard, wigeon and shoveler which move in winter to estuaries; diving ducks, such as eider, common scoter and long-tailed duck are essentially sea ducks, diving for food; lastly, two mainly freshwater diving ducks, scaup and goldeneye, are winter visitors to estuaries. The red-breasted merganser is a fish-eating duck which moves into estuaries in winter.

Eider Anatidae *Somateria mollissima*. **Distribution:** Breed northern half of Britain and Ireland; some summer and winter in south. **Other habitats:** Maritime. **Notes:** Size: 58cm. Diving duck. Common.

Red-breasted Merganser Anatidae *Mergus serrator*. **Distribution:** Breeds N.W. Scotland, Lake District and whole of Ireland. Widespread in winter. **Other habitats:** Breeds fresh water, coastal in winter. **Notes:** Size: 58cm. Large white wing patches in flight.

Greylag Goose Anatidae *Anser anser*. **Distribution:** Breeds N.W. Scotland and established in other parts. Winter visitors in central Scotland. **Other habitats:** Moorland for breeding. Marshes and agricultural land in winter. **Notes:** Size: 76–89cm. Resembles other grey geese.

Goosander Anatidae *Mergus merganser*. **Distribution:** Breeds in northern Britain and Wales. Winters also in the south. **Other habitats:** Fresh water, rarely coastal. **Notes:** Size: 66cm. In flight it appears very white. Feeds by diving.

White-fronted Goose Anatidae *Anser albifrons*. **Distribution:** Winters in Ireland, western Scotland, S.W. England and Wales. **Other habitats:** Marshes, water meadows and saltings. **Notes:** Size: 66–76cm. Immatures lack bars on belly and white bill base.

Shelduck Anatidae *Tadorna tadorna*. **Distribution:** Throughout British Isles. **Other habitats:** Muddy and sandy coasts, sometimes inland waters. **Notes:** Size: 61cm. Late summer moult in Germany but a few go to Bridgewater Bay. Breeds.

Bean Goose Anatidae *Anser fabalis*. **Distribution:** Scarce winter visitor to S.W. Scotland, Northumberland and E. Anglia. **Other habitats:** Marshes and wet meadows. **Notes:** Size: 71–89cm. Browner than other grey geese.

Pink-footed Goose Anatidae *Anser brachyrhynchus*. **Distribution:** Central Scotland, Lincolnshire, E. Anglia. **Other habitats:** Similar to Greylag. **Notes:** Size: 61–76cm. Told from Bean goose by pale blue-grey upper parts. Winter visitor.

Common Scoter Anatidae *Melanitta nigra*. **Distribution:** Few breed N.W. Ireland and Scotland. Winters off all coasts. **Other habitats:** Breeds upland lochs, winters inshore. **Notes:** Size: 48cm. Mainly winter visitor. Diving duck.

Brent Goose Anatidae *Branta bernicla*. **Distribution:** Winter visitor to east and south coasts. **Other habitats:** Mudflats and estuaries. **Notes:** Size: 56–61cm. Completely black neck and head apart from whitish neck patch is important in identification.

Barnacle Goose Anatidae *Branta leucopsis*. **Distribution:** Winter visitor; mainly western Scotland and Ireland. **Other habitats:** Pastures; meadows. **Notes:** Size: 58–69cm. **Notes:** Size: 58–69cm. Easily told by contrasting plumage.

winter

winter

summer

Long-tailed Duck Anatidae *Clangula hyemalis*. **Distribution:** Winter visitor to east coast, some on west coast. **Other habitats:** Mainly maritime. **Notes:** Size: 53cm. Diving duck. White body and dark wings distinctive.

A guide to some other coastal birds

Petrels are small, blackish birds with white rumps and narrow pointed wings. Their flight is erratic, skimming over the waves. The shearwater and the fulmar are larger with gliding and banking flight; their long narrow wings distinguish them from gulls by being held fully and stiffly extended in flight. The bill is heavy and tubular. They are common oceanic birds, visiting land only when breeding, when they can be seen on offshore islands and a few cliffs along the west coast. The fulmar is more widely distributed. Auks (razorbill, puffin and guillemots) are black and white, gregarious diving birds with short necks and short narrow wings. The legs are set well back, giving an upright stance. The bill is pointed and laterally flattened. Flight is fast and direct with rapid whirring wing beats; the feet jut out sideways before landing. They are most frequently seen during the breeding season on rocky coasts and islands. The black guillemot occurs in northern inshore waters throughout the year.

Gannets and cormorants are large diving birds. The gannet is white with black wing tips and pointed beak; the cormorant and shag appear glossy black. The wings are long and, in cormorants, broad. The bill is long and hook-tipped. Flight is rapid and direct with slow, powerful wing beats, and with the neck extended horizontally. The gannet manoeuvres when feeding, and plunges after fish from heights of 30m or more. The cormorant and shag swim and then dive from the surface. They are common off rocky shores throughout the year, cormorants also entering estuaries during the winter. They lack a preen gland, so cannot oil their feathers to waterproof them. Cormorants are characteristically seen standing drying outstretched wings in the sun. The great northern diver is a large diving bird, submerging quickly when alarmed. Flight is swift, on short pointed wings, with the neck drooping slightly. The bird is a winter visitor off the coast of Scotland.

Fulmar Procellariidae *Fulmarus glacialis.* **Distribution:** Breed on coast of Great Britain and Ireland. Winter at sea. **Other habitats:** Breeds on cliffs. **Notes:** Size: 47cm. Ungainly on land, rarely leaving nest vicinity. Wings narrower than a gull's. Stiff-winged, gliding flight. No black wing tips. Voice is a hoarse "ag-ag-ag-arr".

Razorbill Alcidae *Alca torda.* **Distribution:** Coasts of Great Britain and Ireland. **Other habitats:** Breeds on cliff coasts amongst boulder scree and broken cliffs. **Notes:** Size: 41cm. Short neck and laterally compressed bill. Tail cocked up when swimming. In winter throat and sides of head are white. Voice is a growling "aaarr".

Guillemot bridled form

Black Guillemot summer

Black Guillemot winter

Black Guillemot Alcidae *Cepphus grylle.* **Distribution:** Resident on west coast of Scotland and Ireland. **Other habitats:** Rocky coasts with coves, crevices and boulders. **Notes:** Size: 34cm. In winter has mottled head distinguishing it from Guillemot's black head. On land adopts a sloping stance. Voice is a thin, reedy "peeeeee".

Guillemot Alcidae *Uria aalge.* **Distribution:** Coasts of Great Britain and Ireland. Largest colonies in Scotland. **Other habitats:** Inshore in winter. **Notes:** Size 42cm. Call is a trumpeting "arra".

Puffin Alcidae *Fratercula arctica.* **Distribution:** Summer visitor to northern and western coasts. **Other habitats:** Remote island and inaccessible mainland cliffs. **Notes:** Size: 30cm. In winter bill is somewhat smaller. Rapid wing-beats and dumpy outline in flight. Perches upright, but rests horizontally. Voice is a growling "aarr".

Stock Dove Columbidae *Columba oenas.* **Distribution:** Resident in Great Britain and Ireland. **Other habitats:** Breeds in trees, ruins and cliffs. Feeds on open ground. **Notes:** Size: 33cm. Smaller and darker than Woodpigeon, lacking white markings. Flight is rapid, the grey rump and two broken black wing-bars being noticeable. Voice is a gruff "oo-roo-oo".

Gannet juvenile

Gannet adult

Manx Shearwater Procellariidae *Puffinus puffinus.* **Distribution:** Western Britain and Ireland. **Other habitats:** Remote islands. **Notes:** Size: 35cm. Nocturnal at colonies, spends day in nesting burrows or fishing at sea. Long winged, slender-bodied bird.

Gannet Sulidae *Sula bassana.* **Distribution:** Mainly Scotland. **Other habitats:** Breeds on remote islands; rarely found inland. **Notes:** Size: 90cm. Resident. Long wings with black tips. Feeds by diving from heights.

Chough Corvidae *Pyrrhocorax pyrrhocorax.* **Distribution:** Resident in parts of Ireland, Wales, Isle of Man and Inner Hebrides. **Other habitats:** Rocky coasts. Mountainous areas inland. **Notes:** Size: 40cm. Curved red bill and red legs. More slender than Jackdaw. Flight is strong and acrobatic. Sociable. Voice is a high-pitched "kyow".

Rock Pipit Motacillidae *Anthus spinoletta.* **Distribution:** Resident, only winters on low eastern coasts. **Other habitats:** Rocky coasts. **Notes:** Size: 16.5cm. Larger and darker than other two pipits. Call: "tsup". Song is louder than Meadow.

Cormorant Phalacrocoracidae *Phalacrocorax carbo.* **Distribution:** Along all coasts. **Other habitats:** Coastal sometimes inland waters. **Notes:** Size: 90cm. Resident. White patch on thighs in breeding season. Flight swift; rapid wing-beats.

Shag Phalacrocoracidae *Phalacrocorax aristotelis.* **Distribution:** Along most coasts, rare between Northumberland and Solent. **Other habitats:** Off rocky coasts. **Notes:** Size: 76cm. Crest on head in breeding season. Faster wing-beats than cormorant.

Raven Corvidae *Corvus corax.* **Distribution:** Resident in western and northern areas. **Other habitats:** Coastal and upland regions. **Notes:** Size: 64cm. Massive, black bill and shaggy throat feathers. Powerful, often aerobatic flight soars. When overhead, the wedge-shaped tail is obvious. Voice is a deep "kronking".

breeding grounds on the high arctic tundra to Europe and beyond. Most of the dunlin are migrants from the north but some nest on moorland in Britain and move down to the coast in autumn. Other waders which nest inland and move to the coast in winter include curlew, redshank and golden plover. Others such as sanderling, turnstone, grey plover and bartailed godwit nest in arctic regions and occur on the coast as winter visitors. The whimbrel, a relative of the curlew, is only a brief visitor to British mudflats during migration, as it nests in northern Europe, including the Shetlands and Outer Hebrides, and winters in Africa.

These large flocks of waders must remove very large numbers of invertebrates each day and it has been calculated that even a small

Female eider nesting on shingle among rocks. The nest consists of seaweed and is lined with down plucked from the female's breast. Incubation is carried out entirely by the female.

wader such as the knot can consume up to seven hundred molluscs (*Macoma*) in a day. One oystercatcher may consume on average over five hundred cockles daily. Since the oystercatcher gathers in large flocks in many estuaries where cockle beds are often located, the potential damage may be considerable. The significance of beak length in preventing too much overlap in the feeding habits of different waders has already been referred to in the section on sandy and muddy shores. This is especially important where large flocks of waders are feeding in winter. Several species, for example the curlew, whimbrel and godwits, have particularly long beaks which enable them to reach the deeper burrowing bivalve molluscs and worms such as the lugworm. In addition, the legs of waders differ in length, so that the depth of the water also limits certain species to certain areas, again restricting overlap in feeding habits.

Flocks of snow buntings are common along the east coast during the winter, feeding on seeds on sand dunes and other rough ground near the coast. Although a few pairs breed on the highest mountains of Scotland they are essentially winter visitors and return to breed in Iceland and along northern coasts of Scandinavia.

The eider duck, which is the only sea duck breeding in large numbers in Britain, spends the winter offshore in coastal waters, where it feeds by diving for food, especially molluscs. The population tends to be concentrated at a few sites, the largest group occurring at the mouth of the Firth of Tay where it has been estimated that 20,000 birds are concentrated into one flock during the winter. Other diving sea-ducks common off the coast and sheltering in the larger estuaries during bad weather include the scaup, common scoter and long-tailed duck. All three species breed in the Arctic and northern Europe. Diving ducks are well adapted for feeding off the bottom. The long-tailed duck, for example, can dive to depths of 30 metres and stay under the water for more than a minute at a time.

The Cormorants

The two British species of cormorant are the common cormorant and the shag, sometimes called the green cormorant. They are the only web-footed birds which do not produce a waterproofing oil for their feathers and both share a characteristic habit of standing on rocks with wings outspread to dry the feathers every time they come onto land. The cormorants are interesting as they illustrate well how closely related animals often have very different ways of life or ecological niches, thus avoiding competition with one another. Reference has already been made to their different nesting sites and outside the breeding season, the cormorant is found off sandy and muddy shores, especially in estuaries, and even inland on lakes and reservoirs, while the shag is confined to rocky coasts and offshore islands and never goes inland unless driven by storms. Furthermore, the cormorant is a deep diver and feeds mainly on benthic animals such as flat-fish, gobies and shrimps, while the shag feeds in surface waters on herring, sprats and sand eels. The shag has extended its breeding range considerably over the past fifty years and both species now breed round most of the coast of the British Isles except in the south east. Both birds breed in colonies of up to several hundred nests and, unlike most sea birds, the young are blind and naked when hatched. The flight of cormorants is very characteristic as they travel close to the water with a steady flight, rising high in the air as they cross over islands or headlands.

Shag with wings outstretched to dry. The lack of a white face-patch distinguishes this bird from the larger cormorant. This bird is on the Farne Islands.

Feeding methods

The methods used by seabirds to obtain their food vary widely. Most British seabirds are carnivorous, although some gulls, especially those such as the herring gull, which spends some time on land, are omnivorous. The majority catch their food directly from the sea. Gannets and terns plunge into the sea to capture fish near the surface in offshore and coastal waters respectively. The gannet plunges from up to 30 metres with wings folded back like an arrowhead, while the tern hovers close to the water before diving for a fish. The fulmar, a bird of the open sea, glides for long periods and feeds by surface dipping and following trawlers and whalers for discarded offal. Its numbers have increased spectacularly over the past seventy years, which is probably linked with the in-

Herring gull showing trumpeting call in defence of its nesting territory when the head is thrown upwards and a loud call uttered with mouth wide open.

creased amount of waste produced by trawlers. The kittiwake has similar feeding habits to the fulmar and has also shown a small increase in numbers.

Puffins and razorbills pursue fish underwater to depths of over 100 metres and a razorbill has been timed diving under water for 52 seconds. The black guillemot, which differs from the guillemot in that it nests on the lower boulder-strewn beaches, also has a different diet. While the guillemot usually dives in deeper offshore waters and feeds especially on sand eels, the black guillemot feeds nearer inshore over mixed rocky and sandy bottoms, eating mainly inshore species like the butterfish. Petrels normally fly close to the surface, fluttering over an erratic course, rather like large butterflies. When feeding close to the sea they patter along the surface of the water with their feet as if walking, taking planktonic crustaceans and occasionally offal from ships.

One of the greatest hazards to sea birds is oil pollution, particularly from wrecked tankers or leaks from offshore oil-wells. The most vulnerable species in British waters are auks, cormorants, divers, grebes and sea duck. Damage is worst where large flocks of these birds congregate off the coast in bays and estuaries and feed by diving. Birds of the open sea, such as petrels, are more widely dispersed and feed from the air, so that damage to them is not so great. Oil harms birds because it floats and spreads on the water, thus trapping the swimming species. Initially it soaks their plumage, destroying its insulating and water-proofing properties, so that the birds lose their buoyancy and become chilled. Their fat reserves become exhausted as they make increased efforts to remain afloat and keep warm. They may also ingest oil, which damages the digestive and respiratory systems. Feeding grounds and food are also spoilt or even destroyed by oil and by detergents used to disperse the oil.

Coastal Mammals

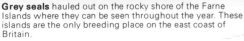
Grey seals hauled out on the rocky shore of the Farne Islands where they can be seen throughout the year. These islands are the only breeding place on the east coast of Britain.

Most British mammals occur at some time within the range of coastal habitats but one group, the seals, belongs exclusively to the coast. Whales are sometimes found stranded on the coast and are described in the section on the sea.

The fox is common throughout Great Britain but is absent from most of the offshore islands. The lack of foxes is important to the large colonies of sea birds nesting on islands; mainland colonies suffer from heavy predation by foxes. Fox dens occur in many rocky coastal areas and on sand dunes and the occupants may be found scavenging along beaches looking for dead birds and other carrion washed up by the tide. The otter occurs in fresh water, but it is also found along the shore and feeding in the sea, especially around Scottish coasts. In fact, a large proportion of the otter population in Scotland occurs along the much indented coasts of the western Highlands and Hebrides. The holt or breeding den at the coast may be located in a dry recess under boulders and rocks or in a sea cave.

In those parts of the Highlands where the hills and moors run down to the sea, red deer feed sometimes on maritime swards and even on sea-weeds along the shore. Herds of deer are found on several of the larger islands off the Scottish coast, including Rhum and Harris. A common coastal herbivore is the rabbit, especially on sand dune systems where it exerts a considerable

effect on the composition of the plant communities. This effect becomes especially marked when grazing ceases after a myxomatosis epidemic. Hedgehogs may also be common on dune systems and may take significant numbers of chicks and eggs from tern and gull colonies.

British waters hold about two-thirds of the world population of grey seals and one third of the European stocks of the common seal. The grey seal occurs along the coasts on both sides of the north Atlantic and its numbers have been increasing at a very rapid rate in recent years both in eastern Canada and in the British Isles. The European common seal is found mainly round the coasts of the North Sea, the Baltic and Iceland. A different sub-species of this seal occurs on American shores, where it is known as the "harbor seal". Both British seals are shy aquatic mammals and prefer to frequent remote and isolated coasts and offshore islands. All seals, however, must come out on to land to produce their young. The grey seal breeds between September and December, depending on the locality, with a maximum number of young (pups) produced in October. There is a concentration of grey seals from the dispersed feeding grounds to localised breeding sites, which are used by only a small fraction of the population at other times of the year. The pups are born on the grassy tops of small islands or on sheltered beaches within a day or two of the cows coming

ashore. They are born with a white coat, which is moulted after several weeks to reveal a coat of the adult type, and grow rapidly, being fed on some of the richest milk produced by any British mammal. After moulting they leave the breeding grounds for a period of feeding at sea. Although neither the grey seal nor the common seal are migratory species, young grey seals can disperse considerable distances. For example, calves tagged on North Rona have been recovered from points as far apart as east Iceland and County Donegal within three months. At the end of the lactation period the cows mate with the bulls, who vigorously defend territories during the breeding season, and the adult population returns to the sea.

The main grey seal breeding colonies in the British Isles are on North Rona, the Outer Hebrides, Orkney and the Farne Islands, but there are also smaller breeding colonies. The large colony on North Rona produces about 2,200 pups annually and that on the Farne Islands about 1,600 pups annually, while the figure for the smaller colony at Ramsey Island is between 150 and 200 per year. Outside the breeding season, grey seals are widely dispersed and may be seen on many parts of the coast, often basking on low rocks just offshore. The long period for suckling the pup has made the grey seal especially susceptible in the past to commercial hunting, especially for the valued pelt of the newly-moulted pup. Both species of seal are now however protected by law and numbers of grey seal are now increasing at such a rate that some control is necessary to maintain healthy stocks and (especially in the case of the Farne Islands) to prevent damage to island ecology. In recent years the grey seal has extended its breeding range as a result of the depopulation of many outlying islands off the Scottish coast.

Common seals breed in mid-summer, between June and July. The pups are usually born on sand and mud banks between tide marks and have an adult-type coat. The pup is active from birth and swims off with its mother as the tide rises, although they return to shore for suckling. This ability of the young seal to enter the water

Common seals hauled out on a bank in Loch Sween showing the characteristic "head up – tail up" position which distinguishes them from resting grey seals. The bank allows immediate access to deep water.

The controversial culling of seals

Seals have few enemies except man, and legal protection extended to seals in the 1930s removed even this control on population growth. Grey seals have consequently increased in numbers to the point where fishermen complained of a threat to their livelihood. Seals eat valuable salmon and tear holes in expensive nets. They also act as a host for the parasitic codworm; more seals mean more infected fish which the housewife is unwilling to buy. However, the greatest threat to fishermen is a decline in fish populations and the seal's contribution to this is probably minor compared to the effects of pollution and overfishing.

Grey seals cause an additional problem on the Farne Islands off the Northumberland coast. They come ashore in the autumn to produce their pups. As the population tripled in the 1960s, to reach a maximum of some 7,000; the beaches became overcrowded.

Disease and aggressiveness increased, so that about 20% of the pups died, (compared with about 3% on uncrowded beaches elsewhere), often in considerable suffering. Moreover females were forced to move off the rocky shores and up to the soft soil on the island tops. Here they caused considerable erosion of the limited depth of soil, leading to loss of plants. Even more important, soil loss deprived puffins of sites for their nest burrows in summer. So more seals meant less puffins; a bird which has already suffered major declines at many of its breeding colonies. Thus, to reduce the seal population many hundreds of females and their pups have been killed; a necessary measure perhaps, but also very controversial as seals are popular animals and the Farne Islands have been a wildlife sanctuary for centuries.

within hours of birth has enabled the common seal to withstand human predation better than the grey seal in the past. Common seals are less gregarious than grey seals and, unlike the latter, do not form large aggregations or show any social behaviour. The tidal sand banks of the Wash support the largest single breeding group of common seals in Europe. Smaller numbers breed off the coast of Norfolk and on the islands of western and northern Scotland. They can be seen outside the breeding season in the sea lochs of the entire west coast of Scotland.

Seals feed largely on fish and spend much of their time in the water hunting their prey. They are coastal feeders, taking those fish which are most abundant and easy to catch. This varies from coast to coast. They probably compete to some extent with commercial inshore fisheries; the total daily consumption of fish by seals round the British coast has been estimated at between 400 and 800 tonnes.

Seal pups are produced on shore and those of the grey seal remain there for at least three weeks; and it is at this stage that culling takes place. The grey seal pelt also provides commercial crop for a small number of licensed hunters.

Grey seal cow hauled out on rocks showing the more pointed head and large irregular dark spots which distinguish it from the common seal.

A guide to British breeding seals

Seals can be recognised by their dog-like head, body covered with thick close fur covering a layer of blubber which throws the skin into folds, and short, thick fin-shaped limbs. The hind limbs stretch backwards and cannot be turned forwards for walking. British seals are mainly active during the day. The two species commonly seen off the coast are the grey seal and common seal.

Adult male grey seals measure up to 2.6 metres in length, the female being about 30cms shorter. The newly born pup is about one metre long. Corresponding measurements for the smaller common seal are up to two metres for the male, 1.6 metres for the female and up to one metre for the pup. The common seal is fairly uniformly mottled with many small dark spots while the grey seal has irregular dark spots and patches. The ground colour of these seals is very variable, the common seal being darkish grey on the back and lighter below while the grey seal bull varies from black to dark brown and the cow from grey to fawn, both being lighter below. The grey seal pup can be identified by its white coat. A useful field character is the shape of the front of the head which is blunt in the common seal and more pointed in the grey seal. Wandering individuals of four migratory Arctic species have been recorded on a few occasions from British coasts. These are the ringed, harp, hooded and bearded seals.

The time of year when the pups are produced is another indication as to the species. Common seal pups are dropped on sand banks during the summer months of June and July. Grey seals produce their pups during the autumn or winter depending on the locality. In the northern part of their range, pups appear in autumn, but in England the pups are dropped in December. Pups on beaches are generally quite accessible and can be approached closely on foot but their mothers may stay on the beach to defend them.

Grey Seal Phocidae *Halichoerus grypus.*
Distribution: Patchy distribution around coasts of U.K. **Notes**: Colour variable. Head large, muzzle high giving a "Roman nose" appearance. Nostrils parallel and separated below.

Common Seal Phocidae *Phoca vitulina.*
Distribution: N. and E. coasts of U.K. **Notes**: Difficult to distinguish from grey seal in water. Nostrils at V angle, almost touching below.

Woodlands

Trees and woodland have always enjoyed a special relationship with human beings. Throughout history forests have been places of shelter, while their wood has been essential to man's development, whether for fuel, for making simple utensils, or building the mighty wooden battleships of the seventeenth and eighteenth centuries. At the same time they have also been places of fear, where dangerous animals were thought to lurk, and their presence has obstructed the growing of crops and grazing for domestic animals.

Our much fragmented forests are still being cleared for agriculture or other more profitable forms of land use, but today we value woodlands not merely as an economic resource but as an amenity. Few places can rival an English oak wood in early summer for peace and beauty: the young oak leaves are just showing brownish-green, while at our feet the last of the primroses are in bloom forming patches of bright yellow in the carpet of bluebells; the air is full of birdsong and the hum of insect activity.

Other types of woodland also have their charm and their own special association of wild plants and animals. From these associations in our remaining relics of near-natural forest we can discover many things about the factors which determine the natural distribution of different plants and animals in the British Isles.

Trees dominate the woodland scene, and it is the combination of climate and soil type which determines the species which grow in a particular area. In turn these trees provide food, shelter and support for a whole range of animals and smaller plants.

Woodland History and Distribution

To understand the distribution and form of today's woodlands we must start at the very beginnings of their development when the vegetation of the British Isles was slowly recovering from the effects of the last ice age. Woodland was gradually replacing the arctic tundra vegetation of low-growing flowering plants, mosses and lichens which can still be seen within the Arctic Circle today. The woodland which started to develop over 10,000 years ago was not the rich mixed oak woodland typical of modern lowland Britain. At first only the most hardy species could survive, and the first woodland cover was almost entirely composed of birch, probably with some hazel, rowan and Scots pine. As conditions improved further the Scots pine slowly became dominant until pinewoods covered much of the country. At this time Britain was still joined to the continent of Europe and we can imagine how the animals associated with these forests spread northwards across Europe with the developing woodland. These would have included red deer, wild boar and red squirrel.

Britain separated from the Continent about 7,000 years ago, preventing further migration except by the more mobile species. By this time the climate had improved to such an extent that oak, elm and ash trees were replacing the Scots pine, and the distribution of trees within the almost continuous forests was coming to resemble that which we see today, with mixed woods dominated by oak throughout the lowlands of the British Isles.

Early woodland development

Remnants of the pine and indeed the pioneer woods of birch and hazel found refuge in the Scottish Highlands, where their descendants can still be seen and where the harsh climate prevents their replacement by oak woodland. Other types of woodland, dominated by trees such as beech, ash and alder occurred locally where conditions were especially suitable. So the woodland which developed after the ice age was not uniform in composition but reflected the many environmental factors which still determine the natural distribution of species. Thus far the development of our forests had been unaffected by the hand of man. This situation did not last long, however, for we were also among the animals which crossed the land bridge before the rising sea level cut Britain off from the Continent. The initial human invasion was reinforced over the centuries by waterborne invaders and colonists, each of whom took a toll of the woodland they found.

These deductions about the spread of woodland across the country can be made as a result of studies of the pollen which is preserved in peat deposits throughout the country. The hard coats of many pollen grains are extremely resistant to decay, enabling the species of the plant from

Relict patches of ancient pine forest persist in a few areas of Scotland. They comprise low-density stands of Scots pine, the only conifer native to Britain. Most conifer woods today consist of introduced species.

Ancient woodland

After the last Ice Age, much of Britain was forested but only a few patches of that primaeval woodland remain today. This is sometimes termed "Primary Woodland", but hardly any of it (and perhaps even none) has survived down the centuries unmodified by man. Strictly speaking, this woodland is thus not comparable to the primary forests of the tropics, which have remained totally unaffected by man. The term "Ancient Woodland" has therefore been suggested (and used in this book) to refer to areas which are likely to have been subjected to some sort of management in the past, but which have never been completely cleared and have been forested throughout historical time. "Ancient" in this context refers to the woodland community being many centuries old, not the individual trees.

Secondary woodlands are those which have developed on land that was once cleared of its natural forest and used for pasture or crops. When this happens, most woodland species die out, so that as the secondary woodland develops it needs to be recolonised from elsewhere. This takes time, and even after hundreds of years, secondary woodland may not regain certain species like the oxslip and small-leafed lime, which have slowly been eliminated as one piece of old woodland after another has been felled.

Wistman's Wood in Dartmoor has survived as a near-relict of ancient woodland because its siting on very rocky land has made it impossible for grazing animals to invade and prevent growth of young trees. However, due to the poor soil and harsh upland climate the trees are stunted in comparison with lowland oaks.

which they originated to be identified. Therefore by counting the number of grains of each species in a given sample, a comparison can be made of the relative abundance of those species when the peat was laid down, with the oldest deposits at the bottom and the youngest at the top. The age can also be determined by carbon-dating. This method tells us not only about the natural spread of species but also about more recent changes observed in the peat record resulting from man's activities. Around 600BC a decline can be seen in most of the forest trees. Tree pollen declines in proportion to an increase in herb and grass pollen, indicating the removal of woodland and its conversion to pasture for domestic animals. Further proof is given by a slight increase in the birch pollen, for birch is a resilient tree and rapidly colonises open land when agriculture is abandoned. Its abundance during this period indicates a nomadic type of agriculture. Studies of peat from Tregarron Bog in Wales confirm relatively short periods of cultivation lasting some forty years, presumably on the drier adjacent land.

In southern Britain much of this early activity appears, from archaeological evidence, to have been on the higher ground where the woodland could be cleared with relative ease, probably by burning. The chalk downs are particularly rich in ancient monuments and appear to have been extensively cultivated by the Celts around the time of the Roman invasion (43AD). The Romans favoured the establishment of towns in the lowlands and agriculture was considerably extended with the use of semi-serf labour. Large amounts of wood were used, particularly in the Weald, for smelting the iron ore which

was then being mined in that area. Even in this early age there is evidence that care was taken not to destroy this valuable resource by too extensive clear-felling. The Saxons who followed the Celts and the Romans were valley farmers and many of the upland chalk fields were abandoned to become naturally reafforested. Today ancient Celtic field systems can be seen in Grovely, Great Ridge and Cranborne Chase Woods, west of Salisbury.

Since then the history of our forests has been one of steady attrition in favour of other forms of land use. Only when the situation became catastrophic were steps taken to conserve the dwindling but vital resource. An indication of the natural distribution of the woodlands which developed after the ice age can still be seen in the relics of ancient forests of the British Isles despite two thousand years of management and modification. The most common woodland type is still one dominated by oak; in many cases its ancestry can almost certainly be traced back to the original climax oak forests which developed over most of the country seven thousand years ago. Those containing pedunculate oak are the typical oak woodlands of the lowlands while a second type, with sessile oak as the dominant tree, is typical of areas of high rainfall down the whole length of the west coast. On highly calcareous soils both oaks are replaced by other trees: beech on the chalk of south east England and ash on limestone in the west and north. In the highlands of Scotland where most extreme conditions occur, woods of Scots pine and birch, remnants of the forest cover of nine thousand years ago, still maintain their supremacy over oak.

A guide to some interesting woodland sites

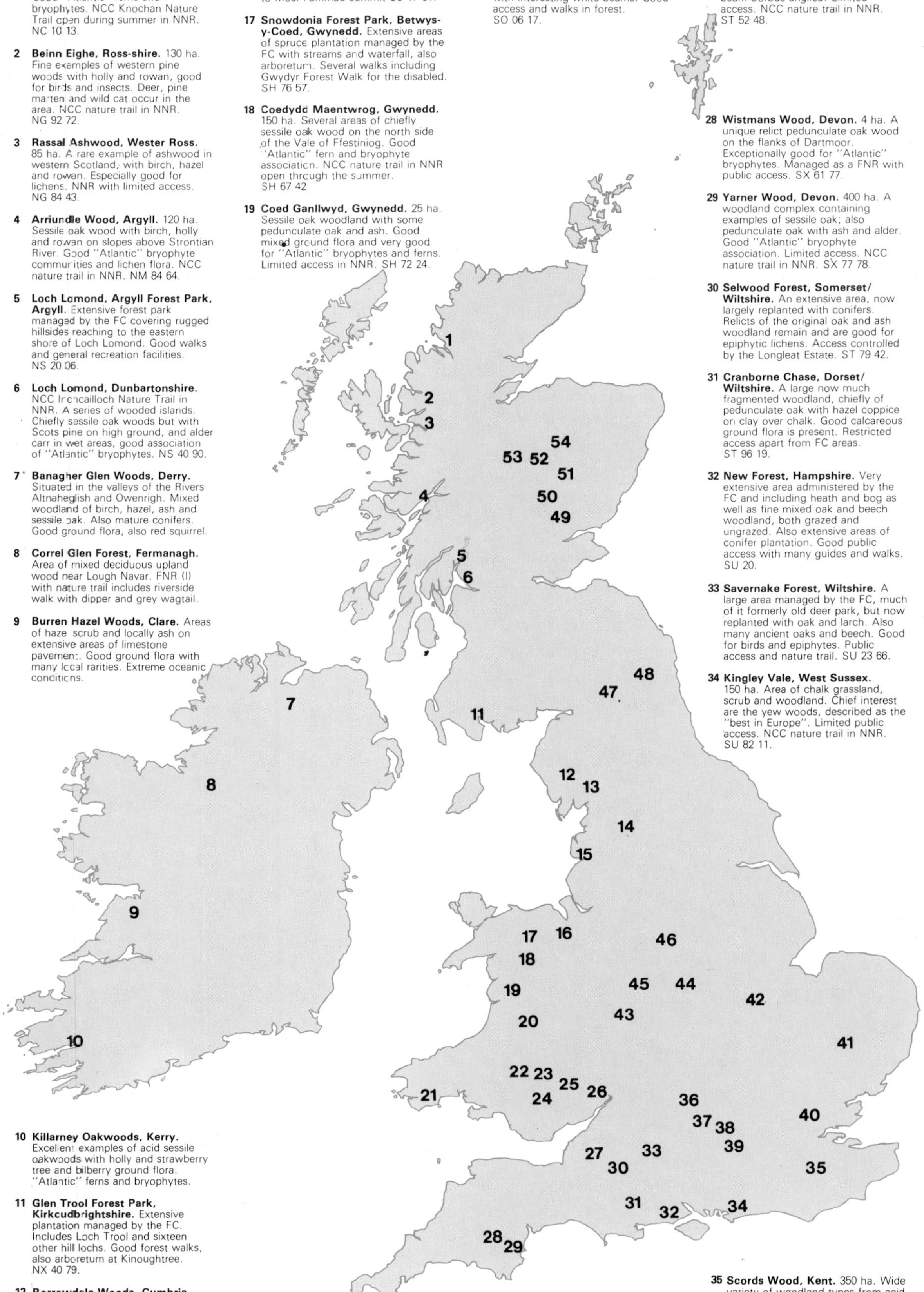

1 Inverpolly, Ross-shire. 300 ha. Good example of primitive birch and hazel woodland with rowan and alder, set in extensive moorland. Good "Atlantic" ferns and bryophytes. NCC Knochan Nature Trail open during summer in NNR. NC 10 13.

2 Beinn Eighe, Ross-shire. 130 ha. Fine examples of western pine woods with holly and rowan, good for birds and insects. Deer, pine marten and wild cat occur in the area. NCC nature trail in NNR. NG 92 72.

3 Rassal Ashwood, Wester Ross. 85 ha. A rare example of ashwood in western Scotland, with birch, hazel and rowan. Especially good for lichens. NNR with limited access. NG 84 43.

4 Arriundle Wood, Argyll. 120 ha. Sessile oak wood with birch, holly and rowan on slopes above Strontian River. Good "Atlantic" bryophyte communities and lichen flora. NCC nature trail in NNR. NM 84 64.

5 Loch Lomond, Argyll Forest Park, Argyll. Extensive forest park managed by the FC covering rugged hillsides reaching to the eastern shore of Loch Lomond. Good walks and general recreation facilities. NS 20 06.

6 Loch Lomond, Dunbartonshire. NCC Inchcailloch Nature Trail in NNR. A series of wooded islands. Chiefly sessile oak woods but with Scots pine on high ground, and alder carr in wet areas, good association of "Atlantic" bryophytes. NS 40 90.

7 Banagher Glen Woods, Derry. Situated in the valleys of the Rivers Altnaheglish and Owenrigh. Mixed woodland of birch, hazel, ash and sessile oak. Also mature conifers. Good ground flora, also red squirrel.

8 Correl Glen Forest, Fermanagh. Area of mixed deciduous upland wood near Lough Navar. FNR (I) with nature trail includes riverside walk with dipper and grey wagtail.

9 Burren Hazel Woods, Clare. Areas of hazel scrub and locally ash on extensive areas of limestone pavement. Good ground flora with many local rarities. Extreme oceanic conditions.

10 Killarney Oakwoods, Kerry. Excellent examples of acid sessile oakwoods with holly and strawberry tree and bilberry ground flora. "Atlantic" ferns and bryophytes.

11 Glen Trool Forest Park, Kirkcudbrightshire. Extensive plantation managed by the FC. Includes Loch Trool and sixteen other hill lochs. Good forest walks, also arboretum at Kinoughtree. NX 40 79.

12 Borrowdale Woods, Cumbria. 500 ha. Fine examples of upland sessile oak woodland in an area of heavy rainfall. Luxuriant fern and bryophyte associations. Access to woods on NT land. NY 27 20.

13 Grizedale Forest, Cumbria. An extensive area largely of conifer plantations established on moorland and managed by the FC. Additional habitats for wildlife have been created. Good public access with guides and trails. NY 37 15.

14 Malham Woods, Yorkshire. 400 ha. These rich woodlands on the Carboniferous Limestone of Upper Wharfedale contain an extensively rich ground flora including many northern species. Good public access within the National Park. SD 98 67.

15 Eaves Wood, Lancashire. 50 ha. An area of ash woodland on Carboniferous Limestone. The ground flora remains of interest, although plantations are present. The wood is managed by the NT with public access. SD 46 76.

16 Clwyd Forest, Clwyd. Extensive areas of conifer and mixed plantation managed by the FC, good for plants and birds. Nature trail and forest trail to Moel Fammau summit SJ 17 61.

17 Snowdonia Forest Park, Betwys-y-Coed, Gwynedd. Extensive areas of spruce plantation managed by the FC with streams and waterfall, also arboretum. Several walks including Gwydyr Forest Walk for the disabled. SH 76 57.

18 Coedydd Maentwrog, Gwynedd. 150 ha. Several areas of chiefly sessile oak wood on the north side of the Vale of Ffestiniog. Good "Atlantic" fern and bryophyte association. NCC nature trail in NNR open through the summer. SH 67 42

19 Coed Ganllwyd, Gwynedd. 25 ha. Sessile oak woodland with some pedunculate oak and ash. Good mixed ground flora and very good for "Atlantic" bryophytes and ferns. Limited access in NNR. SH 72 24.

20 Coed Rheidol, Dyfed. Extensive areas of sessile oak woodland and plantation on the sides of the Rheidol Valley, including falls, and forest walks (FC) from Devil's Bridge, also arboretum. Permit required for NNR. SN 74 78.

21 Slebech Forest (Narberth), Dyfed. Extensive area chiefly of conifer plantation managed by the FC. Good walks overlooking the East Cleddau River and National Park. SN 05 14.

22 Dinas Woodlands (Llandovery), Dyfed. Interesting sessile oak woods on gorge of River Towy, very good for birds including red kite. RSPB reserve with nature trail. SN 78 47.

23 Talybont Forest, Powys. Extensive areas of mixed plantation managed by the FC. Nearby is Penmelallt FNR (7 ha) on Carboniferous Limestone with interesting white beams. Good access and walks in forest. SO 06 17.

24 Cwm Clydach, Powys. 20 ha. Good example of native beech woodland on the western edge of its range, also sessile oak and wych elm/ash woodland. Restricted access, good views from road. SO 21 12.

25 Craig y Viliau Woodlands, Powys. 60 ha. Interesting woodland on Carboniferous Limestone with small-leaved lime and white beams in extensive upland limestone grassland. Public access in NNR. SN 19 15.

26 Forest of Dean. Very extensive area largely managed by the FC. Native types range from pedunculate oak woodland on acid soils to ash limestone woodland with *Sorbus anglica*. Birds include pied flycatcher. Many guides and trails including Symonds Yat and Wyndcliff (FNR). SO 90 10.

27 Ebbor Gorge, Somerset. 45 ha. A fine example of ash woodland on Carboniferous Limestone. Very rich ground flora and endemic white beam *Sorbus anglica*. Limited access. NCC nature trail in NNR. ST 52 48.

28 Wistmans Wood, Devon. 4 ha. A unique relict pedunculate oak wood on the flanks of Dartmoor. Exceptionally good for "Atlantic" bryophytes. Managed as a FNR with public access. SX 61 77.

29 Yarner Wood, Devon. 400 ha. A woodland complex containing examples of sessile oak; also pedunculate oak with ash and alder. Good "Atlantic" bryophyte association. Limited access. NCC nature trail in NNR. SX 77 78.

30 Selwood Forest, Somerset/Wiltshire. An extensive area, now largely replanted with conifers. Relicts of the original oak and ash woodland remain and are good for epiphytic lichens. Access controlled by the Longleat Estate. ST 79 42.

31 Cranborne Chase, Dorset/Wiltshire. A large now much fragmented woodland, chiefly of pedunculate oak with hazel coppice on clay over chalk. Good calcareous ground flora is present. Restricted access apart from FC areas. ST 96 19.

32 New Forest, Hampshire. Very extensive area administered by the FC and including heath and bog as well as fine mixed oak and beech woodland, both grazed and ungrazed. Also extensive areas of conifer plantation. Good public access with many guides and walks. SU 20.

33 Savernake Forest, Wiltshire. A large area managed by the FC, much of it formerly old deer park, but now replanted with oak and larch. Also many ancient oaks and beech. Good for birds and epiphytes. Public access and nature trail. SU 23 66.

34 Kingley Vale, West Sussex. 150 ha. Area of chalk grassland, scrub and woodland. Chief interest are the yew woods, described as the "best in Europe". Limited public access. NCC nature trail in NNR. SU 82 11.

35 Scords Wood, Kent. 350 ha. Wide variety of woodland types from acid sessile oak and beech to pedunculate oak and ash woodland and alder carr. Interesting ground flora. Good public access in NT areas. TQ 48 52.

36 Waterperry Wood, Oxfordshire. 150 ha. A relatively small area of pedunculate oak with hazel coppice within a larger area of conifer plantation, managed by the FC. Good for woodland butterflies. Good public access. SP 60 09.

37 Chiltern Beechwoods (Aston Rowant), Oxfordshire. 300 ha. Examples of the extensive escarpment and plateau beechwoods of the Chilterns. Good association of calcareous shrubs and herbs. Limited public access. NCC nature trail in NNR. SU 75 98.

38 Burnham Beeches, Buckinghamshire. 450 ha. Fine example of beech with pedunculate oak, birch and holly on acidic gravels. An interesting epiphytic flora is present. Good public access. SU 95 85.

39 Windsor Forest, Berkshire. Extensive area of mixed broad-leaved woodland with many ancient trees, also extensive conifer plantations. Especially good for birds, insects and fungi. Public access is restricted. SU 93 73.

40 Epping Forest, Essex. Extensive ancient woodland of beech, much pollarded. Also pedunculate oak with hornbeam coppice. Good general natural history interest. Open access. TQ 42 98.

41 Breckland Forest, Norfolk. An extensive area of "new forest", chiefly of pine but also some hardwoods. All managed by FC. Best area in southern England for red squirrel, also interesting heathland rides. Open access with many guides and trails. TL 85 90.

42 Bedford Purlieus, Northamptonshire and Cambridgeshire. 400 ha. Once part of the Rockingham Forest, the remaining fragments of pedunculate oak woodland on base-rich soils contain an extremely rich ground flora. Public access at Wakerley Great Wood (FC). TL 04 99.

43 Wyre Forest, Worcestershire and Herefordshire. 500 ha. Fine example of sessile oak woodland on acid soils with base-rich conditions present locally. Among the best forest faunas of the Midlands. Limited public access (part NNR). SO 75 76.

44 Charnwood Forest, Leicestershire. A once extensive area of mixed oak woodland, now much fragmented; examples of both sessile and pedunculate types still present and of general natural history interest. Public access at Bradgate Park and Beacon Hill. SK 49 14.

45 Cannock Chase, Staffordshire. 900 ha. Good example of sessile oak, birch and alder woodland among heathland and valley bog and fen among extensive plantations. Good public access in areas managed by the FC. SJ 9818.

46 Derbyshire Dales Woodland, Derbyshire/Staffordshire. 100 ha. Fine examples of ash woodland on Carboniferous Limestone with extremely rich ground flora showing both southern and northern influence. Good public access in National Park. SK 14 53.

47 Kielder Forest Park, Northumberland. A very extensive area chiefly of conifer plantation managed by the FC, among open moorland. Public access with guides and trails. NY 62 93.

48 Holystone Woods, Northumberland. 30 ha. Fragmented examples of sessile oak wood, good northern ground flora, but bryophytes few compared with woods in the wetter Lake District. Public access on NT land. NT 93 01.

49 Tummel Forest, Perthshire. Extensive plantations and other woodland managed by the FC. Walks through woodland and along riverside, also from Kindrogan Field Centre. NN 86 59.

50 Caenlochan, Tayside. Small areas of woodland in extensive moorland and bog. Examples of common birch with rare bryophytes. Also excellent examples of montane willow scrub. Birds include golden eagle. No access to NNR August-October. NO 20 70.

51 Morrone Wood, Aberdeenshire. 100 ha. Best example of a subalpine wood on basic soil with common birch and juniper. Also montane bryophytes. Access in NNR by indicated paths. NO 13 90.

52 Aviemore, Inverness-shire, NCC Loch an Eilien Nature Trail; part of the Cairngorms NNR. Excellent examples of native Scots pine woodland with crested tit, crossbill, etc. NH 89 06.

53 Aviemore, Inverness-shire, Craigellachie Birchwood. 100 ha. Fine pure birch wood, chiefly of silver birch and some alder carr. Good association of northern plants and insects. NNR, public access. NH 88 12.

54 Aviemore, Inverness-shire, Glen More Forest Park. Extensive areas of spruce plantation managed by the FC, but including remnants of Scots pine. Forest walks and nature observation posts. N.B. Also at Aviemore, Loch Garten. RSPB reserve with osprey viewing hide. NH 97 09.

Abbreviations:

NCC	Nature Conservancy Council
FC	Forestry Commission
RSPB	Royal Society for the Protection of Birds
NT	National Trust
NNR	National Nature Reserve
FNR	Forest Nature Reserve
NP	National Park
FNR (I)	Forest Nature Reserve (in Ireland)

Woodland Management

Because woodlands have been so important to the human economy, practically none (in the lowlands at least) have escaped some form of management or exploitation by man. Woodland ecology in Britain is thus a mixture of natural processes, modified by human intervention. Conservation of the resources which woodland can provide is no new phenomenon, although it is only in this century, and particularly the last few years, that conservation has extended to amenity and particularly wildlife conservation. Perhaps the most dramatic conservation measure took place after the Norman Conquest when huge areas were set aside as Royal Forests which were placed under Forest Law. These included the New Forest, Sherwood Forest and the Forest of Dean. The Forest Law protected the game of these forests for the pleasure of the King and his courtiers. Severe penalties were handed out to commoners who killed or even disturbed game within them. A man who killed a hart, a mature six-year old stag, might face mutilation or even death. Afforestation in this sense did not mean, as it does today, the planting of trees to form forests, but merely the placing of tracts of land under Forest Law. Such areas would include scrub, bog and heath vegetation, as can still be seen in the New Forest. At their height these forests included up to one third of England, the excesses of Forest Law being one of the factors which led to Magna Carta in 1215. Even today extensive areas of woodland are conserved for game, including pheasants and deer, by private landowners.

The most significant development of the Middle Ages as far as woodland was concerned was the exploitation of the oak woods through a system called coppice-with-standards, which was ideal for meeting the needs of the local community. The small-diameter underwood coppice provided wattle hurdles, thatching spars and many household utensils, while the standards, squat in profile with branches spreading out almost horizontally above the coppice, produced wood ideal for the timber frames of houses and ships. Vast areas of woodland were also felled to build the "wooden walls of England", the great wooden battleships by which this country once maintained its position as a superpower. Even though metal had replaced wood for ship building, the demand for wood for other purposes during the 1914–18 war still led to the felling of 180,000 hectares of woodland. Such was the depressed state of forestry after the war that the Forestry Commission was formed in 1919 to build up the nation's strategic reserve of timber. It also took over the management of the remaining Royal Forests. Unfortunately the results of this were only just becoming apparent at the outbreak of the 1939–45 War, during which another 160,000ha of woodland were felled. By 1949 much of what woodland remained was described officially as scrub, devastated or felled. The remaining standard oaks of the old coppices, lacking tall straight trunks, were by this time of little timber value. Similarly, with the exception of chestnut, coppice wood was of

little value, so that what remained of these woodlands was unmanaged and derelict. It was therefore necessary for new forests of fast-growing conifers to be planted both by the Forestry Commission and private foresters. This in turn led to mounting concern among nature conservationists who saw the disappearance of many traditional woodland species. Conifer plantations are inhospitable to wildlife, not only because the trees are not native and do not support an elaborate food-chain of insect and other species, but also because when the plantation becomes mature, deep shade is cast throughout the forest. This suppresses or even eliminates the ground flora together with its insect and bird life.

The traditional management of our forests as coppice-with-standards before 1919 had mainly involved the utilisation of the naturally occurring woodlands. These had been modified but not unrecognisably altered. As a result they still teemed with the wildlife which they had contained for thousands of years previously, and only some of the larger animals such as wolf and wild boar had become extinct. The regular cutting cycle which coppice management involved favoured wildlife because of the number of mini-habitats produced. For instance, the ground flora is at its best and is particularly attractive to insects a year after the coppice has been cut. A few years later, when the coppice stools have regrown to form a dense thicket, conditions are at their best for breeding birds. A regularly managed wood therefore contains a

The management of woodland rides

The presence of grassy glades and rides within woodlands provides a most valuable additional habitat for wildlife, but if they are to remain open they must be maintained by regular cutting. A rich flora is often present in the rides, including such attractive plants as devil's bit scabious, centaury, St. John's wort and heather. Many of the insects associated with the early stages of the coppice cycle, such as the pearl-bordered fritillary, will also occur in the rides, while the white admiral butterfly favours rides with bramble flowering along the edges. In nature reserves a method of ride management has been evolved which maximises their potential for wildlife. The rides are first widened by cutting down a narrow strip of woodland on each side. After this one of the

sides is cut every other year, each side thus being cut only every fourth year. By this time the woody growth has just reached the thicket stage of the coppice cycle. This may to a certain extent replace coppicing within such a wood and has the advantage that it can be mechanised and management costs reduced, as no wood is allowed to develop which cannot be cut by a tractor-mounted swipe. This method can also be used to alleviate the effects on wildlife when a broad-leaved woodland is replanted with conifers. Here a strip of the original woodland, including species like hazel and willow, is allowed to grow up again on each side of the rides. It can then be cut at four-yearly intervals as before. The occasional standard tree of oak or ash should also be left.

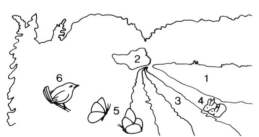

1. Where the trees are cleared and sunlight reaches the ground a profuse and varied flora develops adding diversity and colour to the woodland scene. The specific composition of the flora depends upon how often and at what time of year ride verges are mown.

2. Where scrub and trees are allowed to grow close to the ride, they shade the ground and suppress many colourful flowers. Ultimately the tree crowns meet over the ride which then forms only a gloomy tunnel through the wood.

3. Vehicle wheels, walking and regular close-mowing all have the effect of promoting the growth of grasses and small, prostrate plants which

would otherwise be swamped by taller growth.

4. Grazing animals also help to retard the development of larger plants and maintain a diversity of small grasses and flowers.

5. Many of the flowers along woodland rides provide nectar sources for butterflies and other insects. The surrounding trees also provide shelter from the wind. Open, well-maintained woodland rides are thus an ideal habitat for many insect species.

6. The abundant insects are a rich source of food for insectivorous birds, many of which nest among the taller plant stems and logs from the cleared plants.

Coppice management

The traditional management of woodlands as coppice-with-standards was the one factor which above all benefited the forest wildlife. It was practised in one form or another throughout the British Isles. Coppicing meant the regular cutting of the shrubs and smaller trees, such as hazel, hornbeam or alder, growing under oak. After cutting, the stumps were allowed to regrow, providing thin poles. Above the coppice layer the standards, usually of oak, were allowed to grow to maturity, while a proportion of the saplings were left when the coppice was cut to replace the mature standards when they were felled. Two cycles of management were therefore involved, a short coppice cycle and a long-term one, of perhaps a hundred years, for the standard trees. In up and areas in the west, woods of sessile oak were managed as pure coppice, with no standards, the oak bark being used for the tanning of leather. Over the years many coppices were improved by selecting or planting the most productive species, traditionally hazel, but more recently sweet chestnut. The advantage of this system for wildlife was that each stage of the coppice, from cutting through to dense shade again, encouraged a different set of species, adapted to those conditions, to flourish. A year after the coppice has been cut the ground flora is at its best and particularly attractive to insects, while a few years later the stools have regrown to form a dense thicket which contains a high density of breeding birds, including white throat, garden warbler and blackcap.

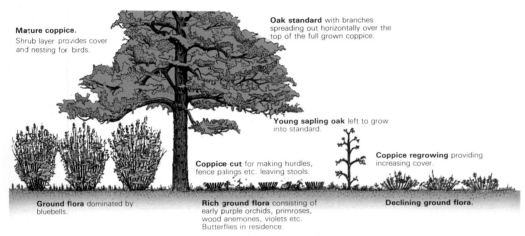

Mature coppice. Shrub layer provides cover and nesting for birds.

Oak standard with branches spreading out horizontally over the top of the full grown coppice.

Young sapling oak left to grow into standard.

Coppice cut for making hurdles, fence palings etc. leaving stools.

Coppice regrowing providing increasing cover.

Ground flora dominated by bluebells.

Rich ground flora consisting of early purple orchids, primroses, wood anemones, violets etc. Butterflies in residence.

Declining ground flora.

great variety of ideal living conditions.

The protection of the last remaining areas of native woodland and the plants and animals traditionally associated with them is now a major objective of nature conservationists. The woodlands richest in all forms of wildlife are those growing on sites which have supported woodland since prehistoric times. These may contain species whose ancestors could have arrived in the locality at the end of the Ice Age, perhaps 10,000 years ago. Such woodlands are described as "primary". Many of these species, especially the plants, do not seem to be able to colonise "secondary" woodland which has been planted on farmland in the last few hundred years or so.

Once the most valuable examples have been selected as nature reserves, they must be managed for their wildlife, for none of our relict ancient forests are large enough to allow nature to take its course. Their structure has also been extensively modified in the past. Relatively small areas of woodland have therefore to be managed intensively for wildlife. The simplest way of maintaining the wildlife diversity is to follow the traditional management regime, especially coppicing. Management aimed at producing a mixed-age, high forest and the creation and management of rides and glades can also be beneficial because of the diversity of habitats which they provide within the wood. Nature conservation in upland woods presents different problems. The presence of farm animals within many of these woodlands has led to the grazing out of the associated ground flora, which is replaced by grass, and the prevention of natural tree regeneration. The priority here is to fence out stock and encourage natural regeneration to rejuvenate the wood.

The Woodland Ecosystem

The type of woodland at any location depends on those physical or "edaphic" factors affecting that particular site. Where the climate or geology is unfavourable the distribution of certain species will be limited. But which species are actually present also depends upon the outcome of biological competition. For example, where oak and pine grow together, they compete with each other for available nutrients, water and light. In the south where the soil and climate are favourable, oak will usually have the advantage, while in the harsh northern environment the more sensitive oak is not competitive and pine is able to become dominant.

Woodland layers

Within most woodlands a number of distinct layers of vegetation are apparent. The upper layer, the canopy, is made up of the leaves and branches of the tall dominant species. These act as the first filter of the light coming from the sun. The vegetation beneath the tree only receives that light which can penetrate from above. Next is the shrub layer, composed of species such as hazel and hawthorn which cannot grow to any height, even in the open. Young saplings of the canopy species should also be

present among these. Below the shrub layer is the herb or field layer, comprising chiefly the low-growing herbaceous plants which typically cover the woodland floor. Because the light is very limited at this level, such plants mostly have adaptations to cope with these shady conditions. In deciduous woodland, for example, they produce leaves and flowers early in the year before the trees are fully in leaf. Below the field layer is the ground layer comprising the lower plants: mosses, liverworts, algae and lichens. The development of these layers is dependent on the extent of the canopy and the light which penetrates through to the layers beneath. In some beech woods, especially where an understorey of yew is present, so little light reaches the ground that it is usually completely bare except for a cover of dead beech leaves and yew needles. In some woods of Scots pine and birch, on the other hand, the shade cast is relatively sparse and a well-developed shrub layer of juniper can grow, as well as a diverse herb layer.

It is often difficult to decide how far these layers are a reflection of the management of the woodland. Management such as coppice-with-standards, for instance, favours the development of such layers, while in an entirely natural

Life and death in the woodland ecosystem. A spider eats a butterfly which had fed on nectar and, as a caterpillar, had eaten leaves. In turn a predating bird or small mammal may eat the spider.

Millipedes are scavenging animals and move slowly across the forest floor eating dead leaves and decaying material, thus helping to recycle nutrients in the woodland system.

The forest layers

The efficiency of the woodland ecosystem depends on how much of the sun's energy can be captured by the green plants and converted into carbohydrate. The tallest trees of the wood, which form the 'canopy', are the first to receive the sun's rays and what grows beneath this layer depends on how much light can filter through to be trapped by other more lowly plants. In beech woodlands this is very little, but oak and ash are relatively light shade-casters and a lush growth of plants can exist beneath them. Immediately beneath the canopy will be tall bushes and small trees which form the second or "shrub layer" of the wood. Growing beneath the shrub layer is a mass of herbaceous plants which form the "herb layer". Many of these come into leaf and flower early in the year or have adaptations such as large flat leaves to make the most of what light is available. The lowest layer of all is the "ground layer" of mosses and liverworts. These remain green throughout the year and are actively growing even in winter. When conifers, which are evergreen, are planted closely together in plantations, the lower layers are shaded out and suppressed or killed.

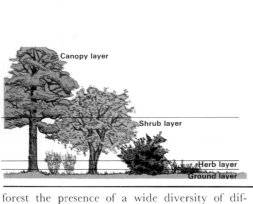
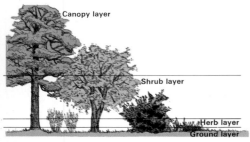

Canopy layer

Shrub layer

Herb layer
Ground layer

The leaves of the tree canopy trap sunlight to produce food for the woodland ecosystem, but in doing so they prevent light reaching the ground and limit plant growth there. Different trees provide varying canopy densities.

forest the presence of a wide diversity of different species, together with the wide range of ages of the trees and shrubs, means that the layer structure is likely to be obscured. The layered structure is particularly beneficial to forest wildlife as each represents a different ecological niche. Each vegetation layer and each plant species in that layer has a different assemblage of insects associated with them, which in turn provide a food source for insect-eating birds. Such a mixed structure is also likely to provide a wide range of nesting habitats for birds. In natural woodland, large amounts of dead wood, in various stages of decay, remain to form an additional, very important niche for other species such as beetles and woodlice.

The forest floor

Although the forest floor may appear devoid of life apart from the plants growing from it, it is in fact a place of intense activity. Even the deep "dead" leaf-litter of a dark beech wood, if carefully examined, will reveal abundant life. Spiders, harvestmen, woodlice, beetles, bugs, ants, slugs and snails are present, all playing their part in breaking down the dead plant and animal material of the forest, or feeding on the other animals present. Larger animals found in this habitat are the long-tailed wood mouse and the bank vole, which feed mainly on fruits such as acorns, hazel nuts or pine cones. These small mammals have runs just below the top layer of dead leaves, and through the roots of the herb layer vegetation.

Leaf litter decomposition is carried out by micro-organisms in the soil, especially bacteria and fungi. They are helped in this by soil animals, including earthworms, which break up the material and therefore increase its surface area for chemical decomposition. The species of decomposers present in the soil fauna vary depending on the soil type. The earthworm, along with springtails, millipedes and nematode worms, is important in woods on calcareous soils, while in woods on acid soils it is less important compared with the springtails and mites. Similarly fungi are relatively more important decomposers than bacteria in these acidic woods. Death and decomposition are vital to the health of the woodland ecosystem,

The speckled wood butterfly (Pararge aegeria) is a characteristic insect of woodland clearings, and is an early resident of glades created by fallen trees. Its coloration matches the sun-dappled forest floor.

for they enable the recycling of nutrients which would otherwise be permanently locked up in wood and leaves. Above ground the forest vegetation is in competition for light, but

The forest floor

The life which teems on and under the forest floor comprises the second of the two main factories of the wood. The first is in the green leaves of the plants, which convert the sun's energy into organic chemicals on which eventually all the life of the wood depends. The chief function of the forest floor community is to take dead wood, leaves and bodies and to break their organic chemicals down into simpler chemical nutrients which can then be taken in by the roots of the plants and used once again. A vast number of leaves fall to the ground each autumn in deciduous woodland, but have largely disappeared by the following spring. This is the result of both physical and chemical decomposition. First the leaves are physically broken up by a host of insects and other invertebrates such as millipedes and earthworms. Following this, chemical decomposition can occur, eighty per cent of which is carried out by fungi and bacteria. By no means all the animals of the forest floor are directly engaged in the task of decomposition, for many, including beetles, spiders and harvestmen are busy eating up those which are. Above ground blackbirds and dunnocks will be methodically going through the leaf litter for the invertebrates which it contains, while below moles will be searching for earthworms. Hence among the organisms of the leaf litter there is an interrelated community making a vital contribution to the whole woodland ecosystem.

Centipedes are fast moving mini-carnivores preying on mites and small insects. Their flattened body enables them to move rapidly through the leaf litter and loose soil of the forest floor. Although the centipede does not eat dead plant material itself, the vast numbers of woodland decomposers provide it with an ample food resource.

underground their roots are competing for water and nutrients. Here biggest is not always best, for the growth of large trees can be inhibited through competition from the roots of dense grass growing around their trunks. This is not always a case of one species simply having a more extensive rooting system than another. There is strong evidence that some, possibly all, plants can exude substances from their roots which actually inhibit the root growth of possible competitors. For instance, heather has been found to have an inhibiting effect on both oak and the much-planted Sitka spruce. It has also been found, however, that if birch is mixed with the oak or if Scots pine is planted with the spruce, these effects almost completely disappear.

Woodland cycles and webs

The ecology of woodlands is essentially one of cycles which in both the short and long term ensure the continuation of the woodland indefinitely, at least while the climate remains stable.

Although trees normally live beyond the age of a human being they are far from immortal. In fact many trees such as birch and beech may deteriorate rapidly when they are less than one hundred years old. Once a mature tree is dead it cannot rapidly be replaced, for as a dominant member of the canopy it has for many decades been suppressing any possible rivals which have been trying to grow beneath it. In many cases, therefore, the death of such a tree, particularly if it is suddenly blown over or loses its crown in a gale, will leave a gap in the forest canopy and create a small glade in the woodland. The first stage of the cycle following the death of a dominant standard tree is a rapid increase in the growth of the herb layer as much more light is suddenly available at ground level. Many species which are well adapted to living under shade conditions, such as primrose and violets, can flower more freely and so are better able to produce viable seed, especially as flowers growing in the light are more likely to be visited by pollinating insects. This phase also benefits many forest insects like butterflies which favour warm sheltered glades where their food plants are readily available.

Over the next few years conditions change rapidly as the more vigorous of the herb layer plants like bramble and bracken form a continuous layer over-shadowing the low-growing plants. With them should come the young saplings which will form the first tree growth to replace the fallen tree. The most abundant will not usually be of the same species as the former dominant. Birch and willow are usually the first to flourish and form a thicket which will also contain the tree which is destined to become dominant. The trees may be protected from the browsing of hares or deer by the dense growth of

Trees produce many seeds which germinate into dense growths of seedlings. Crowding and mutual shading will kill most, and only one or two will ever become mature trees.

Life in dead wood

Although dead wood is an obvious component of most woodlands its significance as an important micro-habitat is often overlooked. Dead and dying wood has been described as one of the greatest resources for animal species in a natural forest, and as many as a fifth of these animal species, chiefly invertebrates, could be lost if all the dead wood were removed. The chief agents of tree decay are fungi, often aided by bark beetles. One of the first signs of decay is that the bark becomes loose and eventually falls away. This is very apparent wherever Dutch elm disease is prevalent. If the back of the bark is examined a maze of tiny galleries will be seen to have been chiselled out by the bark beetle larvae. Also visible are the threads of the fungal mycelia. Many animals are unable to digest wood until it has been partly decomposed by a fungus and the subsequent stages of decay are characterised by a succession of different species. Dead wood, particularly the larger standing timber, is also valuable to many other forms of woodland life. Hollow trees may shelter bats; crevices in the timber and galleries bored by the larvae of beetles may also be used by solitary bees and wasps. Many insects hibernate in holes in dead wood. This wealth of insect life makes dead wood a favourite hunting ground for many woodland birds, particularly woodpeckers. The immense value of this resource is often neglected in woodland management, even in nature reserves, where dead wood is too often tidied up and burnt.

When trees fall down in old age they open a gap in the forest for new plants to colonise. The dead wood is then attacked by decomposers, recycling the tree's constituents in the ecosystem.

Woodlice are characteristic of damp places, and are especially common under rotting logs and loose bark. Here two species are shown, *Oniscus asellus* (shiny) and *Porcellio scaber.*

Wood-boring beetles and their larvae play an important role in breaking down dead trees and recycling the nutrients they contain. They are also an important source of food for birds like woodpeckers.

However, when timber is used for building, these same wood-boring beetles continue to do their job. But by attacking structural timbers they cause considerable damage since there are no natural predators to control them.

bramble around them. This "thicket" stage is particularly favoured by many of the woodland birds, providing good cover for nesting and often abundant food. As the scrub species compete for light and nutrients one after another they are suppressed and eventually killed or take their places in the shrub layer beneath the emerging canopy tree. Finally, perhaps a hundred or more years after the original tree fell, a single one remains once again, usually, but not always, of the same species.

An even more fundamental cycle is that of rainfall and nutrients. Rainfall, itself part of a cycle of precipitation and evaporation, is not a limiting factor in our usually moist climate. However, in the last few years our climate appears to have been drier and this has had a number of distinct effects on our forests. More obviously limiting is the supply of nutrients largely derived from the soil. A lowland oak wood growing on a relatively mineral-rich "brown earth" soil has more nutrients available in the cycle than one growing on a nutrient-deficient "podsol", which has developed on a hard siliceous rock such as slate. The soil is not the only source of inorganic nutrients available, however, for the canopy of the forest acts as a filter of dust particles in the atmosphere. These are washed to the ground and into the soil by rain. Minerals extracted from the tree by microorganisms living on the leaves and branches also reach the soil, again in the downwash of rain falling through the canopy. A percentage of the inorganic minerals from both sources is lost by leaching from the soil into streams and rivers, and eventually the sea. Siliceous podsols will not hold minerals as well as a brown earth derived from sand, silt and clay, and as a result of the constant leaching tend to remain permanently deficient in minerals.

Inorganic materials are taken up by the plants in all layers of the forest and through photosynthesis converted to more complex organic chemicals, including those which form the cells of which the plant is composed. Others are stored as food. When the whole plant, or parts of

Each autumn deciduous trees shed their leaves, providing food and shelter for many forest floor animals. Some dead leaves, like those of beech, do not decay rapidly and may hinder the growth of small plants.

As trees expand their girth their bark develops fissures. These provide sheltered crevices for many invertebrates, especially spiders, and also a substrate for algae and many lichens.

When a large tree dies and falls it provides food for the decomposers and a substrate for mosses and fungi. It also opens a gap in the forest canopy, through which sunlight promotes the growth of wild flowers in the new forest glade. This is a natural part of the woodland cycle and one that is absent from intensively managed forests.

it, die and fall to the forest floor, an annual event in the case of leaves of deciduous trees, decay occurs, releasing the basic minerals once again. This is the most simple "primary" cycle, but throughout its length nutrients may be diverted along an almost endless list of secondary cycles. The parasitic mistletoe, for instance, siphons off the nutrients from the vessels of oak or other trees on which it is growing. Aphids do the same thing and are then "milked" by ants for the sugary juice which they exude. In these cases the nutrients are likely to remain within the forest, for when these organisms die they will fall to the forest floor and be processed. Chiff-chaffs or nightingales, on the other hand, which live through the summer in an English oak wood and feed on caterpillars and other insects, take the nutrients contained in their bodies south to Africa when they leave in late summer. When the same birds return in spring they bring with them nutrients obtained from food collected in their winter quarters. Such cycles are therefore interlocking and overlapping all over the world. Once back in its old breeding quarters a chiff-chaff may be unfortunate enough to be eaten by one of the "top predators" of the wood, such as a tawny owl, sparrowhawk, buzzard or fox. Man may also crop the nutrients of the wood and so form part of the cycle, not only by using the timber, but also by eating blackberries, hazel nuts, pheasant or deer which have grown in the woods.

The woodland nutrient cycle is therefore an intricate food web in which as many of the available nutrients as possible are used and passed from one individual to another, plant and animal, until through death and decay they are reduced again to the basic chemicals which entered the soil through erosion of the underlying bed-rock.

Insects associated with the forest trees

Many woodland trees and shrubs support large numbers of insects which feed either directly on some part of the plant or are specifically parasitic on those which do. The number of insects associated with each tree species varies considerably, from almost three hundred in oak to less than ten in holly. Holly supports so few because its hard green leaves are physically tough and unpalatable. The native holly is in fact an exception to the general rule that the best species for insects are those which arrived naturally after the ice age and have had a long history in this country, giving plenty of time for insects, and other animals to adapt to them. Apart from oak, willow and birch both have well over two hundred species associated with them and even the native Scots pine supports almost one hundred, as does the elm. If a tree is introduced from another part of the world, on the other hand, many of its own special insects are left behind and few of ours will "adopt" it, although introduced trees may be able to support some of the insects associated with related species which are native to the area. For example, sycamore will support a number of insects associated with native field maple, while spruce is acceptable to certain insects of Scots pine.

The purple hairstreak butterfly is one of the many insects dependent on oak.

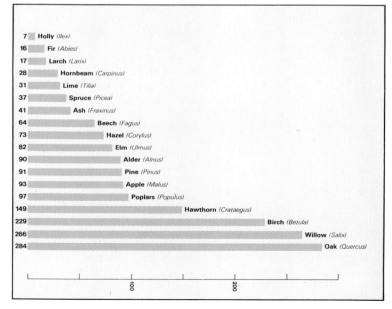

7	Holly (Ilex)
16	Fir (Abies)
17	Larch (Larix)
28	Hornbeam (Carpinus)
31	Lime (Tilia)
37	Spruce (Picea)
41	Ash (Fraxinus)
64	Beech (Fagus)
73	Hazel (Corylus)
82	Elm (Ulmus)
90	Alder (Alnus)
91	Pine (Pinus)
93	Apple (Malus)
97	Poplars (Populus)
149	Hawthorn (Crataegus)
229	Birch (Betula)
266	Willow (Salix)
284	Oak (Quercus)

Deciduous Woodlands and their Trees

Broad-leaved deciduous trees still predominate in most woodlands in the British Isles, at least in the lowlands. Intensive management over the centuries has led to the replacement of the naturally occurring trees by more productive species, firstly by native pedunculate oak and more recently by imported conifers. Even so, the natural distribution of our native trees can still be seen or at least guessed at.

Oak woodlands

The oak is probably the best-known of British trees. With its broad crown and massive trunk it represents an image of strength and endurance which has somehow become a symbol of national character. In this country oak woods have been recorded in every county on the mainland of the British Isles and occur up to 300 metres above sea level. Today only the old county of Caithness contains no recorded oak wood. But oaks occur throughout the northern hemisphere and the two species native to this country are also widespread in Europe and Asia. These are the common or pedunculate oak *(Quercus robur)* and the durmast or sessile oak *(Q. petraèa)*. Other species including turkey oak *(Q. cerris)*, holm oak *(Q. ilex)* and red oak *(Q. rubra)* have also been successfully introduced in the past few hundred years.

The natural regeneration of oak in this country has been the subject of controversy for some time, chiefly because in recent years there has been so little of it. Although in most years plenty of acorns are produced by both native species, few seedling oaks appear, and the vast majority of acorns are eaten by wood pigeons, jays or wood mice. Only a few years ago it was widely considered that because natural oak regeneration was failing, drastic remedial action was required if woodland oaks were to be replaced. Since the drought of 1976 this view has been shown to have been misguided, for at the end of that year a massive mast of acorns was produced and early in the summer of 1977 many woodland floors were covered by young oak seedlings. Although many of these will perish, a small percentage will undoubtedly grow to maturity if allowed to do so. Clearly when we are dealing with a tree which may live for several hundred years, we should not take too short a view of processes such as natural regeneration.

Although the two native species appear to have distinct requirements, the picture is confused because the pedunculate oak has always been planted at the expense of other tree species, including the sessile oak, and therefore may have replaced these species almost entirely in some areas.

Pedunculate oak woodland

Pedunculate oak woodland develops on fairly moist calcareous clay soils in lowland Britain. The tree most often associated with these woodlands is the ash *(Fraxinus excelsior)*. This lofty tree often equals the oak in height and in some woods is almost co-dominant with it. Other trees also commonly found in these oak-ash

Oak trees produce an open canopy allowing plenty of sunlight through to the luxuriant herb layer. In late summer bracken suppresses smaller plants, but in spring there are many early wild flowers.

In one good year a mature oak tree may produce several thousand acorns, but it needs to produce only a single surviving offspring in its lifetime of 2 or 3 centuries to replace itself. The surplus plus the germinating seedlings provide an enormous food resource for many woodland animals.

woodlands are field maple *(Acer campestre)*, wych elm *(Ulmus glabra)*, downy and silver birch *(Betula pubescens* and *B. pendula)*, gean *(Prunus avium)*, crab apple *(Malus sylvestris)*,

The deciduous woodland ecosystem

Timber. There is loss from the ecosystem when timber is removed (formerly through regular removal of coppice poles).

Primary producers. Mainly trees, but in open woodland, substantial productivity by ground flora. Much of the productivity in trees goes into making wood, herbs produce mainly foliage.

Sunlight provides the energy needed for photosynthesis in green plants. Photosynthesis combines water and nutrients from the soil with CO_2 from the air to form plant tissues, proteins, carbohydrates and food stores such as seeds and nectar.

Carnivores. This food source is inaccessible to non-flying predators so the canopy herbivores are mainly preyed upon by birds such as warblers and tits and some bats.

Herbivores. Canopy foliage is consumed by defoliating insects like bugs and caterpillars; nuts, berries and seeds are eaten by birds and arboreal mammals like squirrels. Herbs on the forest floor are available to a different range of herbivores than tree leaves. Mice, slugs and other species of caterpillars, beetles and bugs exploit them.

Many woodland carnivores actually prey on the organisms that live in wood — a major and special feature of the forest habitat. So, woodpeckers (feeding on wood boring larvae) and shrews (eating woodlice) are woodland carnivores which actually rely on decomposers for their food.

Fungi are decomposers which can grow in the absence of light and may provide a minor source of food for rodents and some insects.

Few dead herbivores ever reach the ground before being eaten, but there is a constant rain of faeces from insects in the plant canopy.

Herbivores on the forest floor fall prey to foxes, shrews, carnivorous beetles and ground-dwelling birds.

Leaf litter represents flow of plant productivity from forest canopy to soil. Effect strongly seasonal in deciduous woodland.

Leaf litter is decomposed by worms and especially millipedes. Often they do not manage to consume all the foliage shed by the trees, so there is a small but continuous accumulation of litter. Micro-decomposers like bacteria and fungi disassemble plant tissue molecules.

Dead wood is difficult for many animals to digest and most of this form of plant production feeds the decomposer organisms, not the herbivores. Woodlice and fungi decompose wood on the forest floor; wood-boring beetles and their larvae may attack it here and while the tree is still standing.

Faeces and carcasses of predators are returned to the soil, but the total quantity is not great and is therefore relatively insignificant in the woodland nutrient economy.

A guide to some deciduous trees

Except for three coniferous species all native British trees are deciduous. However (probably since Roman times), other species have been introduced and much of our woodland is now planted non-native fast growing conifers.

The two native British oaks, sessile and pedunculate, were very important in the past and to a lesser extent still are so today. Much timber was cut for building ships and houses, even until the beginning of this century; as they are slow growing species natural woodland has not fully recovered from this depletion.

The other main deciduous species are ash, beech, birch and elm, though the ravages of Dutch elm disease have dramatically depleted the numbers of the latter species during the last few years.

Pedunculate Oak Fagaceae *Quercus robur.* **Distribution:** Throughout the British Isles, but rare to absent in north-western Scotland, and only scattered in western Ireland.

Sessile Oak Fagaceae *Quercus petraea.* **Distribution:** Throughout the British Isles, but more common in the west. **Notes:** Mainly on acid soils; sometimes dominant or co-dominant with *Quercus robur*; forms woods up to 500 metres.

Turkey Oak Fagaceae *Quercus cerris.* **Distribution:** Throughout England, but more common towards the south-east; scattered in Wales, southern and western Scotland and Ireland. **Notes:** Often planted; prefers acid soils; upper surface of leaves rough.

Evergreen Oak Fagaceae *Quercus ilex.* **Distribution:** Scattered throughout central and southern England, but more common in the south and east; rarely in Wales and Ireland. **Notes:** Evergreen; leaves variable in shape.

The flowers of oak are small and insignificant. The numerous small male flowers are on drooping catkins which release their pollen for distribution by the wind, whereas the few female flowers are held in axils or on small erect branches.

aspen *(Populus tremula)*, grey poplar *(P. canescens)* and alder *(Alnus glutinosa)*. Today most of these species are associated with the shrub layer of the oak woodland because they have been widely coppiced in the past. Such mixed coppices were probably common in early times but became rare as hazel *(Corylus avellana)* was selected as the preferred species. Two species which are more locally associated are hornbeam *(Carpinus betulus)* and small-leaved lime *(Tilia cordata)*. The hornbeam is naturally restricted to south east England, while small-leaved lime is most plentiful in the east and west midlands. Both have been exploited in the past for their valuable timber and even today are sometimes cut for pulpwood, used in paper making. Two other species of limited distribution belong to the genus *Sorbus*. They are the white beam *(S. aria)* and the wild service tree or chequer tree *(S. torminalis)*. Neither has any great economic value and both are confined to southern England. Although more abundant on chalk and limestone, white beam does occur occasionally on clay soils, particularly in south east England. The much rarer wild service tree is typically a tree of the clay soils. It is relatively common in the south east, where it is often present with hornbeam, except where the woods are developed on the more calcareous clay-with-flint deposits which overlie much of the North Downs. It also occurs in the East and West Midlands where it often grows with small-leaved lime.

Mixed woodland with sessile and pedunculate oak

Hornbeam, wild service, white beam and the two birches are particularly associated with the extensive areas of "mixed" woodland containing both sessile and pedunculate oak as well as their hybrids. This is the most common type of woodland in parts of south east England. Especially fine examples occur on the more acidic gravels and clays of the Thames Basin, particularly east of London and also in the New Forest. Other trees associated with this type include beech *(Fagus sylvatica)* and rowan *(Sorbus aucuparia)*. Only where neutral or slightly calcareous conditions are present do ash, gean, field maple and hazel become a feature of these woodlands. Woods of mixed composition are not restricted to the south but are found scattered throughout the British Isles, for example the Wyre Forest in the West Midlands, while in Scotland mixed oak woodland is present along the shores of both Cromarty and Dornoch Firths.

A number of species of economic importance has been planted within these native oak woodlands to increase their productivity. Two in particular are sycamore *(Acer pseudoplatanus)* and sweet chestnut *(Castanea sativa)*. Sycamore has been extensively planted since the seventeenth century and now regenerates freely on many soil types, so that the species composition of some woods is being altered; sweet chestnut was introduced much earlier, possibly by the Romans. It is unusual for much viable seed to be produced and so natural regeneration is rare.

A guide to some deciduous trees (continued)

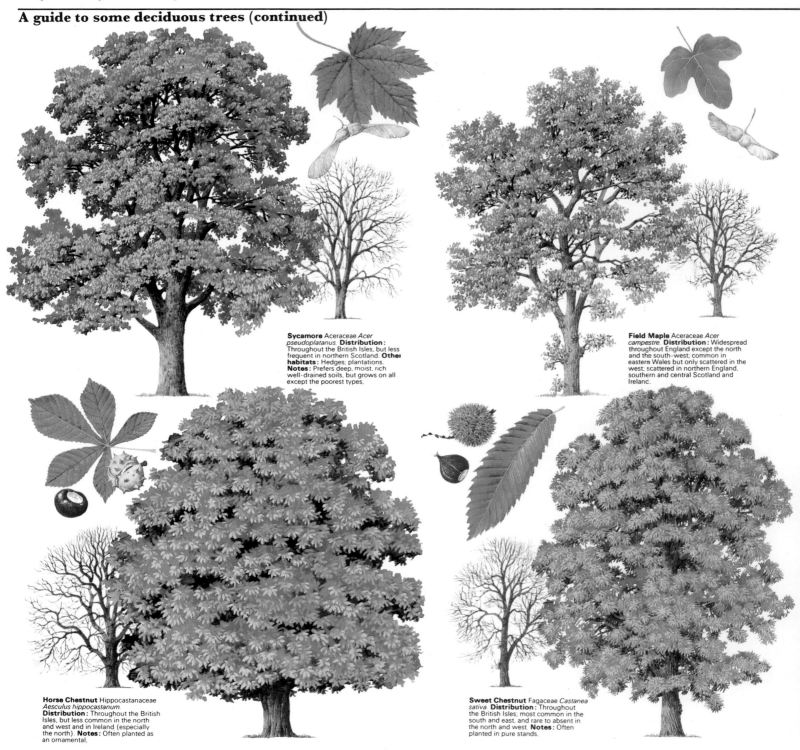

Sycamore Aceraceae *Acer pseudoplatanus.* **Distribution:** Throughout the British Isles, but less frequent in northern Scotland. **Other habitats:** Hedges; plantations. **Notes:** Prefers deep, moist, rich well-drained soils, but grows on all except the poorest types.

Field Maple Aceraceae *Acer campestre.* **Distribution:** Widespread throughout England except the north and the south-west; common in eastern Wales but only scattered in the west; scattered in northern England, southern and central Scotland and Ireland.

Horse Chestnut Hippocastanaceae *Aesculus hippocastanum.* **Distribution:** Throughout the British Isles, but less common in the north and west and in Ireland (especially the north). **Notes:** Often planted as an ornamental.

Sweet Chestnut Fagaceae *Castanea sativa.* **Distribution:** Throughout the British Isles; most common in the south and east, and rare to absent in the north and west. **Notes:** Often planted in pure stands.

The timber is extremely valuable and chestnut coppice is now the only really economic form of this type of management, especially in south east England.

Sessile oak woods

Pure sessile oak woods are a distinctive feature of the wetter, western half of England, Wales and Scotland, and are particularly associated with shallow siliceous soils where pedunculate oak only occurs exceptionally unless planted. Few trees are associated with this type, chiefly birch (*Betula pubescens*), and rowan. Alder may be associated with this woodland type in the wet places such as along stream sides, where ash may also occur. In the north the bird cherry (*Prunus padus*), a small tree which produces a mass of white flowers after the leaves have opened, is also present. In Ireland a feature of sessile oak woods is the presence of the strawberry tree (*Arbutus unedo*).

Sessile oak woods are particularly well-developed in North Devon and Cornwall, central Wales, the Pennines and Lake District. In Scotland these woods may extend as high as 455 metres above sea level. Most were originally managed as oak coppice, in particular for the tannin produced from the bark. This became uneconomic early in this century when, because of the difficulties of transporting the wood and

Field example: Western sessile oak wood: Borrowdale Woodland

Some of the best examples of northern broad-leaved woodland are to be found in Borrowdale in the Lake District. This beautiful valley, much of it owned by the National Trust, is a southwards extension of the Derwentwater valley, and the River Derwent flows through part of the Dale. The rocks of this area, which are of volcanic origin and form the Borrowdale Volcanic Series, produce an acidic soil, although calcareous conditions may occur locally, caused by the presence of mineral calcite. There is a series of hanging woodlands along the steep valley sides. Sessile oak is the predominant type, much of it previously coppiced. The shrub layer is sparse but includes birch, holly and rowan. A fine "Atlantic" community of moisture-loving ferns, mosses, liverworts and lichens is also present. These include Wilson's filmy fern and the liverworts *Scapania gracilis* and *Plagiochila spinulosa*. Over a hundred species of lichens have been recorded from one of the woods.

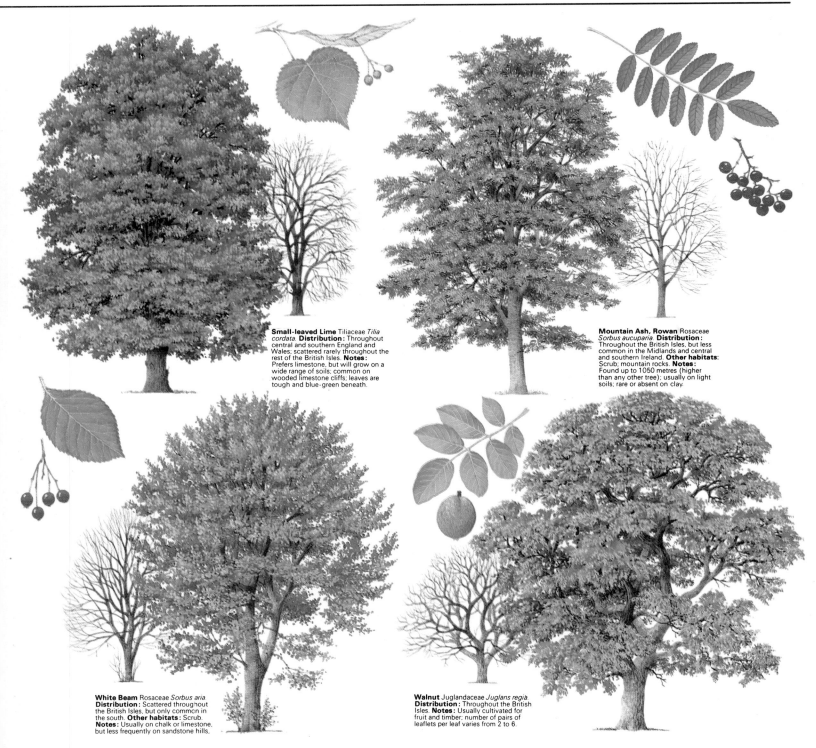

Small-leaved Lime Tiliaceae *Tilia cordata*. **Distribution:** Throughout central and southern England and Wales; scattered rarely throughout the rest of the British Isles. **Notes:** Prefers limestone, but will grow on a wide range of soils; common on wooded limestone cliffs; leaves are tough and blue-green beneath.

Mountain Ash, Rowan Rosaceae *Sorbus aucuparia*. **Distribution:** Throughout the British Isles, but less common in the Midlands and central and southern Ireland. **Other habitats:** Scrub; mountain rocks. **Notes:** Found up to 1050 metres (higher than any other tree); usually on light soils; rare or absent on clay.

White Beam Rosaceae *Sorbus aria*. **Distribution:** Scattered throughout the British Isles, but only common in the south. **Other habitats:** Scrub. **Notes:** Usually on chalk or limestone, but less frequently on sandstone hills.

Walnut Juglandaceae *Juglans regia*. **Distribution:** Throughout the British Isles. **Notes:** Usually cultivated for fruit and timber; number of pairs of leaflets per leaf varies from 2 to 6.

bark along mule tracks, it could not compete with other cheaper sources of tannin. Since then the woods have only been used for the sheltering of stock, or have been replanted with conifers.

A relict oak wood, Wistmans Wood on the flanks of Dartmoor, forms a fascinating exception to the general rule, composed as it is almost exclusively of pedunculate oak, even though sessile oak would be expected. This unique wood provides one example of our need to know much more before we can fully understand the distribution of our natural flora and fauna.

Beech woodland

Although beech woodland is now a familiar sight throughout the British Isles, the natural distribution of beech is in many ways a mystery. Pollen analyses show it to be a relatively late invader of this country, since pollen does not appear in any quantity until about 600BC. The area where beech appears most likely to be native is on the chalk of south east England, especially the North and South Downs and the Chilterns, and also on the oolitic limestone of the Cotswolds. In all these areas the trees grow on both the thin escarpment soils and deeper plateau clays. Beech also appears to be native on limestone at Symonds Yat and in the Wye Valley generally, and on Old Red Sandstone near Cardiff and in Powys. The other main area

Each autumn deciduous trees shed their leaves, providing food and shelter for many forest floor animals.

Some dead leaves, like those of beech, do not decay rapidly and may hinder the growth of small plants.

A guide to some deciduous trees (continued)

Beech Fagaceae *Fagus sylvatica.* **Distribution:** Throughout the British Isles, but less common in the north-west. **Notes:** Often planted; the characteristic dominant of calcareous substrates especially in the south-east; prefers well-drained loams and sandy soils.

Ash Oleaceae *Fraxinus excelsior.* **Distribution:** Throughout the British Isles, but less common in the north. **Other habitats:** Hedges; scrub. **Notes:** Common; forms woods on calcareous soils in the wetter regions; often in oak woods.

English Elm Ulmaceae *Ulmus procera.* **Distribution:** Throughout the British Isles, but rare to absent in central, northern and western Scotland; most frequent in south and east England and south and east Ireland. **Other habitats:** Hedges.

Wych Elm Ulmaceae *Ulmus glabra.* **Distribution:** Throughout the British Isles, but more common in the north and west. **Other habitats:** Hedges; by streams; leaves are rough on the upper surface and hairy on the lower; variable.

where beech is possibly native in the south east is on acid sands which are often podsolised. Examples occur in Windsor Forest, Burnham Beeches, Epping Forest and Blean Woods near Canterbury. In these areas beech tends to be associated with the mixed sessile-pedunculate oak woodland.

Because beech provides a most valuable timber, particularly for furniture making, it has been extensively planted outside the area where it occurs naturally. Even on the chalk in parts of southern England native beech does not form extensive woodlands. Although many beech clumps and hangers are present on the Wessex chalk in Wiltshire, all have been planted in the last few hundred years as an amenity to the landscape, for shelter, or, as in the case of the beech wood on Roundway Hill, Devizes, as a job for the unemployed. It is recorded that this steep escarpment woodland was established in the nineteenth century by the extensive man-handling of top soil to fill the pits in which the young trees were to be planted. After planting they were watered laboriously by hand. This illustrates the difficulty involved in establishing beech, even in a habitat to which the tree is thought to be well suited. Since felling in the 1950s this wood has twice been replanted using conventional forestry techniques, but only a very small percentage of the beech trees have

These trees have been pollarded, an old practice, and effectively "coppicing up in the air" They are cut some three metres above the ground, so that the new growth is beyond the reach of browsing deer and cattle.

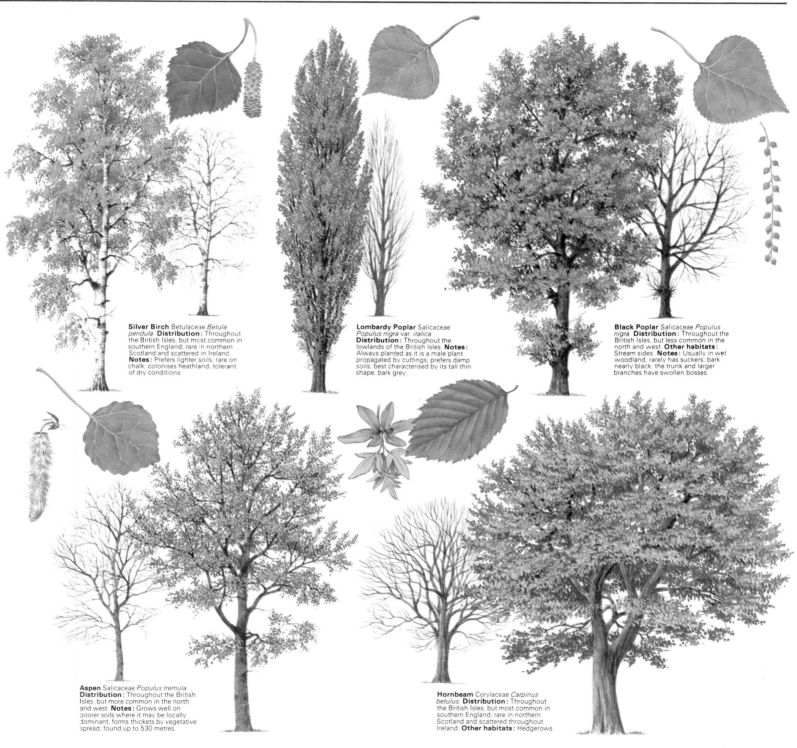

Silver Birch Betulaceae *Betula pendula*. **Distribution:** Throughout the British Isles, but most common in southern England; rare in northern Scotland and scattered in Ireland. **Notes:** Prefers lighter soils; rare on chalk; colonises heathland; tolerant of dry conditions.

Lombardy Poplar Salicaceae *Populus nigra* var. *italica*. **Distribution:** Throughout the lowlands of the British Isles. **Notes:** Always planted as it is a male plant propagated by cuttings; prefers damp soils; best characterised by its tall thin shape; bark grey.

Black Poplar Salicaceae *Populus nigra*. **Distribution:** Throughout the British Isles, but less common in the north and west. **Other habitats:** Stream sides. **Notes:** Usually in wet woodland; rarely has suckers; bark nearly black; the trunk and larger branches have swollen bosses.

Aspen Salicaceae *Populus tremula*. **Distribution:** Throughout the British Isles, but more common in the north and west. **Notes:** Grows well on poorer soils where it may be locally dominant; forms thickets by vegetative spread; found up to 530 metres.

Hornbeam Corylaceae *Carpinus betulus*. **Distribution:** Throughout the British Isles, but most common in southern England; rare in northern Scotland and scattered throughout Ireland. **Other habitats:** Hedgerows.

become established. Virtually no natural regeneration occurred after the wood was felled, although young ash and even some birch is now plentiful. Natural regeneration does occur on both calcareous and acid soils in the south east, however, especially if conditions are improved by the ground surface being broken up or "scarified" by the forester.

Few other trees are associated with pure stands of beech, because of the height and girth which the trees can attain and the very deep shade they cast. But the chalk and limestone escarpment woods often contain areas of more open beech woodland which may include ash, white beam and yew *(Taxus baccata)*. This is considered in the south east to be the penultimate stage in the succession leading to beech becoming the dominant species. However there are many areas, especially in the north and west, where this is obviously the climax stage. The species associated with acidic beech woods in the south east are the same as for mixed oak woods, typically rowan, white beam and occasionally hornbeam.

Alder woods

Woods of alder are found throughout the British Isles, even in the extreme north of Scotland, but only where the soil is waterlogged, and other species are thus excluded. These woodlands are known as "carrs" and can develop under both acid and calcareous conditions, although not in the extreme conditions found in upland peat bogs. When developed under calcareous or fen conditions, the woodlands are referred to as "fen carr". These are best developed in the Norfolk Broads, but relict examples may be found wherever alkaline ground water is present. Alder woodland was certainly much more abundant in the past, for large areas within the primeval woodlands must have been undrained swamp dominated by alder. This would have been especially true in the mild wet conditions which existed 10,000 years ago. Since then extensive clearance and drainage of the woodlands have reduced the carrs to their present fragmented state. Many are fragments indeed, rarely exceeding ten hectares in extent, and often much smaller. In many areas alders are now found only along river banks or around small ponds. Other species, especially birch *(B. pubescens)*, but also oak and ash will quickly invade where the soil of the carr begins to dry out. This may happen naturally over a prolonged period, as the depth of soil is gradually built up above the water table, but today is more often the result of land drainage. Thus the presence of alder on dry ground is a sign of recent drainage. Carr may therefore be considered a stage in the succession from open water to dry oak woodland. Alder is well adapted to living under these soggy conditions. The roots contain nodules which are able to fix nitrogen from the air, so that carrs tend to become nutrient-rich. Its seeds float and so the species is able to distribute itself along water courses. Many carrs were traditionally cut for coppice; the wood, which is resistant to moisture, had a number of uses including the manufacture of clogs.

Elms as a component of woodland

Elm is associated with a number of woodland types in this country. Wych elm *(Ulmus glabra)* is the most widespread as a woodland tree and is especially associated with the ash woods which occur on chalk and limestone throughout the British Isles. It is also sometimes found in oak woods where, on the clay soils of eastern and south east England, it may be present with the rarer smooth-leaved elm *(Ulmus carpinifolia)*. The species, or possibly a closely related subspecies, also occurs in Cornwall where it is known as the Cornish elm. Both of these species produce viable seed but the third species, English elm *(Ulmus procera)*, is sterile. Probably

a hybrid, it has long been encouraged by man because of its vigorous growth and usefulness as a hedgerow tree, where it can replace itself vegetatively by sprouting suckers. It is only a component of woodland where it has spread in from an adjacent hedge, and is most commonly found in coppices where the vigorous suckers can easily compete with the coppice species after they have been cut. There is a danger that because of Dutch elm disease, elms will be lost both as a woodland component and from the landscape as a whole, at least for the next generation. Although the effects are most obvious in the English elm of the hedgerows, the disease also affects the other species.

Birch woodland

Birch appears as a component of every woodland type, but it is only under extreme conditions of climate or, in the south, as a result of man's activities, that it becomes dominant. Both species, common and silver birch, occur throughout the country although silver birch is more usually associated with the lowland pedunculate oak woods and can even regenerate on chalk and limestone soils. Common birch is more abundant in the north and west associated with the sessile oak woods. It is also the species chiefly associated with the true Scottish birch woods which are still scattered through the highlands. Here the subspecies *B. pubescens* ssp. *odorata* gives the woods a pleasantly characteristic smell, especially after rain. In some places, at the extreme range of tolerance of the woodland, the only associated species is rowan, but elsewhere hazel, alder, bird cherry and

Field example: Mixed woodland and alder carr: Scords Wood

Even in the comparatively small woodland areas of south east England a number of woodland types may be found together in one wood where a series of different geological strata are found close together. An example of this is Scords Wood, south of Sevenoaks in Kent. Much of this wood, which belongs to the National Trust, is growing on the relatively high Lower Greensand escarpment which here forms the northern rim of the Weald. The plateau behind the escarpment has an acid podsolised soil, while further down the escarpment a band of calcareous Kentish Ragstone outcrops. At the foot of the escarpment heavy clays typical of much of the Weald form a spring line with the porous rocks above. On the dry acid plateau there are relict areas of sessile oak coppice in a matrix of beech (probably planted) and Scots pine with bilberry, heather and wavy hair-grass in the ground flora. This part of the wood has many features in common with the sessile oak woods in the north and west. Once over the escarpment the character of the wood rapidly changes with pedunculate oak replacing the sessile, although many hybrids are present. In the ground flora the acidic species disappear to be replaced by yellow archangel, the wood violets, bluebell, dog's mercury and bramble. Sanicle, green hellebore and twayblade are associated with the limestone outcrop. In the wet flushes beneath the escarpment a typical alder carr association is present with giant horsetail and both opposite- and alternate-leaved saxifrages.

In October the combination of beech and oak trees in Scords Wood together with the underlying bracken provide rich autumn colours. The dead leaves accumulate in deep drifts at the foot of the slopes in the wood where they harbour many litter-dwelling insects throughout the winter months.

aspen are also present. As conditions become less exacting, oak, ash and wych elm also enter the association. One of the most frequent associates is native Scots pine *(Pinus sylvestris* var. *scotica)*, which also occupies a similar ecological position in an altitudinal and latitudinal zone to the north of oak woodland in the British Isles. Even in these upland areas the activities of man, and particularly his grazing animals, have probably suppressed the upper limit of natural forest, both in total and for individual species, although changes in climate may have also contributed. For instance, sessile oak once appears to have been widespread in Upper Teesdale, but today's woodlands are largely composed of the common birch, more typical of the highlands.

These effects are even more dramatic in the south where birch woods are today relatively plentiful. Where heathlands in the Thames Valley, Hampshire Basin and on the Breckland of East Anglia have been ungrazed, at least since myxomatosis decimated the rabbits in the 1950s, extensive woodlands containing both birch species have developed. Theoretically this stage should eventually be replaced by sessile oak woodland. At present, there is little sign of this happening, possibly because there is no local source of sessile oak seed while the more readily available pedunculate oak does not thrive on these soils. Alternatively, the soils may, because of past cultivation and over-grazing, have become so leached of nutrients that they will not support other tree species until the correct conditions have re-established themselves under the birch woodland. A similar phenomenon following the appearance of myxomatosis is apparent on the chalk in south and south east England, although here ash, pedunculate oak and beech are also regenerating. Another type of birch wood has developed on the peat of several relict fens in East Anglia. The best example of this is at Holme Fen in Cambridgeshire, where the fen was drained and used for agriculture. This was later abandoned, leading to extensive invasion by both species of birch. Associated species include alder and pine. This area is now a National Nature Reserve and so has been saved from further agricultural reclamation.

Ash woodland

Ash occurs as an associate of pedunculate oak, and also on chalk in south east England as a successional stage towards climax beech forest. In much of south, west and north England and also in Wales, ash itself appears to form the climax woodland. Largely because of the calcareous nature of the soils associated with these woodlands and the relatively light shade cast by ash trees, these are amongst the most interesting woodland communities in the country. Typical tree associates include wych elm, white beam, field maple and yew. Examples occur on the western chalk escarpments in Hampshire, Dorset and Wiltshire, but the truly classic ash woods occur on Carboniferous limestone in the Mendips, Wye Valley and Peak District.

In the Pennines, at altitudes of up to 380 metres and in areas of high rainfall, birch *(Betula pubescens)* becomes an associate along with rowan, bird cherry and alder, while white beam and yew disappear under such wet conditions. To add to the interesting features of these woods, a number of local subspecies of white beam may be present. These are almost always associated with sheer inaccessible limestone cliffs where the woods have been least affected by human activity. The Avon Gorge near Bristol is a particularly good example, with no less than five kinds present, including the Bristol white beam *(Sorbus bristoliensis)*. Another, *S. anglica*, is also present in the Mendips and Wye Valley, while in the Peak District and further north another species, the rock white beam *(S. rupicola)* replaces the common white beam.

Chestnut is now the most common form of coppice system in current use. However, chestnut-coppiced woodland supports far less wildlife than an oak and hazel system.

Field example: Ash woodland on limestone: Wye Valley, Forest of Dean

Between Ross-on-Wye and Chepstow, on the borders of England and Wales, the River Wye meanders its way through deep gorges and at Symonds Yat forms a spectacular, almost complete loop. The different geological strata of Old Red Sandstone, Carboniferous Limestone and Coal Measures are crossed several times and these differences are reflected in the dense woodlands which cloak much of the valley sides. The Forest of Dean was once a Royal Forest, but was transferred to the Forestry Commission in 1924. Despite the Forestry Commission policy of planting mixtures of conifers and broad-leaved trees, large areas of the semi-natural broad-leaved woodland remain. On the sandy soils derived from the Old Red Sandstone sessile oak, much of it formerly coppiced, is dominant and is associated with a ground flora which includes bilberry, wavy hair-grass and greater woodrush. The most interesting woodland is developed on the limestone. Although small areas are predominantly beech, more mixed woodlands of ash, yew and white beam are present. Besides the common white beam (*Sorbus aria*) its rare relatives *S. anglica*, *S. eminens* and *S. porrigentiformis* are also present. Small-leaved lime (*Tilia cordata*) is abundant in the Wye Valley woodlands along with the only stand of the much rarer large-leaved lime (*T. platyphyllus*) in the country. An extremely rich shrub and ground flora is associated with these limestone woodlands. There is also much for bird watchers in the Valley, with pied flycatchers and wood warbler as well as dipper along the river itself. Polecat, otter and fallow deer are among the more interesting mammals recorded, and the greater horseshoe bat reaches its northern limit in this area.

Alluvial soils beside the river provide good grazing land, and the river itself is noted for its salmon.

The River Wye meanders extensively through the Forest of Dean, forming large loops especially near Symonds Yat.

Coniferous Woodlands and their Trees

Although coniferous trees and woodland are frequently described as being alien to the British landscape, there are in fact three native species of conifer, all of which can form woodland under certain circumstances. These are the Scots pine (*Pinus sylvestris*), yew (*Taxus baccata*) and juniper (*Juniperus communis*). Of these pine and yew can be considered here, while juniper is more properly regarded as a shrub. It is interesting that of these three species only pine produces cones in the conventional sense, while the other two produce "berries", which is quite exceptional for conifers. Both yew and juniper berries are however modified female cones which have become adapted to encourage attack by birds, which disperse the seed, while the male, pollen-producing cones, carried on separate trees, are conventional in structure.

Yew woods

Yew occurs widely on chalk and limestone where it is usually either succeeded by beech or remains as part of a mixed woodland with ash and white beam. Woods of the latter type, situated on chalk escarpments in west Sussex, Hampshire and Wiltshire present a most attractive picture in early summer, the dark, almost black, evergreen leaves of the yew contrasting strikingly with the almost pure white, newly-opened leaves of the white beam. In these woodlands yew may be locally dominant over substantial areas to the exclusion of other species. The most extensive pure yew wood occurs at Kingley Vale in West Sussex and has long been regarded as the most important wood of its type in Britain and has even been claimed to be the best yew wood in Europe. The yew-dominated woodland, situated on a south-facing chalk escarpment extends to about 40ha, with

Most coniferous woodland today consists of forestry plantations. Because the trees have been deliberately planted, these woodlands consist of single-age stages. reducing their diversity and interest. Conifers cast a dense shade and suppress herbs and shrub growth.

Field example: Native Scots pine: Caledonian Forest

Once much of the Highlands of Scotland was covered by the Caledonian Forest, composed chiefly of Scots pine. This formed the last remnant of the pine forests which covered much of the British Isles 10,000 years ago. Because of extensive exploitation for timber in the past, this once continuous tract of woodland is now fragmented into many separate blocks. Despite this it still forms one of the most extensive wooded areas in Britain. Some of the best remaining examples are along the valleys of the River Dee and Spey and on the lower slopes of the Cairngorm Mountains. Fine examples are included within the Cairngorms National Nature Reserve. The woods extend as high as 640 metres above sea level and occur mainly on coarse sandy gravel soils derived from granite, which are typically acidic and frequently podsolised. Few other trees and shrubs are associated with Scots pine, the chief exceptions being birch, rowan and juniper. Although relatively poor in species the ground flora is highly characteristic. In many woods a luxuriant cover of moss carpets much of the floor, along with heather, bilberry and wavy hair-grass. Species of characteristically northern distribution include chickweed and one-flowered wintergreen, with the lesser twayblade and creeping lady's tresses orchids. The fauna of these woods is also extremely rich, particularly in mammals such as red deer, wild cat and red squirrel, which are absent from much of the south.

The red squirrel is one of Britain's native species and is still common in the Caledonian Forest.

Part of the Caledonian Forest, featuring a mature Scots pine *(Pinus sylvestris)* with bracken and heather.

The coniferous woodland ecosystem

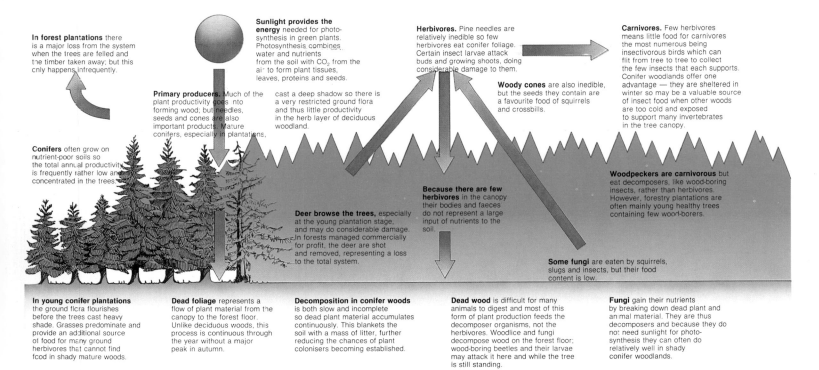

In forest plantations there is a major loss from the system when the trees are felled and the timber taken away; but this only happens infrequently.

Sunlight provides the energy needed for photosynthesis in green plants. Photosynthesis combines water and nutrients from the soil with CO_2 from the air to form plant tissues, leaves, proteins and seeds.

Primary producers. Much of the plant productivity goes into forming wood; but needles, seeds and cones are also important products. Mature conifers, especially in plantations, cast a deep shadow so there is a very restricted ground flora and thus little productivity in the herb layer of deciduous woodland.

Herbivores. Pine needles are relatively inedible so few herbivores eat conifer foliage. Certain insect larvae attack buds and growing shoots, doing considerable damage to them.

Woody cones are also inedible, but the seeds they contain are a favourite food of squirrels and crossbills.

Carnivores. Few herbivores means little food for carnivores the most numerous being insectivorous birds which can flit from tree to tree to collect the few insects that each supports. Conifer woodlands offer one advantage — they are sheltered in winter so may be a valuable source of insect food when other woods are too cold and exposed to support many invertebrates in the tree canopy.

Conifers often grow on nutrient-poor soils so the total annual productivity is frequently rather low and concentrated in the trees.

Because there are few herbivores in the canopy their bodies and faeces do not represent a large input of nutrients to the soil.

Deer browse the trees, especially at the young plantation stage, and may do considerable damage. In forests managed commercially for profit, the deer are shot and removed, representing a loss to the total system.

Woodpeckers are carnivorous but eat decomposers, like wood-boring insects, rather than herbivores. However, forestry plantations are often mainly young healthy trees containing few wood-borers.

Some fungi are eaten by squirrels, slugs and insects, but their food content is low.

In young conifer plantations the ground flora flourishes before the trees cast heavy shade. Grasses predominate and provide an additional source of food for many ground herbivores that cannot find food in shady mature woods.

Dead foliage represents a flow of plant material from the canopy to the forest floor. Unlike deciduous woods, this process is continuous through the year without a major peak in autumn.

Decomposition in conifer woods is both slow and incomplete so dead plant material accumulates continuously. This blankets the soil with a mass of litter, further reducing the chances of plant colonisers becoming established.

Dead wood is difficult for many animals to digest and most of this form of plant production feeds the decomposer organisms, not the herbivores. Woodlice and fungi decompose wood on the forest floor; wood-boring beetles and their larvae may attack it here and while the tree is still standing.

Fungi gain their nutrients by breaking down dead plant and animal material. They are thus decomposers and because they do not need sunlight for photosynthesis they can often do relatively well in shady conifer woodlands.

---

pedunculate oak woodland on adjacent areas where a clay soil is present. Some of the ancient yew trees are at least five hundred years old. Another remarkable and extensive yew wood, known as Great Yews, is situated near Salisbury in Wiltshire. Although some of the trees seem quite ancient, it appears to have been planted and is laid out on a geometrical pattern, following approximately the points of the compass. Like Kingley Vale the woodland is extremely dense and little light reaches the woodland floor which is almost totally devoid of vegetation, a feature which gives such woods a slightly sinister atmosphere.

Yews also occur frequently within areas of mixed oak woodland, especially on the more acid soils in southern England. Here it may be native, certain woods within the New Forest being examples. However, isolated yews in mixed woodland have usually been planted to mark the boundary of a coppice compartment, ownership, parish or even county boundary.

Scots pine

The true Scots pine, which once formed extensive tracts within the ancient Caledonian Forest in the Scottish Highlands, is considered to be a distinct variety *Pinus sylvestris* var. *scotica*. It has a typical pyramidal growth form compared with the flat tops of planted pine in the south. Scots pine seed has been extensively exported from Scotland during the last two or three hundred years to be planted in other parts of the country. The native pine woods of the Caledonian Forest have been extensively cleared and fragmented during historic times in a similar way to the lowland oak woods. However, their relative inaccessibility postponed this process much longer, and it was not until the beginning of the eighteenth century, when the timber resources of the lowland oak woods became severely depleted, that really extensive exploitation of these pine forests took place. Rivers such as the Spey were used to float trunks to the sea. Today remnants of this forest remain on Deeside, Speyside, Rannoch, the Great Glen, Wester Ross and to the north west around the Rhidorroch Forest.

The soils of woodlands where pine is the dominant species are typically siliceous, acidic and frequently podsolised. Where the soil is derived from underlying rocks the pine is usually replaced by broad-leaved species, particularly

A guide to some coniferous trees

Three conifer species, Scots pine, yew and juniper, are native to Britain and may form woodland under specialised conditions, although juniper is more properly regarded as a shrub. Yew occurs widely in woods on chalk and limestone, where it is associated with either beech or ash and white beam. Individual trees may also be found in other woods, even on acid soils, such as in the New Forest oak woods. Scots pine once formed the major component of the ancient Caledonian Forest in the Scottish Highlands. Although now much fragmented, extensive pine woods are still present in Speyside and Deeside. In addition to these three native trees, conifers of many other species have been introduced into the British Isles in recent years chiefly because of their qualities as fast-growing timber producers. In addition some have been introduced for ornamental purposes. In the south, introduced pine has become naturalised in many places, especially on heathland. Of the introduced species larch and Norway spruce have been planted in this country for some four hundred years, while continental Scots pine also used to be extensively grown. Today these have largely been replaced by even faster-growing alien species, which are also tolerant of the poorest soils. Many of these originate from the western seaboard of North America. These include lodgepole pine and Sitka spruce; the latter is now the most extensively planted species. European larch has been superseded by Japanese larch, and by the hybrid between the two species which arose accidentally in 1904; this has been found to be more vigorous than either of the parent trees.

Scots Pine Pinaceae *Pinus sylvestris* **Distribution :** Throughout the British Isles. **Notes :** The dominant tree of the highlands; often forms woods on sandy soils; variable.

Coniferous Woodlands

birch but more rarely by oak and ash. In the western areas where the rainfall is higher, pine woods are found on peat soils. The relationship between pine and birch is complex. Although *Betula pubescens* subsp. *odorata* is typical, both of the usual species *B. pubescens* subsp. *pubescens* and *B. verrucosa* are present. Birch and pine can each form almost pure woodlands or alternatively can be mixed. In general, more extreme climatic conditions appear to favour pine, or more probably put birch at a disadvantage. Pine therefore tends to occur in pure stands on north-facing slopes, especially where the climate is relatively dry or "Continental", as compared with the "Atlantic" or oceanic climate of the west coast. Hence some of the most pure stands occur in Speyside and Deeside. These woodlands, both pine and birch, are developed on mountain slopes and include trees at the highest altitude reached by woodland in Britain although most occur between 300 and 600 metres above sea level.

Even in these remote forests it is difficult to distinguish between natural distribution and the effects of past and present human activities. Birch is certainly more abundant in some pine woods because past exploitation has opened up the woodlands, thereby encouraging its invasion. The chief trees associated with these pine woods are therefore birch, of both species, and rowan. On better soils both sessile and pedunculate oak appear along with ash, while in wetter

Conifers, especially young ones, cast a particularly deep shade, suppressing practically all herb growth. When the trees grow taller or are artificially thinned, conifer woodlands may support more species.

areas along riversides, alder, aspen and bird cherry are associates. The natural regeneration of these native pine woods is rather spasmodic, although the production of seed is often plentiful. The best regeneration appears to take place on disturbed ground, on naturally occurring river gravels, or when the site is burnt or deliberately scarified. As with oak woods management has tended to produce a crop of even age so that it is difficult to picture the structure of completely natural pine woods, although a more mixed age structure would undoubtedly be present.

It is interesting that similar woods exist in south west Norway beyond the natural western limit of spruce *(Picea abies)*. Further east in Europe pine appears to be a succession stage with spruce as the climax. From analysis of pollen it is clear that spruce was present in this country before the last glaciation when it would presumably have been the dominant tree in the north. Spruce did not recolonise this country after the last glaciation and was completely absent until it was planted in recent times.

Naturalised pine woods

Although pine is thought to have become extinct in southern Britain many centuries ago, it is relatively common today in many areas of the south. This recolonisation has come about through the agency of man, who has transported trees south to provide a source of timber, to form

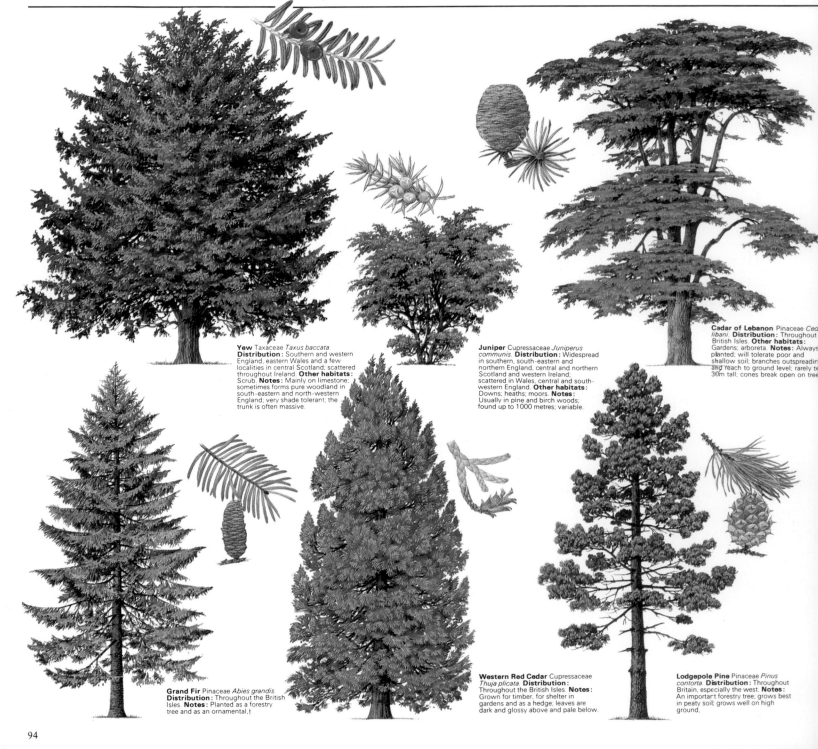

Yew Taxaceae *Taxus baccata*. **Distribution:** Southern and western England, eastern Wales and a few localities in central Scotland; scattered throughout Ireland. **Other habitats:** Scrub. **Notes:** Mainly on limestone; sometimes forms pure woodland in south-eastern and north-western England; very shade tolerant; the trunk is often massive.

Juniper Cupressaceae *Juniperus communis*. **Distribution:** Widespread in southern, south-eastern and northern England, central and northern Scotland and western Ireland; scattered in Wales, central and south-western England. **Other habitats:** Downs; heaths; moors. **Notes:** Usually in pine and birch woods; found up to 1000 metres; variable.

Cedar of Lebanon Pinaceae *Cedrus libani*. **Distribution:** Throughout British Isles. **Other habitats:** Gardens; arboreta. **Notes:** Always planted; will tolerate poor and shallow soil; branches outspreading and reach to ground level; rarely to 30m tall; cones break open on tree.

Grand Fir Pinaceae *Abies grandis*. **Distribution:** Throughout the British Isles. **Notes:** Planted as a forestry tree and as an ornamental.

Western Red Cedar Cupressaceae *Thuja plicata*. **Distribution:** Throughout the British Isles. **Notes:** Grown for timber; for shelter in gardens and as a hedge; leaves are dark and glossy above and pale below.

Lodgepole Pine Pinaceae *Pinus contorta*. **Distribution:** Throughout Britain, especially the west. **Notes:** An important forestry tree; grows best in peaty soil; grows well on high ground.

shelter belts or just to create a visually pleasing landscape. Pine seed from the native forests in Scotland has been extensively exported to England. The trend was possibly set by King James I (who was also James VI of Scotland). In 1621 he had pine seed from the Moir Forest in upper Deeside sent south for planting. Seed may also have been imported from the continent. Another important factor was probably the ability of pine to grow tolerably well on more impoverished soils, where oak could not be established. It is in such areas today that pine appears to have escaped from the plantations and to have re-established itself naturally. The pines typical of the heathland and coast around Bournemouth are now thought so characteristic of the area that the Pines Express was until recently a train linking Manchester with Bournemouth, rather than the Highlands as might be expected. Since myxomatosis decimated the rabbits, pine, like birch, has become even more firmly established on the Tertiary gravels of the Hampshire Basin and Thames Valley and also on the poor sandy soils of the Breckland in Suffolk and west Norfolk. Pine was also planted on chalk in a number of places in the mid-nineteenth century, especially Salisbury Plain. Here an interesting woodland community is now developing, with the natural yew-ash-white beam mixture being supplemented by Scots pine, frequently with an understorey of juniper and other shrubs. All have regenerated

The yew forest at Kingley Vale contains the oldest yew trees in Britain, some being over 500 years old. The forest itself is probably the oldest of its kind in Europe.

Yew grows here on the slopes of the U-shaped valley and part of the valley bottom. The forest is still spreading to cover the slopes at the head of the valley.

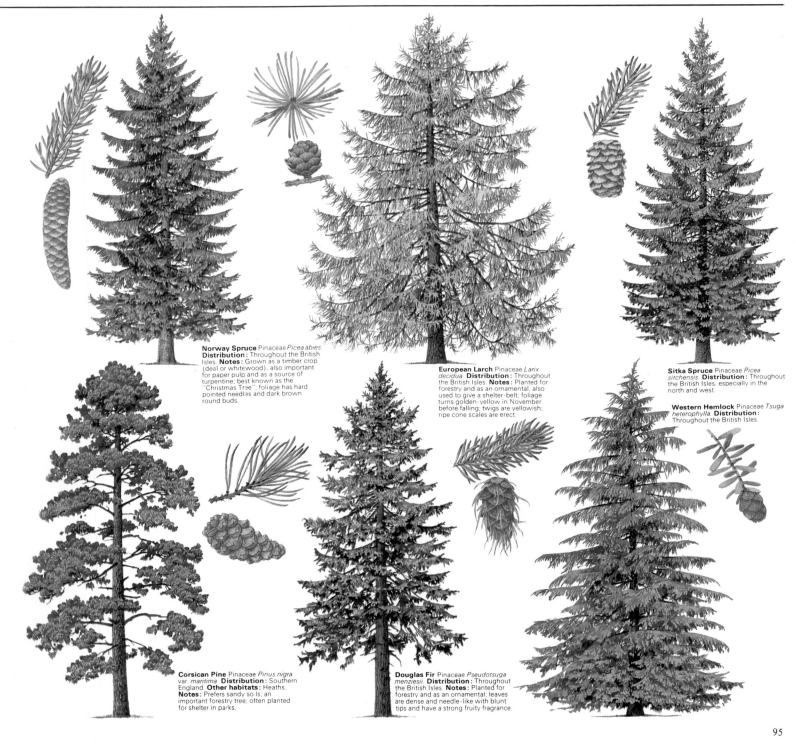

Norway Spruce Pinaceae *Picea abies*. **Distribution:** Throughout the British Isles. **Notes:** Grown as a timber crop (deal or whitewood), also important for paper pulp and as a source of turpentine; best known as the "Christmas Tree"; foliage has hard pointed needles and dark brown round buds.

European Larch Pinaceae *Larix decidua*. **Distribution:** Throughout the British Isles. **Notes:** Planted for forestry and as an ornamental, also used to give a shelter-belt; foliage turns golden-yellow in November before falling; twigs are yellowish; ripe cone scales are erect.

Sitka Spruce Pinaceae *Picea sitchensis*. **Distribution:** Throughout the British Isles, especially in the north and west.

Western Hemlock Pinaceae *Tsuga heterophylla*. **Distribution:** Throughout the British Isles.

Corsican Pine Pinaceae *Pinus nigra* var. *maritima*. **Distribution:** Southern England. **Other habitats:** Heaths. **Notes:** Prefers sandy soils; an important forestry tree; often planted for shelter in parks.

Douglas Fir Pinaceae *Pseudotsuga menziesii*. **Distribution:** Throughout the British Isles. **Notes:** Planted for forestry and as an ornamental; leaves are dense and needle-like with blunt tips and have a strong fruity fragrance.

naturally on open downland since myxomatosis. The end result of this new community is not yet known.

Other conifer plantations

The planting of conifers has been part of forestry in the British Isles for several hundred years. Although the Scots pine was among the first conifers to be widely planted, two other widespread European species, Norway spruce *(Picea abies)* and European larch *(Larix decidua)*, have also been planted for some four hundred years, mainly as small copses or standard trees in coppice woodland. However, it is only since the formation of the Forestry Commission in 1919 that really extensive plantations of conifers have been established, both directly by the state forestry service and, with their financial aid and advice, by the private sector. Other species, particularly those from the north west coast of the USA, have been tried and found to flourish in our relatively wet "Atlantic" climate. The lodgepole pine *(Pinus contorta)* and Sitka spruce *(Picea sitchensis)* both occur naturally along the western seaboard of North America from Alaska to California and are remarkable for their tolerance of nutrient-poor soils. This has led to their extensive use in the afforestation of poor grazing land in upland and coastal areas throughout the western half of Britain. Today more Sitka spruce is planted than any other tree. European larch has now been widely replaced as a commercial species by the Japanese larch *(L. kaempferi)* which grows wild in mountainous areas of Japan and was first introduced to this country as long ago as 1861. It appears better adapted to our climate than the European species and is faster growing. Most productive of all is the hybrid between the two larches, *Larix × eurolepis*, which first arose by accident in 1904, and is now widely planted because of its hybrid vigour. Corsican pine *(Pinus nigra)* from south and east Europe has similarly been found tolerant of a wider range of soils than native Scots pine, and so has largely replaced it commercially. Other widely planted species include Douglas fir *(Pseudotsuga menziesii)*, grand fir *(Abies grandis)*, western red cedar *(Thuja plicata)*, Lawson cypress *(Chamaecyparis lawsoniana)* and western hemlock *(Tsuga heterophylla)*. All these are from North America.

The extensive planting of single species monoculture plantations has led to new problems with pests. Early in the century a species of woolly aphid, *Adelges piceae*, became established in fir plantations, and decimated certain strains of Douglas fir and the European silver fir *(Abies alba)* which had then been widely planted. Because of this problem, silver fir has been replaced as a commercial species by grand fir, which appears not to suffer seriously from the pest. Although the aphid occurs on the continent it is not a pest there, presumably because it is kept in check by natural predators which do not occur in Britain. More recently, attacks by the pine looper moth *(Bupalus piniarius)* on conifer plantations in 1978 have forced the Forestry Commission to treat plantations with insecticide from the air.

The extensive planting of conifers has brought about fundamental changes in the ecology of the upland areas, which were previously open moorland, and in established woodland sites where native broad-leaved trees have been replaced. In particular, changes have occurred in the ground flora and insect associations through shading and the accumulation of needle litter, which produces an acidic soil. Because of this a shrub layer is unable to develop and wild flowers such as primrose and bluebell, typical of broad-leaved woodland, are slowly suppressed and die out. On the bonus side, certain animals are now more abundant than in the recent past because of the extensive new conifer forests, notably the wild cat and the pine marten.

Field example: A conifer plantation: Thetford Forest, Breckland

The Brecklands of East Anglia once formed an extensive stretch of open heathland around the town of Thetford. After the First World War, when agriculture was depressed, the soils were considered too poor to cultivate and the area was largely abandoned. In 1922, 20,800ha were purchased by the Forestry Commission at Swaffham and a start was made on afforesting the area. Scots pine had long ago been extensively planted as windbreaks in the area, and seed was extracted from these trees and sown in nurseries to provide the bulk of the seedlings planted. Other species were tried, including Douglas fir, larch, Corsican pine, beech and oak, but with limited success. Although it was found difficult to establish at the time, Corsican pine has now replaced Scots pine as the favoured species. Although these woods contain very few true woodland plants in the ground flora, they do have a distinctive flora and fauna. Most interesting is the abundance of red squirrel, which has been replaced elsewhere in southern and eastern England by the introduced grey squirrel. Badgers have also colonised the woodlands, along with red and roe deer, while the large areas of conifers have also become breeding grounds for lesser redpoll, crossbill and hobby. To add to the interest, many of the rides contain rare plant species characteristic of the original Breckland heaths; these include the small herbs spring speedwell and Breckland wild thyme.

A ride through a conifer plantation typical of many throughout Thetford Forest. The well-drained sandy soil has been heavily planted by the Forestry Commission making it the largest Scots and Corsican pine forest in England.

The life cycle of conifers

The European larch is a widespread and attractive conifer, which has been planted as a forest tree since the middle of the eighteenth century. On a good soil it may reach twenty metres in as many years, and between thirty and forty metres when fully grown. Although in many ways typical of other conifers, larch has a number of distinctive features, the chief being that it is deciduous and produces fresh green needles every spring. Like most other conifers the seeds of larch are borne in female cones, while the pollen is produced in separate male cones. Both may be present on the same branch. Because the female cones take eighteen months to reach maturity, mature and freshly developing cones also occur together. The young female cones are made up of outer red bract scales; attached to each of these are two ovuliferous scales, each bearing an ovule. Because of their bright colour they are known as 'larch roses'. However they do not attract insects, for like other conifers the larch is wind-pollinated. Each of the pollen grains produced in masses from the small yellow male cones has two air sacs enabling them to be blown long distances. When mature the bract scales are hard and brown. In dry conditions they open to liberate the ripe seeds. Each remains firmly attached to its ovuliferous scale, now dry and papery, which acts as a wing, allowing the seed to be blown far away in the wind. If they land in a suitable site germination is rapid, the seedling eventually growing into a new larch tree.

When conditions are dry the large brown ripe female cones open their bracts to allow wind distribution of the seeds.

The young red female larch cones are here growing on the same shoot as the pollen-containing yellowish male cones.

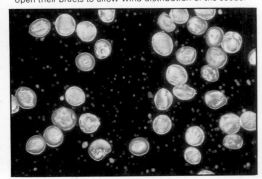

Highly magnified pollen showing the twin air sacs that increase the volume and consequently aid it in its dispersal.

Woodland Shrubs

A holly tree *(Ilex aquifolium)* growing beneath mature trees of a beech wood. The evergreen habit of the holly allows it to undertake photosynthesis and build up its reserves when the canopy has no leaves.

The woodland shrubs described in this section are those which do not normally contribute to the woodland canopy, but are typical of the second or shrub layer of the wood. Under special conditions some of the species may form pure stands of scrub woodland. Normally these are merely a stage in the succession to the climax woodland type appropriate to the site, but they may persist for an extremely long period or even indefinitely. Holly, box, hazel and juniper may all form such scrub woodland.

Holly *(Ilex aquifolium)* is present as a shrub or small tree in many kinds of woodland on both acid and alkaline soils, but perhaps occurs most frequently in the mixed sessile-pedunculate oak woods. Particularly good examples are associated with the Killarney oak woods in Eire where holly forms both an extensive understorey and also pure stands on the adjacent rocky scree slopes. It is probable that the relatively mild moist climate of the region encourages the holly's vigorous growth, along with the strawberry tree which is also an associate of these woodlands. A holly wood is also present on the shingle beach of Dungeness on the Kent/Sussex coast.

Box *(Buxus sempervirens)* is a rare shrub of chalk and limestone soils in the south of England. It has been extensively planted in the past both for its wood, and as cover for game. Like holly, it is an evergreen. It is most unusual to find it regenerating naturally with the other woody colonisers of the chalk. Where it does occur it tends to form extremely persistent scrub woodland stands. So persistent is it that a number of place names throughout the south refer to a box wood occurring nearby. The most famous example is Box Hill in Surrey where pure box woods have developed on slopes which are exceptionally steep for chalk. Extensive box woods still exist elsewhere, in Gloucestershire and in the Chilterns. Box wood is extremely hard and close-grained. It was used for printer's engraving blocks for illustrating such magazines as the Illustrated London News in the mid-nineteenth century, and was then of considerable economic value.

Hazel *(Corylus avellana)* is the commonest and most widespread of the woodland shrubs which because of its past value as coppice was extensively planted and selected for in the woods. It was among the first woody species to colonise this country after the last glaciation, when extensive woods of hazel must have developed. A few hazel woods, particularly on the more calcareous soils, still occur in the Highlands and in the Burren in Eire, and may possibly be a remnant of these pioneer woodlands. Hazel may also rapidly colonise grassland, particularly on chalk if a deep enough soil is present, to form a transient hazel wood in which oak, ash and white beam quickly succeed to dominance.

Juniper *(Juniperus communis)* is the only shrub among our three native species of conifer. In the south of England juniper is a rare and decreasing shrub of calcareous soil, but the populations in the uplands of the north of England and Scotland have a different range of soil tolerance and are not so restricted. Here it is a common member of the shrub layer in woodlands of birch and Scots pine and, more rarely, ash. Under certain conditions in the Highlands the tree layer is unable to develop and a juniper scrub woodland has persisted.

The almost ripe fruit of the hazel, called a hazel-nut or cob-nut, is surrounded by a deeply lobed frill or involucre. Plants in fruit are commonly seen in autumn in woods, scrub and hedges.

Other shrubs

The willows are a complex group of shrubs which although mainly associated with wetter soils, can occur even in dry woodlands on chalk. The distribution of the many different species seems to reflect climate and geology, rather than the type of woodland. For instance, *Salix caprea*, *S. atrocinerea* and *S. aurita* occur with most woodland types throughout the country. Others, notably *S. pentandra*, *S. nigricans* and *S. phylicifolia*, are confined to the north of England and Scotland and are components of the Highland pine and birch woods.

Both blackthorn *(Prunus spinosa)* and hawthorn *(Crataegus monogyna)* are common in the shrub layer throughout the country, but many other shrubs are restricted to a much more southern distribution. These include the closely related midland thorn *(C. oxyacanthoides)* and many of the shrubs associated with the more calcareous soils, notably wayfaring tree *(Viburnum lantana)*, guelder rose *(V. opulus)*, dogwood *(Thelycrania sanguinea)*, wild privet *(Ligustrum vulgare)*, spindle *(Euonymus europaeus)* and purging buckthorn *(Rhamnus catharticus)*. A cousin of the latter species is the alder buckthorn *(Frangula alnus)*. This plant is usually associated with the more acid soils, typically those of the mixed oak woods of south east England, where the purging buckthorn is absent. The two species do however occur together along with guelder rose in the alder carrs in the East

The hawthorns

Two species of hawthorn are native in this country. These are the common hawthorn (*Crataegus monogyna*), also known as the quickthorn, whitethorn or May, and the midland or woodland thorn (*C. oxyacanthoides*). While the common hawthorn occurs on a wide variety of soil types throughout the British Isles, the midland thorn is largely restricted to clay soils in the Midlands and Weald. They are most easily told apart when they are flowering or in fruit, as the midland thorn flowers contain two styles and stigma, whereas the other has only one. Consequently the fruit or haw of the midland thorn contains two pip-like fruits compared with only one in the common hawthorn. The common hawthorn, which has been widely planted as a hedgerow shrub and also occurs on chalk downland, is usually associated with the more open areas of the wood, and does not thrive under deep shade. The midland thorn is a true shrub of the woods and is found in the deepest parts of the oak woods in which it grows. Often hawthorn bushes growing around the periphery will be found to be hybrids which have intermediate characteristics, some of the fruits having one seed, others two. Both the hawthorns are important for the wildlife which they support. The red berries are eaten by redwing and fieldfare, while about one hundred and fifty species of insect are associated with the tree. These include several attractive moth larvae, particularly the lackey, which occur in large numbers in a web which may cover the bush.

Hawthorn berries provide a rich food source for many animals such as this dormouse.

The common hawthorn (above) is easily distinguished from the midland thorn as the flowers have only one style.

Anglian fens. Two rather specialised woodland shrubs are the native elderberry and the introduced rhododendron. Elder *(Sambucus nigra)* occurs in many woods on soils especially rich in nitrates and phosphates. Its presence usually indicates the latrine area of a badger sett or rabbit warren. The evergreen rhododendron *(Rhododendron ponticum)* is a native of Portugal and was introduced for its flowers and possibly for game cover. It is now widely established on more acidic soils, even in the Scottish islands, and has recreated a modified woodland type, with "bushes" nearly 10m tall. The evergreen leaves of rhododendron cast a deep shadow, shading out other plants and thus restricting both tree regeneration and plant diversity. The leaves resist decay and support few soil animals; their thick cuticle makes them unsuitable as food for herbivores and sap-sucking insects and the branches provide a tangled mass which is both an impediment to movement yet an inadequate support for the nests of many bird species. Rhododendron has a tendency to take over large areas and drastically reduce their wildlife potential, and it has been necessary to take steps to eradicate it in many places.

Among the more low-growing shrubs are the native spurge laurel *(Daphne laureola)* and mezereon *(D. mezereum)* which are almost confined to calcareous soils in the south. *D. mezereum* is among our rarest plants and is now legally protected. A further interesting example is the butcher's broom *(Ruscus aculeatus)*, which has evergreen "leaves" which are not really leaves at all but flattened stems on which the flowers and bright red berries develop.

A number of plant species are present in woodland which, although woody, cannot support themselves and instead grow on and over other trees and shrubs. Examples are ivy *(Hedera helix)*, honeysuckle *(Lonicera periclymenum)* and old man's beard *(Clematis vitalba)*, the latter being restricted to calcareous soils.

Rhododendron is an attractive introduced shrub which is now very abundant. It is commonly planted in woods and has become naturalised in many places; but it is an ecological liability, casting dense shade throughout the year and having leaves which are inedible to most woodland animals. It often becomes the dominant species of the shrub layer.

A field guide to shrubs

Shrubs are those woody plants typically to be found growing in the woodland layer beneath the canopy trees. In many broad-leaved woods the most useful species have been encouraged at the expense of others. Thus hazel is the most abundant shrub in many woodlands because of its value as coppice. For the same reason species such as ash and, in some places, hornbeam, which would otherwise be canopy trees, are also found in the coppice layer. Other widespread shrub species include the willows, holly, blackthorn and hawthorn. The much rarer midland thorn, which closely resembles the common hawthorn, is present in woods in the Midlands and south east of England. Elder is often present, usually associated with badger setts or rabbit warrens, where the soil has been organically enriched. Some shrubs are particularly associated with woodland growing on calcareous soils. These include wayfaring tree, guelder rose, dogwood, wild privet, spindle and purging buckthorn. The alder buckthorn, which resembles the latter species, is in contrast confined to acid soils. On drier sites it often occurs with rhododendron; although not native the latter shrub is now widely naturalised. Juniper is associated with many northern woods, particularly the Caledonian pine woods. Under certain conditions woodland dominated solely by shrubs may develop. Holly, for example, forms extensive woods in Killarney, while a few hazel woods occur on the more calcareous soils in Scotland and Ireland. Box is a rare evergreen shrub of chalk and limestone soils in southern England; in one or two places pure box woods have developed, the most famous being at Box Hill in Surrey.

Box Buxaceae *Buxus sempervirens*. **Distribution**: A few scattered localities in southern England. **Other habitats**: Scrub. **Notes**: On chalk or limestone; usually in beech woods; locally abundant; often planted; evergreen.

Hazel Corylaceae *Corylus avellana*. **Distribution**: Throughout the British Isles, but less common in eastern Scotland. **Other habitats**: Scrub; hedges.

Holly Aquifoliaceae *Ilex aquifolium*. **Distribution**: Throughout the British Isles, but less common in northern and eastern Scotland. **Other habitats**: Scrub; hedges; amongst rocks.

Sloe, Blackthorn Rosaceae *Prunus spinosa* **Distribution**: Throughout the British Isles, but becoming rare to absent in northern Scotland. **Other habitats**: Scrub; hedges. **Notes**: On all soils except acid peat; not shade tolerant; grows up to 435 metres.

Hawthorn Rosaceae *Crataegus monogyna* **Distribution**: Throughout the British Isles, but rare in northern Scotland. **Other habitats**: Scrub; hedges. **Notes**: Grows up to 580 metres; the commonest scrub plant on all types of soil.

Elder Caprifoliaceae *Sambucus nigra* **Distribution**: Throughout the British Isles, but rarer in northern Scotland. **Other habitats**: Scrub; roadsides; waste places. **Notes**: Characteristic of base- and nitrogen-rich soils, especially when disturbed; grows up to 516 metres; rarely a small tree to 10 metres height.

Spurge Laurel Thymelaeaceae *Daphne laureola*. **Distribution**: Throughout England, but more common in the south; scattered in Wales and southern Scotland; very rare or absent in eastern Ireland. **Notes**: Evergreen; mainly on calcareous soils.

Spindle(-tree) Celastraceae *Euonymus europaeus*. **Distribution**: Throughout England, especially common in the south; scattered throughout Wales and Ireland and the very south of Scotland. **Other habitats**: Scrub. **Notes**: Grows up to 340 metres; usually on calcareous soils.

Wayfaring Tree Caprifoliaceae *Viburnum lantana*. **Distribution**: Common in southern England, but scattered rarely throughout the rest of the British Isles. **Other habitats**: Scrub; hedges. **Notes**: Usually on calcareous soils; fruit red at first, then turning black.

Gean, Wild Cherry Rosaceae *Prunus avium*. **Distribution**: Throughout the British Isles, but rare in northern Scotland. **Other habitats**: Hedges. **Notes**: Common on better soils; suckers freely; fruit bright or dark red, sweet or bitter.

Dogwood Cornaceae *Thelycrania sanguinea*. **Distribution**: Common throughout England except the north, scattered in southern and central Scotland, Ireland and Wales. **Other habitats**: Scrub. **Notes**: Usually on calcareous soils.

Woodland Wild Flowers

Wild flowers provide the woods with their most attractive feature. Because many are adapted to flowering before the leaves develop in the shrub and canopy layers, they are regarded as the harbingers of spring, and the first celandine and primrose are anxiously looked for as an indication that the short dark days of winter are almost at an end. No doubt to primitive societies this reawakening of the woodland flora contributed to the mystical significance of the many rites and rituals associated with spring. Certainly the woodland flora is at its best from early April until June, by which time many of the species have finished flowering.

Distribution of woodland species

The type of herb layer which will develop in any woodland depends on a number of environmental factors. These include the amount of shade cast by the canopy and shrub layer, and the soil type on which the wood is growing. For instance, neither species of oak casts deep shade and therefore both the shrub and herb layers tend to be well-developed, yet the flora associated with each type of oak is different. This is because sessile oak prefers more acidic conditions which are reflected in the ground flora. The flora associated with the common oak tends to reflect neutral or calcareous conditions. Species also respond to differences in moisture, climate and humidity. Some species are present in woodland growing on similar soils throughout the country. Others are restricted to certain few parts of the country, although within this limited range they may be very common. The primrose *(Primula vulgaris)* is one of the commonest woodland plants on neutral or calcareous soils throughout the British Isles, yet in parts of Cambridgeshire, Suffolk and Norfolk it is replaced by the closely related oxlip *(Primula elatior)* which is nationally rare, but very abundant in certain woodlands growing on the chalky boulder clays in these counties. Another plant with a very localised distribution is the

Many woodland flowers, like these primroses, are adapted to produce their blooms early in the year before the trees develop their leaves and cast a dense shade over the ground. Sights like this have unfortunately become less common due to excessive picking and transplanting to private gardens. However, with the recent increased awareness of the importance of conservation this trend may well be reversed.

The wild arum

The wild arum, cuckoo-pint or lords-and-ladies (*Arum maculatum*) is a common plant of woods and shady hedgebanks, especially on calcareous soils in southern England. The bright green fleshy leaves, often spotted with purple, appear early in spring, growing from an underground tuber. The chief interest of the plant is its very specialised flower which develops in May or June with a complex mechanism to ensure insect pollination. The most obvious part of the flower is the leaf-like sheath or spathe surrounding a purple club-shaped structure, the spadix. The other parts of the flower are arranged round the base of the spadix. The lowest is a group of carpels representing the female part of the flower. Above them is a tight-packed cluster of male stamens and above these a ring of sterile hairs. The whole apparatus functions when flies, attracted to the foetid smell given off by the spadix, pass through the ring of hairs into the hollow, bulbous base of the spathe. Because the hairs radiate downwards escape is prevented. The carpels ripen first and receive pollen from another arum carried in by the flies or midges. A few days later the pollen in the stamens is ripe and falls to the bottom of the hollow chamber where the insects are trapped. The sterile hairs then wither and the insects, dusted with fresh pollen, can escape. After pollination the fruits slowly ripen until the leaves die down, leaving a spike of poisonous fleshy red berries.

The unusual "flower" of the wild arum, commonly seen in early summer in woods and other shaded areas. The purple spadix shows clearly against the background of the pale yellow-green spathe.

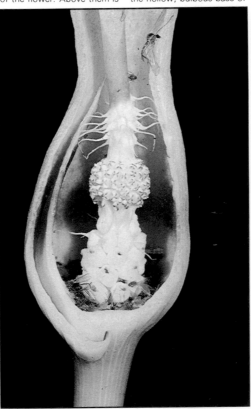

The base of the spathe has been cut away to show the downward pointing hairs (top), the male flowers (centre) and the female flowers with many small pollinating flies (bottom).

The result of pollination. All of the inflorescence has withered and dropped except for the fertilised female flowers which have swollen to form bright red poisonous berries.

coral root *(Dentaria bulbifera)*, which is a member of the cress family Cruciferae. It maintains two isolated populations on calcareous soils in the Chilterns and the Weald. In contrast, the water avens *(Geum rivale)* is quite common in woodland throughout the country, but rather inexplicably is absent from much of the south east, including the Weald, where conditions appear suitable. An example of a plant with a scattered distribution pattern is the yellow star of Bethlehem *(Gagea lutea)*. This is a rare and elusive plant, but maintains small isolated populations on calcareous soils throughout the country.

Influence of soil type

Because oak forms woodland on a wide variety of soils, an assortment of different herb layer associations occur with it which reflect the soil type present. At one end of the spectrum, where oak is growing on a calcareous soil over chalk or limestone, a high proportion of the species associated with these soils is present. These include herb paris *(Paris quadrifolia)*, Solomon's seal *(Polygonatum multiflorum)*, lily of the valley *(Convallaria majalis)* and columbine *(Aquilegia vulgaris)*. The most typical pedunculate oak wood flora occurs on neutral to calcareous lowland clays and sands. Here a rich, and in spring very colourful, ground flora is present which includes celandine *(Ranunculus ficaria)*, primrose

The delicate flowers of the snowdrop *(Galanthus nivalis)* are one of the first signs of spring; often appearing in January when snow still lies on the ground.

(Primula vulgaris), wood anemone *(Anemone nemorosa)*, wood violets *(Viola riviniana* and *V. reichenbachiana)*, sweet violet *(V. odorata)*, bluebell *(Endymion non-scriptus)*, dog's mercury *(Mercurialis perennis)*, early purple orchid *(Orchis mascula)*, greater butterfly orchid *(Platanthera chlorantha)* and twayblade *(Listera ovata)*. The grasses include Yorkshire fog *(Holcus lanatus)* and tufted hair-grass *(Deschampsia cespitosa)*, along with the great woodrush *(Luzula sylvatica)* and wood sedge *(Carex sylvatica)*. In many woods bramble *(Rubus fruticosus)* is a prominent feature of the ground flora, especially on the heavier soils. This plant makes an important contribution to the woodland ecosystem, providing food for deer and many insects, and cover for nesting birds. Taxonomically it is a most complex plant and many sub-species exist.

Where acid conditions occur locally in these woods other species become more prominent, including wood sorrel *(Oxalis acetosella)*, foxglove *(Digitalis purpurea)*, bitter vetch *(Lathyrus montanus)*, tormentil *(Potentilla erecta)*, golden rod *(Solidago virgaurea)*, cow-wheat *(Melampyrum pratense)* and hairy woodrush *(Luzula pilosa)*. These species are also characteristic of the mixed sessile and pedunculate oak woods, including those in south east England. In the most acidic areas where the soil is podsolised they are joined by heath species including wavy hair-grass

A guide to some woodland wild flowers

Few British woods are unaffected by man; felling, planting and coppicing have all served to modify the ground flora. Primrose and bluebell woods are well known, but are not now as frequent as in the past.

Many of the common woodland species flower early in the year before the growth of the leaves of the tree canopy dramatically cuts the available light. Although many of the species illustrated here are only found in woodland, others such as the lesser celandine and ground ivy are frequently encountered in other habitats where they may also be very common.

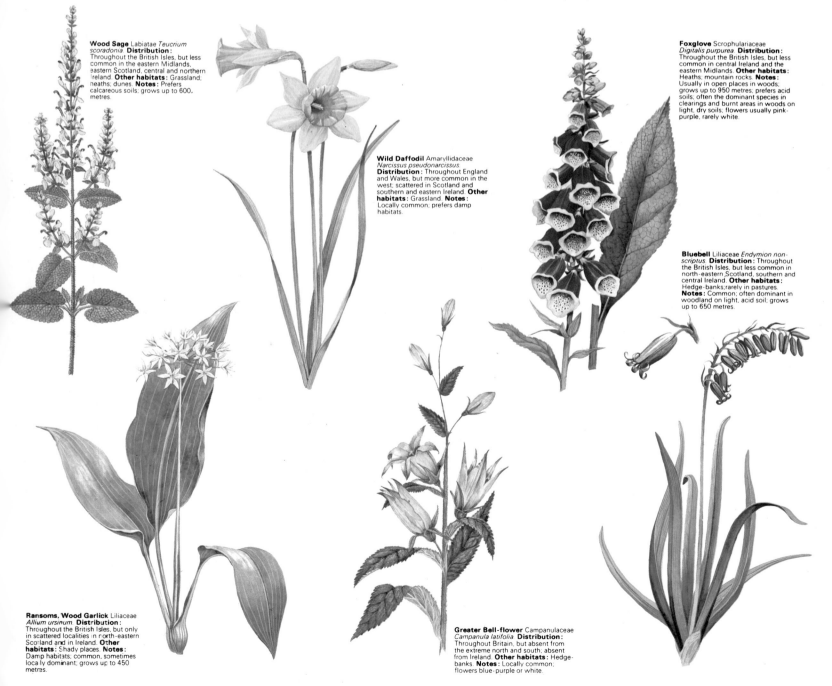

Wood Sage Labiatae *Teucrium scoradonia*. **Distribution:** Throughout the British Isles, but less common in the eastern Midlands, eastern Scotland, central and northern Ireland. **Other habitats:** Grassland; heaths; dunes. **Notes:** Prefers calcareous soils; grows up to 600 metres.

Wild Daffodil Amaryllidaceae *Narcissus pseudonarcissus*. **Distribution:** Throughout England and Wales, but more common in the west; scattered in Scotland and southern and eastern Ireland. **Other habitats:** Grassland. **Notes:** Locally common; prefers damp habitats.

Foxglove Scrophulariaceae *Digitalis purpurea*. **Distribution:** Throughout the British Isles, but less common in central Ireland and the eastern Midlands. **Other habitats:** Heaths; mountain rocks. **Notes:** Usually in open places in woods; grows up to 950 metres; prefers acid soils; often the dominant species in clearings and burnt areas in woods on light, dry soils; flowers usually pink-purple, rarely white.

Bluebell Liliaceae *Endymion non-scriptus*. **Distribution:** Throughout the British Isles, but less common in north-eastern Scotland, southern and central Ireland. **Other habitats:** Hedge-banks; rarely in pastures. **Notes:** Common; often dominant in woodland on light, acid soil; grows up to 650 metres.

Ransoms, Wood Garlick Liliaceae *Allium ursinum*. **Distribution:** Throughout the British Isles, but only in scattered localities in north-eastern Scotland and in Ireland. **Other habitats:** Shady places. **Notes:** Damp habitats; common, sometimes locally dominant; grows up to 450 metres.

Greater Bell-flower Campanulaceae *Campanula latifolia*. **Distribution:** Throughout Britain, but absent from the extreme north and south; absent from Ireland. **Other habitats:** Hedge-banks. **Notes:** Locally common; flowers blue-purple or white.

(Deschampsia flexuosa), bilberry *(Vaccinium myr-tillus)* and ling *(Calluna vulgaris)*. In the pure sessile oak coppices of the extreme west of Britain the ground flora, is often virtually restricted to these, with the addition of such resilient species as wood sorrel and tormentil. In these moist "Atlantic" woodlands a diversity of higher plants is replaced by a rich flora of ferns, mosses, liverworts and lichens.

Rich flora on calcareous soils

The woodlands which have developed on highly calcareous chalk and limestone soils have by far the most rich and varied flora. The presence of beech in many of the chalk escarpment woods in the south east tends to suppress the usual ground flora as a result of the deep shade cast by the trees, but the woods have instead a fascinating selection of plants adapted to living under shady conditions. These include the saprophytic bird's nest orchid *(Neottia nidus-avis)*. Here it is often associated with two other saprophytes which superficially resemble it, the yellow bird's nests *(Monotropa hypopitys* and *M. hypophagea)*. They are not orchids but belong to the family Monotropaceae. Both are plentiful in the south. The two species are difficult to distinguish, the first having stiff hairs inside the flower, while the latter is glabrous. As the whole flower spike, a few inches high, is bent over in the early part of its life, a mirror is required to identify them if picking is to be avoided! A

A typical spring woodland floor flora of a well managed wood on lowland calcareous soil. Here the early flowering early purple orchid and cowslip are in bloom before the leaves of the canopy develop and restrict the available light.

A guide to some woodland wild flowers (continued)

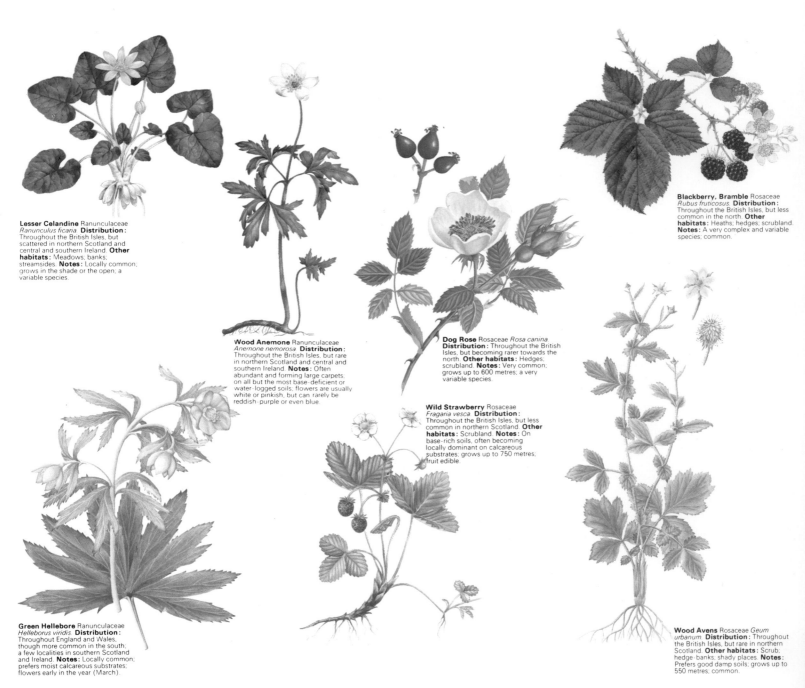

Lesser Celandine Ranunculaceae *Ranunculus ficaria.* **Distribution:** Throughout the British Isles, but scattered in northern Scotland and central and southern Ireland. **Other habitats:** Meadows; banks; streamsides. **Notes:** Locally common; grows in the shade or the open; a variable species.

Wood Anemone Ranunculaceae *Anemone nemorosa* **Distribution:** Throughout the British Isles, but rare in northern Scotland and central and southern Ireland. **Notes:** Often abundant and forming large carpets, on all but the most base-deficient or water-logged soils; flowers are usually white or pinkish, but can rarely be reddish-purple or even blue.

Dog Rose Rosaceae *Rosa canina* **Distribution:** Throughout the British Isles, but becoming rarer towards the north. **Other habitats:** Hedges; scrubland. **Notes:** Very common; grows up to 600 metres; a very variable species.

Wild Strawberry Rosaceae *Fragaria vesca* **Distribution:** Throughout the British Isles, but less common in northern Scotland. **Other habitats:** Scrubland. **Notes:** On base-rich soils, often becoming locally dominant on calcareous substrates; grows up to 750 metres; fruit edible.

Blackberry, Bramble Rosaceae *Rubus fruticosus.* **Distribution:** Throughout the British Isles, but less common in the north. **Other habitats:** Heaths; hedges; scrubland. **Notes:** A very complex and variable species; common.

Green Hellebore Ranunculaceae *Helleborus viridis.* **Distribution:** Throughout England and Wales, though more common in the south; a few localities in southern Scotland and Ireland. **Notes:** Locally common; prefers moist calcareous substrates; flowers early in the year (March).

Wood Avens Rosaceae *Geum urbanum.* **Distribution:** Throughout the British Isles, but rare in northern Scotland. **Other habitats:** Scrub; hedge-banks; shady places. **Notes:** Prefers good damp soils; grows up to 550 metres; common.

further saprophytic plant, the spurred coral root, is among our rarest orchids. It entirely lacks chlorophyll and the presence of the plant is only given away when it flowers, which may be only very occasionally. This has happened in recent years in several beech wood sites in the Chilterns, but in two other localities in Herefordshire and Shropshire it has not been seen since the beginning of the century, although it may still be present. Unlike the bird's nest orchid this plant has no extensive root system and therefore can probably only survive in dense woods where the soil is continually moist. Where a wood is opened to sunlight by felling, it may quickly be exterminated. It is unfortunate that, despite being legally protected, one of the plants flowering in 1978 was dug up, presumably by a thoughtless collector. Another plant lacking chlorophyll, the toothwort *(Lathraea squamaria)*, may also be seen quite commonly on calcareous soils throughout the British Isles, growing closely around the base of a coppiced hazel. It is not a saprophyte, however, but a member of the Orobanchaceae or broomrape family, which are typically parasitic on other plants. The toothwort is no exception, being a parasite of hazel and more rarely elm and other woody species.

The beech woods are also famous for a number of other orchids. The lady orchid *(Orchis purpurea)* is among the largest and most spectacular of our wild orchids and is confined to Kent and the immediately adjacent counties.

Bluebell woodland

A bluebell wood in full bloom is among the most brilliant spectacles of the woodland scene. It is one that we in Britain take for granted, yet it is a particularly British phenomenon. Although the bluebell (*Endymion non-scriptus*) occurs widely in Europe as individual plants, it is only along the north west Atlantic seaboard that it forms a major part of the woodland herb layer. Because of our moist "Atlantic" climate we have the best "bluebell carpets" in the world. Despite this, the bluebell does not readily colonise new woodland, even when this is planted next to an existing bluebell wood. Therefore an extensive area of bluebells usually indicates that the site has been woodland for many centuries. The bluebell leaves emerge from the bulb early in the year, followed in June by the flowers, and the plant's whole life cycle is completed before a full canopy of leaves has developed on the trees. It is therefore ideally suited to deep-shaded woodlands such as beech woods and derelict coppices. While many other plants flourish after coppice has been cut, the bluebell tends to decline.

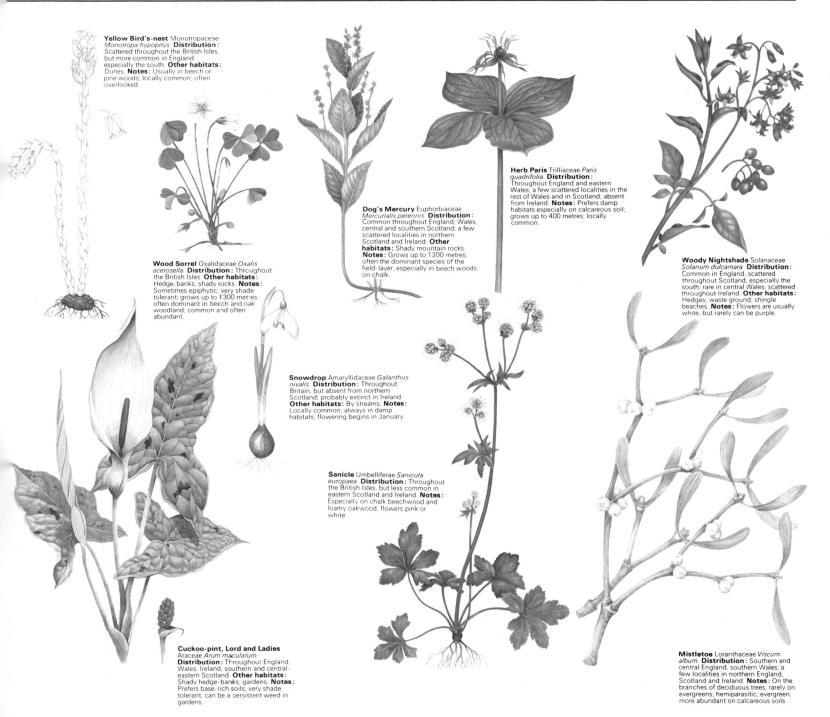

Yellow Bird's-nest Monotropaceae *Monotropa hypopitys.* **Distribution:** Scattered throughout the British Isles, but more common in England especially the south. **Other habitats:** Dunes. **Notes:** Usually in beech or pine woods; locally common; often overlooked.

Wood Sorrel Oxalidaceae *Oxalis acetosella.* **Distribution:** Throughout the British Isles. **Other habitats:** Hedge-banks; shady rocks. **Notes:** Sometimes epiphytic; very shade tolerant; grows up to 1300 metres; often dominant in beech and oak woodland; common and often abundant.

Cuckoo-pint, Lord and Ladies Araceae *Arum maculatum.* **Distribution:** Throughout England, Wales, Ireland, southern and central-eastern Scotland. **Other habitats:** Shady hedge-banks; gardens. **Notes:** Prefers base-rich soils; very shade tolerant; can be a persistent weed in gardens.

Dog's Mercury Euphorbiaceae *Mercurialis perennis.* **Distribution:** Common throughout England, Wales, central and southern Scotland; a few scattered localities in northern Scotland and Ireland. **Other habitats:** Shady mountain rocks. **Notes:** Grows up to 1200 metres; often the dominant species of the field-layer, especially in beech woods on chalk.

Snowdrop Amaryllidaceae *Galanthus nivalis.* **Distribution:** Throughout Britain, but absent from northern Scotland; probably extinct in Ireland. **Other habitats:** By streams. **Notes:** Locally common; always in damp habitats; flowering begins in January

Sanicle Umbelliferae *Sanicula europaea.* **Distribution:** Throughout the British Isles, but less common in eastern Scotland and Ireland. **Notes:** Especially on chalk beechwood and loamy oakwood; flowers pink or white.

Herb Paris Trilliaceae *Paris quadrifolia.* **Distribution:** Throughout England and eastern Wales; a few scattered localities in the rest of Wales and in Scotland; absent from Ireland. **Notes:** Prefers damp habitats especially on calcareous soil; grows up to 400 metres; locally common.

Woody Nightshade Solanaceae *Solanum dulcamara.* **Distribution:** Common in England; scattered throughout Scotland, especially the south; rare in central Wales; scattered throughout Ireland **Other habitats:** Hedges; waste ground; shingle beaches. **Notes:** Flowers are usually white, but rarely can be purple.

Mistletoe Loranthaceae *Viscum album.* **Distribution:** Southern and central England, southern Wales; a few localities in northern England, Scotland and Ireland. **Notes:** On the branches of deciduous trees, rarely on evergreens; hemiparasitic; evergreen; more abundant on calcareous soils.

Many woods on the chalk in Kent, either of beech or oak with hazel and hornbeam coppice, have fine stands of this orchid, presenting a spectacular show in late May. Usually, where the lady orchid occurs, other orchids such as the greater and lesser butterfly *(Platanthera chlorantha* and *P. bifolia)*, fly orchid *(Ophrys insectifera)* and twayblade will also be present.

Although the chalk woodlands of the south east are most famous for their orchids, it is the northern limestone ash woods which contain, or rather once contained, our most spectacular and rarest orchid. This is the lady's slipper *(Cypripedium calceolus)* which used to occur in a number of ash woods in Yorkshire and neighbouring counties. The striking flower produced by this orchid makes it a prize for the plant collector. As a result it has been so extensively picked or dug up that it has become extinct in all but one of its former sites. The few remaining plants are now legally protected, and closely guarded during the flowering season to prevent destruction of this last site. It is hoped that enough seed will be produced to increase the size of the colony.

Ash has developed locally on the western chalk in Wiltshire where beech is not plentiful, but ash woodlands are more typical of the hard limestones throughout the country. Some of the best examples occur on the carboniferous limestone of the Mendips and on the gorges of the Bristol Avon and Wye, both tributaries of the

Honeysuckle most frequently has a scrambling, climbing and twining habit, although it can also grow as a shrub up to 6 metres tall. Pollination is mainly carried out by hawkmoths, though bees also visit the fragrant flowers.

A guide to some woodland wild flowers (continued)

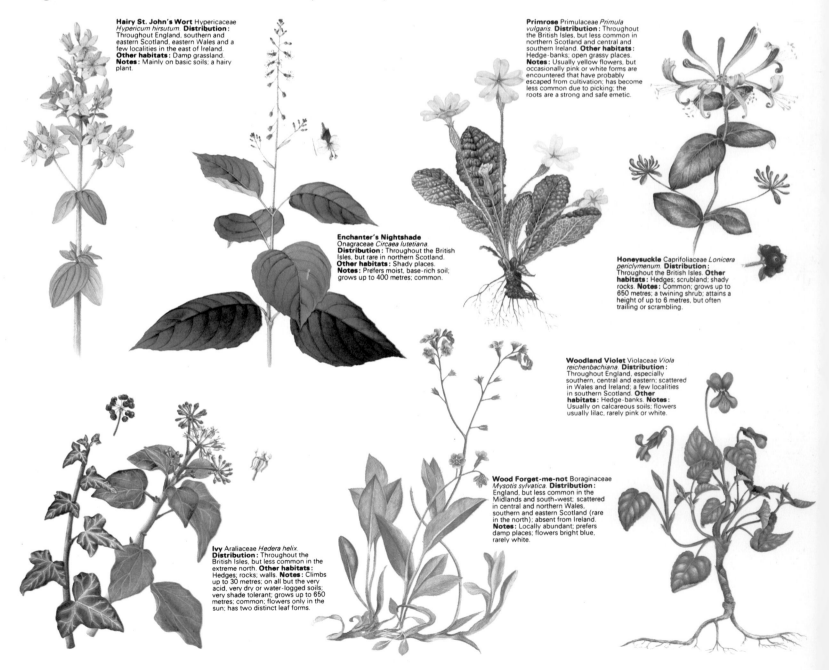

Hairy St. John's Wort Hypericaceae *Hypericum hirsutum.* **Distribution:** Throughout England, southern and eastern Scotland, eastern Wales and a few localities in the east of Ireland. **Other habitats:** Damp grassland. **Notes:** Mainly on basic soils; a hairy plant.

Enchanter's Nightshade Onagraceae *Circaea lutetiana.* **Distribution:** Throughout the British Isles, but rare in northern Scotland. **Other habitats:** Shady places. **Notes:** Prefers moist, base-rich soil; grows up to 400 metres; common.

Ivy Araliaceae *Hedera helix.* **Distribution:** Throughout the British Isles, but less common in the extreme north. **Other habitats:** Hedges; rocks; walls. **Notes:** Climbs up to 30 metres; on all but the very acid, very dry or water-logged soils; very shade tolerant; grows up to 650 metres; common; flowers only in the sun; has two distinct leaf forms.

Primrose Primulaceae *Primula vulgaris.* **Distribution:** Throughout the British Isles, but less common in northern Scotland and central and southern Ireland. **Other habitats:** Hedge-banks; open grassy places. **Notes:** Usually yellow flowers, but occasionally pink or white forms are encountered that have probably escaped from cultivation; has become less common due to picking; the roots are a strong and safe emetic.

Honeysuckle Caprifoliaceae *Lonicera periclymenum.* **Distribution:** Throughout the British Isles. **Other habitats:** Hedges; scrubland; shady rocks. **Notes:** Common; grows up to 650 metres; a twining shrub; attains a height of up to 6 metres, but often trailing or scrambling.

Woodland Violet Violaceae *Viola reichenbachiana.* **Distribution:** Throughout England, especially southern, central and eastern; scattered in Wales and Ireland; a few localities in southern Scotland. **Other habitats:** Hedge-banks. **Notes:** Usually on calcareous soils; flowers usually lilac, rarely pink or white.

Wood Forget-me-not Boraginaceae *Myosotis sylvatica.* **Distribution:** England, but less common in the Midlands and south-west; scattered in central and northern Wales, southern and eastern Scotland (rare in the north); absent from Ireland. **Notes:** Locally abundant; prefers damp places; flowers bright blue, rarely white.

River Severn. Further north there are limestone outcrops in the Peak District, Pennines and Lake District. The ash woods in these areas contain the richest ground flora of any woodland type in the country. Many of the species such as wood vetch *(Vicia sylvatica)*, herb paris, green hellebore *(Helleborus viridis)*, wood brome grass *(Brachypodium sylvaticum)* and wood melick *(Melica uniflora)* are common throughout the range of the woodlands, although certain species are confined to a single region. On the carboniferous and oolitic limestones of Somerset, Avon, Wiltshire, Gloucestershire, Monmouth and Hereford, characteristic species of the region include meadow saffron *(Colchicum autumnale)*, small teasel *(Dipsacus pilosus)*, angular Solomon's seal *(Polygonatum odorata)* and fingered sedge *(Carex digitata)*, while the blue gromwell *(Lithospermum purpurocaeruleum)* is confined to limestone along the Severn estuary. Other species which are also typical although more widespread are lily of the valley and common Solomon's seal. This plant may sometimes hybridise with *P. odorata* to produce *P. × hybridum*, the plant which is usually cultivated in gardens. A plant of particular interest in the woods on oolitic limestone around Bath is the spiked star of Bethlehem *(Ornithogalum pyrenaicum)*. It replaces bluebell as the dominant ground flora species in many woods in this area and is found here in abundance, although extremely rare nationally. The plant produces its pale green leaves in early

The mistletoe

This rather woody, yellow-green evergreen is perhaps the best known of our semi-parasitic plants. It occurs most commonly on trees in the south east and the west Midlands, where it mainly grows high up on the branches of oak and poplar. It also occurs frequently in old orchards on apple trees. More rarely it will grow on beech, birch and plane, but on these trees the smoothness of the bark is probably unsuitable for its establishment. The plant is only semi-parasitic as its leaves contain chlorophyll and it can therefore carry out photosynthesis and produce its own carbohydrates. It is dependent on the host tree for water and inorganic nutrients and well as some extra carbohydrate. These substances are absorbed by means of suckers which are forced into the tissues of the host. Although the flowers are inconspicuous and rarely noticed, fleshy white berries are frequently produced. These berries are attractive to birds, particularly thrushes, hence the name mistle thrush. The seeds may stick to their beaks, and so be carried to another tree. They are then implanted when the bird cleans its beak by rubbing it on the new branch.

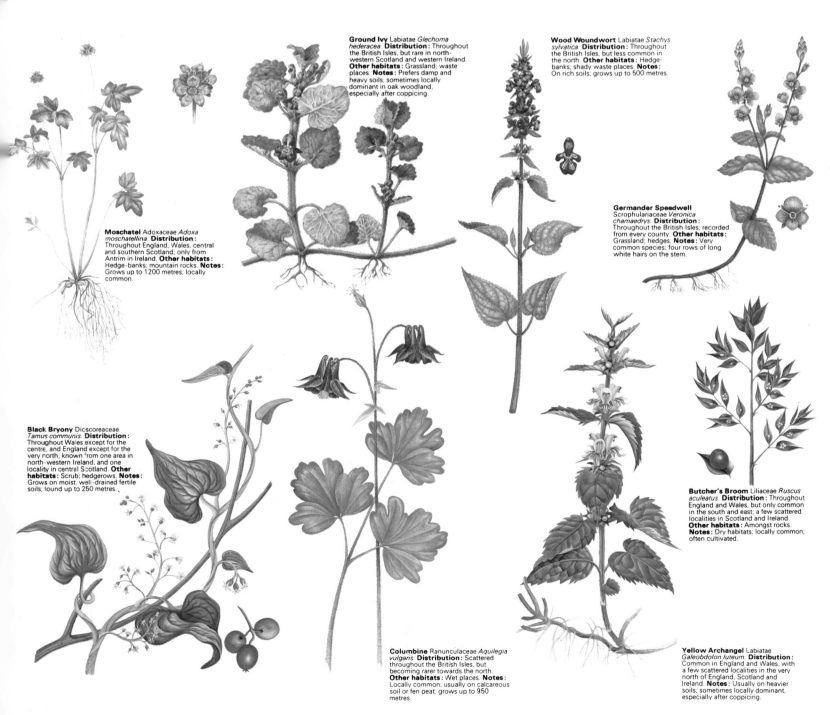

Moschatel Adoxaceae *Adoxa moschatellina*. **Distribution:** Throughout England, Wales, central and southern Scotland; only from Antrim in Ireland. **Other habitats:** Hedge-banks; mountain rocks. **Notes:** Grows up to 1200 metres; locally common.

Ground Ivy Labiatae *Glechoma hederacea*. **Distribution:** Throughout the British Isles, but rare in north-western Scotland and western Ireland. **Other habitats:** Grassland; waste places. **Notes:** Prefers damp and heavy soils; sometimes locally dominant in oak woodland, especially after coppicing.

Wood Woundwort Labiatae *Stachys sylvatica*. **Distribution:** Throughout the British Isles, but less common in the north. **Other habitats:** Hedge-banks; shady waste places. **Notes:** On rich soils; grows up to 500 metres.

Germander Speedwell Scrophulariaceae *Veronica chamaedrys*. **Distribution:** Throughout the British Isles; recorded from every county. **Other habitats:** Grassland; hedges. **Notes:** Very common species; four rows of long white hairs on the stem.

Black Bryony Dioscoreaceae *Tamus communis*. **Distribution:** Throughout Wales except for the centre, and England except for the very north; known from one area in north-western Ireland, and one locality in central Scotland. **Other habitats:** Scrub; hedgerows. **Notes:** Grows on moist, well-drained fertile soils; found up to 250 metres.

Columbine Ranunculaceae *Aquilegia vulgaris*. **Distribution:** Scattered throughout the British Isles, but becoming rarer towards the north. **Other habitats:** Wet places. **Notes:** Locally common; usually on calcareous soil or fen peat; grows up to 950 metres.

Butcher's Broom Liliaceae *Ruscus aculeatus*. **Distribution:** Throughout England and Wales, but only common in the south and east; a few scattered localities in Scotland and Ireland. **Other habitats:** Amongst rocks. **Notes:** Dry habitats; locally common; often cultivated.

Yellow Archangel Labiatae *Galeobdolon luteum*. **Distribution:** Common in England and Wales, with a few scattered localities in the very north of England, Scotland and Ireland. **Notes:** Usually on heavier soils; sometimes locally dominant, especially after coppicing.

spring, but does not flower until July when the woods are dark, and its leaves have died back. The flowering spike, which normally grows to around 45 centimetres, is in the form of a tight bud when it first emerges from the ground. At this stage it used to be regularly gathered and sold in the neighbourhood as Bath asparagus, a trade which, fortunately for the survival of the plant, has now died out. It is not in fact confined entirely to this area, but also occurs in small numbers in widely-separated localities in Berkshire and Cambridgeshire. It is also abundant in some woods on the western chalk of Wiltshire near Swindon, along with meadow saffron, wood vetch, green hellebore and herb paris. It is strange that the plant does not grow further west on the carboniferous limestone or north in the Cotswolds. Conversely, neither angular Solomon's seal nor fingered sedge occur on the chalk.

The northern woods

Further north, in the limestone woods around Dovedale in the Peak District, many of the species of the south western ash woods are also present. With them is a whole range of typically northern species which are unknown or extremely rare in the south. These include the grasses mountain melick *(Melica nutans)*, wood fescue *(Festuca altissima)* and wood barley *(Hordelymus europaeus)*, while the giant bell-flower *(Campanula latifolia)* replaces the nettle-

The white helleborine and bird's nest orchids growing among leaf litter. Both species grow best in humus-rich calcareous soil and are invariably found in shady places, especially beech woodland: the saphrophytic bird's nest orchid grows even in the darkest parts of the wood.

leaved bellflower *(C. trachelium)* of the south. Other northern species include the attractive Jacob's ladder *(Polemonium caeruleum)*, globe flower *(Trollius europaeus)*, melancholy thistle *(Cirsium heterophyllum)*, wood geranium *(Geranium sylvaticum)* and the dark-red helleborine *(Epipactis atrorubens)*. Similar communities typical of the northern limestone are present on both sides of the Pennines, more locally in Scotland, and in Ireland, where extensive outcrops of Carboniferous limestone occur.

While many more plants occur in the southern lowland woods, the Scottish pine woods nevertheless have a distinctive herb layer which includes species confined to Scotland and the north of England. Bilberry and wavy hair-grass however are also typical of sessile oak woods throughout the British Isles, along with other acidic woodland species such as bitter vetch, cow-wheat and hairy woodrush. Typical of the native pine woods are the wintergreens. The most widespread are the lesser *(Pyrola minor)*, medium *(P. media)* and one-flowered winter-green *(Moneses uniflora)*. Species present on peaty soils within these woods include cloud-berry *(Rubus chamaemorus)*, crowberry *(Empetrum hermaphroditum)* and dwarf cornel *(Chamaepericlymenum suecicum)*, while in contrast purple saxifrage *(Saxifraga oppositifolia)*, yellow mountain saxifrage *(S. aizoides)* and Scottish asphodel *(Tofieldia pusilla)* occur on moist calcareous soils. Several orchids are also associated with the

Woodland orchids

Almost half of the British orchid species are frequently if not invariably found in woodland. Many of these grow in a variety of different woodland types, but some are very specific. The bird's nest orchid, a saprophytic species without chlorophyll (and consequently not undertaking photosynthesis) is usually found in dark, mature beech woodland, whereas both violet and white helleborines are found in the younger areas where more light filters through the canopy. In order for orchid seeds to germinate and for the plants to grow well it is necessary for the roots to form a symbiotic relationship with fungal species commonly found in woodland soil.

White Helleborine Orchidaceae *Cephalanthera damasonium.* **Distribution:** Central-southern and south-east England; south Midlands. **Other habitats:** Open grassy slopes. **Notes:** Almost always on chalk or limestone; commonly in beechwood; amount of flower opening depends on the local weather conditions.

Bird's-nest Orchid Orchidaceae *Neottia nidus-avis.* **Distribution:** Throughout the British Isles except north and east Scotland and south Ireland. **Other habitats:** Open grass at wood edges; roadside banks. **Notes:** Usually in dark, bare-floored beech woodland; often on calcareous humus-rich soils; most common in the south.

Broad Helleborine Orchidaceae *Epipactis helleborine.* **Distribution:** Throughout the British Isles except north-east Scotland. **Other habitats:** Hedgebanks; scrub; scree slopes; stabilised dunes. **Notes:** Usually on chalk or limestone with a thin spil cover; will grow in deep shade; commonly in oak woods.

Twayblade Orchidaceae *Listera ovata* **Distribution:** Throughout the British Isles except the extreme south of Ireland. **Other habitats:** Open situations. **Notes:** Prefers calcareous soils; on well drained or wet sites; the most common British orchid.

north, particularly in pine woods. These are the creeping lady's tresses *(Goodyera repens)*, lesser twayblade *(Listera cordata)* and the saprophytic coral root *(Corallorhiza trifida)*. Although typically Scottish, lesser twayblade also grows in south west England where the "Atlantic" climate is to its liking, while the creeping lady's tresses now grows in the large pine forests planted by the Forestry Commission on the Norfolk-Suffolk border. Here it was probably introduced with pine seedlings brought from an area where the orchid occurs naturally.

Surprisingly few of our woodland flowers are confined to woodland habitats. A number of species are regular components of grassland or more strictly old permanent pasture and hay meadows, while on acidic sandy soils heathland species may be present. The hay meadows typical of clay and alluvial soils are remarkable for the number of woodland species they contain. These include wood anemone, meadow saffron, water avens and primrose. These species commence growth and, with the exception of meadow saffron, flower early in the year, before the grasses can form a "canopy" over them. By the time the hay is cut, the woodland species have died down, and do not produce leaves again until the next spring. Other grassland species are associated with woodland edges, glades and rides. Typical examples are devil's bit scabious *(Succisa pratensis)*, betony *(Betonica officinalis)* and lady's mantle *(Alchemilla vestita)*. Because meadows are no longer managed in a traditional way in many parts of the country, the flowers once associated with them are now only found in woodland clearings. These woodland habitats today have developed very largely as the result of management by man. It is however possible that such open conditions occurred in a natural mixed age forest which contained a fairly large population of browsing mammals such as deer. Here these plants would have formed a natural component of the woodland flora.

Wet areas within the woods may contain either bog or fen communities, depending on whether the ground water is acid or alkaline. In the Scottish pine woods conditions may become so acidic locally that tree growth is suppressed, the field layer being dominated by purple moor grass *(Molinia caerulea)* and herbs such as the insectivorous sundews *(Drosera rotundifolia* and *D. intermedia)*, typical of true bog vegetation. Such areas are not confined to Scotland and isolated examples are present throughout the country where conditions are suitable, some of the best examples being in the New Forest. Under the calcareous conditions typical of the alder fen carrs throughout the south, an extremely lush fen vegetation may develop, with species such as yellow flag *(Iris pseudacorus)*, meadow sweet *(Filipendula ulmaria)*, hemp agrimony *(Eupatorium cannabinum)* and greater tussock sedge *(Carex paniculata)*. Other species such as the large pendulous sedge *(C. pendula)*, the opposite- and alternate-leaved saxifrages *(Chrysosplenium oppositifolium* and *C. alternifolium)* and the rather local large bitter cress *(Cardamine amara)* are not found away from woodland.

Plants characteristic of ancient woodland

A feature of many of our native plants is that they appear unable to colonise new habitats, such as woodland which has recently been planted on arable farmland. As a result certain species are only associated with ancient woodland and can be used as indicators of forest antiquity. These are the grass wood melick, bitter vetch, cow-wheat, wood sorrel and the opposite- and alternate-leaved saxifrages. This lack of ability to colonise new sites appears to vary from one part of the country to another, which may indicate that our present climate is a limiting factor. In the clay woodlands of the Midlands, such species as dog's mercury and wood vetch are almost entirely confined to

ancient woodland, while on chalk soils in the south dog's mercury may colonise chalk grassland as soon as invading scrub has created enough shade. Wood vetch, a vigorous climber, may also be associated with such developing scrub. It should be said, however, that in these areas woodland habitats containing these species are usually present nearby, whereas the Midlands woods are often isolated. Nevertheless, in parts of Hayley Wood, near Cambridge, secondary woodland developed long ago on former ridge and furrow ploughland. Even though this is adjacent to ancient woodland, species like bluebell have only colonised parts of the "new" wood, while the rare oxlip, which is a particular feature of the ancient woodland at Hayley Wood, has hardly spread into the secondary wood at all.

The vast amount of seed typically produced by orchids is often responsible for their rapid spread and unexpected appearance in areas where they had not previously been seen. Even so, bird's nest orchid appears to be confined to ancient woodlands in the Midlands, although it occurs in beech plantations, planted less than one hundred years ago, on Salisbury Plain.

A guide to some woodland grasses

Grasses may be found in most British woods with the exception of those with excessive shading and/or a deep litter layer where there is no ground cover. The generally distributed and common ground covering species such as the bents, meadow grasses, couches and creeping soft grass are also found in shady woods.

Most woodland grasses have a tufted habit; they also tend to have large ornamental flowering heads and their leaves are usually a dark green. Most species are perennial. The appearance of many of these species varies due to factors such as the degree of shading, moisture and the aspect or slope of the land.

Woodland Meadow Grass Gramineae (Poaceae) *Poa nemoralis*. **Distribution:** Throughout Great Britain; in Ireland but only common in the east. **Other habitats:** Hedgerows. **Notes:** Delicate grass of shady places; often locally abundant.

Giant Fescue Gramineae (Poaceae) *Festuca gigantea*. **Distribution:** Throughout the British Isles but rare in northern Scotland. **Other habitats:** Shady places. **Notes:** Damp habitats; the only British fescue with long awns.

Hairy Brome Gramineae (Poaceae) *Zerna ramosa*. **Distribution:** Throughout the British Isles except northern and central Scotland. **Other habitats:** Wood margins, hedgerows and persisting on roadsides and ditchbanks that were originally woodland. **Notes:** Grows in the partial shade of open woodland on moist soils.

Wood Sedge Cyperaceae *Carex sylvatica*. **Distribution:** Throughout the British Isles but rare in central and north Scotland. **Other habitats:** Open scrub and grassland (that was probably originally woodland). **Notes:** Grows on heavy, wet (and sometimes chalk with clay) soils.

Wood Millet Gramineae (Poaceae) *Milium effusum*. **Distribution:** Throughout the British Isles but rarer in Ireland, Wales and Scotland. **Notes:** Often abundant in oak and beech woods; prefers damp, heavy, calcareous soil with humus.

Creeping Soft Grass Gramineae (Poaceae) *Holcus mollis*. **Distribution:** Throughout the British Isles. **Other habitats:** Shrubby heaths, hedgerows and other shady situations, sometimes in poor grassland; common weed of sandy arable land. **Notes:** Variable species; often carpets the ground in open woodland.

Wood Melick Gramineae (Poaceae) *Melica uniflora*. **Distribution:** Throughout the British Isles except northern Scotland. **Other habitats:** Shady banks. **Notes:** Often very abundant and loosely carpeting open beechwood floor. Albino form with white spikelets found in south England and south Wales.

Wood False-brome Grass Gramineae (Poaceae) *Brachypodium sylvaticum*. **Distribution:** Throughout the British Isles but less common in north-east Scotland. **Other habitats:** Hedgerows, shady places and persisting in grassland and roadsides that were originally woodland. **Notes:** Ornamental; grows in compact tufts.

Giant fescue   Wood Sedge   Creeping Soft Grass   Wood False-brome Grass

Woodland Meadow Grass   Hairy Brome   Wood Melick   Wood Millet

Woodland Ferns and Lichens

A damp, shaded woodland floor with a rich covering of ferns. Although only a very limited number of species are found in the British Isles, these flowerless plants form an attractive and important part of the flora.

The lower orders of plant life, which include the ferns and horsetails (Pteridophytes), mosses and liverworts (Bryophytes) and lichens, are all characterised by reproducing through spores rather than seeds. Pteridophytes and bryophytes also produce two distinct forms, representing alternating spore- and gamete-producing generations, the sporophyte and the gametophyte. The gametophyte generation involves the release of free-swimming male gametes (spermatozoa) which need water to move in and to survive. Thus, most lower plants are restricted in their distribution by the water requirements of this generation. The relatively high humidity and moisture levels within woods are particularly favourable to the lower plants, many of which have a marked western or "Atlantic" distribution. The south and east of England are therefore poor in these species, although western species may occur where local conditions are favourable. Particularly good examples of such habitats are provided by the small steep-sided valleys or gills which bisect many woodlands in the Weald, and here many of these lower plants are able to maintain isolated populations. Because of their requirement for a high moisture level, plants in these groups are particularly susceptible to the opening up of woodland through clear-felling or even coppicing. This drastically changes the micro-climate and causes a general loss of humidity. Therefore the best woods for them are those which have been largely undisturbed for long periods, or where management such as coppicing has been only on a small scale. As an adaptation to reduce their dampness-dependence, certain species of both bryophytes and pteridophytes have evolved methods of vegetative reproduction which enable them to spread to drier sites. One species of fern which has almost totally overcome this limitation to wet areas is bracken *(Pteridium aquilinum)*. This plant spreads almost entirely by means of underground rhizomes and is common in woodlands throughout the country, and in fact over much of the world, as long as conditions are suitable. It appears to flourish best in a moist clay soil and is unable to tolerate highly calcareous soils, although it readily grows on the chalk even where only small deposits of clay are present. It is not very shade-tolerant but may become the dominant component of the ground flora in more open woodlands and in the early stage of the coppice cycle. It is quickly suppressed when the canopy becomes dense, for the fronds are not fully formed until June.

The pteridophytes include not only the ferns proper but also other spore-bearing plants such as the club mosses and horsetails. Among the horsetails there are a number which are typical of certain woodlands. Dutch or royal rush *(Equisetum hyemale)* and wood horsetail *(E. sylvaticum)* are both species associated with woods on wet acidic soils especially in the north. The wood horsetail is the more widespread of the two, being relatively common in the south west and the Weald, although both are absent from a large part of the agricultural areas of southern Britain. The great horsetail *(E. telmateia)* on the other hand is widespread throughout much of England, Wales and Ireland, wherever a high calcareous water table is present, but is much rarer in Scotland. This fine plant may grow to more than two metres in height, with long slender outward-spreading branches radiating in whorls from the central stem.

Ferns

Three species which illustrate the high humidity requirement for these groups are the "filmy ferns". The Killarney, Tunbridge and Wilson's filmy ferns *(Trichomanes speciosum, Hymenophyllum tunbrigense* and *H. wilsonii)*, are all rather remarkable plants which are characterised by their almost translucent fronds just one cell thick. They occur only in the most shaded humid woodland areas such as beside a waterfall under a dense tree canopy. All are very local species but are most abundant in the west of Britain and Ireland. The only species to be

The life cycle of ferns

Unlike the flowering plants, ferns reproduce by means of spores not seeds. At certain times of year fertile fronds are produced, the undersides of which are sprinkled with a mass of small dark brown outgrowths. These are the ripe fruiting bodies or sori, each covered with a membraneous indusium. The sori are made up of a number of spore-producing bodies or sporangia. When conditions are right the indusium splits open and the sporangia burst, violently ejecting the spores. These require damp conditions to germinate. When they do so a fundamental difference between seed and spore plants becomes apparent. Instead of growing into a little plant like the parent fern, they grow instead into a small prothallus. These may be heart-shaped like a thalloid liverwort, or branched and thread-like. They are usually short-lived. Sexual reproduction is not needed to produce the spores, but this must occur before another spore-producing generation can arise. Male and females organs, the antheridia and archegonia are present, either together or separately on the underside of the small prothalli. When ripe, a mass of minute free-swimming sperm-like antherozoids are liberated from the antheridia These swim in the surface film of water and enter the flask-like archegonia which each contain an egg cell. After fertilisation has occurred this cell commences development to produce a young fern plant again. This alternation between a non-sexual spore-producing (sporophyte) and sexual gamete-producing (gametophyte) plant is referred to as alternation of generations.

The spore-producing organs or sporangia on the frond under-surface are protected by the membranous indusium.

Spores germinate to form a prothallus. Sexual reproduction then occurs giving rise to the sporophyte fern plant.

The characteristic spring growth of a fern with its unfurling fronds. At this young stage the leaves are called croziers.

A guide to some woodland ferns

Many of the British ferns are characteristic species of woodland where the conditions are ideal for their growth; humus is usually plentiful, the soil moist, acid and rich and much direct sunlight is filtered out by the canopy. The dampness is important for the growth and fertilisation of the gametophyte generation (ensuring outbreeding due to sexual reproduction). All species grow only in the soil with the exception of the common polypody which often, but not always, grows as an epiphyte on branches of trees where it is independent of soil factors which may be adverse to its survival.

The male fern is one of the commonest and most widespread of British ferns, and although a woodland species it is frequently found in other places, even in cities: it seems to be very pollution-tolerant. Not surprisingly, as it is able to withstand a wide variety of ecological conditions, it tends to be rather variable in growth: under ideal conditions very large luxuriant plants grow with deeply lobed pinna segments giving the fronds the overall appearance of the lady fern with which it may be confused. However, the coarser nature of the fronds and the different sori allow it to be easily distinguished.

Hart's Tongue Fern Aspleniaceae *Phyllitis scolopendrium* (or genus *Asplenium*). **Distribution:** Throughout the British Isles, but rare in central and northern Scotland. **Other habitats:** Hedgebanks; walls; rock ledges. **Notes:** Common on calcareous substrates.

Lady Fern Athyriaceae *Athyrium filix-femina.* **Distribution:** Throughout the British Isles. **Other habitats:** Hedgebanks; rocky situations in mountainous districts. **Notes:** Common in damp, shady and rocky situations; most abundant in flushes and spring lines.

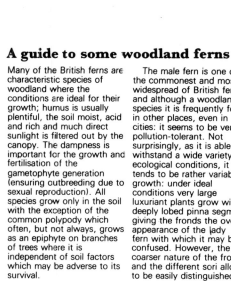

Male Fern Aspidiaceae *Dryopteris filix-mas.* **Distribution:** Throughout the British Isles. **Other habitats:** Hedgerows and roadsides. **Notes:** Has a wide ecological tolerance; often becomes established on walls; frequently planted in gardens.

Broad Fern (Broad Buckler Fern) Aspidiaceae *Dryopteris dilatata.* **Distribution:** Throughout the British Isles. **Other habitats:** Hedgebanks; shady rock ledges. **Notes:** Variable species; often confused with *Dryopteris carthusiana* but differs by having scales dark with pale margins.

Black Spleenwort Aspleniaceae *Asplenium adiantum-nigrum.* **Distribution:** Throughout the British Isles. **Other habitats:** Rocks and rocky soils. **Notes:** Tolerates some exposure; often grows on walls; prefers alkaline substrates.

Hard Shield Fern Aspidiaceae *Polystichum aculeatum.* **Distribution:** Throughout the British Isles; rarer in the north. **Other habitats:** Hedgebanks and rocky mountain ledges; by polluted waterways. **Notes:** Requires a base-rich substrate.

Polypody Polypodiaceae *Polypodium vulgare.* **Distribution:** Throughout the British Isles. **Other habitats:** Walls and rocks. **Notes:** A variable species; grows on the ground or as an epiphyte in trees; common.

Soft Shield Fern Aspidiaceae *Polystichum setiferum.* **Distribution:** Throughout the British Isles, but rare in northern England and in Scotland. **Other habitats:** Hedgerows. **Notes:** Requires base-poor soils; prefers a wet, warm winter.

Oak Fern Thelypteridaceae *Thelypteris dryopteris.* **Distribution:** Scotland, Wales and northern England; rare in the rest of England and Ireland. **Other habitats:** Shaded stream banks; waterfalls. **Notes:** Locally frequent; never on limestone.

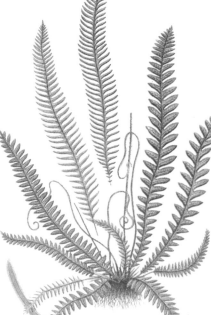

Hard Fern Blechnaceae *Blechnum spicant.* **Distribution:** Throughout the British Isles, but absent or rare in most of the Midlands and East Anglia. **Other habitats:** Heaths; rock ledges. **Notes:** On acid soils; up to 1300 metres; not common in lowland areas.

found in central and eastern England is, as its name suggests, the Tunbridge filmy fern, which typifies the distribution of a large number of "Atlantic" ferns and bryophytes which maintain isolated populations in the Weald, but nowhere else in lowland Britain. Another species with a similar distribution is the hay-scented buckler fern *(Dryopteris aemula)*. This rather rare species is in contrast to the filmy ferns, being typically fern-like in appearance, and belongs to the same genus as the common male fern *(Dryopteris filix-mas)*. It can be distinguished from other species by its yellow-green fronds and purplish stalk or stipe. As the name implies the plant has a scent of hay. This comes from a substance called coumarin produced in glandular hairs on both sides of the frond. A number of other *Dryopteris* species are present in woodland throughout the country. Another widespread species, mainly found in deciduous woodland, and often abundant in wet flushes and along spring lines, is the lady fern *(Athyrium filix-femina)*, whose delicate fronds contrast with the more rugged fronds of its "mate", the male fern.

Two common species of fern which are particularly good indicators of soil pH are the hard fern *(Blechnum spicant)* and the hart's tongue fern *(Asplenium (Phyllitis) scolopendrium)*, the first being an indicator of acid soils, the second of calcareous conditions. They are particularly useful as indicators because they are so readily identifiable. The hard fern with its simply divided dark green fronds is common wherever acid soil conditions occur and it is typically associated with sessile oak woods in the west of the British Isles, and also in the south east of England as well as native pine woods in Scotland. The hart's tongue, by contrast, has a broad, strap-like, undivided frond which is a light shiny green in colour. It is a typical plant of southern woodlands on chalk, limestone and calcareous sandstones such as the Upper Greensand and wherever relatively moist shady conditions occur, on steep banks or even cliff faces. Finally a very easily identified woodland fern is the common polypody *(Polypodium vulgare)* which superficially resembles the hard fern, having only a simple division of the frond. This species is an epiphyte, typically growing high

Leucobryum glaucum forms large cushions on wet moorlands, and in woodland often covers extensive areas. It is easily recognised at a distance by its characteristic colour. The cushions are only loosely affixed to the substrate and can be easily detached; however, the plants continue to grow even when lying loose on the surface.

up on the large branches of oaks. Because it is not directly growing on the soil, soil type does not affect its distribution and it is found throughout the country, except in industrial areas. Its absence from the latter is perhaps because of sensitivity to pollution, or at least physical contamination by soot and grime covering the leaves.

The bryophytes, both mosses and liverworts, form a major component of the ground layer of woodland vegetation. All species in this country are small and confined to moist shady areas. Most of the mosses have short upright stems which grow close together to form tight cushions, but a few species have a more spreading pattern of growth and form mats. As with the ferns and higher plants, some species are very characteristic of certain woodland types and mosses can be used as soil indicators, although they tend to reflect the pH of the surface humus rather than the underlying soil type. *Leucobryum glaucum* is a characteristic species of beech woods on both acidic clays and gravels and also on the chalk, forming quite large pale green cushions. These cushions can survive in comparatively dry areas as the moss has a remarkable ability to retain water through its specialised cell structure. Even in summer, if a small piece is squeezed it will produce moisture like a sponge. Mosses found on true calcareous soils include *Barbula cylindrica* and *B. recurvirostra* and *Tortula subulata*. Although all will grow elsewhere, they are most plentiful in woods on chalk and limestone. The bryophyte flora of sessile and pedunculate oak differ, reflecting the climatic and geological preference of these two trees rather than any effects of the trees themselves. The western "Atlantic" oak woods throughout the British Isles are the richest in the country for bryophytes, including the mosses *Thuidium delicatulum* and *Ulota hutchinsiae* and the liverworts *Plagiochila spinulosa*, *P. punctata*, *Saccogyna viticulosa* and *Scapania gracilis*. These species are absent from much of the south and east, where there is a general lack of suitable habitats, apart from the Weald where the "Atlantic" association including the Tunbridge filmy fern, the hay-scented buckler fern and liverworts such as *P. spinulosa* and *S. viticulosa* are relatively common. This "Atlantic" association also spreads north to Scotland, although many of the species of the south east are replaced by ones typical of northern mountain regions. Mosses characteristic of the native Scots pine woods are *Ptilium crista-castrensis* and *Rhytidiadelphus loreus*, although *R. loreus* occurs elsewhere, sometimes even in the south east. The moss *Hookeria lucens*, which likes moist deeply shaded habitats, has a western and Wealden distribution. It is one of the more delicate mosses and can easily be mistaken for a leafy liverwort. *Scapania nemorosa* and *Plagiochila asplenioides* are both examples of leafy liverworts which occur with this moss. Species of the simpler thalloid liverworts are also common in woodland, but only in the wettest areas. Of these *Conocephalum conicum* and *Preissia quadrata* are typical of moist calcareous rock ledges and rocky stream sides, while *Anthoceros laevis* is common on permanently wet clay banks and slopes and in rides where it is often associated with *Pellia epiphylla*.

The hard fern

The fronds of the hard fern *(Blechnum spicant)* have one of the simplest structures of our native ferns, being divided only once into as many as 100 symmetrical pairs of lobes or pinnae. Each frond is stiff and has a shiny dark green surface with a varnish-like finish. The fronds grow in tufts from a single rhizomatous stock and may be up to 30 centimetres long. The fertile fronds are much taller than the barren ones and have very narrow, more widely-spaced, pinnae. They appear narrow because their margins are rolled over the clusters of fruiting bodies called sori which form a continuous line near and parallel to the margin. These are covered by a membrane known as the indusium. This arrangment contrasts with many other ferns which have their sori scattered on the underside of the pinnae. The pinnae of these fertile fronds are longest in the middle of the frond and get rapidly smaller towards the apex and base. This gives the whole frond a fish-bone appearance, and in Cumberland the plant is known as the herringbone fern. This fern is a very reliable indicator of woodland on acidic soils. It is found throughout the country, but is restricted in much of central and eastern England because suitable soils are not present.

The fertile frond of the hard fern *(Blechnum spicant)* with narrower pinnae is usually held erect above the mass of horizontal sterile fronds with their broader pinnae.

Tree bark bryophytes and lichens

The growing trunks and branches of the larger

trees form one of the most interesting micro-habitats within the forest. Many mosses and liverworts may grow up from the ground on to the dead branches, or the living trunks, but the more specialised true epiphytes including the mosses *Dicranoweisia cirrata* and *Hypnum cupressiforme* var. *filiforme* and the liverwort *Frullania dilatata*, can grow high up in relatively dry conditions on trees such as oak, elm and ash. The bulk of the epiphytic woodland flora is made up of lichens. Over three hundred species, or 22 per cent of the known lichen flora of the British Isles, have been recorded on oak alone. Just as ground-living species are affected by conditions such as soil pH, so lichens are affected by the nature of the bark, including its smoothness, pH and porosity. The species associated with any given species of tree are therefore determined on these criteria. Ash, which supports the second largest number of species after oak, also has a highly fissured bark, providing numerous niches for the lichen to colonise. Trees with a bark of a high (alkaline) pH include oaks, ash, elm, sycamore and field maple, while beech, the birches, elder and Scots pine have acid barks. As well as moisture and pH, light is also a limiting factor, for most species are light-demanding and only occur on trees at the edges of woodland, ride or glade sides, or in ancient deer parks. The ability of these lichens to colonise new trees is extremely slow, and it has been suggested that certain species are unable to produce viable spores at all under modern climatic conditions. Certainly a number of species appear to be found only on the oldest forest trees and also on isolated deer parkland trees. These may be relicts of the old Royal Forests, where the trees are only a generation removed from the ancient forest trees which once occupied the site. Lichens are also extremely susceptible to air pollution and artificial enrichment of the bark. As a result many species are completely absent from industrial and urban areas and also the most intensively cultivated rural areas. Because of these constraints the best remaining woodlands for lichens are now the "Ancient and Ornamental" woodland of the New Forest, and other relict Royal Forests including Savernake and Cranborne Chase, as well as the more undisturbed woods of Devon, west Wales, the Pennines, Lake District and western Scotland. In these damp western and upland areas a distinct association of lichens occurs, along with the "Atlantic" bryophytes. Characteristic lichens in the most exposed regions of these sessile oak woodlands include *Parmelia laevigata*, *Ochrolechia androgyna* and *Sphaerophorus globosus*. In the more sheltered areas of these woods species such as *Parmelia caperata*, *Lobaria pulmonaria* and *Camptothecium sericeum*, typical of lowland oak woods, are present.

Woodland lichens

Most lichens require light and grow more actively when trees are not in leaf, although some species, such as *Graphis elegans*, seem to need both direct sunlight and shade.

Lichens are very pollution sensitive; most of their nutritional requirements are absorbed through their body (or thallus) and in polluted regions the rain and run-off contain toxins in solution, and consequently their numbers are dramatically reduced.

The bark of trees varies in texture, pH and water capacity, and these factors affect the variety of lichen cover. Ash, sycamore and elm have a rich lichen flora, whereas birch and conifers are species poor. Hazel, rowan and beech often have writing lichens growing on them: their pale thalli are covered with black, branching, elongated fruiting bodies resembling hieroglyphics.

A variety of epiphytic lichen species. Such species-rich luxuriant growth is only found in areas with little or no pollution.

The dark greenish-grey beard lichen *Usnea florida* growing with grey *Parmelia physodes*.

Lichens of the genus *Usnea* hanging from a twig show why they are often called beard lichens.

The tree lungwort

If the bark of an oak or ash in an ancient forest is examined it will often be found to be so encrusted with epiphytic lichen that the true colour of the bark cannot be seen. The majority are structurally so minute that they merely appear as a crust on the bark. But the tree lungwort (*Lobaria pulmonaria*) is among the larger of the epiphytic lichens and may be up to 18 centimetres in length. The upper surface of the attractively lobed thallus (or body of the plant) is bright green, while beneath, it is orange with brownish hairs. When dry the whole plant becomes brown and papery. When the lichen is fruiting, small red patches appear on the upper surface of the thallus. Each is composed of a mass of the spore-producing structures called apothecia. The lichen may also reproduce vegetatively through specialised reproductive structures called soredia. This lichen is now chiefly associated with the western and upland oak woods. In the past, however, it had a much wider distribution, and was recorded from Suffolk in the early nineteenth century. Today it can still be found on ancient trees in some southern counties, such as in Longleat Woods in west Wiltshire. This is one of the species of lichens considered indicative of ancient woodland,

Epiphytic lichens on beech bark. The yellow *Parmelia caperata* can grow to a large size, especially on old trees in southern England; it sometimes grows on rocks.

The lungwort (*Lobaria pulmonaria*) is one of the largest lichens found growing on tree bark, particularly on oak and ash in ancient woodlands.

Woodland Fungi

Large and often colourful toadstools may form a striking component of the woodland flora, especially in autumn. These showy fruiting bodies only represent the tip of the iceberg as far as the whole fungal community of the wood is concerned. Each fruiting body is supported by a mass of thread-like mycelia which penetrate the substrate on which it is growing. It is these mycelia which carry out chemical functions, such as the breaking down of organic matter and its absorption into the fungus. In addition to the large fruiting bodies produced by the "macrofungi", there are many smaller "microfungi", including the moulds which remain largely unobserved. Despite their relatively simple biology, fungi represent a complex and vital link in the woodland ecosystem on which all other members are dependent. Because fungi contain no chlorophyll they have to obtain nutrients either as saprophytes from decaying organic matter, or as parasites from other living organisms. It is the saprophytic fungi which, in breaking down organic matter, both plant and animal, release vital nutrients for recycling. Without this process the whole nutrient cycle would almost grind to a halt. Many of the parasites on the other hand are less benign and may cause disease and destruction, bringing early decline and death to forest trees. Many fungus species are particularly associated with microhabitats within the wood such as the dung dropped by animals, or the corpses of the animals themselves. Still others are epiphytes, growing on moss-covered trunks, while a specialised fungal flora is even associated with old birds' nests.

Mycorrhizas

Most intriguing of all are the fungi which have a mycorrhizal association with the roots of higher plants. This is where the vascular plant and the fungus have a close physical and physiological relationship from which both may benefit. The mycorrhizal association between wild orchids and certain fungi is well-known, the usual genus involved being the microfungus *Rhizoctonia*. The relationship may be a truly symbiotic one from which both orchid and fungus benefit: the orchid gains by having dead organic matter broken down by the saprophytic fungus into a form that can be easily absorbed by its roots, while the fungus receives shelter and possibly some nutrients from the plant. Alternatively, there may be a continuing battle between the two plants with the fungus attempting to parasitise the orchid. Certainly the mycorrhizal fungi

of the lady's slipper and early purple orchids are members of the parasitic honey fungus genus *Armillaria*. It is probable that most if not all plants have some degree of mycorrhizal association. Members of the genus *Boletus* are also mycorrhizal, with *B. pseudosulphureus* occurring on the roots of oak, beech and lime. *B. luridus* is associated with hazel, while *Leccinum quercinum* is found with sweet chestnut. Associations between mycorrhizas and their hosts may also change with location. For instance, *Boletus subtomentosus* and *B. chrysenteron* are very commonly associated with oak in the northern sessile oak woods, but they are not necessarily found with oak in the south. Another family which forms extensive associations with both broadleaved and conifer woodland is the Russulaceae, with the two genera *Russula* and *Lactarius* involved.

Bracket fungi growing on the trunk herald the early death of the tree: most old trees are killed by them. Within the wood the fungus attacks the sap and heartwood, digesting its substance and weakening its structure.

Saprophytes

The many saprophytic fungi associated with dead wood, leaf litter and humus are able to break down organic matter extremely rapidly under suitable conditions and play a vital role in the cycle of nutrients through the woodland ecosystem. They make a major contribution to the disappearance by spring of most of the dead leaves which fall in the autumn. The deceiver (*Laccaria laccata*) is an example, and its reddish-brown to brick-red fruiting bodies appear in almost any woodland from summer to the winter months. Two other species which occur on plant debris are *Mycena mucor* and *M. polyadelpha*. Those which grow on dead wood may be characteristic of particular species. For example, species especially associated with oak stumps are *Daedalea quercina*, *Mycena inclinata* and *Coprinus sylvaticus*. The sulphur tuft (*Hypholoma fasciculare*) is an easily recognisable species which forms characteristic bright yellow clumps throughout the year on the stumps of many deciduous and coniferous trees. Other species associated with larger diameter timber, and particularly the tree-trunks themselves, include the bracket fungi, which form large semi-circular fruits or "brackets" on the trunk or stump. These may be very hard and persist from year to year. Many of them are parasitic, but *Grifola frondosa* is saprophytic, usually on oak. This species has been called the "hen of the woods" as the bracket is made up of soft narrow fans which resemble a bunch of feathers.

Other fungi are only found on the smaller branches. *Peniophora quercina* and *Hyphodontia quercina* are particularly associated with oak, while *Leptoporus caesius* and *L. stipticus* are two small bracket fungi associated with the dead wood of conifers. The upper surface of these two species is white, but while *L. caesius* is tinged with blue, *L. stipticus* has a reddish-brown hue at the margin. Extremely small fungi associated with decaying twigs include the coral spot (*Nectria cinnabarina*), which may be common throughout

The advancing front of a mat of fungal mycelium grows over dead wood. The individual hyphae making up the mycelium penetrate and break down the wood into simple and soluble chemicals and these nutrients are then absorbed by the fungus.

A guide to some woodland fungi

Sulphur tuft Agaricineae *Hypholoma fasciculare*. **Distribution:** Mixed woodland. **Notes:** Grows in large clumps on tree trunks; found throughout the year; gills turn brown with age.

Coral spot fungus Nectriaceae *Nectria cinnabarina*. **Distribution:** Mixed woodland. **Notes:** Common throughout the year; on newly fallen twigs and branches; bursts through the bark; densely clustered.

Volvariella bombycina Agaricineae. **Distribution:** Mixed woodland. **Notes:** On trunks of trees, especially knot holes; cap silky and hairy, white, occasionally pale cream; stipe swollen at base.

Puff-ball Lycoperdaceae *Lycoperdon perlatum*. **Distribution:** Mixed woodland. **Notes:** Often in groups; white-grey when young, becoming yellow-brown with age; found in summer and autumn.

Common ganoderma Polyporaceae *Ganoderma applanatum*. **Distribution:** Beech woodland, though found on other trees. **Notes:** Solitary or a few overlapping brackets, especially common on ageing beeches.

Jew's ear fungus Auriculariales *Auricularia auricula*. **Distribution:** Mixed woodland. **Notes:** Found throughout the year, but especially common in the autumn; common on elder; usually grows in groups on living or dead wood.

Red elf-cup Sarcoscyphaceae *Sarcoscypha coccinea*. **Distribution:** Mixed woodland. **Notes:** Very common in south western England; grows on decaying branches on damp ground; common in winter becoming rarer in spring.

Giant polypore Polyporaceae *Grifola gigantea*. **Distribution:** Oak and beech woodland. **Notes:** Grows from summer to winter at the base of trees; fan shaped, often growing in tiers; often up to 1m across.

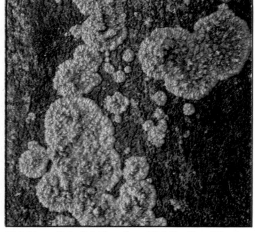

Phlebia radiata Phlebia radiata. **Distribution:** Mixed woodland. **Notes:** Especially on alder; pink to orange-red; around base of trunk or on tree bark; margin free and raised; flesh tough.

Trametes versicolor Polyporaceae. **Distribution:** Usually in birch woodland on a variety of trees. **Notes:** Always on dead wood, causes much decay; colour variable; often grows in tiered clusters; found throughout the year.

Beefsteak fungus Polyporaceae *Fistulina hepatica*. **Distribution:** Oak woodland. **Notes:** Usually on oak and sweet chestnut; hoof, tongue or bracket shaped; appears velvety though the upper surface is sticky and shiny.

Sticky coral fungus Dacrymycetales *Calocera viscosa*. **Distribution:** Conifer woodland. **Notes:** Grows in clumps in autumn and winter on tree trunks; slimy and orange-yellow when growing; orange and horny when old and dry.

A guide to some woodland fungi (continued)

Fly agaric Agaricineae *Amanita muscaria.* **Distribution:** Pine or birch woodland. **Notes:** Usually on poor soils; cap at first red with white scales, but these are often rubbed or washed off.

Lycoperdon pyriforme Lycoperdaceae. **Distribution:** Mixed woodlands. **Notes:** Grows on old stumps and dead roots; becomes brown-grey with age; found in late summer and autumn; smells faintly of herrings.

Death cap Agaricineae *Amanita phalloides.* **Distribution:** Mixed woodland. **Notes:** Especially common in beech woodland; deadly poisonous; yellowish green cap has faint radiating lines; has a faint nauseous smell when mature.

Lepiota cristata Agaricineae. **Distribution:** All woodland. **Other habitats:** Lawns; pastures. **Notes:** By paths in woods; has a strong unpleasant smell; stipe smooth; gills white, crowded.

Coral fungus Hydnaceae *Hericium coralloides.* **Distribution:** All woodland. **Notes:** On dead trunks of trees, especially beech; found only in autumn; much branched from a thick stipe; white to dull yellow.

Cauliflower fungus Clavariaceae. *Sparassis crispa.* **Distribution:** In pine woodlands. **Notes:** Found at base of tree trunks; stem up to 8cm, resembling a root; aromatic; found only in August and September; locally common.

Earth star Geastraceae. *Geastrum triplex.* **Distribution:** Mixed woodland. **Notes:** Especially common in beech woodland; closed fruiting bodies resemble an onion; when first open, rays flesh coloured, later become dark brown.

Amethyst deceiver Agaricineae. *Laccaria amethystea.* **Distribution:** In mixed woodlands. **Notes:** Whole plant deep violet, becoming paler when dry; cap scurfy towards the centre.

Orange-peel fungus Humariaceae. *Aleuria aurantia.* **Distribution:** Mixed woodland. **Other habitats:** Gravel; paths; lawns. **Notes:** On bare soil in woods; no stalk; scarlet-orange inside, downy white outside.

Chanterelle Cantharellaceae. *Cantharellus cibarius.* **Distribution:** All types of woodland. **Notes:** Egg-yolk yellow; smells faintly of apricots; spore-producing layer much folded giving the impression of forked shallow gills.

Edible boletus Boletineae. *Boletus edulis.* **Distribution:** Mixed woodland. **Notes:** Especially common in beech woodland; found from October to December; stipe swollen with a reticulum of raised white veins.

Orange pholiota Agaricineae. *Gymnopilus junonius.* **Distribution:** All woodland. **Notes:** In tufts at the base of trees; gills crowded and narrow; stipe swollen in the middle; cap sometimes minutely scaly.

the year, appearing as a small dark red cushion which bursts through the bark of the newly-fallen branches. A species which has a similar manner of growth and is often found on the dead branches of beech in the winter is *Diatrype disciformis;* the cushion's protruding fruiting bodies or protheca are whitish with black tips at first, turning dark brown or black later.

Parasites

Much of the detailed study of woodland fungi, other than of the structure of their fruiting bodies, has involved the study of pathogenic or disease-causing species, particularly those which cause economic damage to forest trees. Several fungi are particularly damaging to growing trees, causing the death and decay of the living timber. Both the beef-steak fungus *(Fistulina hepatica)* and another bracket fungus *Stereum gausapatum* will cause severe heart rot in oak. Most parasitic species are not host-specific; the honey fungus *(Armillaria mellea)* is a good example. Its toad-stool-like fruiting bodies can be found growing in large clumps at the foot of many trees, both living and dead. Curiously it is weakly luminous at night. It can be a serious pest to many commercial species of tree, not only in the British Isles, but throughout the northern hemisphere and also in Australia. It spreads both by spores and also by root-like cords which can grow through the soil to infect other trees, a feature which it shares with other pathogens. Strangely, although this fungus is often common in native oak wood sites, young trees are apparently able to develop without being badly damaged. Here the fungus appears to act as a secondary agent, affecting older trees which have already been weakened by some other cause. The honey fungus causes further dieback, which assures the death of the tree. On the other hand, if conifers are planted on such a site, severe damage may be caused to the crop. Two bracket fungi, the white rot fungus *(Fomes annosus)* and the red rot *(F. fomentarius),* are also pathogens of pine and birch; the former is of greatest economic significance as it has spread to plantations of introduced spruce.

Although the standing trunk is the most obvious area for attack, almost every part of the tree may be subject to fungal pathogens, often of several species. In oaks this may include disease of the leaves, bark, shoots and roots. While very few species are known to attack acorns, *Ciboria batschiana* being the chief exception, a number of species attack the leaves, either causing mildew, discolouration or spotting. Oak mildew *(Microsphaera alphitoides)* can be a serious foliage disease of oaks in the British Isles. It is particularly common on the leaves of recently coppiced trees. The leaves which are produced on the new shoots in the first two years after cutting are characteristically much larger than those produced on either saplings or mature trees, and it is these which are frequently covered by this greyish-white mildew. The economic significance has diminished, as little oak coppice is now cut commercially. Leaf spotting is a common symptom of fungal attack in many trees, perhaps the commonest being tar spot in sycamore. Yellow spot on the leaves of both sessile and pedunculate oak is caused by the fungus *Sclerotinia candolleana*. The tight masses of small twigs or "witches brooms" so typical of birch trees may also be caused by a fungus (although similar phenomena may be produced by a gall mite or virus). The fungus involved is *Taphrina betulina,* a relative of the common yeast. The catastrophic Dutch elm disease is caused by the fungus *Ceratocystis ulmi* which is spread by bark beetles. A similarly serious disease, oak-wilt, caused by a related fungus *C. fagacearum,* was first reported in the United States in 1942. Fortunately it has not spread to this country and measures have been taken to prevent this in the future.

Fungi thus play a significant if largely unseen

The stinkhorn

Any time from midsummer until late into the autumn the pleasant damp leafy scent of lowland oak woods may be tainted by a nasty "pong". The source of this odour, which is easily mistaken for a rotting corpse, is the stinkhorn fungus, *Phallus impudicus.* Although the fruiting body which produces the odour is quite large and may grow up to 23 centimetres high, it is often quite difficult to locate even when, from the smell, it seems to be close. The stinkhorn belongs to the group of fungi called the Gasteromycetales which also includes the edible puffballs. The spores of this group develop within the fruiting body and are not shed until it is fully mature. In the stinkhorn the mature spore mass is carried up on a tall white stalk. This erupts from a gelatinous white oval body about the size of a large hen's egg, elongation to its full length taking only a few hours. It is at this stage that the jelly in which the spores are embedded breaks down and the conical cap begins to emit its foetid stench. This strong smell has a most important function, that of attracting flies to feed on the decomposing jelly. As they do so, spores stick to their bodies and are carried to other parts of the wood. The structure usually lasts only a few days for it is rapidly attacked by slugs and maggots. The stalk soon collapses and the whole body quickly decomposes, but by then its job is done, the spores having been disseminated even more widely than its smell.

The stinkhorn *(Phallus impudicus)* is the rapid growing fruiting body of a common garden and woodland fungus. Flies distribute its spores; they are attracted by the foetid smell given off by the cap.

part in the woodland ecosystem. Because only the hidden fungus mycelium is present in the soil or wood throughout the year, and is extremely difficult to study, our knowledge of their ecological requirements is extremely meagre, even for the macrofungi, which produce the large fruiting bodies. It appears that few fungi are restricted to any particular woodland type, and although differences have been observed between woods on acid and calcareous soils, it is difficult to know whether this reflects the requirements of the fungi concerned, or merely indicates the presence of higher plants on which they have a mycorrhizal or other relationship. In general the best habitats for fungi are in mixed broad-leaved woodlands on primary woodland sites, where trees are allowed to grow to maturity and die back naturally and where dead wood is not tidied up. Certain species are however characteristic of specific woodland types including beech, birch and pine, and even conifer plantations.

Autumn fungi

Many of the most spectacular of the British fungi grow in woodlands, and an autumn fungus foray is almost always a worthwhile experience, particularly if some of the many edible species can be collected. However it is important to be absolutely sure of their identification, for among the woodland fungi lurk our most deadly species. Those belonging to the genus *Amanita* include both the destroying angel and death cap. The former *(Amanita virosa)* is a rare plant found in mixed woodland, usually on the poorer soils, while the death cap *(A. phalloides)* is relatively common under oak or beech. They are distinguishable from the edible mushroom by their white gills and basal volva (a collar round the base of the stalk). Among the other poisonous members of the genus is the fly agaric *(A. muscaria),* whose white spotted orange cap is commonly associated with gnomes and fairies! It is also typical of pine and birch woods although it may also occur under beech. Not all of the genus is poisonous, and one, the blusher *(A. rubescens),* which grows in conifer woods, is harmless and good to eat (though only when cooked). This species cannot be recommended except for the fungal expert, for a mistaken identification could prove fatal!

The "funnel-shaped fungi" are among the best of the edible woodland species. These have the gills visible on the outside of the horn. The two most sought-after species are the horn of plenty *(Craterellus cornucopioides)* and the chanterelle *(Cantharellus cibarius).* Both make extremely good eating and because of the thinness of its flesh the horn of plenty can be dried and used later for flavouring. The "safest" of the woodland edible fungi are members of the mycorrhizal genus *Boletus.* Although some species such as *B. calopus* and *B. felleus* have a bitter taste, none are actually poisonous. Unlike many toadstools, including the field mushroom, which produce their spores on gills, the *Boletus* produce them from tubes and the underside of the cap looks like a sponge. The *Boletus* are found in many types of woodland but especially pine and birch. The best for eating are *B. edulis* and *B. luteus,* which are often principal ingredients of "mushroom" soup. The Jew's ear fungus *(Auricularia auricula)* is one of the Tremallales or "jelly fungi". It is almost entirely restricted to elder and can be found on both living and dead branches as rubbery pink "ears". Although slightly repulsive to look at, this common fungus is edible and good.

Woodland Invertebrates

Every woodland contains a largely unnoticed host of invertebrate animals which vary in size from single-celled Protozoa to insects several centimetres in length. Many of these animals are unable to survive for long away from moist conditions because their bodies are not well adapted to retaining water. The moist shady conditions within woods are therefore ideal for many species which are not present in drier habitats. The most suitable conditions occur in leaf litter and dead wood, and it is here that the highest invertebrate populations can be found. The most highly developed group among the invertebrates are the insects; large numbers may occur in every microhabitat within the wood from the soil to the tops of the highest oaks. Even so, the number of species associated with British woodlands is small compared with the Continent. It is also worth noting that many more species are present in the south of the British Isles than in the north.

Apart from the microscopic Protozoa which occur within wet leaf litter, the simplest organisms include the nematodes or eel worms. These are tiny, transparent thread-like creatures living in the soil and feeding on diatoms or other algae and fungi. Many such as *Cherilobus quadrilabiatus* feed on decaying vegetation and make a significant contribution to the breakdown of organic matter and the nutrient cycle of the wood. The rather more complex annelid worms, which include the common earthworms and potworms, are also present in large numbers in woodland soils. Unlike eelworms these have clearly segmented bodies and tend to be larger and flesh coloured. The common earthworm (*Lumbricus terrestris*) pulls plant debris and leaves into its "U"-shaped burrow at night where they are digested. The continual burrowing of worms and their burial of leaves considerably speeds the turnover of soil and nutrients in the woodland ecosystem. Worms may be present in extraordinarily large numbers in woodland soils which are not prone to drying out. There can be more than five million to the hectare, moving some 25 tonnes of soil between them.

The molluscs: slugs and snails

The molluscs, which include slugs and snails, are more complex in form and function. Just over one hundred species of land mollusc occur in the British Isles, and of these about half are found in woodland. Molluscs require moisture to produce the thin film of mucus on which they glide, and they lack a waterproof skin so they are especially prone to desiccation. Within woodlands dead wood forms a favoured habitat, providing moist conditions and recesses which can be used for egg-laying and for refuge during the day. In addition to moist conditions, the presence of lime is important, especially for snails, which require it to produce their shell. Climate is also significant to the distribution of molluscs in the British Isles, with most species being present in the milder south, although certain species such as the great grey slug (*Limax maximus*)

A varied woodland flora supports a rich herbivorous insect life. Oak is an indigenous tree and has some 300 insects associated with it, of which this pale tussock (*Basychina pudibunda*) caterpillar is one.

occur in the far north of Scotland. The ash woods on limestone in the south-west have the most suitable conditions and the best mollusc fauna, while the beech woods on chalk and limestone are also very good compared with woods on acid soils, even in the south east. The best woods are usually ancient ones which have been relatively undisturbed by man. Molluscs are unable to disperse quickly to new habitats, and therefore many species may be absent from new woodland and plantations, even when these are only a short distance from an old site. The slugs *Limax cinereoniger* and *L. tenellus* are regarded as indicators of ancient woodland, although occurring in sites as far apart as the Wyre Forest in the Midlands and Rothiemurchus in the Highlands, where they are associated with oak and Scots pine respectively. The closely related *L. maximus* is also a species of old woods, although found in other habitats including gardens. Typical woodland snails include *Zenobiella subrufescens*, *Cochlodina lamellata* and *Ena montana*. While *E. obscura* is restricted to woodlands on calcareous soils, *Zonitoides excavatus* is the only species particularly associated with acid woodlands and appears to be a definite calcifuge. It is most common in the moist "Atlantic" sessile oak woods and is completely absent from East Anglia and east Scotland. Like many "Atlantic" ferns and bryophytes it also has a Wealden distribution.

Slugs and snails are notorious for the damage which they do to garden crops, yet in a natural situation higher plants are very little affected and are not touched at all by some species. Instead slugs and snails are browsers of lower plants, especially algae, lichens and fungi growing on the forest floor and on the trees themselves. Here the molluscs may leave characteristic feeding tracks as they move over the trunks browsing off the minute plants. In turn molluscs are preyed on by small mammals such as shrews and woodmice. The song thrush's preference for snails is well-known, although in woodland it is usually the striped snails that suffer higher predation than those with plain shells, which is the reverse of what happens in grassland areas. Other species which feed on snails include the

glow-worm (*Lampyris noctiluca*), actually the larva of a beetle which occurs in some forest rides in southern England.

The arthropods

The arthropods, which have jointed legs and a segmented body, include some of the most complex and highly evolved invertebrate groups. They also form by far the largest group in the

Slugs are particularly successful woodland animals because the lack of a cumbersome shell enables them to squeeze into small spaces and under logs. This is feeding on a stinkhorn fungus.

Millipedes

Millipedes belong to the class of arthropods known as the Diplopoda, a name which means "double feet" and refers to the fact that the animals have two pairs of legs on nearly every segment. This distinguishes them from the centipedes, which have only one pair of legs per segment. Millipedes can be found in the soil, in leaf litter, under loose bark, and in many other situations where they can find decaying plant material. Some are pests in the garden because they damage plant roots and tubers. Several species, notably those known as flat-backed millipedes, construct simple nests in which they look after their eggs. There are about 45 British species, including the pill millipede (*Glomeris marginata*) which can roll itself into a ball.

×1

Cylindroiulus sp. Iulidae
Distribution: Throughout British Isles **Other Habitats**: Anywhere it can find decaying plant matter and moisture **Adult active**: All year except when really cold **Food**: Assorted plant matter

Centipedes

Centipedes belong to the class of arthropods known as the Chilopoda. They are not closely related to the millipedes, although they are sometimes put with them in a group called the myriapods, meaning "many legs". Centipedes in Britain have a maximum of 101 pairs of legs, but most have far fewer. The fast-running *Lithobius* species, which are often found under stones, have 15 pairs when adult. All centipedes are carnivorous creatures, equipped with a pair of poisonous fangs which they use to capture slugs, insects, and other invertebrates, including other centipedes. There are 44 species in the British Isles, but not all native to these islands. They live in the soil and in leaf litter.

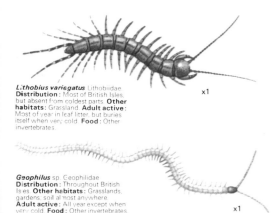

Lithobius variegatus Lithobiidae **Distribution**: Most of British Isles, but absent from coldest parts. **Other habitats**: Grassland. **Adult active**: Most of year in leaf litter, but buries itself when very cold. **Food**: Other invertebrates.

x1

Geophilus sp. Geophilidae **Distribution**: Throughout British Isles. **Other habitats**: Grasslands, gardens; soil almost anywhere. **Adult active**: All year except when very cold. **Food**: Other invertebrates.

x1

The centipede *Lithobius variegatus* is commonly found in the leaf litter and under logs in damp woodlands.

The centipede *Haplophilus subterraneus* is one of the thin thread-like species which are popularly called wireworms.

They usually live in the soil as opposed to under stones and logs which are habitats of other broader-bodied centipedes.

Animal Kingdom. The forest species include the millipedes and centipedes, the arachnids (including the false scorpions, spiders and harvestmen) as well as members of the most important terrestrial arthropod group—the insects.

Millipedes and centipedes

The more primitive animals in these arthropod groups, particularly the myriapods, are principally associated with dead wood and leaf litter. Millipedes such as *Polymicrodon polydesmoides* are almost exclusively vegetarian and are involved in the breakdown of organic matter, particularly in calcareous soils. As they are prone to desiccation they are most active during the winter, when mating takes place. The female constructs a cell where the eggs will be laid which is lined with silk produced from special glands situated towards the rear of the female abdomen. The young take up to seven months to mature, moulting nine times as they grow. Each time the young millipede moults, it builds a silk-lined cell which is afterwards eaten. Millipedes have been found to reach a population peak in certain woodlands in the middle stages of the coppice cycle where a covering of brambles has been a feature of the ground flora. Species recorded include *Tachypodoiulus niger* and *Glomeris marginata*, the latter being the woodlouse-like pill millipede. The small woodlouse *Trichoniscus pusillus* (a crustacean), which is restricted to moist shady woodlands, was also found to be most plentiful at this stage of the coppice cycle.

Centipedes are characteristically fast-moving mini-predators and kill their prey by poison produced from glands situated in the first body segment. One genus *Cryptops* also has appendages on its rear segment used for defence and for clasping prey. All three species of this genus occur in woods, although they are rather rare. A further woodland centipede *Lithobius variegatus* is noteworthy in that it does not occur outside the British Isles.

Spiders and harvestmen

The arachnids are distinguished by having four pairs of walking legs. The best known are the spiders and harvestmen. Many of the common garden spiders such as *Araneus diadematus* are also common in woodland, where their radial webs may be seen in the shrub layer vegetation during the autumn. Members of the genus *Linyphia* are also widespread in woodland, although not always common. *L. triangularis* occurs with *A. diadematus* on shrubby vegetation and bramble, while *L. hortensis* is usually associated with dog's mercury. Species of this genus produce a hammock-shaped web. The crab spiders (of which *Xysticus lanio* is a woodland example, usually occurring on young oak trees) do not build webs, but instead lie in wait for their prey with their front legs stretched out before them. Both web and non web-building spiders are associated with the trunks of forest trees. The deeply-fissured bark of oak appears to be particularly favourable in providing hiding places and shelter for the spiders. More species are therefore associated with oak than either beech, birch or Scots pine which have smoother bark. Although often mistaken for spiders, the harvestmen form a distinct order of arachnids. They are most often found sitting in the trunks of the forest trees. The attractively marked *Megabunus diadema* occurs throughout the British Isles and is found in the highest woodlands up to 675 metres, hunting smaller arthropods and insects. Mites, many of which are parasitic, are also arachnids. In woodland *Bryobia praetiosa* feeds on many plants in the herb layer, and many other species occur (sometimes in vast numbers) among the leaf litter.

Primitive insects: springtails and bristletails

Although insects include the most highly developed of the land invertebrates, the more primitive types, such as the springtails (Collembola) and the bristletails (Diplura), are unable to live in dry habitats and are restricted to the soil, leaf litter and rotting wood. The springtails form a most important and very abundant element in the physical decomposition of organic material, especially on calcareous soils.

Crickets, bushcrickets and grasshoppers

Although only thirty species of Orthoptera are present in the British Isles, they are a most successful group which can colonise the driest habitats. A number of species occur in woodlands, particularly in the south. The wood cricket (*Nemobius sylvestris*) grows to about one

False scorpions

False scorpions are tiny arachnids with greyish bodies and relatively enormous pink claws. The latter are connected to poison glands and they are used to catch mites and other minute creatures for food. Most false scorpions live in the soil or in decaying vegetation such as leaf litter. Many can be found under loose bark, and some inhabit birds' nests. A few are found in buildings, but only where conditions are rather damp, for the animals dry out very easily. False scorpions move forward very slowly with their claws outstretched, but when they are disturbed they pull in the claws and shoot backwards. There are about 26 British species.

x16

Neobisium muscorum Neobisiidae **Distribution**: Throughout British Isles in moss and decaying vegetation. **Other habitats**: Gardens; hedgebanks, river banks. **Adult active**: All year. **Food**: Other small animals.

Harvestmen

Harvestmen resemble spiders in having four pairs of legs, and they clearly belong to the same group of animals—the arachnids. They differ from spiders, however, in having a one-piece body—spiders have a distinct "waist" in the middle. Harvestmen also lack poisonous fangs and they are unable to make silk. They roam over the ground and vegetation relying mainly on their very long second pair of legs to find food in the form of other small animals, both living and dead. Most harvestmen are adult in the autumn, hence their name, but a few species mature in the spring and those species that live in soil and leaf litter can be found at all times of the year. There are 22 British species.

Phalangium opilio Phalangiidae **Distribution**: Throughout British Isles. **Other habitats**: Anywhere with tall herbs or shrubby vegetation. **Adult active**: June to November **Food**: A wide range of insects.

x1

Springtails

Springtails are rather primitive wingless insects which rarely exceed 5mm in length. They feed by chewing living or dead plant material. Some are globular and live on growing plants, but most are elongated and they live in the soil and in leaf litter. They are usually clothed with hairs or scales. A few springtails, such as *Podura aquatica*, live on the surface of weed-covered ponds. All springtails have a forked "spring" at the hind end. This is usually clipped up under the body, but when the insect is disturbed the spring is released; it flicks down onto the surface and sends the insects forward through the air. Young springtails look just like the adults and do not undergo any metamorphosis as they grow up. There are about 300 British species.

x7

centimetre in length and is confined to woodlands. It is relatively common in the New Forest and in woodlands in adjacent counties. Another small member of the Orthoptera, the common ground hopper *(Tetrix undulata)* may be found in woods throughout the British Isles and is present in other habitats too, including moorland and marshland. Both species are omnivores, their diet including algae growing on the ground. Two species of bushcricket also occur in woodlands south of the River Humber. Both are green in colour and resemble rather fat grasshoppers but can be easily distinguished by their much longer antennae. The oak bushcricket *(Meconema thalassinum)* is particularly associated with oak woods, where both adults and nymphs lurk among the foliage, and prey on other insects. The eggs are laid in crevices in the bark or occasionally in empty oak galls. This small bushcricket, some 1.5 centimetres in length, differs from the second species, the speckled bushcricket *(Leptophytes punctatissima)*, in that it has prominent wings. Both species are attracted to light and may be seen on summer nights on house windows in woodland districts. Grassland grasshoppers also occur in woodland rides. These include the common field grasshopper *(Chorthippus brunneus)*. A rather similar but much rarer species is confined to woodlands, particularly ancient woodland in southern England. This is the woodland grasshopper *(Omocestus rufipes)*, which can be identified by the presence of large reddish patches on the underside of the abdomen and white mouthparts.

Bugs and aphids

The British Hemiptera number about 1,650 species, many of which are woodland insects.

Woodland bugs

Bugs (order Hemiptera) are extremely common in woodlands, where the wide variety of plants provides them with plenty of food. Aphids and other homopteran bugs are abundant on the trees, while heteropteran bugs can be found on the trees and the undergrowth. Both plant-feeding and predatory bugs occur, many of them being well camouflaged as they rest on leaves and tree trunks. Four fairly common woodland heteropterans are illustrated here.

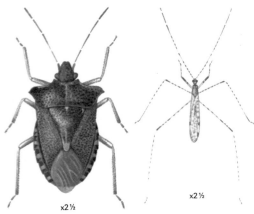

Forest Bug Pentatomidae *Pentatoma rufipes.* **Distribution:** Most of British Isles. **Other habitats:** Hedgerows and gardens. **Adult Active:** July to October. **Food:** Sap from leaves, twigs, and fruit of many trees, especially oak.

Tree Damsel Bug Nabidae *Himacerus apterus.* **Distribution:** Southern half of England and Wales. **Other habitats:** Hedgerows. **Adult Active:** July to October. **Food:** Mites and small insects. **Note:** Individuals with long wings are occasionally found.

Birch Shield Bug Acanthosomidae *Elasmostethus interstinctus.* **Distribution:** Throughout British Isles. **Other habitats:** None. **Adult active:** Spring to late autumn (hibernates in debris). **Food:** Sap of birch (leaves, twigs, and catkins).

Two-pronged bristletails

Two-pronged Bristletails (order Diplura) are primitive, wingless insects with pale bodies no more than 5mm long in the 12 British species. There are two slender "tails" at the hind end. The insects live in soil and leaf litter, where they feed on decaying matter. The young stages are just like the adults except for their size. In warmer parts of the world some diplurans have pincer-like "tails". All British species belong to the genus *Campodea.*

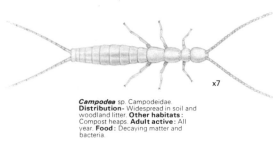

x7

Campodea sp. Campodeidae. **Distribution**- Widespread in soil and woodland litter. **Adult active :** Compost heaps. **Adult active:** All year. **Food :** Decaying matter and bacteria.

Among these are the "heteropteran" and "homopteran" bugs which include the shield bugs and froghoppers respectively. Bugs typically have mouth parts which are adapted for piercing and sucking. The more active heteropterans require a high protein diet which includes other animals, or alternatively pollen. One of the largest families in this group is the Miridae, of which as many as twenty-seven species are associated with oak. Their eggs are typically inserted into the twigs, leaf scars and lenticels; those of *Cyllecoris histrionicus* overwinter in cracks in the young twigs of oak, and hatch in May. The nymphs feed up rapidly on unopened catkins and on other small insects such as aphids, and reach maturity in June. Many of the other woodland shield bugs belong to the family Pentatomidae. They include the forest bug *(Pentatoma rufipes)* which is also associated with oak, while *Palomia prasina* may be found in large numbers on hazel, especially in the south. The flat bug *(Aradus depressus)* belongs to a further family, Aradidae. It is a specialised feeder on fungal mycelia beneath the bark of dead wood. Another related species *A. cinnamomeus* is a sap feeder on pine.

The homopteran bugs or leaf hoppers are also relatively active but are not known to take animal food. One of the largest families of 250 species is the Cicadellidae. These are sap feeders and include many species, all typical of the tree and field layer vegetation of woods. One example, the eared leaf hopper *(Ledra aurita)* can be identified by the pair of ear-like projections situated on the front edge of its thorax. Its flattened and mottled "cryptic" appearance helps this species to blend with lichen-covered branches. While the Cicadellidae are minute insects just a few millimetres in length, the Cicadidae, although structurally similar, are very much larger. Only one species of cicada *(Cicadetta montana)* occurs in this country, where

Most bugs feed on a liquid diet, and the majority are adapted to drink plant sap; but some of the 1600 British species suck blood from animals. Bugs are abundant in woodland and are important food for predators.

it is restricted to the New Forest. Here the song of the male, so typical of warmer climates, can be heard from trees and other vegetation, usually around glades where bracken, the foodplant of the adult, is plentiful. The nymphs spend several years feeding underground on plant roots before emerging to complete their development and adult life as tree dwellers. The adult may reach a length of two centimetres and have a wing span of about five centimetres, but they are small compared with many tropical species.

The aphids ("greenfly" and "blackfly") also belong to the Hemiptera. All are minute, being only a few millimetres in length, and feed on the sap of young leaves. Several generations are passed in a year and parthenogenesis, whereby females can give birth to numerous young without mating, is a special feature of the family. As a result vast numbers of individuals are produced, which are kept in check by predators such as ladybirds, lacewings and hoverfly larvae. Aphids therefore form an important food resource in the woodland ecosystem. In addition to the direct food resource, the sugary "honey dew" which exudes from their bodies in large amounts is used as food by other insects ranging from ants to the purple emperor butterfly. A number of microfungi are also associated with honey dew. These are browsed by small insects such as *Ectopsocus briggsi*, a member of the Order Psocoptera, which particularly favours oak and hawthorn.

Flies

The diptera or two-winged flies encompass a large range of families from small midges to the large and colourful hoverflies. Of the 5,000 or more species which occur in the British Isles, some of the most important and spectacular are woodland dwellers. Many, like the mosquitos, have larvae which develop in puddles and wet holes in trees, whilst other flies have larvae that we would call "maggots", typically associated with dead animal and plant material. Mosquitos, including gnats and midges, abound in most woodlands especially in the late summer and autumn. Among them are the common gnats *Culex pipiens* and *Theobaldia annulata*, both of which are only too ready to feed off an unwary human visitor. More specialised are the small arboreal species which are adapted to living in water-filled rot holes of the mature forest trees. These include the species *Anopheles plumbeus* and *Aedes geniculatus*, relatives of the mosquitos that carry malaria and yellow fever in the tropics. Other Diptera and small beetles such as *Prionocyphon serricornis* also breed in this micro-habitat. A further specialised group includes the fungus gnats, which have larvae adapted for feeding on the fruiting bodies of

Snakeflies

Snakeflies (order Neuroptera) are related to the alderflies and lacewing flies. They get their name from the long "neck", which can raise the head markedly above the body. They are woodland insects that fly rather weakly among the branches and feed on aphids and other small insects. They are especially common in pine woods. The larvae can be found in decaying wood, where they feed on beetle grubs and other small insects. There are just four species in the British Isles, all belonging to the genus *Raphidia.*

x2½

Snakefly Raphidiidae *Raphidia notata* **Distribution :** Pine and oak woods throughout British Isles. **Other habitats :** Occasionally in other types of woodland. **Adult Active:** May to August. **Food :** Small insects. **Note:** Female has long, slender ovipositor.

fungi, while more specialised still are the parasitic gall-producing midges which may attack buds, catkins and fruits of forest trees, especially oak.

The horse flies are blood-suckers, and are mainly associated with pasture and grazing animals, but *Tabanus sudeticus*, the largest British member of the family Tabanidae (also the largest British fly with a wingspan of five centimetres), is a species found in ancient woodland, especially the New Forest. The larvae of this family are soil-dwellers where they prey on annelid worms and molluscs. The robber flies (Asilidae), although harmless to man, are also woodland predators. The adult flies lurk among the foliage of trees and shrubs, waiting to pounce on unwary insects, including some larger than themselves such as bees and wasps. The largest British species *Asilus crabroniformis* occurs occasionally in clearings among conifer woodland in southern England, while another large species, *Laphria marginata*, is restricted to broad-leaved woodland, also in southern Britain. The larvae of these species form part of the very large Diptera fauna of dead wood. Among these are several hoverflies (Syrphidae), the adults of which feed largely on nectar and pollen. These flies are therefore most commonly found in open woodland, particularly where hawthorn and other flowering shrubs are abundant. Harmless hoverflies often resemble bees or wasps, a ruse which dissuades predators. Some hoverflies are also associated with the nests of wasps and bees in woodland. The larvae of *Volucella bombylans* occur as scavengers in bees' nests while *V. pellucens* scavenges in wasps' nests. *Xanthogramma pedissequum*, a species native to woodlands as far north as Lancashire, also occurs in wasps' nests,

where it is thought to feed on the aphid fauna. Although many flies are parasitic on other insects, the number is small when compared with the parasitic Hymenoptera which include the ichneumon "flies". Their range of hosts is also restricted.

Wasps and ants

The Hymenoptera include the bees, wasps, sawflies and ants. Although wasps are instinctively disliked by many people, in natural ecosystems, away from ice-cream wrappers, they have a natural and important role as predators and parasites of other insects. Bees may also be parasites, sometimes of other bees, while also playing an important role as pollinators of flowering plants. One of the largest and most ferocious looking of the woodland hymenoptera is the wood wasp *(Urocerus gigas)*. This species is in fact a harmless sawfly. The large "sting" is only present in the female and is an ovipositor used solely for injecting the eggs deep into the wood of dead or dying coniferous trees. Appropriately this species has an equally spectacular parasite, the ichneumon *Rhyssa persuasoria*. Sawfly larvae, which feed on the leaves of woodland trees and shrubs, are often mistaken for the caterpillars of Lepidoptera, although the rear end of the body is characteristically curled back beneath itself and the larvae cling to the leaves by their six true legs. One of the largest British species is *Cimbex femorata*, the rather dusty green larvae of which feed on birch, while the pine sawflies *Neodiprion sertifer* and *Diprion pini* are common pests of both planted and natural pine wood. Willow is favoured as a food plant by many insect larvae including sawflies. One species, *Pontania proxima*, is responsible for the

Crane-flies

Crane-flies (order Diptera) are slender-bodied flies which are often called daddy-long-legs because of their very long, slender limbs. The adults may lap up a little nectar, but otherwise they do not feed. The larvae, on the other hand, may do a great deal of damage to the roots of trees, cereals, and other plants. These damaging larvae are called leather-jackets. Some crane-fly larvae live in water and feed on debris. The adults use their long legs to hang from grasses and other plants and they sometimes bob up and down on them. They can lose two or three legs without hindrance. There are nearly 300 British species.

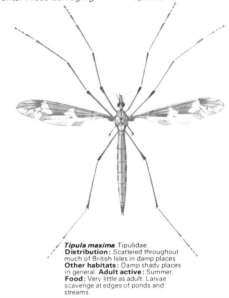

Tipula maxima. Tipulidae. **Distribution:** Scattered throughout much of British Isles in damp places **Other habitats:** Damp shady places in general. **Adult active:** Summer. **Food:** Very little as adult. Larvae scavenge at edges of ponds and streams.

small red bean galls on willow leaves. The larvae feed up on the contents of the gall before pupating in the soil.

The many species of true gall wasps belong to the super-family Cynipoidea. They form galls

Horse-flies

Horse-flies (order Diptera) are stout-bodied flies — some are actually called "stouts" in the New Forest area — whose females are notorious blood-suckers. They plunge their dagger-like mouthparts with equal readiness into horses, deer, cattle, and humans. The males feed mainly on nectar, but both sexes can be found drinking at the edges of pools and streams. Most

horse-flies announce their approach with a loud humming noise, but the cleg-flies approach in complete silence and the first indication we get of their presence is a sharp prick. Horse-fly larvae live in the soil or decaying vegetation and feed on other small animals. There are about 30 species in the British Isles.

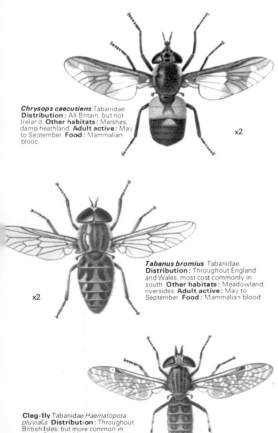

Chrysops caecutiens Tabanidae. **Distribution:** All Britain, but not Ireland. **Other habitats:** Marshes, damp heathland. **Adult active:** May to September. **Food:** Mammalian blood.

x2

Tabanus bromius Tabanidae. **Distribution:** Throughout England and Wales, most commonly in south. **Other habitats:** Meadowland, riversides. **Adult active:** May to September. **Food:** Mammalian blood.

x2

Cleg-fly Tabanidae *Haematopota pluvialis.* **Distribution:** Throughout British Isles, but more common in south. **Other habitats:** Meadows and marshes. **Adult active:** May to September, especially in thundery weather. **Food:** Mammalian blood. **Note:** One of four very similar species.

x2½

These bright iridescent green compound eyes are characteristic of the four species of *Chrysops* which are sometimes called deer flies. As in the horse-flies, it is only the female that bites animals to feed on blood.

Scorpionflies

Scorpionflies (order Mecoptera) get their name from the way in which the tip of the male's abdomen is swollen and turned up — just like the tail of a scorpion, although these insects are quite harmless. They use their jaws, which are at the end of a broad, beak-like process, to nibble dead insects, ripe fruit, and many other soft materials. They inhabit shady places and their caterpillar-like larvae live in the soil. There are just three species of true scorpionfly in the British Isles, and one tiny, wingless relative known as the snow-flea because it comes out in the winter.

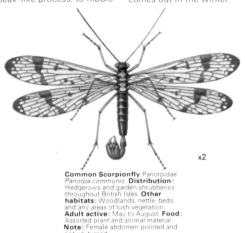

Common Scorpionfly Panorpidae *Panorpa communis*. **Distribution:** Hedgerows and garden shrubberies throughout British Isles. **Other habitats:** Woodlands, nettle-beds, and any areas of lush vegetation. **Adult active:** May to August. **Food:** Assorted plant and animal material. **Note:** Female abdomen pointed and not up-turned.

x2

Scorpionflies are on the wing from May to July, searching the woods for dead insects. These two *Panorpa communis* are feeding on a fly caught in a spider's web. The biting mouth parts (on the right) are at the end of a long snout. In the male the abdomen curves over the back like a scorpion, hence the common name.

on many different plant hosts, although oak is favoured, with as many as 35 species occurring on it in the British Isles, mainly in southern England. The life cycle of these insects is complex, involving two generations in the course of one life cycle; each produces a distinct type of gall (see box). Many bees and wasps are "solitary" in that the larvae are tended by the female alone without the help of workers (as happens in hive bees) and are not insects of dense woodland. They are however abundant along sunny woodland rides and glades. Nesting sites may include sand banks, dead and hollow trees and even the hollow dead stems of bramble. The rarest and also largest of the social wasps is the hornet *(Vespa crabro)*. This is very much a woodland species, usually nesting in hollow trees. It is now almost confined to the New Forest.

Ants are well-known for their social behaviour and once again the largest of the three dozen British species is confined to woodland, usually ones of ancient origin. This is the wood ant *(Formica rufa)* which occurs throughout the British Isles. The extensive nest of this ant is made up of large amounts of plant and animal debris, and forms a microhabitat for other invertebrates, ranging from springtails, which break down the organic matter, to predatory centipedes, spiders and beetles. Many staphylinid or rove beetles are found in ants' nests where they live as scavengers, even preying on the ants' eggs and larvae. Some produce sweet secretions and are therefore welcomed by the ants.

Beetles

The Coleoptera (beetles and weevils) play a most significant role in the woodland ecosystem as adults, larvae or both. Many are nocturnal predators associated with the leaf litter and dead wood habitats. Over a thousand staphylinid beetles alone occur in the British Isles, many in woodland. One of the most common species is the devil's coachhorse *(Staphylinus olens)*. Both larvae and adults are free-roving predators. When attacked the adult raises its abdomen over its back, while opening its jaws in a most aggressive gesture. Other staphylinid beetles are associated with the dung of woodland mammals, where they prey on fly larvae and other insects. Another major family is the Carabidae or ground beetles. Many of these, such as the common violet ground beetle *(Carabus violaceus)*, hunt at night among the ground vegetation and leaf litter for other insects and earthworms, while the large ground beetle *(Calosoma inquisitor)* hunts for caterpillars among the foliage of forest oaks. Research on the insects of coppice woodland has shown that in the early stages of coppice before the ground vegetation develops, carabid beetles such as *Agonum assimile* and *Loricera pilicornis* predominate, while in the middle stages staphylinids such as *Tachinus signatus* are most prominent, their numbers declining once more as the ground vegetation becomes suppressed. Among the more notable of the woodland beetles is the stag beetle *(Lucanus cervus)*, the huge larvae of which feed on rotting wood. This species is confined to southern England, especially the Home Counties, and has declined in numbers in recent years. The longhorn beetles (Cerambycidae) are also wood feeders in the larval stage. Other species which contribute significantly to the woodland ecosystem are the bark beetles and weevils which belong to the super-family Curculionoidea. The bark beetles include *Scolytus scolytus*, the carrier of the Dutch elm disease fungus. The fungus and the beetle have a symbiotic relationship in which the fungus breaks down resistant dead wood enabling the beetles to bury into it, while the fungus is transported to new trees by the beetle, where it causes live trees to die, resulting in the loss of millions of British elms.

Many weevils are foliage feeders while their larvae are root-feeding. *Strophosomus melanogrammus* for instance lays eggs on the shoots of oak on which the adult feeds, its larvae dropping to the ground on hatching. The twig-cutting

The hornet

The hornet is the largest of the British wasps. It is a social insect, living in colonies with up to about 1,000 workers under the control of a single queen. Like the other social wasps, such as the common wasp and the German wasp, the hornet makes its nest with wood pulp, which it chews to form a brittle kind of paper. The nest is generally situated in a hollow tree. Each colony lasts for only one year, and only new queens survive the winter, but a site may be used year after year by a succession of colonies. The nest itself may be re-built several times during the period of occupation.

x1

Hornet Vespidae *Vespa crabro* **Distribution:** Mainly the southern half of England and Wales. **Other habitats:** Occasionally in hedgerow trees and house roofs. **Adult active:** Spring (queen) to autumn. **Food:** Nectar and fruit juices, but young are fed on chewed insects and other animal matter.

Gall wasps and the oak-apple gall

Gall wasps are a specialised group of insects which parasitise plants, particularly oak on which 35 different species have been recorded, each producing its own characteristic gall. The well-known oak-apple gall arises from the abnormal cancer-like growth of an axial bud, induced when numerous eggs are laid into it by the female gall wasp (*Biorhiza pallida*). The wasp larvae feed entirely on the gall tissue. Development is completed within the gall and the adult wasps emerge from it in July. After mating, the wingless females do not remain on the tree, but enter the soil, laying their eggs and producing small brown galls on the oak roots. 16 months elapse before adult wasps emerge from them. This generation is "agamic" as it contains no males, and therefore sexual reproduction does not occur. Instead there are two types of wingless female; one is diploid with a double set of chromosomes, the other is haploid with only a single set. Each type produce galls, the diploid eggs developing into female wasps of the next generation, while the haploid eggs are male.

The tiny gall wasp *Biorhiza pallida* is responsible for many of the galls found on oak.

The large gall on pedunculate oak made by *Biorhiza* has an irregular, globular shape and turns brown with age.

Biting lice

Biting lice (order Mallophaga) are wingless parasitic insects that live mainly on birds. A few live on mammals. The insects are very flat and they have biting mouth-parts with which they chew skin, hair, and feathers. A few ingest blood from the wounds that they make in the skin. Like the sucking lice, biting lice generally keep to one particular area. The eggs are glued to the hairs or feathers of the host and the young lice are just like the adults apart from their size. There are about 500 British species.

x12

Columbicola claviformis
Philopteridae. **Distribution:** Anywhere that wood pigeons live. **Other habitats:** None. **Adult active:** All year. **Food:** Skin and feathers of wood pigeon.

---

weevil *(Rhynchites caeruleus)* lays its eggs in the twigs of many trees and shrubs. These are then severed by the female, the larvae feeding on the dying tissue. Similarly, *Attelabus nitens* rolls up, but does not sever, the leaves of shrubs such as hazel, on which the larvae will later feed. The pine weevil *(Hylobius abietus)* is a harmless inhabitant of native pine woods, but in plantations may be a serious pest, stripping the bark from young pine, larch and spruce.

Butterflies and moths

Although far fewer in number of species, the Lepidoptera form an obvious component of the woodland fauna. Not only are many of the adults large and showy insects, especially the butterflies, but their caterpillars are also largely foliage feeders, and are thus frequently seen. In common with other foliage feeders such as weevils and sawfly larvae, they have a tendency to exploit breaking leaf and flower buds in spring and early summer, when the foliage is physically softer. In oak the tannin content also increases towards autumn and few species are present at this time. Among the larvae of the larger moths found on oak are the buff tip *(Phalera bucephala)*, vapourer *(Orgyia antiqua)*, pale tussock *(Dasychira pudibunda)*, and oak hook-tip *(Drepana binaria)*. The rather remarkable lobster moth *(Stauropus fagi)* is more often associated with beech. One butterfly, the purple hairstreak *(Quercusia quercus)*, occurs exclusively on oak. This species flies in July and August and lays its eggs, which do not hatch until spring, in clusters in the terminal bud. Like many of the moths its caterpillars leave the tree to pupate amongst moss or leaf litter at its base. In contrast, the pale tussock is one of the few species whose caterpillars pupate on the trunks of oak, the pupa being protected by a cocoon of hairs. A smaller species which feeds on the bark of oak is the wasp-like yellow-legged clearwing *(Synanthedon vespiformis)*, while other species feed on the lichen on the trunks of oaks and other forest trees. The larvae of the large goat and leopard moths *(Cossus cossus* and *Zeuzera pyrina)*, the former now almost extinct in the British Isles, feed on the wood of living trees including oak. Other woodland trees,

shrubs and herbs maintain their own distinct fauna, although many species have several alternative food plants. Poplars and willow support around one hundred species of Lepidoptera, almost equalling the oak. Among them are some of the most attractive species, many of which have become common in suburban gardens and parks, where these trees are often planted. They include the poplar and eyed hawk moths *(Laothoe populi* and *Smerinthus ocellata)*, puss moth *(Cerura vinula)*, pebble prominent *(Notodonta ziczac)*, sallow *(Cirrhia icteritia)* and red underwing *(Catocala nupta)*. Wood-feeding species include the hornet and lunar hornet clearwings *(Sesia apiformis* and *Sphecia bembeciformis)*. Wet woodlands with areas of willow are therefore particularly rich in Lepidoptera. Where alder occurs the remarkable larva of the alder moth *(Apatele alni)*, with its black and yellow vertical bands and many black club-like hairs, may sometimes be found sitting prominently on the upper surface of the leaves. A particularly handsome moth of the Highland birch woods is the Kentish glory *(Endromis versicolora)*. This species, the males of which are

The wood ant

The wood ant *(Formica rufa)* is widely distributed but is most plentiful in woodlands in the south. The nests are composed of small sticks, pine needles and other woodland debris, and may reach 75 centimetres in height. Each may contain upwards of 100,000 workers, which will quickly rush to the defence of their nest if attacked, squirting their assailant with formic acid. These quite large ants can be seen in summer foraging for insect larvae from the forest floor to the tree tops. So effective are they as predators that the species has been encouraged in European forests to control woodland insect pests. As with other ants, winged males and females are produced at certain times of the year, and a marriage flight takes place. Some of the fertilised females may return to the parent nest where they lose their wings.

Adult ants *(Formica rufa)* with pupae, often mistakenly referred to as ants' eggs, in the nest. The real eggs are much smaller and are produced only by the queen ants.

Woodlice

Woodlice are land-living crustaceans, more closely related to crabs and shrimps than to insects. They are not fully adapted to life on land, however, and all have to keep to relatively moist places. They are active at night, when the humidity is high. Some species, known as slaters, live on the seashore, but most woodlice live among decaying vegetation. Many can be found in bark crevices. They feed primarily on decaying plant matter, but they will eat young seedlings and also scrape algae from tree trunks and other surfaces. Young woodlice are carried around in a pouch on the mother's body for a few weeks. There are about 30 native British species, and another dozen introduced species.

x2

Porcellio scaber Porcellionidae. **Distribution:** Throughout British Isles. **Other habitats:** Gardens; sand dunes; heathlands; grasslands. **Adult active:** All year except when very cold. **Food:** Assorted vegetable material.

A female ichneumon wasp *(Rhyssa persuasoria)* inserting her ovipositor into the bark of a tree to deposit an egg on to the grub of a horntail which lives below the bark.

Rhyssa persuasoria

Rhyssa persuasoria (order Hymenoptera) is a large ichneumon fly whose larvae feed on the grubs of the horntail. These grubs are well hidden in pine trunks, but the female *Rhyssa* finds them quite easily by running over the trunks and tapping the surface with her antennae. She is guided by the smell of a fungus that is always associated with the horntail tunnels. She then performs the seemingly impossible feat of driving her ovipositor—no thicker than a human hair—4cm or more into the wood. She finds the horntail grub with amazing accuracy and lays an egg on it. When the egg hatches, the *Rhyssa* larva starts chewing away at its host.

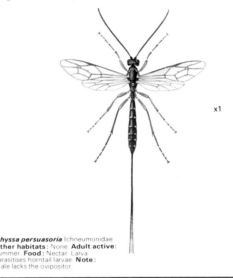

x1

Rhyssa persuasoria Ichneumonidae. **Other habitats:** None. **Adult active:** Summer. **Food:** Nectar. Larva parasitises horntail larvae. **Note:** Male lacks the ovipositor.

The horntail

The horntail (order Hymenoptera) is a sawfly in which the female's ovipositor is more like a drill than a saw. She uses it to drill into pine trunks and to lay her eggs there. The larva takes several years to mature in the trunk, and may not turn into an adult until the tree has been cut and used for building. The emerging adult causes great alarm when it appears in houses, for many people assume that the ovipositor is a powerful sting, but the insect is actually quite harmless.

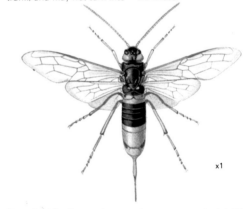

x1

Horntail Siricidae *Urocerus gigas.* **Distribution:** Throughout British Isles in pine woods. **Other habitats:** Timber yards. **Adult active:** Summer, but may emerge anytime in buildings. **Food:** Probably none. Larva eats pine wood. **Note:** Male lacks ovipositor and black on abdomen.

Woodland ants usually build their nests from leaf litter along rides, where they can catch the warmth of the sun. Some of these nests may be as much as 75 cm high and persist for many years.

day-flying, once occurred in south east England, but is now extinct there, although it was found recently in the Wyre Forest in the west Midlands. Although the pine hawk *(Hyloicus pinastri)* occurs in the British Isles, it is restricted to the south and does not occur in the native pine woods. It is nevertheless relatively common on naturalised pine in south east England.

It is clear that the caterpillars of many butterflies and moths are important members of the woodland fauna and provide vital food especially for birds. Many of the larvae have special adaptations to their environment, particularly camouflage patterns and colouring. The same applies to the adult insects, though they are adapted to a completely different role in the woodland system. They too are often camouflaged to blend in with the lichen-covered trees on which they rest, but the adults always have a different type of food from their larvae. Some butterflies do not feed at all; the rest drink nectar. The exception is the purple emperor butterfly *(Apatura iris)*, a rare and most interesting woodland insect (see box). Its larvae feed on sallow, and whereas many other Lepidoptera associated with willows are common in gardens, the purple emperor is restricted to extensive woodlands, or at least well-wooded countryside. Large oaks are essential because the adults gather around them to display and drink honey dew, produced by aphids. This species forms a member of the very attractive butterfly fauna of oak woods in southern Britain.

Many woods, especially overgrown deep-shaded coppices, are disappointing in that the only butterfly to be seen is usually the speckled wood *(Pararge aegeria)*. In more open woodlands however, where the rides are maintained, or best of all, where coppice is still cut in rotation, other species such as white admiral *(Limenitis camilla)* and the woodland fritillaries may also be present. All of these fritillaries, which include the silver-washed *(Argynnis paphia)*, high brown *(Argynnis adippe)* and pearl and small bordered *(Boloria selene and B. euphrosyne)*, are violet

The stag beetle

The stag beetle *(Lucanus cervus)* is the largest British beetle. It may reach five centimetres in length, but its size is very variable. The beetle gets its name from the large antler-like mouthparts or mandibles of the male. The female is slightly smaller, with much smaller mandibles, and was once thought to be a separate species. If disturbed the male will rear up, opening its antlers wide and appearing quite fearsome. This gesture is largely bluff as the muscles of the giant mandibles are not strong enough to exert much force. Apart from this defensive show, the mandibles are used to hold the female during mating. In contrast, the small mandibles of the female are much more practical and can give an unwary assailant a much stronger nip. The mouthparts are not in fact designed for chewing; instead the beetles appear to feed on plant secretions which they gather with their flexible labium. The fat, white larvae eat dead wood and may be found in rotting tree stumps. They reach maturity in three years; the adults emerging in May or June, but only living for a few weeks. The species was once quite common in southern England and could even be found in the London suburbs. It used to rest on pavements or fences during the day, while at night it was sometimes attracted to light. It has unfortunately become much rarer in recent years, but still occurs in well-wooded districts of south east England.

The larva of the stag beetle lives in rotting wood. This species has become much less common, perhaps partly because dead wood is tidied away in many woodlands.

The adult male stag beetle *(Lucanus cervus)* has prominent jaws. It is the largest of the British beetles. The female is smaller and lacks the large "antlers".

feeders as larvae, although the silver-washed has the distinction of laying its eggs high up on the trunk of an oak tree, to which the larvae return to pupate. The white admiral is a honeysuckle feeder, in common with the day-flying broad-bordered bee hawk moth *(Hemaris fuciformis)*. Sadly many of these species, particularly the fritillaries, have declined markedly in recent years, even in south east England. Three species which have always been restricted in their distribution are the heath fritillary *(Mellicta athalia)*, wood white *(Leptidea sinapis)* and large tortoiseshell *(Nymphalis polychloros)*. The heath fritillary, which feeds on cow-wheat, appears especially dependent on the early stages of the coppice cycle, a feature which it shares with the small and pearl bordered fritillaries. Like them it has declined in many former sites, as woodlands have become too shaded. It still maintains isolated populations in Kent and the West Country. In contrast, the wood white prefers deep shaded rides, where its food plants, the woodland vetches, occur. It too maintains isolated populations—in central southern England, the Midlands and the West Country. The large tortoiseshell has recently undergone a mysterious decline and may now be extinct in the British Isles. It is an elm feeder, as is the white-lettered hairstreak *(Strymonidia w-album)*, and the virtual loss of this tree may inhibit its return, although, unlike the hairstreak, it will also feed on willows, poplar, white beam and birch. In contrast the comma butterfly *(Polygonia c-album)* is now common throughout southern Britain,

Some woodland beetles

Everyone knows that the woodworm or furniture beetle breeds in dead wood, but this is just one of a great many beetles (order Coleoptera) whose grubs or larvae tunnel in living and dead tree trunks. Wood is obviously a very tough material, even when partly decayed, and the beetle grubs need their tough jaws to get through it. Most of the species are, in fact, much more common in wood which is partly decayed because such wood is more nutritious on account of the fungi in it. Even then, the beetle grubs have to eat a great deal of wood before they grow to maturity, and many of them take several years to grow up. They usually pupate just under the surface of the wood, leaving the adult beetle to make just a small hole to escape.

Rhagium inquisitor is one of the longhorn beetles. It spends its larval life in decaying logs and tree stumps, but never in healthy trees.

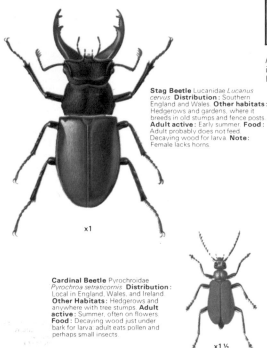

Stag Beetle Lucanidae *Lucanus cervus* **Distribution**: Southern England and Wales. **Other habitats**: Hedgerows and gardens, where it breeds in old stumps and fence posts **Adult active**: Early summer. **Food**: Adult probably does not feed. Decaying wood for larva. **Note**: Female lacks horns.

x1

Cardinal Beetle Pyrochroidae *Pyrochroa serraticornis* **Distribution**: Local in England, Wales, and Ireland. **Other Habitats**: Hedgerows and anywhere with tree stumps. **Adult active**: Summer, often on flowers. **Food**: Decaying wood just under bark for larva, adult eats pollen and perhaps small insects.

x1½

Rhagium bifasciatum Cerambycidae. **Distribution**: Most of British Isles. **Other habitats**: Hedgerows. **Adult active**: Summer **Food**: Decaying wood for larvae; adult eats pollen.

x1½

Wasp Beetle Cerambycidae *Clytus arietis* **Distribution**: Throughout British Isles. **Other habitats**: Hedgerows, gardens. **Adult active**: Spring and summer. **Food**: ? Pollen, but does not eat much as adult. Larva in tree trunks.

x1½

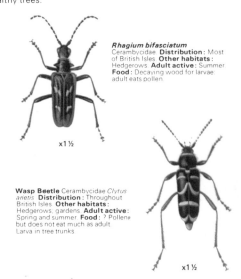

The larva of the lobster moth *(Stauropus fagi)* is a bizarre creature which lives on beech leaves. Unlike most woodland caterpillars it does not pupate in the soil, but overwinters in a silken cradle spun among the twigs. The adult moth is dull brown or grey and emerges in June or July.

A guide to some woodland moths

Large numbers of moths are present in woodland where their larvae are predominantly foliage feeders. Almost every plant within the wood will support at least one species, while well over two hundred species have been found on oak. Many of the larvae feed independently of each other, while others, like the large colourful larvae of the bufftip, live communally. Each small larva of the

tortrix moth rolls a leaf around itself for protection. Although small these larvae may be so numerous as to completely defoliate a tree. They then form a valuable food resource for birds, and even rooks and starlings will forage for them. The eggs of many of these foliage feeders are laid early in the year, or even in the previous autumn and they hatch in early summer. This enables the young larvae to exploit

the tender foliage of the developing leaves. Apart from leaves several species feed on the wood of the growing trees. One of the larger examples is the leopard moth, so called because of the white, black-spotted wings of the adult. Its larvae may take two years to reach maturity, within the tree. Most of the tree—and shrub—feeding species descend to the ground to pupate in the soil and leaf

litter at the foot of the trunks. Here most remain throughout the winter to emerge as adults in the spring.

The majority of moths are nocturnal so few species will be seen on the wing during the daytime. Most woodland moths have adopted camouflage to avoid predation by the numerous birds and their forewings resemble their daytime resting places. Many have

forewings similar to the trunks of trees: the peppered moth is pale to match the trunk of the birch while the merveille du jour is greenish to match lichen-covered bark. The lappet and angleshades resemble dead leaves whereas the green moths, such as the green silver lines and the emeralds, are inconspicuous amongst fresh foliage.

Moths which are active in winter include several

species like the winter moth and the dotted border, in which the male is winged but the female has vestigial wings to avoid being too conspicuous to predators whilst laying eggs on leafless winter twigs. These females can be found crawling on the twigs of hazel and other woodland shrubs during winter evenings.

The Black Arches Lymantriidae-*Lymantria monacha*. **Flight time:** August. Overwinters as ovum. **Foodplant:** Oak. **Distribution:** Throughout southern England; very local in Wales.

The Pine Hawk-moth Sphingidae-*Hyloicus pinastri*. **Flight time:** End June to August. Overwinters as pupa. **Foodplant:** Scots pine, Norway spruce. **Distribution:** Pine forests. Confined to Dorset, Hampshire, Surrey, Norfolk and Suffolk.

The Broad-bordered Bee Hawk-moth Sphingidae-*Hemaris fuciformis*. **Flight time:** May, June. Overwinters as pupa. **Foodplant:** Honeysuckle, bedstraw, snowberry. **Distribution:** Woodland. England and Wales, local and uncommon; apparently decreasing in numbers.

The Goat Moth Cossidae-*Cossus cossus*. **Flight time:** June to August. Overwinters as larva. **Foodplant:** In the trunks of elm, ash, birch and willow; internally, in colonies; feeding for three or four years. **Distribution:** Very local throughout much of Britain; now very rare.

The Swallow Prominent Notodontidae-*Pheosia tremula*. **Flight time:** May, June, August in southern Britain. Overwinters as pupa. **Foodplant:** Poplar, aspen, willow. **Distribution:** Widespread and common throughout the British Isles except Orkney and Shetland.

The Lappet Lasiocampidae-*Gastropacha quercifolia*. **Flight time:** June. Overwinters as larva. **Foodplant:** Hawthorn, blackthorn, sallow. **Distribution:** On chalk and limestone south of the Severn-Wash line; very local elsewhere in Wales and the Midlands.

The December Moth Lasiocampidae-*Poecilocampa populi*. **Flight time:** November, December. Overwinters as ovum. **Foodplant:** Oak, birch, poplar. **Distribution:** Widely distributed throughout Britain except Orkney and Shetland.

The Merveille du Jour Noctuidae-*Dichonia aprilina*. **Flight time:** September, October. Overwinters as ova. **Foodplant:** Oak. **Distribution:** Common throughout England and Wales, more local in Scotland, not reaching the extreme north.

The Light Emerald Geometridae-*Campaea margaritata*. **Flight time:** June, July. Overwinters as larva. **Foodplant:** Oak, birch, beech, elm. **Distribution:** Throughout the British Isles except Orkney and Shetland.

The Four-spotted Footman Arctiidae-*Lithosia quadra*. **Flight time:** August, September. Overwinters as larva. **Foodplant:** Lichens. **Distribution:** Woodland in southern England, elsewhere as an immigrant. Has occurred as far north as Ross-shire. **Note:** Male grey, female white.

The Canary-shouldered Thorn Geometridae-*Ennomos alniaria*. **Flight time:** August to October. Overwinters as ova. **Foodplant:** Birch, alder. **Distribution:** Throughout much of Britain north to Morayshire.

The Poplar Kitten Notodontidae-*Furcula bifida*. **Flight time:** Late May to July. Overwinters as pupa. **Foodplant:** Poplar, aspen. **Distribution:** Widely distributed in England south of the Mersey-Humber line; Wales.

The Green Silver Lines Noctuidae-*Pseudoips fagana*. **Flight time:** June, July. Overwinters as pupa. **Foodplant:** Oak, birch, beech, hazel. **Distribution:** Common throughout much of England and Wales; local in south Scotland.

The Brimstone Moth Geometridae-*Opisthograptis luteolata*. **Flight time:** April to August; October in two broods. Overwinters as pupa (from first brood) and larva (from second brood). **Foodplant:** Hawthorn. **Distribution:** Common throughout the whole of Britain.

The Pine Beauty Noctuidae-*Panolis flammea*. **Flight time:** March to May. Overwinters as pupa. **Foodplant:** Pine. **Distribution:** In pine forests throughout Britain; sometimes a serious forest pest.

The Mottled Umber Geometridae-*Erannis defoliaria*. **Flight time:** October to December. Overwinters as ova. **Foodplant:** Birch, oak and other forest trees. The larva sometimes occurs in great numbers defoliating the trees on which it is feeding. **Distribution:** Abundant throughout Britain to south Scotland.

The Dark Crimson Underwing Noctuidae-*Catocala sponsa*. **Flight time:** July, August. Overwinters as ova. **Foodplant:** Oak. **Distribution:** More or less confined to the New Forest.

The Coxcomb Prominent Notodontidae-*Ptilodon capucina*. **Flight time:** May, June, August, in two broods. Overwinters as pupa. **Foodplant:** Birch, poplar, hazel, willow. **Distribution:** Throughout Britain except Orkney and Shetland.

The Pebble Hook-tip Drepanidae-*Drepana falcataria*. **Flight time:** May, August, in two broods. Overwinters as pupa. **Foodplant:** Birch, oak, sallow. **Distribution:** Widespread in England and Wales, more local in Scotland.

The Pale Prominent Notodontidae-*Pterostoma palpina*. **Flight time:** May and, in southern England, in August. Overwinters as pupa. **Foodplant:** Poplar, aspen, willow. **Distribution:** Common in southern England, local in the north and in Wales.

The Lobster Moth Notodontidae-*Stauropus fagi*. **Flight time:** May to July. Overwinters as pupa. **Foodplant:** Beech, oak, birch, hazel. **Distribution:** Widely distributed in southern England, north-west Wales.

The Green Longhorn Incurvariidae-*Adela reaumurella*. **Flight time:** May, June. Overwinters as larva. **Foodplant:** Leaf-litter. **Distribution:** Widespread throughout deciduous woodland. England and Wales; local in east-central Scotland. **Note:** Male with very long antennae.

x2

The Large Emerald Geometridae-*Geometra papilionaria*. **Flight time:** June, July. Overwinters as larva. **Foodplant:** Birch, hazel, beech. **Distribution:** Throughout Britain except northern Scotland.

although in the 1920s it was restricted to woodlands in the Wye Valley. We may therefore hope that natural fluctuations may bring back other species such as the large tortoiseshell. Two further woodland hairstreak butterflies are restricted to large blackthorn thickets, in glades or along the woodland edges, especially in the Midlands. These are the black and brown hairstreaks (*Strymonidia pruni* and *Thecla betulae*). Both are rare and elusive, although the brown hairstreak is widespread as far north as Cumbria. The black, on the other hand, has always been confined to woodlands in the Midlands, where the population appears fairly stable.

Many of the most attractive woodland butterflies are active in July, when most of the true woodland herbs have finished flowering. The flora of open rides is therefore important to them and the flowers of bramble and the tall marsh thistle *Cirsium palustre* are favoured by the adults. Here they are joined by freshly emerged brimstones (*Gonepteryx rhamni*) and peacocks (*Inachis io*). At this time the woodland rides abound with other flying insects including predators such as dragonflies. These breed away from woodland but seek out the rides for their rich food resource of other insects. Like the brimstone and peacock, dragonflies can be seen well into the autumn, but the butterflies will outlive them by many months. Before winter arrives they will hibernate, to reappear in the first warm days of spring, adding yet another dimension to the visual attraction of the woodland scene.

The handsome, spiny caterpillar of the silver-washed fritillary, like those of most of its near relatives, feeds on violet leaves in woodland clearings.

A guide to some woodland butterflies

Along with wild flowers and birds, butterflies form the most spectacular members of the woodland community. Unfortunately many of the larger more colourful species are confined to the southern half of the British Isles and even here most are rather rare. The king of the woodland butterfly fauna is the purple emperor, which along with our only other purple butterfly, the small purple hairstreak, is found among the upper branches of the oaks. The other forest butterflies are more often found resting on bramble or other flowers along the edges of sunny rides. These include the large silver-washed and high brown fritillaries and the white admiral. The black white-barred wings of this butterfly give it perfect camouflage amongst the dappled shade of the wood. Although much more brightly marked with tawny-brown and black, the outlines of the fritillaries are similarly broken up, making them difficult to follow as they fly gracefully among the overhanging branches of a ride.

The Purple Emperor Nymphalidae-*Apatura iris*. **Flight time**: July, August. Overwinters as larva. **Foodplant**: Goat willow. **Distribution**: Forest clearings. Central southern England.

The White Admiral Nymphalidae-*Ladoga camilla*. **Flight time**: June to August. Overwinters as larva. **Foodplant**: Honeysuckle. **Distribution**: Woodland. England; south of the Severn Humber line.

The Brimstone Pieridae-*Gonepteryx rhamni*. **Flight time**: August to Oct and, after hibernation, March to June. Overwinters as imago. **Foodplant**: Buckthorn, alder buckthorn. **Distribution**: Woodland, hedgerows etc. England and Wales.

The Chequered Skipper Hesperiidae-*Carterocephalus palaemon*. **Flight time**: May, June. Overwinters as larva. **Foodplant**: False brome grass. **Distribution**: Scotland (Inverness-shire, highlands of; Argyll).

The Wood White Pieridae-*Leptidea sinapis*. **Flight time**: May, June, July, August usually in two broods. Overwinters as pupa. **Foodplant**: Tuberous pea and other vetches. **Distribution**: Woodland, cliffs. England; south, south-west and midlands; Wales; south-east.

The Heath Fritillary Nymphalidae-*Mellicta athalia*. **Flight time**: June, July. Overwinters as larva. **Foodplant**: Plantains, cow-wheat. **Distribution**: Coppiced woodland clearings. Very local; Kent, Devon, Cornwall.

The Large Tortoiseshell Nymphalidae-*Nymphalis polychloros*. **Flight time**: July to October and, after hibernation, March to May. Overwinters as adult. **Foodplant**: Elm, also sometimes poplar, aspen, sallow etc. **Distribution**: Woodland edges. Southern Britain.

The High Brown Fritillary Nymphalidae-*Argynnis adippe*. **Flight time**: June to August. Overwinters as ovum. **Foodplant**: Dog violet. **Distribution**: Woodland. Southern England, Lake District; Wales.

The Pearl-bordered Fritillary Nymphalidae-*Boloria euphrosyne*. **Flight time**: May, June. Overwinters as larva. **Foodplant**: Dog violet. **Distribution**: Woodland. South, west and north-west England; Wales; central Scotland.

The Speckled Wood Satyridae-*Pararge aegeria*. **Flight time**: Two broods-April-May; July-September. Overwinters as pupa. **Foodplant**: Grasses such as common couch-grass and cock's-foot. **Distribution**: Woodland, hedgerows etc. England and Wales, as far north as the Mersey; Scotland south-west Highlands.

The Small Pearl-bordered Fritillary Nymphalidae-*Boloria selene*. **Flight time**: June, July. Overwinters as larva. **Foodplant**: Dog violet. **Distribution**: Woodland. South, west and north-west England; Wales; Scotland.

The Silver-washed Fritillary Nymphalidae-*Argynnis paphia*. **Flight time**: June to August. Overwinters as larva. **Foodplant**: Dog violet. **Distribution**: Woodland rides; hedgerows. South and west England; Wales.

♂

♀

The White-Letter Hairstreak. Lycaenidae-*Strymonidia w-album*. **Flight time**: July, August. Overwinters as ovum. **Foodplant**: Wych elm, common elm. **Distribution**: Woodland, wooded lanes. England as far north as the Mersey-Humber line; Wales.

The Black Hairstreak Lycaenidae-*Strymonidia pruni*. **Flight time**: June, July. Overwinters as ovum. **Foodplant**: Blackthorn. **Distribution**: Woodland with old blackthorn thickets. Central England-Leicestershire, Northamptonshire, Huntingdon (Cambridgeshire).

The Purple Hairstreak Lycaenidae-*Quercusia quercus*. **Flight time**: July, August. Overwinters as ovum. **Foodplant**: Oak. **Distribution**: Oak woodland. England; Wales; western Scotland south of the Great Glen.

The Brown Hairstreak Lycaenidae-*Thecla betulae*. **Flight time**: August to October. Overwinters as ovum. **Foodplant**: Blackthorn. **Distribution**: Woodland and hedgerows. Southern and midland England; west Wales.

Woodland Birds

Woodland has the potential to provide one of the richest habitats for birds in the British Isles, with perhaps seven pairs of nesting birds per hectare, compared with three or less per hectare on farmland. But while some woods abound with birds throughout much of the year, many are strangely silent even in the early summer, when elsewhere the dawn chorus is at its height. To provide a favourable habitat for birds a woodland must contain an abundant food source, nesting sites, cover from predators and freedom from general disturbance. Although there are certain exceptions, the species content of different types of woodland is remarkably constant. Birds such as blackbird, robin, wren, blue tit, great tit, chaffinch and in summer, willow warbler and chiffchaff are usually present, and often form 70 per cent of the total bird population whether the wood is of pedunculate or sessile oak, ash, beech, alder carr, Scots pine or even commercial conifers. The species of tree does however affect the density of the bird population and the presence of oak and other species which support large insect populations makes a considerable difference. Some birds are so specialised in their food requirements that they are restricted to certain tree species. The crossbill, which has a bill adapted for extracting seed from cones, is for this reason restricted to conifer woods, while siskin and redpoll have a preference for the catkins and fruit of birch and alder. Other differences can be observed in the bird populations of certain woodland types. The western sessile oak woods of England, Wales and Scotland, for instance, contain a poorer avifauna than pedunculate oak woods in lowland Britain. This does not mean that sessile oak itself is less suitable, but rather that certain aspects of these woods are less favourable. The climate is generally more severe, for example, and their acid soils lead to an impoverished ground flora. Both factors lead to a relative paucity of the insect life which provides the basic food resource of many birds in lowland oak woods. The age of the trees is also important. Young coppice and scrub support many insectivorous warblers, whereas woodpeckers and redstarts need old trees. Mixed-age woods therefore support the greatest diversity.

The population is also affected by the structure of the woods, which in Britain have developed or are developing largely through management by man. The most critical aspect is the availability of nest sites. Woodland birds may be roughly divided into ground, shrub layer or thicket, canopy and hole nesters. Linked with nesting is the requirement for suitable areas for display, and for many species song posts for the males to proclaim their territory. Obviously a woodland providing all of these will have a higher population than one where certain aspects are lacking. The western sessile oak woods are at a disadvantage in this respect also, as they have traditionally been managed as pure coppices, most of which have long been neglected and derelict. No young shrub layer is present and there is often very little ground cover because of grazing. Therefore thicket nesting species such as blackcap or even blackbird are much less abundant. Because the oak stems are largely of coppice origin, they are of relatively small diameter and therefore do not provide good sites for larger hole nesting birds such as woodpeckers. Nevertheless these woods do support populations of smaller hole nesting birds such as pied flycatcher and redstart, two species which are characteristic of this woodland type.

The size of the woodland is a further factor which determines the population of birds within it. Certain species appear to have a size threshold and only occur in large woodlands. Many woodland species, ranging from tawny owl to nuthatch, reach their optimum density in woodland of 100 hectares or more, while some species are almost unknown as breeding species in

smaller woodlands. Therefore, however many small copses are planted to replace one large woodland, many species will be absent. An ideal wood for birds is therefore one of at least 100 hectares. It should include mature oak trees with some ancient trees and dead wood, providing nest sites for both canopy and hole nesting species. Beneath the oaks the coppice should be cut in rotation to provide a range of habitats suitable for the ground and thicket species, along with the rich insect fauna to support them. The edges of the rides and glades will also support these birds. Additional habitats such as small ponds would also be beneficial. Such a woodland is nowadays all too rare outside of nature reserves, and even the majority of our National Nature reserves contain less than 100 hectares of woodland each.

Not all woodland nesting birds rely on the food resources within the wood. In extreme cases, such as rooks and herons, food may never be taken within the boundaries of the wood, while many other larger canopy nesting predators such as buzzard and the rare red kite may also hunt largely outside the wood.

Seasonal changes

The high degree of mobility of birds means that the species content of the woods changes markedly throughout the year. In the spring the arrival of the summer visitors, particularly the *Sylvia* warblers, is heralded by the increasing strength of the dawn chorus. These species commence breeding when the insect food resource, itself geared to take advantage of the tender green foliage, is at its height. In late summer and winter the population structure changes once more. From July onwards the woodland tits form large groups which spend the winter foraging together in the canopy for hibernating insects. These large parties may range widely outside the woodland, and be joined by other species such as tree creeper, goldcrest and more rarely nuthatch. Some of the over-wintering species try to make the most of the available food by storing it; tits may store

berries, for example, while nuthatches store acorns and hazel nuts. Jays are well known for their habit of hiding acorns in the ground, many of which are forgotten and thus contribute to the natural regeneration of the oak woods. During the autumn the indigenous bird population is joined by many visitors from northern Europe, including chaffinches, tits, blackbirds, thrushes and wood pigeons, along with species only present in winter, at least in the south. These include redwing, fieldfare and brambling. Few birds remain in woodland throughout the winter and the more exposed northern sessile oak and native Scots pine woods may become almost devoid of bird life at this time. During the winter, many insectivorous species migrate south to places where more food may be found, the foliage-feeding warblers especially. However some small insectivorous species, such as the wren and tree creeper, manage to survive by searching bark crevices for spiders and hibernating insects.

The woodland bird population may change dramatically over a short period. The hard winter of 1962/63, for instance, brought about a dramatic decline in the population of many over-wintering species, the wren being among the most severely affected. In most cases recovery from such short-term adverse conditions is relatively rapid. A dramatic decline has also occurred recently in several species of summer visitors. The whitethroat has been among the worst affected, in the spring of 1969 a virtual collapse of the population occurred, with very few birds returning to their breeding sites in this country. Here climatic extremes were also involved, in this case the continuing climatic reversal in the southern Sahara, which seems to be preventing this species from migrating across the desert successfully.

Persecution

Other fluctuations have been due to direct action of human agencies, both deliberate and accidental. The brunt of this has been borne by the predatory birds. The increasing emphasis on game preservation during the nineteenth century of pheasants in the lowlands and grouse in the uplands, led to the extinction of tree-nesting avian predators in many areas. The extent of this is shown by the figures for one Scottish estate for the three years up to 1840, when 462 kestrels, 285 buzzards, 275 kites, 63 goshawks, 35 long-eared owls, 18 ospreys and three honey buzzards were killed. Of these, goshawks and osprey became extinct as breeding birds and remained so until recent years, with even now only precariously small populations being maintained. The red kite has never returned to Scotland, and today is found only in mid-Wales. All of these species are now given special protection under the Protection of Birds Acts 1954 and 1967. Illegal control is still regrettably practised by some estates and the absence of buzzards from southern England has been blamed on continuing persecution. The recovery of these species in many areas was seriously affected by the use of toxic chemicals, particularly chlorinated hydrocarbons used as insecticides on seed dressing. These persistent chemicals accumulated in the bodies of the predatory birds from the bodies of smaller birds taken as prey. The sparrowhawk was particularly badly affected, particularly in areas of intensive agriculture in the south and east. The use of these chemicals is nowadays more restricted and the population of these birds is slowly recovering. Today the commonest of the larger woodland raptors are the buzzard and sparrowhawk. Both have a western distribution, although the sparrowhawk is becoming increasingly common in the woodlands of south and east England. Both species are tree nesters, producing bulky structures, often using an old crow's nest as a base. The sparrowhawk frequently hunts within the woods, flying swiftly through the trees to snatch an unsuspecting small bird, but the wider-ranging buzzard takes larger prey such as rabbits. This bird is most plentiful in the western sessile oak woods; in central Wales it occurs there with the rare red kite.

Canopy nesters

The grey heron is a canopy nester in woodland throughout the British Isles. Grey herons nest colonially, often some distance from the water where their food is available. The average colony in England consists of about twenty nests, although in Scotland and Ireland the trend seems to be for a larger number of smaller colonies. The largest British heronry, of about 150 pairs, is at Northwood Hill in north Kent, where the adults find abundant food in the dykes of the nearby Thames-side marshes. The heron starts nesting early and lays its eggs in February. This is about a month earlier than the other colonial, but much commoner, tree-top nester, the rook. A recent survey has shown a decline in the rook population throughout England, Scotland and Wales of about 40 per cent since the mid 1940s, with the greatest decrease, of over 60 per cent, in Wales. Rookery size has also decreased in the same period, with large colonies becoming fragmented, although the average has probably always been below 25 nests. Because, like the heron, rooks nest in isolated clumps of trees and shelterbelts as well as woodland proper, they have been affected by the loss of elms through Dutch elm disease. However, the recent succession of cold springs may have played a more significant element in the rook's decline. Like most of the other corvids which nest in woodland, the rook basically forages for food outside the woodland, but insects such as the oak-feeding larvae of the small moth *Tortrix viridana* may also be taken when plentiful. Other woodland corvids are the carrion crow (replaced in north west Scotland and Ireland by the closely related hooded crow), the magpie, jay and jackdaw. In the north and west ravens may also nest in woodland trees.

The great tit *(Parus major)* is a woodland bird which nests in hollow trees and the stumps of dead branches. It is an important predator of insect larvae and feeds on a wide range of woodland food, including acorns. It is territorial in the breeding season and its loud "teacher, teacher, teacher" call is a characteristic sound.

The green woodpecker *(Picus viridis)* typically nests in trees but feeds a lot on the ground, where it particularly searches for ants. It is more likely to be found along woodland rides and edges rather than in the centre of dense forest. The parents take food back to the young for about three weeks before they are able to fly and fend for themselves.

The corvid which spends most time in woodland, however, is the jay, nesting in various sites from thick undergrowth to the high branches of conifers, 20 metres above the ground. Food consists of young birds and eggs as well as fruits such as acorns.

The three species of pigeon most often associated with woodland are the wood pigeon, stock dove and turtle dove. Only the wood pigeon is found throughout the country and as it feeds extensively on farm crops, it now ranks as the worst avian pest in the British Isles. Wood pigeons breed during any part of the year, building their nests in a wide variety of locations within the wood. They are among the few birds to nest in dark groves of conifers, where the quiet of the woodland may be broken by the clatter of their wings as they are disturbed from their nests or roosting sites. Although it takes similar food, the stock dove is much less destructive. Since the turn of the century this species has extended its range considerably into both Ireland and Scotland, but did not reach south west Ireland until 1951 and has yet to colonise the far north and west of Scotland. In the late sixties a decline took place in lowland Britain, possibly due to use of toxic chemicals, but this has now been largely reversed. The third woodland dove, the turtle dove, is a summer visitor which feeds on various weeds, especially the common fumitory, and nests in thickets and young plantations. Its range only just extends into southern Scotland and the east coast of Ireland. The song of these birds, a purring repetition of its name—tu-r-r, tu-r-r—is a pleasant herald of the arrival of summer. A fourth species, the collared dove, has spread throughout the British Isles since 1955 and now also nests in woodland occasionally, although it is more usually associated with human habitation, particularly farm buildings where grain is stored.

The tawny owl is present in woodland throughout Britain, though absent from Ireland. It is most frequently a hole nester, although old nests of crows or even wood pigeons may be used. While the tawny owl is found in both broad-leaved and conifer woodland, the scarcer long-eared owl is especially associated with conifer woodlands, including plantations. This may be because it cannot compete with the tawny owl in broad-leaved woodland, since in Ireland it is found in both types of woodland. It does not nest in holes, but always makes use of the old nests of other species. Both owls hunt at night for small mammals and birds.

The woodcock is a ground nesting woodland bird. Although quite large, these birds are extremely inconspicuous, sitting tight among cover of bracken or bramble. At dawn and in the evening the breeding males take to the air and repeatedly follow a well-marked flight path along a ride or over a plantation. As they do so, they utter a deep repeated croaking call which changes at intervals to a shrill screech. This display flight is known as roding. Four young are usually produced, and are led away from the nest after hatching. Although for many years regarded as only a folk tale, it has now been established that the adults really can fly from danger carrying their chicks between their legs.

Woodpeckers and hole nesters

The woodpeckers spend most of their lives in trees, where they search for food and excavate their nest holes. The most widespread is the greater spotted, but curiously, like the other two species, it has never bred in the Isle of Man or in Ireland. The similar, but smaller lesser spotted woodpecker is confined to woodlands in the southern half of England and Wales. The attractive green woodpecker or yaffle (see box) is absent from the highlands but is otherwise quite common in open woodland, particularly where ants, its favourite source of food, are present.

The great spotted woodpecker

The great spotted woodpecker is a characteristic woodland bird, but since the 1950s seems to have widened its range to include parks and gardens. It is absent from Ireland and the Isle of Man, and scarce in parts of eastern England where trees are sparse, but is apparently spreading in Scotland, where it had become extinct early in the nineteenth century.

It is a brightly marked black and white bird, with red under the tail in both sexes, a red nape in the male and red forehead in the young. Like other woodpeckers it has sharp hooked claws on its toes, two of which point forwards and two backwards. These grip tree bark firmly, further support being provided by jamming the stiff pointed tail feathers against the tree.

It feeds mainly on woodland invertebrates, particularly wood-boring insect larvae. The woodpecker's tongue is sticky and also barbed so that it can pierce the grubs in their burrows and withdraw them to be eaten. The bird also breaks open nuts and pine cones for food and has earned a reputation for breaking into nest boxes to eat the chicks of other birds.

Great spotted woodpeckers have a loud "pew . . . pew" call, which rings through the woods but they also have a non-verbal means of communication: "drumming" with rapid blows of the beak on a reverberating branch to signal territory ownership.

The great spotted woodpecker is a very typical woodland bird. It excavates a nest hole in the soft wood of decaying trees and feeds extensively on wood-boring insects.

Woodpeckers fly straight and fast with rapid wing beats, avoiding the confined spaces of younger trees at the shrub stage and preferring mature woodland with its nesting sites and food sources. This male bird is carrying away faeces from the nestlings to avoid the nesthole becoming fouled. Both parents care for the young for about three weeks before they fly.

Old woodpecker holes may be used by other woodland birds, ranging from starlings to tits and flycatchers. Starlings use woodland chiefly for nesting and roosting. In winter many thousands of birds use traditional roosts and the accumulation of droppings can considerably modify the ground flora, leading to an abundance of stinging nettles. Other hole nesters are true woodland dwellers, at least in summer. These include the blue, great and coal tits, which are found throughout the British Isles, although the coal tit appears to have a preference for conifer woodland. Like the much rarer crested tit, its beak length and shape is adapted to finding food in bunches of pine needles. The crested tit is also a hole nesting species which occurs typically in open forests of native Scots pine and does not breed outside Scotland. Two further hole nesting tits, the marsh and willow, are both very rare in Scotland and absent from Ireland. While the willow tit uses an existing hole, usually in the stump of a willow or alder, the marsh tit excavates its own hole in very soft or decayed wood. Both species are very similar in appearance and can best be distinguished by their song.

The long-tailed tit is not closely related to the other tits, although often found with them. One of its behavioural differences is that it builds a delicate spherical nest of moss, hair and lichen in thickets and hedgerows. Two other non hole nesting species which join the mixed parties of tits foraging in the woods from July onwards are the tree creeper and goldcrest, both of which occur throughout the British

Isles. The tree creeper is usually associated with broad-leaved woodland, where it nests behind loose bark or other suitable cover. The goldcrest, which is the smallest British bird, usually nests in conifers, with the nest affixed to the lower sides of a branch. It has benefited from the planting of conifer plantations where it may be among the commonest birds present. The closely related firecrest is known to have bred in the British Isles only since about 1962. It is confined to southern England, occurring in a few mixed plantations and other woods where holly and yew are present in the understorey.

Although the nuthatch may accompany these mixed flocks it is rarely seen far from woodland. This attractive bird is confined to England and Wales. It is a hole nester and characteristically reduces the size of its hole with layers of mud. Its chief food is small wood-living insects, although fruits are also taken, especially hazel nuts. These are wedged in a crevice and chiselled until the shell is broken. Among the other hole nesting birds is the pied flycatcher. Like the more widespread spotted flycatcher, this distinctive bird is only a summer visitor. It is restricted to western and northern England, with a scattered distribution in Scotland; it is absent from both Ireland and southern and eastern England. It occurs chiefly in sessile oak woods; in some of these woods numbers have been increased through the use of nest boxes, since nest sites may be a limiting factor under natural circumstances. Unlike the spotted flycatcher, which has declined somewhat in

recent years, the pied flycatcher has generally slowly increased its range northwards since the 1950s.

Songbirds

Two summer migrants which belong to the thrush family are the redstart and the nightingale. The attractively marked redstart frequently occurs with the pied flycatcher in the western sessile oak woods where it may compete with it for nesting sites. Unlike the pied flycatcher it nests in Ireland, although only rarely. In the mid 1960s it was a relatively common summer visitor to woodlands throughout the British Isles, but during the 1970s a dramatic decline has occurred. This may be due, as with the whitethroat, to climatic changes on its migration route in West Africa. In contrast the nightingale, which is restricted to the south east, is still plentiful. Its distribution just overlaps that of the pied flycatcher in the Wye Valley. It is a thicket nester and is renowned for the quality of the male's song. Singing takes place throughout the day, but is more noticeable at night when other species are silent. The birds which make the most significant contribution to the woodland birdsong when they return to breed in the early summer are the *Sylvia* warblers: blackcap, garden warbler and whitethroat. To these should be added the leaf warblers: the willow warbler, chiffchaff and wood warbler, which belong to a different but closely related genus, *Phylloscopus*. All have distinctive and attractive songs which fill the woods where the males are

A guide to some woodland birds

Certain ubiquitous species are likely to be found in woodland and many other habitats, especially various finches and redpolls which often form large flocks in winter and live in the forest canopy. Other species (like the waxwing) will only be seen in the winter and are just as likely to turn up in gardens and hedgerows.

Various tit species are also likely to be seen in winter when they form large mixed-species flocks, conspicuous in the leafless canopy. Many of these birds will also be there in summer in smaller numbers but they are more difficult to see. Warblers and flycatchers will only be seen in the summer and some (like the willow warbler,

wood warbler and chiffchaff) are so alike in appearance that they are best distinguished by their songs. Certain species, notably the capercaillie, crested tit and crossbill are particularly characteristic of coniferous woodlands and are unlikely to be seen anywhere else. The first two will only be seen in Scotland; a few

crossbills breed in the south, though most are winter visitors there. Nightingales are shrub and thicket dwellers (as is the blackbird when it is living in woodland) and may occur in scrubland habitats. Woodcocks and pheasants are birds of the forest floor.

Tawny Owl Strigidae *Strix aluco* **Distribution**: Resident in Great Britain. **Other habitats**: Woods, city parks. **Notes**: Size: 38cm. Eyes black. Mainly nocturnal. In flight large head and broad rounded wings are prominent. Voice is a familiar hooting song and a loud "kee-wick".

Turtle Dove Columbidae *Streptopelia turtur* **Distribution**: Summer visitor and passage migrant. **Other habitats**: Woodlands, copses, large gardens and thick hedgerows. **Notes**: Size: 27cm. Deeply rounded tail, black edged with white. Black and white patch on side of neck. Flicking wing-beats in flight. Voice is a purring "roor-rrr".

Woodpigeon Columbidae *Columba palumbus* **Distribution**: Resident in Great Britain and Ireland. **Other habitats**: Agricultural areas with trees. **Notes**: Size: 41cm. White neck patch with glossy green border. "Explodes" noisily from trees when alarmed. Broad white wing-band. Voice is a "coo-coo-coo".

Long-eared Owl Strigidae *Asio otus* **Distribution**: Resident in Great Britain and Ireland. **Other habitats**: Woodland, especially conifers. **Notes**: Size: 45cm. Eyes orange. Mainly nocturnal. In flight, wings and tail look longer than Tawny's. Elongated "ear" tufts. Voice is a low "oo-oo-oo".

Cuckoo Cuculidae *Cuculus canorus* **Distribution**: Summer visitor in Great Britain and Ireland. **Other habitats**: Woodland and moorland. **Notes**: Size: 33cm. Flight is usually low and hurried and terminating in a long glide. Looks not unlike small hawk or falcon. Wings pointed. Voice is a mellow "cuc-coo".

Sparrow Hawk Accipitridae *Accipiter nisus* **Distribution**: Scotland, western England, Wales and Ireland. Local in eastern England. **Other habitats**: Well wooded, cultivated country. **Notes**: Size: 28–38cm (female larger). Immatures resemble female. Wings rounded unlike other falcons.

Jay Corvidae *Garrulus glandarius* **Distribution**: Resident in Great Britain and Ireland, except northern Scotland. **Other habitats**: Woodland. **Notes**: Size: 34cm. Blue and white wing patches. White rump. Eyes pale blue. Flight is rather jerky with rounded wings. Often in small noisy parties. Voice is a harsh "skraaak".

setting up territories. All of the woodland *Sylvia* warblers are most abundant in the southern half of the British Isles, becoming much rarer in Scotland and in Ireland. All are thicket nesters, normally found in bushes and bramble clumps, and are most abundant along rides or woodland edges and in the early thicket stage of the coppice cycle. The nightingale is an associated species in the south east of England. The chiffchaff is also a thicket nester; although common in Ireland it has a restricted distribution in the highlands of Scotland. The most widespread of the warblers, the willow warbler, is a ground nester, usually building its nest among the vegetation of ditch sides or hedgebanks. This may explain why it is relatively more abundant than the others in the western sessile oak woods, where little thicket cover is present. The wood warbler is also a ground nester particularly associated with the sessile oak woods in both north Britain and the Weald, but almost absent from Ireland. Although a ground nester, the adult spends much of its time foraging in the tree tops.

The three resident species of thrush, mistle thrush, song thrush and blackbird, are among our commonest garden and parkland birds, but woodland is almost certainly their natural habitat. All three may take a wide variety of animal and plant food, berries being particularly favoured. Of the three, the blackbird is most dependent on thicket cover for nesting while the song thrush may occur in upland woods with relatively little cover. The mistle thrush often

The heron is one of several species of birds which nest in woodland but feed elsewhere. They are only normally found in woodlands during the breeding season. where they build large nests out of dead wood and form colonies of ten or more pairs. The same nesting sites are used for many years.

Green Woodpecker Picidae *Picus viridis.* **Distribution**: Resident in England and Wales. **Other habitats**: Deciduous woodlands. **Notes**: Size: 32cm. Flight alternately rises with a few wing-beats and dips with wings closed. Hops heavily in upright position. Voice is a loud, rapid "laughing" call. Seldom drums.

Woodcock Scolopacidae *Scolopax rusticola.* **Distribution**: Resident in Great Britain and Ireland. **Other habitats**: Damp woodlands. **Notes**: Size: 34cm. Mainly crepuscular. Distinguished from Snipe by thicker bill and more rounded wings. Flight noisy and dodging, except during slow display flight above trees. Voice is a "si-wick".

Great Spotted Woodpecker Picidae *Dendrocopos major.* **Distribution**: Resident in Great Britain. **Other habitats**: Woodland. **Notes**: Size 23cm. Strikingly patterned black and white with red undertail coverts. Flight similar to Green. Voice is a loud "tchick". Drums rapidly on resonant dead branches.

Lesser Spotted Woodpecker Picidae *Dendrocopos minor.* **Distribution**: Resident in England and Wales. **Other habitats**: Woodland. **Notes**: Size: 17cm. Distinguished from Great Spotted by sparrow-size, closely barred back and wings and no red under tail coverts. Flutters among twigs in upper branches. Voice a shrill "pee-pee-pee". Drums.

Wryneck Picidae *Jynx torquilla.* **Distribution**: Summer visitor in south-east England. **Other habitats**: Woods, parklands, orchards and gardens. **Notes**: Size: 17cm. Looks more like a grey-brown passerine than a woodpecker. Feeds on ground hopping with raised tail. Crown feathers erectile. Voice is a shrill "quee-quee-quee".

Great Tit Paridae *Parus major.* **Distribution**: Resident in Great Britain and Ireland. **Other habitats**: Woodlands, gardens and hedgerows. **Notes**: Size: 14cm. Black cap. Black band down centre of yellow Underparts. Flight is undulating and of short duration. Voice variable. Main note is a loud, repeated "teacher, teacher".

Blue Tit Paridae *Parus caeruleus.* **Distribution**: Resident in Great Britain and Ireland, except Orkney and Shetland. **Other habitats**: Woodlands, gardens and hedgerows. **Notes**: Size: 12cm. Blue cap. Yellow underparts. Flight is weaker, more fluttering than Great Tit. Voice variable. Main note is a scolding "tsee-tsee-tsee".

Marsh Tit Paridae *Parus palustris.* **Distribution**: Resident in England and Wales. **Other habitats**: Deciduous woods, hedgerows. **Notes**: Size: 12cm. Glossy black cap and plain brown upperparts. Nests in existing holes in trees. Voice is a loud "pitcheew".

Coal Tit Paridae *Parus ater.* **Distribution**: Resident in Great Britain and Ireland, except Orkney and Shetland. **Other habitats**: Woodland, especially conifers. **Notes**: Size 12cm. Black cap with white nape patch. Double, white wing-bars. Flight is similar to Blue Tit. Voice is a piping "tsu-i" and a Goldcrest-like "tsee-tsee-tsee".

Crested Tit Paridae *Parus cristatus.* **Distribution**: Resident in eastern Highlands of Scotland. **Other habitats**: Coniferous woodlands, especially mature Scots Pine. **Notes**: Size: 12cm. Speckled black and white crest. Seeks food on tree trunks. Less sociable than other tits. Voice is a low purring "choor-r-r".

Willow Tit Paridae *Parus montanus.* **Distribution**: Resident in England and Wales. **Other habitats**: Woods, hedgerows but a preference for damp areas. **Notes**: Size: 12cm. Matt black cap. Distinguished from Marsh Tit by pale patch in secondary wing feathers and the harsh, nasal "dzee-dzee-dzee-dzee".

nests conspicuously on the branch of a tree, usually at a good height from the ground. Other common woodland birds, including wren, robin and dunnock, are also familiar visitors to the garden. The wren is at present extremely plentiful and has entirely recovered from the decline it suffered during the severe winter of 1962–63. Its domed nest is built amongst ivy or an upturned tree root. In winter large numbers may roost together in suitable holes, including garden nest boxes. Both robin and dunnock breed in suitable cover near to the ground. They form the most usual woodland hosts of the cuckoo, up to three per cent of their nests may be parasitised.

Woodland finches

A further common garden visitor, the chaffinch, is the most common of the woodland finches, with an average density of 37 nesting pairs per square kilometre of woodland. In some specially-favoured broad-leafed woodland, three times this density may be found. The finches include a number of specialist feeders. The hawfinch is a local breeding species and is absent altogether from most of Scotland and the whole of Ireland. Its exceptionally large strong beak is used to crack the seed of many fruits to feed on the kernels. It is a very shy bird, nesting high above the ground. In the south east, where it is most plentiful, hornbeam is favoured, the nests only becoming visible when the leaves fall in autumn. The siskin and redpoll feed on birch and alder and have both extended their breeding range

The long-tailed tit

Long-tailed tits can be found in any type of woodland and are present throughout the British Isles. Broad-leaved woodland where a good shrub layer is present and the thicket stage of conifer plantations are favoured. Alternatively the nest may be built high above the ground against the trunk of a tree. The nest must rank as among the most remarkable of any British bird. It is a domed structure, delicately constructed of moss, hair and cobwebs, completely covered by lichens, and lined with a bed of about 2,000 feathers. The eggs, usually about ten, are laid in late March; as many as twenty eggs have been recorded, but this is probably due to the nest being used by more than one pair of birds. When this happens the whole breeding party attend to the nest, and defend the territory. Although not closely related to other species of tit, large parties of long-tailed tits join with the other species from July onwards to forage through the woodland and surrounding countryside for insects. In winter the calls of these birds may be the only evidence of bird life in the otherwise silent woods. The presence of long-tailed tits among the party is given away by their high-pitched tinkling "tzee tzee tzee" calls.

The nest of the long-tailed tit (*Aegithalos caudatus*) is made of cobwebs, lichens and feathers, the collection of which requires several thousand journeys by each of the two parents.

A guide to some woodland birds (continued)

Goldcrest Regulidae *Regulus regulus*. **Distribution**: Resident everywhere except Shetland and Orkney. **Other habitats**: Coniferous and locally, deciduous woodland. **Notes**: Size: 9cm. Plump, finebilled, bright crown, double wingbar. Call: high, "zee-zee-zee-zee".

Firecrest Regulidae *Regulus ignicapillus*. **Distribution**: Very rare breeder in south, passage migrant elsewhere. **Other habitats**: Mixed woods and bushy areas. **Notes**: Size: 9 cm. Told from goldcrest by head pattern. Call: less high-pitched "zit".

Blackcap Sylviidae *Sylvia atricapilla*. **Distribution**: Summer visitor except for North. **Other habitats**: Wooded areas, large gardens and hedgerows. **Notes**: Size: 14cm. Call: scolding "tchack". Song is rich and tuneful. May overwinter.

Spotted Flycatcher Muscicapidae *Muscicapa striata*. **Distribution**: Summer visitor everywhere. **Other habitats**: Open woodland, gardens, parks. **Notes**: Size: 14cm. Call: robin-like "tzea". Song: few squeaky notes upright stance.

Pied Flycatcher Muscicapidae *Ficedula hypoleuca*. **Distribution**: Breeds western and northern Britain. Passage migrant on E. coast and Ireland. **Other habitats**: Woodland, often in valleys. **Notes**: Size: 13cm. Autumn male resembles female. Call: "wheet".

Garden Warbler Sylviidae *Sylvia borin*. **Distribution**: Summer visitor. Everywhere except north-west. **Other habitats**: Woods, bushy commons, heaths, gardens, parks. **Notes**: Size: 14cm. Call is harsh, song faster and more uniform than Blackcap.

Redstart Turdidae *Phoenicurus phoenicurus*. **Distribution**: Summer visitor to all areas; rare in Ireland. **Other habitats**: Breeds in deciduous woodland. **Notes**: Size: 14cm. Brief musical song with jangling finish. Call: liquid "looick".

Dunnock Prunellidae *Prunella modularis*. **Distribution**: Resident throughout British Isles. **Other habitats**: Hedgerow, bushy areas, scrub, and open woodland with undergrowth. **Notes**: Size: 14.5cm. Call: shrill "seep".

Willow Warbler Sylviidae *Phylloscopus trochilus*. **Distribution**: Summer visitor everywhere except Shetland. **Other habitats**: Varied; woodland, more open areas, scrub, hedges. **Notes**: Size: 11cm. Pale legs. Call: gentle "hoo-eet". Sweet descending song ending in a flourish.

Nightingale Turdidae *Luscinia megarhynchos*. **Distribution**: Summer visitor, to S. and E. of line from Dorset to Wash. **Other habitats**: Woodland with thick undergrowth. **Notes**: Size: 16.5cm. Sings by day and night. Rich varied song.

Chiffchaff Sylviidae *Phylloscopus collybita*. **Distribution**: Summer visitor; breeds most counties. Local in N.E. **Other habitats**: Mature woodland. **Notes**: Size: 11cm. Call: "hweet". Song: "chiff-chaff". Duller plumage than willow warbler. Black legs.

Wood Warbler Sylviidae *Phylloscopus sibilatrix*. **Distribution**: Summer visitor everywhere. Local in S.E., N.W. and Ireland. **Other habitats**: Mature woodland. **Notes**: Size: 12.5cm. Song: accelerating trill and a repeated "piu". Visible eyestripe.

Robin juvenile

Robin Turdidae *Erithacus rubecula*. **Distribution**: Resident, breeds everywhere except Shetland. **Other habitats**: Varied – needs cover. **Notes**: Size: 14cm. Loud warbly song and a "tic-tic" note.

southwards in the last ten years, possibly owing to the establishment of new plantations which provide a reliable food resource. The siskin is still a rare breeder in England and Wales, but in winter is relatively common and has recently developed the habit of visiting garden bird tables. The parrot-like crossbill is also a finch. In Britain there are two distinct races which can be differentiated by the size of their bills. The Scottish crossbill is confined to the Highlands and especially the relict Caledonian Forest, where it feeds on Scots pine. Elsewhere in Scotland and in scattered locations in England, for example Thetford Chase, the "spruce cross-bill" is present. This has a less powerful bill, more suitable for working on spruce cones.

No review of woodland birds would be complete without including the game birds. The largest species, the capercaille, is confined to Scotland and the Caledonian pine forests in particular. The pheasant, in contrast, is found throughout most of the British Isles and is commonly reared and released in large numbers. It is not a native species, but was probably introduced by the Normans. The measures taken to preserve this species for sport have had significant effects on other woodland wildlife. In order to maintain the population at the highest possible level, large numbers of bird and mammal predators are exterminated, some illegally. On the other hand, copses and areas of cover have been retained for pheasants on many estates, which would otherwise have been cleared.

Birds and woodland layers

CANOPY
Feeding
Willow warbler
Blue tit
Nuthatch

Nesting
Goldcrest
Woodpigeon
Crow

SHRUB AND HERB LAYER
Feeding	**Nesting**
Great tit	Blackbird
Wren	Wren
Goldcrest	Mistlethrush

GROUND LAYER
Feeding	**Nesting**
Woodpigeon	Willow warbler
Blackbird	Woodcock
Woodcock	Pheasant

Woodland is a three-dimensional habitat, offering the opportunity to live both on the ground and at various heights above it. Some birds nest and feed on the ground, others feed on the ground but seek the safety of trees and bushes in which to nest. The tree canopy offers a different range of foods (leaves, seeds, buds, defoliating insects, etc) to the ground (worms, woodlice, small mammals, fallen acorns, etc) but tends to be quite different in winter to what it is in summer. In order to obtain greatest advantage from the different prospects offered at various levels in the forest, the birds need to be suitably adapted. There are indications that their choice of place to live is also genetically determined: experiments with hand-reared blue tits and coal tits show that the former prefer pine branches, the latter oak, just as they do in the wild, even though hand-reared birds have no experience of either. By spacing themselves out vertically in the wood, and seeking preferred tree types, the birds reduce competition between species, share out the many nesting places and food sources and generally make the maximum possible use of all that the woodland habitat offers

Hawfinch Fringillidae *Coccothraustes coccothraustes* **Distribution**-Resident. Local in England, Wales and Scotland. **Other habitats:** Deciduous woods, gardens and orchards. **Notes:** Size: 18cm. Call is an explosive "tzik".

Greenfinch Fringillidae *Carduelis chloris* **Distribution:** Resident everywhere. **Other habitats:** Areas with trees and bushes. **Notes:** Size: 14.5cm. Female browner. Call: Rapid twitter, wheezing "tswee" from male in spring. Song is medley of twitters.

Redpoll Fringillidae *Acanthis flammea* **Distribution:** Breeds everywhere except central southern England. More widespread in winter. **Other habitats:** Birch woods and conifers. **Notes:** Size: 13cm. Call is a nasal "tsweat" and Linnet-like twitter.

Bullfinch Fringillidae *Pyrrhula pyrrhula*. **Distribution:** Widespread resident. **Other habitats:** Areas with thick cover. **Notes:** Size: 14.5cm. Call: a soft piping "peu". White rump visible in flight.

Goldfinch Fringillidae *Carduelis carduelis* **Distribution:** Resident. Breeds everywhere except northern Scotland. **Other habitats:** Similar to greenfinch. **Notes:** Size: 12cm. Call: a repeated liquid note. Song: liquid twittering.

Siskin Fringillidae *Carduelis spinus* **Distribution:** Nests mainly in Scotland. Widespread in winter. **Other habitats:** Breeds in conifers, alder. Birch woods and gardens in winter. **Notes:** Size: 12cm. Females are greyer, no black on head.

Crossbill Fringillidae *Loxia curvirostra* **Distribution:** Resident in Highlands, E. Anglia, New Forest; local elsewhere. **Other habitats:** Coniferous woodland **Notes:** Size: 16.5cm. Call is a loud "chip-chip". Forked tail visible in flight.

Chaffinch Fringillidae *Fringilla coelebs* **Distribution:** Resident throughout British Isles. **Other habitats:** Varied, requires trees or bushes for nesting. **Notes:** Size: 15cm. Has a short, loud, accelerating song. Call is "pink-pink".

Brambling Fringillidae *Fringilla montifringilla* **Distribution:** Widespread winter visitor. **Other habitats:** Woods especially beech, rough areas, stubble etc. **Notes:** Size: 14.5cm. Sexes similar in winter. Conspicuous white rump in flight.

Long-tailed Tit Aegithalidae *Aegithalos caudatus* **Distribution:** Resident in Great Britain and Ireland. **Other habitats:** Hedgerows, bushy heaths, scrub and woodland. **Notes:** Size: 14cm. Small, black, white and pinkish bird with a tail over half its length. Tail black with white edges. Voice is a repeated hard "tut".

Nuthatch Sittidae *Sitta europaea* **Distribution:** Resident in England and Wales. **Other habitats:** Woodland, parks and gardens with trees. **Notes:** Size: 14cm. Climbs trees in short jerks in any direction including downwards. Tail is not used as support. Hammers nuts wedged in bark. Voice is a loud, ringing "chwit-chwit".

Treecreeper Certhiidae *Certhia familiaris*. **Distribution:** Resident in Great Britain and Ireland. **Other habitats:** Woodland, parks and gardens with trees. **Notes:** Size: 13cm. Climbs up trees spirally in short spurts with stiff tail pressed against bark. Extracts insects with long, curved bill. Flight is tit-like. Voice is a thin, high-pitched "see".

Wren Troglodytidae *Troglodytes troglodytes*. **Distribution:** Resident in Great Britain and Ireland. **Other habitats:** Low cover in a variety of country. **Notes:** Size: 10cm. Plump bird with a cocked tail. Extremely active, foraging amongst litter on ground. Flight is straight with whirring wings. Voice is a hard, scolding "tic-tic-tic".

Tree Sparrow Emberizidae *Passer montanus*. **Distribution:** Resident everywhere but local in west. **Other habitats:** Wooded areas; open land in winter. **Notes:** Size: 14cm. Sexes similar. Call includes high pitched "teck".

Woodland Mammals

Mammals remain a largely hidden part of the woodland community, yet the part played by them in the ecology of the woods is highly significant. The majority are herbivores, feeding not only on fruits such as acorns, but also on the foliage of the trees. They therefore affect the natural regeneration of woodland both by eating the fruits and also by browsing off young saplings. Bark also provides food at certain times of the year; a persistent attack by grey squirrel can eventually kill a mature tree. The smaller mammals, such as mice and voles, form an important food resource for the larger predators, such as owls, stoats and weasels. Apart from bats, mammals are unable to cross extensive areas of water. Therefore when the British Isles became separated from the continent after the last glaciation, some seven thousand years ago, new colonisation was effectively prevented. Our present native woodland fauna therefore represents those animals which colonised northwards with the developing forests. Some of these, such as red squirrel and pine marten, are highly adapted to living in conifer woodland, and were no doubt associated with the early forests of Scots pine. Species such as dormouse, which are associated with broad-leaved trees, probably arrived later, and did not reach Ireland before it was separated from the rest of the British Isles. The larger woodland mammals, such as wolf and bear, which were considered undesirable by early man, were exterminated, while even some native species such as the roe deer are only present today in some parts of the country as a result of reintroduction, following earlier extermination. Like birds of prey, all mammal predators suffered extensive persecution during the 19th century from gamekeepers. Today all birds of prey are given special protection, but no mammalian predator has been given such complete protection, and many species are still killed in large numbers by gamekeepers throughout the country.

Several of the mammals which are now extinct must have had a significant effect on the woodland of their time. The wild boar, which remains common in parts of Europe, became extinct in Britain during the 17th century. It is a major consumer of acorns and beech mast. The abundance of this food during the autumn can be used by these animals because of their remarkable fattening ability, which enables them to store nutrients in their bodies during the winter. This ability has been utilised in breeding of modern pigs. Although many fruits are consumed, others are trampled into the soil to regenerate in the spring. They are then subject to browsing by small mammals such as voles, but in the woodlands of the past a much higher population of larger grazers and browsers were present. These included not only deer, but also wild ox or urus *(Bos primigenius)* and European bison *(Bison bonasus)*; both became extinct in

The majority of woodland mammals live on the forest floor, where there is a wide variety of food available to large omnivores such as the badger and specialist feeders like shrews.

Britain in prehistoric times. Although the animals have been extinct here for many centuries, their domestic equivalents have significantly affected woodlands into recent times, and in one or two places, such as the New Forest, still do so today. In the New Forest, commoners, or verderers, retain the right to pasture cattle in the unenclosed woodlands, while in some places pigs are still put out in the autumn for panage. Many smaller "wood pastures" had similar common rights which have only lapsed in recent times. In living memory the young coppice regrowth in Cranbourne Chase woods

As well as catching flying insects, long-eared bats have developed the ability to feed on caterpillars crawling over leaves. Unlike other bats they are able to hover, and their large ears detect their prey by listening for sounds they make and for the echoes of soft high-pitched squeaks, emitted by the bat and reflected by the prey. Bats fly at night when many woodland insects are active, but insectivorous birds are asleep.

had to be protected by brushwood to avoid it being eaten by the cattle which were pastured in the woods.

The only squirrel native to western Europe is the red *(Sciurus vulgaris)*. This is primarily a species of coniferous forest, and in Britain was never an abundant species in broad-leaved woodland. In contrast the grey squirrel *(S. carolinensis)*, in its native USA, is primarily a species of deciduous forest. It is therefore not surprising that since its introduction to Britain, especially in the late 19th century, it has replaced the native red squirrel in deciduous woodland throughout the lowlands of the British Isles. In spring the grey squirrels feed predominantly on tree buds, but in summer strip bark from younger trees and from the smaller branches of older trees, in winter fruits such as acorns are taken. Many are buried, usually singly; it is rare to find a sizeable cache. But it is the bark-stripping which makes grey squirrel a serious pest of woodland. Sycamore, beech, poplar and oak are all affected, sycamore most seriously. Studies on the population of grey squirrels have shown much of this activity to be behavioural rather than merely a feeding exercise. In the most desirable areas of woodland, where food and other requirements are at an optimum, a stable and entrenched resident population is present. Younger squirrels are expelled from these areas and forced to use poorer territories. Where these are young monoculture plantations, serious economic damage may result. Not only is other food in short supply, but the lack of a social structure in the population leads to aggressive behaviour, of which bark-stripping is one symptom. In North America, where little damage occurs, the forests are generally richer and the population is controlled by predators, including man, who hunts squirrels for fur and meat. Grey squirrels are now among the commonest woodland mammals. Their large untidy dreys are built in the branches of the canopy, although holes may also be used. Our native red squirrel has a much better public image than the grey; however, in areas of conifer plantation such as Thetford Forest, it too can cause damage through bark-stripping and has to be controlled. Although pine cones, the favoured food, are available on the trees throughout the winter, large stores of other food, such as hazel nuts, are made in hollow trees, and more rarely in dreys; the latter are typically more compact than those of the grey squirrel. The race indigenous to Britain and Ireland *(S.v. leocotis)* still appears distinct, despite introductions of the continental race, such as that by the Duke of Atholl in 1790 from Scandinavia. It is now confined to the remoter parts of the British Isles, although good populations remain in East Anglia, particularly in the Thetford Forest, and on the Isle of Wight.

Dormice are squirrel-like rodents. Again two species are present in the British Isles, one of which has been introduced. The native species, the common dormouse *(Muscardinus avellanarius)*, is a distinctive mouse-sized animal with a bushy tail. It feeds and breeds in the shrub layer of

The mole *(Talpa europaea)* is normally considered as a grassland animal. In fact, moles are just as common in woodland but their molehills are less conspicuous, being hidden by vegetation and dead leaves.

The dormouse

The common dormouse is about the size of a house mouse, with a tawny coat and bushy tail. It hibernates from October to April, but occasionally interrupts its sleep with a few days' activity. In the nineteenth century dormice were frequently kept as pets, and their reputation for sleepiness as extolled by Lewis Carroll would have been familiar to most Victorian children. During this long period of inactivity the dormouse relies on the fat reserves in its body, and therefore a good supply of food in autumn is critical to its survival. Its favoured habitat is woodland where a thick shrub layer of hazel coppice is present. A variety of fruits, berries and nuts are eaten, especially hazel nuts. It is no longer a common animal, being confined to southern England, particularly Kent, and Wales, and its decline this century has been linked to the loss of actively coppiced woodland. It is active after dark, climbing and feeding in the shrub layer. The day is spent in nests, which are also used for breeding. These may be built up to five metres above the ground and consist of honeysuckle bark, moss and grasses, with a covering of leaves. The animals breed at one year old; up to six or seven young are present in a litter; these later build smaller independent nests. Before hibernation special nests are built at or below ground level in the base of a coppice hazel. Bird nesting boxes have also been utilised in recent years.

The common dormouse is now quite a rare animal and is found mainly in southern counties, particularly in hazel woods. It is nocturnal and spends most of its time in the canopy of trees and shrubs.

broad-leaved woodland. Hazel is particularly favoured, and it is sometimes known as the hazel dormouse. So characteristic is the species of hazel coppice that the disappearance of this form of woodland management has led to the animal's decline and local extinction in many areas. It may however remain unnoticed, for dormice have been found hibernating in bird nesting boxes in areas where they were thought to be absent. It is largely confined nowadays to southern England and Wales. The presence of dormice is often indicated by honeysuckle being stripped of its bark, which is used in nest construction. The fat or edible dormouse *(Glis glis)* is almost twice the size of the native species and looks like a small squirrel. It is widespread in southern and eastern Europe and was introduced at Tring in Hertfordshire in 1902, but since then has only spread to a limited extent to nearby areas of the Chilterns. Unlike the common dormouse it frequently feeds and also nests in the canopy of mature trees. Food includes leaves, buds and occasionally the eggs and young of birds. In autumn fruits are taken but not stored. Apples are a favourite food, and edible dormice have been known to raid attics where they are stored. They have been reported to cause damage by stripping the bark from conifers in plantations in the Chilterns. Both the common and introduced fat dormouse hibernate from October to April, frequently with occasional intervals of activity.

Despite their small size, both the wood mouse *(Apodemus sylvaticus)* and yellow-necked mouse *(A. flavicollis)* may forage in the canopy, 10 metres above ground, for fruits, buds and insects. The rarer yellow-necked species is confined to southern England and Wales, while the common wood mouse is found throughout most of the British Isles. Both are nocturnal, range widely over the ground and also use a complex system of underground passages in or just below the woodland leaf litter. The nest is constructed underground and is composed of leaves and finely-shredded grasses. Neither is confined to woodland, but also occurs in hedge-rows and may even enter houses and outbuildings, especially in country areas. The yellow-necked is however less abundant in open fields than the wood mouse.

The bank vole *(Clethrionomys glareolus)* also occurs in large numbers in woodland. Its food preference is similar to that of the wood mice, but with slightly different emphasis; while the mice eat more insects and seeds, the voles prefer soft fruit, fresh leaves of plants such as bramble, and twigs and bark. Both voles and mice have been found to extract the larvae and pupae of gall wasps from their galls. Bank voles climb less readily than wood mice and are usually restricted to young growth and the shrub layer. They are found throughout the British Isles, but were first recorded in Ireland in 1964, having probably been recently introduced.

These small mammals collectively form a significant component of the woodland ecology and relatively large populations are maintained. The experimental exclusion of small mammals

The fat dormouse resembles a small grey squirrel but is principally nocturnal and largely confined to woodland on the Chilterns, the area to which it was introduced earlier this century.

from areas of oak woodland has led to a great increase in oak regeneration. However, small mammals are only likely to be limiting in years when acorns are scarce; when a good crop is present only a small proportion are removed, leaving plenty to grow unmolested. Both mice and voles store acorns and other nuts under logs and in burrows, and the amount of food available in the autumn appears to have a major effect on the survival throughout the winter. Other small herbivores which may occur in woodland, although chiefly found in other habitats, include the field vole *(Microtus agrestis)*, and rabbit *(Oryctolagus cuniculus)*. Both are more typical of open ground. Where they occur in woodland, rabbits are notorious for preventing the natural regeneration of seeds, such as acorns, which have survived predation by mice, voles and birds such as jays and wood pigeon. Both rabbits and hares browse off young growth within their reach; before myxomatosis rabbits were a serious pest in coppices, where regrowth was seriously suppressed.

Other smaller mammals are major predators on the woodland invertebrates. These include the common and pygmy shrews *(Sorex araneus* and *S. minutus)* and moles *(Talpa europaea)*. Molehills are rarely seen in woodland as the moles use established networks of underground runs. The hedgehog *(Erinaceus europaeus)* is also present in woodland where, because it occasionally takes the eggs of birds, it is persecuted by gamekeepers. Although bats are not obvious members of the woodland fauna, a large proportion of our native species uses hollow trees for breeding and roosting, and bats are often seen flying along the rides in summer evenings

The red squirrel *(Sciuris vulgaris)* is an agile tree-top acrobat. Squirrels eat large numbers of seeds and fruits and assist in the regeneration of forests by burying some of their food uneaten.

The badger

The badger is our largest native carnivore, measuring about 90 centimetres in length, with thick greyish fur and prominent white face with broad black stripes. It is found throughout the British Isles but is most abundant in areas of deciduous woodland, especially where there are sandy banks in which the setts, consisting of a labyrinth of tunnels, can be constructed most

easily. Active setts are quite conspicuous, with large piles of excavated material and discarded bedding of dry grass and bracken around the several entrances. Such extensive setts form the headquarters of badger families or clans. Each clan occupies an extensive territory, which does not usually overlap with those of other clans. The range boundary is marked with conspicuous

dung pits or latrines and is also actively defended. Several females are usually present in the clan; each may produce from one to four cubs within the sett in early spring. These remain underground for about eight weeks. Much food is obtained outside the woodland. A wide variety of plant and animal food is taken, but earthworms, present in large numbers in grassland soil, are often the

staple diet. It is through this association with pasture land that badgers may contract bovine TB from cattle. They may then act as carriers of the disease, and are being controlled by the Ministry of Agriculture in some areas. The badger has been extensively persecuted in the past, particularly through the cruel sport of badger-baiting, which has been illegal only since 1973.

feeding on insects. Species particularly regarded as forest bats include noctule *(Nyctalus noctula)*, barbastelle *(Barbastella barbastellus)* and Leisler's bat *(Nyctalus leisleri)*, the latter tending to be more abundant in Ireland than in mainland Britain. Bechstein's bat *(Myotis bechsteini)*, one of our rarest species, is recorded from Hampshire and Dorset, northwards to Shropshire. It is essentially a forest species in Europe, although the few English individuals have been found hibernating in caves. The population of bats in young coniferous woodland, where no hollow trees are available, has recently been experimentally increased through the use of specially-designed bat boxes.

Persecution of the major mammalian predators of pheasant in the lowlands and of grouse in the uplands has significantly affected the distribution of the larger, more vulnerable species. Thus pine marten *(Martes martes)*, polecat *(Mustela putorius)* and wild cat *(Felix sylvestris)* have been eradicated from the lowland woods and are now found mainly in the uplands, where they have been forced to utilise more barren open habitats. Neither polecat nor wild cat has occurred in Ireland. The polecat was last recorded in Scotland in 1907 but is still present in Wales and has recently spread into the English border counties. The wild cat is now restricted to the higher woodland in Scotland, while the pine marten maintains a number of isolated populations in the Highlands, the Lake District, Wales and part of Ireland. It is the most typically woodland species of the three and appears to favour mixed conifer and broadleaved woodland. It is highly adapted to climbing and hunting among the canopy. Although red squirrel has formed a major part of its diet in the past, birds and small rodents are also significant components. The major predators, fox *(Vulpes vulpes)*, badger *(Meles meles)*, stoat *(Mustela erminea)* and weasel *(M. nivalis)* still maintain reasonably large populations throughout much of the lowlands, despite persecution. The fox would almost certainly be a rarer

The badger *(Meles meles)* is a nocturnal woodland animal. It lives in a large burrow (called a sett) emerging at sundown to feed on acorns, bluebells, blackberries and a

wide variety of other foods as they become seasonally available. Badgers have a keen sense of smell and mainly depend on this to find food.

animal in many country districts if it were not specially protected for the sport of fox hunting. Foxes will take a wide variety of animal food, ranging from ducks and geese to earthworms, although small rodents probably form the main prey. Marked preferences for particular species are often shown, not necessarily reflecting the relative abundance of the species involved. Thus field voles are preferred to bank voles and wood mice, while shrews are only eaten when other food is scarce. Foxes are well known for hiding food and it has recently been shown that most is refound by the individual concerned. Fox earths are usually excavated from disused rabbit warrens or badger setts; occasionally a sett is shared, and four to five cubs are born in early summer.

The badger is a true omnivore and takes much more vegetable food than the fox. Its diet ranges from hazel nuts to bluebell bulbs, but earthworms usually form the staple food. Badgers' underground setts are composed of a labyrinth of tunnels, typically in deciduous woodland on well-drained soils. Unlike fox earths, the chambers are lined with dry grass and other bedding, the remains of which can often be found in the pile of excavated material at the entrance of the setts. The badger is persistent in its use of the traditional runs which radiate from the setts, so much so that foresters find it cheaper to install badger gates, where the runs cross a plantation fence, than to have the fence constantly torn up. The badger is now one of the few mammals which enjoy legal protection, although it is being controlled by the Ministry of Agriculture in some areas because of its role as a carrier of bovine TB.

Woodland deer

Since the extinction of the wolf two hundred and fifty years ago, man has been the only predator of full-grown deer. Of the six species present in the British Isles, only two, the red and roe (*Cervus elaphus* and *Capreolus capreolus*) are native. In both cases the native British race is confined to Scotland and the north of England, while populations elsewhere are the result of introductions. The Scottish red deer spend much of the year high up on the open moors, but in winter herds frequently enter the woods of pine and birch at lower altitudes. Red deer have also colonised many of the extensive conifer plantations in Scotland, where they do considerable damage by browsing. Sometimes they totally suppress sapling growth, particularly of the introduced lodgepole pine. The roe deer occurs in a wide variety of woodland habitats and is

The roe deer

Although the roe deer is native to this country, only in the north of England and in Scotland is the population derived from native stock; the isolated southern and eastern ones have originated from introductions. The roe is a relatively small deer, being approximately the size of a large goat. In summer the coat is bright reddish but becomes darker and greyer in winter. Although introduced in the 19th century the animal has only become abundant in recent years, through the cover and food provided by the extensive new plantations. Roe feed largely by browsing the leaves of trees and shrubs; bramble is particularly favoured in the lowlands, while heather is extensively used in the uplands. They also move outside the woods at dusk to graze on grass and young cereals in adjacent fields. In some woods the large roe population may cause extensive damage to young crops of trees. Rutting, followed by mating, occurs in July and August, but the white-spotted fawns are not born until the following May or June. Twins are usually produced and are left hidden for long periods in the first few days. The males (bucks) have short spiky antlers and, like the females (does), a prominent white patch on their bottoms, with no black markings. Unlike the larger species, roe deer do not form herds but usually live singly or in pairs.

Roe deer *(Capreolus capreolus)* may do considerable damage to young trees by eating growing shoots, stripping bark and rubbing their antlers against small saplings. Foresters therefore cull deer to avoid serious economic loss.

now plentiful in extensive but separate populations in southern England and East Anglia, as well as Scotland and the north. It is not present in Ireland. The southern and eastern populations result from introductions from Germany in the 19th century, but they did not increase until the present century, when they have taken advantage of the many new plantations. Roe will graze on grass and herbs but are chiefly woodland animals, which feed by browsing, with heather and bramble forming an important food where available. Serious damage to young plantations can result from browsing. Fraying is also harmful (the result of bucks cleaning their antlers), it leaves a clearly visible scar of damaged bark. Usually young, springy saplings are chosen, thrashed violently with the antlers and liberally anointed with scent from facial glands. These trees then serve as territorial markers; much of the fraying damage has been found to be caused by animals which are low in the hierarchy of the deer population and which gather in the least suitable habitat. These seek to return to more desirable territories and challenge the dominant males which hold them.

Much of the fraying damage therefore occurs around the traditional rutting stands, where these aggressive demonstrations take place.

The remaining species of deer are all introduced. The two largest species are the fallow *(Dama dama)* and sika *(Cervus nippon)*. The fallow deer was probably introduced from southern Europe by the Normans, while sika was introduced from Japan in the last century. Both species became established as a result of escapes from deer parks, largely during both World Wars, when park fences were not repaired. The fallow is now widely distributed throughout Britain, although it is most plentiful in the south eastern part of England. Sika is restricted to a few isolated populations in England, Scotland and Ireland. Our smallest deer, the muntjac *(Muntiacus reevesi)*, with a shoulder height of less than 50 centimetres, is now fairly widespread in south east England, having escaped from Woburn Park where it was introduced in 1900. The slightly larger Chinese water deer *(Hydropotes inermis)* also originated from Woburn; it is not a woodland species but is found in wet areas of long grass.

The red deer *(Cervus elaphus)* is the largest British deer. Although an open moorland animal, its original home was in the open forests and recently it has begun to colonise plantations in central and western Scotland. Like other deer it feeds mainly by browsing and does considerable damage to growing trees. Where captive deer are kept in wooded park land, they eat the lower branches and foliage of the trees, forming a distinctive "browse line".

Young deer like this fallow fawn *(Dama dama)* are born fully active but spend their first few days hidden in the undergrowth. They normally have a spotted coat which camouflages them on the sun-dappled forest floor.

Lowland Grasslands and Heaths

Open views of lush grasslands are among the finest and commonest components of the scenery of lowland Britain. Our moist climate makes the grass a rich green, causing constant surprise to foreign visitors or holidaymakers returning from drier countries. In summer the meadows, roadsides and rolling hills are spangled with colour from an extraordinary diversity of grassland flowers. We tend to take grass for granted as we walk on it, drive on it and use it to feed animals; but grassland is a rich, living community, full of delicate ecological balances, and not simply a green cloak for the soil.

It is easy to forget that most countries in Europe do not have as much or as varied grassland as Britain, and that even here grassland is a relatively recent historical development following clearance of the ancient forests. In fact all our lowland grass constitutes an artificial habitat, needing constant intervention by man or his grazing animals to stop it returning naturally to forest by way of an intermediate scrubland stage. Superficially, the verdant greens of the grasslands appear totally different from the dull dry purples and browns of lowland heath, but the two habitats share a common origin in forest clearance. Both are characteristically open, lacking trees, and consequently create similar opportunities and pose similar problems for their inhabitants.

The principal difference between heathland and grassland is that the latter is dominated by heathers rather than grass. This is largely due to differing soil conditions. Even where grassland develops, the soil "flavour" still has a major effect in determining the type of plants and animals present. This chapter is thus divided into "calcareous" and "neutral" grasslands, according to soil type. Extensive grasslands are also found on acid soils, but these mainly occur in upland areas and are therefore considered elsewhere.

Early man created most of the lowland grasslands in Britain, by felling trees and grazing with cattle and sheep. Today ancient man and ancient grasslands are still linked because archaeological sites are often only lightly grazed thus preserving the old grassland communities, like here at Maiden Castle in Dorset, but they remain only as fragments within intensively cultivated farmland.

The Physiography of Lowland Grassland

Forest was the natural vegetation cover of Britain before Neolithic man started to clear it for stock-rearing. The open habitats which we see today on chalk downs, in river valleys, on limestone hills and in sandy heaths owe their origins to progressive felling and clearance of this forest, a process which has continued throughout history. Woodland was cleared for conversion to productive arable land, or simply to provide wood for fuel or building purposes. Glades created for grazing animals were extended by the livestock themselves browsing the trees and shrubs. With increasing human populations, there was a demand for still more open ground for arable farming; grassland was also needed to produce hay and fodder for the draught animals used to cultivate the arable land, whose fertility was maintained by using manure from the livestock. These inter-relationships meant that every hectare of arable land needed 1½ hectares of grassland to support it.

During recent history there have been considerable fluctuations in the proportion of arable land to permanent grassland, depending on the relative profitability of arable crops. For example, during the late 19th century cheap wheat was imported from the USA, making the home product unprofitable. This resulted in arable land being allowed to revert to grassland. Conversely during the first and second World Wars much permanent grassland was ploughed up to grow home-produced food. There is still a tendency for all semi-natural habitats such as grassland and heathland to be converted to grass leys or arable grass and heathland.

Although these habitats were artificially created they have been established for so long that they have developed into stable and recognisable associations of plants and animals. Semi-natural habitats rich in plant species and animal life only occur where there has been a relatively long period without ploughing and where modern intensive farming methods have not yet been employed. Not surprisingly, few such places remain.

Grazing management

The character of our grasslands and heathlands has been shaped by their past management, in particular grazing or cutting. Both procedures result in removal of grass material, but preserve the habitat as a whole because grass is adapted to withstand removal of its leaves by animals, while other plants are not. Consequently, continued grazing (or its modern equivalent, mowing) eliminates competitors and preserves grassland from invasion by scrub. Most of the grazing is by cattle, sheep and rabbits, all species which were introduced to Britain by man. This further heightens the artificiality of the grassland habitat, but prolonged grazing can establish a balanced and

Ancient figures cut in the turf, such as here at Cerne Abbas in Dorset, show how little soil covers the underlying chalk. Grazing and mowing prevent encroachment of scrub

diverse plant community of considerable interest. For example, grazing by sheep over many years has created the rich chalk downland grasslands. These are now deteriorating, however, as sheep have become unprofitable and grazing has ceased.

In recent history grazing by rabbits has also had a considerable impact on the species composition of grasslands, particularly on chalk and sandy soils. Rabbits are not native to Britain; they were introduced soon after the Norman Conquest and carefully kept in captivity for their meat and fur. It is only since the 18th century that rabbits have mostly lived outside captivity and have established themselves as widespread feral animals. Their grazing pressure has had a profound effect on the composition of grassland flora, and the sharp drop in the number of rabbits due to the outbreak of deadly myxomatosis in the 1950s has resulted in far-reaching changes in grassland habitats.

Grazed grasslands are usually loosely referred to as "pasture", whereas permanent grassland which is harvested for hay is called "meadow" Some meadow and flood plain grasslands have been maintained by a long history of periodic cutting for hay, sometimes combined with a

little grazing by cattle. Often the productivity was increased in so-called "water meadows" by careful and skilful control of the water regime to flood the grassland in the spring, and produce a rich flush of grass during the early summer. By contrast, some limestone grasslands and heathlands have been managed by periodic burning with the same objective of encouraging more young grass and also keeping invading scrub at bay.

All these types of land management maintain the habitats in a stable state over many years and prevent regression to scrub. Where these management regimes have ceased, or are no longer pursued so intensively, coarse vegetation invades and scrub develops. This forms dark, impenetrable thickets which shade out and suppress the rich grassland flora and the wealth of animal life it supports. Scrub invasion thus heralds an interlude of species impoverishment preceding the later development of woodland on the site. A similar invasion process restores forest on heathland habitats once maintenance by grazing or burning has ceased.

Thus grass and heathland habitats are in a state of unstable equilibrium. So long as the artificial processes which created them continue, they remain balanced, interesting seminatural habitats. But, changes in farming practices and economics alter the balance in favour of natural invasion by scrub. These open habitats are therefore threatened simultaneously on two fronts. On the one hand, less human intervention will allow their obliteration by natural vegetational succession. On the other hand, more human intervention (prompted by the need to extract maximum economic benefit from our limited resources of land) means conversion by the plough or, equally destructive, "improvement" by massive applications of herbicides and fertilizers and consequent transformation into highly artificial communities which support little of the wealth of wildlife seen on semi-natural grassland and heathland. Because grasslands are man-created and only sustained by human intervention they are peculiarly and totally vulnerable even to the smallest changes in management.

Salisbury Plain

This extensive rolling downland plateau in Wiltshire, includes the military ranges of the Salisbury Plain Training Area, covering some 36,000 hectares, which accounts for the Plain surviving as chalk grassland. Much of it was cultivated in early times (Celtic field systems are still visible), and more recently there was sheep grazing and corn cultivation, all resulting in a mosaic of grasslands of different ages, with the more ancient turf being richer in plant species. Interesting turf may also be seen on Silbury Hill and in other situations where the soil is thin and the chalk is near the surface.

Wiltshire has more chalk grassland than any other county, 29,500 hectares in all (69 per cent of the UK total), including 55 Sites of Special Scientific Interest.

This milestone marks the now defunct old Marlborough Road, where the horse-drawn coaches which used to cross the Plain have left deep multiple ruts.

A guide to some interesting grassland sites

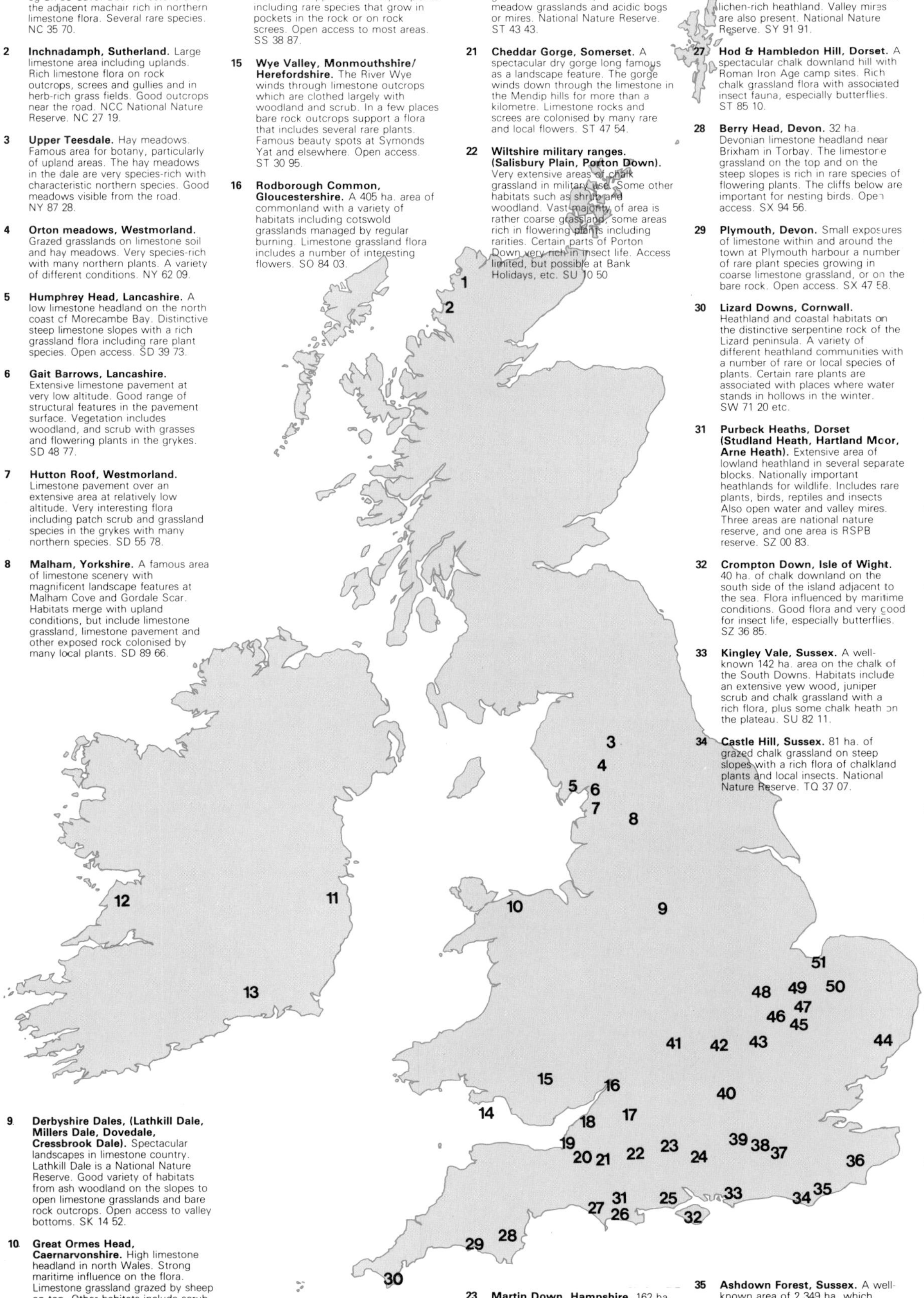

1 **Durness, Sutherland.** Limestone area. Extensive outcrops of limestone on the north coast of Scotland forming spectacular coastal features, eg Smoo Cave. Both limestone and the adjacent machair rich in northern limestone flora. Several rare species. NC 35 70.

2 **Inchnadamph, Sutherland.** Large limestone area including uplands. Rich limestone flora on rock outcrops, screes and gullies and in herb-rich grass fields. Good outcrops near the road. NCC National Nature Reserve. NC 27 19.

3 **Upper Teesdale.** Hay meadows. Famous area for botany, particularly of upland areas. The hay meadows in the dale are very species-rich with characteristic northern species. Good meadows visible from the road. NY 87 28.

4 **Orton meadows, Westmorland.** Grazed grasslands on limestone soil and hay meadows. Very species-rich with many northern plants. A variety of different conditions. NY 62 09.

5 **Humphrey Head, Lancashire.** A low limestone headland on the north coast of Morecambe Bay. Distinctive steep limestone slopes with a rich grassland flora including rare plant species. Open access. SD 39 73.

6 **Gait Barrows, Lancashire.** Extensive limestone pavement at very low altitude. Good range of structural features in the pavement surface. Vegetation includes woodland, and scrub with grasses and flowering plants in the grykes. SD 48 77.

7 **Hutton Roof, Westmorland.** Limestone pavement over an extensive area at relatively low altitude. Very interesting flora including patch scrub and grassland species in the grykes with many northern species. SD 55 78.

8 **Malham, Yorkshire.** A famous area of limestone scenery with magnificent landscape features at Malham Cove and Gordale Scar. Habitats merge with upland conditions, but include limestone grassland, limestone pavement and other exposed rock colonised by many local plants. SD 89 66.

9 **Derbyshire Dales, (Lathkill Dale, Millers Dale, Dovedale, Cressbrook Dale).** Spectacular landscapes in limestone country. Lathkill Dale is a National Nature Reserve. Good variety of habitats from ash woodland on the slopes to open limestone grasslands and bare rock outcrops. Open access to valley bottoms. SK 14 52.

10 **Great Ormes Head, Caernarvonshire.** High limestone headland in north Wales. Strong maritime influence on the flora. Limestone grassland grazed by sheep on top. Other habitats include scrub and rock outcrops. Latter harbour many rare plant species. SH 75 82.

11 **Killiney Hill, Dublin.** A grassland area just to the south of Dublin city.

12 **The Burren, County Clare.** Extensive area of karst limestone country consisting largely of limestone pavements reaching the sea. A unique area of outstanding importance in Europe for flora, with both Arctic and Mediterranean plants.

13 **Nore Valley, Kilkenny.** An area of limestone with some interesting plants, including local whitebeam micro species.

14 **Gower Peninsula, Glamorgan.** Carboniferous limestone forms spectacular cliffs on this popular peninsula close to Swansea. The limestone supports a variety of plants including rare species that grow in pockets in the rock or on rock screes. Open access to most areas. SS 38 87.

15 **Wye Valley, Monmouthshire/Herefordshire.** The River Wye winds through limestone outcrops which are clothed largely with woodland and scrub. In a few places bare rock outcrops support a flora that includes several rare plants. Famous beauty spots at Symonds Yat and elsewhere. Open access. ST 30 95.

16 **Rodborough Common, Gloucestershire.** A 405 ha. area of commonland with a variety of habitats including cotswold grasslands managed by regular burning. Limestone grassland flora includes a number of interesting flowers. SO 84 03.

17 **North Meadow, Wiltshire.** 45 ha. A classic example of lammas land. Meadow grassland which is managed as a hay meadow according to the prescriptions laid down by law. Very rich in flowers including rare species. National Nature Reserve. SU 09 94.

18 **Avon Gorge, Avon.** Spectacular landscape feature where the River Avon carves a gorge through the limestone at Bristol. Vegetation includes woodland, scrub and limestone flowers. Many rare species. A famous site long known to botanists. Partly National Nature Reserve. ST 56 74.

19 **Brean Down, Somerset.** 146 ha. An interesting limestone headland near Weston-super-mare in the Bristol Channel. The steep grassland slopes have rock outcrops and are rich in flowers, especially on the south-facing slopes. Many rare plants. ST 28 58.

20 **Shapwick Heath, Somerset.** A remnant of natural vegetation on the Somerset levels. Fen-like habitats developed on the peat including grazed fen meadows, mown meadow grasslands and acidic bogs or mires. National Nature Reserve. ST 43 43.

21 **Cheddar Gorge, Somerset.** A spectacular dry gorge long famous as a landscape feature. The gorge winds down through the limestone in the Mendip hills for more than a kilometre. Limestone rocks and screes are colonised by many rare and local flowers. ST 47 54.

22 **Wiltshire military ranges. (Salisbury Plain, Porton Down).** Very extensive areas of chalk grassland in military use. Some other habitats such as shrub and woodland. Vast majority of area is rather coarse grassland, some areas rich in flowering plants including rarities. Certain parts of Porton Down very rich in insect life. Access limited, but possible at Bank Holidays, etc. SU 10 50

23 **Martin Down, Hampshire.** 162 ha. An interesting area of grazed grassland that includes chalk grassland, different types of chalk heath and scrub. Rich chalk flora and some interesting insects. SU 04 19.

24 **Butser Hill, Hampshire.** A very high chalk hill with good views from the top. Some of the grazed chalk grassland slopes are very steep. Experimental archaeology in Iron Age camp is a feature of interest. Country Park. Open access. SU 72 20.

25 **New Forest heathlands, Hampshire.** 14,175 ha. Large area of heathlands within an even larger area which forms the whole New Forest. Very important and valuable area of heathland, of international importance for plants, insects, reptiles and birds. A great variety of conditions from dry to wet heath and valley mire. Open access over much of the area. SU 27 09.

26 **Morden Bog, Dorset.** Dry heathland area with decoy ponds. Partially colonised by pines to form pinewood and scrub. Interesting communities include old heather and lichen-rich heathland. Valley mires are also present. National Nature Reserve. SY 91 91.

27 **Hod & Hambledon Hill, Dorset.** A spectacular chalk downland hill with Roman Iron Age camp sites. Rich chalk grassland flora with associated insect fauna, especially butterflies. ST 85 10.

28 **Berry Head, Devon.** 32 ha. Devonian limestone headland near Brixham in Torbay. The limestone grassland on the top and on the steep slopes is rich in rare species of flowering plants. The cliffs below are important for nesting birds. Open access. SX 94 56.

29 **Plymouth, Devon.** Small exposures of limestone within and around the town at Plymouth harbour a number of rare plant species growing in coarse limestone grassland, or on the bare rock. Open access. SX 47 58.

30 **Lizard Downs, Cornwall.** Heathland and coastal habitats on the distinctive serpentine rock of the Lizard peninsula. A variety of different heathland communities with a number of rare or local species of plants. Certain rare plants are associated with places where water stands in hollows in the winter. SW 71 20 etc.

31 **Purbeck Heaths, Dorset (Studland Heath, Hartland Moor, Arne Heath).** Extensive area of lowland heathland in several separate blocks. Nationally important heathlands for wildlife. Includes rare plants, birds, reptiles and insects. Also open water and valley mires. Three areas are national nature reserve, and one area is RSPB reserve. SZ 00 83.

32 **Crompton Down, Isle of Wight.** 40 ha. of chalk downland on the south side of the island adjacent to the sea. Flora influenced by maritime conditions. Good flora and very good for insect life, especially butterflies. SZ 36 85.

33 **Kingley Vale, Sussex.** A well-known 142 ha. area on the chalk of the South Downs. Habitats include an extensive yew wood, juniper scrub and chalk grassland with a rich flora, plus some chalk heath on the plateau. SU 82 11.

34 **Castle Hill, Sussex.** 81 ha. of grazed chalk grassland on steep slopes with a rich flora of chalkland plants and local insects. National Nature Reserve. TQ 37 07.

35 **Ashdown Forest, Sussex.** A well-known area of 2,349 ha. which includes a variety of habitats in addition to open heathland. Wet heathland contains rare plant species. Also some notable insects. Open access. TQ 45 31.

36 **Wye & Crundale Downs, Kent.** 304 ha. of chalk grassland on steep slopes near Ashford. One of the best-known areas of the North Downs for its rich flora including many orchids and other rare species of plants. The Devil's Kneading Trough is a spectacular chalk coombe feature. NCC National Nature Reserve. TR 07 45.

37 **Box Hill, Surrey.** 326 ha. A famous beauty spot on the North Downs near Dorking. Chalk grassland and scrub predominates. Even the popular areas are rich in chalkland flowers and insects including many local species. Box woodland on the steep slopes gives the name to the hill. Many good adjacent areas. National Trust. TQ 17 51.

38 **Chobham Common, Surrey.** A 607 ha. area of dry heathland, relatively close to London, near Woking. The damp valleys have a number of rare and characteristic plants. Also has local birds, insects and other invertebrates. SU 97 65.

39 **Thursley Common, Surrey.** A significant area of heathland, 929 ha. near Godalming in Surrey. Includes a variety of habitats from dry to wet heath with open waters, bogs and pine and birch woodland. Rare plants and rare insects are special features. National Nature Reserve. SU 90 41.

40 **Aston Rowant, Oxfordshire.** 129 ha. of chalk grassland and scrub in the Chiltern Scarp, now separated into two blocks by the M40 motorway cutting. Generally rich in chalk flora with some local plants. Nature Trail on Beacon Hill. NCC National Nature Reserve. SU 72 97.

41 **Pixey & Yarnton Mead, Oxfordshire.** 89 ha. of alluvial meadow grasslands in the River Thames valley. Managed as hay meadows for hundreds of years and subject to changing strip ownership. Very rich flora. SP 48 10.

42 **Totternhoe Knolls, Bedfordshire.** An outlier of the Chiltern Hills near Dunstable. Chalk grassland largely invaded by scrub. Very rich flora including several rare plants. Good for insects. Open access. Local Nature Reserve. SP 97 22.

43 **Therfield Heath, Hertfordshire.** A 20 ha. area of recreational land near Royston which consists of chalk grassland with a good variety of characteristic or rare plants. Open Access. Local Nature Reserve. TL 35 40.

44 **Monewden meadows, Suffolk.** 4 ha. of old grassland meadows with a variety of interesting plants. A notable example of a fritillary field, with other rare species too. TM 22 57.

45 **Devil's Dyke, Cambridgeshire.** A conspicuous land mark feature near Newmarket. An ancient earthwork built of chalk with coarse chalk grassland providing a refuge for many attractive flowers. Open access. TL 60 63.

46 **Woodwalton Fen, Cambridgeshire.** A 208 ha. relict of the fenlands, surrounded by arable agricultural land. Habitats range from damp woodland, birch wood, sallow carr, and open fen to open water in dykes and meres. Mixed fen is very rich in plant species. Also rare insects present. NCC National Nature Reserve. Access by permit. TL 22 83.

47 **Wicken Fen, Cambridgeshire.** Another relict of the fenlands of some 304 ha. Large areas covered by scrub. Open fenland areas rich in plants and insects. Some managed for cutting the sedge litter, some as reed beds. Open water in lodes, dykes and flooded cuttings. National Trust Reserve. TL 55 70.

48 **Barnack Hills & Holes, Cambridgeshire.** 22 ha. of species-rich limestone grassland on the old limestone spoil of ancient quarrying. A rich flora with an abundance of orchids. Open access. National Nature Reserve. TF 07 04.

49 **Ouse washes, Cambridgeshire and Norfolk.** 2430 ha. of meadow grassland area between the parallel old and new Bedford Rivers used as a flood storage area during the winter months. Interesting grassland and aquatic flora but most important for birdlife with large concentrations of wildfowl in winter and some rare breeding species in summer. Managed by Wildfowl Trust, RSPB and Cambridge & Isle of Ely Naturalists Trust. TL 39 75.

50 **Breck heathlands (Lakenheath Warren, Foxhole Heath, Weeting Heath (NNR)).** Extensive remnants of the Breck heathlands. Habitats range from acid heather-covered heathland, through a variety of grassland types to calcareous habitats. Open landscape and bare sandy and flinty areas are characteristic. Dense rabbit warrens on some heaths. Many rare plants, birds and insects. Restricted access. TL 76 80 etc.

51 **Roydon Common, Norfolk.** 232 ha. of typical heathland in west Norfolk, near King's Lynn. Variety of vegetation types including dry and wet heath, birch scrub/woodland and wet bog, with many local plants. TF 69 22.

Abbreviations:

NCC	Nature Conservancy Council
FC	Forestry Commission
RSPB	Royal Society for the Protection of Birds
NT	National Trust
NNR	National Nature Reserve
FNR	Forest Nature Reserve
NP	National Park
FNR (I)	Forest Nature Reserve (in Ireland)

Calcareous Grassland and Scrub

Calcareous soils are formed in chalk and limestone areas and often comprise only a shallow layer on top of the rock itself. A rather specialised calcareous habitat is provided by the chalky boulder clays of East Anglia, which were deposited by receding Ice Age glaciers. Calcareous soils characteristically contain an abundance of calcium carbonate and have a high pH (meaning they are strongly alkaline in nature). These are generally advantageous features so far as plants and animals are concerned, but are offset by the fact that calcareous soils are often very poor in other nutrients like nitrates and phosphates, the lack of which imposes a limiting factor on plant growth. Physical features such as soil depth, slope and aspect (facing the sun or not) also have a profound effect on the actual species present.

Chalk and limestone are very porous, so that the soil which overlies them tends to be dry. This, together with the shortage of crucial nutrients, partially governs the nature of the plant community, but the main controlling factor is land management, both past and present. Grazing is particularly vital in the maintenance of a grassland community; without it the habitat reverts to woodland via an intermediate stage of dense scrub vegetation. Indeed, it may be said that grazing is the factor which, above all others, is responsible for creating and maintaining short turf habitats. Traditional grazing by sheep and cattle creates a short close-grazed sward with some paths and poaching (breaking up by trampling) of the soil on the steeper slopes. Rabbits also play a major role in keeping the grass short and ensuring that the habitat remains suitable for the many species adapted to living in it.

The presence of numerous large anthills is a good indication that the turf is ancient and undisturbed by ploughing; the size and density of the mounds can even be used as a guide to the age of the turf. Where the turf has not been ploughed up for centuries and traditional low-

Open grassland, especially that which is lightly grazed, is not just a carpet of grass, but a very rich plant community, with a dozen or more species in a square metre.

density grazing continues, the grassland turf may be astonishingly rich in flowers, insects, and snails. In fact such sites may be among the most species-rich terrestrial habitats in the whole of Britain. In the best places there may be 30 or more species of plants in one square metre of turf. It is difficult to understand how so many different plants can survive in such close proximity. Perhaps the shortage of water and nutrients, coupled with the unpredictable and irregular impact of occasional grazing, creates such a variety of advantages and setbacks for each species from year to year that no one plant can become dominant. When grazing pressures are removed (for example after the introduction of myxomatosis in 1953) the balance of advantages changes in favour of species previously suppressed and coarser, less varied plants gain

the ascendancy.

A number of plants are so regularly found in calcareous grassland that they may be used as indicators of the habitat type. The grasses include quaking grass, red fescue, sheep's fescue and upright brome grass. The fescues are indicative of old grazed grassland, whereas upright brome grass occurs in coarser grassland which has not been closely grazed. False oat grass indicates periods of past disturbance, while, if the predominant species is rye grass, it is likely that the grassland has been re-seeded by the farmer. The characteristic flowering plants include salad burnet, wild thyme, rockrose, harebell, bird's-foot trefoil, wild carrot and several varieties of orchid.

Areas of grassland which are still managed by grazing, cutting or burning remain as grass, but where management has ceased they develop into scrub. The downland grasslands of today are therefore survivals from a former time when grazing was more extensive. Some are still used as grazing land, particularly in Dorset, Wiltshire and Hampshire. Rough grassland may also be retained for shooting or hunting. Small but interesting patches of grassland and scrub also occur in quite unnatural places such as road and railway cuttings, on embankments and in neglected chalk and limestone quarries. At the time these man-made features were created, natural grassland was more widespread and seed sources were plentiful. Plants characteristic of the district therefore colonised the cuttings and quarries and developed into grasslands similar to those in their surroundings. Nowadays most of the intervening ground is cultivated or developed for building and often only these man-made grasslands remain.

Public pressure

Open grasslands on high downs are attractive places for picnics and outings, and people gather in large numbers at places like Box Hill on the North Downs, Ivinghoe Beacon in the Chilterns, or Butser Hill in Hampshire. The attraction of these places lies in the open grassland, which must be maintained by using sheep, mechanical cutting or burning of the grass. Artificial methods of maintaining grass are rarely so satisfactory as sheep grazing because nutrients are lost from the system, whereas the trampling and dunging by the livestock are beneficial. Public open spaces create other problems of grassland management; visitors' dogs tend to worry the sheep and the visitors themselves physically erode the turf. Some-

Field example: Chalk grassland: Old Winchester Hill

Old Winchester Hill on the South Downs in Hampshire was declared a National Nature Reserve in 1954 to protect an area of chalk grassland with its variety of plant and insect life. It is now one of the few areas left, as much of the surrounding downlands has been claimed for agriculture. Even where grassland persists it is improved turf and not species-rich. Other nearly natural grassland areas still survive at nearby Exton and at Butser Hill.

Part of the hill forms the ramparts of an Iron-Age hill fort, but today the open hilltop and the steep slopes near the road are popular with visitors. The roadside area has suffered from the number of visitors, showing signs or erosion, necessitating some measures to control public access. The reserve is not entirely grassland, also having yew and beech woodlands and scrub. The open grasslands have recently been fenced off and the traditional grazing by both sheep and cattle reinstated in order to maintain short grass turf. The richest flora is on the slope to the south of the hill fort and includes a fine assortment of downland orchids.

Round-headed rampion *(Phyteuma tenerum)*, a rare but locally abundant species found at Old Winchester Hill.

In recent years scrub has invaded large areas of the Winchester Hill grassland. Clearance of this was carried out by the Nature Conservancy Council, using cutting machines followed by stump treatment to prevent regrowth.

The calcareous grassland ecosystem

Grassland develops on richer soils than heathland, but is an unstable habitat because it becomes overgrown by scrub unless grazing animals keep the invading woody plants from getting established. Grasses are adapted to withstand grazing pressures, so the grassland habitat represents collaboration between the grasses and grazers; the former provide food and the latter keep competing plants at bay, maintaining the dominance of the grasses. So long as the grass is kept short by grazing, many sun-loving herbs can also flourish, leading to great diversity of flowers and insects; but reducing grazing and scrub invasion soon result in these being lost because the ground is shaded by taller plants.

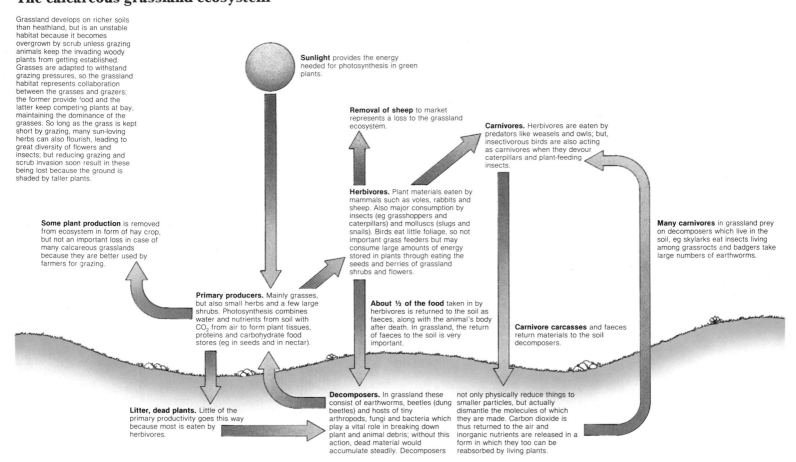

Sunlight provides the energy needed for photosynthesis in green plants.

Removal of sheep to market represents a loss to the grassland ecosystem.

Carnivores. Herbivores are eaten by predators like weasels and owls; but, insectivorous birds are also acting as carnivores when they devour caterpillars and plant-feeding insects.

Herbivores. Plant materials eaten by mammals such as voles, rabbits and sheep. Also major consumption by insects (eg grasshoppers and caterpillars) and molluscs (slugs and snails). Birds eat little foliage, so not important grass feeders but may consume large amounts of energy stored in plants through eating the seeds and berries of grassland shrubs and flowers.

Many carnivores in grassland prey on decomposers which live in the soil, eg skylarks eat insects living among grassroots and badgers take large numbers of earthworms.

Some plant production is removed from ecosystem in form of hay crop, but not an important loss in case of many calcareous grasslands because they are better used by farmers for grazing.

Primary producers. Mainly grasses, but also small herbs and a few large shrubs. Photosynthesis combines water and nutrients from soil with CO$_2$ from air to form plant tissues, proteins and carbohydrate food stores (eg in seeds and in nectar).

About ⅓ of the food taken in by herbivores is returned to the soil as faeces, along with the animal's body after death. In grassland, the return of faeces to the soil is very important.

Carnivore carcasses and faeces return materials to the soil decomposers.

Litter, dead plants. Little of the primary productivity goes this way because most is eaten by herbivores.

Decomposers. In grassland these consist of earthworms, beetles (dung beetles) and hosts of tiny arthropods, fungi and bacteria which play a vital role in breaking down plant and animal debris; without this action, dead material would accumulate steadily. Decomposers not only physically reduce things to smaller particles, but actually dismantle the molecules of which they are made. Carbon dioxide is thus returned to the air and inorganic nutrients are released in a form in which they too can be reabsorbed by living plants.

times spectacular scars are caused on steep slopes where people walk and slide.

Conservation

Nature conservation bodies have bought or leased a number of the more interesting sites on chalk and limestone specifically to conserve their wildlife richness, for example National Nature Reserves like Old Winchester Hill on the chalk in Hampshire, Aston Rowant in the Chilterns and Wye Downs in Kent. The management of such reserves aims to maintain a balance between the open grassland and the subsequent scrub stage. Where too much scrub existed it has been cleared to restore open grassland. This is maintained by grazing or cutting, but since there is no necessity to make a profit the grazing animals are sometimes more decorative than the types used on commercial farms. Soay sheep (from St Kilda in the Hebrides) are among the more unusual breeds used for conservation grazing; they have the dual advantage of being hardy (and thus requiring little attention) and small, so that their hooves do not damage turf on steep slopes.

Rabbit grazing is a welcome additional factor in controlling the growth of coarse grass and scrub; the animals themselves make a pleasing sight and their digging and dunging activities also create special conditions for certain plants. The horseshoe vetch is a plant whose presence is sustained by the activities of rabbits, particularly grazing. It is also the vital food plant of the chalkhill blue, an exceptionally interesting downland butterfly. Loss of rabbit grazing means that the vetch loses out in competition with coarser grasses, the butterfly declines and the habitat is poorer by several species. However, in the farms that often surround nature reserves, economic interests mean that rabbits and their depredations are unwelcome, so that it is often necessary to enclose reserves with costly rabbit-proof fences. Sometimes parts of the grassland are fenced to prevent grazing or cutting to provide some small areas of long coarse grass, which is beneficial to insect life as it provides more shelter. However, as we have seen, removal of grazing pressures reduces the diversity of plants; a similar decline in interest occurs if the turf is improved for modern agriculture. Traditional grazing involves a low

input and a low output in cash terms and is unprofitable in the present economic climate. Profitability can be improved if the density of livestock is increased, but this can be done only if the grassland is made more productive by the application of chemical fertilizers. However, this treatment applied to downland turf favours the growth of certain grasses (as is its purpose) but at the expense of the flowers; the variety of species therefore declines. Regular heavy applications of fertilizer reduce the wildlife interest of grassland to virtually nil after a few years. A more certain way to create even more agriculturally productive grassland with virtually no variety of other plant species is to plough and re-seed the downland with rye grass. Combined with fertilizer treatment, this results in a turf with very low species diversity. These processes repeated all over the country for decades mean that many special grassland-turf plants have become very rare. Similarly, animals like the large blue butterfly, which are critically dependent upon the rich turf ecosystems, are severely endangered by its disappearance.

Anthills and their ecology

Anthills are a characteristic sight on old downland sward. The mounds are built to catch the sun's rays and so provide a warm location for brood chambers. There may be several of these and the worker ants will move the brood to whichever is the warmest.

Mounds are built by the worker ants which heap up soil particles by carrying them to the top of the mound. This provides a loose soil texture which excludes the typical rosette plant form of normal downland turf as these plants cannot tolerate having their growing points covered by soil. In their place trailing plants like rockrose and wild thyme dominate and small annuals, such as wall speedwell exploit the well drained mound tops. Thus the special conditions existing on anthills contribute appreciably to the species diversity of downland turf.

These early purple orchids and cowslips are some of the vulnerable flora of rich calcareous grasslands.

Ants build their anthill nests to provide protection for their colonies, and an improved microclimate; they are also used for storage of food and rearing the brood.

Limestone Cliffs and Pavements

Limestone cliffs and pavements, such as these at Gordale Scar in Yorkshire, support a very specialised flora that would elsewhere be damaged by grazers or swamped by plants.

In areas of chalk and limestone rock the majority of the natural vegetation cover is grassland or scrub, although woodland has sometimes been allowed to develop. A proportion of these areas consists of bare rock, particularly in the case of the harder limestone which outcrops as inland cliffs and scars in many places. These exposures carry special associations of plants which grow in cracks and pockets in the rock. The characteristic flowers include species of both grassland and woodland and also many species which seek the open conditions and freedom from competition which are features of such rocky situations.

Each of the major geographic areas of limestone has its exposures which are rich in plants. Chalk, being a soft rock, has relatively few natural inland exposures. One exception is the cliff overlooking the River Mole at Box Hill, Surrey. Carboniferous limestone has a great many outcrops with important exposures, for example Cheddar Gorge and Avon Gorge at Bristol. Much of the tableland of the Derbyshire Dales includes interesting limestone cliffs and screes in steep-sided winding valleys such as Lathkill Dale, Miller's Dale and Dovedale. Even more extensive exposures of limestone occur in the Craven district of Yorkshire, and further north in Cumbria and Lancashire. Sea cliffs at Humphrey Head, the scars at Gordale and inland cliffs such as Malham Cove are among the more interesting places. Many of the fells have limestone pavements, as on Hutton

Roof and Southern Scales Fell on Ingleborough. Even small areas of limestone may have significant outcrops, for example the Devonian limestone exposures in Torbay and at Plymouth. The most spectacular exposures of bare limestone in the British Isles occur in western Ireland where Black Head and much of the Burren Hills in County Clare consist of limestone pavement.

Limestone pavement is a most distinctive and important formation from the point of view of the wildlife it supports. Pavements consist of relatively level areas of bare limestone which have been smoothed by ice sheets during the Pleistocene age. These pavements have subsequently been eroded by rain water, which, being acidic, has gradually eaten into the surface of the rock, creating surface runnels and deep vertical clefts known as grykes, and leaving regular boulders (or clints) between adjacent clefts. These grykes provide a special habitat for plants by providing a more humid microclimate and shelter from grazing. In places where humus has accumulated in the grykes a pocket of more acid conditions supports a different flora.

Although limestone exposures are, by their very nature, unlikely to be threatened by agricultural developments, they nevertheless need protection from other activities such as quarrying. Weathered "water-worn" surface limestone is an extremely desirable natural product for landscaping rock gardens; in the north of England many of the pavements have suffered

from the removal of stone for garden rockeries. Many glacial boulders have been taken and there has been serious wholesale destruction of the pavement itself by quarrying. Although there is still a substantial area of pavement left unexploited there are few individual pavements which have not suffered some damage through the removal of this decorative stone for commercial purposes.

Many plants grow in the protected cracks in limestone pavements, such as the hawkbit, herb robert, thyme and yellow saxifrage shown here.

Grasses of Calcareous Habitats

Species of grasses are obviously the dominant feature of any grassland; calcareous grasslands commonly contain a number of different species all growing together. They are able to withstand cutting or grazing because grass leaves grow from the base, not from the tip like the shoots of many other plants. Removal of the tips by grazers (or mowing machines) is therefore easily compensated for.

Like flowers, some grasses complete their life cycle in a year, whilst others last from one year to the next. The meadow grass, as its scientific name, *Poa annua*, suggests is an annual, but the majority of grasses are perennials and sprout new shoots from their underground rhizomes indefinitely. Some grasses stay green all the year round, while other species die back and shed their leaves in the autumn, contributing to a colour change in their habitat, like trees at the same season.

Most downland grasses are fine-leaved perennial plants with a tufted growth form and most occur in close turf. Some, such as the fern grass, specialise in colonising bare soil or stony places.

All of the species can survive in well-drained soil and the rather dry conditions of downland slopes. The majority of the calcareous grasses are widespread and occur in many other situations, such as hay meadows and roadside verges. However, blue moor grass is more a plant of the northern limestones, and there are a few rare grasses which occur only in certain areas of the country. Somerset hair-grass, for example, may be seen only on limestones in south west England. Mat grass fescue is another rarity only found in chalk and limestone grassland in the south of England. Quaking grass is a common and highly characteristic species of calcareous grassland. It is very distinctive and one of the few grasses which is readily recognised by the layman. It is not surprising therefore that it has been given many names which refer to the trembling motion of the thin-stalked spikelets of the flowering head. Quaking or totter grass are the most widely used names; others are shivering, trembling, maiden hair, cow quakes, and such intriguing local names as doddering dillies and wiggly wontins. Another very readily recognisable species is fern grass, which has a very stiff wiry growth form, becoming even more stiff and brittle in fruit. Hence it is sometimes called hard meadow grass.

The calcareous sands of the Breckland support a few rather unusual grasses. Purple fescue and interrupted bent grass are slender annual grasses that grow in abundance on track sides and on sandy warrens. Grey fescue forms beautiful tufts of glaucous leaves on some of the Breck heaths.

The fescues are very useful and important grasses of calcareous soils. They form a good close turf in downland and the many cultivated varieties of red fescue also make excellent lawn grasses. In contrast, tor grass, whose loosely tufted light green leaves invade chalk downland turf, is a worthless species that is largely avoided by grazing cattle. The various oat grasses bear a slight resemblance to cultivated oats because the appearance of their spikelets is similar, with their bent awns, but they do not produce useful grains. The yellow oat grass is useful as a grassland constituent as it is highly palatable to livestock.

A guide to some calcareous grasses

Red Fescue, Creeping Fescue Gramineae (Poaceae) *Festuca rubra* Throughout the British Isles. **Other habitats:** Coastal dunes; salt marsh; heaths; open woodland; road verges; railway banks; waste ground. **Notes:** Widespread and often abundant; very common.

Sheep's Fescue Gramineae (Poaceae) *Festuca ovina* **Distribution:** Every county in the British Isles. **Other habitats:** Heaths and moors. **Notes:** Acid or basic soils; open situations where it is often the dominant grass; up to 1300 metres.

Downy Oat Gramineae (Poaceae) *Helictotrichon pubescens* **Distribution:** Throughout the British Isles. **Other habitats:** Gravelly soils. **Notes:** Often locally abundant, especially on damp soils of lowland grassland and lower slopes of hills.

Meadow Oat Grass Gramineae (Poaceae) *Helictotrichon pratense* **Distribution:** Throughout the British Isles. **Notes:** Often locally very abundant; on most natural grassland up to 1000 metres.

Yellow Oat Grass Gramineae (Poaceae) *Trisetum flavescens* **Distribution:** Throughout England and Ireland; less frequent in Wales and rare in Scotland. **Other habitats:** Roadside banks and verges. **Notes:** Tolerates a wide variety of soil types.

Quaking Grass, Totter Grass Gramineae (Poaceae) *Briza media* **Distribution:** Throughout the British Isles, but rare in north and north-west Scotland. **Notes:** More frequent in the south; heavy or light soils in moist or dry situations; up to 650 metres.

Fine Bent Gramineae (Poaceae) *Agrostis tenuis* **Distribution:** Throughout the British Isles. **Other habitats:** Heath; moorlands; waste ground. **Notes:** Grows from sea level to 1300 metres on a wide range of soils, especially poor, dry, acid types; large areas of grassland are dominated by this species.

Creeping Bent Gramineae (Poaceae) *Agrostis stolonifera*. **Distribution:** Throughout the British Isles. **Other habitats:** Salt marshes; roadsides; inland and coastal sands; cliffs; open woodland; a weed of cultivated land. **Notes:** Variable species; grows on light or heavy soil; up to 800 metres.

Fern Grass Gramineae (Poaceae) *Catapodium rigidum* **Distribution:** Throughout England (especially the south); south Scotland; Wales; Ireland. **Other habitats:** Dry banks; walls; stony, rocky and sandy places. **Notes:** Found on well drained soils.

Blue Moor Grass Gramineae (Poaceae) *Sesleria caerulea* **Distribution:** Northern England; central Scotland; western Ireland. **Other habitats:** Cliffs and rock ledges. **Notes:** Up to 950 metres; mainly on dry soils.

Crested Hair-grass Gramineae (Poaceae) *Koeleria cristata* **Distribution:** Throughout the British Isles. **Other habitats:** Sandy places. **Notes:** Common in dry places up to 650 metres.

Field Woodrush Juncaceae *Luzula campestris*. **Distribution:** Throughout the British Isles. **Notes:** A variable species; common in grassy places; grows well on non calcareous soils; wet or dry conditions.

Glaucous Sedge Cyperaceae *Carex flacca* **Distribution:** Throughout the British Isles. **Other habitats:** Calcareous sand dunes. **Notes:** Can withstand some salinity; often found in the estuarine fresh/saltwater marsh zone; variable species; the most common British sedge.

Tor Grass Gramineae (Poaceae) *Brachypodium pinnatum* **Distribution:** Central and southern England; occurring in scattered localities in East Anglia, northern England, southern Scotland, Wales and Ireland. **Notes:** Frequently abundant and spreading.

Upright Brome Gramineae (Poaceae) *Zerna erecta* **Distribution:** Central and southern England; rare in Wales and central Ireland. **Other habitats:** Roadside banks and verges; waste land. **Notes:** Well drained soils; often the dominant species.

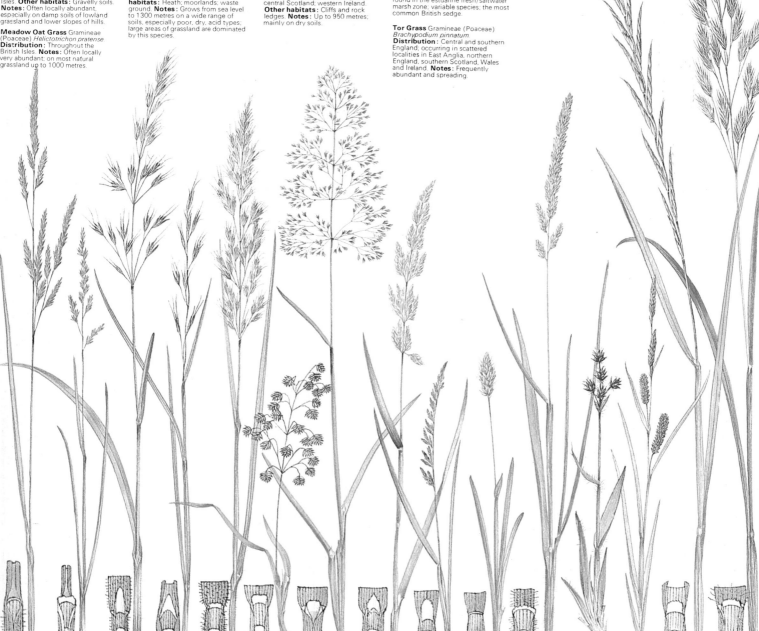

Red Fescue · Sheep's Fescue · Downy Oat · Meadow Oat Grass · Yellow Oat Grass · Quaking Grass · Fine Bent · Creeping Bent · Fern Grass · Blue Moor Grass · Crested Hair-grass · Field Woodrush · Glaucous Sedge · Tor Grass · Upright Brome

Non-flowering Plants of Calcareous Habitats

The well-drained dry soil and dense turf of calcareous grassland do not contain many species of flowerless plants. Only a few mosses and lichens try to compete with the closely-packed flowering plants. More species of fungi are able to grow in these situations as they do not need to compete for light.

The mosses are more obvious during the winter months when they are fresh and green. As with other plants some species are virtually confined to calcareous soils and rocks while others are frequent on alkaline soils but also occur elsewhere. The most conspicuous mosses of chalk and limestone grassland are feather mosses and others which have a sprawling growth under or among the flowering plants. Feather mosses of the genera *Pseudoscleropodium*, *Acrocladium*, *Camptothecium*, *Thuidium* and *Eurhynchium* are frequent and conspicuous. One of the

most attractive is the plumy crested feather moss *(Ctenidium molluscum)* which forms mats of very neat and regular fronds of a beautiful yellow-green colour. The triangular-leaved feather moss *(Rhytidiadelphus triquetus)* has stiff upright branches and scaly triangular leaves which give it a distinctive appearance in downland turf. The cypress-leaved feather moss *(Hypnum cupressiforme)* is a very common plant which grows in many situations. Some of its forms occur on chalk grassland. The leaves have a boat-like shape which gives the shoots a fat appearance.

Shaggy ink caps *(Coprinus comatus)* are found in grassland, on roadsides and rubbish tips and frequently grow in clusters. The older specimen (right) shows the auto-digestion of the rim of the cap.

Lichens do not generally form a conspicuous part of calcareous grassland turf except in places where there is very thin flinty soil and a rather open turf. On the Breck heaths lichens form an important constituent of the grasslands; several species of *Cladonia* are dominant. Some have many repeatedly forked upright stems, while others such as *Cladonia pocillum* form crusts

The dog lichen *(Peltigera canina)* is soft, flexible and brown-green when moist, but brittle, papery and white-grey when dry. The spore-producing structures (apothecia) are the chestnut brown oval areas on the upper surface.

The dung roundhead *(Stropharia semiglobata)* is a fungus of pastures that is usually found growing on old dung (here shown on horses' dung) from spring until autumn. The cap, which can be up to 4cm in diameter, is slimy to the touch as

is the smooth and slender stalk beneath the ring or ring-like zone. The spores and gills are dark brown, whereas the mealy-smelling flesh is pale yellow-white.

of "leaves" on the ground surface, with occasional upright stalked cups.

A variety of fungi is found on downland turf. On closer examination it will be discovered that some of them are actually growing on the dung of grazing animals. This is especially true of species of *Coprinus*, and certain inconspicuous cup fungi.

Puffballs of various types commonly grow in the turf itself. The most frequent on downland are the smaller species of *Calvatia* and *Lycoperdon*. These are white or olive in colour and pear-shaped. When ripe their skin ruptures, releasing clouds of spores like fine dust. Several edible fungi are found on calcareous grassland, although they also occur in pastures and meadows on other soils. The common field mushroom (*Agaricus campestris*) and the more delicate fairy-ring champignon (*Marasmius oreades*) are grassland fungi that appear in late 'summer and autumn. These and similar fungi form fairy-rings in the turf, which are particularly easy to appreciate on downland slopes, where the rings of dark enriched turf can be seen from a distance.

A guide to some grassland fungi

The fruiting bodies of fungi, usually the only part of the plant seen, are a common sight in grassland; most seem to grow and mature very rapidly. However, the mycelium that constitutes the major part of the plant is made up of a complex system of intertwining hyphae usually growing beneath the surface of the soil.

Some species are found growing in so-called "fairy rings" where the mycelium becomes established at a central point and grows outwards in all directions producing fruiting bodies near the advancing front. As growth continues each year a larger ring of toadstools is formed: in some cases fairy

rings can be several metres across. At the edge of the ring where growth is active the fungus often produces chemicals that inhibit or kill the turf plants so that the fruiting bodies appear to grow from a dead or dying ring of higher plants.

Not all fruiting bodies are of the typical toadstool form. Puff-balls, for example, are usually more or less globose structures that contain vast numbers of spores which are puffed out in clouds by the slightest movement.

Common ink cap Agaricineae *Coprinus atramentarius*. **Notes:** Found late summer to autumn; often clustered near trees; gills grey-white, becoming black as spores ripen; cap and gills eventually dissolve into a black fluid.

Shaggy parasol Agaricineae *Lepiota rhacodes*. **Other habitats:** Woodland, especially conifers. **Notes:** Cap ovate at first, then expanding to parasol shape; stipe without scales; cut flesh orange-yellow; stipe ring double.

Parrot toadstool Agaricineae *Hygrophorus psittacinus*. **Other habitats:** Open grassy places in woodland. **Notes:** Grows in summer and autumn; cap shiny and more or less flat when mature.

Wood blewits Agaricineae *Tricholoma nudum*. **Other habitats:** Mixed woodland and gardens. **Notes:** Found in late autumn to early winter; blue-lilac when young becoming brown-violet with age; cap darker towards centre.

Mosaic puff-ball Lycoperdaceae *Lycoperdon caelatum*. **Distribution:** Sandy pastures. **Notes:** Size and shape of a pear; whitish grey turning reddish brown and developing a series of hexagonal cracks; base grey-brown.

Scarlet hood Agaricineae *Hygrophorus coccineus*. **Notes:** Especially common at wood margins; grows from summer to early winter; stipe red at top becoming yellow towards the base; colours fade with age.

Giant puff-ball Lycoperdaceae *Lycoperdon giganteum*. **Other habitats:** Woodland. **Notes:** Sometimes grows in rings; surface smooth, hairy when young; white becoming yellowish when ripe.

Wild Flowers of Calcareous Habitats

Base-rich soils on chalk and limestone are generally very rich in flowering plants. Downland slopes are colourful during early summer, with a great variety of flowers. Limestone outcrops may sometimes look like natural rock gardens, with an abundance of attractive wild plants. These soils are particularly rich in orchids; the great majority of the British species grows on chalk and limestone. The variety of the flora of basic rocks is increased by the fact that pockets of acidic conditions often occur within such areas, supporting still more different species, whereas it is rare to find basic pockets in an acidic area.

The presence of several common flowering plants is indicative of chalk and limestone. These calcicolous plants include rockrose, bloody cranesbill, kidney vetch, dropwort, small scabious and clustered bellflower. All are common and colourful flowers.

Downland slopes often have steep gradients. These result in shallow soil (particularly on the steepest slopes) and influence temperatures, the availability of light and the water content. Water supply is a particular problem for plants growing on such well-drained soil, so that many of these plants are adapted to the dry conditions and can reduce their own loss of water. The adaptations include low growth form to keep the plant within the humid air layer close to the ground surface, and small leaves with thick cuticles. More delicate plants such as orchids may die back soon after flowering to avoid the heat of the summer. Thyme and rockrose are woody perennial plants that are able to withstand dry conditions better. Deep roots are also helpful in reaching water which may be scarce near the surface but is usually available deeper down.

The flowers found on calcareous soils vary widely in different parts of Britain depending on three factors: the geology, the local climate and man's management. The pattern created by the different underlying rock types can be further modified locally by superficial deposits of other materials, such as clay with flints or gravels. The different types of limestone do not appear to differ in their chemical content but the rocks differ in their degree of hardness and in their geographical location; each major type carries a distinctive flora.

The chalk grasslands of south east England are characteristically dominated by salad burnet and rockrose on the south-facing slopes. On the South Downs and in Hampshire, small scabious and devil's bit scabious are conspicuous flowers. Locally ox-eye daisy may become

The locally frequent pyramidal orchid is only found in grassland on chalk or limestone and on calcareous dunes. The pollen-containing organs, the pollinia, have a specially adapted base, or viscidium, that attaches to and tightly coils around the mouth-parts of feeding lepidopteran insects; this increases the chances of cross-pollination.

Parasitic grassland plants

Several downland plants are parasitic and either partially or wholly depend for their growth and development on other host plants. Eyebrights and yellow rattles are two types of semi-parasitic common downland plant. They contain green chlorophyll and are thus able to manufacture some of their own food by photosynthesis, but are also attached to the roots of a range of host species which they parasitise. These partial parasites are able to grow and develop in the absence of host plants but only produce stunted specimens, apparently because their roots are poorly-developed and unable to absorb sufficient water and raw materials to sustain the full development of the plant. When attached to the side roots of the host plants, for example grasses, they develop normally.

Broomrapes, which include a number of species found on chalk and limestone, such as the tall broomrape, thistle broomrape and lesser broomrape, are wholly parasitic. These strange plants lack green chlorophyll and are entirely dependent on their hosts. Their erect stems and flowers are cream, brown or purplish in colour, while their leaves are reduced to brown scales on the stems. They produce enormous numbers of tiny seeds which only germinate in contact with the living roots of a suitable host plant, when they produce a filamentous seedling which penetrates the host's root tissues. The broomrape's absorptive tissue develops in close association with the host, and then develops a tuber which is produced externally. This sends up one or more erect spikes of flowers.

Broomrapes are often very host-specific. Tall broomrape usually occurs only on the greater knapweed. Thistle broomrape thrives only on species of thistle. The lesser broomrape may however be found on a large number of host plants, especially legumes.

The hayrattle, a common hemi-parasitic plant of grassland, is thought to use grasses as host species.

The ivy broomrape (Orobanche hederae) is a locally common parasitic plant that grows only on ivy.

abundant. On the western chalk grasslands in Wiltshire an association of flowers such as sawwort, betony and devil's bit scabious occurs. These abundant flowers give the overall character to a particular chalk grassland but are accompanied by many other less dominant plants. Where the grassland has been partly or completely invaded by scrub, more shade-loving plants may be found; hairy violet, milkworts, fly orchid and wild strawberry favour the shaded conditions on the scrub fringe. There are a number of plants which are confined to the chalk areas of south east England; these include the wild candytuft and Chiltern gentian, which favour disturbed chalk soil, and 2 grassland orchids: monkey orchid and late spider orchid.

The oolitic limestone of the Cotswolds and elsewhere has few special plants but rockrose is very common. There are 2 plant species which are confined to the oolite: perfoliate or Cotswold penny cress and downy woundwort. Both are very rare in Britain and favour the loose disturbed soil of screes and quarry spoil.

The limestones of the north and west of Britain, such as Carboniferous limestone, have many distinctive plants. These rocks are much harder and the grassland areas are frequently interrupted by exposures of the bare limestone rock. The cliffs, outcrops, pavements and loose stony screes which are such a feature of these

Part of Porton Range in southern England covered by a carpet of kidney vetch. In places such as this where there is a shallow, dry, calcareous soil, or near the coast, this species can be abundant or even dominant. As a member of the legume family it plays an important role in increasing the soil's fertility by means of root nodules with nitrogen fixing bacteria that produce useable nitrates from atmospheric nitrogen.

A guide to some wild flowers of calcareous grasslands

The wildflowers growing in calcareous turf are in some cases, such as the rough hawkbit, adapted to heavy grazing by having a rosette growth-form with the growing point protected at the base of the centre of the rosette. Other species, such as bird's-foot trefoil (which also grows in most unshaded habitats throughout the British Isles), can spread vegetatively, survive both grazing and trampling, and flower and fruit well in spite of the adverse conditions.

Many British species, like the common rockrose, are rare or absent in Ireland, due either to the sea forming an impenetrable seed dispersal barrier, or it may be that they were once common but have been eliminated during the post-glacial periods.

Old Man's Beard, Traveller's Joy Ranunculaceae *Clematis vitalba.* **Distribution:** Wales; England, but rare in the north; southern Scotland; south and central Ireland. **Other habitats:** Thickets; wood margins. **Notes:** Always on calcareous soils; can climb up to 30 metres.

Pasque Flower Ranunculaceae *Anemone pulsatilla* **Distribution:** Central and eastern England. **Notes:** On dry slopes; colour varies, purple-violet, reddish or white.

Bulbous Buttercup Ranunculaceae *Ranunculus bulbosus.* **Distribution:** Throughout the British Isles, but less common in Scotland and southern Ireland. **Other habitats:** Fixed dunes. **Notes:** Abundant on dry, especially calcareous substrates; the earliest flowering of the common buttercups; distinguished by reflexed sepals; usually yellow, but sometimes pale or white.

Wild Basil Labiatae *Clinopodium vulgare.* **Distribution:** Throughout the British Isles; common in southern Britain becoming rare to absent in northern Scotland; scattered and rare in Ireland. **Other habitats:** Hedges; wood margins; scrub. **Notes:** Dry soils; found up to 400 metres; scented.

Lady's Bedstraw Rubiaceae *Galium verum* **Distribution:** Throughout the British Isles; but less common in the west of Britain and northern and southern Ireland. **Other habitats:** Hedge banks; stable dunes. **Notes:** Grows on all except the most acid soils; abundantly common; smells of newly cut grass.

Hedge Bedstraw Rubiaceae *Galium mollugo* **Distribution:** Throughout the British Isles, but only common in the south, central and the very north of England. **Other habitats:** Hedge banks; scrub; waste land. **Notes:** Grows up to 400 metres; a very variable species.

Marjoram Labiatae *Origanum vulgare* **Distribution:** Scattered throughout the British Isles, but rare in northern Scotland and more common in southern England. **Other habitats:** Hedge banks; scrubland. **Notes:** Dry habitats; usually calcareous soil; aromatic.

limestones harbour a very different association of plants from that of the grasslands. Many of the distinctive plants are particularly typical of these situations. The Cheddar pink is an attractive rarity which occurs only on the rocks in the vicinity of Cheddar Gorge. Jacob's ladder is similarly confined to limestone screes in the north of England, where it sometimes grows in a profusion of blue flowers.

The limestone pavements are particularly good places to search for some of the more unusual plants. Growing in the shelter of the grykes one can find common flowers like the herb robert, sanicle and dog violet. The pavements of north England may also harbour scarcer species such as the melancholy thistle and the brittle bladder and green spleenwort ferns. The same pavements are also the home of several national rarities which are virtually confined to such places. The unusual baneberry, which is related to the buttercups, and the bluish rigid buckler fern are particularly restricted in distribution. Other rarities typical of the grykes, like the dark red helleborine and limestone polypody fern, also grow elsewhere on screes and in cliff crevices.

One of the most striking areas of limestone pavement occurs in County Clare, Eire. This area, known as the Burren, carries a profusion of luxuriant limestone flora which has made it a Mecca for botanists. The Irish limestone has some surprising absentees from its flora because

Ireland has been separated from the Continent for a longer period than the mainland of Britain. For example the small scabious, a common flower in south east England, is entirely absent, while another "regular" of the English chalk, common rockrose, is present but very rare.

The Burren limestone is also notable for its luxurious growth of maidenhair fern and many attractive flowers such as moss saxifrage, stone bramble, small meadow rue, spring sandwort and bloody cranesbill. Where peaty soil has been allowed to accumulate on top of the limestone there is a different flora, including rare plants which also occur in Teesdale in northern England, for example spring gentian and shrubby cinquefoil. The more widespread mountain avens forms cushions of dark green leaves smothered by cream-coloured flowers. The dense flowered orchid and the Irish sandwort occur nowhere else in Britain.

The great variety of conditions in Britain allows plants from different geographical regions of Europe to thrive where the climate allows. Plants with a southern oceanic distribution, such as the white rockrose, occur on the limestone in south west England. Species of a northern and sub-montane distribution may be found on the limestones of northern England. Spring sandwort and Jacob's ladder are examples of this type and are confined to the north, while the mountain everlasting is common in northern England and Scotland but also reaches the

chalk in southern England. A number of southern continental plants occur in Britain. Honewort and the monkey orchid are rare examples but others, for example the bee orchid and yellowwort, are more widespread, at least in the south. Some species are also widespread but are confined to the south-facing slopes in the north of the country, as in the case of the stemless thistle.

Some of the continental species are not only rare in Britain but have curiously patchy distribution patterns: the tuberous thistle is an attractive rarity that is known only from the chalk in Wiltshire and in Cambridgeshire. Goldilocks is another example which may be found on limestone cliffs as far apart as Berry Head in Devon, Great Orme in north Wales and Humphrey Head in north Lancashire.

Not all the flowers of calcareous soils are restricted to such conditions. The widespread hareharrow, restharrow and lady's bedstraw are common plants on chalk and limestone but need only moderately base-rich conditions and commonly occur in a variety of sites. Certain flowers which are widely associated with calcareous conditions may be variable in form; the more unusual local varieties can be scarce and restricted in distribution. The common milkwort has a striking large-flowered form called *ballii* which occurs on limestone cliffs in western Ireland. Similarly the widespread bladder campion has a red-flowered form which is known in Britain only from the limestone at

A guide to some wild flowers of calcareous grasslands (continued)

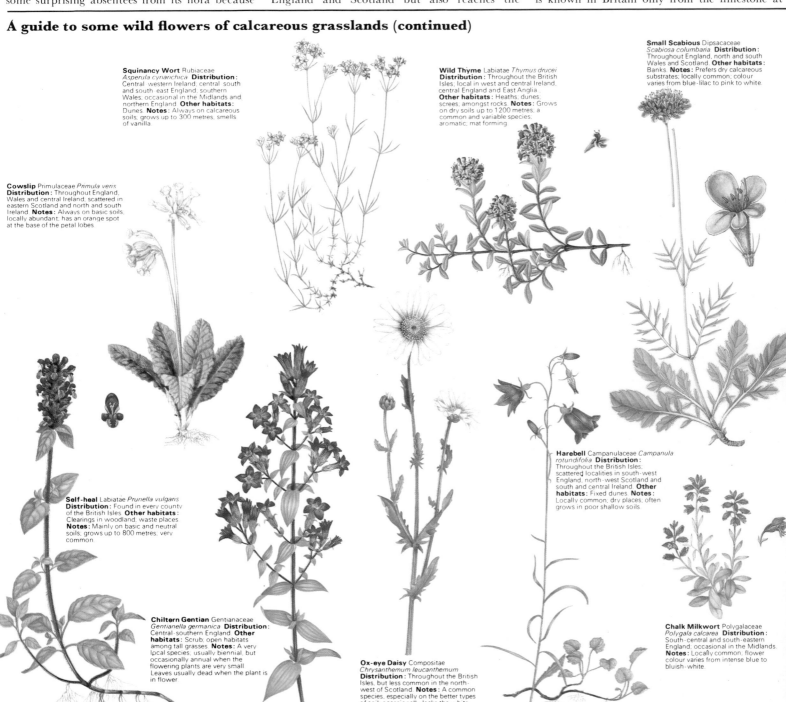

Squinancy Wort Rubiaceae *Asperula cynanchica* **Distribution**: Central western Ireland; central south and south-east England; southern Wales; occasional in the Midlands and northern England. **Other habitats**: Dunes. **Notes**: Always on calcareous soils; grows up to 300 metres; smells of vanilla.

Wild Thyme Labiatae *Thymus drucei* **Distribution**: Throughout the British Isles; local in west and central Ireland, central England and East Anglia. **Other habitats**: Heaths; dunes; screes; amongst rocks. **Notes**: Grows on dry soils up to 1200 metres; a common and variable species; aromatic; mat forming.

Small Scabious Dipsacaceae *Scabiosa columbaria* **Distribution**: Throughout England, north and south Wales and Scotland. **Other habitats**: Banks. **Notes**: Prefers dry calcareous substrates; locally common; colour varies from blue-lilac to pink to white.

Cowslip Primulaceae *Primula veris* **Distribution**: Throughout England, Wales and central Ireland; scattered in eastern Scotland and north and south Ireland. **Notes**: Always on basic soils; locally abundant; has an orange spot at the base of the petal lobes.

Self-heal Labiatae *Prunella vulgaris* **Distribution**: Found in every county of the British Isles. **Other habitats**: Clearings in woodland; waste places. **Notes**: Mainly on basic and neutral soils; grows up to 800 metres; very common.

Chiltern Gentian Gentianaceae *Gentianella germanica* **Distribution**: Central-southern England. **Other habitats**: Scrub; open habitats among tall grasses. **Notes**: A very local species; usually biennial, but occasionally annual when the flowering plants are very small. Leaves usually dead when the plant is in flower.

Ox-eye Daisy Compositae *Chrysanthemum leucanthemum* **Distribution**: Throughout the British Isles, but less common in the north-west of Scotland. **Notes**: A common species, especially on the better types of soil; occasionally lacks the white ray-florets.

Harebell Campanulaceae *Campanula rotundifolia* **Distribution**: Throughout the British Isles; scattered localities in south-west England, north-west Scotland and south and central Ireland. **Other habitats**: Fixed dunes. **Notes**: Locally common; dry places; often grows in poor shallow soils.

Chalk Milkwort Polygalaceae *Polygala calcarea* **Distribution**: South-central and south-eastern England; occasional in the Midlands. **Notes**: Locally common; flower colour varies from intense blue to bluish-white.

Flowers associated with rabbit warrens

Rabbit warrens on calcareous soils create special conditions which favour certain plants to such an extent that they are most commonly found wherever there are rabbit burrows. One of the most conspicuous of these plants is elder. Groups of elder bushes are often found on the site of old rabbit warrens. Their seeds germinate well in the disturbed soil and the growing plants thrive on the high nutrient concentration of the warren soil derived from urine and faeces. Elder can survive while other plants are heavily grazed because the plant is unpalatable to rabbits and is avoided by them.

Many of the colonists which grow in these situations thrive on disturbed soil. Henbane is a distinctive and poisonous weed with medicinal properties; it is rather scarce nowadays. It is readily recognised by its pale yellow flowers with purple veins and sticky foetid foliage. Houndstongue is another plant (avoided by rabbits) which occurs on disturbed chalk. Its strongly-hooked burs readily catch in clothing. Deadly nightshade is nibbled by rabbits but is nevertheless a feature of their warrens, especially on stony limestone soil.

In the calcareous Breck grasslands some of the annuals may be found growing on the loose flinty soil excavated by rabbits. Whole communities of plants occur in this special niche in the grasslands which otherwise only occur where man has disturbed or cultivated the ground. The annuals include common and widespread plants like storksbill and spring whitlow grass and some very rare species. The spring speedwell, which in Britain is confined to a very few places in the Breckland, occurs almost exclusively in these situations.

Grazing by rabbits maintains an extremely short turf, allowing tiny plants to survive that would otherwise be swamped by the more vigorous species around them. Grazing often reveals ant mounds that the rabbits like to sit on and use as latrines, causing a different flora to develop on them, but the mounds in this cliff top picture of Skokholm Island off the Pembroke coast are cushions of thrift.

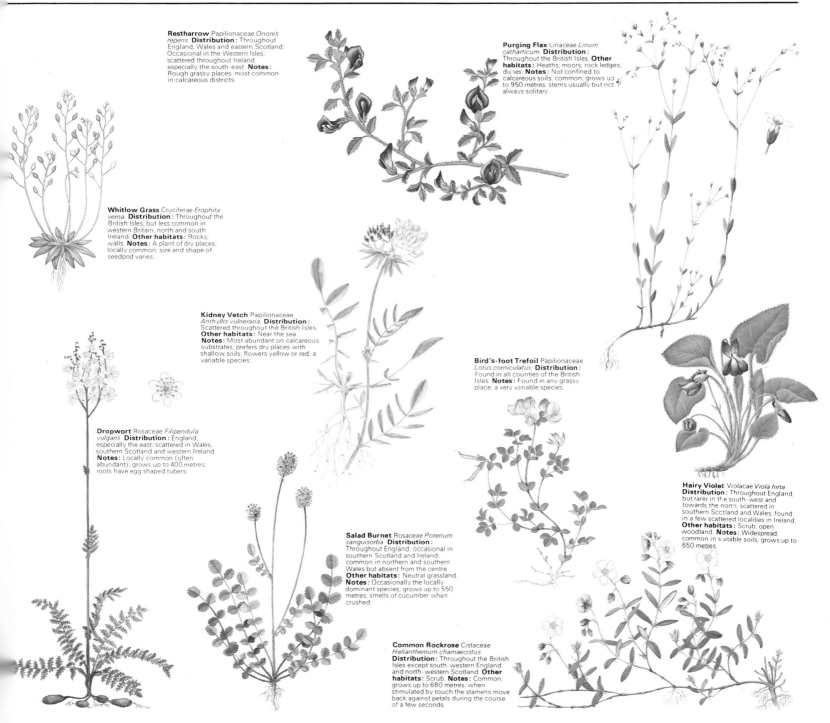

Restharrow Papilionaceae *Ononis repens* **Distribution:** Throughout England, Wales and eastern Scotland; Occasional in the Western Isles; scattered throughout Ireland, especially the south-east. **Notes:** Rough grassy places; most common in calcareous districts.

Whitlow Grass Cruciferae *Erophila verna* **Distribution:** Throughout the British Isles, but less common in western Britain, north and south Ireland. **Other habitats:** Rocks; walls. **Notes:** A plant of dry places; locally common; size and shape of seedpod varies.

Kidney Vetch Papilionaceae *Anthyllis vulneraria* **Distribution:** Scattered throughout the British Isles. **Other habitats:** Near the sea. **Notes:** Most abundant on calcareous substrates; prefers dry places with shallow soils; flowers yellow or red; a variable species.

Dropwort Rosaceae *Filipendula vulgaris* **Distribution:** England, especially the east; scattered in Wales, southern Scotland and western Ireland. **Notes:** Locally common (often abundant), grows up to 400 metres; roots have egg shaped tubers.

Salad Burnet Rosaceae *Poterium sanguisorba* **Distribution:** Throughout England; occasional in southern Scotland and Ireland; common in northern and southern Wales but absent from the centre. **Other habitats:** Neutral grassland. **Notes:** Occasionally the locally dominant species; grows up to 550 metres; smells of cucumber when crushed.

Common Rockrose Cistaceae *Helianthemum chamaecistus* **Distribution:** Throughout the British Isles except south-western England and north-western Scotland. **Other habitats:** Scrub. **Notes:** Common; grows up to 680 metres; when stimulated by touch the stamens move back against petals during the course of a few seconds.

Purging Flax Linaceae *Linum catharticum* **Distribution:** Throughout the British Isles. **Other habitats:** Heaths; moors; rock ledges; dunes. **Notes:** Not confined to calcareous soils; common; grows up to 950 metres; stems usually but not always solitary.

Bird's-foot Trefoil Papilionaceae *Lotus corniculatus* **Distribution:** Found in all counties of the British Isles. **Notes:** Found in any grassy place; a very variable species.

Hairy Violet Violacae *Viola hirta* **Distribution:** Throughout England, but rarer in the south-west and towards the north; scattered in southern Scotland and Wales; found in a few scattered localities in Ireland. **Other habitats:** Scrub; open woodland. **Notes:** Widespread, common in suitable soils; grows up to 650 metres.

The early spider orchid *(Ophrys sphegodes)* is a local species that only grows on calcareous soils. Seed is rarely set as pollination is dependent on the flowers being visited by bees, apparently an infrequent occurrence. This accounts for the rarity and inability of the species to readily spread to and colonise available suitable habitats.

The burnt orchid is a widespread but locally common species that flowers in May and June; it only grows on chalk downs and limestone pastures, mainly in the south.

A guide to some orchids of calcareous grasslands

The orchids, especially of chalk and limestone, are probably the most intensively studied British group of plants. The most commonly encountered species are the fragrant and pyramidal, both of which flower in abundance in June. Others are much rarer and local, with the now almost extinct lady's slipper restricted to one limestone site in Yorkshire. However, the lizard orchid is becoming more common and increasing its range. Others, like the bee orchid, tend to be widespread but only common locally.

Most of the British species are more common in continental Europe and are adapted to warmer and drier conditions than are found here, which explains why most calcareous grassland orchids are more common on the Kent chalk and become progressively rarer towards the north and west.

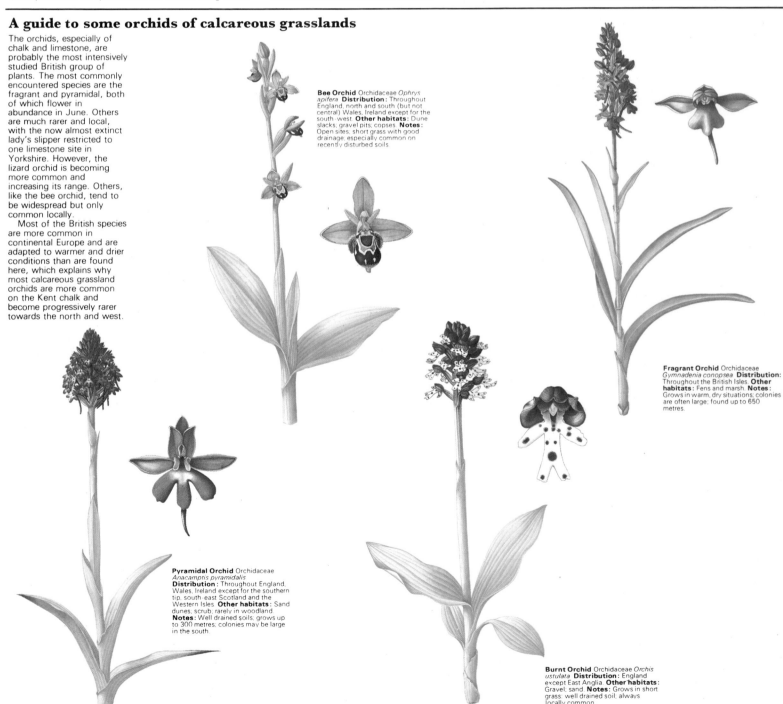

Bee Orchid Orchidaceae *Ophrys apifera* **Distribution:** Throughout England, north and south (but not central) Wales, Ireland except for the south-west. **Other habitats:** Dune slacks, gravel pits, copses. **Notes:** Open sites; short grass with good drainage; especially common on recently disturbed soils

Fragrant Orchid Orchidaceae *Gymnadenia conopsea* **Distribution:** Throughout the British Isles. **Other habitats:** Fens and marsh. **Notes:** Grows in warm, dry situations; colonies are often large; found up to 650 metres.

Pyramidal Orchid Orchidaceae *Anacamptis pyramidalis* **Distribution:** Throughout England, Wales, Ireland except for the southern tip, south-east Scotland and the Western Isles. **Other habitats:** Sand dunes; scrub; rarely in woodland. **Notes:** Well drained soils; grows up to 300 metres; colonies may be large in the south.

Burnt Orchid Orchidaceae *Orchis ustulata* **Distribution:** England except East Anglia. **Other habitats:** Gravel; sand. **Notes:** Grows in short grass; well drained soil; always locally common.

Plymouth. The bee orchid has an unusual form called *trolii*, which has sometimes been called the wasp orchid because of its different flower shape. This plant is found only on oolitic limestone and on the carboniferous limestone near Bristol.

Loose or disturbed soil generally carries a very special flora consisting of plants which are unable to withstand competition but which rapidly colonise bare places. Such situations occur artificially where man has created the disturbance by cultivating the ground or quarrying the rock. Natural sites are provided by screes which occur on steep slopes and below cliffs. Screes on chalk provide a habitat for ground pine, a yellow-flowered member of the mint family which appears sporadically when conditions are suitable. Similarly the screes of the Carboniferous limestone may be colonised by a dainty and diminutive cress called Hutchinsia.

Some of the grasslands of the Breckland have calcareous soils and a flora which has some similarities with chalk and limestone grasslands. The Breckland heaths are situated on sandy soils deposited over chalk. The soils vary from calcareous to acidic, depending on the proximity of the chalk to the surface. The flora is very distinctive and has similarities with the steppe flora of the continent of Europe because of the semi-continental climate and the well-drained sandy soils. The calcareous grasslands contain a number of attractive annual plants which are best seen in the spring. These include fine-

Orchids of calcareous grasslands

A number of species of wild British orchids are confined to chalk and limestone soils. Some of these are common and conspicuous features of these habitats; although it is the spectacularly beautiful flowers which attract people to these plants, there are also many other interesting aspects to their biology.

The seeds are very small and are produced in enormous numbers. Each seed contains very little food reserve, so that its initial growth is slow. The first leaves may not be produced for some years and the first flowers many years later. The bee orchid, for example, takes 6-8 years to produce flowers, while the burnt orchid takes as long as 12 or 13 years. The young orchid plant is dependent in its early stages on an association with a fungus which invades the roots of the developing plant. This association is called a mycorrhiza and is essential for the survival and further development of the orchid. The fungus, which grows as a saprophyte, derives food from dead plant material in the soil. Food substances are passed to those parts of the fungal hyphae in the orchid root, where they are absorbed by the orchid plant. There is throughout a delicate balance between the

tendency for the fungus to invade the orchid root completely and the tendency for the orchid to digest the invading hyphae.

The orchid plant develops at first as a leafless rhizome and later produces leafy shoots which makes it less dependent on the mycorrhiza for food. The plant produces fleshy swollen tubers that provide stored food for the production of the aerial parts of the plant; excess food is returned from the leaves to the roots to form new tubers for the next year's growth.

Many common grassland orchids such as the spotted orchid and twayblade produce flower spikes each year for several years in succession. Other species such as the fragrant and bee orchids store only enough food to permit flowering and fruiting only once before the plant dies. This results in fluctuations in the number of orchid flowers appearing from year to year in one place. A particularly favourable year for seed production or germination will result in the synchronous flowering of many plants some years later.

The common spotted orchid can grow in a variety of habitats as it is very variable and its different forms have differing ecological requirements. Unlike most other orchids its roots are large and branched and resemble human fingers.

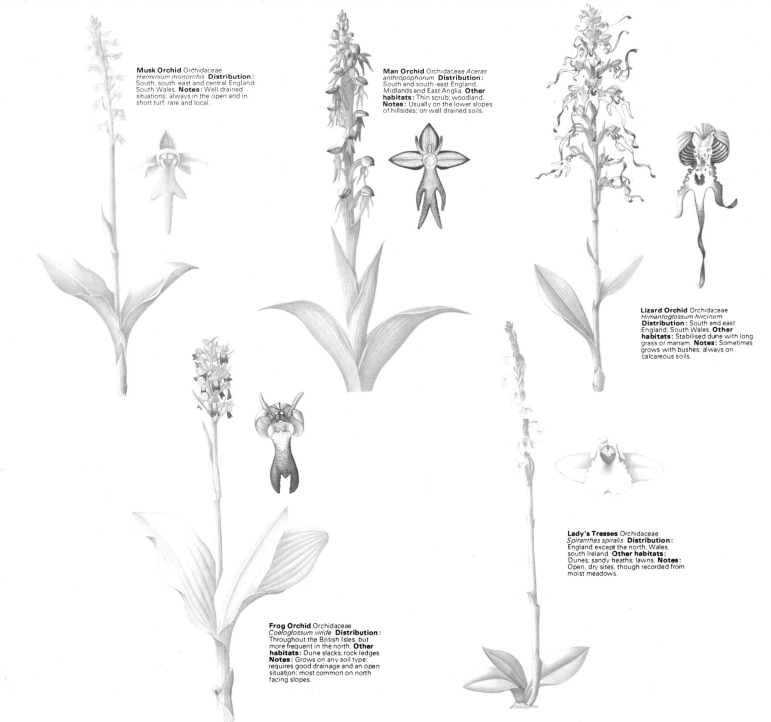

Musk Orchid Orchidaceae *Herminium monorchis* **Distribution:** South, south-east and central England; South Wales. **Notes:** Well drained situations; always in the open and in short turf; rare and local.

Man Orchid Orchidaceae *Aceras anthropophorum* **Distribution:** South and south-east England, Midlands and East Anglia. **Other habitats:** Thin scrub; woodland. **Notes:** Usually on the lower slopes of hillsides; on well drained soils.

Lizard Orchid Orchidaceae *Himantoglossum hircinum* **Distribution:** South and east England; South Wales. **Other habitats:** Stabilised dune with long grass or marram. **Notes:** Sometimes grows with bushes; always on calcareous soils.

Frog Orchid Orchidaceae *Coeloglossum viride.* **Distribution:** Throughout the British Isles, but more frequent in the north. **Other habitats:** Dune slacks; rock ledges. **Notes:** Grows on any soil type; requires good drainage and an open situation; most common on north facing slopes.

Lady's Tresses Orchidaceae *Spiranthes spiralis.* **Distribution:** England except the north, Wales, south Ireland. **Other habitats:** Dunes; sandy heaths; lawns. **Notes:** Open, dry sites, though recorded from moist meadows.

leaved sandwort, fairy flax, meadow saxifrage and the curious fern moonwort. The coarser grasslands contain the rare Spanish catchfly confined in Britain to the Breckland, the maiden pink, and the Breckland mugwort. Trackside and disturbed ground support other special plants of the region, including smooth rupture-wort, sand catchfly and the perennial knawel. The faintly musk-scented wild grape hyacinth is a special feature of the grassland fringing fields and old tracksides. Its dull slatey blue flowers are quite distinct from the bright blue cultivated varieties. The very rare eastern spiked speedwell may still be found in some of the remaining calcareous grasslands. Its relative in western Britain is not so elusive and may be seen on limestone cliffs and outcrops.

Where the Breck grasslands are highly calcareous they produce a magnificent show of common chalk flowers typical of eastern England. In particular the purple milk vetch and wild thyme colour the ground with huge patches of flowers, intermixed with the coral pink of squinancy wort. In places where the grassland is broken, particularly by rabbit activity, there is a wealth of annual plants including more specialities of the Breck like spring speedwell, spring vetch and shepherd's cress, which are among the more local colonists of scrapes in the sand. There are also many commoner plants such as storksbill and common bird's-foot, which abound here and elsewhere.

The stemless thistle *(Cirsium acaulon)* is characteristic of closely grazed calcareous pastures. Usually it has a rosette of spiny leaves with a few sessile flower heads in the centre; occasionally it has a simple or branched stem to 30cm. Seventeenth century herbalists highly prized it as a preventative and cure for the plague.

A guide to some wild flowers of calcareous grasslands (continued)

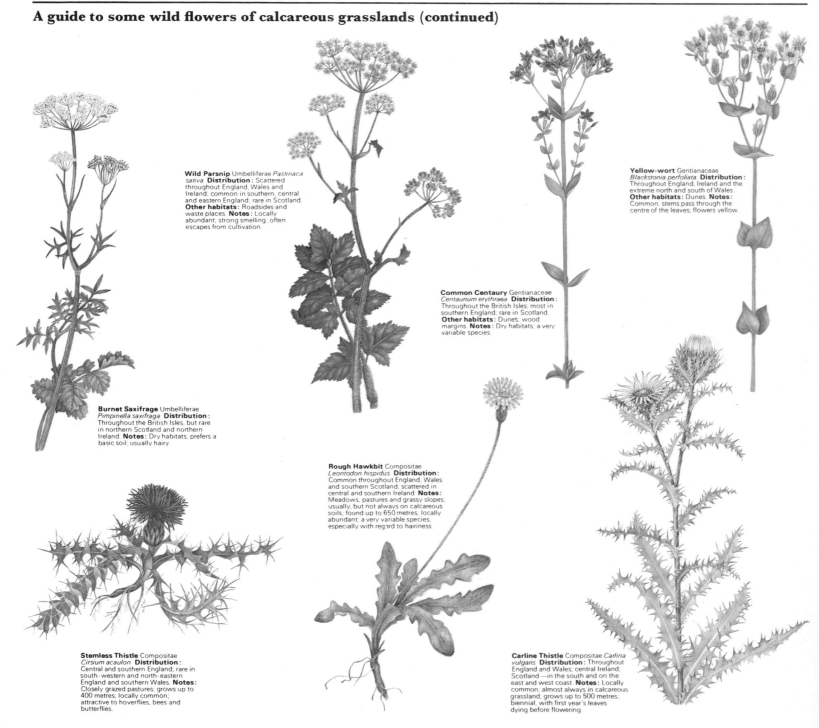

Wild Parsnip Umbelliferae *Pastinaca sativa* **Distribution:** Scattered throughout England, Wales and Ireland; common in southern, central and eastern England; rare in Scotland. **Other habitats:** Roadsides and waste places. **Notes:** Locally abundant; strong smelling; often escapes from cultivation.

Yellow-wort Gentianaceae *Blackstonia perfoliata* **Distribution:** Throughout England, Ireland and the extreme north and south of Wales. **Other habitats:** Dunes. **Notes:** Common; stems pass through the centre of the leaves; flowers yellow.

Common Centaury Gentianaceae *Centaunum erythraea* **Distribution:** Throughout the British Isles; most in southern England; rare in Scotland. **Other habitats:** Dunes; wood margins. **Notes:** Dry habitats; a very variable species.

Burnet Saxifrage Umbelliferae *Pimpinella saxifraga* **Distribution:** Throughout the British Isles, but rare in northern Scotland and northern Ireland. **Notes:** Dry habitats; prefers a basic soil; usually hairy.

Rough Hawkbit Compositae *Leontodon hispidus* **Distribution:** Common throughout England, Wales and southern Scotland; scattered in central and southern Ireland. **Notes:** Meadows, pastures and grassy slopes; usually, but not always on calcareous soils; found up to 650 metres; locally abundant; a very variable species, especially with regard to hairiness.

Stemless Thistle Compositae *Cirsium acaulon* **Distribution:** Central and southern England; rare in south-western and north-eastern England and southern Wales. **Notes:** Closely grazed pastures; grows up to 400 metres; locally common; attractive to hoverflies, bees and butterflies.

Carline Thistle Compositae *Carlina vulgaris* **Distribution:** Throughout England and Wales; central Ireland; Scotland—in the south and on the east and west coast. **Notes:** Locally common; almost always in calcareous grassland; grows up to 500 metres; biennial, with first year's leaves dying before flowering.

The Scrub Habitat

Habitats dominated by shrubs develop as one stage in the process of succession. This is a natural sequence of vegetation communities forming a series of stages in the restoration of Britain's ancient forest cover; the succession may with suitable management be arrested at any stage, from grassland through scrub to forest, so that a mosaic of scrub and grassland may persist, or an impenetrable thicket may develop. Dense scrub may persist if tree growth is inhibited, for example on unstable rock slopes or in exposed maritime habitats.

The most critical phase in the development of scrub is the initial establishment of the shrub species, which cannot tolerate having their young growing points bitten off by grazers. Once small shrubs have become established in the grassland, however, they can withstand more grazing by sheep and rabbits as they get bigger. Shrub species thus rapidly take over grassland to form scrub after some relaxation of grazing pressure, such as occurred after the outbreak of myxomatosis or occurs where sheep grazing is suddenly stopped. Many even-aged stands of scrub can be traced back to events of this type, which allowed the shrubs to first establish themselves.

Speed of development

The type of scrub and the speed of development depend on factors such as the soil type, the management of the grassland and the availability of nearby seed sources. Many of the shrubs of calcareous soils have fleshy fruits distributed by birds such as blackbirds, thrushes, redwings and fieldfares which descend on them in flocks during the winter months. Hawthorn, commonly planted in hedgerows, provides an abundant seed source for colonising open grassland, which accounts for its predominance in scrub. Conversely, species such as juniper and yew are rare hedgerow plants and rarely colonise grassland. Many of the common calcareous scrub species, such as dog rose, juniper and hawthorn, are armed with spines or thorns or are able to form suckers or re-grow from the stem base. These adaptations give a degree of protection against grazing animals. Less well-protected and more susceptible plants tend to occur in the middle of patches of spiny species where they are afforded protection from browsing. Animals which browse the scrub have a considerable influence on the development of the scrub by selecting certain species and avoiding others. For example, elder is often associated with the bare disturbed chalk or limestone of rabbit warrens because it favours loose soil and is avoided by grazing animals.

Establishment of trees

If the scrub is very dense it may prevent or delay the establishment of trees. However, if tree species were originally able to seed into the grassland and establish themselves at the same time as the shrubs they may later grow up through the scrub, and eventually form a woodland canopy. The shrub species then persist as an understorey in the woodland, with the loss of those species, such as juniper, which are intolerant of shade.

Shrub species on calcareous soils include a variety of deciduous and evergreen plants. On deep soils the scrub is dominated more by hawthorn, dog rose and bramble, while on shallow soils plants such as hazel, juniper, dogwood, box and elder may be found. The later stages of succession to woodland are marked by the presence of yew, ash or beech trees. In certain situations, one particular species may predominate. Hazel is a particular feature of the limestone of north and western Britain, where it may be seen on pavements and other outcrops. On the Burren in County Clare it forms a stable community, although elsewhere it develops into ash wood. Juniper, an evergreen coniferous shrub, may predominate on dry shallow chalk

Hawthorn is the common dominant scrub species on most soil types, though it does not thrive on wet peat or poor acid substrates. Here it is shown in flower on chalk downland near Pewsey in Wiltshire.

or limestone. It is commoner in the north of Britain and is often intermixed with yew, white beam and other species; it is usually succeeded by yew wood.

The latter species can itself form scrub in its young stages, developing into woodland later, when it suppresses virtually all ground flora with its dense shade. Another evergreen which occasionally develops as scrub cover is box. It occurs in very few places in Britain on chalk and Jurassic limestone. In two places it contributes to local site names: at Box Hill in Surrey and Box in Gloucestershire, where it occurs on steep slopes.

On the chalk in southern England the scrub is often composed of a variety of species without any plant being conspicuously dominant. In such situations several shrubs produce attractive flowers and fruits. The wayfaring tree, dogwood, privet and spindle are good examples of shrubs which grow mixed with hawthorn, dog rose, white beam and others. Dogwood may dominate the scrub on chalk soils poor in nutrients, or where former arable land has been recolonised.

Alien species can invade grasslands, if there are suitable seed sources nearby, and create a scrub cover in their young stages. The turkey oak and sycamore are particularly invasive alien plants which quickly establish themselves in this way, while buddleja from gardens often dominates the sides of chalk quarries.

Scrub provides a habitat suitable for other plants, which often form a ground flora beneath. However this herb layer may be ephemeral, and is soon altered by developing shade unless maintained by stability of conditions or the existence of a scrub and grassland mosaic. Semi-climbers such as tufted vetch may sprawl over low bushes, while the more woody climbers like old man's beard (especially characteristic of chalky areas in southern England) create a superstructure that can completely cover the shrubs. White bryony and black bryony are unrelated climbing plants which have a less overwhelming growth form.

Grassland is not the natural climax vegetation in most areas, so it tends to be invaded by woody scrub as the first stages of reversion to thickets and forest. This succession is normally kept in check by grazers.

Invertebrates of Calcareous Habitats

Calcareous grassland and scrub habitats generally support a wealth of insects and other invertebrate animal life. This is partly due to the rich variety of plant life and partly due to the diversity of conditions and micro-climates that chalk or limestone hills provide. On downland areas the topography provides many features with different climatic conditions; south-facing slopes are hot and dry in summer and favour sun-loving insects, while north-facing slopes may be moister, favouring species which live, or overwinter, in moss. Deep coombes, which are often a feature of chalk hills, produce a sheltered climate that favours butterflies and other more delicate insects. Mosaics of scrub and grassland produce conditions which are often very favourable to insects because the grassland plants which occur in the glades provide essential food, while the scrub provides sheltered conditions. Steep slopes on chalk and scree slopes below cliffs produce bare stony environments which favour insects needing sparsely vegetated habitats.

In addition to these major ecological niches for the grassland invertebrates there are many more specialised opportunities. The deep grykes of limestone pavement produce dark, damp retreats which contrast strongly with the dry, exposed habitats which predominate in chalk and limestone districts. Rabbit and other mammal burrows produce similarly humid habitats within grassland, while the nests of mammals, birds and insects also provide special conditions for a limited number of creatures. Dung and dead bodies from grazing animals encourage further diversity and not only have a characteristic fauna in open grassland situations, but also attract other insects in times of drought or when moisture is in short supply. Fresh dung readily attracts some of the downland blue butterflies under such conditions, as well as the usual swarms of dungflies.

The invertebrate fauna of grassland may be divided into the species which live in the soil layer and those which feed on the grassland plants. The soil animals may be further divided into those dwelling in the soil itself and those living in the layer of decomposing leaf litter on the soil surface. Some creatures spend all their lives in one particular niche, but there are many

Snails need an abundant supply of calcium carbonate to build up their shells. They are consequently more abundant in chalk and limestone areas than in calcium-deficient habitats such as heathland.

Roman snail

The Roman, or edible snail (*Helix pomatia*) is a large and distinctive mollusc which was almost certainly first introduced into Britain by the Romans as food, but has subsequently been re-introduced as a curiosity to large estates. Its present distribution in Britain centres on the chalk of the North Downs and Hertfordshire and on the limestone in Gloucestershire. It may be found in a variety of places, but steep grassy banks with a south west-facing slope are the favoured habitats. It is equally at home in scrub or grassland and can be found in artificial situations such as railway cuttings and quarries.

In September or October the snail digs into the soil to form a burrow, where it hibernates during the winter months. It seals the mouth of the shell with a chalky plug, which can be pushed off when the animal resumes activity the following April, as soon as the weather turns wet and mild. All snail activity is limited by the weather, particularly rainfall and humidity. The adult snails mate during spells of wet weather in May or June, and lay their eggs from May onwards through the summer after heavy rain has moistened and softened the soil. On average more than 30 eggs are laid in holes excavated in the soil.

These hatch after three to five weeks and the young snails eat their egg shells before emerging to feed on plants. They spend several years increasing in size and and reach maturity when the shell forms a raised lip at the mouth. Thereafter the shell increases in thickness only by annually-added layers. Roman snails are known to live up to nine years, during which time they feed on flowering plants, showing a preference for hardhead and greater knapweed.

Their enemies are relatively few. Mammals and predatory insects probably account for most losses by predation. Rats eat the adult snails, biting away the shell from the mouth to extract the animal. Young snails are eagerly taken by shrews and field mice and by beetles such as the violet ground beetle and the glow worm larva. In European countries they are collected for consumption by man, especially in France, where millions are eaten every year, causing some concern that the snails may become locally extinct through over-collecting.

Individual snails are both male and female (hermaphrodite), but mating still takes place, usually on cool damp nights, in order to fertilise the partner's eggs. These are laid in sheltered places and hatch in a few weeks.

A guide to some snails and slugs

Semi-natural chalk and limestone grasslands, such as occur in the South Downs, the Cotswolds, the Peak District or the Yorkshire Dales, are excellent places for snails and slugs. Richest in species are those with a variety of habitats within a small area: for example, a mixture of sheep-grazed turf, longer moist grass, stone walls, and rocks or broken ground (snails are often prolific in old quarries). The most characteristic snail species are the helicellids (*Candidula*, *Cernuella*, *Helicella*), which are adapted to drought and can survive long periods in dry sunny weather inertly attached to plant stems in order to escape from the heat of the ground. These are common also in coastal sand dunes. Other species find shelter by burrowing, like the round-mouthed snail *Pomatias elegans*, restricted to loose chalky soils. All snails and slugs require moisture and most are nocturnal, so that a close search may be needed to find them, eg by parting the roots of grasses or turning over stones. Only when the humidity is high will they move abroad freely, rock faces for example then becoming temporarily covered with *Clausilia* or *Lauria* emerging from chinks to graze on algae. Some slugs can be strongly seasonal. Remember also that many snails are tiny and the diversity of species is much greater than someone familiar only with a few of the large helicids like the garden or brown-lipped snails might suspect.

x2

Round-mouthed Snail Pomatiidae *Pomatias elegans* 15mm. **Distribution:** Common locally in S. England and Wales. **Habitats:** Hedgebanks, cliffs, screes, always on chalk or limestone; requires a loose friable substrate for burrowing. **Note:** Has an operculum like marine snails but unlike most land shells.

x4

Rounded Snail Endodontidae *Discus rotundatus* 7mm. **Distribution:** Almost ubiquitous, except in the Scottish Highlands. **Habitats:** Common nearly everywhere under ground litter: woods, rocks, hedgerows, waste ground. **Note:** Easily recognised by its regular brown striping.

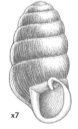

x7

Chrysalis Snail Pupillidae *Lauria cylindracea* 4mm. **Distribution:** Nearly throughout, but much commoner in western areas. **Habitats:** Woods, walls, rocks, often abundant under ivy on tops of stone walls.

x11

Ribbed Snail Valloniidae *Vallonia costata* 2.5mm. **Distribution:** Locally common in lowland Britain and Ireland, absent from the highland zone. **Habitats:** Open grassy calcareous places: chalk downs, walls, rocks. **Note:** The very delicate ribs are easily rubbed off.

x4½

Slippery Snail Cochlicopidae *Cochlicopa lubrica* 7mm. **Distribution:** Almost ubiquitous throughout British Isles. **Habitats:** Catholic: grassland, woods, hedgerows, marshes.

x4

Door Snail Clausiliidae *Clausilia bidentata* 12mm. **Distribution:** Almost throughout British Isles, especially in rocky areas (but absent where air pollution is high). **Habitats:** Woods, walls, rocks; climbs up vertical surfaces in damp weather to feed on algae and lichens.

x2

Lapidary Snail Helicidae *Helicigona lapicida* 17mm. **Distribution:** Local (declining) in S.E. and central Britain, from Devon to Yorkshire. **Habitats:** Rocks, cliffs, woods, stone walls. **Note:** Known by its sharp keel. Hides deep in crevices; difficult to find alive in dry weather.

x1½

Brown-lipped Snail Helicidae *Cepaea nemoralis* 22mm. **Distribution:** Common throughout, north to the Great Glen. **Habitats:** Catholic: woods, fields, hedgerows. **Note:** Very variable in colour and banding (often plain). Predated by thrushes.

x5

Pellucid Snail Vitrinidae *Vitrina pellucida* 6mm. **Distribution:** Almost ubiquitous. **Habitats:** Catholic: fields, woods, hedgerows, sand-dunes. **Note:** Body large and scarcely withdrawable within shell. Often found alive in winter.

x2

Cellar Snail Zonitidae *Oxychilus cellarius* 11mm. **Distribution:** Common throughout, except in the Scottish Highlands. **Habitats:** Sheltered places under ground litter: woods, hedgerows, gardens. Often in caves and cellars.

x1

Common Garden Snail Helicidae *Helix aspersa* 35mm. **Distribution:** Common in S. Britain and Ireland, rarer in north coastal only in Scotland. **Habitats:** Walls, hedgerows, waste ground, gardens. **Note:** Hibernates in crevices and under stones. A garden pest.

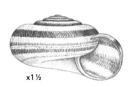

x1½

Heath Snail Helicidae *Helicella itala* 18mm. **Distribution:** Local (declining) in S. and E. England; S. Ireland; elsewhere coastal only. **Habitats:** Dry calcareous grassy and sandy places: chalk downs, hedgebanks, often common on dunes. **Note:** Fastens itself to plant stems in dry, sunny weather.

x2

Striped Snail Helicidae *Cernuella virgata* 15mm. **Distribution:** S. and E. England, and S. Ireland; elsewhere coastal only. **Habitats:** Dry calcareous grassy and sandy places: stubble fields, hedgebanks, chalk downs. **Note:** Fastens itself to plant stems in dry, sunny weather.

x3

Hairy Snail Helicidae *Trichia hispida* 9mm. **Distribution:** Common nearly everywhere, as far north as Perthshire. **Habitats:** Catholic: fields, woods, hedgerows. **Note:** Shell typically covered with fine bristly hairs (often rubbed off in adults).

x2

Strawberry Snail Helicidae *Trichia striolata* 13mm. **Distribution:** Common everywhere, except in N. Scotland and some Midland counties. **Habitats:** Hedgerows, fields, gardens, waste ground. **Note:** Shell never hairy when adult (cf. *T. hispida*).

x1

Kentish Snail Helicidae *Monacha cantiana* 20mm. **Distribution:** Common in S.E. England from Dorset to Yorkshire; very rare elsewhere (not in Ireland). **Habitats:** Hedgebanks, fields, waste ground, mostly on calcareous soils. **Note:** Shell hairy when very young.

x2½

Wrinkled Snail Helicidae *Candidula intersecta* 10mm. **Distribution:** S. England and Ireland, elsewhere mainly coastal. **Habitats:** Dry calcareous grass and sandy places: fields, hedgebanks, chalk downs, dunes. **Note:** Fastens itself to plant stems in dry, sunny weather.

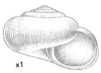

x1

x1½

x1

Black Slug Arionidae *Arion ater* 120mm. **Distribution:** Almost ubiquitous. **Habitats:** Fields, woods, hedgerows, gardens. **Note:** Colouring very variable: red or orange varieties are common in the south, black forms are more typical of mountains and wild places.

Garden Slug Arionidae *Arion hortensis* 30mm. **Distribution:** Almost ubiquitous, except in the Scottish Highlands. **Habitats:** Fields, woods, hedgerows; typical of cultivated places. **Note:** Recognised by its orange sole. A serious pest of crops and gardens.

Field Slug Limacidae *Deroceras reticulatum* 50mm. **Distribution:** Ubiquitous. **Habitats:** Fields, hedgerows, gardens, waste ground. **Note:** Emits an opaque milky mucus if fingered. A serious pest of gardens and crops.

inhabitants which spend only part of their lives in the soil or litter layers. For example, grasshoppers lay their eggs in the soil but live above ground, while crane-flies spend their larval life in the soil feeding on plant roots, but emerge as adults to fly amongst the grassland flowers. Moths may spend only their pupal stage actually in the soil, their eggs, caterpillars and adults being part of the fauna of the vegetation.

The true soil fauna itself consists of small creatures present in enormous numbers and high densities. Mites, springtails, and small worms of different types all dwell in the soil feeding on soil fungi and plant detritus, and contributing to the breakdown of dead plant material and the recycling of nutrients. The litter layer on the soil surface provides shelter and cool humid conditions which favour those invertebrates vulnerable to water loss, such as springtails, woodlice, millipedes and snails.

The grassland plants themselves are devoured by a wide range of herbivorous invertebrate animals. All parts of plants are eaten, often by very specialised feeders. Roots are eaten by the

Slugs and land snails lay quite large eggs, each with a tough white shell to protect the embryos inside from water loss. Pond snails do not have this problem and lay eggs in jelly with no shell.

Ants and anthills

Ants are dominant insects of many habitats, especially grasslands. This is because of the aggressive nature of these predatory insects, combined with their large numbers. Calcareous grasslands are inhabited by a number of species, belonging especially to the genera *Myrmica* (including the red ant *M. rufa*) and *Lasius* (including the meadow ant *L. flavus*).

Myrmica ants generally form small colonies of one to two thousand individuals, often nesting in spaces excavated under the flat stones common in limestone districts. The *Lasius* ants commonly form very large colonies of tens of thousands of individuals. The meadow ant constructs large soil mounds, which are a conspicuous feature of grazed calcareous grassland. The nests of ants are necessary to provide protection for their colonies, and an improved micro-

climate; they are also used for storage of food and rearing the brood. The micro-climate of the nest mounds is more humid than the surroundings, especially in nests under stones, and their temperature is subject to less fluctuation than the outside air.

More than one species of ant may co-exist within a grassland area, as the ants have different foraging habits. *Myrmica* ants feed above the soil surface amongst the herbage, where they prey on bugs, flies,

spiders and other ants. The meadow ant feeds on or below the soil surface preying especially on soil animals such as large mites, beetle larvae and woodlice. All ants are capable of laying chemical trails between the nest and a food source and of communicating with their fellow workers to recruit

support for collecting food.

Grassland ants require nectar or sugary fluids for their energy requirements, and often collect honeydew exuded by aphids for this purpose. Honeydew is a waste product of aphids, consisting of plant sap with some food substances removed and some excretory

products added. The meadow ant farms suitable aphids, storing and tending their eggs during the winter and tending the adult root aphids in cavities in the ground near their nests during the summer. The surface foraging ant species similarly farm aphids on the stems of low herbs.

Worker

x6

x4 **Queen**

Yellow Ant Formicidae *Lasius flavus*
Distribution: Throughout British Isles, but most common in south.
Other habitats: Heathlands and gardens. **Adult active**: Spring to autumn (hibernate deep in soil for winter). **Food**: Mainly other insects on the ground, together with honeydew from aphids.

The yellow ant *Lasius flavus* is a common grassland species. Here the adults are tending their cocoons which are popularly called ants' eggs. Both these and the adult insects are a favourite food of the green woodpecker, which feeds extensively in old grassland areas.

larvae of beetles and moths, such as the crambid grass moths, which feed on grass roots and the bases of stems. The root nodules of leguminous plants are favoured by some beetle larvae; many sawflies and other groups feed on plant stems, generally as stem-borers, feeding inside the stem and hollowing out the soft inner tissues. The eggs of insects such as the speckled bush cricket are also inserted into the stems of plants, but the later stages do not feed there. Leaf blades form the main food supply of many species of insects in both their adult and larval stages. Caterpillars and beetles defoliate plants by biting away whole pieces of the leaves, but some smaller insects are so minute that they can feed in the soft tissues in the middle of the leaves without touching the epidermal layers. These leaf miners, which include the larvae of tiny moths such as *Elachista* and Agromyzid flies, are protected by feeding inside the leaves rather than being exposed on the leaf surface. The buds, flowers, fruits and seed heads of many grassland flowers are also attacked by weevils and other insects; the protein-rich seeds of leguminous

plants are especially popular as food items. The large and persistent seed heads of the knapweeds carry whole communities of insects which feed on the plant materials or parasitise or predate the herbivores.

In these species-rich grassland communities, extreme specialisation among invertebrates is the rule rather than the exception, as one might expect. This particularly applies to certain insects which feed only on plants belonging to one family; sometimes only a single species will do. Whilst the diversity of the habitat persists, these creatures are secure, but they are the first to be affected when circumstances change. Hence the increasing rarity of some of the most extreme specialists as the area of undisturbed ancient grassland in Britain is diminished. Quite small changes in grassland management may thus have far-reaching effects among the invertebrate fauna, reducing both total numbers and the variety of species.

The structure of grassland is particularly crucial for insects. Close-grazed turf clearly provides less food for many herbivorous species

and grazing may drastically reduce the numbers of those that depend on flowers or seed heads. The field grasshopper, however, prefers short grass, while several insect species deposit their eggs in compacted soil. These animals therefore benefit from the effects of grazing, but insects in general do better when grazing stops and allows longer grass to develop. Tall grasses obviously provide more food for plant eaters, but, equally important, they provide a more sheltered and humid micro-climate as well as producing an accumulation of plant litter. The actual structure of the grassland is also more favourable under these conditions, as the long grass allows much vertical movement in the vegetation, protected from the eyes of many predatory birds, as well as movement along the ground surface. Long grass also provides a place for spiders to live and spin their webs, while coarse tussock grasses such as cock's-foot form a specialised protected habitat for insects which spend the winter in their stem bases.

These differences in grassland structure are not only influenced by whether or not there is

Dungflies

Many flies (order Diptera) are attracted to dung—to feed on the associated fluids, to lay their eggs on it, or perhaps to do both. The most numerous flies on cow-pats in the fields are usually the golden yellow males of *Scathophaga stercoraria*. These gather on the dung in large numbers to await the arrival of the less

brightly coloured females. The insects then pair up and mate, usually a little way from the dung, and the female returns there to lay her eggs later. *Scathophaga* is a carnivorous insect in the adult state, feeding on other small flies which it often catches around the dung. It plunges its beak into the prey to suck the juices.

x2

Yellow Dungfly Scathophagidae
Scathophaga stercoraria
Distribution: Throughout British Isles. **Other habitats**: Hedgerow flowers—in search of insects. **Adult Active**: Early spring to autumn.
Food: Other insects.

Dungflies are a common sight on cowpats in summer. Their larvae, together with worms and beetles, clear away

the dung which would otherwise smother large numbers of plants for long periods.

Ground beetles

Beetles (order Coleoptera) are a very large group of insects in which the front wings have become hardened and converted into protective shields called elytra. They usually cover nearly all of the body, and the delicate hind wings are folded up underneath them. Many beetles, however, have no hind wings and cannot fly. Some that live habitually on the ground even have the elytra fused together for extra strength. All beetles have biting mouth-parts and they feed on a wide variety of foods. Those that live on the ground are generally carnivorous or scavengers. True ground beetles of the family Carabidae are all carnivores. Beetle larvae exhibit an immense variety of form, but all have biting mouth-parts and they feed on just as wide a variety of foods as the adults.

The Devil's coach-horse beetle *(Ocypus olens)* is nocturnal. During the day it hides under stones and, when disturbed, arches its body.

Violet Ground Beetle Carabidae *Carabus violaceus.* **Distribution:** Most of British Isles. **Other habitats:** Woodlands; gardens; hedgerows. **Adult active:** All year, but hibernates when very cold. Nocturnal. **Food:** Slugs and other invertebrates.

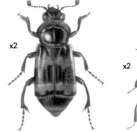

Devil's Coach-horse or **Cocktail** Staphylinidae *Ocypus olens.* **Distribution:** Much of British Isles. **Other habitats:** Woodlands; gardens and buildings; hedgerows. **Adult active:** Most of the year. Nocturnal. **Food:** Other invertebrates.

Pterostichus nigrita Carabidae. **Distribution:** Much of British Isles, especially in damp places. **Other habitats:** Woodlands; hedgerows gardens. **Adult active:** All year, but hibernates when very cold. Nocturnal. **Food:** Slugs and other invertebrates.

Carrion beetles

Many beetles (order Coleoptera) eat and breed in carrion. The most famous are the burying beetles or sexton beetles of the genus *Necrophorus.* These beetles, which are black or black and orange, generally work in pairs on the carcases of voles and other small creatures. They eat small amounts of flesh, but their main job is to bury the carcases by digging out the soil below and allowing them to sink into the ground. Eggs are laid on the carcase when it is buried, and the grubs that hatch out are fed by the mother at first. Later, they begin to eat the fly maggots and other small insects that are themselves eating the decaying flesh.

Necrophorus vespillo Silphidae. **Distribution:** Most of British Isles. **Other habitats:** Hedgerows; woodlands. **Adult active:** Summer. **Food:** Carrion and associated insects. **Note:** One of several similar species, which differ in the orange pattern.

Hister impressus Histeridae. **Distribution:** Much of British Isles. **Other habitats:** Dung almost anywhere. **Adult active:** Summer. **Food:** Carrion, dung, and associated small insects.

Dung beetles

Beetles (order Coleoptera) play a major role in the breakdown of animal dung. Dung beetles actually had to be introduced to New Zealand to help get rid of sheep and cattle dung. There are no native dung beetles there because there are no large native mammals to provide the dung. Some beetles merely eat the dung or lay their eggs in it, but some true dung beetles, such as *Geotrupes* and the famous scarabs, bury pellets of dung and lay their eggs in them. The beetle grubs have just enough dung to last them until they are fully grown. Most dung beetles have broad front legs which they use for tunnelling and shovelling.

grazing but also by its timing. Summer grazing tends to reduce insect numbers by removing food and cover, while autumn and winter grazing generally have less effect on the numbers of insects. Patches of scrub considerably broaden the scope for insect species by providing different species as foodplants and a much larger structured habitat to occupy. In Britain species belonging to the rose family are known to support large numbers of insect species. Bramble, rose, and blackthorn all support more than 100 species, while hawthorn supports more than 200 species. In contrast, the evergreens yew, box and holly each support fewer than 20 species of insects, although juniper and privet have a more diverse insect fauna.

A few groups of invertebrates are most conspicuous in calcareous grasslands. Snails are a particular feature of calcareous districts because they require calcium carbonate for their shells; those found on chalk downland may have especially thick shells. The best sites for snails are semi-natural grasslands which are not heavily grazed or cut for hay. Most species prefer moister, north-facing or shaded slopes; few species can withstand hot sunny locations. The heath snail, a rather flat-spired snail with creamy whorls striped with brown, is a common species of dry pastures often found on grass or thistle stems in dry weather. Some species are very scarce, such as the top snail, a small conical-shelled species that is only known from one or two places in south east England, while others such as glass snails and whorl snails are tiny and insignificant. Limestone pavement, especially at low altitude, is an important habitat for the specialised snails which live in rock crevices. Dry stone walls built of limestone blocks create a similar habitat; the lapidary snail is a flattened species which inhabits these locations in England, Wales and Ireland. Another rock dweller is the craven door snail which occurs in northern England.

Grasshoppers and bushcrickets are large, conspicuous insects particularly abundant in chalk grasslands. Grasshoppers generally deposit their eggs in the soil during the late summer; the larvae hatch in spring to grow into mature

Dung beetles and carrion beetles are nature's road sweepers. They clear away organic material which would otherwise break down only slowly.

Mites

Mites are very small arachnids, with rounded or pear-shaped bodies and eight very short legs in most species. Huge numbers of them live in the soil and in leaf litter, where they feed on fungi and decaying matter or else on other mites and small insects. Some with very round bodies live in water. Red velvet mites are often seen walking on concrete paths and on walls. They feed largely on insect eggs, although the young stages suck fluids from adult insects. Some mites are full-time parasites, infesting the skin of mammals and causing mange.

Mites at nymph stage infest a crane-fly's head. After sucking blood they drop and become free-living, feeding on detritus in the soil, and laying their eggs on the ground.

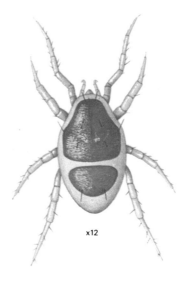

Parasitus coleoptratorum Parasitidae. **Distribution:** Throughout British Isles, on dung and on dung beetles. **Other habitats:** Associated with dung anywhere. **Adult active:** Most of the year. **Food:** Fungi associated with dung.

Dor Beetle Geotrupidae *Geotrupes stercorarius.* **Distribution:** Throughout British Isles. **Other habitats:** Woodlands. **Adult active:** April to October. **Food:** Dung.

Aphodius rufipes Scarabaeidae. **Distribution:** Throughout British Isles. **Other habitats:** Woodlands. **Adult active:** Summer; often flies to light. **Food:** Dung of hoofed mammals.

Philonthus laminatus Staphylinidae. **Distribution:** Throughout British Isles. **Other habitats:** Woodlands. **Adult active:** Summer. **Food:** Dung and associated insects.

Emus hirtus Staphylinidae. **Distribution:** Southern and eastern parts of England. **Other habitats:** Farmyards; anywhere with cows. **Adult active:** Summer. **Food:** Cow dung.

adults from mid-summer onwards. The adult insects draw attention to themselves by their song, the males of each species producing a characteristic song to attract a mate. Grasshoppers particularly like warm conditions and consequently favour south-facing, sunny slopes; two of the rarer species, the stripe-winged and rufus grasshoppers, are restricted to this habitat on chalk hills such as the North Downs and Cotswolds. The meadow and field grasshoppers are more- widespread, while the common green grasshopper occurs all over the mainland and reaches Ireland and the Orkneys. The mottled grasshopper is a smaller insect which also occurs on heathland, where it seems to favour bare places with sparse vegetation; it may also be found on stony or flinty ground in chalk grass-

land. The great green bushcricket is one of the largest insects found in Britain. This omnivorous species lives in many habitats but hedgerows and scrub of chalk and limestone in the south west are amongst the habitats it particularly favours. A much rarer bushcricket is the wart biter, which occurs in a very few sites on chalk and limestone in the extreme south of England.

The butterflies and moths of calcareous grasslands include many attractive and distinctive species. They may be divided into species of the northern Carboniferous limestone and species of the southern limestones and chalk. Particularly characteristic are the micro-moths called crambids, which are grass feeders. The more spectacular small elephant hawk feeds as a larva on bedstraws, especially lady's bedstraw, and is

sometimes attracted to lights. These moths are nocturnal and are probably therefore not so familiar to most people.

The day-flying moths include many colourful species which are common in calcareous districts. The wood tiger, forester moth, six-spot burnet, and cinnabar are all widespread. A colourful micro-moth, the crimson and gold, feeds on wild thyme in its larval stage.

Some moths are very restricted in their distribution in Britain. The feathered-ear moth occurs on the North Downs, and the red harrow on the South Downs, while the least minor moth is restricted to the limestones of western England. In Ireland, on the limestones of County Clare, is found another rarity: the burren green, an attractive moth whose cater-

Bushcrickets

Bushcrickets (order Orthoptera) have long back legs like grasshoppers, but their antennae are much longer than the body. Many can fly well, although they do not often do so. Others have very small wings, especially among the females. The latter can be recognised by the curved, blade-like ovipositor at the hind end. The males "sing" by rubbing the bases of their front wings together. Most species live in hedgerows and among bushes and rough herbage, eating leaves and small insects. The nymphs resemble the adults except for their size and lack of wings. There are 10 British species of which only five can fly.

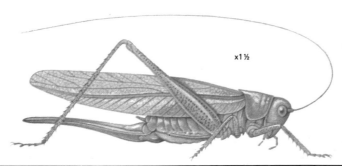

x2½

Speckled Bushcricket Tettigoniidae *Leptophytes punctatissima.* **Distribution**: Hedgerows; garden shrubberies: as far north as Yorkshire. **Other habitats**: Nettle-beds; bramble thickets; woodland clearings. **Adult active**: August to October—flightless. **Food**: Leaves and small insects.

x2½

Dark Bushcricket Tettigoniidae *Pholidoptera griseoaptera.* **Distribution**: Hedgerows and gardens in much of England and Wales. **Other habitats**: Woodland margins and clearings; any scrubby area. **Adult active**: July to November (or first frosts). **Food**: Leaves and small insects. **Note**: Male has saddle-like wings perched on back.

x1½

Great Green Bushcricket Tettigoniidae *Tettigonia viridissima.* **Distribution**: Hedgerows and gardens in southern half of England and South Wales. **Other habitats**: Coastal dunes and cliffs; woodland clearings; scrubby places. **Adult active**: July to October. **Food**: Leaves and small insects.

Female bushcrickets have a very prominent ovipositor. This one is using hers to inject eggs into a plant stem where they will be protected from predators and water loss.

Grasshoppers

Grasshoppers (order Orthoptera) are rather bullet-shaped insects with long, jumping back legs. Their antennae are no more than about one-third the length of the body. Most species can fly, and their wings are folded neatly along the sides of the body when the insects are at rest. Some species have very short wings, especially among the females. Males "sing" by rubbing their hind legs against their wings. The sound attracts the females for mating. Young grasshoppers, called nymphs, look very much like the adults except that their wings are not fully developed. Both young and adults feed mainly on grass. There are 11 British species, all rather variable in colour. They are active only in sunshine.

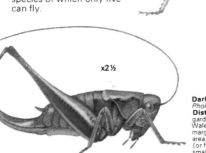

x2

Woodland Grasshopper Acrididae *Omocestus rufipes.* **Distribution**: Woodland clearings and margins south of the Wash, but local. **Other habitats**: Damp and dry heathland. **Adult active**: June to October. **Food**: Grasses and other low-growing plants.

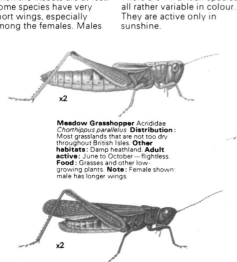

x2

Meadow Grasshopper Acrididae *Chorthippus parallelus.* **Distribution**: Most grasslands that are not too dry throughout British Isles. **Other habitats**: Damp heathland. **Adult active**: June to October—flightless. **Food**: Grasses and other low-growing plants. **Note**: Female shown: male has longer wings.

x2

Common Field Grasshopper Acrididae *Chorthippus brunneus.* **Distribution**: Dry grassland throughout the British Isles. **Other habitats**: Sand dunes and rough ground with some grass. **Adult active**: June to October. **Food**: Grasses and low-growing plants.

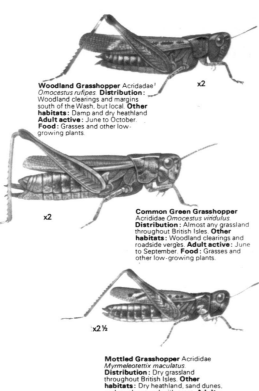

x2

Common Green Grasshopper Acrididae *Omocestus vindulus.* **Distribution**: Almost any grassland throughout British Isles. **Other habitats**: Woodland clearings and roadside verges. **Adult active**: June to September. **Food**: Grasses and other low-growing plants.

x2½

Mottled Grasshopper Acrididae *Myrmeleotettix maculatus.* **Distribution**: Dry grassland throughout British Isles. **Other habitats**: Dry heathland, sand dunes, and rough ground with grass. **Adult active**: June to October. **Food**: Grasses and other low-growing plants.

There are 29 species of British grasshoppers and crickets. Grasshoppers, like this *Chorthippus brunneus*, are active in summer and have short antennae. The antennae of crickets are often longer than the body.

Burnet moths belong to a family of small, brightly coloured, day-flying moths that include the iridescent green forester moths and the black and red burnets. The six-spot burnet is the commonest of the group. Two are shown here pairing on a pupal cocoon. It is a conspicuous insect on chalk downland in late summer. The caterpillar, which is pale green marked with black, feeds on kidney vetch, bird's-foot trefoil and other leguminous plants. When it is fully grown it spins a papery cocoon.

A guide to some grassland moths

Grassland moths include both day-flying and night-flying species. Day-flying moths are usually brightly coloured and are readily attracted to flowers. The forester, burnet and wood tiger moths are all common features of chalk downland grassland during the summer. The night-flying moths tend to have cryptic colours so that they are camouflaged while at rest during the day. They are not generally seen easily as they hide amongst the grass and litter, but they are occasionally flushed out of their hiding places. Some of the species may be found in their larval stage quite easily The mullein moths' distinctively coloured caterpillars may be detected on plants by the extensive damage to their leaves. The caterpillar of the small elephant hawk-moth may be found on bedstraws from dusk onwards as it is a night-feeding species. The larvae of the ghost moth are not so easily found as they feed on the roots of grassland plants. The male is distinctly different from the female, being almost pure white while the female is brown and yellow. The male's conspicuous colour is clearly used for its display flight at dusk. The common swift moth is a closely related species that also feeds on roots in the larval stage but lacks the startling appearance of the ghost.

The Forester Zygaenidae-*Adscita statices.* **Flight time:** Late May to early July. Overwinters as larva. **Foodplant:** Common sorrel. **Distribution:** Local but widespread in Britain as far north as Argyll and Inverness-shire.

Common Grass-veneer Pyralidae-*Agriphila tristellus.* **Flight time:** July, August. Overwinters as larva. **Foodplant:** Grasses. **Distribution:** Widespread throughout the British Isles except Shetland.

The Small Elephant Hawk-moth Sphingidae-*Deilephila porcellus.* **Flight time:** May to July. Overwinters as pupa. **Foodplant:** Bedstraw, willowherb, purple loosestrife. **Distribution:** Most common on chalk and limestone. England and Wales north to Lake District; local in Scotland.

The Mullein Noctuidae-*Cucullia verbasci.* **Flight time:** Late April, May. Overwinters as pupa. **Foodplant:** Mullein, figwort. **Distribution:** Throughout England and Wales as far north as the southern Lake District and Yorkshire.

The Ghost Moth Hepialidae-*Hepialus humuli.* **Flight time:** June, July. Overwinters as larva. **Foodplant:** Roots of grasses, burdock, dead-nettle, docks, dandelion, nettle etc. **Distribution:** Widespread throughout the British Isles. **Note:** Male white. Female yellow.

The Green Carpet Geometridae-*Colostygia pectinataria.* **Flight time:** June, July. Overwinters as larva. **Foodplant:** Bedstraw. **Distribution:** Throughout the British Isles except Shetland.

The Latticed Heath Geometridae-*Semiothisa clathrata.* **Flight time:** April, May; July, August, in two broods. **Foodplant:** Clovers, trefoils. **Distribution:** Common in southern and eastern England; local elsewhere north to the Clyde valley.

The Six-spot Burnet Zygaenidae-*Zygaena filipendulae.* **Flight time:** Mid-June to August. Overwinters as larva. **Foodplant:** Bird's-foot trefoil. **Distribution:** Widespread throughout the British Isles except Orkney and Shetland.

The Common Swift Hepialidae-*Hepialus lupulinus.* **Flight time:** May, June. Overwinters as larva. **Foodplant:** Roots of grasses etc. **Distribution:** Throughout Britain but very local in Scotland.

The Wood Tiger Arctiidae-*Parasemia plantaginis.* **Flight time:** June to August. Overwinters as larva. **Foodplant:** Polyphagous. **Distribution:** Local in southern Britain where it is decreasing; more common from the midlands and north Wales, northwards to Shetland.

The chalkhill blue

The chalkhill blue is a distinctive butterfly, which is highly characteristic of chalk and limestone grassland in the south of England. The butterflies may be found flying in abundance during late July and August on downland slopes where the larval food plant, horseshoe vetch, is abundant. The adult butterflies are active fliers but may often be found basking in the sun or sucking moisture from wet mud or animal dung.

The female butterfly lays her eggs singly on the stems and leaves of various plants in August, but they do not hatch until the following April. During the intervening time the fully-developed larva hibernates within the egg. When the larva hatches it starts to feed on the cuticle of horseshoe vetch leaves, later eating whole leaves. Most feeding takes place after dusk. Like the larvae of other blue butterflies they have a honey gland on the tenth segment, which secretes droplets of a sweet fluid very attractive to ants. Ants constantly associate with the larvae, attending and caressing them, and carry them to plants near their nests. In this symbiotic relationship the ants gain from the sugary secretions, while the butterfly larvae gain from the protection of the ants, which keep parasitic insects at bay. This type of relationship is even more highly developed in other species of blue butterfly such as the large blue.

When fully grown at an age of about ten weeks, the chalkhill blue larva resembles a green slug with yellow longitudinal markings. It ther descends to the base of the food plant to pupate amongst plant debris on the soil surface; after about four weeks the adult butterfly emerges. The males are a pale silvery blue on the upper wing while the females are a dull brownish colour. When they are not flying they may be found sitting with their heads pointing downwards on the stems of grasses and other plants.

A male chalkhill blue basks in the sun.

An ant caresses a chalkhill blue larva for its sugary secretions, an example of their symbiotic relationship.

pillars feed on blue moor grass. The Breckland of East Anglia has a particularly interesting assemblage of moths, with coastal species occurring inland and several local rarities, including pale lemon sallow, marbled clover, and tawny wave moths.

The butterflies are generally better known than the moths. Many species have very specific foodplant requirements but are widespread in chalk and limestone districts. The marbled white is a species which feeds on grasses in the larval stage, but is more or less restricted to calcareous soils, as is the chalkhill blue, which requires horseshoe vetch as a larval foodplant. The much rarer Adonis blue also feeds on this plant but is restricted to southern England, while the small blue is a more local species whose caterpillar feeds in the fruiting flower heads of kidney vetch. The marsh fritillary caterpillar feeds on devil's bit scabious and may be found in a variety of habitats, including downland, in south west England. The larvae live in a communal web in which they overwinter. The dingy and grizzled skippers are common chalk grassland butterflies which fly in the early summer; the silver-spotted skipper is now a relatively scarce species of southern chalk hills and the Lulworth skipper has its headquarters on the Isle of Purbeck in Dorset. The rarest butterfly of calcareous grasslands is the large blue, which is probably now confined to Devon and Cornwall, although it once occurred on limestone in the Cotswolds and Northamptonshire.

Some butterflies, such as the green hairstreak, are more fond of the scrub fringes of grassland. The brimstone butterfly frequents buckthorn bushes to lay its eggs. Adults which survive the winter may be seen during many months of the year feeding on a great variety of flowers from bluebells to meadow saffron. This conspicuous pale yellow species is the one which, as a butter-coloured-fly, was the origin of the group name.

Adult butterflies, as nectar feeders, need different food from their herbivorous larvae and often exploit quite different plants to avoid competing with their own offspring. Thus a single butterfly species may require at least two types of plant, and often many more, in order to provide food at different times. The great range of plants on chalk grassland provides a selection sufficiently diverse to support a considerable variety of even these fussy insects.

The marbled white butterfly has a name which perfectly describes its black and white patterned wings, but the name is nevertheless misleading because it is not a "white" but belongs to the "brown" family. The adult butterfly is conspicuous in grassland areas especially on chalk downland from mid-summer onwards but it is more or less confined to the south.

The larva of the marbled white feeds on the leaves of grasses in common with other related members of the brown family. The young larva hatches in late summer but does not shed its skin before hibernating for the winter.

The strong-flying dark green fritillary may be found in a variety of habitats.

The larva of the large skipper, in common with other skippers, feeds on the leaf blades of grasses.

This brightly coloured distinctive butterfly, the small copper, is widespread in the south.

A guide to some grassland butterflies

The grassland butterflies belong to several families, especially the browns, whites, skippers and blues. They do not emerge as adults at the same time so that you will see different butterflies if you visit the same area in the early summer and again at the end of the summer. Some of the butterflies appear during only one period of the summer, while species like the small copper have two or more generations and so can be seen throughout the season.

The grizzled and dingy skippers, small blue and green hairstreak are amongst the early species. The large blue and marsh fritillary are mid season butterflies while the silver-spotted skipper, chalkhill blue and second brood adonis blue are late comers.

Most of the species do not stray far from their habitats.

The Marbled White Satyridae-*Melanargia galathea*. **Flight time**: July, August. Overwinters as larva. **Foodplant**: Grasses such as cock's-foot and Timothy. **Distribution**: Rough grassland. England, south of the Wash-Severn line.

The Wall Satyridae-*Lasiommata megera*. **Flight time**: May, June, August in two broods. Overwinters as larva. **Foodplant**: Annual meadow grass, cock's foot and probably other grasses. **Distribution**: Grassland. Throughout England and Wales.

The Large Blue Lycaenidae-*Maculinea arion*. **Flight time**: June, July. Overwinters as larva. **Foodplant**: Initially flowers of thyme; then adopted by *Myrmica* ants, feeding on their larvae in the nest. **Distribution**: Confined to a very few localities in Devon and Cornwall.

The Small Heath Satyridae-*Coenonympha pamphilus*. **Flight time**: May to September, probably in two overlapping broods. **Foodplant**: Grasses. **Distribution**: Very common almost everywhere throughout the British Isles.

The Small Blue Lycaenidae-*Cupido minimus*. **Flight time**: May, June. Overwinters as larva. **Foodplant**: Kidney vetch. **Distribution**: Downland, sand-dunes etc. In localised colonies in southern England; very locally in south Wales.

The Green Hairstreak Lycaenidae-*Callophrys rubi*. **Flight time**: April to July. Overwinters as pupa. **Foodplant**: Gorse, bird's-foot trefoil, rock rose etc. **Distribution**: Downland, hedgerows, moorland etc. Throughout much of G. Britain.

The Small Copper Lycaenidae-*Lycaena phlaeas*. **Flight time**: April, May, July, August; sometimes September, October, in two or three broods. Overwinters as larva. **Foodplant**: Docks, sorrell. **Distribution**: Widespread in many habitats.

The Chalkhill Blue Lycaenidae-*Lysandra coridon*. **Flight time**: July to September. Overwinters as ovum. **Foodplant**: Horse-shoe vetch. **Distribution**: Chalk and limestone grassland. England south of the Severn-Wash line. Western limit Somerset.

The Adonis Blue Lycaenidae-*Lysandra bellargus*. **Flight time**: May, June; August, September, in two broods. Overwinters as larva. **Foodplant**: Horse-shoe vetch. **Distribution**: Chalk and limestone grassland. Southern England.

The Common Blue Lycaenidae-*Polyommatus icarus*. **Flight time**: May to July; August, September. Overwinter as larva. **Foodplant**: Bird's-foot trefoil. **Distribution**: Downlands, rough grassland.

The Brown Argus Lycaenidae-*Aricia agestis*. **Flight time**: May, June; July to September in two broods. Overwinters as larva. **Foodplant**: Rock-rose, common stork's-bill. **Distribution**: Downland widely distributed in southern England; north Wales.

The Duke of Burgundy Fritillary Nemeobiidae-*Hamearis lucina*. **Flight time**: May, June. Overwinters as pupa. **Foodplant**: Cowslip. **Distribution**: Woodland, wooded downland etc. Very local except in southern England.

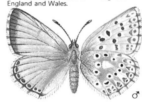

The Marsh Fritillary Nymphalidae-*Euphydryas aurinia*. **Flight time**: May, June. Overwinters gregariously as larva. **Foodplant**: Devil's bit scabious. **Distribution**: Damp meadows; rough hillsides. Local: south and south-west England, west Wales, Cumbria.

The Dark Green Fritillary Nymphalidae-*Argynnis aglaja*. **Flight time**: July, August. Overwinters as larva. **Foodplant**: Violet. **Distribution**: Downland, moorland, sea-cliffs etc.

The Meadow Brown Satyridae-*Maniola jurtina*. **Flight time**: June, July; August, September. in two broods. Overwinters as larva. **Foodplant**: Grasses. **Distribution**: Throughout British Isles, except Shetland. Common almost everywhere except at highest altitudes.

The Grizzled Skipper Hesperiidae-*Pyrgus malvae*. **Flight time**: Late April to June. Overwinters as pupa. **Foodplant**: Wild strawberry, bramble. **Distribution**: Downland, disused railway cuttings, wasteland.

The Large Skipper Hesperiidae-*Ochlodes venata*. **Flight time**: June to August. Overwinters as larva. **Foodplant**: Grasses. **Distribution**: Downland, rough grassland. Throughout England and Wales, local in the north.

The Dingy Skipper Hesperiidae-*Erynnis tages*. **Flight time**: April to June. Overwinters as larva. **Foodplant**: Bird's-foot trefoil. **Distribution**: Downland; rough grassland. Throughout much of England and Wales; very local in Scotland.

The Small Skipper Hesperiidae-*Thymelicus sylvestris*. **Flight time**: June to August. Overwinters as larva. **Foodplant**: Grasses. **Distribution**: Downland; rough grassland. England and Wales as far north as Cheshire and Yorkshire.

The Essex Skipper Hesperiidae-*Thymelicus lineola*. **Flight time**: July, August. Overwinters as ovum. **Foodplant**: Grasses. **Distribution**: Downland; rough grassland. South-east England.

The Silver-spotted Skipper Hesperiidae-*Hesperia comma*. **Flight time**: July, August. Overwinters as ovum. **Foodplant**: Sheep's fescue grass. **Distribution**: Chalk grassland. Confined to south and south-east England. Much less common than formerly.

Heathland

Heathlands occur in lowland Britain on poor dry soils and are dominated by species of heather. In practice, these heaths are usually found on sandy deposits laid down by ancient rivers or glaciers or blown into place by the wind. These sandy soils drain freely, and rain soaks in quickly, carrying away the soil nutrients and minerals. These are often deposited deeper in the soil as a dense "pan" (often of iron salts) which may make a solid and impermeable layer in the soil profile. Above it, the soil is leached (impoverished) of nutrients and cannot support a wide diversity of plants. Soil which has a structure like this is said to be "podsolised" and moreover, it is usually markedly acid (pH 3.4–6.5). Specialised forms of heathland may occur locally on richer soils (eg on Serpentine rock in southern Cornwall) and where chalk is overlain by sandy gravels (eg in parts of Surrey and East Anglia).

Heathland ecology

This combination of rather unpromising soil conditions offers little potential for most plants, and heathlands characteristically have a restricted range of plants and animals. Species of heather can cope with dry, cool, open conditions and thus are able to dominate heathland as they do the drier uplands. Gorse is another dominant shrub which, as a legume, helps to improve the nutrient content of the soil and would thus provide more opportunities for plant colonisation but for the fact that it forms dense thickets in which little else can grow. Both gorse and heather burn readily, but are adapted to fire in the long term. The old plants are burnt off (along with any competitor species) and the heat "primes" their seeds, increasing their germination success.

Fire is in fact an important aspect of heathland ecology. Without it, many less tolerant species are able to invade and alter the habitat. Moreover, if fire is avoided or prevented, large quantities of dead plant material accumulate, especially below heather bushes. Normally this would be broken down by earth worms and other soil organisms, but these are scarce in the dry acid soil. When a lot of dead material has accumulated, if a fire does start, it burns with such ferocity that it may kill even the heather roots, and recovery of the habitat is delayed. A brief, cool fire at regular intervals is far less damaging in the long term and is essential to maintain the heathland habitat.

In fact heathland, like grassland, is an artificial habitat created by man as a result of forest

clearance. Heathland communities are inherently unstable, as are many open habitats, because of the potential changes that can result from natural succession. The natural tendency is to change to woodland with colonisation by trees such as birch and Scots pine, the rate of change depending on the soil and the proximity of seed sources. The perpetuation of heathland depends on the use of suitable management, especially fire, to maintain its character. Traditionally the heaths were burnt, then grazed by free-ranging sheep and cattle which prevented tall woody vegetation from developing and maintained an open habitat. Grazing also favoured the development of grasses, many of which form a significant part of the plant community. Now that casual grazing is no longer widely practised, heathlands are either left alone

Grazing animals like these New Forest ponies are responsible for maintaining the open aspect of heathland. The spiny foliage of the gorse is one of the few things they will not eat, and gorse bushes tend to invade heathland unless they are deliberately excluded.

(in which case they tend to develop as scrub as a stage in reverting to woodland) or they are managed by modern methods to increase their productivity as grazing land.

Heathland can be managed to favour the grasses by the use of nitrogen and phosphorus fertilisers, which increases the growth and dominance of *Agrostis* and *Festuca* grasses. Alternatively it can be converted to grassland by a sequence of stages consisting of burning, adding lime and fertiliser, followed by re-seeding (with or without ploughing). The resultant grassland is much more productive and has been successfully established in many parts of southern England. Heath species can also be replaced by flooding with stream water which brings with it flushed material to enrich the system. In some areas heathland has been used for urban development, for example in the vicinity of Bournemouth and in south west London. Afforestation, with the lodgepole pine *(Pinus contorta)* and sitka spruce *(Pinus sitchensis)*, has provided a further threat to heathlands as an alternative to the low productivity of the traditional management regimes. There is therefore an

The adder (*Vipera berus*) is particularly common on heathland, but also frequently occurs in woodland and hedgerows. It feeds mainly on small mammals and lizards, relying on venom to immobilise its prey

which would otherwise be too active to catch easily. Adders bask in the sun but some heathlands can become too warm on summer days and the snakes then seek shade.

Gorse is characteristic of heaths and rough grassland where it is often the dominant shrub. The leaves are reduced to spines and consequently most photosynthesis is carried out by the stems.

The heathland ecosystem

Heathland develops on poor soils in the lowlands. Rainfall washes nutrients out of porous (usually sandy) soils, leaving the surface layers impoverished and able to support only the heathland plants adapted to these conditions. Accumulation of dead plant material will, in time, enrich the soil and allow other plants to invade unless they are prevented by fires and grazing animals. True heathland plants can withstand these conditions.

Energy from the sun is needed by green plants for photosynthesis, the process by which CO_2 (from the air or water) is used to build up plant tissues.

Carnivores. Mammals (eg fox and weasel) and birds like the buzzard may take larger heathland prey, while the nightjar, hobby, stonechat and several warblers consume heathland insects. Spiders are also important predators of the insect fauna.

Unless kept in check by fire or large herbivores, many shrubs and even trees may encroach on the heathland habitat.

Herbivores. Large herbivores include grazing mammals such as ponies, sheep and rabbits. The major herbivores are probably insects, particularly flies and caterpillars. Bees feed on heather nectar and a number of birds and small mammals feed on plant seeds.

Many carnivorous animals (eg lizards and pipits) depend on the rich fauna of invertebrates (including ants and spiders) found on the soil surface.

Primary producers. The main plants of heathland are heathers and grasses, which use the sun's energy to produce leaves, woody tissue, seeds and other sources of food such as nectar.

Bogs, peat cuttings and shallow ponds harbour animals such as toads and dragonflies whose larvae are aquatic, but whose adults emerge to feed in the heathland ecosystem, mostly as predators.

Periodic fires may result in ash and charcoal being carried away by the wind; a loss of materials from the system.

Dead plant material accumulates and is burnt off periodically, or serves to feed decomposer organisms. However, these do not break down all the available material and it tends to build up as a layer of dry peat. Heath soils are usually somewhat acid, inimical to earthworms, which normally play a major role in decomposing dead plant material.

Faeces deposited on the ground provide food for dung beetles, flies and soil animals.

---

urgent need for conservation of the heathland habitat which has been both reduced in overall area and fragmented by these processes. Conservation is important both for the characteristic heathland wildlife and for the aesthetic appeal of large open spaces dominated by freely-flowering heather plants.

Conservation management requires maintenance of the open character of the heathland by preventing succession to woodland. This may be achieved by clearance of scrub and trees by hand or machines and by occasional rotational burning. The conservation aim is to produce a pattern of various ages in the dominant plant community, while still maintaining some areas of old, or over mature, heather or gorse for its more specialised animal inhabitants. An alternative to regular burning is mechanical cutting of the heather using a "swipe" to remove old shoots and encourage new growth. There is however the problem that cut branches can interfere with plant regrowth if they are allowed to lie where they fall, and they also supply nutrients to the soil. Herein lies the basic paradox of heathland: whereas most habitats are interesting because of their diversity and conservation programmes aim to enhance this, heathland's principal characteristic is its reduced fertility and diversity. The plants and animals that live there are few in numbers of species, but highly interesting because of their ability to survive under difficult conditions and because of their scarcity elsewhere. Heathland conservation therefore seeks to avoid new colonising species becoming established, and avoid enriching the impoverished soil to an extent which will mean that the characteristic species adapted to dry podsols no longer have a clear advantage over would-be invaders which constantly threaten to convert heathland habitat to something else.

Management of heathlands by fire

In order to maintain heathland vegetation the invasion of trees must be prevented. In the traditional form of heathland management this is done by a combination of grazing with livestock and burning the heather. Regular cycles of burning promote the growth of nutritious

Heathland soils are often strongly podsolised: nutrients are washed from the upper layers leaving an impoverished surface soil. Sometimes the mineral salts are re-deposited as a hard pan lower down in the soil profile.

young shoots which are more suitable for grazing stock.

The effects of a heathland fire depend a great deal on the conditions, particularly the temperature reached and the duration of the fire which are governed by the wind, moisture content of the plants and the age of the heather, hence the proportion of woody material or fuel. The temperature may be 500°C in the heather canopy and 250°C at ground level. Normally the fire burns through a given point in less than two minutes, but this depends on whether the fire is burning with the wind, or against it.

In a good clean burn 90 per cent of the fuel is burned, removing most of the surface vegetation. In a poor burn as little as 30 per cent may be burned. The aim of the heathland manager is to prevent a very high ground temperature during the fire as this will be lethal to the stem bases of the heather plants. It is also desirable to burn off the above ground parts of the plants without allowing the temperature to rise too high, because this can result in loss of nutrients in the smoke. Disastrous damage may occur in

very hot fires or in very dry conditions when the dry surface peat may ignite and smoulder down to the mineral soil layer, killing everything.

After burning the heather regenerates; six to ten year old plants grow again better than mature or degenerate plants, but if plants fail to sprout then seed must be relied on. Heather seeds are present in large numbers in the heathland soil and they germinate freely after fires, especially if they are protected just below the soil surface.

Burning affects the types of plants that occur in the heathland by eliminating those species such as young trees which are susceptible to fire and which cannot regenerate quickly. Conversely it allows the gradual dominance of fire-tolerant species such as heather, purple moor grass and bracken which regenerate rapidly after fire, maintaining the characteristic open community of heathland plants devoid of trees.

Heathland Invertebrates

Crab spiders do not catch their prey in a web but lie in wait in flower heads, seizing suitable insects that visit the flowers. These spiders are coloured to resemble the flowers in which they hide,

Heathlands are not rich in variety of insect and invertebrate life but certain groups are quite well represented and are a feature of open heathland habitats. Molluscs, especially snails, are generally not a feature of heathland because of the acidity of the soil and the lack of calcium carbonate for building shells. A number of predatory groups are quite conspicuous, notably dragonflies which often feed over open heathland and woodland edges while breeding in ponds or streams on the wet parts of heaths. Other conspicuous predators include spiders, ants and solitary wasps.

There are few butterflies and moths that occur on heathland. The most typical are the grayling, which likes bare places to fly over in late summer and which feeds on grasses in its larval stage, and the silver studded blue which also flies in late summer, but feeds on gorse and broom as a larva. Other butterflies which occur in heathland are less specific in their requirements and are frequently found in other habitats too. The green hairstreak, for example, feeds on gorse and other leguminous plants and the hedge brown may be found on heathland if there are low thickets of brambles. The small heath occurs in open grassy places together with the small copper, which requires sorrels as the larval food-plant. These common and widespread butterflies occur in many situations and produce more than one brood per year.

There is a similarly limited moth fauna, several of which feed on heather in their larval stage and which consequently occur both on lowland heath and on upland moors. These moths include the true lover's knot, the narrow-winged pug, which has distinctive pointed wings, and the common heath, which are all widespread species. Some heathland moths are more restricted in their distribution, like the beautiful snout, a species of southern England, and the heath rivulet which occurs in the north. A few of the heathland moths are especially large and spectacular. The pine hawk-moth, for instance, occurs where heathland has been invaded by conifers, while on the open heath the large oak eggar *(Lasiocampa quercus quercus)* occurs, together with that most spectacular creature the emperor moth.

Several herbivorous or omnivorous members of the Orthoptera favour the warm sunny heathlands of the south, especially those of the New Forest and the Isle of Purbeck. The small native

The attractively coloured spider, the *Micromata virescens*, is found in grassland in the south where it stalks its prey amongst the grass stems.

species of cockroach *(Ectobius pallidus)* occur in heathland where it flies readily in the sun, and bog bushcrickets *(Metrioptera brachyptera)* are quite large insects that inhabit wet heaths in England and Wales. Their soft "chuffing" song can be heard from late summer well into the autumn, when the adults lay their eggs in plant stems to overwinter.

Grasshoppers favour the grassy parts of heathland. The common green grasshopper is very widespread in Britain and may be found on heathland, but the mottled grasshopper *(Myrmeleotettix maculatus)* is more characteristic of heathland and seems to require bare places on dry heaths. The clubbed antennae, which are conspicuous on the males, are a useful recognition character. The heath grasshopper *(Chorthippus vagans)* is the rarest and may be found on heaths in Dorset and Hampshire only, and even there it is local. Another group of insects that resemble grasshoppers also occur on heathland. These are the groundhoppers which favour heathland and appear in the spring, having overwintered as nymphs, in contrast to other Orthoptera which mature in the late summer and die with the onset of winter.

Dragonflies are a conspicuous and important feature of heathlands. Several of our rarest species occur primarily in heathland areas where they breed in wet heath pools and hunt over the open heath for prey. The golden ringed dragonfly *(Cordulegaster boltoni)* is a common widespread species of upland and lowland heath which breeds in streams where its larvae dwell in the mud. The four spotted libellula *(Libellula*

The emperor moth

The emperor moth is a large distinctive moth which is characteristic of heather-covered heaths and moors. It is the only British member of the silk moth family which includes the atlas and other very large moths of the tropics. Both sexes of the adult moth have four conspicious eye spots, one on each upper wing surface.

The female is larger than the male, greyish in colour and flies at night, while the male has orange hind wings and flies fast by day over open heathland and along woodland edges searching for unmated females. The purpose of the eye spot pattern appears to be to deter attack by predators, especially during emergence

The larva of the emperor moth changes from black and orange as it develops and the full-grown caterpillar appears as shown above, well camouflaged in its natural setting.

Adult emperor moths are on the wing in April. The female lays her eggs in clusters on the branches of the foodplant, usually heather but bramble, blackthorn and sallow are also used. When the larva is ready to pupate, t constructs a cocoon which is cleverly designed to protect the pupal stage. It is pear-shaped with an exit at the narrow end.

Heathland butterflies

There are relatively few species of butterfly which occur in heathland. The butterflies which are characteristic of pure heather areas are the grayling and the silver-spotted blue. Both these species are on the wing in mid to late summer. The grayling favours places where there is bare ground where it often chooses to sit. At rest the underwings show only the cryptic colours, but when disturbed the forewings are raised to expose eyespots. This presumably alarms a would-be predator. The caterpillar feeds on grasses. The silver-spotted blue larva feeds on gorse, heather and broom.

The adult often settles on heather with its wings wide open.

Certain butterflies characteristic of other habitats may also be found on heaths. This is true of butterflies like the hedge brown and dark green fritillary. The strong-flying species such as the small tortoiseshell also occur, especially if there are flowers to attract them.

Heathland moths

Heathland does not harbour a great variety of moths compared to chalk grassland. Heathland moths include both day- and night-flying species. Conspicuous amongst the day-flying moths are the males of the emperor and fox moths which dash about in search of the more sedentary females. Fox moths are large, furry brown moths related to, and closely resembling, the eggars. Their caterpillars are similarly large and furry, armed with irritating hairs. The ruby tige is a reddish coloured moth that flies at night on moorland and heathland. The caterpillars feed on herbaceous plants such as dandelion and dock. An even more attractive moth is the grass emerald, one of several very beautiful green moths. The adult is on the wing in the middle of summer. The larva feeds on leguminous plants of the heathland like the broom, petty whin and gorse.

The Ruby Tiger Arctiidae- *Phragmatobia fuliginosa*. **Flight time**: May, June, occasionally September as second brood. **Foodplant**: Dock, dandelion, golden rod. **Distribution**: Widespread throughout the British Isles except Shetland.

The Grass Emerald Geometridae- *Pseudoterpna pruinata*. **Flight time**: June, July. Overwinters as larva. **Foodplant**: Petty whin, broom, gorse. **Distribution**: Throughout much of England and Wales; south-west Scotland.

The Narrow-winged Pug Geometridae *Eupithecia nanata*. **Flight time**: May, June; July; August in two broods. Overwinters as pupa. **Foodplant**: Heath, heather. **Distribution**: On heathland throughout the British Isles.

The Common Heath Geometridae- *Ematurga atomaria*. **Flight time**: May, June; August, in two broods. Overwinters as pupa. **Foodplant**: Heath, heather, clover, trefo ls. **Distribution**: Abundant on heathland throughout the British Isles except Shet and.

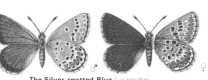

The Silver-spotted Blue Lycaenidae- *Plebejus argus*. **Flight time**: June to August. Overwinters as ovum. **Foodplant**: Bird's-foot vetch, gorse. **Distribution**: Heathland. South and south-west England, Norfolk and Suffolk, north Wales.

The Grayling Satyridae-*Hipparchia semele*. **Flight time**: July to September. Overwinters as larva. **Foodplant**: Grasses. **Distribution**: Heathland; sand-dunes etc. Widespread in southern and western England and Wales; coastal in northern England and Scotland.

The Emperor Moth Saturniidae- *Saturnia pavonia*. **Flight time**: April, May. Overwinters as pupa. **Foodplant**: Heather, bramble, sallow etc. **Distribution**: Widespread throughout the British Isles especially on heathland and moorland.

The Fox Moth Lasiocampidae- *Macrothylacia rubi*. **Flight time**: May, June. Overwinters as larva. **Foodplant**: Heather, bramble, grasses etc. **Distribution**: Widely distributed but local on heathland throughout mainland Britain. **Note**: Male dark brown. Female greyer.

Tiger beetles

Tiger beetles (order Coleoptera) are strong-flying carnivorous insects with large eyes and immense jaws. They are active only in the sunshine and they chase all kinds of insects. They can run rapidly on their long legs, and they can also fly very rapidly, usually with a loud buzzing sound. The larvae live in burrows, with their large jaws just jutting out ready to capture unwary insects. There are five British species of tiger beetles, all associated with sandy soils in which the larvae can burrow.

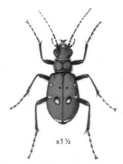

x1½

Green Tiger Beetle Cicindelidae *Cicindela campestris.* **Distribution:** Most of British Isles. **Other habitats:** Sand dunes. **Adult active:** Spring and summer. **Food:** Insects and other small invertebrates

The cardinal beetle (*Pyrochroa coccinea*) is found in southern England.

The large marsh grasshopper (*Stethophyma grossum*) is found only on wet heathland and peat bogs. It is thus much more limited in distribution.

depressa) and common sympetrum (*Sympetrum striolatum*) are pond breeding species that are also widespread. Some of the rare species only occur on southern heaths, for example, the Ashdown Forest heathlands are the home of the brilliant emerald hawker dragonfly. The best areas of Surrey heathland harbour the white faced dragonfly which also occurs in northern Britain. The New Forest, which provides so many habitats in close proximity, has ideal conditions for heathland species to breed on the wet heaths and valley streams. The scarce *Ishnura* is a tiny damselfly which may be found in the New Forest and in a few other places in south west Britain. Most of these species require clear unpolluted water and are threatened in many places by rain water draining off agricultural land which contains a heavy chemical load. In other places they have been eliminated through the destruction of their heathland habitat by agricultural or housing development even though the aquatic breeding sites remain.

The tiger beetle is another insect predator which may be seen running actively along heathland paths, flying when disturbed. Its larvae are also predators, living in vertical burrows in the sand and seizing passing prey with their huge jaws.

Various hunting wasps inhabit heathland and are commonly seen in southern England. Sand wasps (*Ammophila* sp.) are especially characteristic. They may be seen dragging large caterpillars along the ground to their nest holes, where the female wasp lays her egg on the unfortunate paralysed caterpillar and then seals it into the nest hole where the wasp grub devours it. These wasps are unable to fly with the prey because it is so large. Some hunting wasps skim low over the ground in search of spiders, which they despatch with a similar fate. Potter wasps, such as the heath potter wasp (*Eumenes coarctata*), are similar solitary wasps that con-

Heathland bugs

Bugs (order Hemiptera) are common on many heathland plants. Both homopteran and heteropteran bugs are present, but the homopterans tend to be rather small and inconspicuous. Many of the heteropteran bugs are brown in colour, thus matching the heather or ling which dominates much of the surroundings. This is particularly true of the various predatory bugs which crawl over the plants or the ground in search of food. Some of these predators are wingless, or have very short wings, and it is then difficult to distinguish adults from young.

x5

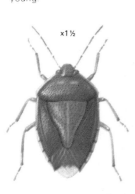

x1½

Heath Assassin Bug Reduviidae *Coranus subapterus.* **Distribution:** Most of British Isles, but not Ireland. **Other habitats:** Sand dunes. **Adult active:** July to October. **Food:** Other insects. **Note:** Fully winged individuals occasionally found.

Gorse Shield Bug Pentatomidae *Piezodorus lituratus.* **Distribution:** Most of British Isles. **Other habitats:** Woods, commons, sea cliffs, and waste places. **Adult active:** All year, but hide in leaf litter if very cold. **Food:** Gorse, broom and related leguminous plants. **Note:** Pink and green in autumn.

Dragonflies are frequent components of heathland invertebrate life. They travel up to 15 km from the surrounding countryside in order to prey on the numerous heathland insects.

Solitary wasps

Solitary wasps of many kinds occur on the heathlands. They all belong to the order Hymenoptera, but to several different families. They are called solitary wasps because each female makes a little nest of her own instead of working for a large family or colony. Species of *Anoplius* and *Ammophila* dig nest burrows in the ground, and the sandy soil of the heathland is very suitable for this. The potter wasp cements sand and clay together with saliva to form little vases for her eggs. The adult wasps feed on nectar, but they provide their grubs with animal food. *Anoplius* fills its nest with spiders, while *Ammophila* and the potter wasp use caterpillars. The prey are paralysed by the wasp's sting before being stored.

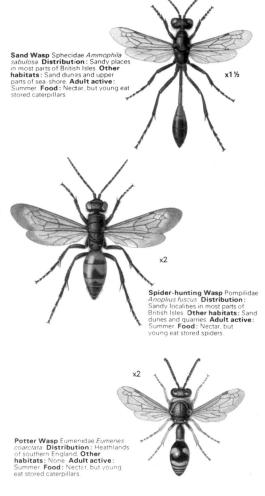

Sand Wasp Sphecidae *Ammophila sabulosa* **Distribution**: Sandy places in most parts of British Isles. **Other habitats**: Sand dunes and upper parts of sea-shore. **Adult active**: Summer. **Food**: Nectar, but young eat stored caterpillars. x1½

Spider-hunting Wasp Pompilidae *Anoplius fuscus*. **Distribution**: Sandy localities in most parts of British Isles. **Other habitats**: Sand dunes and quarries. **Adult active**: Summer. **Food**: Nectar, but young eat stored spiders. x2

Potter Wasp Eumenidae *Eumenes coarctata*. **Distribution**: Heathlands of southern England. **Other habitats**: None. **Adult active**: Summer. **Food**: Nectar, but young eat stored caterpillars. x2

The female sand wasp (*Ammophila*) digs a burrow in sand and then finds a caterpillar to bury in it. She paralyses her victim with her sting then lays an egg on it. The young wasp will then feed on the caterpillar until it emerges.

struct clay flask-shaped nests on heather stems instead of digging burrows.

One of the heathland spiders that is preyed on by the wasps is *Arctosa perita*, a widespread wolf spider that constructs silk tunnels from which it pounces on passing prey. Another characteristic spider of heathland is *Thomisus*, a pink crab spider, which lives on heather flowers, lurking in wait there for visiting insects.

Ants are quite at home in the sandy soils of acid heaths, especially in the well drained grassy areas. They are a special feature of heathland on the Weald and in the New Forest and Poole Basin areas. There are species of *Myrmica* and *Lasius* (some of which are common to chalk grassland) and also species of *Formica* and *Tetramorium*. The latter develop colonies on southern heathlands that occupy and defend many square metres of territory. Heathland ants tend to build deep nests down to one metre below the soil surface, to avoid the drying winds of spring and the heat of summer, and also the occasional heath fire. They favour the lichen covered spaces between bushes on the heath and forage for nectar, which is collected from heather flowers and the nectaries on young bracken fronds. The ants also search in the soil and among the plants for invertebrate prey in the summer months and collect grass and heather seeds in the autumn.

Robber-flies

Robber-flies (order Diptera) are generally long-bodied flies—stout or slender—that feed by catching other insects in mid-air. Some fly to and fro in their search, while others dart out from a perch when they see other insects fly by. The prey is caught by the legs and then stabbed by the robber-fly's horny beak, which sucks out the prey's juices. The robber-flies have very large eyes, with which to detect their prey, and very bristly faces. The bristles protect the eyes from the struggling prey. Robber-fly larvae develop in dung and other decaying matter.

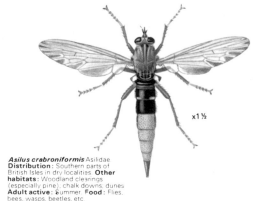

Asilus crabroniformis Asilidae. **Distribution**: Southern parts of British Isles in dry localities. **Other habitats**: Woodland clearings (especially pine), chalk downs, dunes. **Adult active**: Summer. **Food**: Flies, bees, wasps, beetles, etc. x1½

Velvet ants

Velvet (ants) (order Hymenoptera) are not true ants. They are more closely related to the ruby-tailed wasps, but they get their name because the females are wingless and more or less clothed with soft hair. The females wander over the ground and enter the nests of bumblebees, where they lay their eggs. The velvet ant grubs then feed on the grubs and pupae of the bees. Male velvet ants are fully winged and they take nectar from flowers, but the females feed on the honey stored in the nests of their hosts.

Large Velvet Ant Mutillidae *Mutilla europaea*. **Distribution**: Much of British Isles, but mainly southern. **Other habitats**: Woodland margins, hedge banks. **Adult active**: Summer. **Food**: Honey and nectar. Larva eats bumble bee grubs. **Note**: Male similar but winged. x2

The velvet ant (*Mutilla europaea*) is actually a wasp which parasitises bee larvae. Females are wingless, thus resembling ants.

Robber-flies feed by ambushing passing insects. They can leap 50cm on to unsuspecting prey.

Heathland Flora

The heathland flora is not remarkably rich in species. In fact, dry open heath has a very limited flora as a result of the acid soils and the rather dry fire-prone conditions. Variety in the flora is found on the fringes where the heathland merges into other habitats, especially wet heath, which develops a very characteristic flora.

The most characteristic plant of heathland is heather, which dominates the habitat throughout the country in all but the wet heath habitats. Heather or ling *(Calluna vulgaris)* is particularly adapted to the oceanic type climate. Its tiny leaves appear to be related to the commonly overcast conditions of our islands—cloud cover produces scattered light with radiant energy coming from all sides and this can be intercepted better by many small leaves pointing in different directions.

Heathland does not normally remain as open habitat unless the density of browsing animals is very high. The plants that comprise the habitat are therefore only temporary lodgers, colonising the habitat until tree cover is established. Heather shows many of the characteristics of a colonist of open habitats. It has a high reproductive capacity producing large numbers of small seeds which are shed on the soil surface. Under suitable conditions the seeds will germinate quickly, or if they are buried under litter and humus they can remain ungerminated but viable for a long period of time. The heather

plants germinate particularly rapidly after a heath fire, hence they are successful in burned or cleared areas and respond well to management by regular burning. However, if allowed to grow to maturity the heather plants begin to degenerate after about 80 years and collapse, allowing light to penetrate to soil level and stimulate the growth of other plants.

After fires on heathland quite different conditions are created for a time, allowing certain plants to colonise; especially bell heather, rose-bay willowherb and bracken which spreads abundantly. Grasses may be more prevalent in areas where there has been intensive grazing which has reduced the heather and under these conditions certain fine-leaved grasses such as sheep's fescue, brome and fine bent grass and wavy hair-grass thrive.

Other wild flowers

In open spaces among the heather grow a number of other common flowering plants. These include the sheep's sorrel, tormentil, heath bedstraw and heath speedwell. Often these are accompanied by morar sedge and pill sedge whose long thin stalks curve over among the other vegetation. The parasitic dodder frequently attacks heather, gorse and broom, festooning these plants with its thread-like red, leafless stems and clusters of pink flowers. The plant has no leaves as it manufactures none of its

It is the heathers that give heathland its name, and not surprisingly these are usually the dominant plants. Ling, shown here growing with moss, is the commonest species and on well drained acid soils is often the only heather.

own food, deriving all its requirements from the host plant by its probing tentacles.

Certain heath plants are very localised in distribution. The Cornish heath is only really common on the Lizard heathlands, while the Dorset heath has its base on the Isle of Purbeck. In south and west England an attractive tufted grass, bristle bent, is a feature of the heaths, while in Ireland the spectacularly large flowered St Dabeoc's heath occurs on heathland in Connemara.

Heather cannot tolerate wet conditions, so where the drainage is poor it is replaced by cross-leaved heath, which readily hybridises with Dorset heath and with Mackay's heath in Ireland where the habitats of the parents meet. Wetter conditions also provide a habitat for black bog rush, heath rush, cotton grass and purple moor grass. In south western Britain these conditions are ideal for the rarer bog pimpernel, pale butterwort and ivy-leaved bellflower.

The heaths on the Serpentine at the Lizard in Cornwall have a very distinctive flora which is unique. They are dominated by an association of Cornish heath, black bog rush, Devil's bit scabious and the special rarities, dwarf rush and pygmy rush. These very rare species are adapted

to live in shallow depressions that hold water during the winter months, but which are dry in early summer. Cart ruts sometimes provide precisely the right conditions for them.

Lowland heathland merges into upland moor on the fringes of places such as Exmoor. Here bilberry, common club-moss and crowberry begin to appear in the heathland association. On the maritime fringes the species are able to tolerate wind and salt. In these areas the bell heather is prominent together with thyme, creeping willow, and lousewort.

Lowland heaths have relatively few plants which are confined to such habitats; most occur on wet heath in the south west of Britain. One, the early adder's tongue fern, is a very specialised plant that lives in maritime heaths in the very short turf of cliff tops. Marsh club-'moss and marsh gentian are still fairly widespread, but heath lobelia is very restricted in distribution.

Some of the lowland heath plants have undergone dramatic declines in distribution and even local extinctions. This is especially true of wet heath species which have probably become lost through the general improvements in drainage. This probably accounts for the decline of inconspicuous plants like pillwort and flaxseed which favours the wet cart ruts on heaths. The marsh gentian has probably also suffered from habitat destruction by drainage but its attractive violet-blue flowers probably contribute to its decline through people picking the blooms.

The common dodder is a total parasite commonly growing on heathland plants, especially members of the heather family. Here it is growing on ling, though it often grows on gorse.

Bell heather is only common on the drier parts of heaths and moors where it may be co-dominant with ling. Although usually red-purple, the flowers are sometimes white.

A guide to some heathland wild flowers

The very name 'heath' clearly indicates the characteristic group of plants associated with this habitat. The heathers or heaths (members of the Ericaceae) are extremely lime intolerant and invariably found on highly podsolised sandy soils.

Another group of plants well represented here are members of the pea family (Papilionaceae), the most usual being gorse species.

Perhaps the most interesting yet easily overlooked plant is the annual lesser dodder, which parasitises both gorse and heathers: it is completely parasitic and without foliage, its red threadlike stems sometimes smothering the host plant which may be killed.

Heathland usually has only a very limited number of flowering plant species.

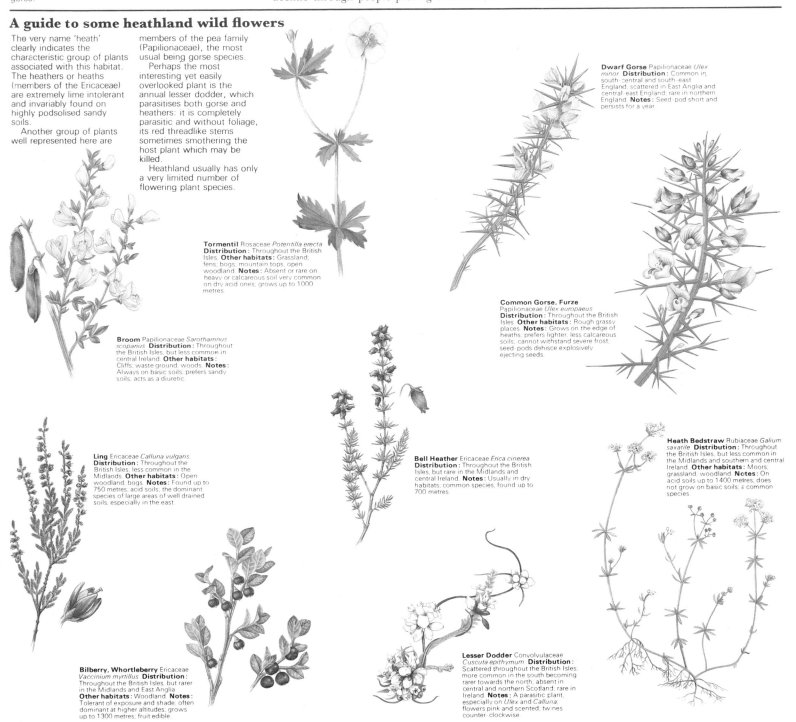

Tormentil Rosaceae *Potentilla erecta* **Distribution**: Throughout the British Isles. **Other habitats**: Grassland; fens; bogs; mountain tops; open woodland. **Notes**: Absent or rare on heavy or calcareous soil; very common on dry acid ones; grows up to 1000 metres.

Dwarf Gorse Papilionaceae *Ulex minor*. **Distribution**: Common in south-central and south-east England; scattered in East Anglia and central-east England; rare in northern England. **Notes**: Seed-pod short and persists for a year.

Common Gorse, Furze Papilionaceae *Ulex europaeus* **Distribution**: Throughout the British Isles **Other habitats**: Rough grassy places. **Notes**: Grows on the edge of heaths; prefers lighter, less calcareous soils; cannot withstand severe frost; seed-pods dehisce explosively ejecting seeds.

Broom Papilionaceae *Sarothamnus scoparius* **Distribution**: Throughout the British Isles, but less common in central Ireland. **Other habitats**: Cliffs; waste ground; woods. **Notes**: Always on basic soils; prefers sandy soils; acts as a diuretic.

Ling Ericaceae *Calluna vulgaris*. **Distribution**: Throughout the British Isles; less common in the Midlands Isles. **Other habitats**: Open woodland; bogs. **Notes**: Found up to 750 metres; acid soils; the dominant species of large areas of well drained soils, especially in the east.

Bell Heather Ericaceae *Erica cinerea* **Distribution**: Throughout the British Isles, but rare in the Midlands and central Ireland. **Notes**: Usually in dry habitats; common species; found up to 700 metres.

Heath Bedstraw Rubiaceae *Galium saxatile*. **Distribution**: Throughout the British Isles, but less common in the Midlands and southern and central Ireland. **Other habitats**: Moors; grassland; woodland. **Notes**: On acid soils up to 1400 metres; does not grow on basic soils; a common species.

Bilberry, Whortleberry Ericaceae *Vaccinium myrtillus* **Distribution**: Throughout the British Isles, but rarer in the Midlands and East Anglia. **Other habitats**: Woodland **Notes**: Tolerant of exposure and shade; often dominant at higher altitudes; grows up to 1300 metres; fruit edible.

Lesser Dodder Convolvulaceae *Cuscuta epithymum*. **Distribution**: Scattered throughout the British Isles; more common in the south becoming rarer towards the north; absent in central and northern Scotland; rare in Ireland. **Notes**: A parasitic plant, especially on *Ulex* and *Calluna*; flowers pink and scented; twines counter-clockwise.

Breckland

The Breckland is an area of about 900 sq km of distinctive undulating landscape on the Suffolk/Norfolk border. It has a semi-continental steppe-like flora and fauna, which result from its sandy soils, open aspect and semi-continental climate, with low rainfall, hot summers and cold winters. Breckland therefore has features which are unique in Britain.

As elsewhere in Britain, the typically open grassland and heathland character of the Breckland is a result of man's influence throughout historical time. Originally the area was covered by forest, but clearance began in Neolithic times, and has been followed by a long history of cultivation and use of the land for grazing. The dry soils of the Breckland are of marginal value agriculturally, so that the extent of cultivation has fluctuated depending on economic conditions. For long periods much of the area was grassland, managed as sheep walks or huge rabbit warrens, thus accounting for some of the local place names, for example Lakenheath Warren. The pine shelter belts which are such a feature of the area were planted in the 19th century to help stabilise the soil and reduce soil erosion caused by the wind sweeping across the otherwise open landscape.

The soils of the area are derived from superficial deposits of glacial material and sand covering underlying chalk. The nature of the soil ranges widely from highly calcareous to highly acidic, depending on the depth of the superficial deposits and the proportion of chalk fragments in the soil. On deep, infertile, acid sands where the vegetation has been disrupted by wind scouring and sand movements in the past, mobile dunes have built up on the original soil surface. The sand movements have created still more variety in the mosaic of different conditions by exposing or burying the chalky material in particular places. Rabbit activity tends to maintain these shifting sands and retard soil stabilisation.

This variety of soil conditions, together with a long history of grazing by sheep and rabbits, has created a range of vegetation, from the deep calcareous soils which are rich in flowers and

The sand dunes of the Breckland are unusual because they occur inland. The majority of the once extensive dunes are now stabilised as heathland or conifer plantation but at Wangford Warren (above) bare shifting sand can be seen.

There are still Breck heathlands where dense rabbit populations create warrens in the sandy soil. This produces areas denuded of vegetation with loose sand and flints. Such areas are attractive to rare breeding birds.

closely resemble the chalk downland to relatively bare acidic grasslands largely dominated by lichen carpets. In the few remaining areas of blown sand there are few plants apart from sand sedge. Some of the moderately acid sands are covered by bracken, while the deep acid soils form open heaths dominated by heather. Many of the special plants of the Breckland are annuals characteristic of disturbed ground, which probably reflects the fact that the open communities originated as a result of cultivation of the sandy soils.

Forestry and cultivation

Recently there have been many changes in Breckland. Since the establishment of the Forestry Commission, huge areas of the relatively unproductive Breck heathlands have been planted with Scots pine and other conifers. The semi-natural vegetation has been further reduced in area and fragmented by increasing cultivation, which has been made more profitable by modern intensive methods involving the

widespread use of chemicals.

Few large areas of grassland and heath remain other than the Ministry of Defence battle training area north west of Thetford. Wherever the heathlands do remain they are undergoing dramatic changes because of the reduction in rabbit numbers caused by myxomatosis. The open, close-grazed, disturbed grassland turf of the past is getting scarce. Generally the grasses have grown luxuriant at the expense of the herbs and annuals. A few of the taller herbs have benefited but many have declined and become very rare. The areas of mobile sand have been colonised by plants and stabilized. The heather has grown taller and coarser in the absence of rabbit grazing. Open heathland has been colonised by birch and pine. All these changes are contributing to a decline in the special wildlife richness of the region.

A guide to some Breckland wild flowers

Breckland, the tree-less grassy heath and rich grassland area of East Anglia, has poor sandy soil, low rainfall and is heavily grazed by rabbits. This grazing not only keeps the area free of trees but also determines if an area is to be grassland or heathland by its intensity. The grassland on less acid soil with comparatively high base status is rich in rare species; however, all these characteristic Breckland species are unable to grow on the more common strongly podsolised acid soils and are thus not seen on much of the Breck. Many are weeds of cultivation requiring a disturbed soil and high lime content; they are intolerant of competition and are annual. Others occur in the heath in areas of locally high lime content. Some, such as shepherd's cress, germinate in autumn or early winter, survive winter as young plants and flower early in spring; by May or June seed has set and the plant withered.

Spring Speedwell Scrophulariaceae *Veronica verna*. **Distribution**: The Breckland of Norfolk and Suffolk. **Notes**: Open habitats in dry grassland; locally common; inflorescence glandular.

Spring Cinquefoil Rosaceae *Potentilla tabernaemontani*. **Distribution**: Scattered throughout Britain. **Other habitats**: Dry basic grassland; rocky outcrops. **Notes**: Prefers to grow on sunny slopes; very local.

Perennial Knawel Caryophyllaceae *Scleranthus perennis*. **Distribution**: The Breckland of East Anglia; Radnor in Wales. **Other habitats**: Rocks. **Notes**: Usually in dry, sandy fields; rare; visited by flies.

Purple Milk Vetch Papilionaceae *Astragalus danicus*. **Distribution**: Eastern England and Scotland; a few localities in the west of England, Scotland and Ireland. **Other habitats**: Short turf on calcareous soils and dunes. **Notes**: Locally abundant.

Field Mouse-ear Chickweed Caryophyllaceae *Cerastium arvense*. **Distribution**: Throughout Britain, especially in the east; scattered in Ireland, especially in the central-east and central-west. **Other habitats**: Dry banks; waysides; grassland. **Notes**: On calcareous or slightly acid sandy soils; variable.

Spanish Catchfly Caryophyllaceae *Silene otites*. **Distribution**: Confined to the Breckland heaths of Norfolk, western Suffolk and Cambridgeshire. **Notes**: Flowers are pale yellow-green; an evening scented species.

Grape Hyacinth Liliaceae *Muscari atlanticum*. **Distribution**: The Breckland of East Anglia; Oxfordshire; Hampshire. **Other habitats**: Dry grassland. **Notes**: Sometimes found as a garden escape, though not often cultivated now; the lobes of the flowers white or pale blue.

Rupturewort Caryophyllaceae *Herniaria glabra*. **Distribution**: Southern Devon; Cambridgeshire; Suffolk; Norfolk; southern Lincolnshire; Cumberland. **Other habitats**: Dry sandy places. **Notes**: Rare; locally common; the shoots are slightly or not hairy; seeds red turning black.

Maiden Pink Caryophyllaceae *Dianthus deltoides*. **Distribution**: Scattered throughout England, Scotland, Wales; one locality in south-eastern Ireland. **Other habitats**: Dry grassy fields, banks and pastures. **Notes**: Locally common; a lowland species; has a variable number of epicalyx scales.

Star of Bethlehem Liliaceae *Ornithogalum umbellatum*. **Distribution**: Scattered throughout Britain, but absent in north-western Scotland. **Notes**: Locally common; the bulb is surrounded by many bulbils.

Spiked Speedwell Scrophulariaceae *Veronica spicata* subsp. *spicata*. **Distribution**: Confined to the Breckland of East Anglia. **Notes**: In dry grassland on basic soil; rare; grows up to 30cm tall; leaves slightly crenate near the middle.

Small Meadow-rue Ranunculaceae *Thalictrum minus*. **Distribution**: Scattered throughout the British Isles, but more common towards the north. **Other habitats**: Limestone rocks and grassland; dunes; lake and streamside gravel and shingle; quarries; scree banks. **Notes**: Very variable; grows up to 1000 metres; tolerant of shade.

Shepherd's Cress Cruciferae *Teesdalia nudicaulis*. **Distribution**: Scattered throughout Britain, though rarer in Scotland; a few localities in north-eastern Ireland. **Other habitats**: Sand and gravel. **Notes**: Locally common.

Neutral Grassland and Meadows

Damp meadows and pastures usually have a rich flora often with characteristic species such as the rare fritillaries (shown above), the probably introduced but naturalized wild tulip *(Tulipa sylvestris)*, the wild daffodil *(Narcissus pseudonarcissus)* and the meadow saffron *(Colchicum autumnale)*.

The cold, wet uplands support extensive areas of grassland containing few, rather coarse, species, growing on poorly drained acid soils. In contrast, the well drained, mineral-rich soils of chalk and limestone areas support rich grassland communities. However, extensive areas of lowland Britain, particularly in agricultural regions, are covered with grass but do not fit into these two categories. These grasslands are usually on neutral soils and owe their existence and character mainly to past farming practices. With a great diversity of farming management, past and present, together with local variations in soil and changes in weather, almost every little patch will differ from others in some small way. Subdivision of neutral grasslands into categories is thus inappropriate, for these communities form a wide spectrum of grassland types. At one extreme are the wet meadows; characterised by a rich green community of grasses, rushes and sedges. Hay meadows, formerly hand-cut, rich in herbs and a mass of bright flowers in early summer are another fairly distinct type. Even grazed meadows can contain a rich assortment of species. These habitats contrast markedly with the "leys" which form the opposite end of the spectrum. Leys often consist of a few specially planted species, richly supplied with fertilisers and are specifically grown as grass crops, destined to be machine-cut for hay or silage. Such grasslands are lacking in biological diversity and are not discussed extensively here.

Neutral grassland communities occur on soils which are neither particularly base-rich nor acidic. In most cases the actual soil types are glacial drift material or alluvial clays and loams. Most neutral grasslands occur at low altitude and have been used for livestock grazing and hay making, often over long periods of time. Wherever species-rich neutral grasslands remain it is because the traditional methods of agricultural management are still practised and there have been no changes in use or attempts at agricultural improvement for many years, perhaps centuries.

Wet meadows

The duration of flooding and the amount of water-logging of the soil particularly affect the types of plants that may occur. Marsh grasslands occur in wet badly drained meadows beside rivers and on flood plains throughout Britain. They are dominated by rushes, water-tolerant grasses such as purple moor grass *(Molinia caerulea)* and flowers such as marsh orchids. Base-rich marshes may be found beside chalk streams in southern England, but more specialised flood meadows may be seen in the fenlands where washlands have been deliberately created to accept flood water overflowing from the Rivers Ouse, Nene, Welland and Witham and their parallel artificial channels. The largest and most important washlands are the Ouse washes, between Earith in Cambridgeshire and Denver

in Norfolk, and which lie between parallel channels of the River Ouse. These washlands are subjected to prolonged winter flooding and then are used for summer grazing. The washland system includes meadow grasslands, with water-tolerant grasses and ditches with marsh vegetation. The high water table, even in summer, keeps invertebrates from burrowing deep in the soil and makes them readily available to predators such as birds. During the winter the washes accumulate great concentrations of wildfowl while in the summer they provide breeding conditions for several rare species of waders and ducks. The other wash systems in Britain are no longer so extensively used as flood storage areas and have been partly or largely reclaimed for agriculture.

Water meadows are valley grasslands that are deliberately flooded; a management method which has been used on chalk streams in southern England from the 16th century onwards. A few water meadows still operate in Hampshire and Wiltshire but most are now disused. Their purpose was to increase the productivity of alluvial meadows by irrigating them with a system of feeder streams in channels, controlled by sluices. The water was made to spill over the edge of the feeders and trickled across the surface of the grassland, collecting in drainage channels at a lower level which returned the water to the river. The chalk stream water, which is warmer than the land in late winter, produced an early flush of grass in these meadows in late winter for early spring grazing. These water meadows have a grass dominated sward with a few flowers such as cushion flower and water forget-me-not.

Hay meadows

Where they still persist, the river valley hay meadows are particularly spectacular and rich in plant life. They are scattered throughout south and east England and are used to grow grass for hay, then grazed for a while after the hay has been cut. It seems strange that cutting should be beneficial to flowers, but the point is that the cutting occurs at a particular time every year. Thus species which flower late in the summer are cut long before they have a chance to seed. After only a few years they are eliminated, leaving room for less competitive species which flower early but are normally crowded out by more vigorous plants. Many of these hay meadow flowers were sought by farmers in the old days because they added sweetness and nourishment to the hay. Today, these additives come from a chemical factory and most hay fields are managed more intensively. The few old-style hay meadows that remain have often been treated the same way every year for centuries, owing to legal complexities and multiple ownership that prevent anyone doing anything else with them. The fritillary meadows of the Upper Thames Valley and the rich meadows at Pixey and Yarnton Meads near Oxford are examples which protect rare botanical specialities whose scarcity is due precisely to the fact that hay plus grazing regimes on unfertilised grasslands are an outmoded form of farming no longer widely practised.

In some places, a "ridge and furrow" pattern was created by ancient cultivation to provide drier growing conditions on the ridges and it persists where the fields have not been deep ploughed in recent years. These pastures occur at scattered localities, mainly in southern England, and where there has been grassland established for a long period of time a rich flora is found. Among flowering plants one of the most characteristic is the cowslip which cannot tolerate the water-logged conditions of the wetter meadows.

Grasslands in northern areas of Britain are different in character to those in the south and have a different species composition. Northern hay meadows occur mainly in upland valleys, especially in limestone districts or on ungrazed river banks at altitudes of up to 300 metres. Similarly the permanent pasture of the south has its counterpart in the north and west of Britain with grazed grasslands which have a different species composition, including plants such as the globe flower (*Trollius europaeus*).

Basic slag was the first material applied to old grasslands to increase their clover content, leading to improved grass yield, but in more recent times many different methods have become available for the agricultural improvement of grassland. Most of the species-rich neutral grassland communities have been eliminated in Britain through the use of fertilisers, ploughing and with agriculturally better species, reseeding the grassland or converting the fields to arable land. The result is that the wildlife diversity of traditional hay meadows and rich grazed pastures is now more seriously threatened than in any other major habitat type. Neutral grasslands persist in widely scattered locations where measures have been taken to ensure their survival or where some other circumstances have protected them. In many cases they persist simply because the owners or tenant farmers belong to an older generation of farmers who are not under economic pressure

Flood meadows are allowed to flood in the winter to accommodate water from storms which might cause damage if it unexpectedly inundated crops or towns downstream.

and who continue to use the old farming methods out of habit. The younger farmers who will replace them will not be able to ignore economic realities so easily. Some grasslands survive because they are remote from the farms to which they belong and are less accessible or less used than they might otherwise be. Certain hay meadows which have legal status as Lammas Lands have their management laid down by law, which hinders implementation of modern methods. Common land or other situations where multiple ownerships are involved have also survived as any change would require unanimous acquiescence of all the parties involved and it is not worth the trouble of trying to obtain the necessary agreement.

Drainage is another improvement which threatens the marsh fields. In the past it has been a costly operation. Today the technology is available to dig ditches and sink pipes quickly and relatively cheaply, so the high value of arable products makes it realistic to improve fields that could not be economically drained in the past. Similarly there are major drainage schemes carried out by the Water Authorities, which assist individual farmers over large areas in achieving improvement of their badly drained

grasslands, at the expense of the wildlife which had become specially adapted to the conditions which have persisted for centuries previously.

Agricultural improvement

Virtually all the species-rich grasslands, whether cut for hay or grazed by livestock, or both, are an anachronism on modern farms. Until the last century the production cycle on mixed farms was a closed circuit. The farms produced meat, wool and wheat for sale; they grew fodder crops for their livestock (including hay and roots); they put the manure from the livestock on the arable fields and used draught animals to pull the plough. This system resulted in a dependence on old grassland for the well-being of the farm and its essential animals. When imported foodstuffs were brought in and when inorganic chemical fertilisers became widely available, the old grasslands were no longer crucial to the farm system and were developed for other purposes or "improved" to gain higher yields.

Hay meadows are a traditional form of land use. Even though modern machinery is now used, the effect of cutting grass regularly at the same time of year is the same now as in centuries past. It encourages the development of a particular association of grasses and herbs, which is often enriched as a result of grazing later in the year.

The Flora of Neutral Grassland and Meadows

Semi-natural neutral grassland occurs mainly on clays and loams where the soil is neither very alkaline nor very acid. This type of grassland grades into other types such as fenlands on peat, and salt marsh grassland on the coast. The variety of types of neutral grassland have different plant communities which are determined by the soil type and its pH, the water regime and the type of management.

Wet grasslands

The various types of neutral grasslands may be recognised by their management regimes and each produces a flora adapted to the different conditions. Washland grasslands which receive flood water during long periods in the winter months are poor in flowering plants but contain several grasses. Reed canary grass, marsh foxtail and flote grass can all tolerate these conditions while reedsweet grass grows in the wettest spots.

Water meadows also have a rather undistinguished grass-dominated flora which is often rich in intergeneric hybrids between rye grasses and fescues. A few flowers occur in these places especially lady's smock, marsh ragwort, water avens and water forget-me-not, which may be concentrated along the minor water courses.

The amount of water considerably affects the flowers that are able to thrive. Greater burnet can tolerate some flooding, for example, but cannot exist in the washlands; while cowslip cannot tolerate flooding at all and only occurs in well drained pastures. Dry grasslands characteristically contain red fescue, sweet vernal grass, cowslip and green-winged orchid. Wetter grasslands have different grass species such as meadow foxtail and Yorkshire fog and the flowering plants include greater burnet and

lady's smock. Grasslands which are wetter still have a fen type community of sedges and rushes with marsh orchids, ragged robin and marsh bedstraw.

The commonest plantain of neutral grassland is the ribwort or black plantain *(Plantago lanceolata)* named after the ribbed leaves or black immature flowerheads. From the rosette of leaves arise erect stalks bearing the flower heads and from which in turn are produced great quantities of seed. New leaves are produced in the autumn and last through the winter in fresh green condition.

Grasslands in areas of flooded land or poorly drained soil are colonised by rushes, whose natural niche is in the transition zone between water and moist mud. Their tiny seeds are readily dispersed by water and hence arrive in the places where they can thrive with the flood-

A guide to some meadow grasses

Cocksfoot Gramineae (Poaceae) *Dactylis glomerata* **Distribution:** Throughout the British Isles. **Other habitats:** Roadside, rough grass; occasionally in open woodland. **Notes:** Coarse grass; often abundant; sometimes cultivated.

Tufted Hair-grass Gramineae (Poaceae) *Deschampsia caespitosa* **Distribution:** Throughout the British Isles. **Other habitats:** Rough grass and moorland. **Notes:** Wet badly drained soils; abundant in marshy fields; a coarse and variable grass; up to 1300 metres.

Crested Dog's Tail Gramineae (Poaceae) *Cynosurus cristatus* **Distribution:** Throughout the British Isles; has been found in every county. **Notes:** Common, often abundant; on a wide range of soils, acid to basic, light to heavy, wet to dry; up to 650 metres.

Sweet Vernal Grass Gramineae (Poaceae) *Anthoxanthum odoratum* **Distribution:** Throughout the British Isles. **Other habitats:** Heaths and moors; hill grassland; open woodland. **Notes:** Very variable; early flowering; strongly smelling of cut grass (coumarin).

Perennial Rye Grass Gramineae (Poaceae) *Lolium perenne* **Distribution:** Throughout the British Isles. **Other habitats:** Roadsides and waste land. **Notes:** Especially common on rich, heavy soils; extensively sown for the formation of new pastures; variable in structure.

False Oat Grass Gramineae (Poaceae) *Arrhenatherum elatius* **Distribution:** Widespread in the British Isles. **Other habitats:** Rough grassland; hedgerows; roadsides; gravel and shingle banks; waste ground. **Notes:** A coarse grass; very common.

Meadow Foxtail Gramineae (Poaceae) *Alopecurus pratensis* **Distribution:** Throughout the British Isles. **Notes:** Abundant in low lying areas and river valleys, especially water meadow and old grassland; rich moist soils.

Meadow Fescue Gramineae (Poaceae) *Festuca pratensis* **Distribution:** Throughout the British Isles but rare in northern Scotland. **Other habitats:** Roadsides. **Notes:** Most common on loamy or heavy soils; usually present in water meadow and low lying grassland.

Smooth Meadow Grass Gramineae (Poaceae) *Poa pratensis* **Distribution:** Throughout the British Isles. **Other habitats:** Road sides; cultivated land; waste land; walls; shaded places. **Notes:** Found up to 1300 metres; mainly on well drained sandy, gravelly or loamy soils; a variable species; an important hay and pasture grass.

Rough Meadow Grass Gramineae (Poaceae) *Poa trivialis* **Distribution:** Throughout the British Isles; has been found in every county. **Other habitats:** Waste and cultivated land; pond and stream margins. **Notes:** Sometimes found in partial shade; common on moist, rich soils.

Timothy Grass Gramineae (Poaceae) *Phleum pratense* **Distribution:** Throughout the British Isles, but less common in north-west Scotland. **Other habitats:** Field margins; road sides; waste places. **Notes:** Grown extensively for grazing and hay; shallow rooting; prefers heavy soil.

Reed Canary Grass Gramineae (Poaceae) *Phalaris arundinacea.* **Distribution:** Throughout the British Isles, but less common in north-west Scotland. **Other habitats:** By rivers, streams, lakes, pools; marshes. **Notes:** Often forms a large mass of vegetation; always grows in wet soils.

Wood Small-reed Gramineae (Poaceae) *Calamagrostis epigejos.* **Distribution:** Throughout England, sparse in Scotland and Wales, rare in north and west Ireland. **Other habitats:** Open places in damp woods; thickets; ditches; fens. **Notes:** Grows in heavy soils; occasionally very abundant.

Common Rush Juncaceae *Juncus conglomeratus.* **Distribution:** Throughout the British Isles. **Other habitats:** Bogs; damp woodland. **Notes:** Prefers wet, acid soils; easily distinguished by its rough feeling, coarsely ridged stem with a short spathe above the inflorescence

Cocksfoot   Crested Dog's Tail   Perennial Rye Grass   Meadow Foxtail   Smooth Meadow Grass   Timothy Grass   Wood Small-reed

Tufted Hair-grass   Sweet Vernal Grass   False Oat Grass   Meadow Fescue   Rough Meadow Grass   Reed Canary Grass   Common Rush

The meadow foxtail starts growth early in the year and is one of the first grasses to flower. It is most abundant on rich, moist soils where it is leafy and succulent and produces a valuable hay crop.

water. The clump-forming rushes are particularly serious weeds of grassland, where hard rush *(Juncus inflexus)* favours rather calcareous areas while soft rush *(J. effusus)* prefers more acid soils which are poor in nutrients. The latter species grows branched flower heads that in turn produce large numbers of fruit capsules containing phenomenal numbers of tiny seeds. These are mucilaginous and become sticky when wet so that they readily adhere to animal's and bird's feet and the muddy wheels of vehicles and are thus dispersed widely.

Effects of farming
Most of the traditionally managed pastures, rich in herbs, have been improved to increase their agricultural productivity by the use of inorganic chemical fertilisers. Nitrogen treatment in particular produces an increased growth in species such as perennial rye grass, cocksfoot and meadow fescue by encouraging the production of more shoots. These grasses are thus invigorated and compete strongly at the expense of most of the flowering plants which are progressively eliminated from the sward. The use of chemicals has also led to changes away from the traditional

A guide to some orchids of neutral grasslands and meadows

Meadow or pasture can be artificial or naturally occurring. In both cases, however, orchids are able to fill rapidly any available or suitable niche because they produce masses of fine dust-like seeds that are easily wind-transported in adequate numbers to the new site. On cut and heavily grazed pasture orchids do not grow well, but in protected areas they flourish. It is in the ungrazed moist water meadows that most orchids will be seen, though the early purple orchid flowers in hay meadows before cutting takes place — it cannot tolerate too wet conditions. The marsh helleborine is usually as illustrated here, but it is occasionally found with white-lipped yellow flowers. Both the common spotted and marsh orchids are variable species: the former has several clear-cut varieties that only occur in the extreme north and west, whereas the many varieties of the latter tend to interbreed and merge.

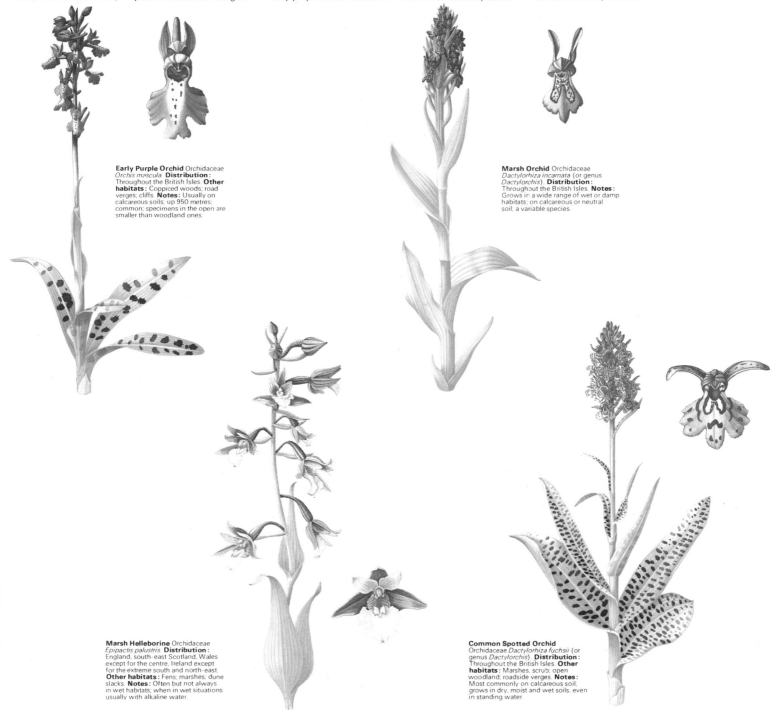

Early Purple Orchid Orchidaceae *Orchis mascula*. **Distribution:** Throughout the British Isles. **Other habitats:** Coppiced woods; road verges; cliffs. **Notes:** Usually on calcareous soils; up 950 metres; common; specimens in the open are smaller than woodland ones.

Marsh Orchid Orchidaceae *Dactylorhiza incarnata* (or genus *Dactylorchis*). **Distribution:** Throughout the British Isles. **Notes:** Grows in a wide range of wet or damp habitats; on calcareous or neutral soil; a variable species.

Marsh Helleborine Orchidaceae *Epipactis palustris*. **Distribution:** England, south-east Scotland, Wales except for the centre; Ireland except for the extreme south and north-east. **Other habitats:** Fens; marshes; dune slacks. **Notes:** Often but not always in wet habitats; when in wet situations usually with alkaline water.

Common Spotted Orchid Orchidaceae *Dactylorhiza fuchsii* (or genus *Dactylorchis*). **Distribution:** Throughout the British Isles. **Other habitats:** Marshes; scrub; open woodland; roadside verges. **Notes:** Most commonly on calcareous soil; grows in dry, moist and wet soils, even in standing water.

farming methods, with effects on the flora. For example, the use of nitrogen fertilisers on grassland in late winter produces a flush of grass which can be grazed in spring and this is followed by the application of more fertiliser to produce a hay crop in the summer. By contrast, the traditional hay meadow management did not allow for spring grazing because the meadows were shut to livestock from February to July to allow the hay crop to grow. The spring grazing affects early flowering species such as the fritillary by removing their flowers or fruits before they have had time to set seed.

Prolonged grazing affects the flora by eliminating species that are unable to withstand it like false oat grass, while the coarse leaves of tufted hair-grass are avoided by grazing stock in preference for the more palatable fescues and bent grasses, so that this species persists as tussocks in grazed grassland. Over-grazing may lead to poaching or breaking up of the turf. This process allows weed species like ragwort and creeping thistle to colonise. The excessive disturbance of treading and dunging around feeding troughs and gateways encourages the growth of knotgrass and rayless chamomile and in wet spots may encourage more attractive species such as the pink flowered bog pimpernel.

Weeds

A number of the flowering plants that colonise agricultural grasslands, including the perennial

The autumnal crocus *(Crocus nudiflorus)* is rare and often confused with the meadow saffron *(Colchicum autumnale)* as both species rapidly put up flowers, but no leaves, in the autumn; in both cases the leaves appear the following spring. However they can be easily distinguished as the autumnal crocus has three stamens and the saffron six.

A guide to some wild flowers of neutral grasslands and meadows

To the farmer, meadow and pastureland should consist only of perennial grasses and species of clover; all other plants are classified by him as weeds because they reduce the yield of hay. To most other people, however, it is the brilliant variety of flowers that make meadows most attractive. Many species, like the dandelion, daisy and clovers are well known to all.

Little or no grazing or cutting takes place in water meadows and this allows taller species like marsh thistle and water avens to grow and flourish. This also allows biennial species, such as hemlock (a poisonous umbellifer) to grow.

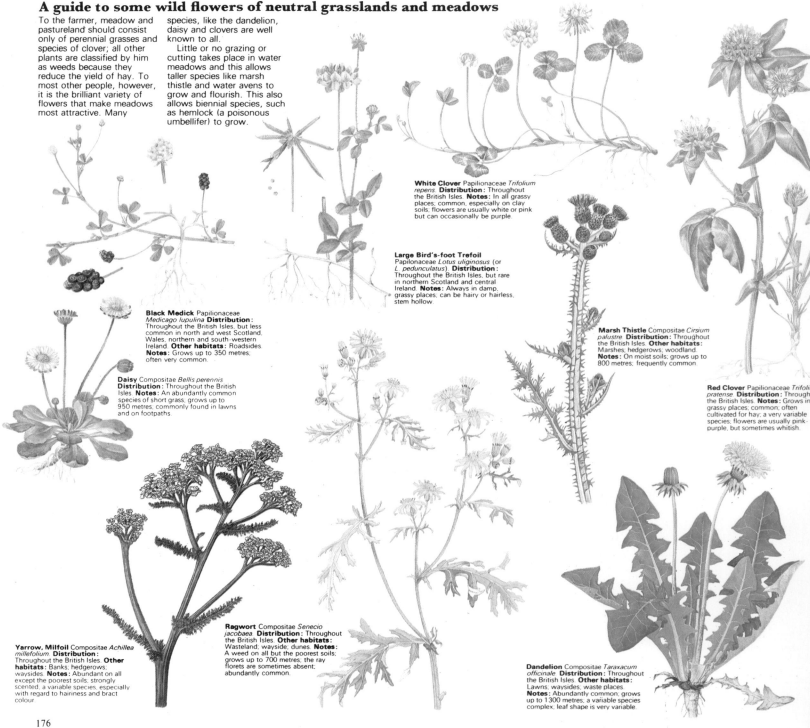

White Clover Papilionaceae *Trifolium repens.* **Distribution:** Throughout the British Isles. **Notes:** In all grassy places; common, especially on clay soils; flowers are usually white or pink but can occasionally be purple.

Large Bird's-foot Trefoil Papilionaceae *Lotus uliginosus* (or *L. pedunculatus*) **Distribution:** Throughout the British Isles, but rare in northern Scotland and central Ireland. **Notes:** Always in damp, grassy places; can be hairy or hairless; stem hollow.

Black Medick Papilionaceae *Medicago lupulina* **Distribution:** Throughout the British Isles, but less common in north and west Scotland, Wales, northern and south-western Ireland. **Other habitats:** Roadsides. **Notes:** Grows up to 350 metres; often very common.

Daisy Compositae *Bellis perennis* **Distribution:** Throughout the British Isles. **Notes:** An abundantly common species of short grass, grows up to 950 metres; commonly found in lawns and on footpaths.

Marsh Thistle Compositae *Cirsium palustre.* **Distribution:** Throughout the British Isles. **Other habitats:** Marshes; hedgerows; woodland. **Notes:** On moist soils; grows up to 800 metres; frequently common.

Red Clover Papilionaceae *Trifolium pratense* **Distribution:** Throughout the British Isles. **Notes:** Grows in all grassy places; common; often cultivated for hay; a very variable species; flowers are usually pink-purple, but sometimes whitish.

Yarrow, Milfoil Compositae *Achillea millefolium.* **Distribution:** Throughout the British Isles. **Other habitats:** Banks; hedgerows; waysides. **Notes:** Abundant on all except the poorest soils; strongly scented; a variable species, especially with regard to hairiness and bract colour.

Ragwort Compositae *Senecio jacobaea* **Distribution:** Throughout the British Isles. **Other habitats:** Wasteland; wayside; dunes. **Notes:** A weed on all but the poorest soils; grows up to 700 metres; the ray florets are sometimes absent; abundantly common.

Dandelion Compositae *Taraxacum officinale.* **Distribution:** Throughout the British Isles. **Other habitats:** Lawns; waysides; waste places. **Notes:** Abundantly common, grows up to 1300 metres; a variable species complex; leaf shape is very variable.

rye grass and cocksfoot leys, may be regarded as weeds by the farmer, who places little value on such plants. Certain species are actually toxic to cattle and other livestock and so are particularly unwelcome. This is true of the buttercups which contain an acrid poison which is harmful to cattle. Creeping buttercup *(Ranunculus repens)* is a feature of damp meadows where it may form large colonies; meadow buttercup *(R. acris)* forms tufted plants in long herbage; bulbous buttercup *(R. bulbosus)* prefers pasture on dry soils. Ragwort, a troublesome weed of pastures on lighter soils, contains an alkaloid poison that can be fatal to horses and cattle if eaten. Creeping thistle is a nuisance because it produces inedible foliage and covers large areas of ground. The tall prickly flowering stems develop from buds on lateral roots: it is this that makes the weed so invasive as it tends to form formidable spreading patches of plants that are connected below ground and so is difficult to eradicate. It also produces prolific quantities of fruits which bear a parachute of feathery hairs and are blown everywhere to cause fresh nuisances to grow.

Hay meadows

Meadows which are cut by traditional methods for hay and occur on loam or peaty soils are wonderfully rich in flowering plants in addition to many grasses. The dominant grasses are sweet vernal, meadow fescue, red fescue, crested

Probably the best known British wild flower is the dandelion, here growing profusely in a meadow. It is widespread and very variable and able to set seed without pollination. Its ability to regenerate from fragments and the numerous seeds ensure it is successful and able to colonise suitable and available habitats.

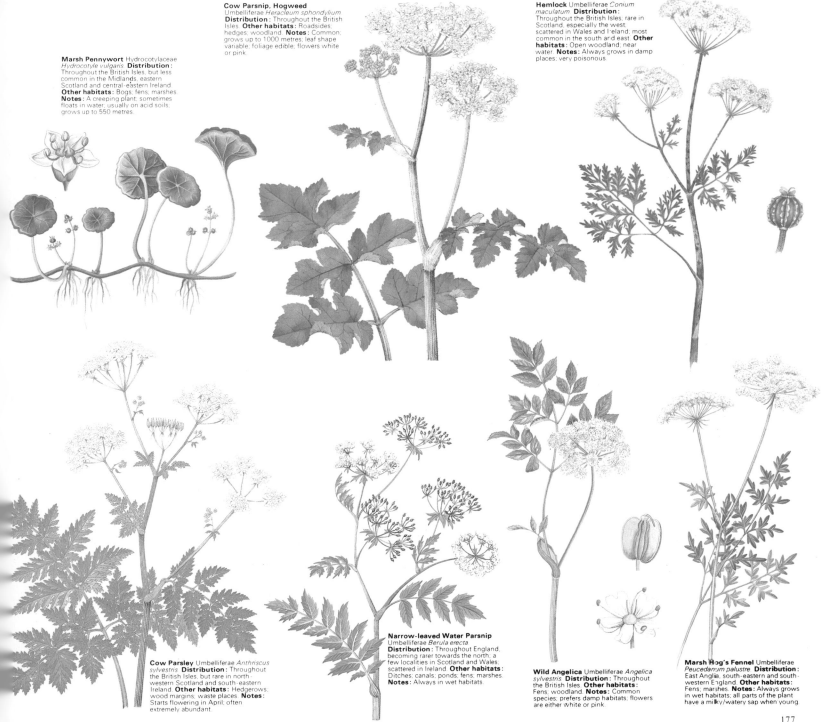

Marsh Pennywort Hydrocotylaceae *Hydrocotyle vulgaris.* **Distribution:** Throughout the British Isles, but less common in the Midlands, eastern Scotland and central-eastern Ireland. **Other habitats:** Bogs; fens; marshes. **Notes:** A creeping plant; sometimes floats in water; usually on acid soils; grows up to 550 metres.

Cow Parsnip, Hogweed Umbelliferae *Heracleum sphondylium.* **Distribution:** Throughout the British Isles. **Other habitats:** Roadsides; hedges; woodland. **Notes:** Common; grows up to 1000 metres; leaf shape variable; foliage edible; flowers white or pink.

Hemlock Umbelliferae *Conium maculatum.* **Distribution:** Throughout the British Isles, rare in Scotland, especially the west, scattered in Wales and Ireland, most common in the south and east. **Other habitats:** Open woodland, near water. **Notes:** Always grows in damp places; very poisonous.

Cow Parsley Umbelliferae *Anthriscus sylvestris.* **Distribution:** Throughout the British Isles, but rare in north-western Scotland and south-eastern Ireland. **Other habitats:** Hedgerows; wood margins; waste places. **Notes:** Starts flowering in April; often extremely abundant.

Narrow-leaved Water Parsnip Umbelliferae *Berula erecta.* **Distribution:** Throughout England, becoming rarer towards the north; a few localities in Scotland and Wales; scattered in Ireland. **Other habitats:** Ditches; canals; ponds; fens; marshes. **Notes:** Always in wet habitats.

Wild Angelica Umbelliferae *Angelica sylvestris.* **Distribution:** Throughout the British Isles. **Other habitats:** Fens; woodland. **Notes:** Common species; prefers damp habitats; flowers are either white or pink.

Marsh Hog's Fennel Umbelliferae *Peucedanum palustre.* **Distribution:** East Anglia, south-eastern and south-western England. **Other habitats:** Fens; marshes. **Notes:** Always grows in wet habitats; all parts of the plant have a milky/watery sap when young.

The fritillary

The fritillary is a native lily with many local names. Growing from a bulb, it has a smooth stem 30cm high and after four years a single nodding bell-shaped flower, usually chequered purple and white, is produced, though occasionally it may be entirely white.

The species is characteristic of traditional hay meadows in the alluvial flood plains of some areas of southern England. Once widespread, it has now disappeared from most of its former sites, especially in the lower Thames Valley, though a few meadow populations survive in Suffolk, Berkshire, Wiltshire and Gloucestershire. The plant's decline is attributed to widespread picking, but the major cause has in fact been the loss of suitable habitats.

It depends for survival on the traditional (and now obsolete) practice of hay making. The plants flower in late April/early May and ripen seed by the time the hay is cut: the disturbance of hay cutting helps distribute the seeds. Agricultural changes of recent years have resulted in the disappearance of traditional hay meadows through ploughing, the use of inorganic fertilisers and by permitting summer grazing.

Most of the flowers of the fritillary are chequered dark and pale dull purple; however, entirely cream-white flowers are often found. Although rare in the wild it is often cultivated in gardens from where it frequently escapes. It is usually found in damp meadows.

dog's tail *(Cynosurus cristatus)*, meadow foxtail, Yorkshire fog and perennial rye grass with scarcer species such as quaking grass *(Briza* sp.). The flowering plants are mostly species that flower early in the summer, their fruits ripening at hay cutting time. The most characteristic are lady's smock, dandelion, buttercups, bird's-foot trefoil, meadowsweet, pepper saxifrage, and meadow rue. Rarer species such as the fritillary also occur together with interesting plants like devil's bit scabious *(Succisa pratensis)*, the name of which derives from the tap root which has a truncated appearance as if bitten off.

Grasslands on well drained medium to heavy soils, which are cut or grazed, are characteristic of the Midlands and eastern England. Again these meadows contain many grasses like downy oat, catstail, meadow brome and tall fescue in addition to the more widespread species like red fescue and perennial rye grass. The characteristic flowers are cowslip, green-winged orchid, betony, saw-wort, greater burnet, lady's bedstraw, hardhead and more locally the meadow saffron. When the pasture occurs on lighter soils other species may be found depending on the acidity such as creeping bent grass, pignut (which yields an edible rootstock) and meadow saxifrage.

The hay meadows in the northern parts of Britain contrast strongly in botanical composition. They contain some plants that are scarce

A guide to some wild flowers of neutral grasslands and meadows (continued)

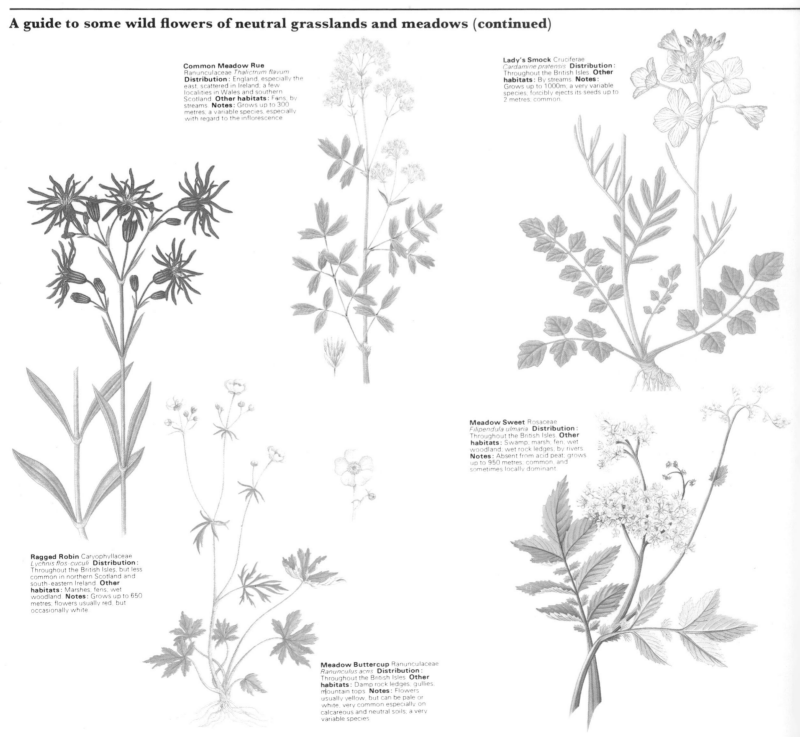

Common Meadow Rue Ranunculaceae *Thalictrum flavum* **Distribution**: England, especially the east, scattered in Ireland, a few localities in Wales and southern Scotland. **Other habitats**: Fens, by streams. **Notes**: Grows up to 300 metres, a variable species, especially with regard to the inflorescence.

Lady's Smock Cruciferae *Cardamine pratensis* **Distribution**: Throughout the British Isles. **Other habitats**: By streams. **Notes**: Grows up to 1000m; a very variable species; forcibly ejects its seeds up to 2 metres; common.

Ragged Robin Caryophyllaceae *Lychnis flos-cuculi* **Distribution**: Throughout the British Isles, but less common in northern Scotland and south-eastern Ireland. **Other habitats**: Marshes, fens, wet woodland. **Notes**: Grows up to 650 metres; flowers usually red, but occasionally white.

Meadow Sweet Rosaceae *Filipendula ulmaria* **Distribution**: Throughout the British Isles. **Other habitats**: Swamp, marsh, fen, wet woodland; wet rock ledges; by rivers. **Notes**: Absent from acid peat; grows up to 950 metres; common, and sometimes locally dominant.

Meadow Buttercup Ranunculaceae *Ranunculus acris* **Distribution**: Throughout the British Isles. **Other habitats**: Damp rock ledges, gullies, mountain tops. **Notes**: Flowers usually yellow, but can be pale or white; very common especially on calcareous and neutral soils; a very variable species

in the south like the melancholy thistle and wood cranesbill, which replaces the meadow cranesbill of southern hay meadows. Another conspicuous feature is that plants which are familiar as woodland species in southern England become meadow plants in these northern hay meadows. This is particularly true of the greater butterfly orchid and early purple orchid.

Grazed grassland in northern Britain also contains very different species like the blue moor grass, lady's mantle, and bitter pea. Wherever there are springs and flushes special conditions are created that favour birds' eye primrose, grass of parnassus (which is not a true grass but a flowering plant with white flowers), and very locally alpine bartsia, in addition to a wealth of sedges.

Within most grasslands the picture is more complicated than this account implies. Even a series of adjacent fields can have different associations of plants depending on their precise soil conditions and past management history. Even in a single field the flora can vary in different parts depending on the level of the ground, degree of flooding, presence of springs and wet hollows, ponds or water courses. The flora of a very large meadow can be affected by many influences over the years, such as disturbances for river improvement works and laying pipelines, which can all alter or modify the botanical composition in small areas.

Biennial cow parsley flowers from April to June and is the commonest early-flowering umbellifer in the south. Its zygomorphic flowers may be white, cream or, rarely, yellow.

Caterpillars of the cinnabar moth feed on ragwort. Experiments have been undertaken to use these caterpillars as a biological control against this damaging weed.

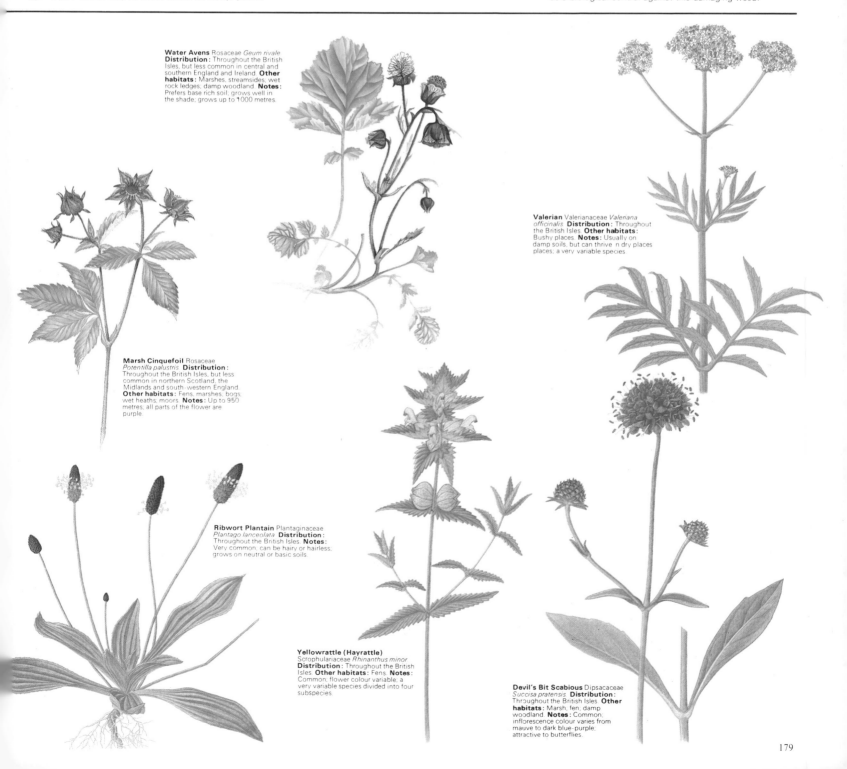

Water Avens Rosaceae *Geum rivale* **Distribution:** Throughout the British Isles, but less common in central and southern England and Ireland. **Other habitats:** Marshes, streamsides, wet rock ledges, damp woodland. **Notes:** Prefers base rich soil; grows well in the shade; grows up to 1000 metres.

Valerian Valerianaceae *Valeriana officinalis*. **Distribution:** Throughout the British Isles. **Other habitats:** Bushy places. **Notes:** Usually on damp soils, but can thrive in dry places; a very variable species.

Marsh Cinquefoil Rosaceae *Potentilla palustris* **Distribution:** Throughout the British Isles, but less common in northern Scotland, the Midlands and south-western England. **Other habitats:** Fens, marshes, bogs, wet heaths, moors. **Notes:** Up to 950 metres; all parts of the flower are purple.

Ribwort Plantain Plantaginaceae *Plantago lanceolata* **Distribution:** Throughout the British Isles. **Notes:** Very common; can be hairy or hairless; grows on neutral or basic soils.

Yellowrattle (Hayrattle) Scrophulariaceae *Rhinanthus minor* **Distribution:** Throughout the British Isles. **Other habitats:** Fens. **Notes:** Common; flower colour variable; a very variable species divided into four subspecies.

Devil's Bit Scabious Dipsacaceae *Succisa pratensis* **Distribution:** Throughout the British Isles. **Other habitats:** Marsh, fen, damp woodland. **Notes:** Common; inflorescence colour varies from mauve to dark blue-purple; attractive to butterflies.

Reptiles

There are six species of reptile indigenous to Britain: three snakes and three species of lizard. All of these are more or less associated with heathland or grassland habitats but most have fairly wide habitat requirements and either occur in a variety of habitats or require more than one habitat type during a full year.

The smooth snake *(Coronella austriaca)* and sand lizard *(Lacerta agilis)* are rare and en-

dangered in Britain and are protected by the Conservation of Wild Creatures and Wild Plants Act (1975). Both of these species are very restricted in distribution, occurring together on the sandy heaths of Dorset, Hampshire and parts of Surrey. The sand lizard requires dry, well drained sandy banks with mature heather bushes in which to clamber. It also occurs on sand dunes in Dorset and on the Lancashire

The grass snake (*Natrix natrix*) lays about 30 eggs, usually in decaying vegetation; the decomposition of which keeps them warm and speeds development of the embryo.

coast and is thus less restricted than the smooth snake, which is only found in the south.

The grass snake *(Natrix natrix helvetica)* occurs in England and Wales where it is widely distributed and may be found in a variety of habitats that include grassland, open woodland, hedgerows and marshland. It feeds particularly on frogs so has a preference for places near water and may be readily seen in fenland districts on the sides of dykes.

Both the slow worm *(Anguis fragilis)* and the adder *(Vipera berus)* occur throughout the mainland of England, Scotland and Wales. The slow worm prefers well-vegetated sites with plenty of ground cover, and favours rough pasture with long grass, scrubland, heathland and hedge-banks. It especially enjoys warm damp spots. The adder generally prefers dry localities ranging from heathland and open woodland to upland moors. Their habitat preferences change during the seasons: they seek dry sites to hibernate over winter but prefer damper summer feeding localities.

The most widespread of the British reptiles is the common or viviparous lizard *(Lacerta vivipara)* which is found throughout Britain including Ireland, but not the remoter islands such as Orkney or the Outer Hebrides. Within its range the common lizard may be found on heaths, grasslands, in woodland clearings, in gardens and hedge-banks and many similar habitats.

All these reptiles are warmth-loving animals that are generally commoner in the south of the country and seek sheltered sunny positions such as south facing banks to bask in the sun. Slow worms more frequently bask beneath flat stones

The female common lizard (*Lacerta vivipara*) retains the eggs within her body, and they hatch immediately after they are laid. Less than 10 young can be produced each year, but their survival rate is enhanced. Moreover, the female can bask in the sun to speed embryo development, even in relatively cool places.

or sheets of discarded metal. Common lizards, which are agile climbers may choose logs, tree stumps or walls on which to sun themselves. However, these reptiles do not enjoy the intense heat of the direct mid-day sun and will retreat under cover or into burrows when they become too hot.

Generally these species are inactive during the winter months when it is too cold and availability of food is much reduced. Most species hibernate in burrows or other sheltered places between the autumn and spring. The more southern species such as the sand lizard hibernate for the longest periods of time (September to April). The hardier species may be seen surprisingly early in the year if there are suitably warm and sunny days to tempt them out; adders, for example, may be seen regularly on bright days in March and may even emerge in February if conditions are suitable. Both adders and slow worms commonly hibernate in large clusters which may be discovered in hollows in the ground, under tree roots or in holes in walls.

All the reptiles are predators and generally show definite preferences for certain food organisms. The slow worm searches for prey by slow deliberate movements at dusk onwards or after rain, seeking out live invertebrates, especially slugs, snails, worms, insects and their larvae, which live in the soil and litter and under logs and stones.

Predation

The common lizard feeds mainly on insects, spiders and other invertebrates on the ground, and in vegetation and on walls and tree trunks. The sand lizard has similar food requirements, feeding especially on insects and other vertebrates in the tangled stems of old heather bushes. It will also eat slugs, snails and worms and will take dead prey or meat.

The snakes have a preference for vertebrate prey but will take some invertebrates. The grass snake swims readily and pursues much of its prey in water, taking frogs and their tadpoles, newts and small fish. In addition grass snakes may raid bird's nests for fledglings and take some small mammals.

The adder feeds mainly on small vertebrates such as young birds, frogs, newts and small mammals. It kills its prey by striking with its poison fangs and then following the prey until it dies. Adders do not bite things they cannot eat except in self defence. Thus humans have little to fear from this attractively marked snake—provided it is left alone. The risk of stepping on one by accident is not great as all snakes are shy creatures and avoid contact with humans when possible. The danger of adder bites needs to be kept in perspective; only about a dozen people have died from adder venom in Britain this century, practically all of them children. For a healthy adult, the adder poses no serious threat and it is a pity that so many snakes, including harmless ones (and even slow worms!) are killed by people for reasons of hysterical prejudice.

The smooth snake is non-venomous and feeds on small vertebrates especially lizards and slow worms. All snakes swallow their prey whole and probably feed more on invertebrates early in their lives.

The various British reptiles reproduce either by giving birth to live young (as in the case of the common lizard and adder), by producing eggs which are laid in burrows in the sand (in the case of the sand lizard), or in warm rotting vegetation (as in the grass snake). The young reptiles are particularly vulnerable to predation either by other larger reptiles, or by predatory birds and mammals. In areas where the heathland habitat has been exploited for building development, for example around Bournemouth, the reptiles are also threatened by domestic cats that kill them and children who collect them as pets.

A guide to British reptiles

Most reptiles are found on heathland; some also inhabit various types of greassland. The smooth snake and sand lizard are very rare, localised in distribution and protected by law. The adder is widespread, boldly marked and often sluggish. Males have a pale creamy ground colour, females are browner; black or reddish variants are sometimes seen. Grass snakes always have a pale, usually yellow, patch on each side of the neck and no zig-zag pattern down the back. The smooth snake also lacks the zig-zag pattern of the adder, has a narrower head and also lacks the yellow of the grass snake. Male sand lizards are bright green, females are browner and both have a much more bulky head than the common lizard. Common lizards are widespread, abundant and variable in colour. Males are often dark and brightly patterned on the back, with an orange belly. Females are pale yellow underneath and are a pale, plainer brown above. The slow worm is actually a type of lizard (having eyelids and ear holes unlike snakes) capable of shedding its tail if held by it, as the common and sand lizards also do. Male slow worms are bronze all over, the females and young having a very dark belly sharply contrasting with the pale brown back. Blue spotted males are occasionally found.

Grass Snake Colubridae *Natrix natrix helvetica.* **Distribution:** Widely distributed over England and Wales. **Notes:** Has distinctive yellow collar, hibernates from October to the beginning of March.

Slow Worm Anguidae *Anguis fragilis.* **Distribution:** All over England, Wales and Scotland. More abundant in the south. **Other habitats:** Hedgerows, gardens. **Notes:** Hibernates mid-October to late-February.

Common/Viviparous Lizard Lacertidae *Lacerta vivipara.* **Distribution:** Common over all of England and Wales, most of Scotland and parts of Ireland. **Notes:** Hibernates mid-October to late February.

Adder Viperidae *Vipera berus.* **Distribution:** Common in England and Wales, sparsely distributed in Scotland. **Notes:** Has characteristic zig zag markings. Hibernates from early October to late February.

Sand Lizard Lacertidae *Lacerta agilis.* **Distribution:** Rare, only found in localised areas in South West and North West. **Notes:** Hibernates from early October to late-March.

Smooth Snake Colubridae *Coronella austriaca.* **Distribution:** Very rare, only found in localised areas in the South West. **Other habitats:** Wooded areas. **Notes:** Hibernates from early October to late March.

Birds of Grassland, Scrub and Heathland

The barn owl (*Tyto alba*) has sensitive ears and eyes to allow hunting in the dark. Its soft plumage permits silent flight, giving the prey no warning of the bird's approach; powerful feet with sharp claws kill small mammals in seconds.

Where grassland is maintained by heavy grazing, few birds can find enough cover in which to nest. However some species actually prefer these conditions, relying on their own alertness and the perfect camouflage of their eggs to avoid predation. The rare stone curlew is probably the best example, as it actually chooses bare stony ground on which to nest in the south and east. Where there is insufficient grazing, especially by rabbits and vegetation begins to grow taller, stone curlews are displaced.

Longer grass, especially scattered tufts, provides food and home for many more species, the skylark being one of the most characteristic. The exuberant song, delivered only in flight, is a characteristic sound of open grassy country and the skylark is one of Britain's most widely distributed birds. In a good habitat, there may be 70 or more pairs in a square kilometre. In wet grassland, various wader species may be found, especially snipe. The long probing beak of these birds is well suited to seeking out invertebrate food among the grasses and soft mud of water meadows and pasture land. Snipe make a characteristic rasping alarm call as they fly

away from an intruder, zig-zagging sharply in flight. In the spring they make another very characteristic sound in their display flight. The two outer tail feathers are stuck out at right angles to the body and make a loud whirring noise in the airflow as the bird repeatedly dives towards the ground.

Many birds feed in the grassland habitat but do not nest there, swallows for example. The green woodpecker is particularly fond of raiding the ant nests that characterise old grassland and many other species come to feed as winter visitors. Some of these are seasonal fugitives from the harsh uplands, like the merlin and golden plover; others migrate in from more northerly latitudes, notably geese. Seven species of geese visit Britain in winter to partake of our grass and may be seen, particularly in coastal areas, grazing in flocks of a thousand birds or more.

The corncrake is a rather special grassland bird, being particularly associated with hay meadows, but like the special flowers of this habitat, the corncrake has suffered as a result of changes in farming methods. When hay was cut by men using scythes, the birds could easily

escape and the cutters would spare nests and chicks. Mowing machines are more methodical and lack such compassion. Moreover, the modern trend is towards cutting hay earlier in the year when birds are still on eggs. Corncrakes were common a century ago but have declined drastically, and seem doomed to disappear from mainland Britain unless they can adopt a new habitat in which to live.

Many other grassland birds are particularly associated with farmland and influenced by agricultural management, and some of these are considered later in "Man-made habitats".

Scrubland birds

As scrub begins to invade grassland, a mixed habitat develops, allowing a greater variety of species to find both food and nest sites. The advent of bushes offers somewhere for birds to nest off the ground and also provides a selection of prominent song perches from which to declare territorial ownership. A mixture of bushes and grassland is particularly favoured by warbler species, whose varied songs are often the main clue to their presence and identity. Early stages in the growth of pine plantations also provide fine scrub habitat with high populations of up to six different warbler species. One particularly characteristic scrub warbler is, or was, the whitethroat, whose grating song could be heard from almost any patch of bushes or rank vegetation. However, in 1969 less than a quarter of Britain's normal whitethroat population returned from their migration to west Africa. They were victims of the widespread drought in the southern Sahara and, despite the abundance of food and habitat in Britain, after ten years the species has still not restored its previous population size.

Warblers are summer visitors and during the winter, their place may be taken by large parties of mixed species. Elegant long tailed tits flit from bush to bush looking for food, whilst blue tits, coal tits and others methodically search the branches and twigs, forming a large mixed-species foraging party. Similarly, assorted species of finches gather in large flocks in bushes and scrub. Hawthorn, blackthorn, wild rose and some of the other species that lead the scrub invasion of grassland offer rich pickings of bright red berries for birds in winter. Some species like the fieldfare, redwing and waxwing come to Britain from Scandinavia to enjoy the winter food provided by our bushes, and in return spread the seeds of those bushes in their droppings helping to advance the invasion of grassland by scrub.

If scrub development continues, dense thickets develop which are often not very good bird habitats. Nightingales like thick scrub, but desert it when it becomes too old and dark. Dense hawthorn and blackthorn may prove attractive to magpies which like to build their large domed nests in such situations, as do many hedgerow species, but these are considered elsewhere in this book.

Heathland Birds

In areas where heathland is colonised by species of heather, to the near-exclusion of everything else, there are relatively few birds to be found. The red grouse is the only British bird which actually feeds mainly on heather, but it prefers the cooler, wetter parts of the country, not the warm dry areas where typical heathland develops.

The little owl

The little owl *Athene noctua* is a small compact owl with dappled grey plumage and fierce yellow eyes. It can often be seen perching in prominent places like hedgerow trees, on fence posts or on rocks. When disturbed or alarmed it bobs in a characteristic way. The owl is highly characteristic of agricultural land with hedgerows, trees and buildings. Elsewhere the little owl occurs in bare open habitats, shunning densely wooded regions and the built up areas of inner cities, though it may be found in parkland.

It preys on a variety of animals ranging from small mammals and birds down to invertebrates such as worms, beetles and slugs. The owl hunts chiefly at dusk and dawn but is readily seen in daylight. It frequently carries its prey to a hollow tree to dismember it and uneaten food may accumulate in such places. Hollow trees are also favourite nesting sites but a variety of other situations may be chosen including holes in walls, buildings, cliffs and even rabbit burrows. A clutch of three to five white eggs is laid in the spring, with sometimes another clutch later.

The species is well established in Britain yet it was introduced to the country in the nineteenth century.

The little owl (*Athene noctua*) is the smallest British owl. It hunts over grassland and is most often seen perched on a fence post or dead tree beside a field.

The most typical heathland bird is probably the nightjar, though it may also be found in open woodland and on some grassy areas. In common with other heathland species, the nightjar has suffered a decline in numbers and is now very scarce in Scotland. It is a summer visitor to Britain (May–August) and on warm nights its purring call, like a distant motorbike, is a particularly distinctive feature of the lowland heaths. Nightjars feed on insects, snapped up in flight with their very broad mouth, and overcome the problem of nesting on open heathland by laying two well camouflaged eggs on to the bare ground, with no nest. The young are also well camouflaged, and are fed by their parents for about a month.

Where heathland is composed of a mosaic of heather and bushy scrub, the habitat becomes much more attractive to birds in general. Bushes not only support a wider selection of insect food, but more importantly, provide protected nest sites up off the ground. Gorse is a common heathland shrub and this has the extra advantages that it is evergreen (and so provides shelter at all times of the year) and is very spiny, an effective deterrent to most nest robbers. Where gorse occurs, the linnet, stonechat and red-backed shrike are characteristic inhabitants.

Linnets are seed eaters, so do well in many open habitats, including farmland and are one of the most abundant and widespread small breeding birds in Britain, despite the depredations of 19th century trappers working to supply the cage bird trade. The stonechat is similarly not

Song thrushes feed on snails, smashing them against a stone to break open the shells. Examination of the debris around such an "anvil" shows what species have been most frequently taken.

The nightjar (*Caprimulgus europaeus*) is a typical heathland bird, feeding on large numbers of insects caught at night on the wing. Nightjars nest on the ground, usually laying two eggs in early summer directly on to the soil surface. Both the eggs and the adult birds are beautifully camouflaged to match the surrounding dead plant material; a necessary protection in the open habitat of heathland. Nightjars are becoming rare as their habitat is lost.

confined to heaths, being typical of many open habitats especially around the coast. However, the red-backed shrike is a much scarcer bird, now almost entirely confined to bushy areas on heathland in the south and east. It was formerly widespread and fairly abundant, but the total British population may now be less than 100 birds. The decline is attributed to climatic deterioration in the last few decades. Shrikes particularly need an abundance of large insects for food, and warm heathlands abound in these (especially dragonflies and damselflies in damper patches). A recent trend towards cooler, wetter summers has apparently reduced the abundance of insects, with unfortunate consequences for shrikes. If shrikes are present in an area, they should be fairly easily seen as they characteristically keep watch from a prominent perch for potential food. Shrikes also have a distinctive habit of impaling uneaten food on thorns to form a ghoulish larder; perhaps, quite literally, as provision for a rainy day when fewer insects might be active.

The Dartford warbler is another rare species, almost entirely confined to lowland heath in the south of England. It especially prefers areas with scattered gorse bushes 1–2 metres high. Unlike other British warblers, this species stays in its breeding area over winter and does not migrate.

It is not surprising that severe weather has caused drastic reductions in the population in some years. It is also very vulnerable to fires in the nesting season and at one time practically the whole population of the Surrey heaths was wiped out by fires.

Dartford warblers were once fairly widespread, breeding in at least 15 southern counties; but they are now confined to a mere six with a total of perhaps 1,100 birds. The size of the British population appears to be limited by the restricted and decreasing area of suitable habitat, but an interesting and encouraging recent development is the discovery of some pairs found breeding in young conifer plantations.

The woodlark is another species especially associated with lowland heaths. Its range has shrunk in recent years so that it is now confined to heaths in Hampshire, Surrey and Sussex, and a quarter of the British population now breeds in the New Forest.

Where heathland is invaded by scattered trees, especially pines, the hobby may nest. This elegant falcon is one of our most aerial acrobats feeding on large insects and small insectivorous birds (even fast fliers like swifts) caught on the wing. Again this is a species that relies heavily on the abundance of insect food (for itself or its preferred prey) available on lowland heaths and

is now less widespread than previously. There would be insufficient prey to enable hobbies to be resident like the Dartford warbler, so they migrate south for the winter, only returning with fine weather in May, later than most of our migrant birds.

Lapwings are typical of the ground-nesting plovers and waders which lay large pointed eggs that can be fitted closely together for efficient brooding. Lapwings nest in all types of grassland and open ground including the uplands and also arable fields.

The hobby (*Falco subbuteo*) is a typical hawk of the southern heaths. It feeds on the larger species of heathland insects, which are caught on the wing whereas the closely related kestrel catches most of its insect food on the ground. Hobbies also catch small birds in flight and carry them back to a favourite perch to be plucked and then eaten.

A guide to some birds of lowland grasslands and heaths

Kestrel Falconidae *Falco tinnunculus* **Distribution**: Resident throughout British Isles. **Other habitats**: Almost ubiquitous. **Notes**: Size: 33–36cm. As with other raptors female larger than male. Habitually hovers.

Stone Curlew Burhinidae *Burhinus oedicnemus*. **Distribution**: Summer visitor in south-east England. **Other habitats**: Sandy heaths, waste land and chalk uplands. **Notes**: Size 41cm. Slow wing-beats with trailing legs. Two whitish wing-bars obvious in flight. Runs furtively. Voice is Curlew-like.

Nightjar Caprimulgidae *Caprimulgus europaeus*. **Distribution**: Summer visitor in Great Britain and Ireland. **Other habitats**: Woodland, broken hillsides, dunes and moorland. **Notes**: Size: 27cm. Crepuscular. Spends day crouched motionless along branch, or on ground. Flight is light and floating with aerobatic dashes after flying insects. Voice is a loud "churring".

Hobby Falconidae *Falco subbuteo*. **Distribution**: Summer visitor to southern England. **Other habitats**: Downland, heaths and agricultural land, with small woods. **Notes**: Size 30–36cm. Short tail and long wings resemble Swift in flight. Female is the larger.

Barn Owl Tytonidae *Tyto alba*. **Distribution**: Resident in Great Britain and Ireland. **Other habitats**: Agricultural country. **Notes**: Size 34cm. Eyes black. Unstreaked, white underparts. Slow flapping in flight, at times wavering on rounded wings. Voice is wild shrieks various hissing and snoring noises.

Skylark Alaudidae *Alauda arvensis*. **Distribution**: Resident in Great Britain and Ireland. **Other habitats**: Open country. **Notes**: Size 18cm. Tail has white sides. Flight is strong and undulating. Performs the well-known song-flight. Voice is sustained often from great height. Flight note "chirrup".

Whitethroat Sylviidae *Sylvia communis*. **Distribution**: Summer visitor throughout British Isles. **Other habitats**: Open areas with thick cover. **Notes**: Size 14cm. Female has brown hood. Call: scolding notes. Rapid chattering song. Rufous patch on wings.

Lesser Whitethroat Sylviidae *Sylvia curruca*. **Distribution**: Summer visitor. Mainly in S.E., local elsewhere. Absent from Scotland and Ireland. **Other habitats**: Prefers taller undergrowth to Whitethroat. **Notes**: Size 13.5cm. Call: "tchak". Song a fast rattle, sometimes a warble.

Little Owl Strigidae *Athene noctua*. **Distribution**: Resident in England and Wales. **Other habitats**: Agricultural areas. **Notes**: Size 22cm. Eyes bright yellow. Regularly hunts by day. Perches on telegraph poles etc. Flight is low and rapid with deep undulations. Voice is a shrill "kiw".

Stonechat Turdidae *Saxicola torquata*. **Distribution**: Resident, mainly western and northern coastal counties. **Other habitats**: Gorse, commons, rough hillside, heath. **Notes**: Size 12.5cm. Male has white rump. Call: harsh "tsak-tsak".

Red-backed Shrike Laniidae *Lanius collurio*. **Distribution**: Rarish summer visitor to S.E. England. **Other habitats**: Scrubby commons and thickets. **Notes**: Size 17cm. Pointed wings and long tail. Is able to hover.

Dartford Warbler Sylviidae *Sylvia undata*. **Distribution**: Resident mainly Hants. and Dorset. **Other habitats**: Heathland with gorse. **Notes**: Size 12.5cm. Call: a scolding "tchir-r". Whitethroat-like song.

Grasshopper Warbler Sylviidae *Locustella naevia*. **Distribution**: Summer visitor everywhere except northern Scotland. **Other habitats**: Marshlands, heaths, conifer plantations. Thick undergrowth important. **Notes**: Size 12.5cm. Characteristic reeling song. Has a rounded tail.

Meadow Pipit Motacillidae *Anthus pratensis*. **Distribution**: Widespread resident. **Other habitats**: Rough open country. **Notes**: Size 14.5cm. Song: repeated thin notes ending in a trill, often sings in a climbing flight and parachute descent.

Tree Pipit Motacillidae *Anthus trivialis*. **Distribution**: Widespread summer visitor but not Ireland. **Other habitats**: Heaths and commons with scattered trees, woodland edges. **Notes**: Size 15cm. Loud, shrill song, sweeter than Meadow.

Linnet Fringillidae *Acanthis cannabina*. **Distribution**: Resident throughout British Isles. **Other habitats**: Breeds in thickets and hedgerows, open areas in winter. **Notes**: Size 13cm. Rapid twittering call. White feather edgings in wing and tail.

Twite Fringillidae *Acanthis flavirostris*. **Distribution**: Breeds western Scotland and Ireland. Local in northern Britain also winter visitor to E. and S.E. coast. **Other habitats**: Breeds moorland. Coastal areas in winter. **Notes**: Size 13.5cm.

Mammals of Grassland Habitats

Generally mammals are not restricted to one particular vegetation type but occur in a variety of situations. Most of the species which are commonly found in grassland and open heathland habitats are distributed widely in the British Isles, although several are absent from Ireland.

The brown hare is perhaps the only species which is at home in completely open, short-grazed turf. It relies on staying well away from cover so that no predators can approach unobserved and can thus be seen in large fields and on open downland. They never use burrows, and their young (leverets) are born furry and alert out in the open unlike the helpless babies produced by a rabbit in the safety of her underground nest. In early spring, hares may be seen wildly chasing about, occasionally stopping to rear on their hind legs and "box" each other. This behaviour, inspiration for the expression "Mad as a March hare" is in fact part of the territorial contest between males.

Rabbits are also important grassland mammals and are crucial to the maintenance of the habitat. They normally live in communal burrow systems called "warrens" within which an elaborate social hierarchy develops, and individuals rarely wander more than 200 metres from home. Females produce up to 30 young in a year in a series of litters beginning as early as January, but at least 70 per cent of these babies die within a year. The British population still suffers badly from the introduction of myxomatosis in the 1950s which killed over 90 per cent of rabbits in most areas.

Rabbit droppings are a common sight on grazed turf. They are hard spherical pellets about 8mm in diameter. It is often not realised that these are in fact "second faeces"; rabbits actually eat their first faeces. This is because grass is difficult to digest; a meal passes into their huge intestine largely unaffected by digestive juices. Here, masses of bacteria and other micro-organisms complete the breakdown of the food but by then it is too late for most of the nutrients to be absorbed by the rabbit and there is considerable loss in the faeces. The droppings are soft, moist and black and, as they contain some 25 per cent of protein from the microbes, the rabbits eat them. They pass through the system again, all the nutrients are reclaimed by the rabbit, and when the double-digested food is finally excreted as the familiar dry pellets little nourishment remains. They are still useful to the rabbit as scent and territory markers and are carefully deposited in strategically located latrines as a signal to other rabbits.

Other grassland animals prefer the grass to

The rabbit (*Oryctolagus cuniculus*) is one of the most important landscape formers other than man. Their grazing maintains short turf and the death of over 90 per cent from myxomatosis in the 1950s resulted in great loss of grassland.

be long enough to provide them with shelter. The short tailed vole is probably the most typical species of old grassland as it eats grass, makes its nest of grass and lives its whole life in a maze of tunnels among the stems and roots. It is rarely found in other habitats, whereas the three shrew species may also occur in woodlands and hedgerows. Shrews are insectivores and eat large numbers of beetles, grubs, woodlice, worms and spiders as they scurry about in runs among the grass roots. They are constantly active and die of starvation if deprived of food for more than a few hours. They die anyway after about 12 months (unlike other small mammals which often live well into their second or even third year) and shrews are often found dead on footpaths in the autumn. The largest species is the black and white water shrew which, despite possessing adaptations for aquatic life, is not confined to water and may be found even on dry downland.

Moles also live in grassland, though are rarely seen. They do appear on the surface, but mainly at night. Their prominent "hills" are a common sight and in early spring extra large "fortresses" may be thrown up to accommodate the nest in which the young are born. Moles are solitary creatures, each living in its own burrow system.

Harvest mice

Areas where the vegetation becomes very rank, perhaps including nettles and cow parsley, are suitable for harvest mice. This attractive species is popularly considered to be a cornfield creature,

but as corn is reaped annually, it cannot provide a good long-term habitat. In fact harvest mice are like little grassland monkeys, scrambling about among stiff stalked vegetation. They are excellent climbers and are the only British mammal with a prehensile tail; which can be curled round a stalk to support the animal's whole weight. Harvest mice therefore favour the "stalk zone" of old grasslands and hedge-bottoms and are equally at home in reed beds. The reed canary grass is a favourite material for nest building and breeding nests may be found constructed among its tall stems. In the winter, grasses tend to die back, and the mice build fresh nests nearer the ground and also in the more permanent security of bushes.

Stoats and weasels, though not confined to grasslands, feed extensively on the other mammals there. They usually hunt along regular routes retreating into dens in hollow trees or under rocks during periods of inactivity. Both animals stand erect on their hind legs to survey their surroundings. They pursue their prey, which consists mainly of mammals, by scent and they kill by biting their prey at the back of the neck. Their long slender bodies give them access to the narrow tunnels used by their prey species. Stoats especially may hunt in small parties or family groups and tend to feed mainly on rabbits and other mammals but usually avoid shrews. They also take some birds and may resort to reptiles and amphibians or even insects if really hungry. Weasels prey on smaller animals especially voles and some young birds.

The stoat (*Mustela erminea*) is one of the most ferocious of all mammalian predators, regularly attacking prey several times larger than itself. Its main food used to be rabbits and it was a common grassland and hedgerow species. The loss

of rabbits due to myxomatosis severely affected the stoat population, but numbers are now recovering. Stoats will also kill birds, particularly nestlings, and are consequently persecuted by gamekeepers.

The short tailed vole (*Microtus agrestis*) not only feeds on grass but nests on it, too. Litters of four to six young are produced there throughout the summer. The young leave the nest when they are three to four weeks old.

A guide to grassland mammals

The mole is unmistakable with its huge digging hands, but it is less often seen than its excavations, though young moles spend considerable time at the surface, especially in late spring. Shrews are small and have a very long pointed snout. Their teeth are red tipped; their eyes and ears are small. The pygmy shrew is the smallest British

mammal and has a tail which is at least three quarters the length of the head and body. The common shrew's tail is usually less than half the body length. Both are often found dead as they do not normally live more than a year; they also have distasteful skin glands so when caught by cats they are usually rejected uneaten. The water shrew is larger,

has boldly contrasting colours and a flange of bristly hairs along the underside of the tail. The brown hare has black ear tips, grizzled fur and much more orange coloured flanks than rabbits. The yellow harvest mouse is a very tiny inhabitant of long grass and coarse vegetation where it suspends its spherical nest. It is the only British mammal

with a prehensile tail. The field, or short tailed, vole is a plump greyish animal with small ears, small eyes and short pinkish tail. The stoat is larger than the weasel, and always has a black end to its tail and a yellowish belly. Weasels are white underneath, with a more irregular junction between this and the brown of the flanks.

Pygmy Shrew Soricidae *Sorex minutus.*
Distribution: Throughout mainland Britain and Ireland. Absent from Shetlands, Scilly and Channel islands. **Other habitats:** All types of habitat with plenty of ground cover. **Notes:** Paler than common shrew. Tail as long or longer than body and rather thick. Active day and night.

Water Shrew Soricidae *Neomys fodiens.*
Distribution: All mainland Britain but patchy in N. Scotland. Absent from Ireland and many offshore islands. **Other habitats:** Streams, ponds, watercress beds, beaches, woodlands. **Notes:** Very black, pale belly. Tail brown above, white below with a keel of hairs. Similar long hairs on margins of feet. Active day and night.

Mole Talpidae *Talpa europaea* **Distribution:** All mainland Britain. Absent from Ireland and most offshore islands. **Other habitats:** Woodland. **Notes:** Cylindrical body, short black coat. Large forefeet. Small eyes, no external ear. Lives underground and is active day and night. Avoids shallow, stony, wet or acidic soils.

Field Vole Cricetidae *Microtus agrestis.*
Distribution: Throughout mainland Britain but absent from Ireland and most islands. **Other habitats:** Woodland, hedgerow, bog, dune, moorland. **Notes:** Rather shaggy fur, greyish brown above, pure grey below (occasionally tinged with buff). Blunt face, small ears, very short tail. Active day and night.

Common Shrew Soricidae *Sorex araneus.*
Distribution: Throughout mainland Britain and most offshore islands. Absent from Ireland. **Other habitats:** Hedgerows, woodland, scrub, bracken, heather. **Notes:** Almost black back, pale flanks, grey belly with yellow tinge. Young are paler. Pointed nose, small eyes and ears. Tail shorter than body. Active day and night.

Harvest Mouse Muridae *Micromys minutus.*
Distribution: South of a line from the Humber to the Bristol Channel. Occasionally as far north as Edinburgh. Not Ireland. **Other habitats:** Tall dense vegetation (hedgerows, reedbeds etc). **Notes:** Small animal with small ears, long tail with prehensile tip. Young lack white front of adult. Makes spherical nest 30–60cm up in vegetation.

Brown Hare Leporidae *Lepus capensis.*
Distribution: Throughout mainland Britain on low ground. Absent from Ireland, Hebrides, Shetlands. **Other habitats:** Edges of woodland. **Notes:** Warm brown back usually, but black, white and sandy coloured animals occur. Underside white, ears long and black tipped. Top of tail dark. Long hind legs and loping gait. Mostly nocturnal.

Stoat Mustelidae *Mustela erminea.*
Distribution: Whole of Britain and Ireland except a few islands. **Other habitats:** Marsh, woodland, moorland and mountains. **Notes:** Summer coat brown above, yellowish below. Winter coat (in north) white. Tail tip always black. Active day and night.

Weasel Mustelidae *Mustela nivalis.*
Distribution: All of mainland Britain. Not Ireland and most islands. **Other habitats:** Marsh, hedgerows, moorland and mountains. **Notes:** Back colour rusty red to light sandy tan, underparts white, sometimes blotchy brown. Tail rather short, tip never black. Active day and night.

The Uplands

The mountains and moorlands of the north and west provide some of the most spectacular scenery in Britain. The distant views and dramatic peaks contrast sharply with the dissected landscape of the intensively cultivated and inhabited lowlands. The scenic value of the uplands is evident from the fact that all the British National Parks are situated in such areas.

Modern man, as he increasingly uses the uplands for outdoor recreation, may see them as wide open and treeless but they were not always like that. At one time or another in the last 10,000 years, every bit of our open moorlands, except the very tops of the mountains, was covered by forest. The present open aspect is due to climatic change and to the activities of man and his grazing animals.

The uplands are composed of older, harder rocks. Because they are hard, these rocks resist erosion and remain as mountains; but equally the slowness of weathering means that upland soils often contain few nutrients derived from the underlying rocks. These poor soils are also often waterlogged, owing to the high rainfall in upland areas and such conditions give rise to a rather specialised flora of relatively few species. The exposure of the higher, better-drained areas also limits the diversity of species found there.

Although they are regions of harsh climate and limited resources, the mountains and moorlands of Britain are a refuge for rare and interesting species of wildlife, many of them remnants of communities which were widespread during the last Ice Age. The extreme conditions found in the uplands mean that many plants and animals just cannot exist there, while those that do live at the very limits of survival.

Y Garn, Snowdonia, shown here, graphically illustrates the harsh reality of the upland habitat where, because of the increased altitude and steep slopes, there is no support for trees and crops, and instead gives way to moorlands, open grassland and bare rock.

The Physiography of the Uplands

The great age of the rocks which form Britain's uplands means that they have been slowly eroding away for tens or hundreds of millions of years. The effects of rain, wind and snow, and of alternating periods of heat and cold have all been to reduce once massive mountain ranges to the relatively diminutive ones of today. Thus the present-day summit of Snowdon was once at the bottom of a valley, but the surrounding mountains have since been eroded away, leaving what is now the highest peak in Wales. The last great period of change has been the past two million years, from the near tropical climate of the Tertiary era to that of the Quaternary, with periods of glacial conditions alternating with temperate inter-glacials such as the present one.

During the ice ages snow falling on upland areas accumulated as ice to form glaciers. As accumulation continued the glaciers merged to form ice sheets, at times over a thousand metres thick. These flowed out into lowland regions, covering as they went all but the highest mountain summits. In the major regions of glacier formation, such as the highlands of Scotland, the Lake District and Snowdonia, the ice carved its mark on the landscape. Corries were scooped out by the great weight and thrust of ice at the glacier heads and valleys were deepened, giving them a "U"-shaped profile. The steepened valley sides gave rise to unstable rock and scree habitats, which still remain. The moving ice sheets rounded the profiles of the lower hills and carried enormous quantities of rock and soil far from their origins, depositing them as drift and moraine and as great outwash plains of sand and gravel stemming from melting glacier fronts. At their maximum extent ice sheets covered all of upland Britain and Ireland with the exception of Dartmoor and Exmoor in the south west.

The geography of upland Britain

The uplands of south west England are fairly low. Exmoor rises less than 450m while the granite of Dartmoor just reaches 600m at its highest point, both areas consisting of rounded hills covered by moorland and rough grazing. The southern part of the Pennine chain, the upland backbone of England, rises to just over 600m in the rounded, peat-covered hills of the Peak District, formed by millstone grit overlying Carboniferous limestone. The Craven district of the mid-Pennines is formed mainly from Carboniferous limestone, the horizontal bedding of which has eroded to give the characteristic step-like profile of the higher peaks, such as Ingleborough. Some of these rise to about

The higher parts of Dartmoor and Bodmin Moor are formed from granite. Where this outcrops at the surface, wind and frost action sculpts the rock into characteristic tors. Although these look like piles of flat boulders they are actually weathered from the solid rock mass.

700m and were probably high enough to protrude above the ice of the last glaciation. The northern Pennines run as a long chain of rounded, moor-covered, hills as far as the Cheviots and the southern uplands of Scotland. Many summits reach about 600m, but the highest point, Cross Fell, is 893m. The highest point in England, nearly 1,000m high, is Scafell in the Lake District, where many of the summits are over 800m and glacial action has resulted in steep rocky peaks bearing true mountain vegetation on their upper slopes. Similarly, the peaks of Snowdonia in north Wales, several of which are at or above 1,000m, provide a rocky mountainous contrast to the lower, more rolling moorland of the mid-Wales uplands.

In Ireland the highlands surround the great central plain. The highest point is in the south west, where the Mountains of Kerry rise to 1,041m. In the west the Connemara summits reach over 800m, while the Mountains of Mourne and the Wicklow mountains in the east have several summits between 700 and 900m. However, the mountain flora of Ireland, like that of the lowlands, tends to be less diverse than that of the other British mountain regions.

It is in the highlands of Scotland that Britain's highest and most extensive mountain habitats are to be found. Ben Nevis, in the west of the Grampians, is the highest point in Britain and rises to 1,347m, while in the east the granite mass of the Cairngorms forms the largest area in Britain above 1,100m. Many of the peaks of the north western highlands, such as Beinn Eighe, reach over 1,000m and bear truly montane plant communities.

Upland Britain since the last Ice Age

The ice sheets had melted from most of Britain by about 10,000 years ago, lingering longest in the uplands of the Lake District and the Highlands. The resulting landscape was at first open with disturbed soils and tundra-like vegetation. As the climate slowly became warmer, woodland developed, first in the lowlands and later spreading into the uplands. Birch woods were usually the first to form, followed by Scots pine. In the

Glacier valleys, such as here at Great Langdale in the Lake District, are relatively straight with smooth sides where the ice planed off the rocks in its path.

more northern parts of Scotland and on the higher hills birch woodland persisted, as did pine in much of the highlands, but mixed forests including oak, elm and ash came to cover almost all of lowland Britain and most of the valleys and lower summits of the uplands as well.

This dense forest blotted out all the plants of the open, late glacial, environment, which would only have remained in areas for some reason left uncolonised by forest, such as Upper Teesdale and the very tops of the mountains.

About 7,500 years ago, by which time the development of forest was virtually complete, the climate became markedly wetter. This led to the development of blanket bogs on the higher uplands, in which dead plant material did not rot away but slowly accumulated as a spongy mass of peat. In the southern Pennines, for example, peat formation occurred at heights over 400m, where it was wet enough to swamp the forests, wood from which may still be found buried at the base of the peat deposits in very good condition. Later the climate slowly became drier and warmer again, and the period up to about 3,000 years ago marks the maximum development of forest. In the uplands oak woods were present higher up. The climate was probably warmer than now, since woodland remains have been found up to heights of 900m, some 200m higher than today. About 3,000 years ago the climate again became wetter, leading to fresh extension of the blanket bogs on the uplands, and these wetter conditions have on the whole persisted until the present.

Until Roman times the effect of man on the uplands was probably limited, although there is some evidence for local forest clearance from about 2,000BC onwards in north west England and in Scotland. Some of the woodland on the lighter limestone soils may have been more extensively cleared in Bronze Age times, but major clearance of upland forests probably did not begin until the Mediaeval period. The

A guide to some interesting upland sites

1 Beinn Eighe, Ross-shire. Part of the north west Highlands, 1,052 m high. A richer mountain flora than nearby peaks, with moss beds and dwarf heath. Pine wood at base. NNR 4758 ha.

2 Rhum. Island managed by the Nature Conservancy Council for research on red deer. NNR 10,684 ha.

3 Ben Nevis, Inverness-shire. Highest point in Britain, at 1,347 m. Mainly granite. Snow may remain all year in some places, only melting in hot summers. NN 17 71.

4 Rannoch Moor, Argyll/Perthshire. Large area of complex upland peat bogs surrounded by the Grampian Mountains. Remains of pinewood on its edge. NNR 1499 ha.

5 Connemara Mountains. Very wet climate has led to blanket bog growth over much of the range. Several arctic/alpine species found near sea level here.

6 Mountain of Kerry. Sandstone mountains which include the highest point in Ireland, Macgillycuddy's Reeks, at 1,041 m.

7 Wicklow Mountains. High rounded granite mountains reaching 926 m dissected by steep valleys.

8 Mountains of Mourne. Granite mountains reaching 852 m. Rounded profiles with moorland and blanket peat.

9 Lake District, Cumbria. Steep glaciated peaks rising to 978 m, with deep valleys and lakes. Arctic/alpine vegetation and high level woodland present. NP including NNRs and FC. NY 22 07.

10 Craven Uplands, North Yorkshire. Carboniferous limestone mountains capped with Millstone Grit. Hills have 'step-like' profile and are covered by moor and peat. Part of Yorkshire Dales NP. Includes NNRs, nature trails. SD 85 75.

17 Peak District. Millstone Grit hills rising to 636 m. Extensive blanket peat, much of it eroded, dominated by cotton grass. NP includes NNRs, nature trails. SK 09 98.

18 Colt Park Wood, Yorkshire. Ash-dominated woodland developed on limestone pavement on the lower slopes of Ingleborough. NNR 8 ha. SD 77 77.

19 North Yorkshire Moors. Most easterly of the uplands. A smooth plateau mainly covered with heather moor, rising to 454 m. North Yorkshire Moors NP includes nature trails. SE 70 99.

20 Upper Teesdale, Durham. An area of sugar limestone and whin-sill which has a remarkable flora, possibly through having remained unforested for over 10,000 years. NNR 3,497 ha. NY 85 27

21 Cross Fell. Highest point in the Pennines at 893 m (NY 69 35). Extensive blanket peat, rough grassland on some lower slopes.

22 Cheviots. Rounded volcanic rocks rising to 816 m (NT 91 20). The tops are mainly covered with heather moorland with upland grassland on lower slopes. Within Northumberland NP.

23 Southern uplands. Mainly rounded grassy hills rising to 830 m on Broad Law (NT 15 24). Some upper slopes covered with peat or heather moor.

24 Ben Lawers, Perthshire. Soft mica-schists rising to 1,214 m. Has little peat but extremely rich mountain-top and alpine meadow vegetation. NNR.

25 Grampians. The main mountain range of the central Highlands contains numerous peaks over 1,100 m, many with rich mountain vegetation. Several NNRs.

26 Cairngorms. High dissected granite plateau rising to 1,311 m. Extensive mountain-top vegetation and persistent snow patches. High-level pine present. NNR 25,947 ha.

27 Rothiemurchus Forest, Inverness-shire. Largest remaining semi-natural Scots pine forest. Open structure with rich shrub layer including juniper. NH 89 06.

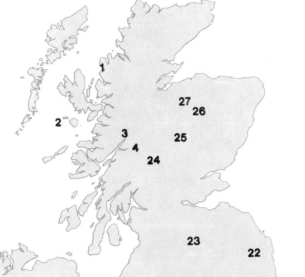

11 Snowdonia, Gwynedd. North end of Cambrians' high rocky mountains much eroded by glaciation. Snowdon reaches 1,062 m. True mountain vegetation on the peaks. NP includes NNRs, nature trails. SH 60 55.

12 Cambrian Mountains. Large areas of peat and heather moor in mid-Wales. Breeding area of the red kite. Highest point Plynlimon, 752 m. NP includes NNRs, nature trails. SN 78 87.

13 Brecon Beacons. Rounded hills formed from the Coal Measures, reaching 886 m. Mostly covered by moor and blanket peat. NP includes NNRs, FNRs, nature trails. SO 01 22.

14 Exmoor, Somerset/Devon. Red sandstone hills rising to 520 m at Dunkery Beacon. Mostly heather moor with rough grassland in the valleys. NP. SS 75 42.

15 Wistman's Wood, Devon. Semi-natural oak woodland at 400 m on Dartmoor. The trees are stunted and grow between large boulders which protect them from grazing. FNR. SX 61 77.

16 Dartmoor, Devon. Rounded granite hills rising to 613 m at Yes Tor. Mostly heather moor and rough grazing, with some blanket peat and valley bogs. NP includes NNRs (3), FNRs (2), nature trails. SX 60 80.

Abbreviations:

NCC	Nature Conservancy Council
FC	Forestry Commission
RSPB	Royal Society for the Protection of Birds
NT	National Trust
NNR	National Nature Reserve
FNR	Forest Nature Reserve
NP	National Park
FNR (I)	Forest Nature Reserve (in Ireland)

great expansion of the wool industry which then took place led to extensive clearance of the upland woodlands to provide grazing for sheep on the hills, especially in the Pennines. This, combined with continued demand for timber for fuel and for ship-building, resulted in the virtual elimination of the English upland forests, leaving the open scenery we see today.

In Scotland extensive woodland remained until much later, but from the 17th century onwards increasing amounts of timber were used for charcoal, particularly in industries such as iron smelting. From the 18th century there was further widespread and rapid clearance of the highland forests to provide open areas for sheep and, later, moorland for shooting grouse and red deer. This resulted in almost complete destruction of the great pine forests of the Scottish uplands and their replacement with open heather moor.

The physical environment

Physical conditions in the uplands are so harsh and demanding that many things cannot live there at all, and those that do must fight a constant battle for survival against the elements.

The ancient hard rocks of our upland areas weather only slowly, releasing few nutrients to the soil. "Soil" is itself a rather misleading term for the rock fragments and splinters which support some of the upland flora. Many plants must grow on bare rock; others live in ground that is permanently saturated because rain cannot drain away into solid bedrock. Steep, often unstable slopes compound the problems for both plants and animals. To all this must be added the climatic difficulties which stem from the effects of altitude.

The most obvious problems are exposure to wind, rain and cold, the effects of all of which are exacerbated by altitude. The change in mean temperature with heights above sea level varies from place to place, but in Britain it represents a decrease of about 1°C for every 150m increase in altitude. This is well illustrated in the contrast between the summit of Ben Nevis

The upland environment

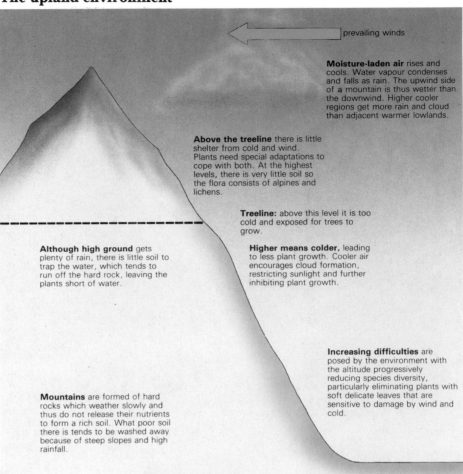

prevailing winds

Moisture-laden air rises and cools. Water vapour condenses and falls as rain. The upwind side of a mountain is thus wetter than the downwind. Higher cooler regions get more rain and cloud than adjacent warmer lowlands.

Above the treeline there is little shelter from cold and wind. Plants need special adaptations to cope with both. At the highest levels, there is very little soil so the flora consists of alpines and lichens.

Treeline: above this level it is too cold and exposed for trees to grow.

Although high ground gets plenty of rain, there is little soil to trap the water, which tends to run off the hard rock, leaving the plants short of water.

Higher means colder, leading to less plant growth. Cooler air encourages cloud formation, restricting sunlight and further inhibiting plant growth.

Increasing difficulties are posed by the environment with the altitude progressively reducing species diversity, particularly eliminating plants with soft delicate leaves that are sensitive to damage by wind and cold.

Mountains are formed of hard rocks which weather slowly and thus do not release their nutrients to form a rich soil. What poor soil there tends to be washed away because of steep slopes and high rainfall.

(1,347m) where the July mean temperature is 6°C and its base at Fort William (10m) where the average July temperature is 15.5°C.

Precipitation (in the form of rain or snow) increases markedly with altitude, especially in the west of Britain. In the Lake District annual rainfall at sea level averages some 90cm, but at 150m this rises to about 140cm per year, and by 900m may reach 300cm. On the drier eastern side of the Pennines, a rainfall of 140cm per year does not occur below a height of 600m.

The higher rainfall of the uplands is associated with more cloud and less sunshine, which not only results in lower temperatures but also reduces still further the growth and productivity of the plants living there.

The absence of trees on the open uplands means that plants are not sheltered from the increased winds of higher altitudes. The wind not only buffets the plants, and may even tear them free, but also causes them to dry out. A further problem stems from the "chill factor", whereby winds cause an increase in the effects of cold. The physical conditions found in upland Britain are thus more extreme than elsewhere and pose a major challenge to survival which relatively few plants and animals can overcome.

Soil conditions have a profound effect in determining what type of plant community can develop. Much of the land, providing it is not too steep, may be covered with glacial drift. This is debris left by the ice sheets of the last glaciation, often derived from rocks far distant from its final location. Drift often contains much clay as well as coarser soil material and so may be poorly drained, directly affecting the nature of the plant communities which develop. Where the drift is absent or only very thin, the nature of the underlying rock becomes more significant. Soils on relatively soft rocks, such as the Carboniferous limestone of the Craven uplands in the Pennines, or the mica-schists of Ben Lawers, usually bear more diverse plant communities than those on hard, slowly-weathering, rocks.

The main community types

At first sight most of the uplands appear uniformly wet, windy and bleak, but they do in fact contain a surprising range of different habitats and wildlife communities. On the highest peaks, where there is little soil, truly alpine conditions are found, while lower down, especially in sheltered regions, extensive woodland may grow. Most of the open ground is covered by upland grassland habitat or heather moor, with the wettest patches developing into bogs.

The uplands frequently show signs of past glacial activity. The weight of ice gouged depressions in the underlying rock and shown here is a typical corrie lake formed at the head of a glacier at Cwm Idwal in Snowdonia. Such lakes are usually lacking in nutrients and their cold waters support little life.

The Alpine Zone

On the higher mountain tops the grasslands give way to a more open community of plants capable of growing among the broken rocks which usually cover most of the summits. Many of the species found here are mosses and lichens and flowering plants with a dwarf or cushion-type growth form which helps them to survive conditions of extreme exposure. This not only lessens exposure to the wind but also makes it more likely that the plant will be covered by protective snow during the cold winter months. Snow is an effective insulator and beneath a snow patch the plants will be shielded from the wind and experience temperatures only a few degrees below freezing, rather than the much colder conditions out in the open.

On the rocky summits plant cover is often incomplete, with plants mainly growing in between the broken boulders which usually cover such sites. The physical state of these areas which are being colonised by mountain plants varies widely. The stability of the substrate varies from fixed and bare rock-faces to constantly shifting gravel on both steep unstable scree slopes and in gullies among cliffs. In the exposed and stable conditions most of the plants are short or prostrate, many, such as the moss campion *(Silene acaulis)*, adopting a protective cushion growth form. The few woody plants that are present are dwarf species, such as the heart willow *(Salix herbacea)*. The reindeer "moss" *(Cladonia rangiferina)* is actually a tufted lichen and is usually abundant on and between the rocks, whilst the large woolly hair moss *(Rhacomitrium lanuginosum)* is one of the most common plants of the summits. However, where the substrate is constantly shifting, mosses and other cushion plants seem unable to colonise successfully, probably because they cannot grow fast enough to keep pace with the moving gravel. Under such conditions more robust species like tufted hair-grass, *(Deschampsia caespitosa)* become established, followed by other species as the substrate becomes more stable.

Many of our mountain plants are known as "arctic/alpines". This is because outside Britain some species are only found on mountains such as the Alps and Pyrenees or in the far north and the Arctic, growing there at low altitudes in conditions at least similar to those of the moun-

The mountain tops of the Cairngorms are exposed and bleak. Some remain snow-covered throughout the year but even those that do not are cold and inhospitable to all forms of wild life.

Field example: Mountains and moorlands: The Cairngorms

The Cairngorms, the eastern section of the Grampian mountain range of Scotland, are the upper part of a granite plateau, rising to its highest point, 1,309m, at Ben Macdui, forming the largest continuous area in Britain over 1,000m. Erosion has created valleys and the action of glaciers has greatly steepened them and has led to the creation of corries. Short arctic/alpine plants, lichens and *Rhacomitrium* moss grow between the shattered rock fragments known as mountain-top detritus. On the less exposed slopes, dwarf shrubs of the heather family are abundant, and many of the lower saddles and spurs are peat-covered. Trees occur up to heights of between 500 and 600m, those at the higher levels, mainly Scots pine and birch, being slow-growing and stunted. Below the western slopes of Cairn Gorm, the Rothiemurchus Forest, one of the largest remnants of the great Caledonian Forest, is an open Scots pine woodland with larches and a rich shrub and herb layer, sheltering rare birds such as the crested tit and capercaillie. A large part of the Cairngorms is a National Nature Reserve, but other areas are under intense recreation pressure.

Reindeer, re-introduced in 1952, grazing on the snow-covered Cairngorms.

tains of Britain. For example, the alpine lady's mantle *(Alchemilla alpina)* is widespread in the Arctic, but in Britain is now almost confined to mountains. Some of our arctic/alpines are found at lower altitudes in the west of the country than in the east. On the extreme west coast of Ireland a number of species, such as mountain avens *(Dryas octopetala)*, are found growing almost down to sea level.

The richest assemblages of arctic/alpine plants are to be found on sites which are below the exposed summits and protected from grazing, such as stabilised scree and rock ledges. Here, particularly on mountains composed of relatively soft rocks, may be found a great variety of mountain plants, including saxifrages, the mountain sorrel *(Oxyria digyna)* and mountain avens. The constituent rocks of scree slopes are often fairly large and able to offer a good deal of shelter in an otherwise exposed habitat. This allows flowering plants and ferns to become established early in the colonisation cycle, though the actual species are dependant on the underlying rock type. On millstone grit, sandstone and most granites the first colonising species are usually woolly hair moss, reindeer "moss" and rock moss *(Andreaea rupestris)*, quickly followed by the first flowering plants which in these examples are limited to cowberry *(Vaccinium vitis-idaea)*, bilberry *(V. myrtillus)*, crowberry *(Empetrum nigrum)* and the fir club-moss *(Lycopodium selago)* with its rhizome creeping beneath and the shoots growing through the moss cushions. All of these species are usually associated with raw humus and leached soils. On slate and metamorphosed igneous rocks more species are likely to become established. In addition to those above, parsley fern *(Crytogramma crispa)*, mountain fern *(Thelypteris limbosperma)*, dwarf willow and alpine ladies mantle are also to be expected. On a mica schist one would expect to find mountain lady fern *(Athyrium distentifolium)*, brittle bladder-fern *(Cystopteris fragilis)* and beech fern *(Thelypteris phegopteris)* as well. It is noticeable that the number of ferns increases when the slope is

north facing. On the strongly basic igneous rocks of some of the Western Isles of Scotland, flowering plants often become established before the mosses and lichens. The pioneering species are often rock cress *(Cardaminopsis petraea)* and stone bramble *(Rubus saxatilis)*, soon followed by alpine saw wort *(Saussurea alpina)* and alpine meadow rue *(Thalictrum alpinum)*. Where springs and seeping water provide a steady supply of

Alpine lady's mantle, moss campion, alpine forget-me-not *(Myosotis alpestris)* and mossy cyphel *(Cherleria sedoides)* growing on a rocky ledge on Ben Lawers. This is, however, only a small part of the rich alpine flora that grows there.

minerals a characteristic small pocket of rich vegetation, or "flush community" develops. This may include mosses and liverworts as well as rushes, sedges and alpines such as the starry saxifrage *(Saxifraga stellaris)*.

Alpine flowers

True alpine flowers are only found on the highest mountains of the British Isles. Many of these upper regions have a poor uninteresting flora consisting mainly of grasses and heaths. However, in some cases, such as Cader Idris in Wales and Ben Lawers in Scotland, there is a wide range of alpine plants; this richness is due to the differing geology and soil types and also to the local climatic conditions, all of which may vary considerably from neighbouring mountains. Prerequisites for such a rich flora are an adequate supply of nutrients and an annual rainfall of at least 125cm.

Because conditions for growth are difficult, most species are small and have a cushion growth form; however, in many cases, such as those illustrated here, the flowers are large and attractive.

The trailing or alpine azalea *(Loiseleuria procumbens)* is a small creeping evergreen plant.

The purple mountain saxifrage *(Saxifraga oppositifolia)* forms either loose mats or dense cushions of vegetation.

The moss campion *(Silene acaulis)* is so named because its growth habit resembles bright-green dense moss cushions.

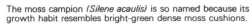

Rose-root *(Sedum rosea)* grows in mountain rock crevices and also on sea cliffs.

The yellow mountain saxifrage *(Saxifraga aizoides)* has creeping vegetative stems with upturned tips

Blanket Bogs and Peat

The uplands attract a high rainfall, and extensive areas are poorly drained. Consequently, many places are permanently wet, too soggy even for the mountain grassland species to survive. These permanently wet places develop as blanket bogs, so called because they smother everything with a spongy blanket of wet vegetation and peat.

In normal, well-drained soils dead leaves and other debris are quickly broken down and decomposed by soil animals such as earthworms and by micro-organisms such as bacteria and fungi. Where the soil is badly drained and is usually water-logged there will be very little oxygen available, so there will be few decomposers present. The cold and acidity of the ground water also inhibit decomposition. Dead plant material will thus tend to accumulate, forming peat: a mass of relatively undecayed dead plant material which may be several metres deep. Blanket peat is characterised by being rather acid and poor in minerals. The most important plant forming bog peat is the bog moss, Sphagnum. This not only draws up water with itself as it grows, rather like a sponge, but can also make the surrounding water acid (for details see: Wetlands—peat bogs), thus helping to perpetuate the conditions required for peat formation. Most plants cannot grow in acid, water-logged, oxygen-deficient conditions, since plant roots require oxygen for respiration just as do the leaves and stems. Once blanket peat formation begins, therefore, the existing vegetation is killed and smothered. Thus, provided cool, wet conditions continue, blanket bogs can obliterate even mature woodland and replace it with layers of peat, capped by a living layer of Sphagnum moss. But peat can only form and accumulate where there is enough water to

keep it saturated for most of the year. If it dries out through a change in climate or because of deliberate drainage by man, its formation ceases, the Sphagnum is replaced by plants of drier places and the peat itself may begin to erode away.

The peat is mostly formed from the spongy dead remains of bog-moss Sphagnum. Some species such as S. papillosum continue to grow

in the wetter regions as a fairly complete greenish yellow carpet over the bog surface. Other mosses are sometimes present on drier peats and on hummock tops, including the robust dark green Polytrichum commune, which may itself form hummocks. Small leafy liver-

Blanket bogs develop in cool, permanently wet areas, and are characterised by the presence of bright green bog moss (*Sphagnum*) and the cotton grass (*Eriophorum*).

Peat consists of undecayed plant material, and when it is dried out can be used as a fuel. Peat cutting for this purpose is an important local industry in many upland and boggy areas.

worts such as *Odontoschisma sphagni* may be easily overlooked amongst the other plants. Compared with many habitats, the list of higher plants growing in blanket bogs is relatively short, indicating the ecological difficulties posed by these bogs. Generally the bogs in the wettest parts of Britain, such as the west coast of Ireland and western Scotland, have the greatest species richness.

The sedge family, the Cyperaceae, is particularly abundant, especially the deer grass *(Trichophorum cespitosum)* and the sedge known as "cotton grass" *(Eriophorum vaginatum)*, which has tufts of rounded leaves and a single seed head looking like a wisp of cotton wool. This is particularly characteristic of wet areas in the Pennines. In Irish and western areas the black bog rush *(Schoenus nigricans)* is typically found, as are the purple moor grass *(Molinia caerulea)* and the shrubby bog myrtle *(Myrica gale)*. The beautiful yellow-flowered bog asphodel *(Narthecium ossifragum)* is common on most sites, while the straggling cranberry *(Vaccinium oxycoccus)* is found in wetter areas. In late summer the delicious orange fruits of the cloudberry *(Rubus chamaemorus)* may sometimes be found on the blanket bogs of the Pennines and Scotland, although it is rare in Ireland.

Blanket bogs have only low levels of mineral nutrients available for plant growth because the hard rocks of which the uplands are formed weather only slowly. Furthermore, because dead vegetation is not decomposed and recycled, much of the mineral content of the blanket bog is locked up in the deeper layers of peat, unavailable to plants growing on top. Insectivorous plants, notably sundew *(Drosera rotundifolia)* and also species of butterwort *(Pinguicula)*, overcome the problem by utilising nutrients from their animal "prey". But generally the main mineral input is not from the ground but from the rain (except for some biological nitrogen fixation by micro-organisms). Phosphorus and potassium are two important minerals which are often in short supply in blanket bogs; on some sites they are probably being lost in drainage water faster

than they are being supplied in the rain. The vegetation of the bogs thus usually has a lower mineral content than that found in more mineral-rich conditions, and provides little sustenance for herbivores. In fact herbivore production on blanket bogs is even lower than on the upland grasslands. At Moor House, in the northern Pennines, for example, less than one per cent of the plant production is eaten by herbivores, usually sheep, grouse and minute

Upland soils are deficient in nutrients and some plants acquire organic material by trapping insects. In the butterwort *Pinguicula vulgaris* this is done by the leaves.

bugs called psyllids or jumping lice. Most of the plant production goes to form litter and peat. Some of this is eaten by soil animals such as enchytraeid potworms and cranefly larvae or decomposed by micro-organisms, but about 10 per cent of the annual plant production is not consumed and accumulates as additional peat.

The upland ecosystem

The uplands are not very sunny, even in summer. Their plant productivity is further limited by the lack of nutrients released from hard, impervious rocks to the moorland soil. Strong winds and low temperatures hamper plants and animals alike. Upland moors are thus not highly productive habitats, have a low density of animals and reduced diversity of species. However those things, especially certain ericaceous plants, which can tolerate the difficult conditions may completely dominate the habitat.

Sunlight provides the energy needed for photosynthesis in green plants.

Carnivores. A few large predators such as golden eagle and peregrine kill food the bigger herbivores; but food production on moorland is generally too low to support many large carnivores and most predatory birds feed on moorland only during the summer, migrating to the lowlands when winter conditions make things even more difficult

Herbivores. Sheep, mountain hares, voles (and, in Scotland, red deer) feed directly on the shrubby vegetation. In many areas the red grouse is particularly important and unusual as a herbivorous bird feeding directly on heather shoots; other birds usually only eat seeds. Insects also exploit the heather — caterpillars eat the plants, bees and flies take nectar.

The most numerous carnivores which frequent moorland throughout the year are small. The meadow pipit, various spiders and beetles and the pigmy shrew feed on the abundant invertebrates which live at the soil surface. Crows and foxes survive by scavenging for much of their food and thus effectively become detritus feeders.

Primary producers. Green plants use the sun's energy to build up leaves, wood and other plant tissues. **On open moorland** the principal plants are heather and similar woody shrubs; there are a few grasses, especially in wetter areas.

In blanket bogs the main plant is sphagnum moss, which few things eat and which grows on top of a layer of dead moss.

Accumulation. Cold, wet conditions do not favour decomposition and, in bogs especially, little takes place. Consequently, partially decomposed materials accumulate as peat. Dry peat even forms out in the open more because of the lack of earthworms and other major agents of plant decomposition.

Carcasses of dead sheep and other mammals are a major source of food for scavenging crows, ravens and foxes. In lowland habitats this food source would be used to a much greater extent by insects such as beetles and fly larvae.

Detritus feeders. Dead plant material may be eaten by insects before it becomes buried by more debris. These tiny animals may be among the most abundant moorland creatures.

Moorland

Moors are tracts of uncultivated, poor soil which are generally treeless; however, in this moorland region of Perthshire a single pine tree has managed to survive.

Where the blanket bog has dried out or been burnt or drained, it may tend towards a type of upland heath or dry moor. Moor is also found on the more freely draining acid soils of the uplands, occurring over a wide range of altitudes and, especially in Scotland, often on the sites of former woodlands.

In some plant communities a remarkably high proportion of the flowering species belongs to just a few families. Good examples are the moors and drier blanket peats, which are usually dominated by members of the heather family, the Ericaceae, especially *Calluna* and species of *Vaccinium* and *Erica*. All the British Ericaceae grow in acid or montane habitats and several species are found only on mountain tops in Scotland. These include such plants as the arctic bearberry *(Arctous alpinus)* and the alpine azalea *(Loiseleuria procumbens)*.

Heather moors, whether on dried peat or on acid mineral soils, are almost always dominated by heather or ling *(Calluna vulgaris)*; where the moor is regularly burnt, there may be few other plants present, except in areas where the *Calluna* has yet to regenerate. The bilberry *(Vaccinium myrtillus)* is common on dry moor but is intolerant of fire. On dry sites bell heather *(Erica cinerea)* may be found, but in damper places it is replaced by the cross-leaved heather *(E. tetralix)*. The heath bedstraw *(Galium saxatile)* and the tormentil *(Potentilla erecta)* occur regularly, and the wavy hair-grass *(Deschampsia flexuosa)* is particularly common. These are all plants found on lowland heaths, and the same is true of many of the lichens and of the mosses. They are discussed further under "Heathlands" elsewhere in this book.

The productivity of moorland is relatively low, which means that the density of animals,

particularly the larger types, is not high. Grouse eat virtually nothing but young heather and are clearly the most important plant-eating bird of the moorlands, but generally the heather moors are notable for the relatively large proportion of the live plant material which is eaten by small invertebrates. These tiny herbivores are mainly insects, such as thrips, psyllids (bugs) and leaf-hoppers, many of which have piercing mouth parts and feed on plant sap. This is not to imply that herbivorous mammals are absent, only that they are not the major consumers of heather. Characteristic upland species like red deer and mountain hare may spend a lot of time among the heather, but usually seek out more palatable and nutritious plants if they can. Sheep and voles likewise prefer grass to heath.

Among the dead plant litter on the soil surface are enormous numbers of small detritus feeders, such as springtails and mites, together with tiny carnivores such as spiders, shrews and insectivorous birds such as meadow pipits.

Most of the large moorland carnivores are birds. They kill small birds and mammals, but many also feed extensively on carrion such as dead sheep. For example, crows (both carrion and hooded) feed on dead animals as well as on larger insects and on the eggs of other birds such as the grouse; short-eared owls on the other hand normally take only live prey such as voles, shrews and birds like meadow pipits. The other important moorland predators are birds of prey, ranging from the merlin and kestrel (feeding on small birds and some large insects) to the peregrine, which will kill grouse, and the buzzard and golden eagle, which take quite large animals such as rabbits as well as carrion.

Moorland management

As heather plants (*Calluna vulgaris*) age they form a dense ground cover of woody stems with a reduced growth rate, opening out in the centre allowing other plants to invade, and providing a poor food supply for the grouse. To prevent this, the heather is usually burned before it becomes too old and woody, usually at between 10 and 15 years. Burning allows new growth from old stem bases and may encourage the germination of seeds, which show an increased germination rate after a short exposure to high temperatures. The quality of the heather plants will influence the breeding success of the grouse

Large areas of moorland are burned at the end of winter. The fires are carefully controlled so that they do not become too hot and ignite the underlying peat.

Upland Flora

The vast majority of Britain's mountain vegetation would be described as moorland. This is a term used commonly to describe wild open countryside and includes several vegetation types; moorland is perhaps best defined as land which is too poor to cultivate. It is usually a closed community as far as vegetation is concerned and is dominated by heather or grass. The remaining mountain vegetation is mainly woodland. There are some areas of montane plants that are only found at higher altitudes.

The most common upland vegetation is grassland, the most characteristic being that dominated by sheep's fescue (*Festuca ovina*) and fine and creeping bent (*Agrostis tenuis* and *A. stolonifera*). This *Festuca/Agrostis* grassland is generally found on the steeper, well drained slopes where the soils are acid brown earths. These grass species cover between 65 and 75 per cent of the sward so that, although many other species are found in the community, they are not numerous. They include tormentil (*Potentilla erecta*), heath bedstraw (*Galium saxatile*) and the common speedwell (*Veronica officinalis*). Several mosses are commonly present, especially *Rhytidiadelphus squarrosus*, *Pleurozium schreberi* and *Hypnum cupressiforme*. The presence of heath grass (*Sieglingia decumbens*), heath woodrush (*Luzula multiflora*) and wavy hair-grass (*Deschampsia flexuosa*) indicates an acid humus in the soil.

Other plants are remnants of earlier cultivation – mainly ribwort plantain (*Plantago lanceolata*), creeping buttercup (*Ranunculus repens*) and self-heal (*Prunella vulgaris*). Heavy grazing upsets the balance of the community and the *Festuca* tends to be suppressed in favour of the *Agrostis* until eventually mat grass (*Nardus*) dominates.

Nardus grassland is most commonly found between 300 and 600m where rainfall is higher and the soils are more thoroughly leached and therefore more acid. This type of grassland is much less species-rich than that dominated by *Festuca* and the only species commonly associated with *Nardus* is *Juncus squarrosus*, the heath rush; this may be replaced in drier areas by wavy hair-grass.

There is one other grass species which can be found dominating an area of upland grassland;

this is the purple moor grass (*Molinia caerulea*) and in the west of Britain it is one of the most widespread plants. *Molinia* is mainly found growing on peat and has a preference for damp, but not wet, soils, and thus often marks a transition to bog. In bog habitats it becomes small and non-tufted and is generally found with bog myrtle (*Myrica gale*) and deer grass (*Trichophorum cespitosum*).

On the mountain summits a "montane grassland" develops as a natural succession to *Rhacomitrium* (or woolly hair moss) heath. With a build-up of humus from the colonisation of the moss, grasses become more widespread, particularly the viviparous sheep's fescue (*Festuca vivipara*). These montane grasslands have far fewer flowering plant species than the lower grasslands; this is mainly because they are heavily grazed by sheep and is especially noticeable in areas in Wales and the Lake District.

On acid upland soils the vegetation is usually composed of ericaceous shrubs, especially heathers and bilberry (*Vaccinium myrtillus*). These bilberry moors cover fairly small areas and are especially characteristic of the gritstone edges among the cotton grass (*Eriophorum*) moors of the Pennines. As the name would suggest the dominant plant is bilberry, but the cowberry (*Vaccinium vitis-idaea*) is also often present. There is usually a rich moss flora, including *Pleurozonium schreberi*, *Rhytidiadelphus loreus*, *Dicranum majus* and *Hylocomium splendens*. *Vaccinium* moor is a remnant of previous woodland and is usually found on the edges of existing woods; it is easily destroyed by the removal of the trees or by burning, when heather moor will quickly take over.

Heather moorland is by far the most common and widespread type of moorland in Britain, but is usually confined to areas of pronounced slope and high annual rainfall. The vegetation may be entirely ling (*Calluna vulgaris*), or it may be a mixture of heaths including ling, bell heather (*Erica cinerea*) and cross-leaved heath (*E. tetralix*). Other species likely to be found are heath rush (*Juncus squarrosus*), wavy hair-grass, bilberry, *Hypnum cupressiforme* and *Campylopus*

flexuosus.

These two forms of moorland occur where there is some drainage, but as the moors of Britain are in the highland areas they necessarily have high rainfall, and on the less porous substrates soils become waterlogged and peat is formed: these areas are covered by bog vegetation. This is a very characteristic community and is dominated entirely by the bog mosses (*Sphagnum* spp.). Also to be found are many grasses and sedges, mainly purple moor grass, deer grass and the cotton grasses. The bog asphodel (*Narthecium ossifragum*) adds a welcome and unexpected colour to the community. Heathers from the surrounding moors may also be found growing here, but are very much reduced in size and rarely exceed 15cm. Bog is also a very good place to find insectivorous plants, commonly sundew and great sundew (*Drosera rotundifolia* and *D. anglica*) and the

Upland grasses

The commonest form of upland vegetation is some form of grassland. In regions of vegetation colonisation the woolly hair moss is sometimes accompanied only by the mountain sedge, but more frequently has sheep's fescue and wavy hair-grass as well. Above 3000ft however, crowberry often pioneers, with woolly hair moss, lichens, bilberry and the three leaved rush growing through it. On areas showing stone stripes and polygons cotton grass is often the pioneering species.

Summit grasslands usually have a variety of species as the substrate on which they are growing is unstable due to frost heaving and solifluction. Only when stabilised and sheep grazed is a uniform turf of limited species developed. This blends at lower altitudes, in the lower uplands, with the extensive *Festuca/Agrostis* grasslands that cover much of the lower mountain slopes, and it is this turf that is the main foodstuff of all British grazing animals.

Three Leaved Rush Juncaceae *Juncus trifidus*. **Distribution** : West Scotland. **Notes** : Grows in detritus and on rock ledges on mountain tops; often forms circular patches.

Mountain Sedge Cyperaceae *Carex bigelowii*. **Distribution** : West and central Scotland; north England; north Wales; scattered in Ireland. **Notes** : Usually found above 650 metres in damp, stony places.

Mat Grass Gramineae (Poaceae) *Nardus stricta*. **Distribution** : Throughout the British Isles; has been recorded from every county; more common in the north and west. **Notes** : From poor, dry to damp, sandy soils; from low elevation to 950 metres; often abundant and dominating large areas.

Hare's Tail, Cotton Grass Cyperaceae *Eriophorum vaginatum*. **Distribution** : Scotland; Wales; north, north-west, south-west and central southern England; Ireland except for the south-east. **Notes** : Damp, peaty places, especially blanket bogs; often locally abundant.

Deer Grass Cyperaceae *Trichophorum cespitosum*. **Distribution** : Throughout the British Isles except for the Midlands. **Notes** : Damp, acid, peaty places, especially blanket bogs and heaths; often locally dominant; absent from base-rich soils.

Shady ravines provide cool, damp habitats ideal for the growth of ferns, liverworts and mosses. Some species additionally require certain soil types, so they tend to be very localised in their distribution.

Three Leaved Rush   Mat Grass   Deer Grass

Mountain Sedge   Hare's Tail

common butterwort *(Pinguicula vulgaris)*.

The third main vegetation type found in the upland areas of Britain is woodland. There is little doubt that it was once much more extensive than it is now and has been replaced on the higher slopes by moorland. What remains falls into five groups: four of single species and one of mixed woodland.

Oak woodland is one of the most distinctive of the upland woods. In the few remaining natural oak woods at higher levels the sessile oak *(Quercus petraea)* is dominant, but other species occasionally present include downy birch *(Betula pubescens)*, rowan *(Sorbus aucuparia)* and holly *(Ilex aquifolium)*. Most of the old natural oak woods show evidence of coppicing or heavy grazing; here the main growth continues from the lateral branches, there being no main trunk. Past grazing has also determined the ground flora, which tends to be grassy.

On the lower slopes the soils tend to be drier and the ground flora of the oak wood changes, grasses become softer and the bluebell *(Endymion non-scriptus)* and bracken *(Pteridium aquilinum)* are common. This again changes when the rainfall exceeds 150cm a year, as in the west. Here the wood sage *(Teucrium scorodonia)*, wood sorrel *(Oxalis acetosella)*, honeysuckle *(Lonicera periclymenum)*, foxglove *(Digitalis purpurea)* and numerous ferns and mosses occur. Such woods also have a rich epiphyte flora growing on the trees themselves; this may include the common polypody *(Polypodium vulgare)*, lichens, and liverworts such as *Frullania tamarisci*. The ground flora may also be dominated by ferns or bilberry.

The upland birch woods probably mark the sites of former oak woodland or pine woods. It is not unusual to find birch fringing either of these communities. Downy birch is the most common species, but *Betula pendula*, the silver birch, is found locally in the eastern Highlands. The ground flora is often very similar to that of oak woodland, but the epiphytic flora contains more fungi: *Exoascus turgidus* often causes the trees to become misshapen and damaged, and such trees are likely to be colonised by bracket fungi.

Many of Britain's upland wooded areas are today covered by coniferous forest, the majority of which has been planted. The only naturally occurring coniferous forest in these areas is pine and these native woods are now confined to small areas of the Grampians where *Pinus sylvestris*, the Scots pine, occurs. These forests are remnants of what were at one time very extensive stands, most of which have now been replaced by heather moor.

The fourth single-species woodland type is alder *(Alnus glutinosa)*, but this is now very rare;

A field guide to some upland ferns

'Upland' is a broad category encompassing a wide variety of habitats. Such regions are frequently wooded (the woodland ferns are covered elsewhere).

Ferns play an important role in the colonisation of bare rock: on modified slate and volcanic ash block scree, parsley and mountain ferns are frequent and on mica schists mountain lady, brittle bladder and beech ferns are also found. *Asplenium viride* is characteristic of Pennine limestone.

On the lower grasslands of upland regions where the dominant species are *Festuca* and *Agrostis*, bracken often invades if the soil is at least 20 cm deep. The spread of this fern has accelerated since the introduction of sheep to the exclusion of cattle that eat the young shoots, and also due to the expense of labour of cutting—three or four cuttings in a year kill it. Fortunately it is now coming under control due to herbicides.

Brittle Bladder-fern Athyriaceae *Cystopteris fragilis* **Distribution:** Throughout the British Isles; less common in central and south England, central and south Ireland. **Other habitats:** Woods. **Notes:** Usually basic rocks; very variable species; found up to 1300 metres.

Wilson's Filmy Fern Hymenophyllaceae *Hymenophyllum wilsonii* **Distribution:** Scotland; north, north-west, south-west England; scattered throughout Ireland. **Notes:** Rocks, rock ledges and tree trunks; always in moist atmosphere; found up to 1000 metres.

Rusty-back Fern Aspleniaceae *Ceterach officinarum* **Distribution:** Throughout the British Isles, but becoming less common towards the north. **Notes:** Crevices in limestone and mortar in walls; found up to 450 metres.

Mountain Fern Thelypteridaceae *Thelypteris limbosperma*. **Distribution:** Throughout the British Isles, but less common in central England and Ireland. **Other habitats:** Woods. **Notes:** Common in pastures and screes, especially on steep banks above streams; absent from limestone; found up to 950 metres; prefers ground-water flowing through its root system.

Moonwort Ophioglossaceae *Botrychium lunaria* **Distribution:** Throughout the British Isles, but more common in north England and Scotland. **Other habitats:** Fixed sand dunes. **Notes:** Dry grassland and rock ledges; well drained soils; up to 1000 metres.

Parsley Fern Cryptogrammaceae *Cryptogramma crispa*. **Distribution:** Scotland; north, north-west, south-west England; Wales; scattered in Ireland. **Notes:** Only on calcium-free siliceous soils and rock screes; rarely on stable substrates; only in mountainous districts.

Holly Fern Aspidiaceae *Polystichum lonchitis*. **Distribution:** North Wales; north England; central and north Scotland; a few places in west Ireland. **Notes:** Rocky fissures on higher mountains; rare; requires a base-rich substrate; found growing up to 1000 metres.

much more common is mixed woodland. This is usually found on unstable flushed soils and as the name suggests consists of a wide variety of species. Many new tree species are now being introduced and grown in large numbers by the Forestry Commission. These cannot be considered as natural woodland, but both the trees and their management have a marked effect on the ecology of the area.

With the high rainfall found in the British mountains it is not surprising that there are large numbers of springs present. Where these arise there is a constant downwards movement of water and soil from higher up the slope, causing continual erosion and deposition. Such areas are known as "flushes" and they support a rich and varied vegetation. Naturally there is a high proportion of species needing water in their environment such as rushes (*Juncus* spp.) and sedges (*Carex* spp.), and in the more open flush areas the bryophyte population may be dominant: *Philonotis fontana* often forms a charac-teristic silver-green carpet, and *Dicranella palustris, Bryum alpinum* and, in lime-rich areas, *Cratoneuron commutatum* add to the moss flora.

The flowering plants of flushes can be very varied and may include plants normally expected at much higher or lower altitudes. This includes many alpine species, often growing slightly larger here than in their normal habitat, notably the saxifrages, starry, purple and Dovedale moss (*Saxifraga stellaris, S. oppositifolia* and *S. hypnoides*). Further up the mountain flush vegetation may also be found on damp ledges. Here there is a different pattern of colonisation, terminating in a very species-rich community.

Most species restricted to higher altitudes are mainly found in open soil and rock crevices where competition is scarce. These plants include those normally restricted to an arctic/alpine distribution and, surprisingly, some maritime species such as thrift (*Armeria maritima*) and sea campion (*Silene maritima*).

Montane species are often found on nutrient-deficient and immature soils; availability of mineral salts does little to determine distribution, but limestone can. In the Pennines the typically montane plants are confined almost entirely to the narrow bands of limestone: here are found the yellow mountain saxifrage (*Saxifraga aizoides*), purple saxifrage, Dovedale moss, alpine poa (*Poa alpina*), hoary whitlow grass (*Draba incana*), green spleenwort (*Asplenium viride*) and numerous rare mosses.

In Snowdonia too, the alpine species are confined to areas of Ordovician limestone, and on outcrops of calcareous lava species of very limited distribution in Wales are found, such as mountain avens (*Dryas octopetala*), moss campion (*Silene acaulis*) and purple saxifrage. In fact, the rich montane floras of these calcareous extrusions are a marked contrast to the species-poor surrounding areas. In the Scottish Highlands the most species-rich areas are found on the lime-rich mica schists, while in the Lake District they are confined to volcanic rocks.

A field guide to some upland wild flowers

The upland flora of Britain is limited mainly by the adverse conditions. With increasing altitude the average temperature falls, exposure to strong winds increases and the growing season is usually short as snow covers the ground for several months of the year. Despite this, some plants are adapted and thrive: they are mainly low shrubs or perennial herbs whose buds survive the winter conditions protected by a layer of snow. They are frequently cushion plants whose habit protects shoots by bunching and the whole plant by having only low wind resistance. Many of these plants (like the mountain avens) are characterised by producing large showy flowers on dwarf stems. Annuals overwintering as seeds are very uncommon, the snow gentian, a rare plant of Scottish mountains, being the best known: the uncertain conditions make seed setting a risky business. The perennials depend mainly on vegetative reproduction in order to spread and survive.

Cowberry Ericaceae *Vaccinium vitis-idaea* **Distribution**: Wales; northern England; Ireland; common in Scotland. **Other habitats**: Woodland. **Notes**: Evergreen plant, on moorland, always grows on acid soils; occasionally the dominant species.

Mountain Sorrel Polygonaceae *Oxyria digyna* **Distribution**: Snowdonia and the west coast of Ireland; common in Scotland and the Lake District. **Notes**: Damp rocky places, especially beside streams, often locally common.

Heart Willow Salicaceae *Salix herbacea* **Distribution**: Scotland, especially common in the west; Lake District; scattered in Wales and Ireland. **Notes**: Mountain tops and rock ledges; often abundant; found from 95 to 1400 metres.

Alpine Lady's Mantle Rosaceae *Alchemilla alpina* **Distribution**: Northern Scotland, Lake District; scattered in southern Ireland. **Notes**: Grows in grassland, rock crevices and screes; often the locally dominant species; up to 1300 metres.

Starry Saxifrage Saxifragaceae *Saxifraga stellaris* **Distribution**: West-central and north-west Wales; northern England; common in Scotland; scattered throughout Ireland. **Other habitats**: By streams and in springs. **Notes**: Wet rock ledges and wet stony ground; habitat must always be wet; found at the highest British altitudes.

Crowberry Empetraceae *Empetrum nigrum* **Distribution**: Throughout Scotland, northern England, Wales and Ireland; occasional in south-west England. **Notes**: Moors, mountain tops and the drier parts of blanket bogs; often common and sometimes the dominant species.

Mountain Avens Rosaceae *Dryas octopetala* **Distribution**: Scattered in northern England, northern Wales, west and central Scotland and western Ireland. **Notes**: Grows on ledges and crevices of mountains; always on basic rocks; locally common; found from sea level to 1000 metres.

Cloudberry Rosaceae *Rubus chamaemorus* **Distribution**: Pennines in England; throughout Scotland; Snowdonia in Wales; Tyrone in Ireland. **Notes**: On mountain moors and blanket bogs; locally common; found up to 1300 metres.

Upland Invertebrates

With the low temperatures, frequent high winds and heavy rainfall, it is hardly surprising that few of the great variety of invertebrate animals found in the lowlands occur in mountain and moorland areas. Apart from the climate, other factors also influence the distribution of many invertebrates. Much moorland soil is of an acid nature, lacking base minerals such as lime (calcium carbonate). As snails require lime to manufacture their shells, few are found over large tracts of moorland. The type of invertebrate species present in the uplands varies throughout the British Isles, largely as a result of differing rock and soil types, which also influence the vegetation at the beginning of the food chain. Where limestones, dolerites and basalts occur, the variety of herbaceous plants in the uplands tends to be greater than on more acid rocks and thus the range of invertebrate species increases. These rich habitats (especially grasslands) provide a suitable habitat for snails; in many of the drier, warmer situations ants are also found. If the soils are deep, mole hills often appear, indicating the presence of both moles and the earthworms on which they feed. As the soils become more acid, moor grass *(Molinia)* and mat grass *(Nardus)* become more abundant. Where these grasses are associated with heather *(Calluna)* the hairy, dark brown and black, fox moth caterpillar *(Macrothylacia rubi)* is seen regularly. But as a general rule, increasingly acid soil conditions are accompanied by a reduction in invertebrate and plant diversity.

Several species of invertebrate found in mountain and moorland environments are quite spectacular. Perhaps top of the list in this respect is the emperor moth *(Saturnia pavonia)*, in which both the caterpillar and moth are beautifully marked. Day flying moths, like the large chocolate-coloured northern eggar *(Lasiocampa quercus callunae)*, make an impressive sight as the males quarter the moorlands in search of females.

Some of the most impoverished upland

Upland butterflies

In Britain there are few butterflies in upland habitats because the climatic conditions do not favour these sun-loving insects and there are few suitable foodplants. The typically upland species are all browns, feeding on the leaves of grasses and sedges, and they produce only one generation each year as the summer is relatively short in the uplands. They may be seen on the wing in the middle of summer (June and July).

The Small Mountain Ringlet Satyridae-*Erebia epiphron* **Flight time:** Late June, July. Overwinters as larva **Foodplant:** Mat grass. **Distribution:** Grassy mountain tops.

The Large Heath Satyridae-*Coenonympha tullia* **Flight time:** June, July. Overwinters as larva. **Foodplant:** Grasses and sedges. **Distribution:** Acid peatbogs. Local in north Wales and northern England; widespread in Scotland.

The Scotch Argus Satyridae-*Erebia aethiops* **Flight time:** late July, August. Overwinters as larva **Foodplant:** Blue moor grass. **Distribution:** Grassy hillsides. England, Cumbria only; widespread in mid- and west Scotland.

The large black slug *Arion ater* is a common sight in wet upland pastures. In places it may be so abundant that at certain times of the year slugs consume more of the grass than the sheep. Slugs do not have large shells like snails so they are less dependent upon calcium-rich soils and can thus be found in the mineral-deficient soils of upland areas.

Stoneflies are characteristic inhabitants of fast-flowing cool streams, which contain plenty of oxygen in the water. The larvae spend up to three years in water before turning into the adult form. Some stoneflies emerge as early as February and a few species, like this *Dinoceras cephalotes* do not feed once they are mature.

habitats are the very acid grasslands and heather moors. Such habitats cover large expanses and are dominated by a few plant species. Because the soil is frequently water-logged and lacking oxygen, the soil fauna is frequently reduced or almost absent. Those species which do occur are often microscopic, such as animalcules and rotifers. A few small mites and springtails are also found in the plant litter on heather moorland. Where *Sphagnum* is present, the grasshopper *(Mecostethus grossus)* can be found, while the long-horned grass-hopper *(Metrioptera brachyptera)* occurs where there is cross-leaved heath *(Erica tetralix)*.

Few snails occur in the more acid parts of the uplands though some species can be found, especially if there are woodland remnants. The rounded snail *(Discus rotundatus)* is an example, but it is not confined to upland areas. Several other species, such as the rock snail *(Pyramidula rupestris)* and the craven door snail *(Clausilia dubia)*, inhabit the more calcareous uplands, but generally the shortage of calcium is a limiting factor for these shelled molluscs. Their place is taken by the slugs, which do not need to produce a shell and are thus less dependent upon mineral availability.

Most of the upland spiders are small, dark-coloured species, easily overlooked, but there is one related invertebrate which may be seen after an upland walk, the sheep tick *(Ixodes ricinus)*. This is probably the commonest tick in Britain. Although usually found on sheep, it does occur on many other warm-blooded animals and will occasionally attach itself to a dog. Its life cycle takes about three years to complete, during which time the animal has only three meals of blood and spends less than a month attached to a host. The eggs hatch in the autumn into a small six legged larva. In the following spring, the larva climbs to the top of some vegetation and waits for a passing animal, which will act as its host. It feeds before again falling to the ground, where it changes to an eight legged nymph and remains in this condition until the next spring, when it hopes to find another host. If successful it has another large feed before dropping to the ground again. In the spring of the third year, the adult finds a host to feed on prior to mating.

Dragonflies

Many upland areas are too exposed and un-suitable for dragonflies and damselflies but species such as *Aeshna juncea* and the black sympetrum *(Sympetrum danae)* will hunt in up-land localities. The goldringed dragonfly *(Cordu-legaster boltoni)*, which breeds in fast flowing streams, is an upland species. There are three dragonflies which are confined to Scotland but they are very rare or local in distribution. Perhaps the most montane of these is the blue aeshna *(Aeshna caerulea)* which breeds in upland pools and slow streams and probably feeds on the swarms of midge larvae which abound in such situations. One of the more widespread dragonflies, which may occasionally be seen in upland terrain, is the four-spotted libellula *(Libellula quadrimaculata)*.

There are many bugs which inhabit moor-lands, especially where there is scattered pine forest or birch nearby. The birch flatbug *(Aradus betulae)*, the mountain shieldbug *(Elas-mucha ferrugata)*, and the parasitic heath bug *(Rhagognathus punctatus)*, which feeds on the larvae of the heather-leaf beetle *(Lochmaea suturalis)*, are examples. The spectacular plant bug *(Zicrona caerulea)* is another, while one or two species of gall wasps, scale insects and bees also occur. The characteristic bilberry bumble bee *(Bombus lapponicus)*, with its orange-tipped abdomen, is very noticeable.

In view of their low productivity, it is often surprising how many of the small upland peat pools contain water beetles and water-boatmen. A small whirligig beetle, *Gyrinus minutus*, is

Upland moths

There are relatively few species of moths in the upland because of the low temperatures, unsuitable climatic conditions and the scarcity of suitable foodplants. However, although few species are involved there may be large numbers of individual moths in montane habitats. Several species of northern moth are not restricted to one species of foodplant, but feed on a number of different plants, or on common, widespread plants. Where such moths are rare or restricted in range other factors limit their spread. Some normally nocturnal moths take on diurnal forms in the uplands to take advantage of higher day temperatures. Another adaptation to low montane temperatures is found in moths like the Northern Eggar and Northern Dart which have extended their development over two years, overwintering as larvae in their first and second winters.

Upland moths may be separated into groups such as lowland species that also occur on mountains, sub-montane species that occur on the lower levels of hills and the truly montane species, such as the Northern Dart, which are confined to the higher parts of the hills.

The Small Dark Yellow Underwing Noctuidae-*Anarta cordigera*. **Flight time:** May, June. Overwinters as pupa. **Foodplant:** Bearberry. **Distribution:** Confined to the Scottish Highlands where it is very local.

The Netted Mountain Moth Geometridae-*Semiothisa carbonaria*. **Flight time:** April, May. Overwinters as pupa. **Foodplant:** Birch, sallow, bilberry, heather, bearberry. **Distribution:** At high altitudes in the mountains from Perthshire to Ross-shire.

The Twin-spot Carpet Geometridae-*Perizoma didymata*. **Flight time:** July, August. Overwinters as larva. **Foodplant:** Primrose, red campion, bilberry. **Distribution:** Common throughout almost the whole of the British Isles.

The Northern Eggar Lasiocampidae-*Lasiocampa quercus callunae* **Flight time:** End May, June. Overwinters as larva in first winter, pupa in second winter. Life cycle two years. **Foodplant:** Heather, bramble and other herbaceous plants. **Distribution:** Moorland; widely distributed from the south Pennines northwards to Orkney.

The Rannoch Sprawler Noctuidae-*Brachionycha nubeculosa*. **Flight time:** Late March, April. Overwinters as pupa. **Foodplant:** Birch. **Distribution:** Confined to the Scottish Highlands.

frequently found above 300 metres. One of the most colourful and interesting moorland beetles is *Plateumaris discolor*, a reed beetle which feeds on the roots of cotton grass, *Eriophorum* spp. It has been recorded up to 600 metres above sea level; the adult exhibits a range of metallic colouring from brassy through coppery to black. Another beetle which may be found on the moors is the heather-leaf beetle, which fre-quently kills large tracts of heather by eating the bark and leaves and stripping young stems. A striking carabid beetle, *Carabus nitens*, is also regularly seen on moorlands. This is another metallic insect, this time green being the most prominent colour. The elytra are bordered with bright red.

Butterflies are nowhere near so abundant as they are at lower altitudes. Nevertheless a few species do occur on the uplands. The large heath butterfly *(Coenonympha tullia)* does occur in some localities where there is suitable grassland habitat, but the mountain ringlet *(Erebia epiphron)* is our only exclusively montane butter-fly. Where moorland grades into birch or pine woodland characteristic butterflies such as the green hairstreak *(Callophrys rubi)*, Scotch argus *(Erebia aethiops)* and dark-green fritillary *(Argyn-nis aglaja)* are likely to be found.

Several species of moth found in montane conditions have adapted their way of life to the severe conditions. For example the engrailed clay *(Diarsia mendica)* has an upland subspecies which is seen on the wing during the day, while in other situations it is a nocturnal moth. It thus avoids the lowest night temperatures. Moths such as the northern eggar, foxmoth and the northern dart *(Xestia alpicola)* over-winter as caterpillars and thus have the best part of two seasons for development, important in a situation where their foodplants have very short growing seasons. There are many other common and widespread moths such as the drinker *(Philu-doria potatoria)*. Where bilberry and cowberry are present the small dark yellow underwing *(Anarta cordigera)* is frequently seen. The moun-tain equivalent of the more familiar six-spot burnet is the Scotch or mountain burnet *(Zygaena exulans)*. The diminutive black moun-tain moth *(Psodos coracina)* is often found in dwarf shrub habitats on the highest Scottish mountains.

Flies (Diptera) are relatively numerous as upland species go. Two species of daddy long-legs, *Tipula excisa* and *T. macrocera*, can be found right up to the summit of some mountain ranges. If there is a large hatch of these tipulids, considerable numbers of birds may be attracted to feed on such abundant short-term food supplies. After fledging, family parties of rooks and jackdaws pay frequent visits to montane grasslands where they capitalise upon sudden hatches of insects. In summer large swarms of midges (chironomides) frequently occur in sufficient numbers to attract swifts, swallows and martins to the mountain tops.

Just as insects should be considered in relation to the vegetation they eat, so they should be related to their position in upland food chains. Many of the most widespread and abundant upland birds, such as skylark, meadow pipit and wheatear, exploit this invertebrate food source. As winter approaches and many invertebrates either pupate or seek the shelter of deep litter, these birds must also leave the uplands to seek alternative food in lowland and coastal situations or migrate to warmer climates.

Ticks

Ticks are blood-sucking arachnids closely related to the mites. They have short legs and a very strong beak or rostrum with which they attach themselves to their hosts. Ticks generally inhabit grassy places where there are plenty of mammals—small rodents, rabbits, deer, cattle, dogs, or even humans. The eggs are scattered on the ground, and produce tiny six-legged youngsters called seed ticks. These sit on the grass and wait for passing animals. They climb on, and immediately stick in their beaks to suck blood. They become bloated in a few days and fall off. After moulting to eight-legged forms, they attach themselves to fresh hosts and feed again. Then they drop off and moult a second time to produce adults. There may be weeks or even months between the feeding periods. Adults climb on to fresh hosts and mate. The females swell enormously as they take in blood, and then they drop off to lay their eggs.

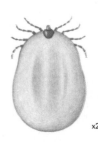

x2

Sheep Tick Ixodidae *Ixodes ricinus* **Distribution:** Most of British Isles, but most common in hilly regions of north and west. **Other habitats:** Woodland edges and clearings. **Adult active:** Spring and summer. **Food:** Mammalian blood.

Upland Birds

There are several very different species of birds which are particularly characteristic of upland areas, for example the dotterel, golden plover, wheatear, black grouse, merlin, hen harrier and golden eagle. The ptarmigan is not seen below 300 metres, except in the very north of Scotland, and usually lives above 750 metres, but pride of place must go to the red grouse. This is a specific associate of heather moorland. Well-managed moors with mineral-rich soils will support 50–60 pairs of birds per square kilometre. Their noisy chucklings and defiant "go-back, go-back, go-back!" call are among the most distinctive sounds of the uplands. Formerly the red grouse was thought to be the only bird unique to Britain, but it is now considered to be a national race of the widespread willow grouse found across northern Europe and America.

The uplands provide a very open habitat in which it is difficult for a nesting bird to hide. It is important therefore that the adult be well camouflaged and that the eggs and chicks should also match their surroundings. It is therefore not surprising that some of the most effectively camouflaged eggs are produced by upland birds which must nest mostly on the ground. The chicks of grouse, plovers and waders are able to scatter and hide almost as soon as they hatch. Smaller birds usually manage to nest between boulders or in grass tussocks; their chicks remain in the nest to be fed by the adults.

Some cliff nesters find convenient crags in the uplands, with the result that species like the peregrine falcon, chough and raven, normally found along rocky coasts, are also among the species of birds which breed in the uplands.

The shortage of food in upland environments limits the population density of birds. But during the summer months insects may be relatively abundant, enabling meadow pipits, for example, to live at 1,000m or more. This species is usually the commonest passerine above 500m, with about 20 nesting pairs per square kilometre; there are far less on very poor moorland, but twice as many on new forestry plantations. Despite the fact that meadow pipits nest on the ground, where they and their chicks seem very vulnerable to the wet, they seem to prefer the wetter parts of Britain.

The wheatear is another bird which is characteristic of open habitats, especially uplands where sheep have grazed the grass to a very short turf. Lowland wheatears usually have two broods a year but those in the uplands (up to 1,200m) only manage one. They nest among boulders and loose scree; with pale blue eggs they cannot afford to nest out in the open like skylarks or meadow pipits. Wheatears overcome the problem of food shortage by only living in upland areas for a short period in the summer. A similar strategem is employed by several wader species, for example curlew and redshank. Their clear calls are a distinctive feature of the uplands in summer, but soon after their chicks are fledged they depart to spend the winter in large flocks feeding in estuaries. These larger birds must find it difficult to obtain enough food and population densities above 500m are low. Perhaps the greatest advantage the uplands provide for these ground nesting birds is the relative freedom from predators and disturbance

The merlin is probably the most characteristic upland bird of prey. It hunts mainly small birds,

---

A field guide to some upland birds

The ptarmigan is one of the few birds resident in the uplands during the winter. At that time it is pure white, but in summer it is a mottled grey-brown with white wings. It and the dotterel are rarely seen below about 600 metres; few other birds share their rocky alpine habitat. The red grouse is a dark chocolate-brown; it is usually associated with heather, and is distinguished by its characteristic "go-back, go-back" and gurgling alarm note. The harriers are difficult to tell apart, especially the females, but are rarely seen; the red kite is another rare species, which is restricted to central Wales. The ring ouzel resembles a blackbird and frequents rocky screes; whinchats are normally associated with more scrubby habitats. The wheatear is a common small bird with a quiet trilling song and flashes a characteristic white rump patch as it flies away. It is one of the first of the migrants to appear in the uplands each summer.

Grey Plover winter

Golden Plover winter

Grey Plover summer

Golden Plover summer

Golden Plover Charadriidae *Pluvialis apricarius*. **Distribution**: Breeds from southern Pennines northwards but winters in all districts. **Other habitats**: Moors, and, in winter, also fields, seashores and estuaries. **Notes**: Size: 28cm. Under-surfaces of wings white. Flight is rapid, often in flocks. Voice is a liquid "tlui" when in flight.

Grey Plover Charadriidae *Pluvialis squaterola*. **Distribution**: Passage migrant and winter visitor. **Other habitats**: Estuaries, sandy beaches and shores. **Notes**: Size: 28cm. Usually seen in winter plumage. Conspicuous black axillaries in flight. Has dejected, hunched appearance. Voice is a high-pitched "tlee-oo-ee"

Red Grouse Tetraonidae *Lagopus lagopus*. **Distribution**: Resident in northern Britain, Ireland, parts of Wales, Devon and Cornwall. **Other habitats**: Heather moors. **Notes**: Size: 32–41cm. Male larger. Round, unforked tail. Call: "kowk, kok-ok-ok ok"

Ptarmigan winter

♂

Ptarmigan autumn

Ptarmigan Tetraonidae *Lagopus mutus*. **Distribution**: Mainly Scottish mountains over 900 metres. **Other habitats**: Barren mountain tops. **Notes**: Size: 32–36cm. Male larger. White wings in all plumages.

♀

Short-eared Owl Strigidae *Asio flammeus*. **Distribution**: Resident in Scotland and northern England. Winters elsewhere. **Other habitats**: Open country. **Notes**: Size: 38cm. Eyes yellow. Regularly hunts by day. Perches chiefly on ground, adopting a slanting rather than upright inclination. Harrier-like flight. Voice is a high "kee-ow"

♂

♂

winter

Snow Bunting Emberizidae *Plectrophenax nivalis*. **Distribution**: Few nest in northern Scotland; widespread winter visitor. **Other habitats**: Breeds on mountain tops, more coastal in winter. **Notes**: Size: 16.5cm. Female resembles winter male. Summer male has black and white plumage.

♀

Black Grouse Tetraonidae *Lyrurus tetrix*. **Distribution**: Northern Britain, parts of Wales, Exmoor, Quantocks. **Other habitats**: Moorland fringes, sparsely wooded heaths, young conifers. **Notes**: Male 53cm. Female 41cm. Females are browner than red grouse.

♂

summer

♂

♀

Wheatear Turdidae *Oenanthe oenanthe*. **Distribution**: Widespread summer visitor except central and S.E. England. **Other habitats**: Moorland, heath, downs, coastal turf. **Notes**: Size: 14.5cm. White rump and tail pattern distinctive.

♀

Dotterel Charadriidae *Eudromias morinellus*. **Distribution**: Summer visitor, breeding in the central Highlands. **Other habitats**: Barren mountains above 780 metres. **Notes**: Size: 22cm. Winter adults are paler but retain eye-stripes and pectoral band; often very tame. Flight is rapid. Voice is a trilling "wit-e-wee"

Capercaillie Tetraonidae *Tetrao urogallus*. **Distribution**: Resident of eastern highlands. **Other habitats**: Mature coniferous forest. **Notes**: Male 86cm. Female 62cm. Unmistakable. Female larger than female black grouse, has a rufous breast patch and rounded tail.

Whinchat Turdidae *Saxicola rubetra*. **Distribution**: Summer visitor to all British Isles, local in Ireland and south-east England. **Other habitats**: Rough grassland, heath, moor, young conifers. **Notes**: Size: 12.5cm. Pale eyestripe and white on tail distinguishing.

♂

especially meadow pipits, and benefits considerably from drainage and land improvements associated with young plantations. However, old plantations deprive it of open hunting and nesting habitat and are responsible for the decline of this tiny falcon. Even good moorland habitats do not usually support more than two nesting pairs per ten square kilometres. In winter the loss of potential prey, as migrating species depart, compels the merlin to travel to the lowlands where it harries the birds of marshes and estuaries, before returning to its traditional nesting site in early spring. Similar habits are exhibited by the short-eared owl. Like the merlin it nests on the ground (unusually for a ground nester, the eggs are pure white), but unlike other owls hunts mainly in daylight. Competition with merlins is avoided because short-eared owls prey on small mammals, mainly the short-tailed vole but also the common shrew. The absence of these species from Ireland probably accounts for this owl not being found there. Short-eared owls, like the merlin, benefit from the early stages of upland forestry.

The short-eared owl is a bird of open country. It can therefore often be seen in the uplands, particularly in summer, but in the winter-time may be forced by the weather and by food shortage to migrate to lower altitudes, where it may be found in marshland and in open estuarine habitats.

Peregrine Falconidae *Falco peregrinus.* **Distribution:** Breeds Scottish highlands, western Britain and parts of Ireland. More widespread in Britain. **Other habitats:** Open country and marshes. **Notes:** Size: 38–48cm. Female is the larger.

Peregrine juvenile

Golden Eagle Accipitridae *Aquila chrysaetos.* **Distribution:** Breeds in upland areas of Scotland and Lake District. **Other habitats:** Mountainous and coastal regions. **Notes:** Size: 75–88cm. Colouring of nape varies, immatures have white tail. Broad slotted wings. Soars and glides.

Buzzard Accipitridae *Buteo buteo.* **Distribution:** Scotland, N.W. and S.W. England, Wales and Ulster. **Other habitats:** Barren hills, coastal districts and woods. **Notes:** Size: 51–56cm. Variable plumage. Broad rounded wings and tail.

Merlin Falconidae *Falco columbarius* **Distribution:** Breeds northern Britain, central Wales, S.W. England. Winters in coastal areas. **Other habitats:** Hills, open moorland; saltings and dunes in winter. **Notes:** Size: 27–33cm. Female is browner than female kestrel.

Hen Harrier Accipitridae *Circus cyaneus.* **Distribution:** Breeds in Scotland, northern England, N. Wales and Ireland. Widespread in winter. **Other habitats:** Moorland, young conifers, heaths, pasture and marshes. **Notes:** Size: 43–51cm. White rump noticeable.

Red Kite Accipitridae *Milvus milvus.* **Distribution:** Breeds central Wales. **Other habitats:** Hill country with wooded slopes. **Notes:** Size: 62cm. Long wings with large, whitish patch and forked tail distinctive.

Ring Ouzel Turdidae *Turdus torquatus.* **Distribution:** Summer visitor in northern and western areas. **Other habitats:** Breeds on mountain and moorland. Coasts when on passage. **Notes:** Size: 24cm. A white gorget on breast and a pale wing patch. Flight is rapid, dodging behind rocks when approached. Voice is a loud "tac-toc-tac".

Montagu's Harrier Accipitridae *Circus pygargus.* **Distribution:** Rare summer visitor to S.W. England. **Other habitats:** Marshes, common, moorland and sand dunes. **Notes:** Size: 41–46cm. Female resembles female Hen. No white rump in male.

Upland Mammals

Although the bleak montane environment imposes a severe limitation on the number of warm-blooded species that can live there, none of our mountains is high enough to preclude all mammals. The smallest British mammal (the pigmy shrew) is found on high moors, and even at the very top of Ben Nevis, our highest mountain. The wood mouse, normally considered an inhabitant of forests and hedgerows, has been found close to the summit of Snowdon, over 900 metres above sea level. It is likely that these mountain-top small mammals are at least partially sustained by apple cores and other picnic debris left by tourists in the summer.

Only one British mammal, the mountain hare *(Lepus timidus)*, is exclusively montane in its distribution, being found in the Scottish Highlands and on various other mountainous areas as far south as Derbyshire. However, in Ireland it also extends into the lowlands, doubtless because of the absence there of competition from the brown hare. In Ireland the species usually remains brown throughout the year but in the mountains on the mainland it moults three times a year, and grows a white coat to last over winter. The timing and extent of the moults are very variable, being influenced by age, altitude and temperature. It feeds mainly on heather (90 per cent of the diet in winter) and cotton grass; each hare has a usual range of about 20 hectares of open moorland.

As described elsewhere, the upland habitat is poor in nutrients and its vegetation is consequently not very nourishing. Moreover, the short growing season reduces the amount of plant food available, so that it is perhaps surprising that the largest British land mammal, the red deer, is a frequent inhabitant of the Scottish moors. This may be due to the fact that it is primarily a forest animal; when the uplands were deforested it had either to adapt to life on the open moorland or become extinct. In fact the upland populations are only seasonal: the deer tend to migrate to lower, richer ground for the winter and may then become a nuisance to farmers. An experiment begun in 1952 aimed at establishing a population of reindeer on the upper slopes of the Cairngorms. The idea was that they would be well adapted to the arctic/alpine conditions and would not compete with anything else at those high altitudes, feeding on lichens and heather as they do. Although reindeer used to live in Britain during the last Ice Age, the modern herd seems not to have flourished particularly, though it still survives. Small herds of wild goats are found in many upland regions, over 60 separate populations in Scotland alone. However, these are not truly wild but "feral", having gone wild from the domestic state. Even so, they appear well able to sustain viable populations, even above 1,000 metres. They are smaller and shaggier than modern breeds of domestic goat.

The polecat was formerly widespread but persecution by gamekeepers has now reduced its range considerably. It is not primarily an upland animal, but its present stronghold is the upland region of central and western Wales.

Many of the upland grasslands provide extensive areas of ideal habitat for the characteristic small rodent of rough grass, the short-tailed vole *(Microtus agrestis)*. Where the grasslands have been drained and converted to conifer plantations, the voles often benefit from the improved conditions to such an extent that their populations increase rapidly to plague proportions, often resulting in considerable damage from their gnawing of the young plantation trees. However, once the trees are big enough to shade the ground and suppress the grass, short-tailed voles are reduced and become confined to the plantation edges and open areas. They are very hardy and can live at altitudes up to 1,300m. They are an important source of food for many upland predators, particularly birds such as the short-eared owl.

The fox and wildcat are the major large mammalian predators regularly found in the uplands, though stoats, weasels and (locally) polecats and pine martens may occur at all altitudes. Foxes are especially abundant in young plantations with high vole populations, but also live out on open moors. Here, food may be infrequent, so home ranges may extend to 10 square kilometres or more. A fox needs about 500 grams of food daily.

The mountain hare is found in the upland of Scotland and parts of the Pennines, where it turns white in winter. In Ireland, where the brown hare is absent, mountain hares are also found at lower altitudes

Red deer, such as this herd on the move in the Scottish Highlands, live in upland areas for only part of the year, migrating to lower ground in search of food in the winter. They often feed on crops and are therefore regarded as pests by man — a result of the disappearance of the red deer's natural habitat. The stags and hinds live separately, only coming together during the rutting season from mid-September to the end of October.

Wetlands and Freshwater

Several strikingly different habitats, ranging from rushing streams to artificial reservoirs and squelchy fens, all have one feature in common: their major component is water. The extent and nature of the water will govern the type of wildlife community which develops, and it is often difficult to draw a hard and fast distinction between various habitats and communities which grade into one another through their common dependence upon water.

Habitats such as lakes, ponds, rivers, gravel pits and reservoirs which consist primarily of open water are here classified as freshwater. These are differentiated from wetlands (which include river banks, fens and bogs) where there is relatively little open water and a much higher proportion of soil and vegetation in the habitat. Reedswamps growing at the edges of lakes and slow moving rivers could be put into either category and illustrate important features of wet habitats in general. Especially towards the edges of lakes and rivers and in wetlands the plant and animal communities may show zonation, different communities occurring, for example, at different water depths or at different heights above the water table. Over a long time, too, the environment may change, as when a lake silts up, and the community at a given place will also change into one characteristic of the new conditions. This process is known as succession and is of considerable importance in lakes and wetlands.

Most of our freshwaters have been profoundly modified by man. The lower reaches of nearly all our major rivers have been confined within embankments, and they may also be polluted by sewage, industrial waste and agricultural chemicals washed from the land. Many water bodies are almost entirely artificial, such as reservoirs and our network of canals. New artificial lakes, such as clay and gravel pits, are still being created, partially compensating for the loss of freshwater habitats resulting from natural succession and artificial drainage or infilling.

Many wetland habitats, particularly those like shallow ponds, provide a range of conditions from open water, through marsh to dry land. They thus support a great assortment of plant species which in turn are the food and home for an equivalent diversity of insects, birds and other animals.

The Physiography of Lakes and Rivers

Thirlmere in the Lake District is one of the many lakes in the north west of Britain that fill valleys gouged by glaciers.

The lakes, ponds and rivers of Britain cover a wide range in terms of age, area, depth and water type. Most of the larger and deeper lakes are to be found in upland Britain, in the north and west. This is partly because the older and harder rocks of this region are often more impermeable than those of the lowlands, and also because the glaciers of the last ice-age, which were responsible for the formation of many of our lakes, were mainly confined to upland Britain.

Glaciers flowing down from the hill tops gouged into the valley floors and steepened the valley sides. When the ice melted, these great hollows filled with water. Lakes formed in this way are characteristically deep and much narrower than they are long. Many of the lochs of the Scottish highlands are of this type, including the deepest lake in Britain, Loch Morar, which goes down to 310m at its deepest point and yet is only just over 1km wide for most of its 17km length. The long, thin northern arm of Loch Lomond, almost 200m deep in places, has a similar origin.

Similar features are shown by lakes in the other main areas of glacier formation, such as in the English Lake District and in north Wales. These valley basin lakes were not the only types to be formed by glacial action. Where glaciers started to form, high up on the mountains the weight of ice and snow carved out bowl shaped depressions in the mountainsides, giving rise to corries. Where these were deep enough they filled with water and, although some have since filled with silt or peat, some still remain small rather rounded lakes. Good examples are found in the Cairngorms and below the summit of Snowdon.

Ice was also responsible for the formation of lakes of a quite different type. When the ice sheets melted they deposited enormous amounts of sand, gravel and clay which had been carried by the ice, forming layers of glacial drift or boulder clay. In some places large blocks of ice melted more slowly than the surrounding ice and so became surrounded by drift. When these blocks finally disappeared they left a depression (a "kettle hole") which filled with water to become a lake. Such lakes are usually quite shallow and not much longer than they are broad. A good example is Loch Leven, which is only 6km long by 4km wide and on average less than 5m deep. The numerous meres of the Cheshire and north Shropshire plain are much smaller but formed in a similar way. Many of these have been invaded by vegetation and some, such as Chartley Moss in Cheshire, have become completely covered by a floating layer of bog peat.

The Great Glen

Much older are the few lakes associated with geological faults. The Great Glen of Scotland is a fault which has resulted in a deep tear in the earth's crust. This has created two large lakes, Loch Lochy and Loch Ness, which are typically long, narrow and deep. Loch Ness is on average 130m deep and less than 2km wide and yet is 35km long. But even lakes of this depth would have been ice filled in the last ice-age, making the survival of Loch Ness Monsters from an earlier geological epoch highly improbable.

The largest lake in the British Isles is Lough Neagh, in Northern Ireland, covering an area of 400 square kilometres. It was formed by the subsidence of a great sheet of volcanic larva which left a shallow basin which filled with water, less than 20m deep at its deepest point.

Many of Britain's lakes are man made. Dams have been built across valleys in the wetter uplands to form reservoirs and in lowland Britain most of the larger water bodies are artificial. Some are reservoirs formed, like Grafham Water near Huntingdon, by damming a shallow valley. Others, such as the large reservoirs west of London are entirely surrounded by embankments and so are raised above the surrounding countryside. The other main artificial lakes result from the continuing demand for sand and gravel. This has given rise to numerous water filled gravel pits which in some areas, such as parts of the Thames Valley, cover a significant proportion of the land surface. In other areas, flooded claypits are abundant. The continued creation of such new lakes represents a steady increase in the amount of open water in Britain. Perhaps the most natural looking man-made lakes are the Norfolk Broads. These were formed from extensive peat cuttings in the river valleys of East Anglia which were flooded in the fourteenth century as the rising sea level caused the river waters to spill over into the peat workings, forming the extensive shallow lagoons and wetlands we see today.

Britain's rivers are also very diverse and often highly modified by man. Those that flow through the uplands are usually steep splashing torrents because mountains are formed of hard rock and retain steep slopes despite the erosive force of water over the years. Turbulent flow ensures thorough oxygenation of the water, but causes severe problems associated with avoiding being swept away. Hard rocks do not weather rapidly, so liberate few nutrients into the water; upland streams and lakes thus often have low nutrient levels compared to waters in the lowlands. Where rivers flow over softer deposits such as sand and clay, the waters are often muddy, making it difficult for animals and especially plants, to live because of silt deposition and lack of light penetration. Moreover, river banks of soft deposits are worn away easily, so rivers may be shallow and the silt they carry tends to fill up lowland lakes and ponds. Shallow water is easily warmed by the sun and will then hold less oxygen.

Wetlands: a transitional habitat

Wetland habitats are also very complex and diverse. Essentially they represent transitional zones between open water and dry land, so they have many interesting plants and animals contributed by each habitat type. In addition, certain wetlands (especially fens) have special features which support unique species. Such habitats are thus frequently rich in wildlife and of great interest; but under permanent threat of changing into another less interesting habitat type just through drying out a little more. Wetlands also share many features with habitats such as blanket bogs and water meadows described elsewhere in this book.

Lakes, Reservoirs and Ponds

Lakes, ponds and reservoirs are characterised not only by having relatively still water but also by most of the water body being open, away from the immediate influence of the banks. Water itself warms and cools only slowly, so that organisms living in it are not subject to the rapid environmental changes suffered by terrestrial plants and animals. However, the greatest single factor governing the life of lakes is a unique property of water: it is most dense at a temperature of 4°C. As the water cools in winter, it becomes more dense; but continued cooling only affects the surface layers because freezing water is less dense and floats on top of water at 4°C. Ice is even less dense (ie it takes up a greater volume of space than the water from which it is made; hence the bursting of water pipes in winter) so it forms at the surface and then helps insulate the waters below. If water were densest at 0°C, then lakes would freeze solid from the bottom up. In fact, the bottom layers stay at 4°C, providing a constant (if chilly!) environment for plants and animals over winter which could not survive freezing or the

When a pond freezes in winter birds retreat to the centre where their activity keeps a patch of open water free of ice long after the rest of the pond has frozen.

even colder air temperatures above.

The rising and sinking of water in response to changes in its temperature is not merely a feature of winter conditions; it affects deeper lakes throughout the year. Measurements of the summer water temperature at different depths in a fairly deep lake such as Windermere will show that there is a relatively shallow upper layer which is much warmer than the rest of the water lying below it. The upper warm layer is called the epilimnion and floats on the lower, cooler layer known as the hypolimnion. The region where these two layers meet is one of abrupt temperature change, and is known as the thermocline.

Stratification

The temperature phenomenon is known as stratification. It is found in most deeper lakes, especially in hot and calm summers and is caused by the heating of the upper water by the sun. At temperatures above 4°C, water becomes less dense so the upper layers of the lake continue to float on the colder hypolimnion. The warmer the surface water gets the more the density difference makes it difficult to mix the two layers of water and they remain more or less separate until later in the year, when the epilimnion has cooled and winds cause mixing of the whole water body—the "winter turnover". In some lowland water storage reservoirs special efforts may be made to stir the water to prevent stratification. At least this stops the development of a static and possibly stagnant hypolimnion.

Most of the sunlight is absorbed in the epilimnion and little reaches the hypolimnion, so the upper layer is the site of most algal growth and also of most animal plankton activity and dead plant and animal material tends to sink down into the hypolimnion. Because there is little mixing across the thermocline there is only a limited oxygen supply to the decomposition organisms of the hypolimnion, and as the summer progresses all the oxygen in the lower layers may sometimes be used up. This is especially true in productive lakes and in

A fine show of macrophytes (big aquatic plants) in a New Forest pond in late summer. Water lilies, yellow flags and bur-reed are prominent, but the comparatively invisible algae are the most important source of plant food.

The grass snake feeds mainly on frogs and newts, so it is a common wetland animal. It is also fully capable of swimming and searching for its prey in the water.

shallow lakes where the volume of the hypolimnion is small and where there is a plentiful supply of detritus. One effect of these anaerobic conditions is to cause the release of minerals trapped in the organic muds on the lake floor, but it is only on mixing, or turnover, later in the year that the minerals in the hypolimnion are made generally available again to the whole water body.

Light can only penetrate a few metres at most into lake water, and so photosynthesis can only take place in the surface layers, known as the photic zone. Thus except in small ponds or shallow lakes with extensive rooted vegetation growing on the bottom, most of the primary production takes place in the open water. The plants of the photic zone are suspended in the water, floating freely with the water currents, and are known as the phytoplankton. They consist of green algae, blue-green algae and diatoms.

Algal growth is very uneven over the year. As the water warms and the days become longer in the spring there is often a rapid and spectacular burst of growth (known as "blooms"), often of a few or only one species, such as the diatom

The ecosystem of ponds and lakes

Water chemistry is all-important in this ecosystem. Where the water has come from hard upland rocks and nutrient-deficient soils, a lake will have clear water which supports a low density of algae and animal life. Where sediment and nutrients enrich the water (sometimes excessively when agricultural fertilisers are washed off the land) a greater density and diversity of organisms develops.

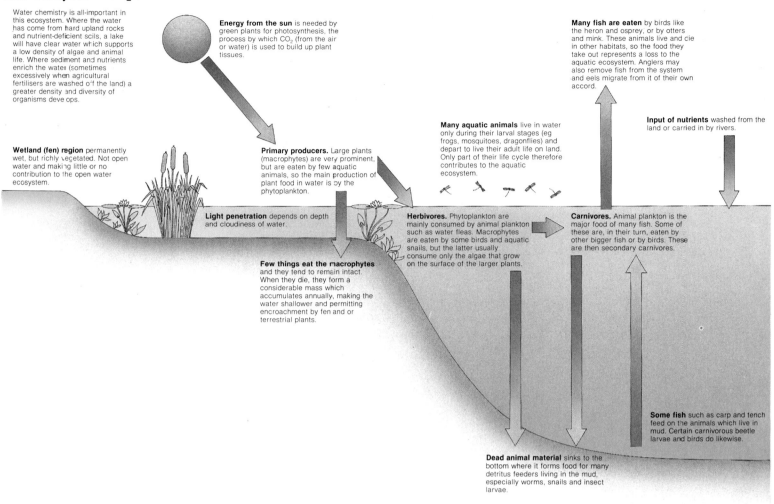

Energy from the sun is needed by green plants for photosynthesis, the process by which CO_2 (from the air or water) is used to build up plant tissues.

Many fish are eaten by birds like the heron and osprey, or by otters and mink. These animals live and die in other habitats, so the food they take out represents a loss to the aquatic ecosystem. Anglers may also remove fish from the system and eels migrate from it of their own accord.

Many aquatic animals live in water only during their larval stages (eg frogs, mosquitoes, dragonflies) and depart to live their adult life on land. Only part of their life cycle therefore contributes to the aquatic ecosystem.

Input of nutrients washed from the land or carried in by rivers.

Wetland (fen) region permanently wet, but richly vegetated. Not open water and making little or no contribution to the open water ecosystem.

Primary producers. Large plants (macrophytes) are very prominent, but are eaten by few aquatic animals, so the main production of plant food in water is by the phytoplankton.

Light penetration depends on depth and cloudiness of water.

Herbivores. Phytoplankton are mainly consumed by animal plankton such as water fleas. Macrophytes are eaten by some birds and aquatic snails, but the latter usually consume only the algae that grow on the surface of the larger plants.

Carnivores. Animal plankton is the major food of many fish. Some of these are, in their turn, eaten by other bigger fish or by birds. These are then secondary carnivores.

Few things eat the macrophytes and they tend to remain intact. When they die, they form a considerable mass which accumulates annually, making the water shallower and permitting encroachment by fen and or terrestrial plants.

Some fish such as carp and tench feed on the animals which live in mud. Certain carnivorous beetle larvae and birds do likewise.

Dead animal material sinks to the bottom where it forms food for many detritus feeders living in the mud, especially worms, snails and insect larvae.

Asterionella. This peak of growth may last a few weeks and is followed by a rapid decline. In the case of diatoms, which have silica in their shells, this decline is partly brought about by the depletion of silicates in the water as it is incorporated into the diatom cells. When they die many of the diatoms sink to the bottom layers of water where the silicates and other minerals will effectively remain trapped until the winter turnover. Other species of algae may form later blooms so that there is often a succession through the year, with green and blue-green algae usually occurring after the diatoms. However, these later blooms are not so large as that in the spring and these too decline as essential nutrients such as nitrogen and phosphorus are used up. If autumn storms occur early enough to mix the lake waters and redistribute the minerals from the hypolimnion whilst the days are long enough to allow algal growth, there may be another peak of growth in the autumn, but this is not usually as great as that in the spring.

Copepods and cladocera

In the open water phytoplankton is grazed by small invertebrate animals of the zooplankton. Many of these are members of the Crustacea, such as copepods and cladocera (water fleas). Many of these are filter feeders and may be quite specific as to the size of food particles they can take in. Most of them tend to feed only on the smaller algae, bacteria and tiny particles of detritus. The larger algal cells, such as many of the diatoms, are less intensively grazed, although rotifers and protozoans may take some. Peak numbers of algae tend to be followed by those of the zooplankton but the latter are normally more spread out in time. Some of the zooplankton species are carnivores, but most of the predation on the zooplankton is by fish.

Much of the dead plant and animal remains will fall as detritus to the lake floor where it forms the food source for the bottom dwelling organisms, collectively known as the benthos. Many of these are burrowing animals, such as oligochaete worms, chironomid fly larvae, and

molluscs such as the pea-mussel. Some of the benthos are carnivores, but most are scavengers which have the vital effect of breaking down detritus and, with the help of micro-organisms, release minerals back into the water to supply nutrients for the next phytoplankton bloom.

Measurements of how far light can penetrate the water of different lakes reveal enormous differences between them, from the clear waters of many highland lochs (except where the water is stained with peat) to the murky waters of shallow productive lakes such as Loch Leven. The main lakes of the Lake District form a distinct series from the clear waters of Wastwater to those of Windermere and Esthwaite Water in which light penetration is rather limited. The absorption of light by lake water is partly because of the algae and other organisms present, as well as suspended solid material and coloured substances in solution. Thus the most transparent waters are those of low fertility and are usually those with only low concentrations of mineral nutrients. Such waters are known as oligotrophic, (meaning "little food"), as distinct from eutrophic waters which are mineral rich and fertile. Oligotrophic lakes are characteristic of parts of Britain where geologically older rocks predominate (ie the uplands, the north and west). Such rocks are harder and thus do not dissolve away and release nutrients into the water. Such lakes are thus chemically barren and support fewer species of plants and animals as well as a lessened density of both. In the Lake District the oligotrophic lakes such as Wastwater and Buttermere receive their water as drainage mainly off rocky mountainsides with little farming or housing in the catchments, whilst the more eutrophic lakes such as Esthwaite Water receive much of their water as drainage from richer agricultural soils.

Such differences in lake fertility have not always existed. Cores taken from the sediments on the lake beds have revealed that soon after they were formed the waters of the lakes were rich with minerals washed out of the freshly exposed rocks of the surrounding areas. As time

passed this source of minerals was exhausted and the lakes became oligotrophic. But over the last two centuries there has been a marked increase in the richness of what are now more eutrophic lakes. They show an increase in organisms characteristic of rich waters, such as the diatoms *Asterionella* and *Fragilaria*. The reasons for this increase in nutrient richness are probably related to human activities, especially to the expansion of agriculture. Recently the use of inorganic fertilisers on farms in the lake catchments, has lead especially to nitrates being washed off the land into the lakes.

Human influences

This process of enrichment is a common feature of lakes which are influenced by human activity. In some lowland lakes the results have been unfortunate because the increased productivity often leads to extensive algal blooms, which may block filters in reservoirs. Normally oxygen is produced as a useful by-product of photosynthesis, so excessive algal blooms might not be considered harmful. However, photosynthesis only takes place in the light; during the night these algal cells actually *consume* oxygen, and thus compete with fish and other animals for this essential of life. Heavily eutrophic lakes are therefore threatened by their own successful productivity and are liable to suffocation, especially in late summer because warm water will hold less dissolved oxygen than normal, making the problems still worse. When the algae die their decay may exhaust the oxygen in the water, leading in some cases to fish deaths and unpleasant smells.

Such conditions are of concern not only to the water engineer and the biologist, but also to the many different groups of people who use lakes for recreation. Water has always had an attraction for man and is now used by groups as diverse as anglers and swimmers, sailors and water-skiers and also by those who simply sit by the lakeside and watch. Reconciling the differing demands of such people with wildlife conservation is an ever increasing problem.

Water Margins and Wetlands

The banks of rivers and the shores of lakes are good examples of ecotones, habitats which form the boundary between two others and which show special characteristics as a result of the two sets of sometimes conflicting environmental factors. The overriding feature of water margins is the gradient in wetness from the water itself to the dry land, and the positions of the plant species growing on the bank will reflect this. Although most river and lake shores are usually damp, the tops of banks built up above the surrounding land may in the summer be very dry places indeed.

Many of the plants on the upper parts of the banks will also be those of the surrounding land, but lower down many of the species will be those characteristic of damp meadows. Closer to the water's edge grow many plants typical of very damp places, and where the river water is reasonably rich in calcium, a specialised fenland community develops. The water level may often vary in streams and rivers and even in lakes, so that the plants of the lower bank must be able to tolerate periods of flooding. In particular they must be able to withstand low levels of oxygen in the soil around their roots when they are inundated with water.

In still, shallow water, extensive areas of fringing vegetation develop forming a complete gradation from truly aquatic plants to those of fens or wet meadows. The most conspicuous plants are the reeds and sedges and indeed the fringing community is often loosely termed a "reedbed", due to the dominance of the common reed *(Phragmites communis)* in this type of habitat. This can grow in water up to a metre deep, or on almost dry land.

The common reed is a particularly important plant of wetlands and water margins. It dies back during the winter so that reedbeds turn yellow in the autumn and fresh green growth grows up among the old stems the following spring. This leads at first to a mixture of yellows and greens in the reedbed, which becomes entirely green as the summer progresses, dotted with the feathery purple flower heads. Sedges and rushes remain green throughout the year and are thus conspicuously different from the dead winter reeds. Neither normally grows more than a metre tall, half the height of some reeds. Some reedbeds are very extensive and form a habitat in their own right providing a home for a great variety of animals, especially insects, and birds. Reeds provide protection and shelter for birds like the reed warbler, which build their nests up in the stems, and also for those that build floating nests or nests near water level, such as the great crested grebe and mute swan. Hollow reed stems provide a shelter for over-wintering insects, and the tall plants offer convenient perches for dragonflies in summer. In some lakes the reedbeds may be important in taking up mineral nutrients washed off the surrounding land. This reduces the amounts reaching the open water, at least until the reeds die back in winter, and so reduces the chance of dense algal blooms occurring.

In fast flowing rivers and streams the zonation or sequence of plants from the submerged species of the deep water through to the emergents of the shallows and the bank flora is often fairly static. The water speed prevents a significant build up of mud or silt and so a change in the types of plants, but where the water is slow flowing or still, the accumulation of silt and plant remains leads to a steady shallowing of the water. The gradual build-up of mud and dead plants slowly creates dry (or at least marshy) land where once there was open water. The drier conditions then offer an opportunity for invasion by land plants and by trees (eg willows and alder) which can tolerate wetland conditions. These in turn contribute to the build-up of humus, allowing yet more new plants to become established.

Succession: from water to dry land

This general process of change of communities in time is called succession, and the specific succession from open water to some sort of terrestrial community is known as the hydrosere. In more detail, this is what happens: in the deepest waters that receive enough light at the bottom for plant growth the plants present are those which can grow completely submerged. As silting up occurs the water will eventually become shallow enough, about 2 to 3m, to allow rooted plants with floating leaves, such as water lilies, to grow in places sheltered from wave action. Further accumulation will raise the bottom closer to the surface until the water is shallow enough to allow emergent plants to grow, plants rooted on the bottom but with at

River banks

The nature of a river bank will be determined not only by the type of soil from which it is formed but also by the speed of the river. Rivers will cut deeply into sands and gravels and will frequently erode away their banks, especially on the outsides of bends. Sometimes this forms steep 'cliffs' of bare soil, ideal for the nest burrows of kingfishers, but unsuitable for most plants. Unstable eroded banks will support much less life than those of more gently flowing rivers. Highland streams and rivers are subject to sudden and severe spates after heavy rain, which will not only erode the banks but will often wash away most of the vegetation, even that growing at some considerable height above the normal water level. Banks can be eroded and vegetation damaged through other causes. Cattle trample and puddle the banks where they have access to the water and anglers may flatten the taller patches of vegetation in order to avoid entangling their lines. The wash from rivers used by power boats, if these are travelling at speed, has a considerable effect.

For burrowing animals, such as the water vole and the water shrew, the river bank affords shelter and protection. Animals that build nests in the open, however, are more likely to find protection amongst the emergent vegetation.

Not only is the water shallower close to the banks, but the current will also be less swift there, because of the drag caused by the banks. Emergent plants will themselves further slow down the water, but in all but shallow and wide rivers the band of emergent vegetation will be fairly narrow, especially if the river deepens sharply away from the bank. Most of the common reedswamp plants, such as *Phragmites*, *Typha* and *Sparganium erectum*, may be present, usually as separate clumps formed by the spread of underground stems. Other tall grasses frequently occur, especially the reedsweet grass *(Glyceria maxima)* and the reed canary grass *(Phalaris arundinacea)*. During the summer colour may be added by such species as the yellow flag *(Iris pseudacorus)*, growing with long sword-like leaves close to the water's edge, and the flowering rush *(Butomus umbellatus)*. This is, in fact, not a rush at all, and bears three-petalled pink flowers between July and September. It occurs mainly in central and southern England and at scattered sites in Ireland.

On the bank itself the flora may be quite diverse. Not only will there be a great variety of damp meadow and water meadow plants, especially broad-leaved species, but also some narrow-leaved, Monocotyledon, species. For example, creeping bent-grass *(Agrostis stolonifera)* is a common pasture grass which is frequently found growing on river banks, sometimes even submerged. On poor soils or at the edges of slightly acid waters the soft rush *(Juncus effusus)* may often be found, but in richer conditions it is often replaced by the hard rush *(J. inflexus)*. On the lower bank, species of sedge may grow, such as the lesser pond sedge *(Carex acutiformis)* which is common, especially in lowland England on rich soils.

least some of their leaves held up through the water into the air. This stage in the succession, which is often represented by reedbeds, is known as reedswamp. The plants of the reedswamp will still further slow down the water, enhancing the deposition of silt, and will themselves be adding dead leaves, stems and roots to the silt, which thus becomes more organic.

In time the organic silts reach a level close to that of the water surface, often above it in summer but flooded in winter. Although some reedswamp plants may still be present they are gradually replaced by other species typical of less flooded conditions, giving rise to a fen community discussed later. The fen may be colonised by trees such as willows or alder, to give fen carr, or if the mineral supply has been reduced, be eventually invaded by the bog-moss, *Sphagrum*, to form a bog. Silting is now much less important and most of the accumulating soil is formed from dead plant remains which remain more or less undecayed in the waterlogged conditions, forming peat.

The various stages in succession form clearly marked vegetational zones at any one point in time. Over a long period, these zones gradually extend outward from the dry land to encroach on open water unless prevented by wave action or water flow. Shallow, static waters, particularly small ponds, thus tend to be transient in the long term; gradually strangled out of existence by the very life they support. Hence the need for conservationists to dredge ponds and slow moving waters if their biological interest as fresh

The feathery mauve flower heads of *Phragmites* are a characteristic sight in summer, while in autumn they give way to the fluffy seed masses. Reedbeds provide a habitat for a wide variety of animals and birds, among them the great crested grebe. The stems, when dead and hollow, are used by over-wintering insects for hibernation.

Wetland and Freshwater Flora

The large plants that grow in fresh water are collectively known as macrophytes. Most of the obvious representatives of this group are large, such as the water-lilies, pondweeds and reeds, but there are also many smaller species, like the diminutive duckweed relative *Wolffia arrhiza*, a free-floating flowering plant without roots which has an oval body or thallus that rarely exceeds a diameter of 1mm. Macrophytes also include non-flowering plants like the quillwort (*Isoetes lacustris*), a submerged fern ally, and bryophytes, especially liverworts. Despite often being large and prominent, these macrophyte species usually make only a slight contribution to the aquatic food-web because so few animals eat them in any quantity. It is the tiny, free-swimming, drifting or sedentary algae that are the basis of the freshwater ecosystem, and it is upon them that the aquatic food-web depends. The macrophytes, however, are important as they play a major role in modifying the habitat, as well as providing food and shelter for a myriad of animals and small plants that would be unable to survive the conditions in open water.

It should be stressed that macrophytes are a special feature of still and shallow water and the richest selection of species is usually found in clear shallow ponds. The species that are rooted to the bottom can grow in both still and flowing

The submerged leaves of *Ranunculus aquatalis*, a water crowfoot, have a finely dissected form, in contrast to the leaves floating on the surface which are circular but deeply cut. Intermediate varieties between these two forms are, however, common. The species can often be found growing in abundance locally.

A guide to some aquatic plants

Water plants can be conveniently categorised into free-floating, like duckweed; submerged (and usually rooted), like Canadian pondweed; and rooted, with floating or aerial leaves like the water lilies and bog bean: the distinction between this last group and reedswamp plants is not clear cut. Those like the water lilies are adapted for growth in still water and produce showy flowers with many seeds. However, many water plants flower and set seed irregularly and rely mainly on vegetative reproduction for survival and spread: they are nearly all perennial.

In still or very slow flowing water free-floating plants like duckweed or rooted plants with large, floating leaves like water lilies occur, whilst in moving water only plants with long, thin submerged stems and leaves which bend and sway with the current are found. Some species, like the water crowfoot, have different morphological forms so that they can survive in still or flowing water.

Reedmace Typhaceae *Typha latifolia* **Distribution:** Throughout the British Isles, but becoming rarer and eventually absent in north-western Scotland. **Notes:** Reed-swamps, where it is often abundant and dominant; lakes, ponds, canals and slow flowing rivers.

Branched Bur-reed Sparganiaceae *Sparganium erectum* **Distribution:** Throughout the British Isles, but rare in north-western Scotland. **Notes:** On mud, shallow water in ponds, ditches, slow flowing rivers and ungrazed marshland; common; variable.

Water Lobelia Lobeliaceae *Lobelia dortmanna* **Distribution:** Lake District; throughout Wales, especially the north; Scotland, especially the north and west; Ireland, especially the north and west. **Notes:** In stony lakes and tarns with acid water; locally common.

Bog Bean Menyanthaceae *Menyanthes trifoliata* **Distribution:** Throughout the British Isles, but more common in the west. **Notes:** In ponds, lake margins and the wetter parts of bogs and fens; grows up to 1000 metres; occasionally locally dominant in shallow water.

Frog-bit Hydrocharitaceae *Hydrocharis morsus-ranae* **Distribution:** Throughout England and central Ireland; rarely in southern Wales. **Notes:** Floating in ponds and ditches; usually in calcareous districts; locally common; in dry seasons has a land form.

Water Plantain Alismataceae *Alisma plantago-aquatica* **Distribution:** Throughout the British Isles, but less common in central and northern Scotland. **Notes:** On muddy soil by slow flowing rivers, ponds, ditches and canals; in damp ground or shallow water.

Mare's Tail

Water Lobelia

Bog Bean

Water Plantain

Frog-bit

Reedmace   Branched Bur-reed

water as they are anchored securely enough to withstand the current. In contrast, the free-floating species can only survive in still water where they cannot be swept away, or in slow-flowing water where they are lodged (usually between other rooted plants). Invariably this is a precarious existence as there is always the possibility of being dislodged and swept away by the current, especially when the river or stream is in flood.

Both the depth and clarity of the water are crucial factors in determining macrophyte growth. The bottom-rooted plants that grow in both still and moving water are limited by the available light: they are unable to grow in deeper water as light penetration is inadequate for photosynthesis, and in deep lakes these species are limited to a narrow fringe around the shore. On the other hand, the free-floating species can grow in both shallow or deep water, though in the latter only when it is still; when lodged between other (bottom-rooted) plants in moving water they are restricted to the shallow regions where these rooted species are able to grow. The bottom-rooted species also have the advantage that they can take in the nutrients that they require from the substrate in which they are growing; often this is mineral-rich whereas the water in which they are growing has only a low mineral content.

The bog bean (*Menyanthes trifoliata*) grows in water up to about a metre deep, but its leaves and flowers are held clear of the water surface.

This restricts the growth of the free-floating species as they are dependent on absorbing their nutritional requirements directly from the water in which they are growing. However, many of the free-floating plants are able to absorb their mineral requirements not only by means of roots (if they have them), but also through all of their surfaces. The bottom-rooted species take in nearly all of their requirements by means of their roots and little or none through their other surfaces. The problem of sufficient light affects both free-floating and bottom-rooted plants. In water where there are solids, such as mud or silt, held in suspension, or where dissolved substances colour the water (as in the run-off from peat), light cannot easily penetrate; consequently the plants cannot grow at the depths they would be able to if the water was clear.

Herein lies a fascinating mechanism by which microscopic planktonic plant algae (the phytoplankton) can suppress the growth of, and in certain circumstances even kill, large plants many thousands of times larger than themselves. In the spring the sudden surge of phytoplankton growth often gives rise to a "bloom" or very dense population of algae that completely permeates the water. When early and very dense it can in fact stop the growth of the macrophytes in deeper water as it impedes the penetration of light. Usually, how-

Mare's Tail Hippuridaceae
Hippuris vulgaris. **Distribution:** Scattered throughout the British Isles. **Notes:** In lakes, ponds and slow flowing streams; grows up to 580 metres; prefers base-rich water; locally common.

Water Soldier Hydrocharitaceae
Stratiotes aloides. **Distribution:** Scattered in northern and central-southern England, East Anglia, south-western Scotland and a few places in Ireland. **Notes:** Broads, ponds and ditches in calcareous districts; very local; northern plants female; southern plants mainly male.

Floating Bur-reed Sparganiaceae
Sparganium angustifolium. **Distribution:** West of Britain and throughout Ireland. **Notes:** Peaty lakes; mainly mountainous districts.

Shoreweed Plantaginaceae
Littorella uniflora. **Distribution:** Throughout the British Isles, but more common in the north and west. **Notes:** In shallow or deep water, or just exposed on sandy and gravelly shores of non-calcareous ponds and lakes; often forms an extensive turf in shallow water.

Hornwort Ceratophyllaceae
Ceratophyllum submersum. **Distribution:** Scattered throughout central and southern England, rarely in the north. **Notes:** Ponds and ditches; very local.

Spiked Water Milfoil Haloragaceae
Myriophyllum spicatum. **Distribution:** Throughout the British Isles, more common in the south and east. **Notes:** In lakes, ponds and ditches; grows up to 500 metres; locally common, especially in calcareous water.

Lesser Duckweed Lemnaceae
Lemna minor. **Distribution:** Throughout the British Isles, but rare in the north. **Notes:** Floating, often forming a green carpet, in all still water; only flowers in ditches exposed to the sun.

White Water Lily Nymphaeaceae
Nymphaea alba. **Distribution:** Throughout the British Isles, but rare in south-eastern Ireland. **Notes:** Lakes and ponds; grows up to 350 metres; variable in size.

Arrow Head Alismataceae
Sagittaria sagittifolia. **Distribution:** Throughout England, except the very north; scattered in eastern Ireland, Wales and southern Scotland. **Notes:** Shallow water in ponds, canals and slow flowing rivers; on muddy soils, locally common.

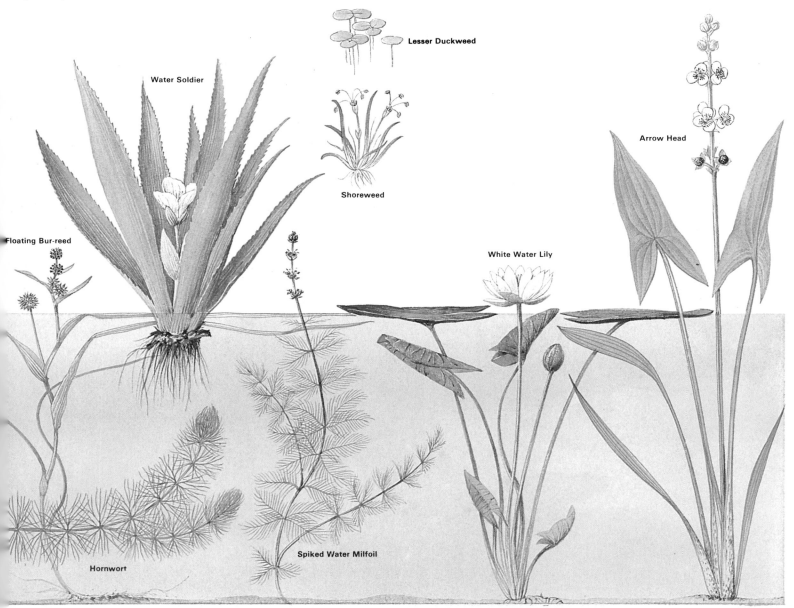

Lesser Duckweed

Water Soldier

Shoreweed

Arrow Head

Floating Bur-reed

White Water Lily

Hornwort

Spiked Water Milfoil

order to obtain the highest economic yield. In a situation where a pond or small lake has no outlet, but relies upon evaporation and ground seepage to remove water, the macrophytes can, under certain conditions, be threatened and even exterminated. Where there is an excess of decaying organic material (fertiliser, raw sewage, plant remains, etc.), and especially where light levels are low (usually due to shading by trees), the level of oxygen dissolved in the water, which is necessary for respiration, can be minimal. Under these conditions microscopic anaerobic organisms, mainly bacteria, saprophytic phytoplankton and blue-green algae, become established and they produce substances that inhibit the growth of the ordinary phytoplankton and the macrophytes. This means that even those plants with floating or emergent leaves which are able to utilise and absorb atmospheric gaseous oxygen, as well as the submerged plants that are dependent upon dissolved oxygen in the water, are unable to grow. They will then usually rapidly sicken and die, leaving the water in a stagnant condition.

Different aquatic species are able to grow at differing intensities of light and there is thus a zonation of species. This zonation is most marked around the margin of a lake or pond because further from the shore, in the areas of deep water, the free-floating plants predominate. These may be like the duckweeds (*Lemna*) or the tiny water fern (*Azolla*) that have their leaves spread out and floating on the surface. This ensures that they get all of the light that they need but is often detrimental to the rest of the ecosystem, as they cast such heavy shade and blot out most of the light from the plants and animals living below. This inhibits phytoplankton growth and consequently the food-web dependent upon it, and duckweed-smothered ponds are often stagnant and more or less lifeless. These floating macrophytes are not used as food by many other organisms (especially affected are the small animal plankton or zooplankton species that only feed on phytoplankton), so do not represent a fair exchange for the algal species that they suppress. Some other species of free-floating plants grow with submerged leaves and stems in a zone just beneath the water surface, to a depth of

In certain areas orange water in ditches and ponds may be caused by rusting tins but more often by bacteria oxidising iron salts dissolved by rain from surrounding soils.

A guide to some wetland wild flowers

At the margins of lakes, ponds and ditches a transition zone between open water and dry land is often found. This may be entirely colonised by tall reed-swamp plants whose intensely competitive character ensures a very limited variety of species. Alternatively, a broad spectrum of wetland flowering plants may grow.

Many of these, like the yellow flag iris and kingcup, have large attractive flowers. Several, including the lesser spearwort and water forget-me-not are perennial, spreading both vegetatively and by seed, whereas others like the wild balsam are annual and depend on seed for survival. In this latter species dispersal of seed is very specialised: when ripe

the walls of the seed capsule are strongly tensioned, and will explode at the slightest touch, ejecting the seeds about two metres. Two types of flower are produced; one that remains as a bud and pollinates itself and another that opens and allows insect pollination.

Creeping Yellow Cress Cruciferae *Rorippa sylvestris.* **Distribution:** Scattered throughout England, southern Scotland, Wales and southern, central and eastern Ireland; more common in the east. **Other habitats:** A garden weed. **Notes:** Moist ground by streams and brooks, and areas with standing water only in winter; frequent, but not common.

Lesser Spearwort Ranunculaceae *Ranunculus flammula.* **Distribution:** Throughout the British Isles. **Notes:** Common in all wet places; a variable species divided into three subspecies.

Kingcup, Marsh Marigold Ranunculaceae *Caltha palustris.* **Distribution:** Throughout the British Isles; less common towards the south in Ireland. **Notes:** In marshes, fens, ditches and wet woodland; grows well in partial shade; rare on base-poor peat; grows up to 1200 metres; very variable; can be creeping or erect.

Great Water Dock Polygonaceae *Rumex hydrolapathum.* **Distribution:** Throughout central and southern England, scattered in Wales, southern and central Scotland, Ireland and south-western England. **Notes:** Wet soils and shallow water; the leaf margin can be flat or undulate; frequent, but not common.

Water Forget-me-not Boraginaceae *Myosotis scorpioides.* **Distribution:** Throughout Britain, but less common in central and northern Scotland. **Notes:** Usually by streams and ponds; common.

Water Betony Scrophulariaceae *Scrophularia aquatica.* **Distribution:** England, but less common in the north; scattered in Wales and Ireland and a few localities in south-eastern Scotland. **Notes:** Edges of ponds and streams, in wet woodland and meadows; common; petioles and stems are winged; usually visited by wasps.

Water Mint Labiatae *Mentha aquatica.* **Distribution:** Throughout the British Isles, but less common in central and northern Scotland. **Notes:** Swamps, marshes, fens, wet woodland and by rivers and ponds; found up to 500 metres; a common and variable species.

Brooklime Scrophulariaceae *Veronica beccabunga.* **Distribution:** Throughout the British Isles, but less common in northern and western Scotland. **Notes:** In streams, ponds, marshes and water meadows; common.

several metres.

The assemblages of higher plants growing in still water are determined not only by water depth and light penetration, but also by the type of lake bottom (stones, silt or organic matter) and especially by the chemistry of the water. In fact the two main factors that affect all aquatic vegetation are the presence or absence of sufficient dissolved oxygen and the deficiency or adequacy of mineral nutrients in solution, which are usually derived from silt. Floating vegetation that is not rooted on the bottom is dependent on the water for all or nearly all of its requirements and any deficiencies may result in a scanty growth or even none at all. Where many macrophytes have become established their photosynthesis provides sufficient oxygen for all the plants and animals of the habitat, but in areas where there are few plants, adequate oxygenation of the water depends upon solution of the gas from the air by

The hemlock water dropwort Oenanthe crocata (right) is one of the most poisonous British plants. It grows in damp places, but can also be found in shallow water.

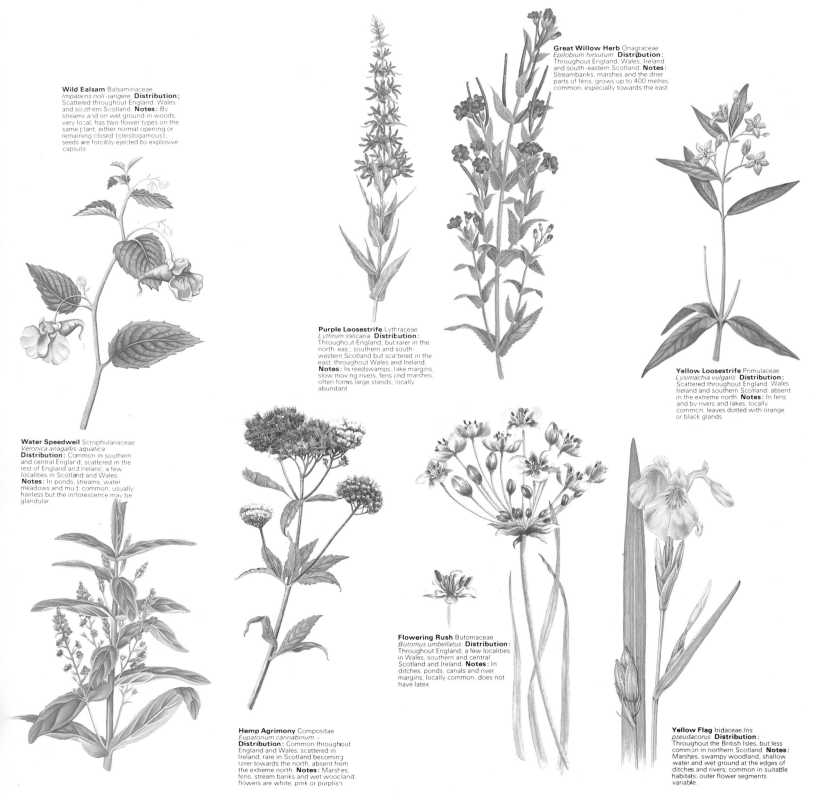

Wild Balsam Balsaminaceae *Impatiens noli-tangere*. **Distribution:** Scattered throughout England, Wales and southern Scotland. **Notes:** By streams and on wet ground in woods; very local; has two flower types on the same plant, either normal opening or remaining closed (cleistogamous); seeds are forcibly ejected by explosive capsule.

Great Willow Herb Onagraceae *Epilobium hirsutum*. **Distribution:** Throughout England, Wales, Ireland and south-eastern Scotland. **Notes:** Streambanks, marshes and the drier parts of fens; grows up to 400 metres; common, especially towards the east.

Purple Loosestrife Lythraceae *Lythrum salicaria*. **Distribution:** Throughout England, but rarer in the north-east; southern and south-western Scotland but scattered in the east; throughout Wales and Ireland. **Notes:** In reedswamps, lake margins, slow moving rivers, fens and marshes; often forms large stands; locally abundant.

Yellow Loosestrife Primulaceae *Lysimachia vulgaris*. **Distribution:** Scattered throughout England, Wales, Ireland and southern Scotland; absent in the extreme north. **Notes:** In fens and by rivers and lakes; locally common; leaves dotted with orange or black glands.

Water Speedwell Scrophulariaceae *Veronica anagallis-aquatica*. **Distribution:** Common in southern and central England; scattered in the rest of England and Ireland; a few localities in Scotland and Wales. **Notes:** In ponds, streams, water meadows and mud; common; usually hairless but the inflorescence may be glandular.

Flowering Rush Butomaceae *Butomus umbellatus*. **Distribution:** Throughout England; a few localities in Wales, southern and central Scotland and Ireland. **Notes:** In ditches, ponds, canals and river margins; locally common; does not have latex.

Hemp Agrimony Compositae *Eupatorium cannabinum*. **Distribution:** Common throughout England and Wales; scattered in Ireland; rare in Scotland becoming rarer towards the north, absent from the extreme north. **Notes:** Marshes, fens, stream banks and wet woodland; flowers are white, pink or purplish.

Yellow Flag Iridaceae *Iris pseudacorus*. **Distribution:** Throughout the British Isles, but less common in northern Scotland. **Notes:** Marshes, swampy woodland, shallow water and wet ground at the edges of ditches and rivers; common in suitable habitats; outer flower segments variable.

223

to these will be plants usually only found in still waters, such as the water violet *(Hottonia palustris)* a member of the primrose family with lilac and yellow flowers, and also the carnivorous bladder-wort. Lowland ponds on mineral-rich substrates, especially those collecting the run-off from agricultural land, often rapidly become choked with vegetation unless they are constantly cleared out.

Where the water is not too deep and the shore is not too exposed to wave action, plants with floating leaves may occur. The two most conspicuous species are the yellow and white water lilies; the former *(Nuphar lutea)* being less common in Scotland but more generally distri-buted in England than the white *(Nymphaea alba)*. These are not the only native water lilies in Britain; the least water lily *(Nuphar pumila)* has a yellow flower and grows at scattered sites in Scotland and Shropshire, and the fringed water

The pale archegonia (right), the female reproductive organs of the liverwort *Marchantia polymorpha*, lie beneath the canopy of the erect umbrella-like reproductive stems.

A guide to some wetland grasses, sedges and rushes

Saw Sedge Cyperaceae *Cladium mariscus* **Distribution**: Scattered throughout the British Isles, but common only in Norfolk. **Notes**: Forms dense, pure stands in reed-swamp and fenland, usually on neutral or basic soil.

Common Cotton Grass Cyperaceae *Eriophorum angustifolium* **Distribution**: Throughout the British Isles, but less common in the Midlands. **Notes**: Prefers very wet and acid conditions, grows best in water; does not survive in drained areas.

Bulrush Cyperaceae *Scirpus lacustris* (or genus *Schoenoplectus*). **Distribution**: Throughout the British Isles, but less common in Wales. **Notes**: In rivers, lakes and ponds, grows in very silty conditions.

Bulbous Rush Juncaceae *Juncus bulbosus* **Distribution**: Throughout the British Isles. **Other habitats**: Woodland. **Notes**: Always on acid soils; variable species; grows in or out of water.

Soft Rush Juncaceae *Juncus effusus* **Distribution**: Throughout the British Isles. **Notes**: Often the dominant species in wet pastures, bogs and wet woodland; especially common on acid soil; stem feels smooth; spathe above inflorescence long.

Blunt-flowered Rush Juncaceae *Juncus subnodulosus* **Distribution**: Throughout England, but only common in the east; occasional in Wales and southern Scotland; frequent in west and central Ireland. **Notes**: Fens, marshes and dune-slacks with ground water; usually on calcareous peat.

Black Bog Rush Cyperaceae *Schoenus nigricans* **Distribution**: Throughout the British Isles, but widespread in west Scotland, west Ireland and East Anglia. **Other habitats**: Salt marsh. **Notes**: On damp and usually peaty base rich soils; especially common near the sea.

Lesser Pond Sedge Cyperaceae *Carex acutiformis* **Distribution**: Throughout England and central Ireland, but less common in Wales, Scotland and south-west England. **Notes**: Locally abundant, often forming dense stands; on peaty or clayey base rich soil, growing by the side of rather than in water.

Carnation Sedge Cyperaceae *Carex panicea* **Distribution**: Throughout the British Isles. **Other habitats**: Mountain grassland; heathland. **Notes**: Acid soils; most common on areas receiving continuous irrigation.

Reedsweet Grass Gramineae (Poaceae) *Glyceria maxima* **Distribution**: Throughout the British Isles, but rare in south-west England, Wales and northern Scotland. **Notes**: On the banks of running water and in still water; forms large, pure stands in suitable habitats; a useful fodder grass.

Greater Tussock Sedge Cyperaceae *Carex paniculata* **Distribution**: Throughout the British Isles, but infrequent in Scotland. **Notes**: In fens and slow flowing water; prefers peaty, base rich soil where the water level is seasonally high; can withstand some shading; forms very dense tussocks.

White Beaked Sedge Cyperaceae *Rhynchospora alba* **Distribution**: Scattered throughout the British Isles; mainly in western Scotland, west, central and northern Ireland. **Notes**: Wet and usually peaty, acid soils; locally common.

Common Reed Gramineae (Poaceae) *Phragmites communis* **Distribution**: Throughout the British Isles. **Notes**: Very wet areas, usually growing in water; often covering large areas of swamp and fen; especially common in the lowlands. This is the tallest British grass and is often used for thatching.

Saw Sedge · Common Cotton Grass · Bulrush · Bulbous Rush · Soft Rush · Blunt-flowered Rush · Black Bog Rush · Lesser Pond Sedge · Carnation Sedge · Reedsweet Grass · Greater Tussock Sedge · Common Reed · White Beaked Sedge

lily *(Nymphoides peltata)* has rounded but slightly notched leaves 3 to 10cm across, small yellow flowers and is largely confined to the fens of East Anglia and parts of the Thames Valley. As well as pondweeds such as *Potamogeton lucens* and *P. natans* there may be present members of one of the most interesting groups of floating leaved and emergent plants of still or very slow water, the Alismataceae, the water plantain family, the most widespread of which is the water plantain *(Alisma plantago-aquatica)*. However, not all of the species found are flowering plants; the liverworts *Riccia fluitans, Ricciocarpus natans* and species of *Hypnum* may occur. The first two have differing growth forms, depending on whether they are growing on land or floating on the surface of the water. On land they have rhizoids that penetrate the mud at the water's edge, whereas when floating they have none, but instead have long pendulous scales that hang beneath the plant improving its stability as well as increasing the area available for both absorption and photosynthesis.

Free-floating plants tend to be found only on sheltered waters protected from wave action, and this means that they are often found amongst the emergent plants of the reedswamp. Only the extraordinary water soldier *(Stratiotes)* with its variable buoyancy is of any size, and this is con-

fined as a native plant to East Anglia and the Vale of Trent, although it has been introduced elsewhere. The most common free-floating plants are the duckweeds *(Lemna)* comprising small pale green leaf-discs with one or more (depending on the species) roots dangling in the water.

Where the water is reasonably shallow and where the shore is protected from wave action on large lakes, the predominant plants are emergent species forming a reedswamp. This may contain a variety of species of the lower river bank or of the fen, and indeed blends imperceptibly with the latter habitat; but in many places large areas of reedswamp may be composed of only one plant species. Such reedswamps in fact form some of the most extensive single-species stands of vegetation to be seen in Britain. In upland tarns one of the most common reedswamp plants is *Carex rostrata*, growing in waters to a depth of about 50cm, but in richer waters the most emergent plant is *Phragmites*, capable of growing in depths of up to 2m in places. The reedmace *(Typha latifolia)* also often forms extensive beds in reasonably rich waters in most of lowland Britain and is wrongly often referred to as a bulrush.

Many of the emergent plants have two distinct morphological forms. In one their leaves are adapted for the aerial habitat and in the other they are adapted for the submerged. The two

Catkins, the fluffy male flowers of the pussy willow *(Salix caprea)* appear early in the year. In the absence of insects, the pollen is dispersed on the wind.

A guide to some wetland trees and shrubs

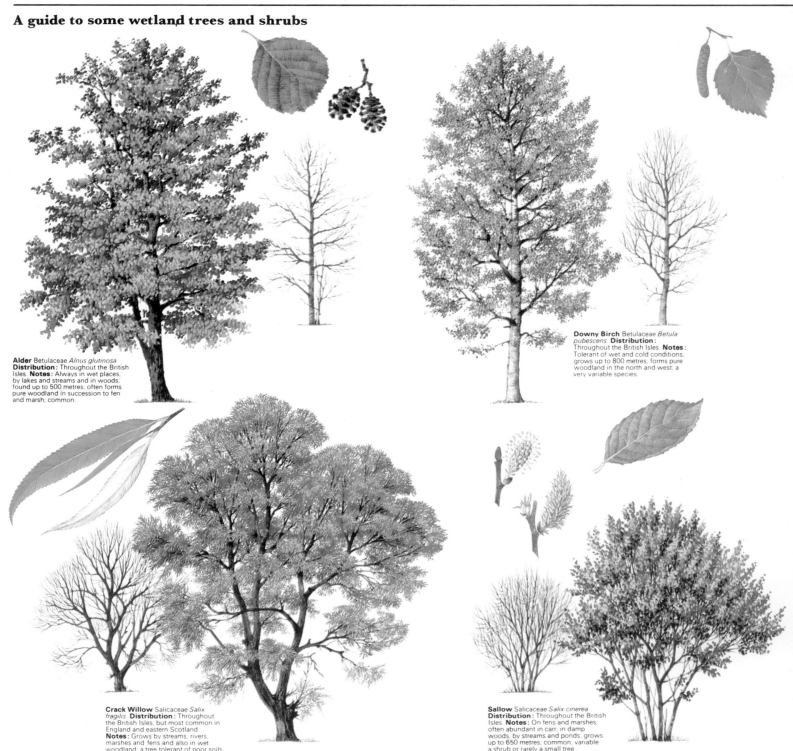

Alder Betulaceae *Alnus glutinosa* **Distribution:** Throughout the British Isles. **Notes:** Always in wet places; by lakes and streams and in woods; found up to 500 metres; often forms pure woodland in succession to fen and marsh; common.

Downy Birch Betulaceae *Betula pubescens* **Distribution:** Throughout the British Isles. **Notes:** Tolerant of wet and cold conditions; grows up to 800 metres; forms pure woodland in the north and west; a very variable species.

Crack Willow Salicaceae *Salix fragilis* **Distribution:** Throughout the British Isles, but most common in England and eastern Scotland. **Notes:** Grows by streams, rivers, marshes and fens and also in wet woodland; a tree tolerant of poor soils.

Sallow Salicaceae *Salix cinerea* **Distribution:** Throughout the British Isles. **Notes:** On fens and marshes; often abundant in carr; in damp woods, by streams and ponds; grows up to 650 metres; common; variable; a shrub or rarely a small tree.

leaf-forms may grow on the same plant as happens in arrowhead *(Sagittaria sagittifolia)* which has long strap-shaped submerged leaves that can bend or move with the water currents, and emergent arrowhead shaped leaves on long but fairly substantial leaf-stalks. In other species like the bulrush *(Schoenoplectus lacustris)* and the bur-reed *(Sparganium ramosum)*, plants grow with their leaves either all emergent or all submerged. In both of these species the submerged form is sterile and so unlike the well-known emergent form that identification is very difficult or impossible. These amphibious species can be divided into two groups; those that are more or less terrestrial but can exist in water, and those that are aquatic but can exist almost or just out of water. The adjustment of form and function in response to the different medium varies greatly from species to species.

In nearly all cases where species have submerged foliage the leaves are either thin and flat, or finely dissected. This structure has two distinct advantages. Firstly, all of the cells of the plant are near the water from which oxygen and (mainly in the case of free-floating types) nutrients are obtained, and secondly, these shapes offer the least resistance to water movement and as a result are less likely to be damaged or, in the case of the bottom-rooted species, torn free.

Sallow *(Salix cinerea)*, a member of the willow family, is a common shrub or small tree in fenland and marshy areas, although it will thrive in damp conditions anywhere. It is the foodplant for the eyed hawk-moth *(Smerinthus ocellata)*, whose effectively camouflaged larva is here seen feeding on the leaves.

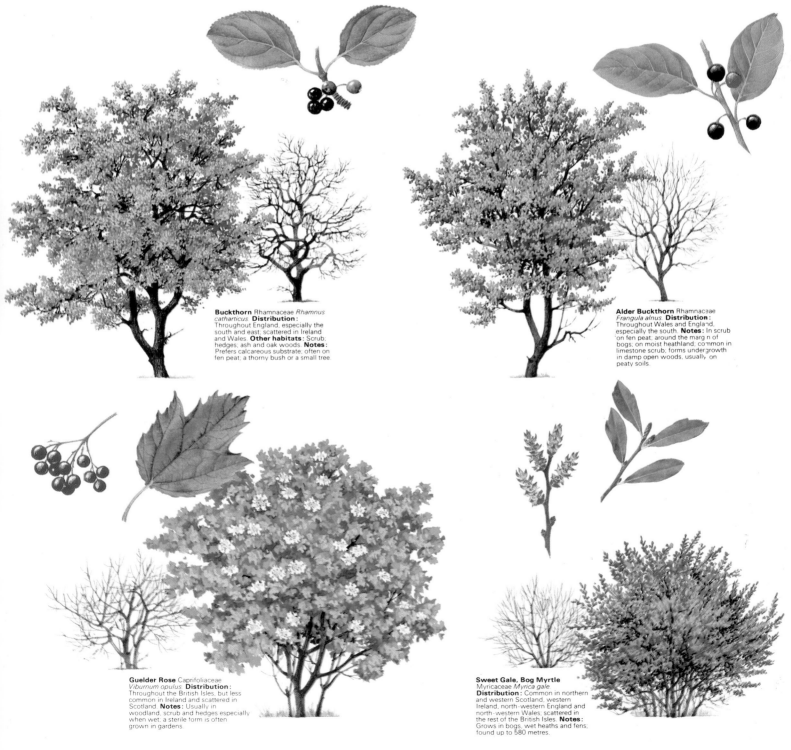

Buckthorn Rhamnaceae *Rhamnus catharticus.* **Distribution:** Throughout England, especially the south and east; scattered in Ireland and Wales. **Other habitats:** Scrub; hedges; ash and oak woods. **Notes:** Prefers calcareous substrate; often on fen peat; a thorny bush or a small tree.

Alder Buckthorn Rhamnaceae *Frangula alnus.* **Distribution:** Throughout Wales and England, especially the south. **Notes:** In scrub on fen peat; around the margin of bogs; on moist heathland; common in limestone scrub; forms undergrowth in damp open woods, usually on peaty soils.

Guelder Rose Caprifoliaceae *Viburnum opulus.* **Distribution:** Throughout the British Isles, but less common in Ireland and scattered in Scotland. **Notes:** Usually in woodland, scrub and hedges especially when wet; a sterile form is often grown in gardens.

Sweet Gale, Bog Myrtle Myricaceae *Myrica gale.* **Distribution:** Common in northern and western Scotland, western Ireland, north-western England and north-western Wales; scattered in the rest of the British Isles. **Notes:** Grows in bogs, wet heaths and fens; found up to 580 metres.

227

Wetland and Freshwater Invertebrates

Wetlands and freshwater provide habitats for a tremendous diversity of invertebrates including minute protozoa, sponges, worms, rotifers, moss animals, molluscs, crustaceans, arachnids and numerous insect species. Many of the microscopic creatures are widespread and occur in vast numbers; other invertebrates have a very restricted distribution. The largest British freshwater invertebrate is the crayfish *(Astacus pallipes)*, one of the crustaceans.

In the main groups, or phyla, it is unusual to find all the members of the group living in freshwater; for example, there are marine and terrestrial molluscs as well as the freshwater ones. Coelenterates such as corals, jellyfish and sea-anemones are marine, whereas there are also several species of *Hydra* found in freshwater. Many freshwater invertebrates spend part of their life cycle in the aquatic environment and part on land, like the nymphs of dragonflies which spend their life underwater, but develop into adults which emerge to become free-flying insects. Many adult beetles, although spending their larval stages underwater, are equally at home on the water surface, swimming underwater or flying through the air.

All invertebrates are "cold-blooded" so that their body temperature closely resembles that of the medium in which they find themselves. It is for this reason that many, but not all, freshwater and wetland invertebrates are more obvious in summer than in winter. As winter approaches many insects and other invertebrates either change to a less active form or are forced to reduce their level of body activity as their temperature drops with that of the surrounding medium. Stonefly nymphs are exceptions and may be active all winter. As spring arrives and the environment warms up many invertebrates which have spent the winter in the mud at the bottom of ponds, lakes and rivers in a cold-resistant stage, become more active, grow and quickly breed so that their numbers increase rapidly. The process can be very evident when, for example, large swarms of midges, mayflies or other insects hatch in response to the rise in temperature.

As with other ecosystems, one type of aquatic environment is suitable for some invertebrates but not for others. Species found in rushing upland, acid or oligotrophic rivers usually differ from those in slow flowing lowland rivers and chalk streams. Frequently closely related species of invertebrate have adapted to different modes of life, thus each is able to exploit a niche which is not fully utilised by other animals. The may-

Dragonflies like this *Aeshna cyanea* are fast flying predators on smaller insects. Young dragonflies, called nymphs, lack wings and live in the water.

flies (the Ephemeroptera) exhibit a range of forms: there are burrowing nymphs in slower streams and creeping nymphs on muddy and sandy surfaces. Perhaps the most spectacular of the flattened nymphs belong to the genus *Ecdyonurus*, which can withstand the rushing waters of upland torrents and the buffeting caused by the turbulent waters on exposed lake shores. The many kinds of free-swimming mayfly nymphs generally have cylindrical bodies which are more efficient for this mode of life. They can be found in habitats as diverse as small streams, ponds, lakes and tarns; whilst other forms are found amongst marsh vegetation.

All of these aquatic creatures face the problem of obtaining sufficient oxygen for their needs. Many develop special feathery gills, either projecting from the body or lining a special gill cavity. Those that live in well-aerated streams have little difficulty, but some (like the stonefly larvae) are unable to tolerate low oxygen concentrations often found in ponds and sluggish rivers. Gills are very sensitive structures and are prone to damage by detergents which pollute many waters.

An alternative to aquatic respiration using gills is to breathe air, as many freshwater insects do. This requires visits to the surface, where air may be taken in through special breathing tubes which are pushed through the surface film. Some insects (notably beetles) trap a bubble of air close to the body and carry it with them as they swim. The water spider, *Argyroneta aquatica*, does the same. It produces an underwater web which is then "inflated" with air taken down by the spider. The inflated web produces the characteristic glistening underwater "bell" in which the animal lives. Oxygen levels are a major factor determining which species will or will not be present in the water; and are a significant feature in causing the fauna of streams to differ from that of ponds and sluggish rivers. Pollutants, especially organic material (which decomposes and uses up oxygen) may cause the elimination of some oxygen-sensitive species; as will warm water from factories because less oxygen will dissolve in water at higher temperatures.

There are very many microscopic freshwater invertebrates and their importance should not be overlooked just because they are small. They form an essential link in the majority of aquatic and wetland food chains. Hold up a jar of water taken from most natural freshwaters and you will soon be aware of the life it contains. Particularly characteristic are the water fleas (cladocerans and copepods) which jerk through the water. Though tiny, it should be noted that many are algal feeders. They filter individual phytoplankton cells from the water and thus form the first stage in a food chain. In their turn, they provide food for fish, especially the young. Cladocera and copepods form the major element

The hydra lives underwater attached to submerged stones and the stems and leaves of water weeds. If disturbed it shrinks to a jelly-like blob, but is normally clearly visible and grows up to 3 cm in height. It feeds on small aquatic animals caught in its crown of tentacles. A hydra is seen here snaring a passing water flea.

These bloodworms are the larvae of midges. They are common in shallow water, where they provide an important source of food for many small predators.

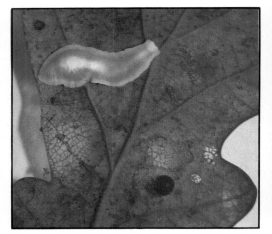

Flatworms like this *Dendrocoelum lacteum* may be found crawling over stones, dead leaves and other detritus on the beds of lakes or slow moving water.

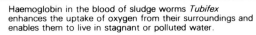

Haemoglobin in the blood of sludge worms *Tubifex* enhances the uptake of oxygen from their surroundings and enables them to live in stagnant or polluted water.

The medicinal leech *Hirudo medicinalis* draws blood from vertebrate prey with its powerful sucker. It produces an anti-coagulant to ensure that the blood flows freely.

The fish leech *Pisciola geometra* feeds on the blood of fish and may even cause death, as in the case of this baby trout.

Freshwater worms and leeches

Worms and leeches belong to the phylum Annelida. This group includes all the segmented worms which are so abundant in seashore habitats. However, the marine worms are polychaetes which do not venture into freshwater. Here the segmented worms (eg *Tubifex*) are oligochaetes which are circular in cross-section or leeches (flat with a sucker at each end). Some small worms may be seen which are not segmented and have only one sucker (at the front). These are planarians or flatworms and belong to a different phylum. Blood worms are not worms at all, but are the larvae of flies.

Leeches feed by sucking blood from fish and other vertebrates. They produce a special substance which prevents clotting so that their victim's blood continues to flow freely. The other worms are bottom-dwelling scavengers and detritus feeders. In turn they provide important food for many predators. Fish feed extensively on the worms in rich mud, as do some diving ducks and carnivorous beetles.

of the freshwater animal plankton (zooplankton). Because their algal food is seasonally abundant, forming "blooms", the zooplankton population densities also fluctuate widely through the year. The greatest numbers are present in late spring, following the early phytoplankton bloom; then a decrease occurs as they use up their algal food. Another population peak may develop following an autumnal algal bloom.

The animal groups

Of all the microscopic invertebrates, Protozoa of the genus *Amoeba* are animals which many people have heard of but few have seen. There are several species found in Britain and they can sometimes be seen moving over the surface of the mud as minute greyish or opaque specks, but a microscope is necessary to see them in detail. A number of other Protozoa are often found in great abundance even in small water bodies such as farm ponds and ditches. Some of these contribute to the green colouring often associated with stagnant waters. Animals such as *Euglena* and *Ceratium* are two of the most widespread. Slipper animalcules, stentors and vorticellids (bell-shaped animals attached to plants, sticks or

stones under water) are a few examples of the Protozoa.

Sponges belong to the phylum Porifera. The majority are marine creatures, but there are two British types that inhabit freshwater. The river sponge *(Ephydatia fluviatilis)*, although found in rivers, also occurs in the shallow waters of many lakes as a greyish or yellowish encrusting growth on logs, posts or plant stems. The pond sponge *(Euspongilla lacustris)* is found in deeper, stiller waters and has a branching, finger-like form.

The only common representatives of the phylum Coelenterata found in freshwater are species of *Hydra*; long slender invertebrates with a crown of tentacles. *Hydra* are often found attached to the underwater stems or leaves of aquatic plants, or to submerged stones. When disturbed, they usually shrink into a small blob of jelly, but if left alone in water, will eventually "reform" into a clearly visible creature extending up to two or three centimetres in height. The colour (green or brown) gives the names to two species. The slender hydra is a third species which is generally smaller than the other two. Although *Hydra* are probably more widespread

in eutrophic standing waters, they are found in a wide range of habitats. They even occur in some upland rivers, often in large numbers especially where there is a suitable micro-habitat such as among dense growths of aquatic plants.

Flatworms

So far the freshwater invertebrates considered are all minute and with the possible exception of *Hydra* and the water fleas will usually be overlooked without careful examination with a lens or a microscope. The flatworms, of the phylum Platyhelminthes, are much more obvious. There are three classes of flatworm; the turbellarians, of which the planarians are the largest; the flukes or trematodes and the tapeworms or cestodes.

There are ten kinds of British planarian occurring in still and running water. They look like blobs of stiff jelly, ranging from white to black in colour. They move by elongating and gliding over the surface of submerged plants and stones. It is not easy to identify species of planarians in the field as the arrangement of the eyes, not always easily seen, and the sex organs

Freshwater molluscs

Although they live in water, most pond snails are air breathers and have to visit the surface in order to refill their lung. This is a large cavity just inside the shell aperture. Pond snails differ from land snails in having eyes at the base of their tentacles instead of at the tips. Freshwater mussels, like their marine relatives, obtain oxygen from the water through gills. These are extremely large, occupying most of the space within the shell, because they are used for trapping food particles as well as for respiration.

Great ram's-horn snail *Planorbis corneus*. Body usually black, though red varieties are sometimes found. Often introduced into garden ponds.

Whirlpool ram's-horn snail *Anisus vortex*. Common in quiet unpolluted rivers and drainage ditches in England, especially among dense pondweeds.

Amber snail *Succinea putris*. Virtually amphibious, found typically out of water on emergent vegetation at the edges of rivers and lakes.

Great pond snail *Lymnaea stagnalis* with egg rope on shell (laid by another great pond snail). Britain's largest water snail. An omnivorous feeder.

Wandering snail *Lymnaea peregra*, browsing on pondweed (*Potamogeton*). Britain's commonest freshwater snail, and very variable in shape and size.

Painter's mussel *Unio pictorum*, found in canals and large rivers in England. Note frilly edge of siphons projecting beyond valves on right.

are the main determining features. It is perhaps interesting to note that each planarian is both male and female at once (hermaphrodite) but nevertheless it is still necessary for two individuals to come together for successful fertilisation of the eggs. Planarians are very widespread, some like *Crenobia alpina* occurring on the stones in rushing upland streams, while *Polycelis nigra*, a dark coloured planarian with a row of eyes arranged

The red water mite *Arrhenurus* is seen here with its egg-mass. These tiny, fast swimming mites are often found among pond weeds and also inside the protective shelter of freshwater mussels.

around its anterior margin, is common in lowland lakes and streams. Planarians feed in a variety of ways; *Dendrocoelum lacteum*, very common in many lowland lakes, feeds largely on the freshwater louse, while *Dugesia polychroa*, identified by its rounded head, pronounced neck, and eyes placed far back, is widespread and feeds upon water snails. Other species feed on fish eggs or young fish; one species preys on *Hydra* while others are to be found eating decaying plant or animal matter.

The parasitic flukes or trematodes are distinguished from planarians by the sucker or suckers on their underside. The suckers enable flukes to cling to their hosts; a common and widespread fluke is often found on the gills of the three-spined stickleback. Perhaps the best known fluke is the liver·fluke, which lives in several vertebrate hosts and spends part of its life cycle in water snails, but as an internal parasite. Care should be taken not to confuse the flukes with the leeches, which also attach themselves to their hosts by suckers. However, leeches are true worms – in the same phylum as the earthworm. Leeches are common in all types of freshwater habitat; they have two suckers, one at each end, and they do not attach themselves to their host for any great length of time so they can be seen frequently moving over stones or water plants. Unlike planarians which glide over the substrate, leeches stretch forward, attach themselves by their front sucker, then by a looping movement, draw the rear sucker to-

wards the front one, attach it to the substrate and repeat the process.

Moss animals

Moss animals, freshwater members of the phylum Ectoprocta, have confused naturalists for centuries as to where they should be placed in the classification of animals. Most moss animals are marine and the few freshwater examples are easily overlooked. They are beautiful creatures; a number of individuals or zooids are joined together and resemble a mossy growth on underwater stones and tree roots. Once again a microscope is required to view the animals at their best. Even their scientific names have a touch of magic about them; *Plumatella* and *Lophopus crystallinus* are both elegant, beautiful animals with their delicate translucent crowns of tentacles waving gently in still water.

Molluscs

There are two classes of the large phylum Mollusca found in freshwater and wetlands in Britain. They are the single shelled gastropods such as the freshwater snails and limpets, and two shelled bivalves such as the freshwater mussel. Snails of one species or another have colonised the great majority of freshwater habitats, except for bogs and acid peat pools which are found throughout much of upland Britain and in one or two lowland localities such as parts of the New Forest. Such pools are usually devoid of aquatic macrophytes upon

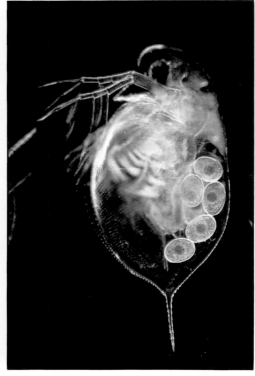

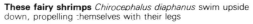

These fairy shrimps *Chirocephalus diaphanus* swim upside down, propelling themselves with their legs

The water flea *Daphnia* swims by using its large antennae to produce a jerky motion.

which most of the 36 species of freshwater gastropod found in these islands feed. In addition, the minerals required to construct the snail's shell are often lacking or only present in minute quantities in such waters.

Many molluscs are widespread and common; for example, the nerite (*Theodoxus fluviatilis*) is found in many rivers and also on wave washed lake shores. If the water current is not too strong then the freshwater winkles, *Viviparus viviparus* and *V. fasciatus* may be encountered throughout much of southern Britain. In still waters *Bithynia tentaculata* is common. All these molluscs have a horny plate or operculum attached to the foot. When the snail withdraws into its shell then the operculum conveniently closes the shell opening. For this reason they are known as operculate snails. One of the most interesting operculates is Jenkins' spire shell (*Potamopyrgus jenkinsi*) a tiny dark coloured snail, no more than five millimetres long, which has spread throughout the country during this century. It is thought that its spread from brackish estuarine waters may have been accelerated by being transported on the feet of birds.

Most of the larger plants grow in the shallower zones of lakes and so it is here that many of the gastropods will be found. In upland lakes, where there is frequently little calcium in the water, species such as the wandering snail (*Lymnaea peregra*) and the ram's-horn snail (*Planorbis atba*) are most abundant. As the nutrients and calcium content of the water

increases additional species occur, examples being *Planorbis contortus* and the bladder snail, *Physa fontinalis*. Many other species of mollusc become more numerous with increasing nutrients and calcium in the water.

Although many species found in lakes may still be found in slow flowing rivers, there is a tendency for them to disappear as water speed increases. In faster flowing waters species especially adapted to clinging to stones become increasingly abundant. The small freshwater limpet (*Ancylus fluviatilis*), is often the most abundant mollusc in such situations. The richest aquatic molluscan fauna probably occurs in the chalk streams of the south.

The pulmonate snails, unlike the operculates, have no operculum and no gills through which oxygen can be absorbed. They obtain their main supply of oxygen by taking it directly into a cavity within the shell. They must, therefore, come to surface for oxygen and as a result are usually found in stiller waters; the pond snails belong to this group. The great pond snail (*Lymnaea stagnalis*) is common in ponds and sheltered lakes throughout Britain, and several other pulmonates like the very much smaller dwarf pond snail (*L. truncatula*) live in wetlands such as marshes. Many other pulmonates are found in large ponds, sheltered lakes and slow flowing waters, particularly canals. The ram's-horn snail (*Planorbis planorbis*) is common and

widespread, but perhaps not quite so familiar as the larger (25cm) great ram's-horn (*P. corneus*) which, although more restricted in its distribution, is frequently kept in aquaria. Several aquatic molluscs are highly adapted to cope with drying out; a frequent problem in small ponds.

There are fewer than 30 freshwater bivalves (lamellibranchs) found in Britain. They are less mobile than the snails and feed by filtering food particles from the water. The most familiar is the large swan mussel (*Anodonta cygnea*), but there are several other species found in slower flowing rivers, canals and lakes.

There are also four species of orb-shell cockles (*Sphaerium*) and 15 species of pea-shell cockle (*Pisidium*), of which *P. cinereum* is probably the most widespread. A bivalve which was introduced into this country during the last century is the strikingly marked zebra mussel, *Dreissena polymorpha*, which lives in groups attached to submerged objects and became widely distributed throughout the British canal network through being carried on barges.

Leeches

Leeches are true worms (phylum Annelida) with a segmented, flattened body and are very common in all kinds of freshwater. Although they feed upon other animals they spend much of their time attached to water plants or to the substrate. The small "snail-leeches" (*Glossi-*

A pair of water lice or water slaters (*Asellus aquaticus*). Related to the terrestrial woodlice, these creatures are crustaceans and spend their lives on the bottom of ponds and under stones feeding on detritus. The female can often

be distinguished by the presence of a white swelling on her underside in which she is carrying her eggs.

The freshwater crayfish *Astacus pallipes* resembles a miniature lobster. It is normally found in clean lowland rivers, particularly in the south east. A larger species, *A. aquatalis*, has been introduced into the Thames.

phonia) parasitise molluscs but will also feed on worms and insect larvae. Another common species which feeds upon insects is *Helobdella stagnalis* while the closely related *Theromyzoa tessutatum* is usually found in the nasal cavities of water fowl. The horse leech *(Haemopis sanguisuga)* is the largest British leech and occurs in a number of freshwater habitats feeding mainly by swallowing its prey whole—even small snails, worms and tadpoles!

Arthropods

The phylum Arthropoda includes the creatures possessing a hard exoskeleton, segmented body and jointed legs. The principal freshwater representatives are the Crustacea and the insects. The latter have a waterproof covering and, as a group, are therefore able to live on dry land, but crustaceans are more or less restricted to water and wet habitats because they cannot prevent the loss of moisture from their body. The freshwater shrimp *(Gammarus)*, a crustacean, is one of the most widespread and best known aquatic invertebrates. The crayfish, *(Astacus fluviatilis)* also a crustacean, is found in base-rich rivers and lakes, particularly in the south, and is frequently found in a number of northern lakes where the water source is from limestone areas. The crustaceans exhibit an ability to colonise a wide range of habitats, and one of the most remarkable species in this context is the fairy shrimp *(Chirocephalus diaphanus)*, which is found in very small temporary water bodies. Following periods of heavy rain it will suddenly appear in situations like flooded wheel ruts, having survived long periods of dryness in the form of drought-resistant eggs.

Perhaps the commonest and most widespread crustaceans are the water fleas (cladocerans like *Daphnia* and *Bosmina)* and tiny copepods *(Cyclops).* They are found in most waters from peat bogs and oligotrophic lakes of the north to the chalk streams and marl lakes of the south, but the actual species often change from one locality to another, and larger lakes tend to contain more species. Water fleas move in a series of jerks, shooting upwards for a few millimetres with a great burst of activity, then slowly sinking before repeating the process. The most noticeable feature of the copepods is the one or more masses of eggs carried towards the rear of the body. The eggs of *Daphnia* are carried in a pouch on the animal's back, from which the young are born after a few weeks.

Water lice *(Asellus)* are much larger crustaceans and resemble aquatic woodlice. They are

Damselflies

Damselflies (order Odonata) are slender-bodied dragonflies with relatively weak powers of flight. Many of them appear to drift from plant to plant, and, in contrast to the stouter-bodied dragonflies, they generally rest with their wings closed vertically above the body. Young damselflies live in water, but can be distinguished from other dragonfly nymphs by their slender shape and by the three leaf-like gills extending from the hind end of the body. There are 16 British species of damselfly, rarely found far from water.

A pair of the small red damselfly *Ceriagrion tenellum*. These two insects are seen mating and may remain joined together even during flight.

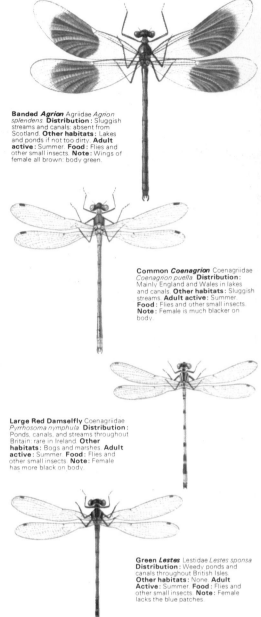

Banded *Agrion* Agriidae *Agrion splendens*. **Distribution:** Sluggish streams and canals; absent from Scotland. **Other habitats:** Lakes and ponds if not too dirty. **Adult active:** Summer. **Food:** Flies and other small insects. **Note:** Wings of female all brown; body green.

Common *Coenagrion* Coenagriidae *Coenagrion puella*. **Distribution:** Mainly England and Wales in lakes and canals. **Other habitats:** Sluggish streams. **Adult active:** Summer. **Food:** Flies and other small insects. **Note:** Female is much blacker on body.

Large Red Damselfly Coenagriidae *Pyrrhosoma nymphula*. **Distribution:** Ponds, canals, and streams throughout Britain; rare in Ireland. **Other habitats:** Bogs and marshes. **Adult active:** Summer. **Food:** Flies and other small insects. **Note:** Female has more black on body.

Green *Lestes* Lestidae *Lestes sponsa*. **Distribution:** Weedy ponds and canals throughout British Isles. **Other habitats:** None. **Adult Active:** Summer. **Food:** Flies and other small insects. **Note:** Female lacks the blue patches.

From this aquatic larva the adult damselfly *Coenagrion mercuriale* will develop and spend warm summer days flying round the margins of lakes and rivers.

The male demoiselle agrion *Agrion virgo* is a dark bottle-green and has a slow heavy flight. It may be seen perched on waterside vegetation on warm sunny days. Each male has a favourite perch and defends the surrounding area against other males by darting after any that approach too closely.

Dragonflies

Dragonflies (order Odonata) fall into two main groups — the weak-flying damselflies and the faster-flying hawkers and darters. Hawkers fly to and fro for long periods, snatching smaller insects from the air as they go. Darters spend much of their time resting on perches, from which they dart out to catch insects that pass by. The young dragonflies live in water, where they feed on a variety of small animals. Some bury themselves in the bottom deposits, while others crawl on the vegetation. They may take several years to grow up. There are about 5,000 species of dragonflies, including damselflies, of which about 40 live in the British Isles. Small species rarely fly far from water, but the larger species may fly miles from the nearest pond or stream.

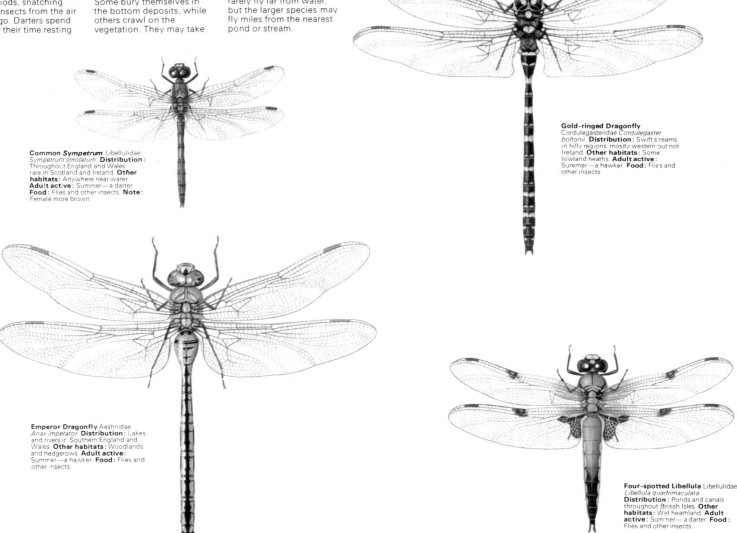

Common Sympetrum Libellulidae *Sympetrum striolatum* **Distribution:** Throughout England and Wales; rare in Scotland and Ireland. **Other habitats:** Anywhere near water. **Adult active:** Summer—a darter. **Food:** Flies and other insects. **Note:** Female more brown.

Gold-ringed Dragonfly Cordulegasteridae *Cordulegaster boltonii.* **Distribution:** Swift streams in hilly regions; mostly western but not Ireland. **Other habitats:** Some lowland heaths. **Adult active:** Summer—a hawker. **Food:** Flies and other insects.

Emperor Dragonfly Aeshnidae *Anax imperator* **Distribution:** Lakes and rivers in Southern England and Wales. **Other habitats:** Woodlands and hedgerows. **Adult active:** Summer—a hawker. **Food:** Flies and other insects.

Four-spotted Libellula Libellulidae *Libellula quadrimaculata.* **Distribution:** Ponds and canals throughout British Isles. **Other habitats:** Wet heathland. **Adult active:** Summer—a darter. **Food:** Flies and other insects.

Mayflies

Mayflies (order Ephemeroptera) are weak-flying insects that spend their early lives in water. They have two or four very flimsy wings and two or three slender "tails" at the hind end. The adults do not feed and they rarely live more than a few days. Some do not live for more than a few hours as adults —just long enough to mate and lay eggs. They are rarely found far from water. The nymphs may take a year or more to grow up in ponds and streams, where they burrow in the mud or crawl over the bottom and feed mainly on plant debris. They all have three "tails". When fully grown, the nymph floats to the surface and the winged insect breaks out, but it still has one moult to go—it quickly sheds its dull, hairy coat for a much shinier one. No other group of insects moults once the wings have developed. There are 47 British species.

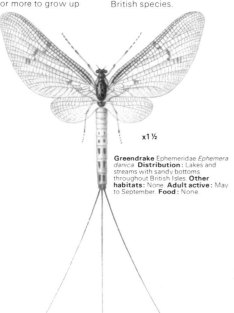

x1½

Greendrake Ephemeridae *Ephemera danica* **Distribution:** Lakes and streams with sandy bottoms throughout British Isles. **Other habitats:** None. **Adult active:** May to September. **Food:** None.

Mayflies like this *Ephemera danica* spend most of their time as aquatic nymphs. The adult insects emerge from the water to find a mate but do not live more than a day or two. Consequently they have no need to feed. The food canal is actually filled with air to lighten the insects, thus enabling them to fly more efficiently.

Caddisflies

Caddisflies (order Trichoptera) are moth-like insects whose wings are densely clothed with hairs. Most are brown or grey, and they rest with their wings held roofwise over the body and the antennae, which may be very long, held out in front. Some species may feed on nectar, but most adult caddisflies probably do not feed. Larval caddisflies live in water and many of them construct tubular cases around themselves, using silk from their own bodies together with sand grains and pieces of plant debris. Each species makes its case to a particular pattern, and most carry the cases around with them. Some caddis larvae are free-living, and some live in silken nets which trap food particles in the water. The larvae eat both plant and animal matter. There are about 190 British species.

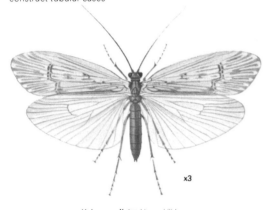

x3

Halesus radiatus Limnephilidae. **Distribution:** Running water throughout the British Isles. **Other habitats:** Adult may fly to lights at night. **Adult active:** Autumn. **Food:** ? Nectar.

mainly scavengers feeding on a wide range of decaying organic matter, particularly among the detritus on the bottom of ponds and lakes. There are many species but *A. aquaticus* and *A. meridianus* are the commonest and most widespread.

The water flea

The water flea is not a true flea (which is an insect) but a small cladoceran crustacean belonging to the family Daphnidae, of which there are over 20 species in Britain. Most *Daphnia* move through the water by a series of jerky movements which makes them conspicuous, although few are more than three millimetres in length.

The head is slightly separated from the main part of the body and has a large single eye. *Daphnia* has a short first pair of antennae and a much more prominent branched pair of second antennae. The former are used largely as sensory organs while the latter pair serve as "limbs" for locomotion.

The main part of the body is enclosed in a carapace or kind of shell which is a single structure, folded along the middle of the dorsal surface but is not joined in front. The feet are also covered by the carapace in *Daphnia*, but in other genera they protrude somewhat.

Although most Cladocera are semi transparent or transluscent in water they can appear a brownish colour when they contain ephippia with "winter" eggs. Under a good lens or a

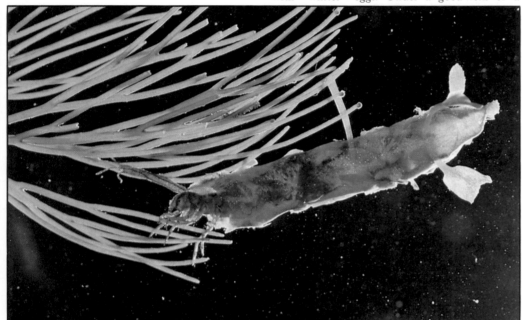

The larvae of some caddisflies construct a protective home from bits of twig, leaf and other debris which they carry with them as they move along lake and river beds. This one has built its home out of duckweed.

microscope other internal organs, gut, heart, liver and eye muscles, can be seen. Water fleas lay their eggs into a brood pouch on the dorsal side of the female. The eggs develop and hatch into miniature adults which live for up to six months in shallow, still waters and form the food of many other aquatic animals.

Insects

Aquatic insects are very diverse in form and habits: some have restricted geographical or habitat preferences, others are widespread; some are predators, others omnivores, while others are herbivores. Some are parasitic, others scavengers. The range of life cycles exhibited is very varied, some species having more than one generation in a year; others taking several years to reach breeding maturity (some have up to four different kinds of life form or stages between egg and adult). Many aquatic insects have their larval or immature stages underwater with adults emerging to become free flying. A few groups, such as some water beetles and water bugs, have the ability to live as adults both above and below the water. Aquatic insects are so varied that it is possible to consider only the most important groups here.

Mayflies and true flies

Mayflies emerge from their immature stages in vast numbers in late May or early June. There are 47 British species of which many occur in the chalk streams of southern England, but changes in substrate will often lead to a change in species. In shallow waters, where silt has collected, *Caenis horaria* is often found but if the substrate changes to sand then *C. moesta* is more likely to be present. Many flies have larval stages which are aquatic and many more species are associated with wetland habitats: some tipulids or daddy-long-legs are examples. The best known aquatic flies are the Culicidae or gnats and mosquitoes, and the chironomids or midges. The larvae of several species of horse-flies are found in wet ground and one of the most obnoxious insects, the rat-tailed maggot (*Eristalis*) lives in rich decomposing muds at the bottom of stagnant pools.

Dragonflies and damselflies

These include a number of beautiful and elegant species; for example, the banded agrion (*Agrion splendens*) and the demoiselle (*A. virgo*) damselflies have metallic blue and green bodies and dark wing markings. These damselflies have a slower, fluttering flight. Dragonflies can be classified as either hawkers or darters; hawkers feed by patrolling a regular "beat" in

Alderflies

Alderflies (order Neuroptera) are related to the snakeflies and the lacewing flies. They fly weakly and rarely travel far from the water in which they grow up. They spend most of their time clinging to the waterside vegetation, with their wings held roofwise over the body. They could be confused with caddisflies, but the latter never have so many cross-veins on the wings. Alderflies probably eat little or nothing in the adult state, but some may chew pollen or the algae covering waterside tree trunks. The larvae live in water and prey on other small animals. Their abdomens bear 7 pairs of feathery gills, which look rather like extra pairs of legs. There are only two British species.

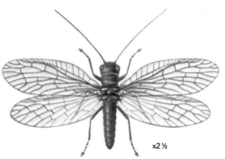

x2½

Common Alderfly Sialidae *Sialis lutaria*. **Distribution:** Edges of ponds, canals, and slow rivers throughout British Isles. **Other habitats:** None. **Adult active:** May to July. **Food:** ? Pollen and algae.

Long-headed flies

Long-headed flies (order Diptera) get their name because, when seen from the side, the head appears much taller than it is broad. The flies are rarely seen far from the water and they can generally be seen scuttling about on the mud at the edge of a pool or stream. Sometimes they skate about on the water surface. At rest, the front end of the body is raised above the rest on the long legs. The flies catch other small insects that approach them. They crush them in their specially adapted mouthparts before sucking up the juices. The larvae, which live in the water or wet mud, are also carnivorous. There are about 250 British species.

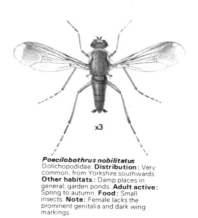

x3

Poecilobothrus nobilitatus Dolichopodidae. **Distribution:** Very common, from Yorkshire southwards. **Other habitats:** Damp places in general; garden ponds. **Adult active:** Spring to autumn. **Food:** Small insects. **Note:** Female lacks the prominent genitalia and dark wing markings.

Soldier-flies

Soldier-flies (order Diptera) are slow-flying insects, often with brilliant metallic coloration and rather flattened bodies. They get their name from their bright "uniforms". The flies spend much of their time sitting on waterside plants with their wings folded flat over their bodies. They may take a little nectar from flowers, but do not feed a great deal. Soldier-fly larvae or maggots live either on land or in the water. Aquatic larvae are generally carnivorous and eat other small creatures. The terrestrial larvae live in the soil or rotting matter. There are about 20 British species.

x3

Chloromyia formosa Stratiomyidae. **Distribution:** Much of British Isles. **Other habitats:** Damp woods and hedgerows; gardens. **Adult active:** May to July. **Food:** Nectar. Larvae terrestrial, in decaying matter. **Note:** Male has gold abdomen.

The water boatman *Notonecta* swims with its large paddle-like legs, hence the name backswimmer. It makes frequent journeys to the surface to replenish its oxygen.

The water scorpion *Nepa cinerea* is a carnivorous freshwater bug. It is seen here sucking out the juices from the carcass of a damselfly larva it has killed.

search of insect prey, while darters rest on a perch most of the time and dash out to seize prey as it comes past.

Stoneflies

In contrast to the dragonflies, which prefer still or gently flowing waters, the stoneflies are characteristic of rapidly flowing waters, free from silt and fine detritus. They are also common in clear water along wave-washed lake shores. There are over 30 species in Britain and one of the commonest is *Nemoura cinerea*.

Bugs

Many aquatic bugs live on the surface of the water but others will submerge, and marginal and marshland vegetation is a favourite habitat of a number of species. The water measurer (*Hydrometa stagnorum*) and the familiar pond skater (*Gerris najas*) are representative of the water surface bugs, whereas the water scorpion (*Nepa cinerec*) is found underwater. The water boatmen, of which *Notonecta glauca* is the most common and widely distributed, and the corixids or lesser water boatmen are also very familiar freshwater bugs.

Lacewings and beetles

The ungainly alderfly (*Sialis lutaria*) can be found from the oligotrophic waters of the north to sluggish lowland rivers and streams in the south, wherever there are suitable muddy substrates in which the larvae live.

Water bugs

Water bugs belong to several different families of bugs (order Hemiptera) and there are about 60 species in the British Isles. They fall into two distinct groups—those that walk or skate on the surface film with the aid of water-repellent hairs on their feet, and those that live under the surface. Some of the latter group can absorb all their oxygen from the water, but most have to surface periodically. The water scorpion and water stick insect draw air down their long breathing siphons, while others trap air among the fine hairs that coat their bodies. This trapped air gives the bugs a silvery appearance. Almost all of the water bugs are predatory insects, both as nymphs and adults. The nymphs look much like the adults except that they have no wings, although many adults are also wingless.

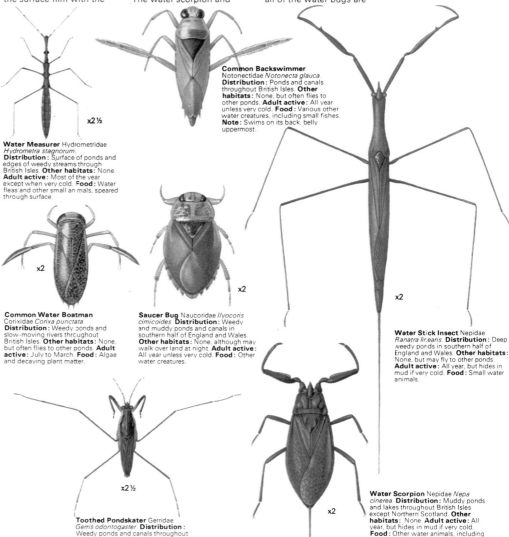

Water Measurer Hydrometridae *Hydrometra stagnorum*. **Distribution:** Surface of ponds and edges of weedy streams through British Isles. **Other habitats:** None. **Adult active:** Most of the year except when very cold. **Food:** Water fleas and other small animals, speared through surface.

Common Backswimmer Notonectidae *Notonecta glauca*. **Distribution:** Ponds and canals throughout British Isles. **Other habitats:** None, but often flies to other ponds. **Adult active:** All year unless very cold. **Food:** Various other water creatures, including small fishes. **Note:** Swims on its back, belly uppermost.

Common Water Boatman Corixidae *Corixa punctata*. **Distribution:** Weedy ponds and slow-moving rivers throughout British Isles. **Other habitats:** None, but often flies to other ponds. **Adult active:** July to March. **Food:** Algae and decaying plant matter.

Saucer Bug Naucoridae *Ilyocoris cimicoides*. **Distribution:** Weedy and muddy ponds and canals in southern half of England and Wales. **Other habitats:** None, although may walk over land at night. **Adult active:** All year unless very cold. **Food:** Other water creatures.

Water Stick Insect Nepidae *Ranatra linearis*. **Distribution:** Deep weedy ponds in southern half of England and Wales. **Other habitats:** None, but may fly to other ponds. **Adult active:** All year, but hides in mud if very cold. **Food:** Small water animals.

Toothed Pondskater Gerridae *Gerris odontogaster*. **Distribution:** Weedy ponds and canals throughout British Isles, on surface. **Other habitats:** None. **Adult Active:** Spring to autumn. **Food:** Other insects stranded on water surface.

Water Scorpion Nepidae *Nepa cinerea*. **Distribution:** Muddy ponds and lakes throughout British Isles except Northern Scotland. **Other habitats:** None. **Adult active:** All year, but hides in mud if very cold. **Food:** Other water animals, including small fishes.

Stoneflies

Stoneflies (order Plecoptera) are rather weak-flying brownish insects that are normally found on stones and vegetation around streams. The wings are folded flat or rolled around the body when the insects are at rest. Most species have two long cerci or "tails" at the hind end. Adult stoneflies rarely feed, but some species nibble algae and lichens or take pollen from flowers. The young stages (nymphs) live in clear streams and may be carnivorous or vegetarian. They are very flat, with strong legs and two long cerci. They may take three years to grow up, and then they crawl out of the water ready for the adult to burst out of the nymphal skin. There are about 3,000 species of stoneflies, of which only 34 live in the British Isles.

Mosquitoes

Mosquitoes (order Diptera) are slender-bodied blood-sucking flies, notorious for spreading malaria and other human diseases in many of the warmer parts of the world. Only the females actually suck blood, which they need for the proper formation of their eggs. The males, which can be distinguished by their very furry antennae, prefer nectar. Eggs are laid on water, and the larvae live in the water, where they feed on microscopic organisms. They pupate in the water too, forming little comma-shaped pupae which swim about when disturbed. There are about 30 British species, distinguished from most other small flies by the scales on the wing veins.

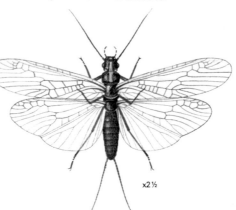

Large Stonefly Perlodidae *Perlodes mortoni*. **Distribution:** Stony rivers throughout British Isles. **Other habitats:** None. **Adult active:** March to July. **Food:** Probably none.

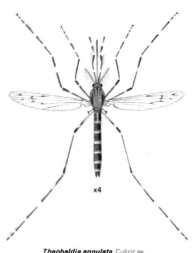

Theobaldia annulata Culicidae. **Distribution:** Most of British Isles. **Other habitats:** Female sometimes hibernates in houses. **Adult active:** Most of year except when very cold. **Food:** Blood (female only) and nectar. **Note:** The largest British mosquito.

The water spider

Most web-spinning spiders use their webs for catching food, but the water spider makes an underwater web in which it stores bubbles of air. The spider lives in this "diving bell" and darts out to catch small water animals that swim by. The prey is always taken back to the diving bell to be eaten. When the air supply begins to run low, the spider makes a number of visits to the surface and brings back more bubbles of air, trapping them between her hairy back legs and her body until she can release them into the bell.

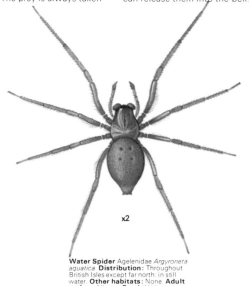

x2

Water Spider Agelenidae *Argyroneta aquatica* Distribution: Throughout British Isles except far north: in still water. Other habitats: None. Adult active: All year. Food: Various aquatic animals, mainly insects.

The water spider *(Argyroneta aquatica)*, like other spiders, breathes air and does not get its oxygen from the water. It carries a bubble of air round its abdomen and returns periodically to the surface to replenish it.

There are many spectacular carnivorous and omnivorous water beetles. Some of the carnivorous larvae are amongst the most ferocious creatures in the freshwater environment. Probably the most characteristic and best adapted water beetles belong to the same family as the great diving beetle *(Dytiscus marginalis)*. Another spectacular species is the great silver beetle *(Hydrophilus piceus)*. The familiar whirligig beetles *(Gyrinus)*, have very shiny wing cases and are frquently seen in late summer whirling round and round on the surface of ponds and sluggish streams.

Caddisflies

There are nearly 200 different caddis species in Britain. They spend their immature stages underwater and the adults usually take to the wing at dusk. There are two main groups, those whose larvae build themselves a protective case and those that do not. The former collect sand grains and plant fragments and stick them together to form a delicate, precisely constructed case. Each species constructs a characteristic case, which the larva carries about as it walks along the river or lake bed. If disturbed or removed from water, the larva hides inside its house. The non case-building caddis larvae are nearly always restricted to running waters. They live under stones and spin a net, the mouth of which faces up-stream so that it is able to catch microscopic food particles washed in by the water current.

Water beetles

Water beetles belong to several different families and there are several hundred species in the British Isles. Some are fierce carnivores: others feed on plants and detritus. Many are good swimmers, with broad, hair-fringed legs, while others crawl on submerged plants. Most have to surface periodically to renew the air supplies carried under the wing cases or elytra. Some also trap air between the hairs on the underside of the body. Some small species never have to surface: the air trapped around the body acts as a physical gill, absorbing oxygen from the water and passing it on to the breathing pores. Most water beetles are fully winged and able to fly from pond to pond. The young stages (larvae) are exceedingly variable, but all have strong, biting jaws. Many species which are plant-eaters in the adult state have carnivorous larvae.

The larvae of the great diving beetle will readily attack tadpoles and even fish.

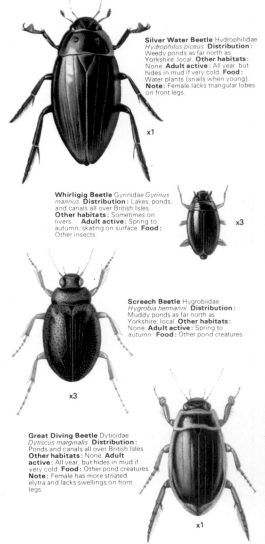

Silver Water Beetle Hydrophilidae *Hydrophilus piceus.* Distribution: Weedy ponds as far north as Yorkshire: local. Other habitats: None. Adult active: All year, but hides in mud if very cold. Food: Water plants (snails when young). Note: Female lacks triangular lobes on front legs.

x1

Whirligig Beetle Gyrinidae *Gyrinus marinus.* Distribution: Lakes, ponds, and canals all over British Isles. Other habitats: Sometimes on rivers. Adult active: Spring to autumn, skating on surface. Food: Other insects.

x3

Screech Beetle Hygrobiidae *Hygrobia hermanni.* Distribution: Muddy ponds as far north as Yorkshire: local. Other habitats: None. Adult active: Spring to autumn. Food: Other pond creatures.

x3

Great Diving Beetle Dyticidae *Dytiscus marginalis.* Distribution: Ponds and canals all over British Isles. Other habitats: None. Adult active: All year, but hides in mud if very cold. Food: Other pond creatures. Note: Female has more striated elytra and lacks swellings on front legs.

x1

The great diving beetle *Dytiscus* is a carnivorous creature but will also feed on organic debris collected from the mud at the bottom of a pond or river. It is well adapted to life in water, although it must still surface for air.

The swallowtail butterfly

In Britain the English race of the swallowtail butterfly is confined to the fenlands of the Norfolk Broads. Occasionally specimens of the Continental race may appear on the south coast as migrants from the mainland of Europe.

In its larval stage the native race feeds almost exclusively on a rare wetland plant, the milk parsley, and may be found at dusk at the tops of stems. The adult butterflies are on the wing in the early summer and are readily attracted to meadow thistles and other pink flowers.

The **Swallowtail** Papilionidae-*Papilio machaon.* **Flight time:** May, June, sometimes August, September, in two broods. **Foodplant:** Milk parsley. **Distribution:** Fenland. Confined to the Norfolk Broads and Wicken Fen where it has recently been re-introduced.

Swallowtail butterflies *Papilio machaon* mating. Swallowtails have become very rare in England, largely because their wetland habitats have been lost by land drainage.

The swallowtail caterpillar feeds only on milk parsley, a plant confined to wetlands. Boldly marked, in order to deter predators, it often pupates on the stem of a reed.

Butterflies and moths

Generally butterflies and moths prefer wetland to aquatic habitats; few actually live in water, though some of the Pyralidae or china mark moths do spend their larval and pupal stages underwater in watertight cases and cocoons. The caterpillars of many butterflies and moths are very specific in their food requirements and will only eat a few species; sometimes only a single type of plant will do. This means that if the plant becomes rare, as a result of wetland drainage or vegetational succession, then the insect becomes scarce too. Certain characteristic wetland butterflies like the swallow tail *(Papilio machaon)* have declined with the loss of wetland habitat, and the British race of the large copper *(Lycaena dispar)* became extinct when the final stages of fen drainage were complete in Cambridgeshire about 1850.

The caterpillar of the red underwing moth *Catocala nupta* feeds on willow and poplar leaves. It is found throughout the south and east of England, the adults flying in August and September.

A guide to some wetland moths

Marsh and fen grasslands, with their varied plant life, support many attractive species of moth. Wainscots feed on the stems of grasses and sedges. They include the bulrush wainscot which spends its larval stage tunnelling in the stems of the reed mace. The larva of the drinker moth feeds on coarse grass and reed and has a liking for drinking dewdrops — hence the common English name. The narrow-bordered bee hawk is a spectacular mimic of bumble bees that flies over wet grasslands in early summer.

The Marsh Carpet Geometridae *Perizoma sagittata.* **Flight time:** June, July. Overwinters as pupa. **Foodplant:** Meadow-rue. **Distribution:** Confined to a few fens in East Anglia.

The Brown China Mark Pyralidae *Nymphula nymphaeata.* **Flight time:** June to August. Overwinters as larva. **Foodplant:** Pondweed, frogbit, bur-reed. **Distribution:** Common throughout much of Great Britain.

The Cream-bordered Green Pea Noctuidae *Earias clorana.* **Flight time:** May, June. Overwinters as pupa. **Foodplant:** Osier, willow. **Distribution:** Very local; south, south-east and east England; mid-Wales; south Scotland.

The Narrow-bordered Bee Hawk-moth Sphingidae *Hemaris tityus.* **Flight time:** May, June. Overwinters as pupa. **Foodplant:** Devil's-bit scabious, field scabious. **Distribution:** Throughout much of Britain but local and uncommon; decreasing in numbers.

The Drinker Moth Lasiocampidae *Philudoria potatoria.* **Flight time:** July, August. Overwinters as larva. **Foodplant:** Grasses. **Distribution:** Widespread in southern and mid and England and Wales; local in northern England and in the western high ands of Scotland.

The Cream-spot Tiger Arctiidae *Arctia villica.* **Flight time:** Late May to early July. Overwinters as larva. **Foodplant:** Herbaceous plants. **Distribution:** Locally common in southern England and south Wales.

The Bulrush Wainscot Noctuidae *Nonagria typhae.* **Flight time:** July to September. Overwinters as ovum. **Foodplant:** In stems of bulrush. **Distribution:** Locally common throughout Britain to southern Scotland.

The Red Underwing Noctuidae *Catocala nupta.* **Flight time:** August, September. **Foodplant:** Willow, poplar. **Distribution:** England and Wales as far north as the Mersey-Humber line; absent from the south-west.

The Scarce Burnished Brass Noctuidae *Diachrysia chryson.* **Flight time:** July, August. Overwinters as larva. **Foodplant:** Hemp agrimony. **Distribution:** Very local in southern England, East Anglia and south Wales.

Freshwater Fish

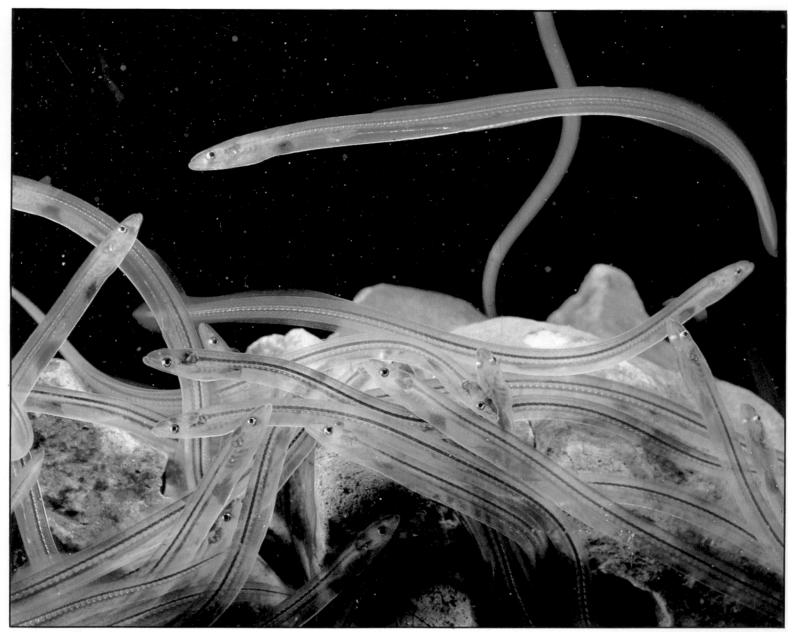

There are over 50 British freshwater fish species distributed the length and breadth of these islands. Fish do not normally occur in waters at high altitudes, in acid peat pools or in water with low oxygen concentrations and high levels of pollution. Our understanding of the distribution of fish has been complicated by the transfer of fish from one water to another by man for both sporting and commercial purposes, but several generalisations can be made about the distribution of freshwater fish, particularly those found in rivers. Basically there are five major zones in river systems, each characterised by a different fish fauna, but there is considerable overlap both in terms of river structure and the fish that each zone is capable of supporting. Very few river systems have a static structure and conditions vary from season to season and from year to year, causing changes in their fish populations.

The three main divisions of a river system are fast waters, medium waters and slow waters, with two intermediate zones. The fast zone is known as the torrent, or trout zone, and has very clear, well oxygenated, unpolluted water flowing over rocky substrates. As the name suggests, the current is fast and the gradient very steep and salmonids like trout *(Salmo trutta)* and salmon *(S. salar)* are most abundant. In some trout zones, the minnow *(Phoxinus phoxinus)* stone loach *(Noemacheilus barbatulus)* and bullhead *(Cottus gobio)* are present although they are much more typical of the intermediate region. This is known also as the grayling *(Thymallus thymallus)* zone, and is characterised by a number of other species which are found in this and also in the middle zone. Barbel *(Barbus barbus)*, chub *(Leuciscus cephalus)*, dace *(L. leuciscus)*, gudgeon *(Gobio gobio)* and bleak *(Alburnus*

alburnus) are examples. In the grayling zone, sometimes known as the minnow zone, the current is fast and the gradient steep; so the splashing waters are well oxygenated and they will support trout and salmon too.

The middle zone is ideal for barbel and chub, so these two species give it its name. In addition there are dace, gudgeon and bleak. Roach *(Rutilus rutilus)*, rudd *(Scardinius erythrophthalmus)*, perch *(Perca fluviatilis)*, ruffe or pope *(Gymnocephalus cernua)* and the pike *(Esox lucius)* are also present. The common eel *(Anguilla anguilla)* is probably present in all non-polluted waters at some time or other so of course it too is found in the barbel zone.

The lower intermediate zone, that between medium and slow waters, is the characteristic zone of the bream *(Abramis brama)*. Here there is a gentle gradient and sluggish current and in addition to pike, ruffe, perch, rudd and roach are white bream *(Blicca bjoerkna)*, carp *(Cyprinus carpio)*, tench *(Tinca tinca)* and the three-spined stickleback *(Gasterosteus aculeatus)*.

The fifth zone is the flounder or mullet zone, where there is little or no gradient, the current is tidal (two way flow) and the water brackish. Apart from the sticklebacks and flounder *(Platichthys flesus)*, thick and thin-lipped mullet *(Crenimugil labrosus* and *Liza ramada)* and common goby *(Pomatoschistus microps)* are found.

Species of the mullet zone can tolerate sea water as can migratory species such as eels, salmon and trout. This facility must have been a considerable advantage to these species in colonising new waters and in recolonising areas following natural, or man-made, disasters.

Several species of fish are confined to running water although in some instances these species have been successfully introduced into lakes.

Migrating elvers of the common eel *Anguilla anguilla* reach the shores of Britain in this transparent form.

Typical running-water species are grayling, barbel, bleak, dace, chub, bullhead, the stone loach and the very rare burbot *(Lota lota)* which is a freshwater member of the cod family and is confined to east Yorkshire and East Anglia. Where trout and grayling are found in the same river then the latter favours the deeper pools. Grayling are particularly abundant in the Hampshire chalk streams such as the Itchen, Avon and Test but also occur in the Severn, Yorkshire Ouse and several Scottish rivers.

Not all the zones are present in every river. In many hill streams in Wales and the western highlands only the trout zone may be present, and in parts of lowland England only the chub, bream and flounder zones will be present because there are no mountains in which the rivers can originate.

It is more difficult to classify standing waters according to their fish communities. Oligotrophic (nutrient-poor) lakes in upland Britain are dominated by the salmonids, trout and char *(Salvelinus alpinus)*. Char inhabit deep upland lakes from which several races described as individual populations have developed noticeable differences. It is thought that each race has probably developed from a common ancestral stock which, at the time of the last Ice Age, was able to colonise many upland lakes but has since become isolated. During the 10,000 years of isolation the populations in each lake have evolved slight structural or anatomical differences. The char is distributed throughout much of Scotland, including Shetland and Orkney, parts of the Lake District and north Wales. In Lake Windermere the race *Salvelinus alpinus willughbii* is interesting in that some individuals come into shallow water to breed, whilst others lay their eggs in deep water. Ennerdale is another lakeland water which contains char and it is interesting to note that two marine relicts, a shrimp *(Mysis relicta)* and a copepod *(Limnocalanus macrurus)* also occur here, over 125 metres above sea level!

Wastwater in Cumbria, the least productive of the lakeland waters, also contains char, the only other fish being brown trout, though a few salmon eels pass through on their migrations. In the deeper lakes of Snowdonia, such as Bodlyn, Cwellyn, Padarn and Peris, the char is known as the torgoch or "red-bellied". Further east in Bala Lake (Llyn Tegid in Welsh), is the gwyniad *(Coregonus clupeoides pennanti)*, a local variety of the European whitefish. In fact the genus *Coregonus* has two British freshwater species; the lavaret *(C. clupeoides)* and the vendace *(C. albula)*. All the populations of both species are confined to their own particular lake and like the char, each has its own local name; the powan is confined to Loch Lomond and Loch Eck and the schelly is from the Lake District where it occurs in Hawswater, Ullswater and Red Tarn. The local names for the vendace are lochmaben, from a loch of that name; the Cumberland vendace, from Bassenthwait and Derwentwater; and the pollan from Ireland. Char do not seem able to compete with coregonids so the two are not usually found together. Bala Lake, in addition to the gwyniad, has a population of grayling which is a species more characteristic of rivers than lakes. Other species of oligotrophic lakes, particularly where there is access from the sea, are salmon and sea trout which are on their way to and from the spawning grounds, eels, lampreys, and the three-spined stickleback. Where streams enter the lake, species such as the stone loach and bullhead may be found and sometimes the minnow. As lakes become more alkaline and richer in minerals, species characteristic of

The river lamprey *Lampetra fluviatilis* spends most of its life in the open sea where it exists as a parasite on fish, attaching itself to them with its powerful sucker and feeding on their blood supply. Adult lampreys come into freshwater during the autumn and breed there the following spring, after which they die.

The salmon

The salmon is, to many anglers and naturalists, one of the best known and most prized species of fish. It is a marine fish which comes to freshwater in the autumn to breed, the eggs being laid in a shallow depression in the gravel bed in the upper reaches of a fast flowing river. After the male has shed sperm or milt over the eggs, they take about three months to develop. The newly hatched salmon (called alevins) spend their first month attached to the yolk-sac of the egg until the food supply has been used up. The young salmon, now known as fry, then feeds on plankton until it is about 18 months old. As the fry grow they develop "parr marks", which are dark blue-grey transverse bands. When the parr is three or four years old, these disappear and the silvery young salmon (now, known as a smolt) migrates to the sea. When at sea many British salmon spend their time at feeding grounds off the west coast of Greenland.

Salmon return to breed in freshwater at various stages. Some come back after only a year in the sea, others do not return for up to several years. After the adults have bred they attempt to make the journey back to the sea, but most are too weak to make the return journey and die on the spawning grounds. The post-breeding adults are called kelts.

Salmon lay their eggs in exactly the same part of the same river in which they themselves hatched years previously. It is still not fully understood how they find their way "home" so precisely, although there is a theory that they are imprinted with the smell of their birthplace.

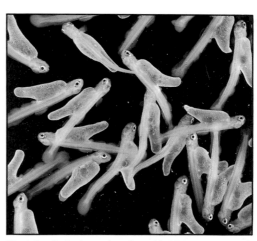

Newly hatched salmon, four days old, still have their yolk-sac attached to provide them with nourishment.

fry

parr

smolt

male adult

female adult

In early summer adult salmon (*Salmo salar*) migrate from the sea into rivers to breed, but the exertion makes the fish very susceptible to disease and many die.

lowland rivers like perch, pike and roach may occur. Indeed in some of the more productive lakes these three species become more abundant than the salmanoid species and eventually replace them.

The cyprinids (including carp, barbel, gudgeon, tench, bream, bleak, minnow, rudd, roach, chub and dace) are only found in freshwater, but many of the species are widespread and abundant. Some of them are particularly adapted to cloudy and eutrophic waters and use a sense of "smell" rather than sight to find their food. Many cyprinids, unlike the salmonids, spawn in beds of rooted water plants and so are much more likely to be encountered in lakes in southern lowland Britain than in the uplands where aquatic macrophytes have difficulty in establishing themselves in fast flowing water.

The carp favours ponds and lakes but is also found in slow flowing rivers and canals, and may occasionally be found in quite stagnant places where it can withstand considerable deoxygenation of the water. Carp, like tench, are bottom feeders, and were originally introduced into Britain in the sixteenth century as a source of food and later for angling. A relative, the bitterling carp *(Rhodeus sericeus)* is now fairly widespread in southern Britain having been first introduced into ponds in Cheshire and Lancashire. In lowland eastern Britain the crucian

Male and female of the three-spined stickleback *(Gasterosteus aculeatus)*. During the breeding season in May and June the male stickleback develops a bright red throat and belly. As well as proving strongly attractive to the female these vivid colours also serve the purpose of repelling rival males.

A guide to freshwater fish

Fish need to be inspected closely in order to identify them. Usually this means catching them or handling dead specimens. Certain species are bottom dwellers (bullhead, loach, gudgeon) and likely to be found under stones. Other bottom dwellers, such as tench and ruff, frequent still, muddy water, and are thus unlikely to be seen unless caught on rod and line. Eels often occur in isolated ponds and ditches because they will travel over land. Lampreys look eel-like, but are not true fish and are easily distinguished by the large fleshy sucker around the mouth. Of the fish shown here, the ones most likely to be seen or caught by anglers are pike, trout (in clean water), perch, roach, dace, chubb, rudd and barbel. Most of these are fairly distinctive, especially if fin colour is noted. Stickleback, minnow, bullhead and gudgeon are often dismissed as 'tiddlers' and may sometimes be difficult to tell from young specimens of larger fish.

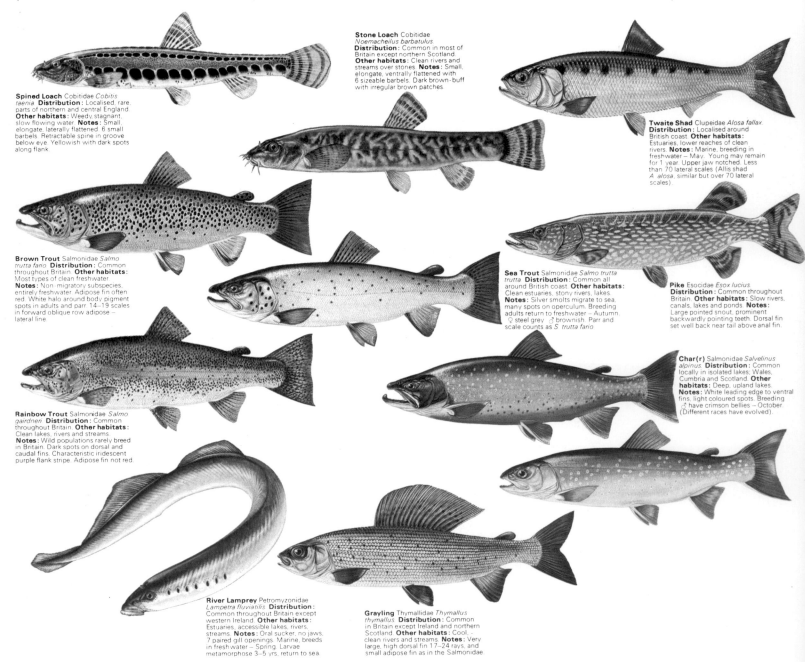

Spined Loach Cobitidae *Cobitis taenia*. **Distribution**: Localised, rare, parts of northern and central England. **Other habitats**: Weedy, stagnant, slow flowing water. **Notes**: Small, elongate, laterally flattened, 6 small barbels. Retractable spine in groove below eye. Yellowish with dark spots along flank.

Stone Loach Cobitidae *Noemacheilus barbatulus*. **Distribution**: Common in most of Britain except northern Scotland. **Other habitats**: Clean rivers and streams over stones. **Notes**: Small, elongate, ventrally flattened with 6 sizeable barbels. Dark brown-buff with irregular brown patches.

Twaite Shad Clupeidae *Alosa fallax*. **Distribution**: Localised around British coast. **Other habitats**: Estuaries, lower reaches of clean rivers. **Notes**: Marine, breeding in freshwater – May. Young may remain for 1 year. Upper jaw notched. Less than 70 lateral scales (Allis shad *A. alosa*, similar but over 70 lateral scales).

Brown Trout Salmonidae *Salmo trutta fario*. **Distribution**: Common throughout Britain. **Other habitats**: Most types of clean freshwater. **Notes**: Non-migratory subspecies, entirely freshwater. Adipose fin often red. White halo around body pigment spots in adults and parr. 14–19 scales in forward oblique row adipose – lateral line.

Sea Trout Salmonidae *Salmo trutta trutta*. **Distribution**: Common all around British coast. **Other habitats**: Clean estuaries, stony rivers, lakes. **Notes**: Silver smolts migrate to sea, many spots on operculum. Breeding adults return to freshwater – Autumn. ♀ steel grey ♂ brownish. Parr and scale counts as *S. trutta fario*.

Pike Esocidae *Esox lucius*. **Distribution**: Common throughout Britain. **Other habitats**: Slow rivers, canals, lakes and ponds. **Notes**: Large pointed snout, prominent backwardly pointing teeth. Dorsal fin set well back near tail above anal fin.

Rainbow Trout Salmonidae *Salmo gairdneri*. **Distribution**: Common throughout Britain. **Other habitats**: Clean lakes, rivers and streams. **Notes**: Wild populations rarely breed in Britain. Dark spots on dorsal and caudal fins. Characteristic iridescent purple flank stripe. Adipose fin not red.

Char(r) Salmonidae *Salvelinus alpinus*. **Distribution**: Common locally in isolated lakes: Wales, Cumbria and Scotland. **Other habitats**: Deep, upland lakes. **Notes**: White leading edge to ventral fins, light coloured spots. Breeding ♂ have crimson bellies – October. (Different races have evolved).

River Lamprey Petromyzonidae *Lampetra fluviatilis*. **Distribution**: Common throughout Britain except western Ireland. **Other habitats**: Estuaries, accessible lakes, rivers, streams. **Notes**: Oral sucker, no jaws, 7 paired gill openings. Marine, breeds in freshwater – Spring. Larvae metamorphose 3–5 yrs, return to sea.

Grayling Thymallidae *Thymallus thymallus*. **Distribution**: Common in Britain except Ireland and northern Scotland. **Other habitats**: Cool, clean rivers and streams. **Notes**: Very large, high dorsal fin 17–24 rays, and small adipose fin as in the Salmonidae.

carp (*Carassius carassius*) may be found, and in some places the goldfish (*C. auratus*) has become naturalised as a result of people liberating unwanted pets into the nearest stream or lake. In such cases, the goldfish may form a permanent, breeding population, though its members revert to a dull greenish colouring. Certain species of tropical aquarium fish have similarly become established in some canals where the water is warmed by industrial discharges. However, such populations are likely to be exterminated by a cold winter.

Tench also frequent ponds and lakes, even those low in oxygen content. Tench can survive a certain amount of desiccation and in quite shallow waters will survive drying out or freezing in severe winters providing there is a good depth of mud. They are most abundant in the Trent, Thames and rivers of Hampshire, East Anglia and the Midlands. Other species found in similar standing waters are the silver bream and common bream. The spined loach (*Cobitis taenia*) is also normally found in slow flowing or stagnant water.

A number of marine species feed or breed in the lower reaches of rivers, the twaite shad (*Alosa fallax*), for example. In the lakes of Killarney there is a land locked form which is now rather rare and has suffered from polluted rivers. An even rarer species, the allis shad (*A.*

The pike (*Esox lucius*) is the largest British fish resident in freshwater. It lurks among water weeds ready to lunge at its prey, using the grooves on its snout like the sights of a gun. Pike feed mostly on other fish, but often take water voles, ducklings and moorhens. Their backward-pointing teeth hold the prey until it can be swallowed head first.

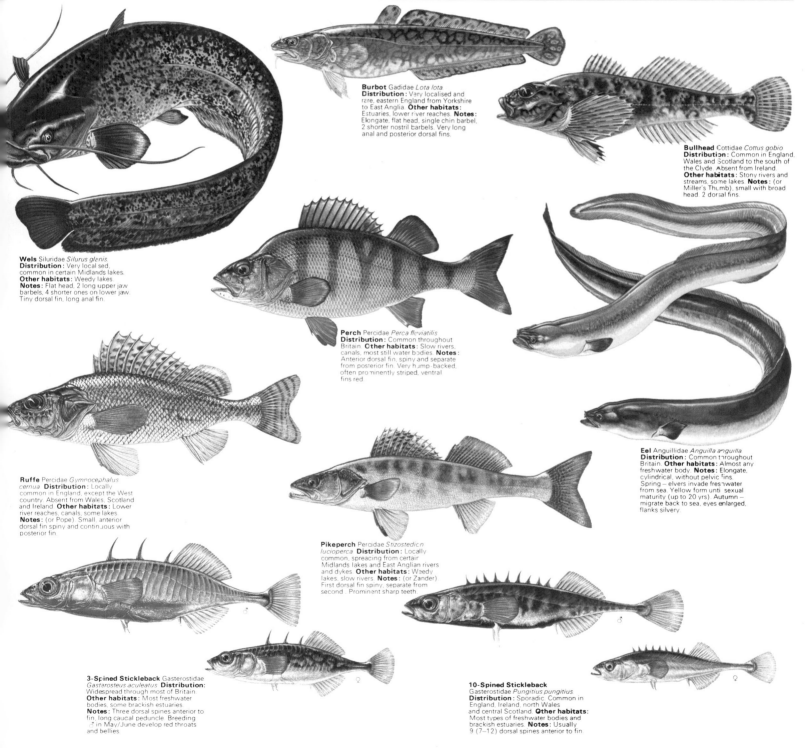

Burbot Gadidae *Lota lota*
Distribution: Very localised and rare, eastern England from Yorkshire to East Anglia. **Other habitats:** Estuaries, lower river reaches. **Notes:** Elongate, flat head, single chin barbel, 2 shorter nostril barbels. Very long anal and posterior dorsal fins.

Bullhead Cottidae *Cottus gobio*
Distribution: Common in England, Wales and Scotland to the south of the Clyde. Absent from Ireland. **Other habitats:** Stony rivers and streams, some lakes. **Notes:** (or Miller's Thumb), small with broad head. 2 dorsal fins.

Wels Siluridae *Silurus glanis*.
Distribution: Very localised, common in certain Midlands lakes. **Other habitats:** Weedy lakes. **Notes:** Flat head, 2 long upper jaw barbels, 4 shorter ones on lower jaw. Tiny dorsal fin, long anal fin.

Perch Percidae *Perca fluviatilis*
Distribution: Common throughout Britain. **Other habitats:** Slow rivers, canals, most still water bodies. **Notes:** Anterior dorsal fin, spiny and separate from posterior fin. Very hump-backed, often prominently striped, ventral fins red.

Eel Anguillidae *Anguilla anguilla*
Distribution: Common throughout Britain. **Other habitats:** Almost any freshwater body. **Notes:** Elongate, cylindrical, without pelvic fins. Spring — elvers invade freshwater from sea. Yellow form until sexual maturity (up to 20 yrs). Autumn — migrate back to sea, eyes enlarged, flanks silvery.

Ruffe Percidae *Gymnocephalus cernua* **Distribution:** Locally common in England, except the West country. Absent from Wales, Scotland and Ireland. **Other habitats:** Lower river reaches, canals, some lakes. **Notes:** (or Pope). Small, anterior dorsal fin spiny and continuous with posterior fin.

Pikeperch Percidae *Stizostedion lucioperca* **Distribution:** Locally common, spreading from certain Midlands lakes and East Anglian rivers and dykes. **Other habitats:** Weedy lakes, slow rivers. **Notes:** (or Zander). First dorsal fin spiny, separate from second. Prominent sharp teeth.

3-Spined Stickleback Gasterosteidae *Gasterosteus aculeatus* **Distribution:** Widespread through most of Britain. **Other habitats:** Most freshwater bodies, some brackish estuaries. **Notes:** Three dorsal spines anterior to fin, long caudal peduncle. Breeding ♂ in May/June develop red throats and bellies.

10-Spined Stickleback Gasterosteidae *Pungitius pungitius*. **Distribution:** Sporadic. Common in England, Ireland, north Wales and central Scotland. **Other habitats:** Most types of freshwater bodies and brackish estuaries. **Notes:** Usually 9 (7–12) dorsal spines anterior to fin.

alosa) enters rivers, sometimes in large shoals, to spawn. The young remain for about a year in freshwater, and the river Severn is one river where this species may be caught in the spring.

Fish feed on a wide range of aquatic flora and fauna. Some are herbivorous (though they do not normally eat large plants, only phytoplankton and algae), others carnivorous, a few omnivorous. They frequently change their diet as they grow larger. Some species, such as the grayling, will feed upon whatever food is most readily available, although freshwater shrimps, molluscs and insect larvae are the preferred food. A number of species like young trout and tench, feed on plankton and at the other extreme, some species will feed on amphibia, rodents and young birds; pike being the best example. Many fish are able to survive long periods without much food and species such as bream can fast for considerable periods during prolonged cold weather, having laid down large quantities of fat during the summer months.

Breeding, by one species or another, takes place throughout the year. Lavaret spawn in January, followed by smelt and dace in February. Smelt continue into March when grayling start. As more food becomes available in the spring so the number of species spawning in-

The grayling *(Thymallus thymallus)* is a species characteristic of upland rivers since it requires well-oxygenated water associated with strong currents. It also abounds in the Hampshire chalk streams such as the Itchen, the Avon and the Test. It spawns from March to May on gravel on the beds of shallow streams.

A guide to freshwater fish (continued)

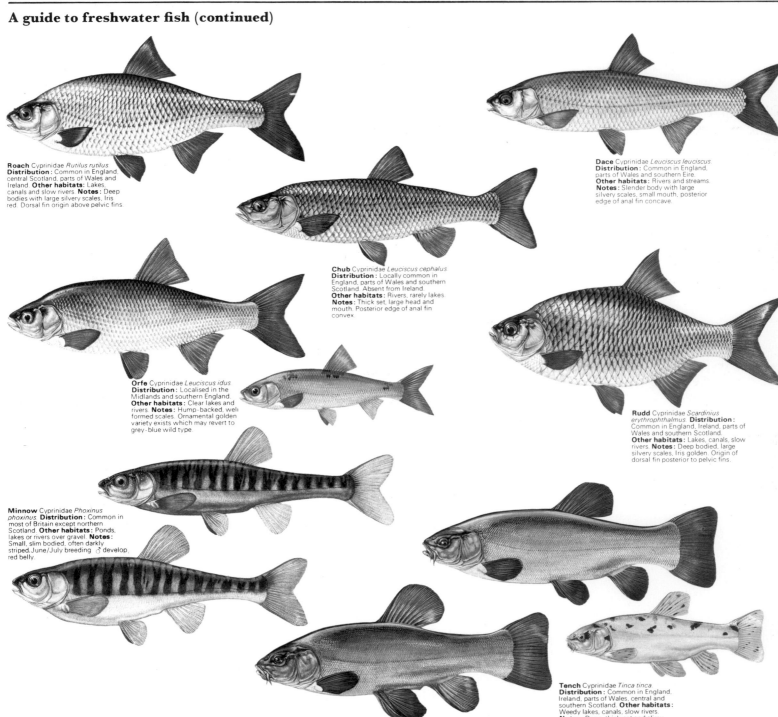

Roach Cyprinidae *Rutilus rutilus.*
Distribution: Common in England, central Scotland, parts of Wales and Ireland. **Other habitats:** Lakes, canals and slow rivers. **Notes:** Deep bodies with large silvery scales. Iris red. Dorsal fin origin above pelvic fins.

Chub Cyprinidae *Leuciscus cephalus*
Distribution: Locally common in England, parts of Wales and southern Scotland. Absent from Ireland. **Other habitats:** Rivers, rarely lakes. **Notes:** Thick set, large head and mouth. Posterior edge of anal fin convex.

Orfe Cyprinidae *Leuciscus idus.*
Distribution: Localised in the Midlands and southern England. **Other habitats:** Clear lakes and rivers. **Notes:** Hump-backed, well formed scales. Ornamental golden variety exists which may revert to grey-blue wild type.

Minnow Cyprinidae *Phoxinus phoxinus.* **Distribution:** Common in most of Britain except northern Scotland. **Other habitats:** Ponds, lakes or rivers over gravel. **Notes:** Small, slim bodied, often darkly striped. June/July breeding ♂ develop red belly.

Dace Cyprinidae *Leuciscus leuciscus.*
Distribution: Common in England, parts of Wales and southern Eire. **Other habitats:** Rivers and streams. **Notes:** Slender body with large silvery scales, small mouth, posterior edge of anal fin concave.

Rudd Cyprinidae *Scardinius erythrophthalmus.* **Distribution:** Common in England, Ireland, parts of Wales and southern Scotland. **Other habitats:** Lakes, canals, slow rivers. **Notes:** Deep bodied, large silvery scales, Iris golden. Origin of dorsal fin posterior to pelvic fins.

Tench Cyprinidae *Tinca tinca*
Distribution: Common in England, Ireland, parts of Wales, central and southern Scotland. **Other habitats:** Weedy lakes, canals, slow rivers. **Notes:** Deep, thick-set and slimy. One pair of barbels. An ornamental golden variety exists.

creases. April sees pike and carp breeding, joined in May by tench; gudgeon usually start in June, barbel in July. Tench are often still spawning in some waters in August. The salmonids spawn throughout the autumn and the year ends with vendace in December. One of the most interesting species is the bitterling. In the breeding season (April–May) the female develops a long external tube through which the eggs are introduced into a freshwater bivalve mollusc such as *Anodonta*, or *Unio*. The eggs pass down the tube, into the mussel's gill chamber where they await the sperm from the male bitterling. The sperm are deposited over the mussel's inhalent siphon and make their way through the mollusc to the waiting eggs. The young fish remain protected inside the mussel for about three or four weeks after hatching, before escaping to live independent lives. The bitterling, in return, often acts as host to the larvae of the mussel. These are called glochidia and are ejected from the parent and swim about until they become attached to a fish like the bitterling. They live as parasites, obtaining their food from the blood of the fish, for about three months before dropping off their host as small perfect mussels to complete their life on the river or lake bed.

The **bullhead** *(Cottus gobio)* is a bottom-dwelling fish found in clear lakes and stony streams. The female lays about 100 eggs in a nest on the bottom where they are guarded by the male for three to four weeks before they hatch. Bullheads are small fish (up to 18cm long) and do not live for much more than five years.

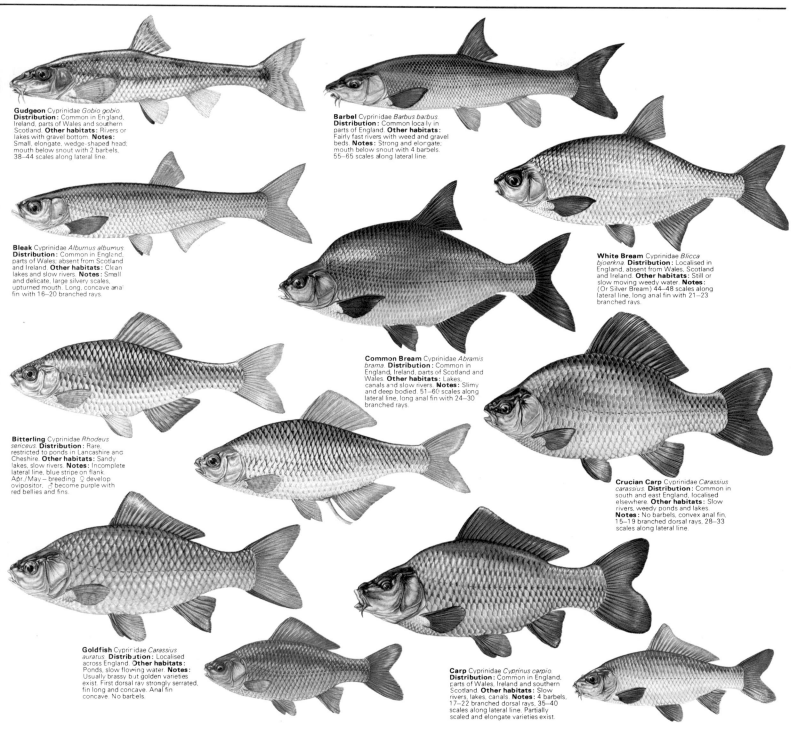

Gudgeon Cyprinidae *Gobio gobio*. **Distribution:** Common in England, Ireland, parts of Wales and southern Scotland. **Other habitats:** Rivers or lakes with gravel bottom. **Notes:** Small, elongate, wedge-shaped head; mouth below snout with 2 barbels, 38–44 scales along lateral line.

Barbel Cyprinidae *Barbus barbus*. **Distribution:** Common locally in parts of England. **Other habitats:** Fairly fast rivers with weed and gravel beds. **Notes:** Strong and elongate; mouth below snout with 4 barbels, 55–65 scales along lateral line.

Bleak Cyprinidae *Alburnus alburnus*. **Distribution:** Common in England, parts of Wales; absent from Scotland and Ireland. **Other habitats:** Clean lakes and slow rivers. **Notes:** Small and delicate, large silvery scales, upturned mouth. Long, concave anal fin with 16–20 branched rays.

White Bream Cyprinidae *Blicca bjoerkna*. **Distribution:** Localised in England, absent from Wales, Scotland and Ireland. **Other habitats:** Still or slow moving weedy water. **Notes:** (Or Silver Bream) 44–48 scales along lateral line, long anal fin with 21–23 branched rays.

Common Bream Cyprinidae *Abramis brama*. **Distribution:** Common in England, Ireland, parts of Scotland and Wales. **Other habitats:** Lakes, canals and slow rivers. **Notes:** Slimy and deep bodied. 51–60 scales along lateral line, long anal fin with 24–30 branched rays.

Bitterling Cyprinidae *Rhodeus sericeus*. **Distribution:** Rare, restricted to ponds in Lancashire and Cheshire. **Other habitats:** Sandy lakes, slow rivers. **Notes:** Incomplete lateral line, blue stripe on flank. Apr./May – breeding ♀ develop ovipositor, ♂ become purple with red bellies and fins.

Crucian Carp Cyprinidae *Carassius carassius*. **Distribution:** Common in south and east England, localised elsewhere. **Other habitats:** Slow rivers, weedy ponds and lakes. **Notes:** No barbels, convex anal fin, 15–19 branched dorsal rays, 28–33 scales along lateral line.

Goldfish Cyprinidae *Carassius auratus*. **Distribution:** Localised across England. **Other habitats:** Ponds, slow flowing water. **Notes:** Usually brassy but golden varieties exist. First dorsal ray strongly serrated, fin long and concave. Anal fin concave. No barbels.

Carp Cyprinidae *Cyprinus carpio*. **Distribution:** Common in England, parts of Wales and southern Scotland. **Other habitats:** Slow rivers, lakes, canals. **Notes:** 4 barbels, 17–22 branched dorsal rays, 35–40 scales along lateral line. Partially scaled and elongate varieties exist.

Amphibians

Eight species of amphibian are found in Britain; six are native and two are recent introductions which only survive in the south. Even though amphibians spend much of their time on land, they must return to the water to breed because their eggs do not have a protective covering like those of birds.

Newts

There are three species of newt, all widespread throughout Britain with the smooth newt (*Triturus vulgaris*) probably the commonest, and the only one recorded in Ireland. The largest is the crested or warty newt (*T. cristatus*) which reaches a length of 15cm. The third species is the palmate newt (*T. helveticus*).

Newts spend much of their time on land, hiding under stones, fallen logs or other objects by day and venturing out to feed mainly at night. They hibernate for much of the winter so the best time to observe them is during the breeding season when they return to water. They prefer ponds and very slow moving waters, and are not found in rushing streams.

The crested newt is the darkest of the three species, with a distinctly warty skin, hence its other vernacular name. The "warts" secrete a strong, unpleasant tasting substance which probably serves to deter predators. It breeds mainly in deeper pools, usually starting in March. The adult male quickly develops a high, serrated crest along its back; he then follows a female, pressing his snout against her, and after some excited behaviour drops a sperm capsule, or spermatophore, beside the female. The female lays between 200 and 300 eggs, which are fertilised from the spermatophore. On completion of their metamorphosis from the tadpole the young newts leave the water and do not return until they are ready to breed, which may be when they are two years old but is more often at three.

The palmate is the smallest of the British newts and may be found in brackish pools at sea level and in high altitude mountain tarns. It is also found on Bardsey, Skomer and Skokholm islands. Although it is often difficult to distinguish the female palmate newt from that of the smooth newt, the male is easily recognised, particularly in the breeding season, by a thread-like filament at the end of his tail and the swollen webs of the hind feet. In the breeding season the male has a prominent ridge along each side of the back which is a glandular pad that develops under the skin. The dorsal crest is lower than that of smooth newts and is straight, not convoluted, along its edge. After the breeding season the crest reduces, the webs on the feet almost disappear and only a small tail filament remains. In several respects the display of the male during courtship is similar to that of the crested newt.

The smooth newt is mainly confined to the lowlands and especially frequents weed filled ponds. The female is dull brown but the male is much more brightly coloured. The brilliance of the colour increases in the breeding season when there are contrasting black spots over the body, a reddish belly, and a pronounced serrated crest. The courtship is not unlike the previous species with the tail of the male doubled back

This female great crested newt *Triturus cristatus* is laying her eggs. Newt eggs are produced singly and attached to water weeds, unlike the floating masses of frogspawn.

along the body on the side nearest the female. After courting for a short period the male deposits his spermatophore near the female, who grasps it with her vent so that the sperms are forced into her body, thus fertilising the eggs before laying. The tadpoles hatch from the eggs and develop until August before they are ready to leave the water. However, some will remain in or very near the water until the following year.

The food of newts is made up of the larvae of many aquatic invertebrates. As they develop and leave the water they will feed upon terrestrial invertebrates such as worms, insects and spiders.

Frogs and toads

Perhaps the best known amphibian is the common frog (*Rana temporaria*), alas nothing like so common as it was a few decades ago. It is widely distributed throughout Britain from sea level to well up into the mountains where they have been seen spawning in small mountain streams well over 1,000 metres above sea level. Water in small peat pools as well as in high-productivity calcareous lakes is suitable, and ditches, slow flowing streams, ponds, lakes, artificial habitats and even temporary water supplies are all acceptable. Frequently vast numbers of frogs will "migrate" to a central breeding area, and they have even been known to halt traffic on busy roads in their quest to return to water. The eggs of frogs, surrounded by a transparent jelly, are laid in solid masses rather than in ribbons like those of the toad. They may be laid as early as January in some areas and it is not unusual for frogs to have their breeding interrupted by a period of cold weather which covers their pond with ice.

The common toad (*Bufo bufo*) is well known to many gardeners and seems better able to tolerate dry soil conditions than the frog which normally only frequents damp areas. Although widely distributed, the common toad is not usually found at high altitudes like the frog. Toads are

A guide to newts

Male newts develop bright colours in spring and a very broad tail. Females lack these features and may be difficult to tell apart, while outside the breeding season even males can be hard to identify. The great crested newt is about 10cm long, much larger than the other species. It has a warty skin and orange belly. The common newt also has a yellow or orange underside, with dark spots. Male palmate newts have large black hind feet, especially in the breeding season.

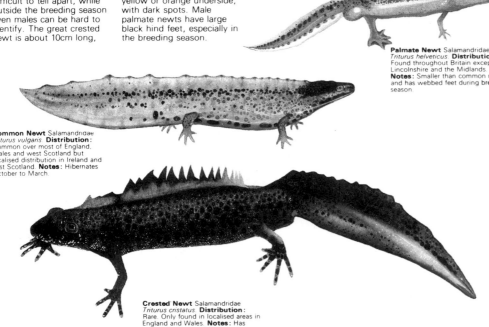

Palmate Newt Salamandridae *Triturus helveticus* **Distribution**: Found throughout Britain except Lincolnshire and the Midlands. **Notes:** Smaller than common newt and has webbed feet during breeding season.

Common Newt Salamandridae *Triturus vulgaris.* **Distribution**: Common over most of England, Wales and west Scotland but localised distribution in Ireland and east Scotland **Notes:** Hibernates October to March.

Crested Newt Salamandridae *Triturus cristatus.* **Distribution**: Rare. Only found in localised areas in England and Wales. **Notes:** Has warty skin, largest British newt. Hibernates September to March.

A mating pair of the common toad *Bufo bufo*. The long strings of toad spawn are usually tangled round underwater obstacles, whereas frog spawn floats freely.

easily identified from frogs by their shorter legs, which means that they crawl rather than hop or jump, and by their dryer, dull, warty skin. Like the newts and frogs, the toad hibernates during the winter months.

The natterjack toad *(Bufo calamita)* is now a rare species restricted to a few localities. It prefers pools on sandy heaths and wet patches among coastal sand dunes, and it is much more agile than the previous species and can run rapidly because the hind limbs are much shorter than those of the frog and common toad. The yellow centre back line immediately distinguishes it from the other British species. If alarmed the natterjack's skin changes so that the dark blotches become even darker and the background colour paler. Toads, including this species, have two additional defence mechanisms to discourage predators; by inflating the lungs, a toad can increase its body size by up to 25 per cent and appears even larger by standing up on straightened hind legs and lowering its fore legs. In addition toads secrete a white, pungent, poisonous fluid in the skin glands, which deters most predators.

The natterjack burrows into the sand during the day and a requirement for mobile dunes or sand may be one of the causes of its decline and scattered distribution, because it has now disappeared from most of its former haunts in Surrey, Hampshire and Dorset. Its decline has been sufficiently marked that the natterjack is the only British amphibian to be favoured with legal protection.

During the breeding season, usually late April to June, the noise made by natterjacks is impressive. Only the males croak, beginning about dusk. The croaking is carried out from within the water, the male lifting his head well above the surface expanding his vocal sacs, then forcing air into the lungs across the vocal chords, the inflated sac acting as a resonator. The noise is a continuing, rapidly repeated

hum-m-m-rup . . . hum-m-m-rup. The croak serves to invite the female into the water for mating. The spawn is produced in a distinctive double band which splits into a single band as it absorbs water. The spawn and tadpoles develop more quickly than in the other frogs and toads, the young leaving the water in six to eight weeks.

Various foreign amphibians have been introduced to Britain, including the European tree frog and the midwife toad, but they do not thrive and colonies rarely persist for long, even in the south. However, the edible frog *(Rana esculenta)* has successfully maintained viable colonies in several ponds in the Home Counties, though many have now been lost as a result of pollution or pond drainage. The marsh frog *(Rana ridibunda)* is the only really successful introduced amphibian. In 1934 a few, left over from a physiology class at University College, London, were released in a garden pond near Romney Marsh in Kent. In 20 years they spread through the dykes and ponds on the marsh and now are very numerous, having apparently displaced the common frog. Both edible and marsh frogs are very noisy in the breeding season (May–June), when the males emit drawn-out croaking noises in a loud chorus which is audible from over 200 metres away.

A guide to frogs and toads

Frogs have a smooth skin, pointed nose and a generally lean and athletic appearance. Toads are more robust, with a warty skin and prominent lumps behind the head. Toads tend to be more tolerant of dry conditions whereas frogs need wetter

areas; both have to return to water to breed.

Marsh frogs are only likely to be found in the Romney Marsh area of Kent, to which they were introduced in the 1930s. The males call loudly in late spring. Common frogs are

widespread but becoming scarce in urbanised areas and arable land.

The common toad is abundant, even in town gardens. It is most likely to be found under logs and stones or lurking in a cool damp spot awaiting passing

prey. The natterjack is localised in distribution. Small colonies are found in parts of the southern counties and also in certain sand dune systems in Norfolk and Lancashire.

Common Frog Ranidae *Rana temporaria*. **Distribution:** Throughout Britain. Very common in Ireland. **Other habitats:** Parks and gardens. **Notes** Hibernates mid-October to late February.

Marsh Frog Ranidae *Rana ridibunda ridibunda*. **Distribution:** Replaced Common frog in Romney Marsh area, (common) there but absent elsewhere. **Notes:** Hibernates mid-October to early April.

Natterjack Toad Bufonidae *Bufo calamita*. **Distribution:** Very rare; only found in localised areas in North West England. **Notes:** Has yellow strip along its back. Hibernates October to February.

Common Toad Bufonidae *Bufo bufo*. **Distribution:** Common in England, Wales and Scotland. Only amphibian found on Orkney. **Other habitats:** Gardens, parks. **Notes:** Hibernates mid-October to mid-March.

Tadpoles of the common frog *Rana temporaria* begin life as herbivorous feeders and later become carnivorous, developing legs before turning into the terrestrial adult form.

Wetland and Freshwater Birds

Most British birds have a need to visit water at some stage, whether it be for drinking or bathing. However, there are many species which are particularly adapted to exploit the aquatic habitats; ducks, geese and swans, the waders and several species such as the kingfisher, dipper and grey wagtail come readily to mind.

Many birds which do visit wetlands perform several necessary or important functions in the maintenance of ecological diversity in freshwater habitats. For example, the pondweed *(Potamogeton natans)* has seeds which germinate more successfully if they have been eaten and passed through the gut of waterfowl, and it is thought that the small snail *(Potamopyrgus jenkinsii)* has spread throughout freshwater in Britain as a result of being carried on the feet of birds. There is evidence to show that many other groups of animals like crustaceans, water mites and rotifers can be transported by birds. Birds which feed on land but roost on water (eg geese and gulls) may provide an important source of nutrients to the aquatic ecosystem through their faeces. Not all waters are equally attractive to birds; many isolated mountain lakes have no fish, and so are unattractive to fish-eating birds, and upland lakes in general have such low levels of productivity that they offer little food of any kind. Similarly, fast flowing streams are frequented by only a few birds; for example, on the River Ogwen, 400m above sea level, only the dipper, common sandpiper and grey wagtail are regularly found, compared with over a dozen species lower down.

Large ponds, overgrown gravel pits and lowland rivers support many more birds; and some wetland habitats like fen carr and certain reedbeds are alive with birds, especially in summer. Even bleak city reservoirs may be attractive in their own way because they provide a safe place for water birds to spend the night. Over 100,000 gulls use the west London reservoirs in this way during the winter, and dozens of species use them as "staging posts" during their migration periods. Many species of waterfowl visit Britain in the autumn because their summer haunts in Scandinavia and the Arctic are frozen for part of the year. In Britain's oceanic climate, many lakes, rivers and reservoirs remain ice-free for the winter months; so it is worthwhile for species like Bewick's swan to fly in from as far away as Siberia each winter.

Divers

Divers are exceedingly well adapted to aquatic life. Not only are their feet webbed and set well

The kingfisher feeds almost entirely on fish caught by plunging into the water. Ice in winter prevents feeding and causes serious reductions in population.

back on the body for most efficient propulsion, but their legs are flattened to present a knife edge to the water offering little impediment during the forward stroke of the paddling movement. However, these adaptations are a liability on land and the birds are hardly able to walk ashore. They must therefore nest close to the water's edge.

In Britain divers are restricted to Scotland as breeding birds although they visit a number of inland waters in England on passage and during the winter. The red-throated diver breeds on many lochs in north west Scotland; often very small peaty pools are chosen, the nest usually being on the bank or upon a small island. The black-throated diver also breeds in north west Scotland, but is absent from Orkney and Shet-

land and does not breed in north west Ireland. Although most of the passage of these birds is along the coasts, occasionally a diver will turn up on an inland lake or mere. In winter, when divers are most likely to be seen in southern Britain, they are in a dull brownish grey plumage and the species are often difficult to tell apart.

Grebes

Unlike ducks and divers, grebes have the feet only partially webbed; the webbing extends separately along each toe as in the unrelated coot.

The grebes are entirely aquatic, with six species having been recorded in Britain. As a breeder the Slavonian grebe is confined to the highlands where it is a bird of shallow freshwater lochs. The first British nest was recorded in 1908 in Grampian, and since then it has spread slowly until the population reached 50 pairs in the early 1970s. At the turn of the century the black-necked grebe was first noticed breeding in Britain, but for a number of reasons this species hasn't made the steady progress of the Slavonian grebe. A large population in Ireland was eliminated after the Shannon hydro-electric scheme was completed. Both these species can be seen on many inland waters as passage and winter visitors. Black-necked grebes, particularly, may be seen regularly on the reservoirs surrounding London during the winter months, but at this time grebes are in their nondescript winter plumage and the species are difficult to differentiate.

The little grebe is more widespread than other British grebes. Unlike the Slavonian grebe which breeds in marginal sedges along the banks of oligotrophic highland lakes, the little grebe is usually associated with denser aquatic vegetation so is widespread on richer waters throughout the British Isles. The little grebe is found on slow flowing rivers, canals, lakes and ponds. It does also occur on some more acid moorland pools.

The heron

The heron *(Ardea cinerea)* spends hours of the day standing motionless or quietly stalking its prey at the water's edge. There are two standing poses which are most frequently used, first with body in the near horizontal axis and head held forward, slightly pointing towards the water, and second with almost vertical axis and head sitting on the shoulders. The stalking attitude is a slow progression with one or two steps between pauses, again with head forward and lowered towards the water surface. The stalking birds are much more successful catching fish than the standing birds.

Herons feed over a very wide range of habitats, from estuaries and mudflats to upland tarns, bogs, marshes and even grasslands. Shallow rivers of both lowland and upland type are also 'fished'. The diet is varied, although fish form a high percentage of the total. When stalking fish the success rate of adult herons is about 50 per cent, with young birds being far less successful.

The heron is an ambush predator, standing motionless at the water's edge waiting until a fish or frog comes within striking distance of its beak.

The larger great-crested grebe occupies many of the same waters as the little grebe, but favours the larger lakes and meres provided they are not too deep. It is particularly numerous on the meres of Cheshire and Shropshire and the Norfolk Breads where dozens of pairs will frequent the same water. However, it is not confined to standing water and is regularly seen on larger slower-flowing rivers such as the Thames and Hampshire Avon. In contrast to other grebes, this species feeds mainly on fish, caught during brief (30 second) dives. Reed-beds are the most favoured nesting sites fringing lowland lakes. Great crested grebes nearly became extinct in Britain during the last century, but have benefited considerably from the provision of new habitats in the form of flooded gravel pits.

Bitterns and herons

The bittern is a localised rare breeder with its main concentration in the Norfolk Broads and an isolated colony at Leighton Moss in the north west, with other sites occasionally containing one or two pairs. The streaky plumage of bitterns provides excellent camouflage in reedbeds, where they spend most of their time. The grey

The great crested grebe at one time became extremely rare, but now probably over 3000 pairs breed in Britain.

They prefer to build their nests among the reeds and vegetation fringing shallow lakes and disused gravel pits.

A guide to some freshwater birds

Most water birds are fairly distinctive and, by virtue of their open habitat, relatively easy to see. Some are quite difficult to tell apart, especially the grebes in winter when they lose their bright colours and all look alike. Similarly the three divers are difficult to distinguish in winter, at which time they are more likely to be seen near the coast. Many of the waders are also coastal birds in winter. Some of the birds shown here swim (ducks, swans, grebes, divers) but others will be seen walking by the water's edge (waders, wagtails, herons). Coot and moorhen do both and, like the water rail and snipe, also frequent wetlands. Certain species (especially dipper, grey wagtail, common sandpiper) are characteristic of clean, fast flowing waters. Others, such as swans and grebes, are birds of lakes and ponds. Some of the species here are rare and specialised: the phalarope is a northern bird and the spoonbill an irregular summer visitor from the Continent to marshy places in the east and south. The reedling (bearded tit) is a bird of extensive reedbeds and the corncrake (now declining rapidly in numbers) is more a species of old-established meadows and long grass, mostly in the north and west.

Great Crested Grebe Podicipitidae *Podiceps cristatus*. **Distribution:** Widespread, south of central Scotland. **Other habitats:** Areas of water, also coastal in winter. **Notes:** Size: 48cm. In flight conspicuous white wing patches. Resident.

Red-necked Grebe Podicipitidae *Podiceps grisegena*. **Distribution:** East coasts. **Other habitats:** Coastal. **Notes:** Size: 43cm. Winter visitor. Distinguished in winter from Great Crested Grebe by darker neck and black-tipped yellow bill. Flight is like Great Crested Grebe.

Black-necked Grebe Podicipitidae *Podiceps nigricollis*. **Distribution:** Breeds central Scotland; winters E. and S. coasts. **Other habitats:** Shallow lakes and coasts. **Notes:** Size: 30cm. In flight longer white wing-patch than Slavonian and dark wing-tips. Slightly uptilted bill.

Little Grebe Podicipitidae *Tachybaptus ruficollis*. **Distribution:** Widespread breeder. **Other habitats:** Variety of water, more marine in winter. **Notes:** Size: 27cm. In flight no wing-patch. Stockier than other grebes. Resident.

Slavonian Grebe Podicipitidae *Podiceps auritus*. **Distribution:** Rare breeder in N.E. Scotland; winters off all coasts. **Other habitats:** Shallow lakes and coasts. **Notes:** Size: 33cm. In winter told from Black-necked Grebe by white cheeks and straight bill.

Black-throated Diver Gaviidae *Gavia arctica*. **Distribution:** Local in north and west Scotland; winters S.E. England. **Other habitats:** Lakes in summer, more coastal in winter. **Notes:** Size: 56–58cm. Bill is more slender than that of Great Northern Diver.

Great Northern Diver Gaviidae *Gavia immer*. **Distribution:** Scotland, Ireland, S.W. England. **Other habitats:** Lakes in summer, coasts in winter. **Notes:** Mainly winters. Very occasionally nests. Size: 68–81cm. Flight is strong but take off is difficult.

Red-throated Diver Gaviidae *Gavia stellata*. **Distribution:** Highlands and islands of Scotland; Co Donegal. **Other habitats:** Nests on moorland lakes, in winter coastal. **Notes:** Uptilted slender bill and whiter appearance distinguishes it from other divers. Size: 53–58cm.

heron is widespread, breeding in woods in colonies. Herons are very vulnerable to long cold winters because their feeding sites freeze over, and their total population has varied from 2,250 to 5,000 pairs in England and Wales during this century—with up to 11,000 pairs probably occurring in the British Isles.

Geese, ducks and swans
The geese, swans and ducks form the family Anatidae, perhaps the most characteristic of freshwater birds. Some species only come to Britain as winter visitors, others breed here and have their populations boosted in winter by an influx of their continental relatives. Only one species, the garganey, is a summer visitor.

The ducks differ markedly in their feeding habits. Some like the pochard and tufted duck can dive to considerable depths and feed on bottom-dwelling invertebrates. They can therefore live on quite deep water (eg reservoirs and many upland lakes), whilst the mallard and mute swan which "up-end" to reach the bottom are more common on shallow lowland waters with plenty of plant food. Ducks like the shoveller filter food from the floating debris at the water surface.

There is a similar diversity of nesting habits. Many species prefer reedbeds and emergent water plants, but some like the introduced mandarin use holes in trees and may thus breed some distance from open water.

The most widespread and numerous duck is the mallard, which occurs throughout the length and breadth of Britain. It nests in a great variety of situations from upland stream sides at 600 metres to coastal, brackish marshes, from village ponds to the largest lakes in the country. The drake mallard has a distinctive glossy bottle-green head, but in summer it is almost uniform dull brown; the "eclipse" plumage. The teal is the next most widespread breeding duck, but nevertheless it is thinly distributed and the total numbers are not great. It breeds on some lowland waters but also on upland bogs, moorlands and peat mosses. The tufted duck is also a widespread breeding species, occurring on lakes, artificial waters such as old gravel pits, lochs and reservoirs. It is one of the most obvious ducks on many waters as the dark females and the black and white drakes sleep out in the middle of the lake.

In the uplands the wigeon is found breeding on oligotrophic lakes and along river banks, and there are a few scattered breeding localities in the south east on coastal marshes or on wetlands away from the coast. In the winter large numbers of additional birds arrive in this country and although the majority are attracted to the coast, they will feed regularly on suitable grass and wetland areas. Like the last species the goldeneye is mainly a winter visitor to our coasts. However, it visits freshwaters in small numbers and occasionally pairs stop to breed in Scotland. It nests in holes in trees and this is probably the prime factor restricting its spread as a breeding bird, because it will readily take to artificial nest sites in the form of nest boxes. The sawbills are fish eating species frequently found. Both the red-breasted merganser and the goosander have been spreading as breeding species in recent decades; formerly they were restricted to Scotland but now they are well distributed in northern England and north Wales. The goosander is more a bird of freshwater and there are favourite winter feeding lakes which regularly support a few birds in several parts of England. A third sawbill, the smew, takes refuge on a number of freshwater lakes, reservoirs and rivers as a winter visitor. Some of the reservoirs and gravel pits to the west of London are regular haunts of this species.

With the increasing numbers of bird watchers rare visitors are seen in increasing numbers. Species such as the ruddy shelduck, blue-winged teal, American wigeon and ferruginous duck are all birds which have been seen on fresh-

A guide to some freshwater birds (continued)

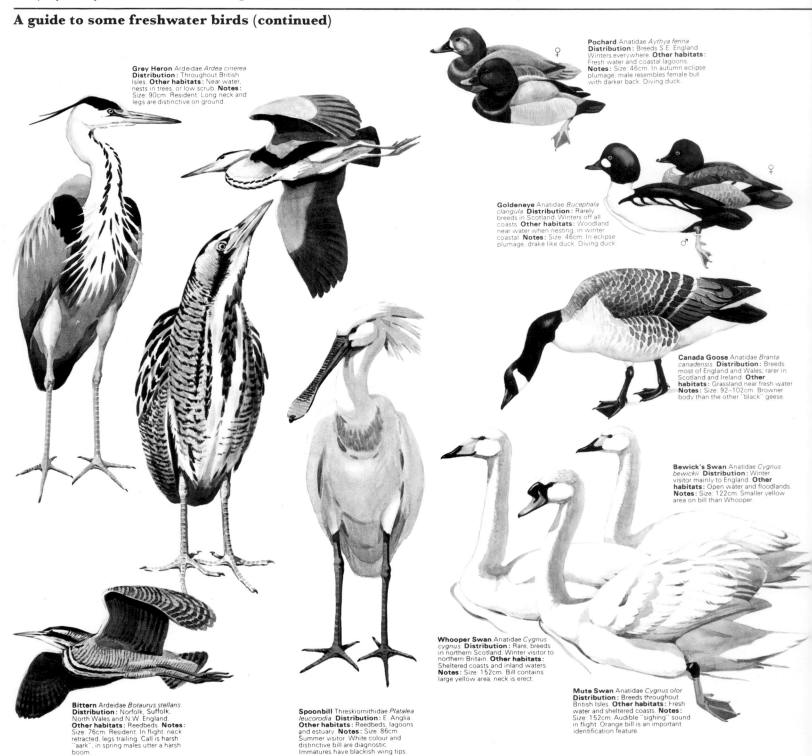

Pochard Anatidae *Aythya ferina* **Distribution**: Breeds S.E. England. Winters everywhere. **Other habitats**: Fresh water and coastal lagoons. **Notes**: Size: 46cm. In autumn eclipse plumage, male resembles female but with darker back. Diving duck.

Grey Heron Ardeidae *Ardea cinerea* **Distribution**: Throughout British Isles. **Other habitats**: Near water, nests in trees, or low scrub. **Notes**: Size: 90cm. Resident. Long neck and legs are distinctive on ground.

Goldeneye Anatidae *Bucephala clangula* **Distribution**: Rarely breeds in Scotland. Winters off all coasts. **Other habitats**: Woodland near water when nesting; in winter coastal. **Notes**: Size: 46cm. In eclipse plumage, drake like duck. Diving duck.

Canada Goose Anatidae *Branta canadensis* **Distribution**: Breeds most of England and Wales, rarer in Scotland and Ireland. **Other habitats**: Grassland near fresh water. **Notes**: Size: 92–102cm. Browner body than the other "black" geese.

Bewick's Swan Anatidae *Cygnus bewickii* **Distribution**: Winter visitor mainly to England. **Other habitats**: Open water and floodlands. **Notes**: Size: 122cm. Smaller yellow area on bill than Whooper.

Whooper Swan Anatidae *Cygnus cygnus* **Distribution**: Rare, breeds in northern Scotland. Winter visitor to northern Britain. **Other habitats**: Sheltered coasts and inland waters. **Notes**: Size: 152cm. Bill contains large yellow area; neck is erect.

Bittern Ardeidae *Botaurus stellaris* **Distribution**: Norfolk, Suffolk, North Wales and N.W. England. **Other habitats**: Reedbeds. **Notes**: Size: 76cm. Resident. In flight: neck retracted, legs trailing. Call is harsh "aark", in spring males utter a harsh boom.

Spoonbill Threskiornithidae *Platalea leucorodia* **Distribution**: E. Anglia. **Other habitats**: Reedbeds, lagoons and estuary. **Notes**: Size: 86cm. Summer visitor. White colour and distinctive bill are diagnostic. Immatures have blackish wing tips.

Mute Swan Anatidae *Cygnus olor* **Distribution**: Breeds throughout British Isles. **Other habitats**: Fresh water and sheltered coasts. **Notes**: Size: 152cm. Audible "sighing" sound in flight. Orange bill is an important identification feature.

waters in recent years. However, the large number of ornamental wildfowl collections in the country means that there is always a chance that such rarities are in fact escaped rather than wild birds. Nevertheless the mandarin and ruddy duck, now firmly established as a resident breeding species, originated as escapes and are now able to survive competition with our native species and the rigours of our weather.

The geese are another group of wetland birds, and as with the ducks there are several escapes or introduced species which are now well established. Perhaps the most successful and best known of these is the Canada goose, one of the only two geese in Britain and whose numbers are not swelled by winter visitors. The other is the much more recently established Egyptian goose which is a native of Africa brought to England for waterfowl collections. The Norfolk population is the only one which has really established itself, although the bird is occasionally seen from Devon to Northumberland. The Canada goose, originally brought as a curiosity from North America, was already breeding wild in Britain by 1785, but even well into the twentieth century was still mainly associated with park lakes and similarly protected sites. The bird has increased rapidly in the past 30 years (the population trebled in the two

Bewick's swan is the smallest and rarest of the three species of swan found in Britain. Each winter a few hundred fly to this country from their breeding grounds in Siberia, returning in March.

Mallard Anatidae *Anas platyrhynchos*.
Distribution: Resident all areas.
Other habitats: Inland waters and estuaries in winter. **Notes:** Size: 58cm. In autumn eclipse moult male resembles female. On the wing there is a blue speculum with white border.

Gadwall Anatidae *Anas strepera*.
Distribution: Breeds E. Anglia. Winter visitor in most areas. **Other habitats:** Ponds and lakes. **Notes:** Size: 51cm. Dull plumage with black tail coverts. Black and white speculum. Surface feeder.

Pintail Anatidae *Anas acuta*.
Distribution: Few breed in Scotland and eastern England. Winter visitor to most areas. **Other habitats:** Freshwater in summer and estuaries in winter. **Notes:** Size: 26cm. Male – green and white speculum, female – brown speculum.

Smew Anatidae *Mergus albellus*.
Distribution: Winter visitor to S.E. England. **Other habitats:** Large open fresh water. **Notes:** Size: 41cm. Diving duck. Female distinct from grebes by white throat and cheeks.

Teal Anatidae *Anas crecca*.
Distribution: Breeds mainly in the north, more numerous in south in winter. **Other habitats:** Winters on inland waters and estuaries. **Notes:** Size 35cm. In autumn male resembles female. Both sexes have green speculum.

Shoveler Anatidae *Anas clypeata*.
Distribution: Breeds throughout British Isles. **Other habitats:** Shallow water with cover. **Notes:** Size: 51cm. In flight both sexes have a blue forewing and green speculum. Enormous bill distinctive. Male has "eclipse" plumage.

Garganey Anatidae *Anas querquedula*. **Distribution:** Summer visitor to S.E. England. **Other habitats:** Shallow pools and creeks with cover. **Notes:** Size: 38cm. Fairly rare. Both sexes have blue-grey forewing and green speculum in flight.

Wigeon Anatidae *Anas penelope*.
Distribution: Breeds northern Scotland. Winters throughout British Isles. **Other habitats:** Breeds near fresh water, in winter more coastal. **Notes:** Size: 46cm. Conspicuous white patch and green speculum on wings in flight. Surface feeder.

Scaup Anatidae *Aythya marila*.
Distribution: Rarely breeds in Scotland, winters in most areas. **Other habitats:** Nests near lochs and rivers, winters on coasts. **Notes:** Size: 48cm. Diving duck.

Tufted Duck Anatidae *Aythya fuligula*. **Distribution:** Breeds eastern Britain. Winters everywhere. **Other habitats:** Fresh water. **Notes:** Size: 43cm. Male distinguished from Scaup by black back. Female has smaller white facial mark than Scaup. Diving duck.

decades following the last war) largely as a result of new habitats becoming available from gravel and clay pits. These geese are now a major nuisance in many areas because of damage to crops and consumption of grass intended for farm animals.

In recent years the greylag goose has become a more widespread breeding species following its re-establishment by wildfowlers. It is our only indigenous goose, a small population surviving on Loch Druidibey, now a National Nature Reserve, in the Outer Hebrides. No other geese (apart from Canada and Egyptian) breed in Britain but large numbers of white-fronted, pink footed and some bean geese feed on wetlands and grasslands during the winter months. Birds like the pink footed goose use freshwater lakes mainly for roosting by night, and by day fly out to feed on surrounding land. Occasionally barnacle geese and brents will feed on wetland grasslands close to the coast, but they are essentially estuarine birds and rarely visit freshwaters inland.

Of the three British swans only the widespread mute swan is resident and is a familiar sight of many a village pond. It is a widespread breeding species, occurring over much of lowland Britain and the total population is about 15,000 birds with a further 5,000 or more in Ireland. Neither of the other two species, the whooper swan or Bewick's swan, breed in this country although

very small numbers of whooper swan have been known to spend the summer in the Outer Hebrides and northern Scotland. Hard weather brings increasing numbers of Bewick's to Britain and if this is prolonged then large numbers of birds from the Ouse Washes may move westwards towards the Severn, Anglesey and Ireland.

The rails

Rails and crakes are compact, skulking marsh birds with short rounded wings. Moorhens and coots are more aquatic than most in their habits and both swim well. The water rail is a secretive bird which is more often heard than seen and is found amongst dense vegetation on the margins of lakes, rivers and canals and in marshland where there is plenty of cover.

The moorhen and coot are two of the most familiar waterbirds. Moorhens can be found on almost any water from field ponds to the largest lakes; from field ditches to large rivers it is only missing from the high ground of Dartmoor, Exmoor, Wales and the Scottish Highlands. There are also very few in the Outer Hebrides and on Shetland. The coot is also widespread but generally requires larger waters than the moorhen. Both moorhens and coots graze grasslands, particularly in winter, but coots also dive for submerged vegetation and so they favour shallow rather than deep lakes. Submerged vegetation is more abundant in rich

lowland lakes, so these tend to support more coots, which also like to use this material to construct their floating nests.

Waders

One of the biggest groups of wetland birds is the waders. The oystercatcher, usually a bird of the shore, feeds on invertebrates, particularly worms, on many wetland grasslands and in recent decades has spread its breeding range along many rivers so that it can now be found as a breeding species in most of Scotland and the north west of England. Of the plovers, the lapwing or green plover is the most widespread of those associated with wetland habitats. Mainly a bird of the farmlands, the lapwing is common in uplands, wet pastures and marshes, but the plover most closely associated with freshwater is the little ringed plover. In France it breeds on the wide gravel and sand banks on the lower reaches of the major rivers, but in Britain it has adopted a man-made substitute: sand and gravel pits. It first nested here in 1938 and now there may be 500 pairs nesting in Britain during the summer in wet pits and beside rivers and lakes. The closely related ringed plover is much more a bird of coastal habitats, but it will visit the shores of inland waters on passage.

The sandpipers, godwits, curlews and snipe are groups which are more frequently attracted

A guide to some freshwater birds (continued)

Green Sandpiper Scolopacidae *Tringa ochropus* **Distribution:** Passage migrant and winter visitor in Wales and England. **Other habitats:** Beside lakes, ponds, and ditches. **Notes:** Size: 23cm. In flight dark upperparts, white rump and blackish under-wings are obvious. Tail barred with black near tip. Voice is a ringing "weet-a-weet".

Wood Sandpiper Scolopacidae *Tringa glareola*. **Distribution:** Breeds in north-east Scotland. Passage migrant. **Other habitats:** Swampy woodlands. Visits pools, creeks, sewage farms and lake margins. **Notes:** Size: 20cm. In flight white rump and projecting feet are obvious. No wing-bars. Does not look so "black and white" as Green Sandpiper. Voice is an excited "chiff-iff".

Common Sandpiper Scolopacidae *Tringa hypoleucos*. **Distribution:** Summer visitor, breeding mainly in northern and western Britain, north of mid-Wales. **Other habitats:** Stony shores of upland streams and lakes. Seen at coast and in wetlands during migration. **Notes:** Distinctive bobbing behaviour, perched on a stone. Prominent white flash under tail as it flies.

Redshank Scolopacidae *Tringa totanus* **Distribution:** Resident in Great Britain and Ireland. **Other habitats:** Breeds on grassy meadows, coastal saltings and low moorlands. Also on estuaries. **Notes:** Size: 28cm. In flight white hind edge of wings and white rump are conspicuous. When uneasy, often "bobs". Voice is a loud "tew-hee-hee".

Black-tailed Godwit Scolopacidae *Limosa limosa*. **Distribution:** Breeds in Cambridgeshire. Winter visitor in south. Passage migrant elsewhere. **Other habitats:** Rough damp pastures and water meadows. Estuaries in winter. **Notes:** Size: 40cm. In flight feet project beyond tail, broad white wing-bars and white tail with black band being obvious. Voice is a loud "wicka-wicka".

Greenshank Scolopacidae *Tringa nebularia*. **Distribution:** Breeds in the north-west Highlands. Elsewhere a passage migrant and winter visitor. **Other habitats:** Breeds on moorlands with pools. Winters on estuaries. **Notes:** Size: 30cm. Distinguished from Redshank by lack of wing-bar and white rump extending up the lower back. Legs project beyond tail in flight. Voice is a loud "tew-ew-tew".

Spotted Redshank Scolopacidae *Tringa erythropus*. **Distribution:** Passage migrant, over-winters in south. **Other habitats:** Coastal areas and inland pools. **Notes:** Size: 30cm. Black plumage is unmistakable in summer. Distinguished from Redshank by lack of wing-bar and projecting legs beyond tail in flight. Voice is a clear "tchu-it".

Curlew Sandpiper Scolopacidae *Calidris ferruginea*. **Distribution:** Passage migrant. **Other habitats:** Estuaries and sometimes inland. **Notes:** Size: 19cm. Distinguished from Dunlin by white rump, more elegant, upright posture, paler breast and brighter eye-stripe. Voice is a soft "chirrup".

Red-necked Phalarope Phalaropodidae *Phalaropus lobatus*. **Distribution:** Breeds in northern Scotland. Elsewhere, a scarce passage migrant. **Other habitats:** Breeds on marshy ground. **Notes:** Size: 17cm. Distinguished in winter from Grey by darker back and white wing-bars. In summer female is much brighter coloured than the male. Voice is a low pitched "whit".

to wetlands and freshwater than plovers, but like so many wading birds and ducks in winter the birds fly off to estuarine and coastal habitats when a rapid temperature drop leads to a reduction in the available terrestrial and aquatic invertebrate food supply. Species such as the dunlin, redshank, greenshank, curlew and snipe, are all found breeding on or near wetlands, frequently on higher ground but not exclusively so. At the onset of cooler weather, or when the young are able to fly they begin to collect into flocks and return to lower lying wetlands and estuaries. The lapwing is one of the earliest birds to aggregate in this way but it is quickly followed by curlew, so that by the end of July quite large parties of this species are seen along muddy shores. It may be, however, that it is the non-breeding or unsuccessful breeders that return first, leaving the available food in the uplands to the rapidly developing young.

Among the waders, the most widespread summer visitor to this country is the common sandpiper, which breeds along the banks of clear upland rivers and streams, or on the shores of upland lakes. The black-tailed godwit, for so long absent as a British breeding species, tried to breed on the Ouse Washes in 1952, succeeded the following year and has bred there ever since. From this small beginning other scattered pairs have bred in the south east and

The cuckoo

This handsome bird, which in flight superficially resembles a hawk, winters in Africa and, as the traditional rhyme suggests, "comes in April", although earlier soundings are frequently recorded. The distinctive call of the cuckoo is by no means confined to wetland and, except for urban areas, may be heard in almost any habitat. The cuckoo does not build a nest of its own, but is parasitic on other species. The female keeps suitable nests under observation until the right stage is reached by the selected host parents, then removes one of the host's eggs and replaces it with one of her own. The whole operation takes only a few seconds, and may be repeated up to a dozen times in different nests, only one egg being laid in each. When the egg hatches the young cuckoo pushes any unhatched eggs or nestlings out of the nest. The adults depart southwards in July, but it is not until much later that the young are ready to leave, and they must therefore rely entirely on instinct to find their winter quarters.

The cuckoo is not usually considered a wetland bird, but reed warblers and sedge warblers are among its most frequent victims. After the cuckoo egg has hatched the baby cuckoo will push any eggs and nestlings from the host bird out of the nest. Here a young 14-day-old cuckoo is seen being fed by a sedge warbler.

Water Rail Rallidae *Rallus aquaticus.* **Distribution:** Resident in Great Britain and Ireland. **Other habitats:** Reedbeds, swampy margins of ponds, rivers and overgrown ditches. **Notes:** Size: 28cm. Long red bill. Dangling legs in flight. Voice is a variety of groans, grunts and squeaks. Often heard at night.

Corncrake Rallidae *Crex crex.* **Distribution:** Summer visitor, breeding mainly in Scotland and Ireland. **Other habitats:** Lush grasslands and crops. **Notes:** Size: 27cm. Chestnut wings and dangling legs are obvious in flight. Prefers to run. Voice is a rasping, continuous "crek-crek". Often heard at night.

Moorhen Rallidae *Gallinula chloropus.* **Distribution:** Resident in Great Britain and Ireland. **Other habitats:** All waterside areas with cover. **Notes:** Size: 33cm. Jerks tail when nervous. Swims with jerking head. Flight is laboured with legs dangling or projecting behind the tail. Voice is a loud "kr-r-rk".

Coot Rallidae *Fulica atra.* **Distribution:** Resident in Great Britain and Ireland. **Other habitats:** Large open waters and estuaries in winter. **Notes:** Size: 38cm. Legs have large "scalloped" toes projecting in flight like long "tail". Patters along the water before taking off. Voice is a high pitched "kowk".

Dipper Cinclidae *Cinclus cinclus.* **Distribution:** Resident in western and northern areas. **Other habitats:** Fast flowing streams and rivers. **Notes:** Size: 18cm. "Bobs" on rocks in water. Wades, and can feed under water. Flight is rapid and usually low, following streams. Voice is a metallic "clink".

Bearded Reedling Timaliidae *Panurus biarmicus.* **Distribution:** Resident in East Anglia. **Other habitats:** Large reedbeds for breeding. **Notes:** Size: 17cm. Tawny brown, long-tailed with males having conspicuous black "moustaches". Flight is laboured on whirring wings. Voice is a metallic "tching-tching".

Pied/White Wagtail Motacillidae *Motacilla alba.* **Distribution:** Pied: Resident all counties. White: Passage migrant (rarely nests in north). **Other habitats:** Open country with buildings, banks etc for nesting. **Notes:** Size: 18cm. Females browner and similar. Males duller in winter.

Grey Wagtail Motacillidae *Motacilla cinerea.* **Distribution:** Resident most areas; rarely winters in eastern England. **Other habitats:** Nest near water; variety of wet sites in winter. **Notes:** Size: 18cm. Female lacks black chin.

Snipe Scolopacidae *Gallinago gallinago.* **Distribution:** Resident in Great Britain and Ireland. **Other habitats:** Boggy areas. **Notes:** Size: 27cm. Secretive and rarely seen until flushed. Zig-zag flight. Tail has white on edges. Voice is a persistent "chick-ka". Tail feathers produce vibrating sounds in display flight.

Jack Snipe Scolopacidae *Lymnocryptes minimus.* **Distribution:** Winter visitor in all areas. **Other habitats:** Marshy areas. **Notes:** Size: 19cm. Distinguished from Snipe by smaller size, relatively shorter bill and slower more direct flight. Lack of white on tail. Normally silent.

Yellow/Blue Headed Wagtail Motacillidae *Motacilla flava.* **Distribution:** Yellow: Summer visitor to much of England. Blue Headed: Breeds locally in S.E. **Other habitats:** Lowland meadows and marshes. **Notes:** Size: 16.5cm. Greenish-brown back.

on the Solway Firth and several have spent the summer in suitable habitats. One of the most spectacular wader courtship displays is that of the ruff, as males sport their summer ruffs in the most elaborate of leks (or courtship arenas). Like the black-tailed godwit the ruff has returned recently to Britain as a breeding species in a few wetland areas, the first positive evidence of nesting being in 1963.

One of the attractions of bird watching on freshwaters and wetlands is the variety of passage migrants or rare American, Siberian or Asiatic visitors which are recorded from time to time. The little stint, curlew sandpiper, spotted redshank and jack snipe, are regularly encountered, and in some coastal areas large flocks of bar-tailed godwit can be seen roosting on flooded fields and marshlands.

Gulls and terns

The gulls and terns are birds which most people associate with the coast, but they are also characteristic of many wetlands and freshwater habitats. Two species are particularly characteristic of land adjacent to northern oligotrophic lakes; the common gull, which usually nests in small colonies, and the black-headed gull, whose colonies can reach several hundred individuals. The black-headed is much more widespread, breeding in Wales and on the east

The coot nests among the marginal vegetation of lakes and rivers. The nest itself is a floating mass of twigs and reeds. Surrounded by water, the nest is relatively safe from land predators.

A guide to some freshwater birds (continued)

Reed Bunting Emberizidae *Emberiza schoeniclus.* **Distribution:** Resident throughout British Isles. **Other habitats:** Damp areas, farmland and heaths. **Notes:** Size: 15cm. Call is a loud "chink"; short, squeaky song.

Kingfisher Alcedinidae *Alcedo atthis* **Distribution:** Resident in Great Britain and Ireland, except northern Scotland. **Other habitats:** Slow flowing rivers and streams. **Notes:** Size: 17cm. Solitary. Flight is rapid and usually low. Hovers when fishing. Perches alertly with nervous "bobbing" action. Voice is a piping "chee".

Sand Martin Hirundinidae *Riparia riparia.* **Distribution:** Summer visitor in Great Britain and Ireland. **Other habitats:** Open country with river banks, cuttings and gravel pits for nesting. **Notes:** Size: 12cm. Distinguished by brown upperparts and a distinct brown chest band. Feeds mainly over water. Flight is more fluttering and erratic than Swallow. Voice is a harsh "tchrrip".

Marsh Harrier Accipitridae *Circus aeruginosus.* **Distribution:** Rare breeder in E. Anglia (sometimes winters). **Other habitats:** Reedbeds, marshes. **Notes:** Size: 48–56cm. Variable colouration of plumage. Note lack of white rump.

Reed Warbler Sylviidae *Acrocephalus scirpaceus.* **Distribution:** Summer visitor to England and Wales. Local in north and west. **Other habitats:** Reedbeds. **Notes:** Size: 12.5cm. Call a low "churr"; song is repetitive and harsh.

Sedge Warbler Sylviidae *Acrocephalus schoenobaenus.* **Distribution:** Summer visitor. Most of British Isles. **Other habitats:** Thick vegetation near water. **Notes:** Size: 12.5cm. Call: loud "tuc-tuc". Song: more varied than reed warbler. Has conspicuous white eyestripe.

Osprey Pandionidae *Pandion haliaetus.* **Distribution:** Summer visitor to Scottish Highlands; elsewhere on passage. **Other habitats:** Lakes and rivers in wooded areas. **Notes:** Size: 51–58cm. Distinctive contrasting plumage.

and south coasts of England, and has a number of inland colonies in the English Midlands. One of the largest colonies is near the Beaulieu River, where there are between 20,000 and 30,000 pairs!

One of the most familiar British birds is the herring gull, which breeds in large colonies round most coasts and can also be seen scavenging on city rubbish tips or following the plough. Outside the breeding season it frequents many inland waters and may be seen returning in long lines of birds to roost on reservoirs and lakes. Similar in size is the lesser black-backed gull, which is more frequently seen inland during the breeding season, nesting on many bogs and moorlands as well as in coastal dune systems. This species feeds much more on terrestrial and aquatic invertebrates than the herring gull and so is associated more with freshwaters. Occasionally the great black-backed gull breeds within colonies of other gulls on freshwater sites, and is sometimes seen in winter on a few waters inland.

Of the terns, only two have a close affinity with freshwater and wetlands; the common tern and the black tern. There has been an increase in inland breeding of the common tern in recent years, particularly on islands in gravel and sand pits. In some places they have been encouraged to breed for the first time by anchoring rafts, covered with shingle, out in open water. Thus common terns now breed on old claypits near Peterborough, 80km from the sea. Terns of several species are regularly encountered on passage over lakes and meres, and the black tern is especially characteristic in spring and autumn as it bobs up and down in flight to pick floating food off the surface of the water.

Insect feeders

Many British birds feed by catching insects in flight, and they are particularly attracted by the abundance of gnats and midges to be found over water and wetland habitats. The mass emergence of adult mayflies in early summer from their aquatic larval stage also provides a great feast. Consequently swifts, swallows and martins are seen in great numbers hawking over water. Their nest sites are not normally chosen with regard to the proximity of water, but the sand martin burrows into sandy and earth banks which are frequently formed by rivers or gravel pit excavation. Thus, fortuitously, this species often has its food and nest site provided indirectly by water. Reedbeds provide swallows and martins (and also other birds like starlings, not normally associated with water at all) with a safe roosting site in early autumn. The same reedbeds are also the home for various warblers, sedge and reed warblers, which are in turn, major hosts for the cuckoo. Thus the cuckoo becomes an associate of a wetland habitat, even though it is not normally thought of as a water bird. The bearded tit is also a special reedbed bird; it is called the "reedling" in some places. The reed bunting is another species which is characteristic of tall vegetation in wetland sites.

Other waterside species

The grey wagtail is a bird of upland fast flowing rivers, while the yellow wagtail favours wet lowland meadows and streams and the pied wagtail has a very varied habitat preference, but is usually found near to water.

Two birds particularly adapted to water are the kingfisher, and the dipper. The former is found hunting fish on all kinds of slow moving waters from rivers, canals, streams and ditches to ponds and lakes while the dipper is confined to fast flowing streams unless it is driven to an estuary in severe weather. While the dipper hunts for its food by swimming underwater, the kingfisher prefers to sit on a perch above the water watching for a fish to swim by before plunging in to get it. This method of feeding is precluded by ice, which in turn is most likely to form on the relatively still waters favoured by the kingfisher. This species is thus very badly hit by prolonged cold winters.

The osprey

The osprey (Pandion haliaetus) is a common species worldwide but in Britain it is a rarity. It was formerly more abundant here but because of persecution by gamekeepers and egg-collectors it ceased to breed in Britain about 1916. A migratory species (wintering in Africa), it continued to be recorded here as an occasional visitor until, in the early 1950s, a pair bred in Scotland. Since then, despite repeated set-backs, due to disturbance and egg-collectors, ospreys have bred with increasing frequency. This success is confined to Scotland, and at Loch Garten and Loch of the Lowes public hides allow two pairs to be observed through all stages of the breeding season by many thousands of people. These nests are continuously guarded and about 20 pairs of ospreys now nest in Scotland.

The osprey normally nests in trees, close to water, and it is our only fish-eating hawk. It hunts by day, catching fish in its long, curved talons, and will drop from as much as 60 metres to the surface of the water. The spiky pads with which its very strong feet are equipped enable it to grip slippery fish, which are then carried head-first as the osprey flies. Many species of fish are taken either from the sea or freshwater, particularly those, such as pike, which bask near the surface.

Ospreys returned to Britain as breeding birds in the 1950s and at least 12 pairs now breed in Scotland every year.

The osprey is a fish-eating bird of prey. The fish are caught with the feet, which bear hooked spines on the underside giving a good grip on the slippery prey.

Wetland Mammals

If the introductions, escapes and occasional visitors to freshwater and wetlands are excluded, there are only three British freshwater mammals; the otter *(Lutra lutra)*, the water vole *(Arvicola terrestris)* and the water shrew *(Neomys fodiens)*. The coypu *(Myocastor coypus)* and the American mink *(Mustela vison)* occur in some parts of the country as escapes and of course, many mammals pay frequent visits to lakes and rivers for drinking. A number of terrestrial mammals are excellent swimmers when the necessity arises, red deer being an example.

Perhaps the freshwater mammal which excites most interest is the otter which, unfortunately, has disappeared from most lowland waters, but is still reasonably abundant in some upland areas and along the coasts and rivers of Scotland. The otter is rarely seen, partly because of its now restricted distribution and partly because of its nocturnal habits. The males are known as dogs and the females as bitches. They construct a shelter or "holt" under the roots of trees or under large bank-side boulders. Their presence on a river can frequently be detected by their tracks or signs; the footprints in mud are particularly distinctive, as the otter has five toes on each foot and these are joined by a web— a characteristic feature of so many animals and birds adapted to the aquatic habitat. On soft mud the outline of the web can be seen between the toes, but the claw marks are very small and show only as small points beyond the toes. The otter normally moves over land in leaps and there is considerable variation in the placing of the feet. In many instances the belly and tail can leave a trail, especially in soft mud or in snow. Occasionally the otter will walk, in which the hind foot is placed behind the fore-foot, or at other times it will trot, in which case the hind foot can be placed in such a way that it overlaps the print of the fore-foot. Otters, particularly when they have young, love to slide down clay, snow or icy banks into the water and their "chutes" can sometimes be found. They use regular feeding places on the banks of rivers and lakes. The faeces (called "spraints") are often diagnostic, the otter's being black, slimy and with an oily smell. The remains of fish scales and fish

bones are often visible. Otters use their droppings to mark out territories, so they are often deposited in clusters on tussocks of grass or sedge or on rocks and tree stumps.

Otters emerge at dusk and swim at the surface. They will eat crayfish, frogs, voles and birds, but when they catch a fish they bring it to the bank to eat. The head or back is usually eaten first and the tail end is discarded intact. As potential predators of salmon and trout they have become unpopular in some places, but otters in

Escapes from fur farms, mainly during the 1950s, led to the American mink *(Mustela vison)* becoming widespread over most of mainland Britain. It is found particularly on river banks.

fact prey mainly on slower moving species which are easier to catch.

The smallest of the aquatic mammals is the water shrew, which is widely distributed in mainland Britain. Like so many mammals it is usually nocturnal and as in the last species has a number of features which make it particularly adapted to an aquatic life; for example, the ear is completely hidden by fur, the tail has a keel formed by a double row of stiff hairs and the large hind toes have a fringe of stiff hairs which are a considerable advantage when swimming. The black upper side with silver-white underside is characteristic and is a colour distribution found in a number of aquatic animals. Although the water shrew is found in a great variety of types of water it is closely associated with slow flowing rivers and streams. At the other extreme it has been observed crossing deep, rapid flowing, upland rivers. Besides swimming it is adept at diving and walking underwater. Although found in many types of water, the water shrew is absent from the Highlands of Scotland. Despite its association with water and special adaptations, the water shrew is not confined to aquatic or even wetland habitats. It may be encountered in hedgerows or even on the dry tops of downland hills.

The water shrew feeds mainly on small invertebrates, but can kill creatures like fish and frogs which are bigger than itself. There is evidence to suggest that this may be accomplished, at least partly, as a result of having toxic substances in its saliva which effectively poison the prey when it is bitten.

The commonest aquatic mammal in Britain is the water vole *(Arvicola terrestris)* which unlike the last species is found in the Highlands. Unlike the water shrew, the water vole is mainly active by day and can be seen frequently nibbling at emergent vegetation. There can be few people who have walked along the banks of a river or canal who have not heard the "plop" of the water vole as it enters the water. The presence

The otter

Otters, which at the beginning of this century were widespread and common, have now declined in numbers, particularly in lowland Britain. The decline has been so marked that the otter is now legally protected under the Wild Creatures and Wild Plants Act.

Otter cubs are very small at birth, their body being only 5-6cm in length, with the tail about the same. The eyes are closed at birth and take a long time, about a month, to open. After about two months the cubs make their first journeys towards the entrance of the holt, but it is another two to three weeks before they take their first swim. During this time they have been suckled by the mother, as well as being brought fish. Once in the water the young soon show an innate ability to hunt and this is then developed by experience and learning from the mother.

Otters seize their fish prey from underneath with their front feet, and kill it before swimming to the bank or to shallow water to eat it. In Scotland, otters frequently live in coastal habitats and feed along rocky shores at low tide. This habitat offers particular advantages in cold winters, because rockpools do not freeze over and offer food at all times, unlike ponds and shallow lakes.

The otter's fur is closely set and waterproof, while air, trapped in the fur, acts as an insulating layer.

The otter *(Lutra lutra)* has become very scarce in most of lowland Britain and is now legally protected. It has suffered greatly from disturbance to its riverside habitat but in some areas otters are still quite common, particularly in western Scotland.

of water voles can be established in many cases by the entrances to tunnels low down in river banks. Frequently such holes are underwater, with a ventilation shaft higher up on the bank. Other signs include chewed water plants, cylindrical droppings and tiny footprints in waterside mud. The water vole is also ideally adapted to its aquatic surroundings, having thick water-repellent fur and ears which are modified to keep out water. The brown rat (*Rattus norvegicus*) is often found in similar waterside situations to the water vole, but the more pointed snout and prominent ears distinguish the rat from the vole.

The coypu (*Myocastor coypus*) was introduced from South America as a fur bearer to be kept in captivity. However, enough escaped to establish the species in the wild, where it did considerable damage by eating crops and burrowing into river banks. Despite attempts at eradication, the coypu is still abundant, though now confined to East Anglia and subject to very high mortality in cold winters.

The American mink (*Mustela vison*) was also brought to Britain to be kept in fur-farms. It too escaped, and since the 1950s has become one of the most widespread British carnivores. It is principally a river-bank species and feeds on fish, small mammals and birds. Despite attempts to exterminate mink, the species now seems permanently established and is certainly far more likely to be seen in most parts of England and Wales than our native otter.

The Chinese water deer

This small deer, barely 60cm high at the shoulder, was introduced to Woburn Park in Bedfordshire about 1900. Escapes from there have now established a wild population of this species in parts of Norfolk and the east Midlands. It is extremely shy and retiring and easily escapes detection in the reed-beds and long grass where it lives. The males do not have antlers like other deer but instead grow prominent curved tusks. These are extremely sharp and may be up to 8cm long. They are probably, like antlers, used for fighting and social display during the rut. This occurs in mid-winter and the young are born in May and June.

The Chinese water deer *(Hydropotes inermis)* has become widespread in Britain as a result of escapes from captivity in Woburn Park, Bedfordshire. It is found, particularly in wetland habitats in the east Midlands and East Anglia.

A guide to some wetland mammals

The otter is now rare in the south and east where the mink is more likely to be seen. The mink has a very pointed nose and prominent ears, both of which are distinctive when swimming. The otter is much larger and on land its webbed feet, broad flat head and heavy, short-haired tail are characteristic. Mink occur in various colour forms, from white to black; otters do not. The coypu is restricted to East Anglia. It has a heavy build and squarish head and prominent whiskers. It might be mistaken for an otter in the water but the latter is now very scarce in East Anglia and also more sinuous in its movements. The water vole is rat-sized and sometimes confused with the brown rat which readily takes to water. Rats have a pointed face and greyish brown fur; the water vole is chocolate brown, with a pinky-orange belly and flanks. Water shrews are sometimes found near clean water, but also occur widely elsewhere. They are a boldly contrasting black, above, and white below.

Water Vole Cricetidae *Arvicola terrestris.* **Distribution:** Mainland Britain but local in N. Scotland. Some islands. **Other habitats:** Grassland. **Notes:** Rat sized but tail, ears and muzzle shorter. Fur shaggy, brown or black. Swims and dives well.

Chinese Water Deer Cervidae *Hydropotes inermis.* **Distribution:** Bedfordshire and adjacent counties. **Other habitats:** Grasslands and adjoining cover. **Notes:** Larger than Muntjac but paler, large rounded ears. Male lacks antlers but upper canines may be visible. Tail same colour as body, no prominent rump patch. Fawns have parallel lines of white spots on coat. Active dawn and dusk.

Coypu Capromyidae *Myocastor coypus.* **Distribution:** Norfolk and East Suffolk. **Notes:** A large rodent, shaggy brown fur on back, front fur grey. Webbed hind feet. Prominent orange incisors. Almost hairless tail. Mainly nocturnal.

Mink Mustelidae *Mustela vison.* **Distribution:** Patchy throughout mainland Britain and Ireland. **Notes:** Dark brown, sometimes with white patches. May be pale brown, grey or white. Slightly bushy tail. Mainly nocturnal.

Otter Mustelidae *Lutra lutra.* **Distribution:** Widespread but rare throughout mainland Britain. Ireland. **Notes:** Long body, short legs, flat head, small ears, prominent whiskers. Long tapering tail. Webbed feet. Brown coat with pale throat. Swims smoothly with V-wake. Nocturnal.

Man-made Habitats

Hardly any of Britain remains unaffected by man except some mountain tops and a few parts of the coast. In that sense, most of the habitats described in this book may be described as "man-made". However, these are better considered as "semi-natural" or "man-modified" habitats to distinguish them from habitats actually created by man, such as towns, rubbish tips and gardens.

Similarly, although pastureland and meadows owe their existence to man, their ecological relationships are still semi-natural; whereas arable farmland is an almost wholly artificial habitat. It is ploughed, harrowed, sown, fertilised, weeded, harvested and manipulated almost daily to ensure that all its biological productivity is channelled into supporting a single species, the crop, for man's use. Wildlife is an irrelevance at best; at worst it is a competitor—a "weed" or "pest" to be eliminated; indeed efficiently farmed arable land contains less wildlife than an equivalent area of urban land. Hedgerows provide its one redeeming factor. These are rich in wildlife and are of great interest; yet again, they are artificial man-created and man-managed habitats.

This section reviews, very briefly, the general ecology of some of the great diversity of very specialised habitats created by man which are quite different from any natural habitat which might have preceded them.

For thousands of years man had a steadily increasing impact on the landscape, and in the last 200 years his influence has become almost universal. Poplar-shielded orchards set amidst arable farmland at Chingley Wood, Kent, exemplify man's manipulation of the landscape.

Arable Farmland

Nearly a third of all land in Britain is used for arable farming. The intensity of agricultural production and the type of cultivation varies greatly in different areas depending on the soil type, topography and climate among other factors, and generally, the more efficiently the land is farmed, the less wildlife it supports.

Arable land predominates in the lowlands; the most favourable areas being those with flat fertile land, warm summer weather, low rainfall and a lack of high winds. Eastern England, especially East Anglia has a suitable climate and a base-rich soil but in the west the climate is more oceanic, the topography is steeper and the soils are more acidic, leading to a predominance of permanent grassland. In the arable areas wheat and barley are the main crops, together with peas and beans, potatoes, sugar beet and fodder crops.

The agricultural methods of the past were compatible with a variety of wildlife and many farms supported a great diversity of plants and animals. Modern agricultural practice is very different and major impacts are caused by mechanisation, chemicals and specialisation in farming technique. Changes on modern farms are often rapid and there is little time for animal life to adjust. The change from old-fashioned to modern farming involves such things as enlarging fields for arable crops by the removal of hedgerows and the lowering of water tables by major drainage schemes to enable more land to be cultivated.

In spite of these trends there are still many niches on farmland which can be occupied by plants and animals. Field edges and odd corners are usually inhabited by weeds like grasses and fat hen, but are much influenced by the chemicals used on crops. Waysides on farms are often semi natural grassland with interesting species

but they may be affected by spray drift, or are even deliberately sprayed to create a tidy appearance on the farm. Further pockets of diversity are provided by ponds which are most common in livestock areas because they originated as watering places for the animals.

The principal aim of arable farming is to concentrate plant productivity in one plant species, ruthlessly eliminating competing 'weeds' and thus greatly reducing species diversity in the habitat.

The flora of such places is not usually outstanding but there are several rare plants which are characteristic of the cattle trodden mud of pond margins including small fleabane, orange foxtail grass, mudwort, least water pepper and black cyperus sedge. The fauna of farm ponds may also include the common dragonflies, frogs, toads and newts; and the moorhen is also a regular feature.

Weedkillers, pesticides and frequent intrusions by farm machinery are all inimical to wildlife; indeed that is their purpose, to concentrate all production into a single species, the crop itself. However, cornfields, vegetables and other crops may still harbour a few survivors which will benefit from the provision of abundant food (in the form of fertilizers or the crop plant) and also gain by the eradication of less adaptable competitors. Those plants which have been successfully adapted to the challenge of the new habitat are branded as "weeds" and about 200 species have been found growing on arable land, the most successful being those adapted to living in disturbed soil. About 90 species depend heavily on arable farmland for a home and a few are virtually unknown in other habitats.

Cornfield weeds exploit the disturbed soil and lack of competition in cultivated fields. Their association with man can be traced back into antiquity and in some cases the species' natural origins are unknown. Characteristically the weeds are annual plants that spread by seeds shed by last year's generation, or else they are introduced as impurities in imported seed corn. Harvesting imposes a type of artificial selection on these plants, favouring the species that ripen seed before the harvest or those that are short or prostrate in form and survive the harvest to produce ripe fruit in the stubble.

The chalky soils have a number of attractive and characteristic weeds like venus looking-glass, scarlet pimpernel, lesser toadflax, fumitory and cornflower. Sandy soils have a quite different and specialised weed flora capable of tolerating the dry, well drained and well aerated soil which is usually calcium deficient or acidic in nature. Common weeds of sandy fields include the corn marigold, storksbill, vipers bugloss, sheep's sorrel and corn spurrey.

Arable weeds

Modern agricultural methods have brought about the decline of some of these plants while others are still troublesome weeds. Improved seed cleaning and screening has caused the disappearance of some plants from our fields and new practices such as stubble burning have probably caused the decline of spreading bur-parsley and other species that ripen in the stubble. The use of chemical herbicides provides effective control from which there is practically no escape.

In spite of effective modern methods of weed control certain plants contrive to be a nuisance both in arable fields and in horticultural ground. They often have adaptations that enable them to produce enormous numbers of offspring. Common adaptations involve the production of several generations per year and huge numbers of seeds that remain viable for a long time. For example, shepherd's purse produces self-pollinated flowers, ripens seed a few weeks after germination and produces up to three generations in a season. Moreover the seeds have a mucilaginous surface layer which becomes sticky when wet enabling them to adhere to feet and wheels and thus be spread from place to place. Groundsel is another familiar weed of cultivated ground. It produces up to three generations a year which yield wind-borne fruits that can germinate without delay. The potential output averages about 1,000 offspring per plant!

Couch grass is an unusual weed because it is

The corn poppy

The corn poppy, *Papaver rhoeas* is the commonest of a number of species of poppies which are weeds of arable crops. It occurs especially on lighter soils where it grows in temporary leys grown for hay or among corn and other arable crops. L ke a number of other arable weed species this poppy has a long association with man's cultivated land. so much so that its natural habitat and origins are not known.

A conspicuous feature of the plant is its ability to appear in abundance very soon after soil is disturbed because the buried seeds can remain viable for a very long period, probably more than 100 years. This results in spectacular shows of its scarlet flowers on construction sites and new road works which are on the site of former arable land. Seed production is very high with the fruits producing more than 1,000 tiny lightweight seeds per capsule and the total seed output per plant probably averages 17,000 seeds. Some of the seeds can germinate immediately while others will not germinate for a while even under ideal conditions.

In spite of the fact that the plant can now be controlled by the use of herbicides it can still be seen in crops, sometimes appearing in patches or along certain crop rows where, perhaps, the chemicals were not effective. This is in contrast to many other cornfield weeds that are now very scarce and difficult to find.

Poppies are well adapted to arable land because their seeds can remain dormant in the soil for years, until ploughing encourages them to grow. Modern harvesting, however, often removes the plants before they seed.

perennial. It produces wiry underground stems that spread rapidly in light soils and if the stems are broken up, (by ploughing for example) even small portions can produce new plants.

While there is a small number of weeds that remain common and troublesome there are many others that are becoming increasingly rare and species such as the corncockle, hedge hog parsley and pheasant's eye are virtually extinct. It is likely that in the future the majority of cornfield weeds will exist only in special places where they are deliberately sown and encouraged.

The habitats and ecology of a farm

1 Hedges on farm perimeter often coincide with ancient boundaries and hence tend to be species-rich.

2 Internal hedges largely removed or replaced by wire fences.

3 Farm buildings. Habitat for nesting birds and mammals

4 Grassland paddocks adjacent to farm may be species-rich even if other grassland is improved.

5 Trackside in farmyard harbours many weeds. Even nettles may be valuable as foodplant for butterflies.

6 Trees round farmyard may include elms containing rookeries or nesting pigeons.

7 Permanent grassland may attract lapwings and contain cowslips.

8 Dew pond. Traditional means of collecting run-off water (not dew) for cattle.

9 Copses retained or planted for shooting provide cover for game birds.

10 Pond, originally for watering livestock, now replaced by troughs, etc. May contain frogs and newts.

11 Flood meadows. Flooded too regularly to be cultivated, but used for hay and grazing cattle.

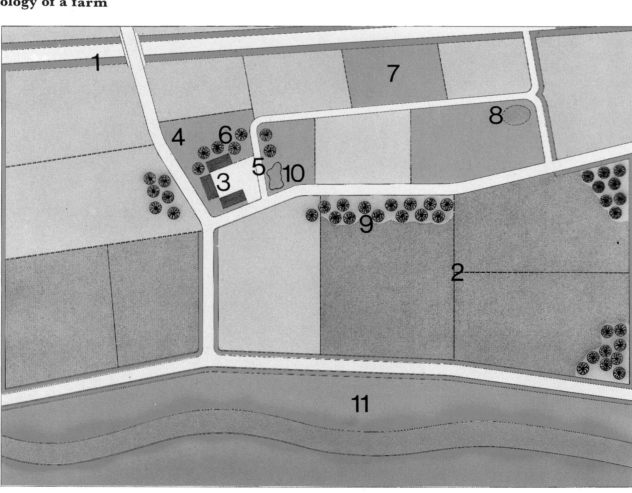

Hedgerows

Hedgerows were probably originally planted to mark ancient boundaries, to estates and parishes for example, and certain hedges still serve this purpose centuries later. However, the majority of hedges were planted especially in the eighteenth and nineteenth centuries to enclose patches of land in order to establish ownership or retain livestock. The hedges are formed from woody shrubs which are (or should be) cut regularly to maintain a bushy structure near the ground and prevent them becoming too tall and loose to stop cattle and sheep forcing their way through. Hedgerows are very extensive in Britain; estimates suggest a total length of about a million kilometres.

The density of hedges in the landscape, the type of management treatment and the basic species content, are all very variable. The lowest number of hedges is found in the arable areas of East Anglia where the fenland counties average only about 16 metres of hedge per hectare of farmland in some areas. In the west of the country where mixed farming or stock farming predominates the density of hedgerows is greater and their management is more regular.

The modern trend shows a general pattern of hedge removal especially in arable districts where the hedge no longer serves any useful function on the farms but takes up space and impedes the efficient use of large farming machinery. Generally the oldest and richest farm boundary hedges survive while the more recently planted internal hedges are removed. The rate of hedge removal is now slowing down because there are few hedges left to remove in some areas and there is little to gain by taking

out the last remnants.

Formerly the management of hedges was done by hand. The shrubs would be trimmed and the taller stems cut partially through, bent down and woven into the base of the hedge. This process produced a dense low hedge, but is very labour intensive. The modern trend is towards increasingly mechanised management of hedges especially in East Anglia where tractor mounted machines are used to regularly trim hedgerows

Hedgerows are an ancient part of the English countryside, providing food and cover, as well as convenient paths. Here, they connect Widdecombe with wild moorland.

down to low well clipped barriers. The hedges in these areas are often allowed to develop gaps and are not replanted. They also suffer from damage periodically through rampant stubble fires in the adjacent fields.

Hedges consist of a variety of shrubs and trees together with flowering plants. Hawthorn is the

Natural history of hedgerows

Hedges are particularly rich habitats for wildlife because they combine the features of woodland and open fields with particular opportunities of their own. Habitats like this, formed at the junction of two or more different habitat types, are known as "ecotones" and are characterised by their richness. Furthermore, the constant growth and continued cutting of hedgerows mean that the habitat is constantly changing — a further encouragement to species diversity. Much depends on just when the hedge is cut — a difference of a few weeks can greatly alter the composition of the flora and the special insects that depend on it. The variety of hedgerow plant and insect life supports a wide range of birds, whose numbers are enhanced by the many species which feed in adjacent fields but retire to the seclusion and shelter of hedges in order to nest. In some parts of the country, where little woodland remains, many species would be entirely absent but for the havens offered by hedgerows. The actual species present depends much upon the structure of the hedge and the types and ages of trees within it. A

kilometre of mixed hawthorn and elm hedge may support over 40 pairs of nesting birds.

It takes a long time to establish a good hedgerow, and it is the oldest ones (perhaps established for several centuries) which support the greatest variety of wildlife; hence the importance of conserving them, for they cannot be quickly replaced or regrown. Hedges, however, take up space and cost money to maintain, so many have been removed. An estimated 200,000 kilometres of hedgerow have been lost since the last war, a process encouraged by government grants to improve farming efficiency. This financial incentive to destroy hedges has now been discontinued and hedgerows may be seen to benefit agriculture by providing wind breaks and shelter belts. In areas where many hedges have already gone, those that remain are often vital to prevent valuable topsoil being blown from the fields during winter gales. The hedges also provide a home for insectivorous birds which help control pests in the adjacent crops; they may, in addition, support many species of beneficial insects without harbouring extensive populations of pests.

3. Some hedgerow shrubs are allowed to grow into full-sized trees, a prominent feature of the English landscape. The majority of British elms are found in hedges; so are many oaks, some of which become 'stag headed' with dead branches protruding from their canopy.

4. Tall hedges are important as sheltered feeding and nesting places for many species of birds. Closely trimmed hedges may have more small birds nesting in them, but do not harbour the larger species.

5. In arable areas the hedgerow is of little use to the farmer and costs money to maintain. Hedges are often removed to make room for farm machinery and to increase the size of the fields.

6. Because hedgerow planting and maintenance are so expensive, wire fences are often put up as a cheap substitute. These serve the farmer's purpose, demarcating fields and keeping animals from straying,

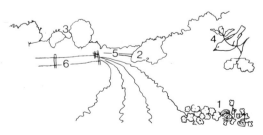

1. Where hedgerows and roadsides are kept cut back, many colourful flowers flourish in summer. These herbs include many of the special food plants required by insects and other invertebrates.

2. Where the hedge is allowed to sprawl outwards, it shades the ground underneath, suppressing herb growth and reducing plant and animal diversity.

commonest basic constituent but sometimes mixed hedges are planted using blackthorn and holly in addition. Other species may arrive as seed; in a young hawthorn hedge, rose, blackthorn and ash soon appear while other shrubs like hazel and field maple are very slow to colonise even if seed sources are readily available nearby. The presence of hazel and woodland herbs like dog's mercury, bluebell, wood anemone, primrose and yellow archangel are all good indications that a hedgerow originated as part of a wood as these species spread very slowly and do not readily colonise hedgerows.

A hedge planted as pure hawthorn slowly acquires additional species as it gets older and studies of the species diversity of hedgerows in relation to their age, (where this can be reasonably accurately dated from historical records) have shown that there is a more or less direct relationship between the number of species established in a hedge and its age. As a general rule one new species colonises the hedge every hundred years, so that a two-species hedge could be 200 years old and a ten-species hedge 1,000 years old, but this is only a rough guide; there are many local features which modify the situation.

Hedgerow trees

Sapling trees commonly sprout from hedges, especially ash, sycamore, beech and oak, but are often trimmed off before reaching full size. Elms are highly characteristic hedgerow trees, and were important in the past as forage plants and as a source of timber. Several climbers thrive but are favoured by particular types of

Hedgerow flowers in early summer: bluebells and red campion predominate here, but earlier or later in the year, in spring and autumn, other species may be prominent.

management, for example, woody nightshade and white bryony are both more abundant in unmanaged hedges, but clipped hedges favour rose and honeysuckle.

Some five or six hundred species of plants have been recorded from hedgerows but probably only about half of these regularly occur. Certain wayside plants like hedge garlic, cow parsley, hedge woundwort, wild arum and hogweed are common hedge bottom species. Many of these have associated insects which are abundant in hedgerows, but generally occur elsewhere too. Several butterflies are common as associates of hedgerow plants, for example the brimstone which feeds on buckthorn as a larva; the orange tip whose foodplant is hedge garlic and the gatekeeper that feeds on bramble. Two species are more restricted to hedgerows: the white letter hairstreak, that is dependent on elm, and the brown hairstreak which feeds on young blackthorn in hedges near woodland, but is less common within woodland itself. The latter species over-winters in the egg stage attached to twigs and is adversely affected by intensive management and trimming of the hedgerow.

Hedgerows are important reservoirs of wildlife, especially on arable land where little other shelter exists, but they are also important as routes for dispersal of species. Many isolated copses and patches of habitat in field corners can be reached by species moving along the hedgerow, and without its shelter they might never spread to their new home. Hedgerows are thus not just homes but vital highways for wildlife, linking many different and separate habitat units in the countryside.

The Urban Habitat

At first sight, cities appear inimical to wildlife, but many of our major cities lie on rivers which permit survival of fish, birds and other aquatic species.

Urban habitats pose a severe challenge to wildlife. The constant passage of wheels and feet exclude ground nesting birds and also prevent the development of many plants. In turn, the lack of plants means less food for animals, fewer insects and thus less prey for insectivorous creatures. Large areas of ground are covered by bricks and concrete, further reducing the potential for plant growth and, to cap it all, the air may be heavily polluted with oil fumes and toxic gases (like sulphur dioxide) which are particularly damaging to plant tissues.

As a result of these difficulties, urban wildlife tends to be rather sparse. However, for those things that can come to terms with the problems there may be considerable advantages in town life, not least being the exclusion of their less adaptable competitors.

Advantages of city life

The concrete jungle, unlike a real one, actually generates and traps heat. Cars, people, factories, central heating systems; all produce warmth which is trapped in the stonework of streets and buildings. Bricks and concrete also absorb the sun's warmth during the day and release the heat at night. As a result, towns are 5°C or more warmer than the surrounding countryside,

with fewer frosts and a longer growing season. This is why daffodils in town parks bloom a week or two earlier than those only a few kilometres away out in the country.

The food problem is lessened by the fact that many people put out food for birds (or pets) in their gardens; others make a point of feeding the birds in parks and town squares. Dustbins and street markets provide rich pickings for those animals which are prepared to scavenge. Formerly the nose bags and dung of city horses provided plenty of food for house sparrows, and the change to motor transport has meant that sparrows are less numerous now than a century ago.

Despite the general disturbance of the hurly-burly of towns, there are many quiet nooks for plants and animals that require little space in which to live. There are derelict buildings, waste ground, builder's yards and many odd corners where people rarely go. The main problem for a plant or animal is how to reach such a spot. It is here that railway embankments, canals and road verges may play a vital role in providing access, deep into the heart of a city. Foxes in particular have invaded many cities, so have grey squirrels and even muntjac deer. These creatures seem able to survive in small

The presence of young tawny owls in cities shows that families can be reared in urban conditions.

growing even high above the ground on top of buildings and walls in the dirt that tends to accumulate from the dusty town air.

gardens and parks, but need railway banks and other avenues for urban penetration in order to reach these havens surrounded by streets and buildings. Many cities are built on major rivers which often provide important access routes. In the past 100 years, gulls have developed the habit of moving inland up major rivers during the winter and often benefit from the warmth and shelter of town parks. The river Thames is responsible for many exotic creatures, from whales to puffins and otters being seen close to

The European scorpion, brought in from the Continent by container traffic, has become established locally in seaports and spread by the motorway network. One colony has been discovered in a London Underground station! Unlike its many relatives, the species is harmless.

the very centre of London.

Plants too need access routes, though many have the advantage that they can be wafted in on the wind. Plants with wind borne seeds are usually the first to appear on derelict ground, and some like the ragwort and rosebay willow herb are so successful that they can be found

Pollution problems

Rivers, ditches and ponds in urban areas (where they still exist) tend to be polluted by rubbish and oily run-off from roads and pavements. As a consequence, many of the more intolerant plants and animals are displaced – there are only two colonies of frogs left in central London for example. If the polluted water is cleaned up, there may be a spectacular improvement in wildlife diversity; the best example being the return of fish to the Thames. Millions of pounds spent on improved sewage works and other forms of pollution control have meant that salmon have appeared in London's river for the first time in a hundred years and over 95 other species of fish have now been recorded in the Thames. Only a decade or so ago there were stretches of the river which had practically no fish at all.

The pollution of city air is mainly by gases from engines and chimneys. Sulphur dioxide is the principal problem because plants are especially sensitive to it. Some lichens for example, are killed by concentrations of only a few parts per million. Indeed lichens can be used as indicators of urban pollution, especially those that grow on trees which are not buffered by a stony substrate which helps to neutralise acidity in the air. Few tree bark lichens survive in central city areas but one, *Lecanora conizaeoides* seems to have become much more tolerant than its relatives and has thus become far more abundant at their expense in the last hundred years or so.

Town air is also laden with soot and dust which darken the surfaces of trees and buildings. Pale coloured moths and other invertebrates are very conspicuous against such a background and are soon picked off by birds. Thus, over the past 100 years certain species which occur both as pale and dark coloured varieties have undergone marked population changes. The best example is the peppered moth *Biston betularia*, the dark form of which was rare a century ago and still is in unpolluted rural areas. However, in grimy towns, the pale forms were constantly eliminated, giving the dark form a chance to proliferate to an extent not seen elsewhere. However, the Clean Air Act and the efforts of municipal authorities to clean up dirty buildings have meant that the dark moths now once again have no particular advantage and their paler brethren are becoming more numerous in cities once more.

Indoor animals

The greatest variety of indoor animal life is provided by invertebrates, most of which are regarded as pests. Some species are parasites of man, such as bed bugs and fleas. Many others are scavengers seeking food scraps or poorly stored food materials. They include exotic insects from warmer countries which are able to live in Britain in artificially heated indoor environments, like crickets, various species of cockroach and pharoah's ants. Insects that eat dead wood, (like the death watch beetle) have colonised man's homes to become serious pests. Carpet beetles, larder beetles and clothes moths have all turned their attention to animal products in the home ranging from furs and woollen clothing to stored meat. A number of insects also enter houses for shelter, especially during the winter months when small tortoiseshell butterflies, peacock butterflies, queen wasps and lacewing flies may be found in the attic.

Rats and mice have been so successful in colonising man's own personal environment that they have been transported all over the world. House mice are even sufficiently adaptable to thrive inside cold storage plants among frozen sides of beef; while brown rats are at home in the permanent darkness of sewers.

Distribution of the Oxford ragwort

The case of Oxford ragwort, *Senecio squalidus*, makes an interesting study of the way in which a plant can be introduced into Britain by man and soon become established as an accepted member of our flora, with a widespread distribution.

The plant is a native of Sicily where it grows on volcanic ash. It was introduced to this country at Oxford Botanic Garden from whence it has spread. It was recorded as growing on old walls in Oxford at the end of the eighteenth century. Within a hundred years the plant had spread to seven other counties in southern England and during the twentieth century the plant has become widely distributed in England and Wales and occurs both in Ireland and Scotland. The plant forms a low sprawling bushy growth with bright yellow flowers and deeply divided deep green leaves. During and after the war it became common on bomb sites in London and is now a very familiar plant of waste ground, railway ballast and sidings, and old walls. It usually chooses stony, well drained places which are presumably similar to its natural habitat. The plant is a prolific producer of fruits which are wind dispersed and bear a parachute of hairs. The way in which the plant has spread and the pattern of colonisation in particular areas, suggest that railways have been responsible in part for the distribution of this alien. Presumably the seeds are readily sucked along by the draft of passing trains while the tracks and associated railway yards provide suitable habitats *en route*.

Oxford ragwort is a plant that grows in the wild on volcanic sites. It arrived in Britain accidentally and proved ideally suited to buildings and rubble.

The Flora of Man-made Habitats

As man's demands for housing and transport, and for industry and agriculture, continue to increase, so too do the areas of man-made habitats that result. Even in the most apparently inhospitable of sites, such as the sides of railway bridges or industrial waste tips, plant life still thrives. Most of us now live in towns or cities, but if we care to look there is a surprising wealth of plants to be found, quite apart from those deliberately grown in our gardens.

The most critical stage in the life history of most plants is the initial establishment of the young plant, and this is achieved through a great variety of methods. Rapid establishment is especially important in ground that is frequently disturbed, such as waste tips and arable land. Many of the weeds of arable land are plants characteristic of open conditions, which today are largely confined to man-influenced habitats and to coasts. There are two main strategies for plant success in such conditions, involving seed production and vegetative reproduction respectively. Many weeds are annuals capable of rapid germination, growth and flowering, so that there is a good chance of seeds being produced before the ground is disturbed again. A good example is the scarlet pimpernel (*Anagalis arvensis*) which may produce up to 12,000 tiny seeds from one plant and which flowers early enough for the

Plantains (*Plantago* spp.) are normally regarded as weed species and are well adapted to man-made environments. Although able to grow in most types of soil, as well as in cracks in paving and walls, they usually require an open aspect. They have a rosette growth habit which protects the growing plant.

A guide to some arable weeds

Plants classified as weeds of arable land are those that grow in direct competition with the crop. They have two main life-forms, either as ephemerals or creeping perennials. The former complete their life cycle in a few weeks and produce masses of seed (such as shepherd's purse), while the latter rely on their ability to regenerate entire plants from fragments of the underground organ (such as creeping thistle). In some areas parasitic plants (such as dodder) can be a nuisance.

Few weeds are found growing in the crop nowadays due to the purity of seed and the action of selective weedkillers: often the borders of fields are not treated and it is in such places that the richest assemblages of weed plants are to be found.

Hairy Bitter Cress Cruciferae *Cardamine hirsuta* **Distribution:** Throughout the British Isles. **Other habitats:** Bare ground; rocks; screes; walls. **Notes:** Very common species; grows up to 1300 metres; seed pods erect; usually self pollinated.

Shepherd's Purse Cruciferae *Capsella bursa-pastoris* **Distribution:** Throughout the British Isles, but less common in north-west Scotland. **Notes:** Very common; very variable; often forms distinctive local populations.

Slender Tare Papilionaceae *Vicia tenuissima*. **Distribution:** South England, mainly central and east. **Other habitats:** Grassy places. **Notes:** Locally common species; tendrils are usually simple.

Soft Cranesbill Geraniaceae *Geranium molle*. **Distribution:** Throughout the British Isles, but less common in Wales, Scotland and Ireland. **Other habitats:** Dry grassland; dunes; waste places. **Notes:** Grows up to 550 metres; plant covered with long, soft, white hairs.

Creeping Thistle Compositae *Cirsium arvense*. **Distribution:** Throughout the British Isles. **Notes:** Very common; grows up to 650 metres; visited by hoverflies and butterflies, often in large numbers; often grows in gardens.

Petty Spurge Euphorbiaceae *Euphorbia peplus*. **Distribution:** Throughout the British Isles, but less common in northern Ireland and Scotland. **Notes:** A very common species of arable and cultivated land; grows up to 450 metres.

seeds to produce a second generation of plants later in the same year. Other plants rely largely on vegetative reproduction. Couch grass (*Agropyron repens*) is not only deep rooted but spreads by long underground stems which may grow out more than 3 metres in one year. Even if these rhizomes are broken up by digging or ploughing they are still capable of producing new plants. The diversity of arable weeds is less today than in the past, partly due to the use of herbicides; but in some cases it may be due to the greater purity of agricultural seed. The corn cockle (*Agrostemma githago*) was a common contaminant of seed in the last century and was a widespread weed. With the cleaner seed of today it is now quite rare.

Many garden weeds show similar adaptations to life in disturbed ground. Plants such as groundsel (*Senecio vulgaris*), shepherd's purse (*Capsella bursa-pastoris*), and hairy bittercress (*Cardamine hirsuta*), are all able to colonise rapidly by producing large numbers of seeds and by rapid growth and flowering, features that allow them to seize new opportunities quickly and establish themselves on even the smallest patches of newly exposed soil.

A common weed of verges and farm gateways also illustrates the importance of human transport in the spread of plants. The rayless chamo-

Red valerian (*Centranthus ruber*), which blooms from June to October, is an introduced plant that usually has red or pink flowers. It is frequently cultivated but also occurs widely in the wild, especially on old walls, cliffs, dry banks and waste places. Pollination is carried out by long-tongued insects, mainly Lepidoptera.

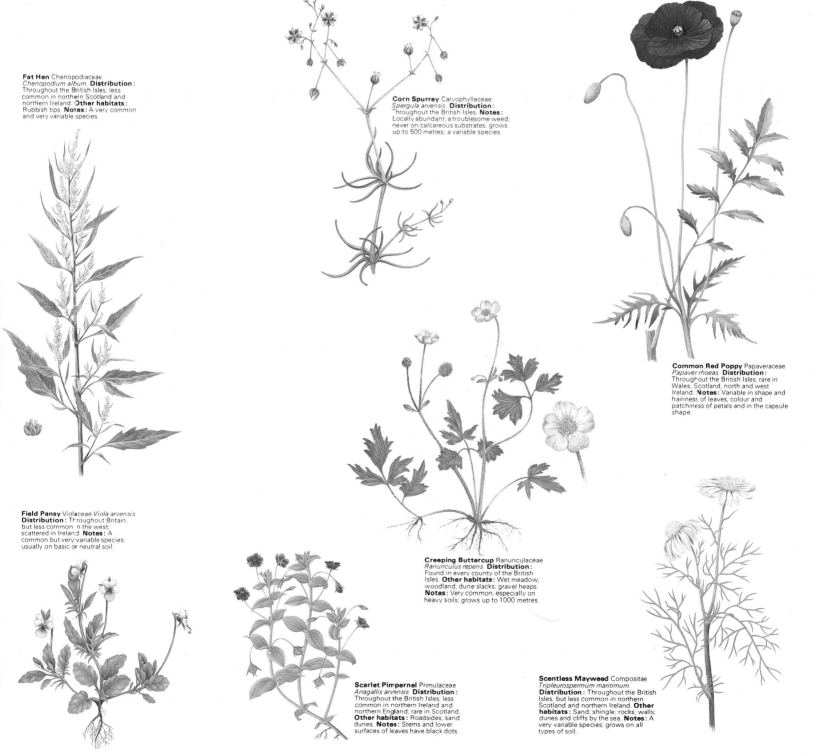

Fat Hen Chenopodiaceae *Chenopodium album.* **Distribution:** Throughout the British Isles; less common in northern Scotland and northern Ireland. **Other habitats:** Rubbish tips. **Notes:** A very common and very variable species.

Corn Spurrey Caryophyllaceae *Spergula arvensis.* **Distribution:** Throughout the British Isles. **Notes:** Locally abundant; a troublesome weed; never on calcareous substrates; grows up to 500 metres; a variable species.

Common Red Poppy Papaveraceae *Papaver rhoeas.* **Distribution:** Throughout the British Isles; rare in Wales, Scotland, north and west Ireland. **Notes:** Variable in shape and hairiness of leaves, colour and patchiness of petals and in the capsule shape.

Field Pansy Violaceae *Viola arvensis.* **Distribution:** Throughout Britain, but less common in the west; scattered in Ireland. **Notes:** A common but very variable species; usually on basic or neutral soil.

Creeping Buttercup Ranunculaceae *Ranunculus repens.* **Distribution:** Found in every county of the British Isles. **Other habitats:** Wet meadow; woodland; dune slacks; gravel heaps. **Notes:** Very common, especially on heavy soils; grows up to 1000 metres.

Scarlet Pimpernel Primulaceae *Anagallis arvensis.* **Distribution:** Throughout the British Isles; less common in northern Ireland and northern England; rare in Scotland. **Other habitats:** Roadsides; sand dunes. **Notes:** Stems and lower surfaces of leaves have black dots.

Scentless Mayweed Compositae *Tripleurospermum maritimum.* **Distribution:** Throughout the British Isles, but less common in northern Scotland and northern Ireland. **Other habitats:** Sand; shingle; rocks; walls; dunes and cliffs by the sea. **Notes:** A very variable species; grows on all types of soil.

mile *(Matricaria matricarioides)* is an introduction to Britain, probably from north east Asia via North America. It was first recorded in 1871, and in the 30 years after 1900 spread virtually throughout Britain. Unlike other members of the daisy family its seeds do not possess a downy parachute for wind dispersal, but are spread by mud and rain – the plant's spectacular spread is almost certainly due largely to the seeds being carried in the mud-caked tyres of early motor cars. The Oxford ragwort *(Senecio squalidus)* is now a widespread plant of waste ground and railway embankments. It escaped from the Oxford Botanic Gardens before 1800 and its spread seems likely to have been in part aided by the railway system. Embankments and cuttings, which were frequently burned and ash covered, provided a habitat in some ways similar to the volcanic ash soils of its native Sicily. Modern motorway verges are another new source of relatively undisturbed land and may in the future provide valuable sites for plants of open and grassland habitats.

Plants of tracks and pathways must be able to withstand both crushing and abrasion by trampling and a hard compacted soil. Typical is the fast growing annual meadow grass *(Poa*

Horsetails *(Equisetum* spp.) are fern allies that are well adapted to growth in man-made habitats. They are perennials with creeping underground rhizomes from which the stems arise at intervals. This means that they are able rapidly to invade and colonise suitable sites. There are eleven species in Britain, of which five are widespread.

A guide to some urban weeds

Urban weeds are those plants that are not wanted in the garden. Apart from competing for light, minerals and water, many have a more sinister effect in that their roots produce toxins designed to inhibit the growth of plants around them.

As with arable weeds, these plants are mainly either ephemerals (like shepherd's purse) or perennials (such as ground elder), though "normal" annuals (like rayless chamomile) are also frequently encountered. Urban weeds are restricted in their distribution by both climatic and soil conditions.

Japanese Polygonum Polygonaceae *Polygonum cuspidatum.* **Distribution:** Scattered throughout the British Isles, but rare in the extreme north of Scotland. **Notes:** A commonly cultivated species.

Stinging Nettle Urticaceae *Urtica dioica.* **Distribution:** Throughout the British Isles. **Other habitats:** Hedge banks; woodland; grassy places; fens; stony soils. **Notes:** Abundant up to 900 metres; covered with stinging hairs.

Broad-leaved Dock Polygonaceae *Rumex obtusifolius.* **Distribution:** Throughout the British Isles, but less frequent towards the north. **Other habitats:** Field margins; hedgerows. **Notes:** Especially common on disturbed ground.

Oxford Ragwort Compositae *Senecio squalidus.* **Distribution:** England and Wales; local in Scotland and Ireland. **Notes:** On old walls, embankments and waste ground; this species is now spreading rapidly.

Rose Bay Onagraceae *Epilobium angustifolium.* **Distribution:** Very common in Britain except north Scotland; scattered throughout Ireland, especially in the east. **Other habitats:** Rocky places; scree slopes; wood margins; wood clearings; disturbed ground. **Notes:** A very variable species; found up to 1000 metres.

Coltsfoot Compositae *Tussilago farfara.* **Distribution:** Throughout the British Isles. **Other habitats:** Arable fields; waste places; banks; landslides; dunes; screes; streamsides; shingle; flushes. **Notes:** Grows up to 1000 metres; prefers stiff soils; flowers close at night; flowers appear before the emergence of the leaves.

Rayless Chamomile Compositae *Matricaria matricarioides.* **Distribution:** Throughout the British Isles. **Notes:** Especially common on tracks, paths and much used gateways; strongly aromatic; abundant, and becoming more so.

Mugwort Compositae *Artemisia vulgaris.* **Distribution:** Throughout the British Isles; very common in the south, but much less so in the north. **Other habitats:** Roadsides; hedgerows. **Notes:** Has a variable leaf and inflorescence shape.

annua) which frequently grows in the cracks in pavements. Other track plants may form small tough cushions, such as the pearlwort *(Sagina procumbens)*, or have rosettes of tough leathery leaves, such as the daisy *(Bellis perennis)* and the plantain *(Plantago major)*. Towards the edges of paths two grasses may be common, the perennial rye grass *(Lolium perenne)* and wall barley *(Hordeum murinum)*.

Derelict sites and other urban wastelands often have a rich and colourful plant life. This may include many species which would be unwelcome in our gardens but which provide a splash of colour on wasteland, emphasising that perhaps the best definition of a weed is simply that it is a plant growing in the wrong place!

To be successful, such wasteland plants must be able to establish themselves whilst the ground is still open, for there may be only a limited number of sites on the surface suitable for seed germination. Many do this by the production of enormous numbers of seeds, as in the case of the rosebay willow-herb *(Epilobium angusti-folium)* which lends such a brilliant mauve colour to many waste sites and areas which have been recently burned. Once established from seed, the coltsfoot *(Tussilago farfara)* can spread

extensively by its underground rhizomes, while its large leaves cast a dense shade. The seeds of fat hen *(Chenopodium album)* show another adaptation to an unstable environment. They have varying dormant periods so that germination may be spread over a number of weeks, increasing the chance of at least some seeds germinating in favourable conditions. Many of our urban wasteland plants are introductions. Typical is the Canadian fleabane *(Erigeron canadensis)* which came from North America about 1700. It spread only slowly until this century, when railways and bomb-sites greatly extended its range. In fertile soils stinging nettles *(Urtica dioica)* are abundant. They are especially characteristic of soils with high nitrate levels caused by dung and domestic wastes.

If a waste site is left undisturbed the early colonising plants are soon shaded out by larger species, such as the scrambling brambles *(Rubus* spp), or woody species such as buddleja *(Budd-leja davidii)*. This is a garden escape, introduced from China only at the end of the 19th century, but which is now one of the commonest urban woody plants. Buddleja is also one of the several plants able to grow on walls, its roots exploiting crevices in the brickwork.

Wall-rue *(Asplenium ruta-muraria)* is a common fern that is usually found growing on walls and basic rocks throughout the British Isles.

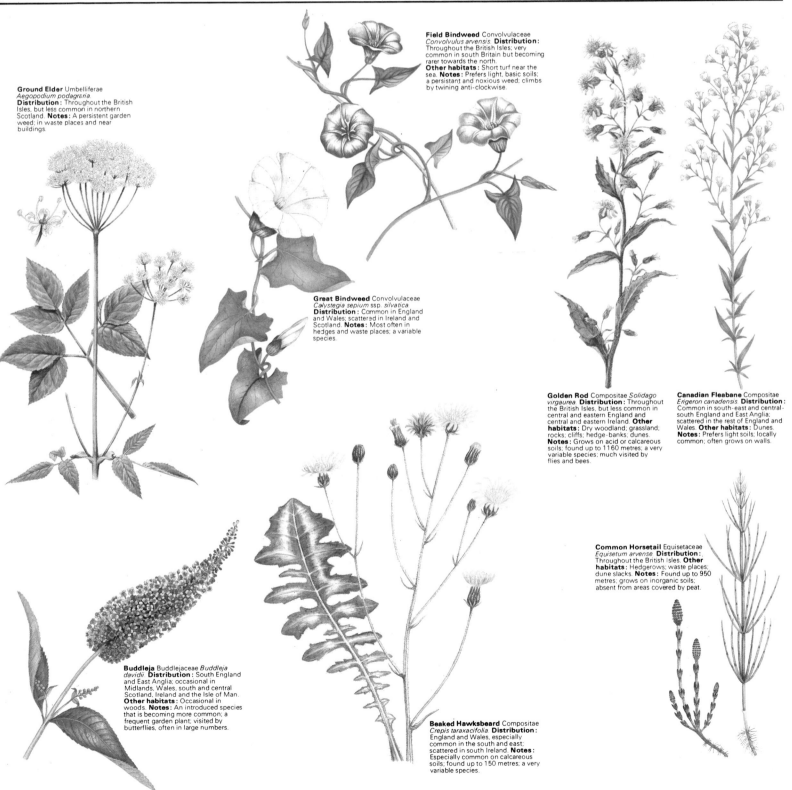

Ground Elder Umbelliferae *Aegopodium podagraria*. **Distribution:** Throughout the British Isles, but less common in northern Scotland. **Notes:** A persistent garden weed; in waste places and near buildings.

Field Bindweed Convolvulaceae *Convolvulus arvensis*. **Distribution:** Throughout the British Isles; very common in south Britain but becoming rarer towards the north. **Other habitats:** Short turf near the sea. **Notes:** Prefers light, basic soils; a persistant and noxious weed; climbs by twining anti-clockwise.

Great Bindweed Convolvulaceae *Calystegia sepium* ssp. *silvatica*. **Distribution:** Common in England and Wales; scattered in Ireland and Scotland. **Notes:** Most often in hedges and waste places; a variable species.

Golden Rod Compositae *Solidago virgaurea*. **Distribution:** Throughout the British Isles, but less common in central and eastern England and central and eastern Ireland. **Other habitats:** Dry woodland; grassland; rocks; cliffs; hedge-banks; dunes. **Notes:** Grows on acid or calcareous soils; found up to 1160 metres; a very variable species; much visited by flies and bees.

Canadian Fleabane Compositae *Erigeron canadensis*. **Distribution:** Common in south-east and central-south England and East Anglia; scattered in the rest of England and Wales. **Other habitats:** Dunes. **Notes:** Prefers light soils; locally common; often grows on walls.

Buddleja Buddlejaceae *Buddleja davidii*. **Distribution:** South England and East Anglia; occasional in Midlands, Wales, south and central Scotland, Ireland and the Isle of Man. **Other habitats:** Occasional in woods. **Notes:** An introduced species that is becoming more common; a frequent garden plant; visited by butterflies, often in large numbers.

Beaked Hawksbeard Compositae *Crepis taraxacifolia*. **Distribution:** England and Wales, especially common in the south and east; scattered in south Ireland. **Notes:** Especially common on calcareous soils; found up to 150 metres; a very variable species.

Common Horsetail Equisetaceae *Equisetum arvense*. **Distribution:** Throughout the British Isles. **Other habitats:** Hedgerows; waste places; dune slacks. **Notes:** Found up to 950 metres; grows on inorganic soils; absent from areas covered by peat.

Invertebrates of Man-made Habitats

Aphids have sucking mouthparts with which they withdraw sap and juices from plant leaves, causing withering.

Whiteflies

Whiteflies (order Hemiptera) are small homopteran bugs allied to the froghoppers and the aphids. Their wings are covered with a white, waxy powder, giving them the appearance of minute moths. They all feed on plant juices, which they suck with the needle-like beak typical of all the bugs, usually while sitting on the undersides of leaves. The young nymphs move about to start with, but then they lose their legs and remain motionless, just sucking plant sap until they turn into adults. Whiteflies are mainly tropical insects. There are about 14 British species, and a number of introduced species can also be found in greenhouses.

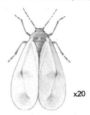

Cabbage Whitefly Aleyrodidae *Aleyrodes proletella.* **Distribution:** Much of British Isles. **Adult Active:** Summer. **Food:** Cabbages and related wild and cultivated plants.

Hedgerow bugs

Bugs (order Hemiptera) are a very large and variable group of insects, but they all possess needle-like, piercing beaks through which they suck liquid food. There are two distinct sub-orders—the Heteroptera and the Homoptera. In the Heteroptera, the front wings, if present, are horny near the base and membranous near the tip. They are folded flat over the body at rest. The homopteran front wing, if present, is of uniform texture throughout—either tough or membranous—and folded roofwise over the body at rest.

Lygus pratensis Miridae. **Distribution:** Throughout British Isles. **Other habitats:** Woodlands; gardens; heathlands. **Adult active:** March to October. **Food:** Wide variety of shrubs and herbaceous plants.

Pied Shield Bug Cydnidae *Sehirus bicolor.* **Distribution:** Hedgerows in southern half of Britain (not Ireland). **Other Habitats:** Woodlands; gardens; and waste places. **Adult Active:** April to September (hibernates underground). **Food:** White deadnettle and related plants.

Many plants and animals (especially insects) which are common in natural habitats also occur in man-made habitats, often in even greater numbers. This is because man generates a complex mosaic of communities (e.g. hedgerows, gardens, road verges etc.) which frequently support a greater diversity of wildlife than a natural habitat of comparable area.

Because people are much more likely to see such insects in these man-made habitats this section reviews a particularly wide range of insect groups and species.

Bugs and aphids

There are over 1,500 species of bug in Britain, most of which feed by sucking juices out of plants or animals, using piercing mouthparts. Many species make themselves a nuisance, particularly in gardens by damaging plants and by carrying virus diseases.

The eggs of bugs hatch directly into miniature wingless adults which moult as they increase in size and develop progressively into the adult form. There is no major transformation stage comparable to the pupa of a butterfly.

About a third of the British species are heteropterans in which the wings are thick and hard at their bases and soft and transparent towards the tips. The fore wings are crossed over the back and do not lie side by side as in beetles (but like the latter, the hind wings are used for flight). Shield bugs belong to this group and characteristically have a wide, squarish front end, giving them a "broad shouldered" appearance. Other species include squash bugs, whose name is not derived from the characteristic flat shape of bugs in general but owes its origin to the squash gourd on which it feeds in its native America. Squash bugs were introduced to Britain, but are not a serious nuisance because they do not feed on commercially valuable plants.

The 200 species of capsid bugs are mostly long, thin brown or green creatures which form the largest family of Heteroptera. Most feed on grasses by piercing the seeds, injecting saliva and sucking out partially digested food. One species feeds on apples in this way, the saliva causing discoloration of the fruit.

Two thirds of the British bugs belong to the Homoptera, in which the whole of the fore wings is either hard (as in froghoppers) or soft and transparent (as in aphids). The aphids are probably the most familiar bugs, with 500 species which reproduce at a phenomenal rate. The females lay their eggs in the autumn and these hatch the following spring into wingless females. These actually bear live young, again all females. Some have wings and fly to soft garden plants where they produce yet another generation of wingless females. Each aphid can produce perhaps 50 female offspring each of which will produce 50 of their own in the three weeks or so in which they will live. In five years, if they were left unchecked, it is said that they would outweigh the human race! It is not until the autumn that males are produced who will mate with females to produce the eggs, which last over winter. Aphids form an important food source for many carnivorous insects and small birds. They are also carefully tended by ants, which like to collect a sugary secretion called honeydew. Lime trees growing along city streets may support huge numbers of a particular aphid species (perhaps 10 million on a single tree) which will produce so much of this material that it drips to the ground where it forms a sticky mass.

Woolly aphids produce a waxy secretion which forms a protective mass in which they hide – rather like a solid smoke screen. These white fluffy masses are a common sight on apple trees. White flies, which attack cabbages, resemble minute moths but are relatives of the aphids.

Aphids

Aphids (order Hemiptera) are small bugs belonging to the sub-order Homoptera. They may be winged or wingless, but most can be recognised by their pear-shaped bodies and by the two slender tubes, called cornicles, sticking up from the hind end. All feed by plunging their slender beaks into plants. They breed very rapidly in summer, when all the aphids are parthenogenetic females. They give birth to one or more offspring every day, and the offspring are ready to give birth themselves within a week or so. Dense clusters thus build up on the plants, although some of the aphids are winged and fly to other plants to start up again. Males appear in autumn and mate with the females, which then lay over-wintering eggs—often on trees and shrubs, even though the summer forms may occur on herbaceous plants. There are about 530 British species, in seven families.

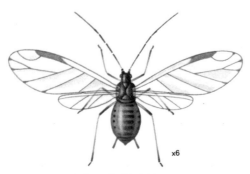

Lachnus roboris Lachnidae. **Distribution:** Most of British Isles, wherever oaks grow. **Other habitats:** None. **Adult active:** Spring to autumn. **Food:** Sap of oak trees.

Lacewings

Lacewing flies (order Neuroptera) are delicate insects, usually with green or brown wings. Most eat aphids in both adult and larval stages. The eggs of the green lacewings have slender stalks attaching them to plants. The larvae are spiky, shuttle-shaped creatures, often covering themselves with the skins of the aphids that they have sucked dry. Many green lacewings come into the house to hibernate in the autumn, and some turn a rather dirty pink colour at this time. There are over 50 British species, in five different families. Some have aquatic larvae. Twelve are green lacewings.

Chrysopa sp Chrysopidae.
Distribution: All over British Isles.
Other Habitats: Everywhere with good vegetation cover. **Adult Active:** Spring to Autumn. **Food:** Aphids and other small insects.

Lacewing larvae are carnivorous. This young *Chrysopa vittata* is performing a useful role by eating garden aphids.

The almost vertical take-off of the adult lacewing is revealed here through ultra-high-speed photography. These green insects, with their characteristic filmy wings, are frequently found about the house.

Aphids are a pest because of their sheer numbers. Even though each only consumes a minute amount of plant sap, collectively this removes enough to cause wilting. They also transmit viruses among vegetables and valued garden plants.

Lacewings

Lacewings are usually nocturnal and are most often seen in houses because they hibernate indoors over winter. They are slow flyers and have large, elegant, net-like wings.

Both the adult and the larvae of the common green lacewing feed avidly on aphids and are thus a gardener's ally. In a macabre kind of insect scalp collecting, the adult lacewing impales the empty skins of its victims on the hairs of its back. These shrivelled remains help break up its outline and serve as camouflage.

Butterflies and moths

There are about 70 species of British butterflies and some 2,000 species of British moths, so the division of the insect order Lepidoptera into these two groups is somewhat disproportionate. The butterflies are more familiar to us because their bright, distinctive colours make them conspicuous and easy to identify. Moreover, they fly during the day, whereas most moths are nocturnal. Over half the moths are small and nondescript brown in coloration. These are generally dismissed, almost despairingly, as "micromoths" because their more precise identification is a job for the expert. They include many small brown species like the clothes moth.

Butterflies are easily distinguished from moths because they have knob-ended antennae (moth antennae are usually feathery). They also have a thin body and hold their wings together vertically above the back when at rest.

The species of moths outnumber butterflies by nearly 300 to 1, but because they are mostly small, drab and fly at night, they are much less well known. They do include some colourful species, notably the cinnabar and tiger moths and others which are superbly camouflaged against the bark or rock on which they rest during the day. The yellow and the red underwings are good examples; in these species the forewings provide a camouflaged covering for the

The butterflies represent ten families. The ones most frequently seen in gardens are probably the whites (Pieridae); blues (Lycaenidae) and browns (Satyridae) are common grassland species. Two members of the Nymphalidae, the peacock and small tortoiseshell, are often seen inside houses or outbuildings. This is because they hibernate indoors over winter. Most of the other butterflies survive winter as a dormant chrysalis hidden in soil or thick vegetation.

Hoppers

Hoppers (order Hemiptera) are jumping bugs belonging to the sub-order Homoptera. They feed by plunging their needle-like beaks into plant tissues and sucking the sap. Many spread virus diseases as well as causing physical damage with their beaks. The nymphs feed in the same way as the adults, but they often look rather different because they lack wings. Some froghopper nymphs live in frothy masses known as cuckoo spit. They produce this themselves by pumping air into a fluid secreted from the hind end of the body. The froth helps to protect the nymphs from predators and from desiccation. There are several different families of hoppers, with about 350 British species.

Elymana sulphurella Cicadellidae.
Distribution: Throughout British Isles in hedgebanks. **Other Habitats:** Almost any dryish habitat with grass.
Adult Active: July to October.
Food: Various grasses.

Cercopis vulnerata Cercopidae.
Distribution: Widespread in England and Wales in hedgerows. **Other Habitats:** Woodlands. **Adult Active:** April to July. **Food:** Various plants. Nymphs on roots in hardened froth.

Common Froghopper Cercopidae
Philaenus spumarius. **Distribution:** Throughout the British Isles. **Other Habitats:** Anywhere with varied plant cover. **Adult Active:** June to October. **Food:** Wide variety of plants. Nymph in cuckoo spit.

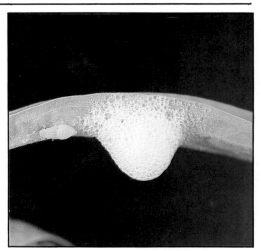

"Cuckoo spit" is produced by tiny froghoppers (*Philaenus*) and provides a protective hiding place for the insect.

brightly coloured hind wings. The hawk-moths are certainly the most spectacular species. They range from the death's-head hawk-moth, Britain's biggest insect, to the tiny bee hawk which darts between flowers. The elegant green of the lime hawk, the pink and black of the privet hawk and the lurid pink of the elephant hawk are all particularly striking.

Adult butterflies and moths feed mainly on nectar or other liquid diets; it is their larvae which wreak havoc among clothes, carpets, flower beds and cabbage patches. The caterpillars hatch from eggs in spring or early summer, feed voraciously and grow very rapidly, moulting their skin several times as they do so. Most caterpillars feed on fresh green vegetation (though there are exceptions such as the wood-boring goat-moth caterpillar) and often will only eat a particular plant or a few species closely related to it. This is why caterpillars can

be a major menace in man-made habitats. Where man has chosen to plant very large numbers of a species for his own benefit (eg cabbages, pine trees) they provide an artificially extensive food source for caterpillars, which then do considerable damage and it is necessary to resort to insecticides to control them.

Many man-made habitats, especially hedgerows, contain a very high diversity of plant species. These will include many of the special

A guide to some butterflies of man-made habitats

The range of butterflies found in man-made habitats is generally restricted, since many other British species are heavily dependent not merely on individual foodplants but also the way their habitats have been managed.
Of the species that

are present in man-made habitats some, such as the large and small whites exploit the vast food resources presented to them by fields of crops such as cabbages, and this in turn produces extraordinary numbers of individual specimens.

Other species such as the comma, the gatekeeper, the orange-tip and the ringlet enjoy hedgerow habitats where there is a fine mixture of foodplants, nectar and sunny spots in which to bask.
The peacock and the small tortoiseshell are frequent

visitors to gardens, where they enjoy taking nectar from garden plants, especially buddleja and sedum. Unfortunately these butterflies are dependent on nettles for their foodplant and since few gardeners are prepared to devote space to this plant, their numbers are

limited. It is ironic that gardeners often blame farmers for the loss of butterflies when they themselves could provide the most valuable habitat for these two species. Both types hibernate as adults during the winter and can often be found in sheds and

roof spaces. The hollyblue is a most welcome sight in towns and breeds around the sites of old-established holly trees and ivy. Although they are not over-common in the countryside, there are many colonies within central London, not least around Buckingham Palace.

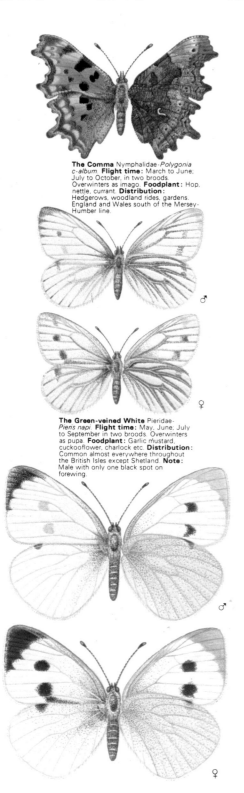

The Comma Nymphalidae-*Polygonia c-album*. **Flight time:** March to June; July to October, in two broods. Overwinters as imago. **Foodplant:** Hop, nettle, currant. **Distribution:** Hedgerows, woodland rides, gardens. England and Wales south of the Mersey-Humber line.

The Green-veined White Pieridae-*Pieris napi*. **Flight time:** May, June; July to September in two broods. Overwinters as pupa. **Foodplant:** Garlic mustard, cuckooflower, charlock etc. **Distribution:** Common almost everywhere throughout the British Isles except Shetland. **Note:** Male with only one black spot on forewing.

The Large White Pieridae-*Pieris brassicae*. **Flight time:** April to June; July to September in two broods, later as a third brood in some years. Overwinters as pupa. **Foodplant:** Cabbages, nasturtium. **Distribution:** Common almost everywhere in the British Isles. Resident population sometimes re-inforced by large scale immigration.

The Gatekeeper Satyridae-*Pyronia tithonus*. **Flight time:** July to September. Overwinters as larva. **Foodplant:** Grasses. **Distribution:** Hedgerows, woodland rides. England and Wales as far north as the Lake District except the Pennines and the north-east.

The Small White Pieridae-*Pieris rapae*. **Flight time:** March to May; June to September in two broods. Overwinters as pupa. **Foodplant:** Cabbages, nasturtium. **Distribution:** Common almost everywhere throughout the British Isles except the extreme north where it is local.

The Orange Tip Pieridae-*Anthocharis cardamines*. **Flight time:** May, June. Overwinters as pupa. **Foodplant:** Cuckooflower, hedge mustard, garlic mustard. **Distribution:** Hedgerows and gardens. Common throughout England and Wales except Lancashire and the north-east; Scotland only in Aberdeenshire and adjacent counties. **Note:** Female without orange tip to forewing.

The Ringlet Satyridae-*Aphantopus hyperantus*. **Flight time:** June to August. Overwinters as larva. **Foodplant:** Grasses. **Distribution:** Hedgerows, woodland rides. Widespread in southern and central England and Wales; local in north-west England.

The Holly Blue Lycaenidae-*Celastrina argiolus*. **Flight time:** April, May; July to September in two broods. Overwinters as pupa. **Foodplant:** Flowers, buds and berries of holly, ivy, snowberry. **Distribution:** Gardens and open woodland. Widely distributed in southern England and Wales; local in northern England. **Note:** Female only with black tip to forewing.

The Peacock Nymphalidae-*Inachis io*. **Flight time:** March to November, in two broods. Overwinters as imago. **Foodplant:** Nettle. **Distribution:** Common throughout England and Wales except the north-east; local in Scotland where it is spreading.

The Small Tortoiseshell Nymphalidae-*Aglais urticae*. **Flight time:** March to November, in two or more broods. Overwinters as imago. **Foodplant:** Nettle. **Distribution:** Very common almost everywhere throughout the British Isles except Shetland.

food plants of a wide assortment of caterpillars, which will then produce to a large and varied butterfly population in these habitats.

Caterpillars are large and soft-bodied. Lacking the tough armour plating of beetles or the mobility of adult Lepidoptera, they are very vulnerable to predation. Many birds (leaf warblers, tits and several garden birds) feed extensively on them. As a defence, some caterpillars (especially of moths) have long irritating hairs which are a deterrent to predators. Others have bold coloration to warn of distasteful substances in their body and some have elaborate camouflage or predator confusion devices. Few of these tricks are a defence against the ichneumon wasps which lay their eggs directly into the caterpillar's body where their larvae develop, surrounded by living food.

In late summer, most caterpillars pupate. Some moth species have a silken cocoon which the caterpillar spins around itself first. Butterflies do not do this, but often produce a camouflaged chrysalis instead. This may be suspended from the vegetation or hidden among leaves. Many caterpillars produce a chrysalis which lies in the surface layer of soil, often covered by falling leaves.

In this inactive state the animal passes the winter and, at the same time, undergoes transformation to become an adult insect. This

A guide to some moths of man-made habitats

The Garden Tiger Arctiidae-*Arctia caja*. **Flight time**: July, August. Overwinters as larva. **Foodplant**: Herbaceous plants. **Distribution**: Widespread throughout the British Isles except Shetland.

The Cinnabar Moth Arctiidae-*Tyria jacobaeae*. **Flight time**: Late May to July. Overwinters as pupa. **Foodplant**: Ragwort, groundsel. **Distribution**: Well drained soils. Widespread in southern and midland England and Wales; mainly coastal in northern England and Scotland.

The Elephant Hawk-moth Sphingidae-*Deilephila elpenor*. **Flight time**: June; occasionally later as a second brood. Overwinters as pupa. **Foodplant**: Willowherb, bedstraw. **Distribution**: Throughout England and Wales; local in Scotland.

The Poplar Hawk-moth Sphingidae-*Laothoe populi*. **Flight time**: May, June; occasionally later as a second brood. Overwinters as pupa. **Foodplant**: Poplar, sallow. **Distribution**: Throughout the British Isles.

The Garden Carpet Geometridae-*Xanthorhoe fluctuata*. **Flight time**: May, June; August, September, in two broods. Overwinters as pupa. **Foodplant**: Many herbaceous plants, currant, gooseberry etc. **Distribution**: Common throughout the British Isles.

♂

♀

The Vapourer Lymantriidae-*Orgyia antiqua*. **Flight time**: July, August; September, October, in two broods: one in the north. Overwinters as ovum. **Foodplant**: Most deciduous trees and shrubs. **Distribution**: Throughout the British Isles.

The Turnip Moth Noctuidae-*Agrotis segetum*. **Flight time**: May, June; occasionally as second brood in September, October. Overwinters as larva. **Foodplant**: Roots of turnip, beet, swede, carrot etc. **Distribution**: Common throughout the British Isles except Orkney and Shetland.

The Small Magpie Moth Pyralidae-*Eurrhypara hortulata*. **Flight time**: June, July. Overwinters as larva. **Foodplant**: Nettle, mint, white horehound, woundwort. **Distribution**: Common and widespread in Britain as far north as Lancashire and Yorkshire; local further north to south Scotland.

The Privet Hawk-moth Sphingidae-*Sphinx ligustri*. **Flight time**: June, July. Overwinters as pupa. **Foodplant**: Privet, lilac, ash. **Distribution**: South and south-east England; scarcer in Midlands and Wales.

The Large Yellow Underwing Noctuidae-*Noctua pronuba*. **Flight time**: June to September. Overwinters as larva. **Foodplant**: Many herbaceous plants and grasses. **Distribution**: Abundant throughout the British Isles.

The Golden Plusia Noctuidae-*Polychrisia moneta*. **Flight time**: June, July; sometimes as a second brood in August, September. Overwinters as larva. **Foodplant**: Larkspur, monkshood. **Distribution**: Common, especially in gardens, throughout much of England and Wales; very local in south Scotland.

The Winter Moth Geometridae-*Operophtera brumata*. **Flight time**: October to February. Overwinters as imago. **Foodplant**: Many trees and shrubs. **Distribution**: Common throughout the British Isles. An important orchard pest.

x2

The Currant Clearwing Sesiidae-*Synanthedon salmachus*. **Flight time**: Late May to July. Overwinters in stems of blackcurrant; possibly feeding for two years. **Distribution**: Widely distributed in Britain as far north as Dumfries.

The Peach Blossom Thyatiridae-*Thyatira batis*. **Flight time**: June, July; sometimes August, September as a second brood. Overwinters as pupa. **Distribution**: Widespread throughout Britain except the far north of Scotland.

The White Ermine Arctiidae-*Spilosoma lubricipeda*. **Flight time**: Late May to July. Overwinters as pupa. **Foodplant**: Herbaceous plants. **Distribution**: Widespread throughout the British Isles except Shetland.

The Magpie Moth Geometidae-*Abraxas grossulariata*. **Flight time**: July, August. Overwinters as larva. **Foodplant**: Blackthorn, hawthorn, heather etc., currants, gooseberries on which the larva is sometimes a serious pest. **Distribution**: Throughout the British Isles.

x2

The Large White Plume Moth Pterophoridae-*Pterophorus pentadactyla*. **Flight time**: June, July. Overwinters as larva. **Foodplant**: Bindweed. **Distribution**: Common throughout England and Wales.

The Swallow-tailed Moth Geometridae-*Ourapteryx sambucaria*. **Flight time**: July, August. Overwinters as larva. **Foodplant**: Hawthorn, blackthorn, elder, etc. **Distribution**: Throughout England and Wales; south Scotland.

The Burnished Brass Noctuidae-*Diachrysia chrysitis*. **Flight time**: June to September. Overwinters as larva. **Foodplant**: Nettle. **Distribution**: Common throughout the British Isles except Shetland.

The Peppered Moth Geometridae-*Biston betularia*. **Flight time**: May to July. Overwinters as pupa. **Foodplant**: Oak, birch, elm, beech, sallow etc. **Distribution**: Throughout Britain north to central Scotland. The black form (ab. *carbonaria*) occurs especially in industrial areas.

The Buff Tip Notodontidae-*Phalera bucephala*. **Flight time**: Late May to July. Overwinters as pupa. **Foodplant**: Many deciduous trees. **Distribution**: Common and widely distributed in England and Wales; local in Scotland.

emerges in the spring by dissolving part of the chrysalis around the head and breaking out from the weak point. The newly emerged adult has crumpled, wet wings. These are expanded by pumping blood into them and they harden as they dry. The wings are just one of the features found in the adult but not in the larva. The adult also has long legs, large compound eyes, quite different internal organs and a long coiled tongue or proboscis to replace the caterpillar's stout jaws. The wings are covered by fine scales, another new feature. These provide the colours and patterns, but are easily rubbed off or lost during flight. Many insects live only a few weeks.

Once the newly emerged adult can fly, it is important to find a mate. The sexes are brought together by scent. Females emit a special attractant which is detected by the male of her species, who may be several hundred metres away. Detection is by special sensory cells on the antennae and the large feathery antennae of moths are particularly sensitive. Often a single female will draw in many males from the surrounding countryside, each of which has not only to detect and recognise minute quantities of scent, but somehow locate its source. These powerful sex attractants can now be synthesised to produce an efficient and deadly new method of insect control. Only the chosen pest species is attracted by the artificial scent, so there are no innocent victims as with random pesticide use. The males are lured to their death in traps "baited" with a source of fake female scent, leaving few or none to breed and continue the species.

Female butterflies lay about 200 sticky eggs, either singly or in small batches. Often they have a very elaborately sculpted surface. The eggs usually hatch in a few days, but in some species it is the egg which forms the over-wintering stage and it will not hatch till it has been chilled for some time.

Butterflies and moths thus have a four-stage life cycle: egg (ova), caterpillar (larva), chry-

The caterpillar of the puss moth displays its "tails". These can be used as whips against parasitic ichneumon flies. The larvae emerge as tiny black creatures, subsequently turning into the handsome form shown above.

salis (pupa) and adult (imago). There must be considerable advantages in this system or it would not have evolved. Certainly it ensures that the adults, feeding on fluids, do not compete with their own offspring for food, because the latter chew solid materials. There is also a separation of other roles: the caterpillar just feeds and grows; it never reproduces. Usually it becomes bigger than the adult, too big to fly perhaps. The transformation inside the pupa remodels the body, using the food stored up inside the caterpillar from its feeding. The adult, when it emerges, can fly and reproduce (things the larva cannot do), but it does not grow. Within a few days, months at most, mating will have taken place and new eggs laid. The cycle is then complete; the individual insects are dispensable and die.

Flies

Although we think of the housefly (distastefully!) as being the typical fly, there are many other types found in man-made environments, including hoverflies in the garden, mosquitoes and gnats in and around ditches and water butts, and many tiny flies which are common in crops

Hedgerow flies

Flies (order Diptera) are extremely common around any hedgerow from early spring until the last days of autumn. Most of them are seeking nectar from the flowers and sucking it up with mop-like tongues. Others, such as *Empis*, use the hedgerow as a hunting ground where they can catch various insects to eat. The bee-fly may simply sun itself on the plants in the hedge bottom in spring, but it is more likely to be searching for the burrow of a solitary bee near which to drop its eggs, for the bee-fly grubs are parasites in the nests of the bees. Hoverflies are very common visitors to hedgerow flowers.

Household flies

Adult flies (order Diptera) feed by sucking or mopping up various fluids. They have many different types of mouths. Some feed on nectar, some suck animal blood, while others prefer to feed on rotting materials. Many have become firmly associated with man, existing on the abundant food and waste in and around the home. The larvae are all legless maggots and the domestic ones usually feed on dung and rotting meat. The adults often enter houses to feed or to find somewhere to lay their eggs, although the cluster-fly comes in to find winter quarters in lofts and attics.

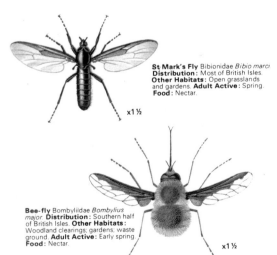

St Mark's Fly Bibionidae *Bibio marci*. **Distribution**: Most of British Isles. **Other Habitats**: Open grasslands and gardens. **Adult Active**: Spring. **Food**: Nectar.

×1½

Bee-fly Bombyliidae *Bombylius major*. **Distribution**: Southern half of British Isles. **Other Habitats**: Woodland clearings; gardens; waste ground. **Adult Active**: Early spring. **Food**: Nectar.

×1½

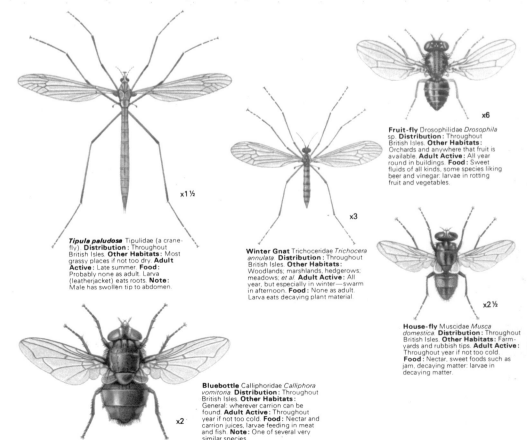

×1½

Tipula paludosa Tipulidae (a crane-fly). **Distribution**: Throughout British Isles. **Other Habitats**: Most grassy places if not too dry. **Adult Active**: Late summer. **Food**: Probably none as adult. Larva (leatherjacket) eats roots. **Note**: Male has swollen tip to abdomen.

×2

Bluebottle Calliphoridae *Calliphora vomitoria*. **Distribution**: Throughout British Isles. **Other Habitats**: General: wherever carrion can be found. **Adult Active**: Throughout year if not too cold. **Food**: Nectar and carrion juices, larvae feeding in meat and fish. **Note**: One of several very similar species.

×3

Winter Gnat Trichoceridae *Trichocera annulata*. **Distribution**: Throughout British Isles. **Other Habitats**: Woodlands; marshlands; hedgerows; meadows; *et al.* **Adult Active**: All year, but especially in winter—swarm in afternoon. **Food**: None as adult. Larva eats decaying plant material.

×6

Fruit-fly Drosophilidae *Drosophila* sp. **Distribution**: Throughout British Isles. **Other Habitats**: Orchards and anywhere that fruit is available. **Adult Active**: All year round in buildings. **Food**: Sweet fluids of all kinds, some species liking beer and vinegar: larvae in rotting fruit and vegetables.

×2½

House-fly Muscidae *Musca domestica*. **Distribution**: Throughout British Isles. **Other Habitats**: Farm-yards and rubbish tips. **Adult Active**: Throughout year if not too cold. **Food**: Nectar, sweet foods such as jam, decaying matter: larvae in decaying matter.

Hoverflies

Hoverflies (order Diptera) are a very diverse group of insects, but most can be recognised very easily by the false margin to the wing, formed by the abrupt bending of the veins to run parallel to the true margin.

They are superb hoverers and often 'hang' in shafts of sunlight between the trees. Many gain protection by mimicking bees and wasps. *Volucella bombylans* actually exists in several forms, each resembling a

different kind of bee. Hoverflies can be found in just about every kind of habitat as long as there are some flowers on which they can feed. They mop up nectar, and some actually crush and eat

pollen grains. Their larvae are even more variable than the adults. Some live in bulbs, others in dung and rotting vegetation, and several more live as scavengers in the nests of bees and wasps. Another

group crawl over plants and eat aphids, while yet another group live in water. The rat-tailed maggot, which is the larva of *Eristalis*, has a telescopic tail that it pushes up to the water surface in order to

breathe. There are about 250 species of hoverflies in the British Isles.

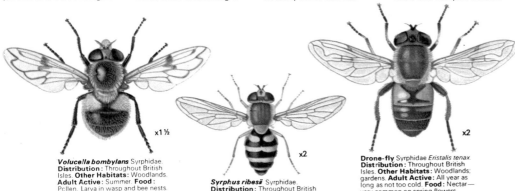

Volucella bombylans Syrphidae. **Distribution:** Throughout British Isles. **Other Habitats:** Woodlands. **Adult Active:** Summer. **Food:** Pollen. Larva in wasp and bee nests.

Syrphus ribesii Syrphidae. **Distribution:** Throughout British Isles. **Other Habitats:** Woodlands; gardens. **Adult Active:** Summer. **Food:** Nectar, especially of umbellifers. Larva eats aphids.

Drone-fly Syrphidae *Eristalis tenax*. **Distribution:** Throughout British Isles. **Other Habitats:** Woodlands; gardens. **Adult Active:** All year as long as not too cold. **Food:** Nectar — very common on spring flowers. Larva in muddy water. **Note:** Pale marks on abdomen very variable.

Xylota lenta Syrphidae. **Distribution:** Local in midlands and south. **Other Habitats:** Woodlands. **Adult Active:** Summer. **Food:** Nectar and exuding tree sap. Larva in rotting wood.

and among the rotting fruit littering orchards.

The true flies belong to the insect order Diptera; a word meaning "two wings" which refers to their most characteristic feature. Insects typically have four wings, but in flies the rear pair are reduced to small stubs which act as balancing organs. The presence of only one pair of wings helps to distinguish hoverflies and beeflies from the wasps and bees which they resemble. These harmless flies have no sting but copy the bold black and yellow warning colours of the stinging insects which warn predators to leave them alone. Thus they mimic unpleasant creatures and survive by bluff. Humans too are easily deceived by these "sheep in wolves' clothing" and are reluctant to catch or handle hoverflies just in case they turn out to be wasps after all! Hoverflies are particularly characteristic garden insects, and get their popular name from their habit of hovering in front of a flower and then darting off to another so quickly as to be invisible. This characteristic agile behaviour immediately distinguishes them from the lumbering wasps.

The largest flies are also very characteristic of man-made habitats, particularly gardens and houses in late summer. These are the crane flies, whose thin wings and spindly appendages have earned them the name "Daddy Longlegs". Again, they are quite harmless though their larvae (called "leather jackets") are a serious pest in arable crops and may even damage pastureland through their habit of attacking the grass roots. The wheat bulb fly is another fly which can be a major nuisance in farmland.

All flies have a life cycle which involves a complete metamorphosis (like the butterflies and moths). The egg develops into a larva which then pupates and abruptly changes into the adult form. Earwigs, cockroaches and grasshoppers are among the insects with an "incomplete" metamorphosis. Their young (called nymphs) pass through a succession of stages which progressively become more and more like the adult at each moult. There is no single major transformation inside a pupa. Fly larvae (which we call maggots) usually have no distinct head, just a sausage-shaped body. These grow very fast because they emerge from eggs normally laid on a mass of food, so the larvae do not have to travel to feed but can use all their energy to grow. The maggots of the bluebottle are typical and familiar to anglers as "gentles", widely used as bait. They are kept and sold in sawdust, which is why they do not smell – normally such maggots live and feed on rotting food and meat, adding their own digestive juices to speed up the decay and liquefaction of their food. Like other insect larvae, the development of these maggots is very temperature-dependent and they can be retarded by keeping them cool.

Houseflies are a hazard to health because they walk over both filth and food, carrying bacteria from one to the other. As their popular name suggests they are characteristically indoor insects, though they like to visit gardens, yards and streets to bask in the sun on warm surfaces. They are strong fliers and for house-dwellers they can be surprisingly well travelled. One marked individual was recaptured over 20km from home! But perhaps the most intriguing feat performed by the housefly is walking up the smooth face of a vertical pane of glass or hanging from the ceiling. This is accomplished by the use of pads of tiny hairs on the feet which can grip the most minute irregularities in a surface – even glass.

Adult flies feed on fluids (though some eat pollen), taking a liquid diet or pouring digestive juices on to more solid food, then drinking the partially digested slime that results. Dungflies can be seen doing this on cow pats and houseflies feed in the same way on food in the kitchen. Horseflies get their liquid food in the form of blood, but is is only the female that irritates horses (and holidaymakers) by biting them; the males feed on flowers. This is an unusual example of the two sexes avoiding competition with each other for food.

The mosquitoes and gnats form an important group of flies which are characterised by having aquatic larvae. These have a large and distinct head (unlike terrestrial maggots) and their tiny transparent bodies, twitching in the water of puddles, garden ponds and rainwater butts, are easily mistaken for baby fish. Mosquito larvae breathe air through tiny tubes thrust above the surface film from which they hang, but chironomid midge larvae are red worm-like creatures (often called "blood worms") which live in mud. They are particularly characteristic of polluted rivers and ponds.

Aquatic larvae turn into adult gnats, swarms of which may be seen whirling over the surface of still water. Such swarms often only consist of males, whose communal display serves to attract females.

Some midges may be found flying even in midwinter, when they are an important source of food for many insectivorous birds.

Mosquitoes (like horseflies) are best known for their blood sucking, but again, it is only the females that are responsible; the males feed on nectar. Relatively few species attack man; most draw their blood from other warm-blooded creatures, including birds. The whining noise made by mosquitoes is almost as irritating as their bite. Like the buzz of a bee, the sound is generated by the wings moving at very high speed; thousands of beats per minute. This consumes vast amounts of energy and despite the aerial abilities of flies and other insects, their

Sawflies

Sawflies (order Hymenoptera) get their name from the saw-like nature of the ovipositor in most species. This is used to cut little slits in plants before laying the eggs there. Although they belong to the same order as bees and wasps, the sawflies never have the wasp-waist of these other insects; the thorax is joined to the abdomen on

a broad front. Some sawflies eat smaller insects, but the majority feed on pollen. Most of them are rather sluggish insects and do not fly a great deal. Most sawfly larvae feed on leaves and look rather like the caterpillars of butterflies and moths, but they have at least six pairs of stumpy legs on the abdominal region. There are about 450 British species.

Gooseberry Sawfly Tenthredinidae *Nematus ribesii*. **Distribution:** Throughout British Isles. **Other Habitats:** Woodlands and scrub. **Adult Active:** April to September. **Food:** Pollen. Larvae eats gooseberry and currant leaves. **Note:** Female has orange body and is broader.

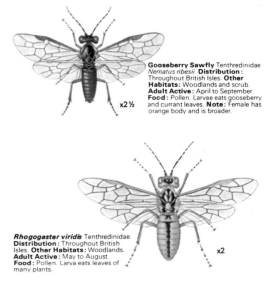

Rhogogaster viridis Tenthredinidae. **Distribution:** Throughout British Isles. **Other Habitats:** Woodlands. **Adult Active:** May to August. **Food:** Pollen. Larva eats leaves of many plants.

flying is an inefficient and costly form of locomotion. A bluebottle may burn up food reserves equivalent to a third of its body weight to fuel an hour's flying. Reversing the direction of wing beat 200 times a second throws a great strain on the wing articulation, emphasising the enormous strength of the insect exoskeleton.

Bees and wasps

The bees and wasps (together with ants) form the insect order *Hymenoptera*. Commonly seen in gardens and other man-made habitats, they are of particular interest because some of them are social animals.

The honey bee (*Apis mellifera*) is also one of the very few invertebrates domesticated by man. Its colonies, made up of some 50,000 individuals, are highly organised around the queen, the only breeding female present. The majority of the colony are sterile females (workers) plus some males (drones). These three castes within the hive all have specialist roles to play. The

Parasitic wasps

Many members of the order Hymenoptera are parasitic in their early stages, living in or on the bodies of other young insects—the hosts—and gradually destroying them. The hosts are not destroyed, however, until the parasites are fully fed and have no further use for them. Among the best known of these parasites are the ichneumon flies, such as *Netelia*. These often come into houses at night. They lay their eggs mainly in the caterpillars of butterflies and moths. Chalcid wasps are much smaller parasites. Some actually grow up inside the eggs of other insects. The female *Torymus* uses her long ovipositor to drill into galls to lay eggs on the gall wasp grubs. The ruby-tailed wasps are parasites in the nests of solitary bees and wasps.

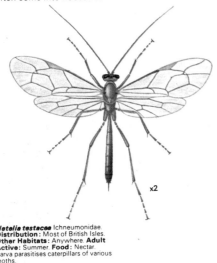

Netelia testacea Ichneumonidae.
Distribution: Most of British Isles.
Other Habitats: Anywhere. **Adult Active:** Summer. **Food:** Nectar.
Larva parasitises caterpillars of various moths.

workers collect nectar, feed the larvae and also produce and store honey to maintain the colony over winter. Workers die after a few months but the queen lives four or five years. During that time she mates only once, then returns to the hive to lay eggs (at an average rate of one a minute) for the rest of her life. The drones are produced in limited numbers and their sole function is for one of them to mate with the queen. Communication within the hive is by scent, unique to each colony, and also by a kind of "dance" through which the workers tell each other where to find food.

The 16 species of furry bumble bee live in smaller colonies which survive for only one season because all their members (except young queens) die in the autumn. The following spring, the queens re-establish colonies by building new nests among grass tussocks or in a mouse burrow.

Cuckoo bees, as their name suggests, take advantage of the highly organised social life of their relatives. The female takes over a bumble bee nest by ousting the queen and getting the workers to look after her own eggs and young.

Not all bees are social; several species are solitary, including the leaf cutter bee which slices out small discs from the leaves of garden plants in order to construct a nest, usually in rotting wood. Mining bees are also solitary. The female excavates a small burrow, leaving a ring of fine soil surrounding the entrance. The eggs are laid in the burrow on a mass of pollen and nectar which will serve as food for the larvae when they hatch.

Generally bees are viewed favourably because they are useful to man. Apart from the masses of honey (up to 200kg per hive in one season) produced by the domestic species, bees are important pollinators of fruit trees and many garden flowers.

Like the bees, wasps include solitary, social and parasitic species. Only five species are social; all of these are banded in black and yellow and include the familiar common wasp (*Vespula vulgaris*) which frequently builds its large spherical nest in attics and under floors. Wasps construct their nests by chewing up scraps of dry wood which, mixed with saliva, forms a paste and dries into a kind of paper. The colony is founded by the queen who lays a

Wasps

Wasps of various kinds, both social and solitary, are very common in hedgerows. Social wasps are those that live in large colonies, each of which is ruled by a queen. The most frequent species in the hedgerow are the common wasp and the very similar German wasp (*Paravespula germanica*), both of which nest in holes in the hedgebank. Large numbers of worker wasps can be seen flying in and out. Solitary wasps nest in the ground and in the hedgerow plants themselves. *Odynerus* species generally excavate tunnels in the banks, while *Ancistrocerus* species often use hollow stems for their nests. These wasps store caterpillars or beetle grubs in their nests. *Ectemnius* tunnels in dead wood and stocks its nests with flies.

Common Wasp Vespidae
Paravespula vulgaris. **Distribution:**
Throughout British Isles but less common in north. **Other habitats:**
Anywhere that it can nest underground without getting waterlogged; also in roofs and hollow trees. **Adult active:**
Spring (queen) to late autumn. **Food:**
Nectar and sweet juices, but young fed on other insects.

few eggs which hatch into grubs. These are fed by the queen on dead insects and grow into worker wasps in a week or two. They then take over the job of enlarging the nest and raising more young, leaving the queen to concentrate on egg laying. The colony increases to perhaps 2,000 insects by late summer.

For most of the time wasps are beneficial to the gardener because of the many caterpillars and destructive insects they kill as food for their developing grubs. The workers collect the prey and in exchange the grubs produce a sweet substance for the workers. However, in late summer the queen stops laying, no more grubs are produced and the workers are deprived of their sweet secretions. It is then that they become a nuisance by seeking out substitutes like jam and soft fruit.

Solitary wasps are usually slender insects, often coloured black and red, which use their sting to paralyse caterpillars and spiders before laying an egg on the carcass. Parasitic wasps lay their egg into the body of a living host. Sometimes this is a plant and results in the formation of a gall like the familiar oak apple. Ichneumon wasps are parasites on caterpillars and the larvae develop inside the host, eating away the tissues, before emerging in adult form.

Only female wasps possess a sting, a modification of their egg laying structure, the ovipositor. Unlike bees, wasps can use the sting many times.

Beetles

There are about 3,700 species of British beetles. Most of them live in the country, but some are particular associates of man and draw attention to themselves by becoming a nuisance.

Beetles range in size from the stag beetle (60mm) down to the flea beetle (1mm). Some are carnivores, like the ladybird which is a good friend of the gardener because of its voracious consumption of greenfly. There are also plant feeders, including the weevils and the notorious Colorado beetle, and various scavengers (mostly ground and dung beetles) which are frequently found under stones and debris in gardens. A few species are adapted to life in water.

It is the wood-eating beetles that play the greatest role in man-made habitats. In natural habitats they, and their larvae, play an important part in recycling the nutrients contained in the wood of dead trees. However, in buildings they can cause considerable damage. The larvae of the death-watch beetle (*Xestobium rufovillosum*) live in wood for up to three years, chewing the hard material and reducing it to powdery faeces and empty space. The larvae pupate and hatch into adults in the autumn. These spend the winter immobile in the wood, but the following spring

Individual cells inside a wasp nest each harbour a single egg which will turn into a grub; both stages are seen here.

The fully developed wasp will emerge to become a full member of the colony.

Hedgerow beetles

Huge numbers of beetles (order Colecptera) can be found in gardens and hedgerows. Many are leaf beetles belonging to the family Chrysomelidae. These are generally brightly coloured and often very shiny. The weevils, belonging to several different families, can be recognised by the long "snout" on the head. Both leaf beetles and weevils feed mainly on the leaves in the adult state, and leaf beetle larvae also nibble the leaves. The large number of plant species in the garden and hedgerow allows many beetle species to survive.

Chrysolina polita Chrysomelidae. **Distribution:** Most of British Isles. **Other habitats:** Damp places in general. **Adult active:** Summer. **Food:** Plants of mint family. x2½

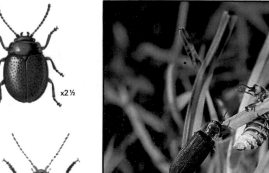

Glow worms, now increasingly rare, are in fact beetles. Seen here is the male, with wings, and the wingless female.

x3

Green Tortoise Beetle Chrysomelidae *Cassida viridis*. **Distribution:** Much of British Isles, in damp places. **Other habitats:** Marshlands; damp woodlands. **Adult active:** July and August. **Food:** Both larvae and adults feed on leaves of mints and related plants.

x5

Lema melanopa Chrysomelidae. **Distribution:** Throughout British Isles. **Other habitats:** Arable fields. **Adult active:** Most of the year—often sunbathes on walls in spring. **Food:** Grasses and other herbaceous plants.

x1

Cockchafer Scarabaeidae *Melolontha melolontha* **Distribution:** Most of British Isles, but not common in north. **Other habitats:** Woodlands; parks. **Adult active:** May and June—called may-bug by many people. **Food:** Tree leaves. Grubs eat roots of all kinds of plants.

x2

Soldier Beetle Cantharidae *Cantharis rustica* **Distribution:** Most of British Isles. **Adult active:** Summer—often on flowers. **Food:** both larvae and adults eat other insects.

x2

Otiorhynchus clavipes Curculionidae (a weevil). **Distribution:** Much of British Isles. **Other habitats:** Woodlands. **Adult active:** Summer. **Food:** Leaves of a wide variety of trees and other plants.

x5

Apion miniatum Apionidae. **Distribution:** Much of British Isles, but local. **Other habitats:** Waste ground; coastal and damp places in general. **Adult active:** Summer. **Food:** Leaves of docks.

♂ ♀

x2   x2

Glow-worm Lampyridae *Lampyris noctiluca*. **Distribution:** England and Wales, mainly southern, associated with chalk and limestone. **Other Habitats:** Grasslands; open woodlands. **Adult active:** July and August. **Food:** Larvae eat snails; adults rarely feed.

x2

Click Beetle Elateridae *Agriotes obscurus*. **Distribution:** Throughout British Isles. **Other habitats:** Grasslands (including arable land); woodlands. **Adult active:** May to July. **Food:** Larvae (wireworms) eat roots; adults chew pollen.

Only the female glow worm actually glows, emitting a cold greenish light at night which serves to attract the male.

Bees

Bees belong to the very large order of insects known as the Hymenoptera. This order also includes wasps, ants, sawflies, ichneumon flies and many other groups which seem to have little in common apart from their membranous wings with relatively large cells. The bees all feed on nectar and pollen from the flowers, and they store these materials in their nests for their larvae to eat as well. Most bees are solitary insects, with each female making her own small nest and stocking it with food for her offspring.

Bumblebees are social insects, in which a mated female—the queen— starts a nest in the spring. Most of her offspring are workers, which enlarge the nest and collect food for later broods of young bees. Later in the year males and new queens are produced, but only the mated queens survive the winter to start new colonies. Honey bees are even more social: the queen cannot do anything apart from lay eggs and she depends on her workers all her life. There are about 250 species of bees in the British Isles.

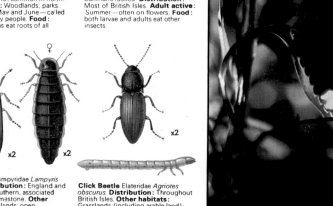

Honey Bee Apidae *Apis mellifera*. **Distribution:** Throughout British Isles, usually living in hives. **Other Habitats:** Occasionally nests in hollow trees in warmer parts; bees scour all habitats for food. **Adult active:** Early spring to autumn. Social. **Food:** Nectar and pollen. **Note:** Several races, with different abdominal colours. x2

Buff-tailed Bumble Bee Apidae *Bombus terrestris*. **Distribution:** Most of British Isles but absent from N. Scotland. **Other habitats:** Almost anywhere; nests under ground. **Adult active:** Early spring to summer. Social. **Food:** Nectar and pollen. x1½

Andrena albicans Andrenidae. **Distribution:** Throughout British Isles. **Other Habitats:** Woodland margins; grasslands. **Adult active:** Early spring. Solitary. **Food:** Nectar and pollen: especially fond of sallow and dandelion. x2

Honeybee workers are sterile females. They are seen here tending the special cell in which the queen bee will be reared, and it is she who will be fertile and lay the eggs to produce the next generation.

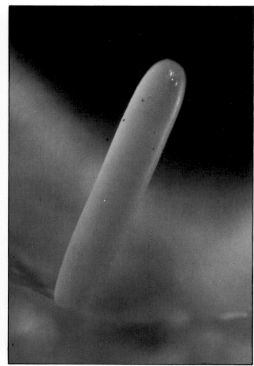

The newly laid egg of the honeybee is laid in a single hexagonal cell in the 'honeycomb' within the nest.

Ladybirds

Ladybirds are beetles (order Coleoptera) belonging to the family Coccinellidae. There are 42 members of the family in the British Isles, but only about twelve are generally called ladybirds. These are brightly coloured and very shiny beetles, with domed, rounded bodies. They are all carnivorous insects, feeding mainly on aphids and other small bugs. Both adults and larvae eat these pests and destroy large numbers for the gardener. Many ladybirds are extremely variable in colour and pattern. They often hibernate indoors in vast numbers.

Eyed Ladybird Coccinellidae *Anatis ocellata.* **Distribution:** Scattered through most of British Isles in vicinity of pine and fir trees. **Other habitats:** Coniferous woodlands. **Adult active:** Summer. **Food:** Aphids.

Seven-spot Ladybird Coccinellidae *Coccinella 7-punctata.* **Distribution:** Throughout British Isles. **Other habitats:** Almost anywhere with vegetation. **Adult active:** Spring to autumn. **Food:** Aphids.

Two-spot Ladybird Coccinellidae *Adalia bipunctata.* **Distribution:** Throughout British Isles: black ground colour more common in northern regions. **Other habitats:** Almost anywhere. **Adult active:** Spring to autumn. **Food:** Aphids.

Ten-spot Ladybird Coccinellidae *Adalia 10-punctata.* **Distribution:** Throughout British Isles. **Other Habitats:** Almost anywhere. **Adult active:** Spring to autumn. **Food:** Aphids. **Note:** Very variable, but always distinguished from 2-spot ladybird by yellow legs.

22-spot Ladybird Coccinellidae *Thea 22-punctata.* **Distribution:** England, Wales, and Ireland. **Other Habitats:** Almost anywhere, especially with nettles. **Adult active:** Spring to autumn. **Food:** Aphids.

14-spot Ladybird Coccinellidae *Calvia 14-guttata.* **Distribution:** Much of British Isles, associated with hawthorn and some other trees. **Other habitats:** Woodlands. **Adult active:** Summer. **Food:** Aphids.

14-spot Ladybird Coccinellidae *Propylea 14-punctata.* **Distribution:** Southern half of England and Wales; Ireland. **Other habitats:** Almost anywhere. **Adult active:** Summer. **Food:** Aphids.

The ladybird (*Coccinella 7-punctata*) is among the most useful of insects to the gardener. It is carnivorous and finds its food supply among the aphids — greenfly and blackfly — which are major garden pests.

they become active and start tapping their heads against the wood. The woodworm is the larva of the furniture beetle *(Anobium punctatum)*; some 5mm long, it reduces wood to dry powder. The larvae pupate after three years, just below the surface of the wood. From here the adults can bore their way out after hatching, leaving their familiar round exit-holes in furniture and house timbers. The adults do not travel far and only live a month, dying after they lay their eggs.

In the case of the Colorado beetle it is again the larvae that are the main pest. They attack potato crops, but strict control over imported vegetables and prompt attack on outbreaks of this pest have kept infestation to a minimum, for the beetle is not native to Britain. The adult is about the same size as a ladybird and the females lay about 500 eggs which hatch in a few days. The larvae grow quickly and pupate to form adults, which are themselves breeding after six weeks.

The cockchafer *(Melolontha melolontha)* is one of our larger beetles, and often called "June bug" because the adults emerge at that time of year from pupae in the soil. On warm summer nights they can be heard crashing against window panes, attracted by lights indoors. The cockchafer is one of the dozen or so garden beetles that are almost certain to be present even in heavily urbanised areas. Its larvae live in the soil, feeding on grass roots, and can do considerable damage to crops and pastureland.

Not all beetles are pests, or even a nuisance. Many are quite neutral in their effects on man's interests, including most of the common garden

Bark beetles

Bark beetles are a group of beetles (order Coleoptera) whose larvae tunnel just under the bark of various trees. They feed on the nutritious tissues there or else on fungi that grow there after the beetles' invasion. The parent beetles, often working in pairs, bore into the bark and nibble out a chamber or a tunnel in which the eggs are laid. When they hatch, the grubs continue tunnelling. They pupate when fully grown and new adults bore their way out through the bark. The tunnelling grubs make patterns in the bark, and each species has its own pattern based on the original spacing of the eggs. But the tunnels are not seen until the bark falls. This happens when the infestation is particularly heavy and it can severely damage the tree, but the greatest damage is done by various fungi which the beetles carry from tree to tree. Dutch elm disease, which has destroyed millions of elm trees in Europe and North America, is spread by a bark beetle called *Scolytes scolytes.*

Elm Bark Beetle Scolytidae *Scolytes scolytes* **Distribution:** Throughout British Isles. **Other Habitats:** Wherever elms grow. **Adult active:** Late spring to autumn. **Food:** Elm bark.

Elm bark beetle larvae, as adult beetles, are the principal carriers of the Dutch elm disease organism.

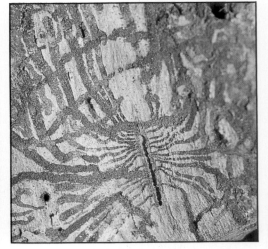

Beetle larvae eat the bark of elms and form tunnels which cause it to become detached from the tree.

beetles. The scavenging devil's coach horse beetle *(Ocypus oleus)* is one of the common garden species, easily recognisable by its long abdomen which is arched forwards over the head (like a scorpion's tail) if the beetle is disturbed. It is a harmless scavenger, though its powerful jaws can deliver a sharp nip. Ground beetles are also common in gardens. Most are black with a green or purple gloss. They cannot fly and feed at night on small invertebrates like worms and caterpillars.

The large bloody-nosed beetle is another conspicuous species, especially during the summer in hedgerows. It is a slow moving creature, but predators do not take advantage of this because of its unusual defence mechanism. When attacked it produces a red acrid-tasting liquid from the mouth (hence its name).

Ladybirds have a similar defence mechanism which protects them from birds despite their conspicuous colouring. Indeed it is the bold pattern of red and black which warns the birds to leave them alone. The familiar black spots of the ladybird are on its wing cases (or elytra), which are developed from the front pair of wings and form a protective shield over the hind pair. These elytra are a characteristic feature of beetles and are raised clear of the hind wings in flight. This can be clearly seen in a ladybird as it takes off.

Spiders

There are about 600 species of British spiders; quite a few of them are found in gardens and many more live in buildings, hedgerows and other man-made habitats. All are carnivorous but have only a tiny mouth and no proper jaws. They feed principally by sucking juices from their insect prey. Many spiders catch their food by spinning a web, seen at its most elegant on a dewy morning. The typical spiral web with radiating supports is made by the common (and most distinctive) garden spider *(Araneus diadematus)*. Not all webs are of this pattern; household cobwebs are an untidy silken mass and some webs are in the form of hammocks slung between grass stems close to the ground. Some

A **close up** of the face of the garden spider (*Araneus diadematus*). Its eight eyes give it good vision, and its large hollow fangs have poison glands at their base which are used for killing or paralyzing its prey.

spiders make no web at all. The silk is produced in special glands at the rear of the abdomen and exuded through tiny nozzles called spinnerets. It is not squeezed out like toothpaste, but has to be pulled out by the spider's legs or as it moves along. The thread is also used as a lifeline, anchored at one end and paid out as the spider walks. The spider can also drop and hang suspended on its silken thread. It can climb back later, eating the silk as it goes so that its materials are not wasted.

Females produce a special silk for wrapping up the eggs. This fluffy coccoon is either carried or guarded by the female until the young hatch. A few days later these develop eyes, spinnerets and claws. They disperse by climbing to a vantage point, spinning a silk thread and waiting for the wind to catch it and whisk them away.

Spiders live for a year; some may survive longer, moulting their skin annually to grow a new one. The dry, empty skins of the large, long-legged house spider *(Tegenaria)* are often found tangled in dusty cobwebs behind cupboards and in other dark little-disturbed nooks. The three species of *Tegenaria* do not live solely in houses, but often inhabit gardens. They have the familiar and disconcerting habit of coming into the house, especially in the autumn, via the bath overflow pipe, when the onset of cold weather encourages them to seek a more sheltered home.

Spiders are very numerous; several hundred may live in a square metre of old grassland. They also consume huge quantities of insects. They are thus likely to be beneficial to man, and certainly do no harm.

Earwigs

Earwigs (order Dermaptera) are easily recognised by the pincers at the hind end. These are primarily defensive organs, and they differ in shape from species to species. They are usually straighter and more slender in females than in males. Many earwigs are completely wingless, but some fly well with the aid of their very thin hind wings. These wings are hidden away under the short, square front wings or elytra when the insects are at rest. Some earwigs have elytra, but no hind wings. Most earwigs are scavenging creatures, feeding at night and hiding under stones and bark by day. The mother looks after her eggs and actually feeds her youngsters for a while. The nymphs are paler than the adults and their cerci are very slender. There are only four British species, although some others are occasionally found in dockland areas.

x3

Common Earwig Forficulidae
Forficula auricularia. **Distribution:**
Gardens, hedgerows, and buildings
throughout British Isles. **Other
Habitats:** Virtually anywhere that is
not too wet. **Adult Active:** Spring
to autumn (hibernates under ground)
Food: Almost any plant or animal
material. **Note:** Female has straighter
and more slender cerci

The cross spider (*Araneus diadematus*) is a familiar sight in British gardens. Often called simply the garden spider, it ensures its food supply by spinning a large web to trap passing insect prey.

A guide to some spiders of man-made habitats

Spiders are often mistaken for insects, but they are really very different. They belong to the group known arachnids and they have four pairs of legs compared with the three pairs of an insect. With very few exceptions, they have poison fangs around the mouth, and they all feed on other small animals, mainly insects. Some spiders ambush their prey by hiding on plants and grabbing the prey when it comes within range. Other spiders are fast-running hunters, with very good eyes to help them see their prey. The best-known spiders, however, are the trappers, which make various kinds of webs to catch their prey. Most webs catch flying insects, but some trap those walking on the ground. Young spiders are just like the adults except for size and they feed in the same way. There are about 600 species in the British Isles.

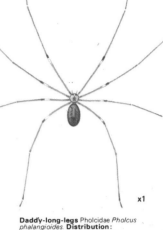

x1

Daddy-long-legs Pholcidae *Pholcus phalangioides.* **Distribution:** Southern half of England; Wales; southern Ireland; in buildings. **Other habitats:** None. **Adult active:** All year, but may become dormant in winter. **Food:** Flying insects. A trapper.

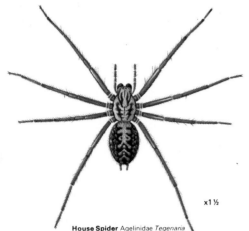

x1½

House Spider Agelinidae *Tegenaria saeva.* **Distribution:** Most of England and Wales; rare in Scotland. Usually in buildings. **Other habitats:** Dry, overhanging banks; rocks and walls; caves. **Adult active:** All year in buildings. **Food:** Flying insects. A trapper.

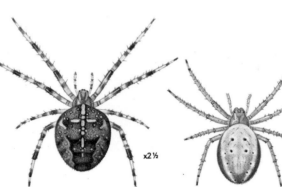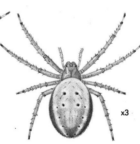

x2½

Garden Spider Argiopidae *Araneus diadematus.* **Distribution:** Throughout British Isles; on vegetation and fences. **Other habitats:** Everywhere there is somewhere to somewhere to hang orb web. **Adult active:** Late summer and autumn. **Food:** Small insects. A trapper.

x3

Araneus cucurbitinus Argiopidae. **Distribution:** Throughout British Isles on trees and bushes. **Other habitats:** Woodland. **Adult active:** May to July. **Food:** Small insects. An orb-web trapper. **Note:** Young may be brown.

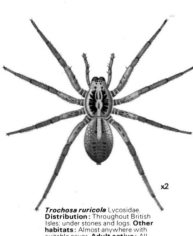

x2

Trochosa ruricola Lycosidae. **Distribution:** Throughout British Isles: under stones and logs. **Other habitats:** Almost anywhere with suitable cover. **Adult active:** All year. **Food:** Insects and other spiders. A nocturnal hunter.

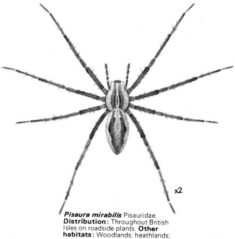

x2

Pisaura mirabilis Pisauridae. **Distribution:** Throughout British Isles on roadside plants. **Other habitats:** Woodlands; heathlands; grassy areas anywhere. **Adult active:** May to July. **Food:** Insects and other spiders. A hunter.

x5

Zebra Spider Salticidae *Salticus scenicus.* **Distribution:** Throughout British Isles except N. Scotland: on walls. **Other habitats:** Rocky places and exposed tree trunks. **Adult active:** May to September. **Food:** Insects. A hunter which jumps on to prey.

Earwigs

Earwigs are very distinctive insects, having what appears to be a pair of jaws at the rear end of the body. These are straight in the female and curved in the male, and are brandished vigorously when the insect is alarmed. Earwigs are heavy animals for the size of their wings and hardly ever fly. But they do have wings; these are double-folded to accommodate them below the fore wings and may be extended to form a semicircular fan. Earwigs lay eggs which are guarded by the female, who constantly cleans them to prevent infestation by mould. They hatch in the spring and the young are fed and tended by their mothers. Earwigs are active mainly at night and feed largely by scavenging. Their name is derived from the ill-founded belief that they live in people's ears.

Invertebrates in the home

Houses are homes for man, but they are also inhabited by a considerable variety of animal lodgers. In seeking to make our homes as comfortable as possible we provide cosy conditions for beetles, bugs, mice and a host of other creatures – not to mention the occasional flea or louse that lives on man himself. Central heating provides warmth throughout the winter and allows insects such as house crickets to survive which could not withstand the cold outside.

Cockroaches

Cockroaches (order Dictyoptera) are flattened insects with long, spiky legs. There are about 3,500 species, most of them living in tropical regions. Some fly well, but many have short wings and cannot fly at all. In many species the males have longer wings than the females. Cockroaches are rather greasy and smelly insects that scavenge any kind of plant or animal food that they can find. There are three small native species in southern England, but most of the cockroaches that are seen are foreigners that have become established in warm buildings. They hide by day, but do a lot of damage to food when they come out at night. The females lay their eggs in little horny 'purses', and the nymphs that hatch out look just like the adults except that their wings are undeveloped. The wings grow gradually, getting larger each time the cockroach moults.

x1

Common Cockroach Blattidae *Blatta orientalis.* **Distribution:** In buildings throughout British Isles. **Other habitats:** On rubbish dumps during the summer. **Adult Active:** All year round in buildings. **Food:** Anything. **Note:** Flightless female almost wingless.

x1

American Cockroach Blattidae *Periplaneta americana.* **Distribution:** Widespread in buildings, but mainly in ports and large towns. **Other Habitats:** Common on ships. **Adult Active:** All year round in buildings. **Food:** Anything.

Ducted hot-air central-heating systems have been a particular boon to these animals and also to cockroaches, not only because they provide warmth but also because of the free access they offer to all parts of the house with little risk of being seen and killed.

Household warmth does have drawbacks; in particular the environment is extremely dry. Creatures such as flour beetles and carpet beetles survive without water in what must be among the driest habitats on earth. Small wonder that they are close relatives of the beetles to be found in deserts. Other beetles such as the death-watch and furniture beetles inhabit the dry timbers of buildings and do considerable damage.

Elsewhere in the building, damper conditions may prevail, particularly in basements and kitchens. Here may be found the silverfish (actually a primitive wingless insect) and cockroaches. There are several species of domestic cockroach, all of them very dependent upon the warmth and shelter of buildings for survival and showing a strong preference for kitchens. They do no real harm, but are repulsive and highly unwelcome.

Clothes moths (or more correctly, their larvae) feed on fabrics. Their natural home is in birds nests and owl pellets where they are adapted to eat fur and feathers; garments (especially woollen ones) are made of similar materials and offer an alternative home. A particular advantage for these and many other household creatures is that the domestic environment is often devoid of predators. The few that do live indoors, (spiders, for example) are frequently killed on sight, leaving the far more damaging pest animals to get on with their mischief unhindered.

The nuisance value of our lodgers varies considerably from the relatively harmless booklice (primitive insects) which live in damp houses, to weevils, beetles and mites which consume and disfigure food, culminating in animals which spread disease and may cause human fatalities. Among the latter may be included the rat flea responsible for spreading the Black Death in the Middle Ages; during one major epidemic in the 13th century, a quarter of the people of Europe died. Fortunately this disease is no longer a serious problem in Europe owing to cleaner houses and the eradication of the black rat from most places. It is usually replaced by the brown rat, but this does not carry plague. Rat fleas are not the most common household species; these are probably cat and dog fleas brought in by pets. Fleas are characteristic of animal nests (their larvae live in the debris of the nest lining before invading the host to suck its blood). Humans make "nests" too so it is not surprising to find the human flea *(Pulex irritans)* sharing it. However, modern homes are generally too clean and dry for it to survive. Similarly, bed bugs and body lice are among the once common species of British fauna which have undergone a major decline in recent years – although nobody regrets it! Even clean houses collect debris and dust in odd corners and between floorboards. Here may be found bed mites (which also live in bedding). They are minute and generally harmless, but may be inhaled when the dust is disturbed or beds are made. They then cause an allergic reaction in some people, resulting in attacks of asthma.

Considerable effort is expended in trying to rid our homes of unwelcome animal guests. This poses problems because the use of poisons and insecticides carries the risk of contaminating our food or killing pets. Certain insecticides designed specifically for use in the home because they are harmless to humans and other warm-blooded animals, are nevertheless lethal to goldfish. Even where special poisons have been developed to kill only the pest species, the intended victims may become resistant to its effects after a few hundred generations.

Life in human habitations poses many prob-

Crickets

True crickets (order Orthoptera) are related to the bushcrickets, but their bodies are flatter and their hind legs are shorter. They generally live on the ground and they scuttle about rather rapidly. There are two long "tails" or cerci in both sexes, and the female also has a long, needle-like ovipositor. The hind wings, when present, are furled like umbrellas and they protrude from the hind end of the body like an extra pair of tails. Of the four British crickets, only the house cricket has hind wings and only this species can fly. Males "sing" by rubbing the bases of the front wings together. Crickets are generally scavenging insects, although some are largely vegetarian. The nymphs are just like the adults except that they lack wings.

House Cricket Gryllidae *Acheta domesticus.* **Distribution:** Houses, bakeries, etc all over British Isles (an introduced species). **Other Habitats:** Rubbish dumps, especially in summer. **Adult active:** All year in buildings—mainly nocturnal. **Food:** Almost anything. **Note:** Female has slender ovipositor at hind end.

Bristletails

Bristletails (order Thysanura) are primitive, wingless insects whose tapering bodies are clothed with shiny, metallic scales. There are three slender 'tails' at the hind end. Nearly 600 species are known, most of them living in the soil and leaf litter. Several live amongst the debris on the sea-shore, while the familiar silverfish and the firebrat live in domestic premises. They are all scavenging insects, the domestic species being especially fond of starchy foods. Apart from size, the young insects are almost identical to the adults. There are nine British species.

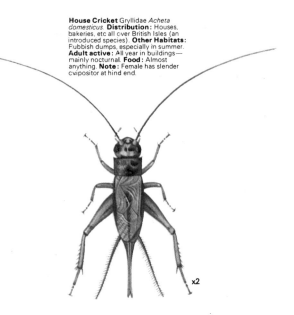

Silverfish Lepismatidae *Lepisma saccharina.* **Distribution:** In buildings throughout British Isles. **Other habitats:** None. **Adult Active:** All year. **Food:** Flour and other starch-rich materials.

lems for animals, not least being our many and ingenious methods of extermination. However, any creature which can avoid destruction can find food, warmth and shelter in all seasons and throughout the world; an ecological opportunity which some have exploited to the full – unfortunately for us!

Household beetles

Many beetles (order Coleoptera) are scavengers in nature, being particularly common in the nests of birds and small mammals, where they feed on scraps of food and also on the fur and feathers. Not surprisingly, a number of these beetles are also found in our houses and other buildings, where just the same kinds of materials can be found. The woodworm or furniture beetle is really a scavenger on dead wood: in nature, it breaks down the wood and returns it to the soil. It also breaks down wood in houses, often doing a great deal of damage.

The carpet beetle larva, in particular, is a household pest. It chews carpets and other fabrics, causing disintegration.

The two-spot carpet beetle (*Attagenus*), like the clothes moth, has benefited from the food supplied by man.

Tenebrio molitor Tenebrionidae. **Distribution:** Throughout British Isles, where cereal products are stored. **Other habitats:** None. **Adult active:** Spring. **Food:** Adults and larvae, known as mealworms, eat flour.

Churchyard Beetle Tenebrionidae *Blaps mucronata.* **Distribution:** Throughout British Isles. **Other habitats:** None. **Adult active:** Most of year. **Food:** Vegetable debris in stables, kitchens, stores, etc.

Fur Beetle Dermestidae *Attagenus pellio.* **Distribution:** Throughout British Isles. **Other Habitats:** Animal nests: adults on flowers. **Adult active:** Spring. **Food:** Adult takes nectar and pollen; larva eats flour, fur, wool, etc.

Woodworm or Furniture Beetle Anobiidae *Anobium punctatum.* **Distribution:** Throughout British Isles. **Other Habitats:** Woodlands and anywhere with dead wood. **Adult active:** Mainly early summer. **Food:** Larvae tunnel in dead wood; adults may sip nectar.

Carpet Beetle Dermestidae *Anthrenus verbasci.* **Distribution:** Much of British Isles away from large towns. **Other habitats:** Bird nests: adults on flowers. **Adult active:** Spring and early summer. **Food:** Larvae (called woolly bears) eat wool, fur, etc; adults sip nectar and pollen.

Birds of Man-made Habitats

There are probably few insects specifically associated with cornfield weeds and those that feed on the actual crop plants are generally regarded as pests and are vigorously controlled by the farmer. Similarly, few mammals live in arable fields. Moles are eradicated because their mounds impede the farm machinery and rabbits which make raids into the crop from their home at the edge of a field, are eliminated whenever possible.

Birds of farmland

Birds have a better chance of using arable fields; they can fly away from machines to return later, and many of them do not compete with the farmer but may help him by reducing insect pests. The most welcome to the farmer must be the game birds, especially that popular sporting bird the grey partridge *(Perdix perdix)*. The species is widespread in Britain but most characteristic of mixed farming areas with hedges and marginal land in addition to cultivated fields. The bird is suffering a steady decline in numbers due to modern agricultural practices, especially stubble burning, removal of hedgerows and the use of pesticides, all of which affect the supply of insect food. The partridge favours farms with small fields and plenty of cover in early spring. The quail *(Coturnix coturnix)* is also typical of hayfields and corn crops but it is much rarer. It is a summer visitor that breeds on farmland, especially on the chalk downland of southern England. The males are heard readily but the nests are difficult to locate.

The lapwing *(Vanellus vanellus)* was once more typical of farmland than it is today. It still occurs in permanent grassland, ploughed land and young corn, but is now much more sparsely scattered. Its decline in south east England is probably due to loss of permanent pasture, drainage of wet grassland and regular use of machinery during the nesting season.

The rook *(Corvus frugilegus)* is widespread in lowland Britain and Ireland where it is characteristic of tree clad agricultural land. This gregarious bird nests in dense colonies early in the year and is very beneficial to the farmer in feeding largely on the invertebrates of arable land; many of which are serious agricultural pests.

The collared dove *(Streptopelia decaocto)* is an interesting species that is increasingly regarded as a pest. The species has undergone an explosive expansion in Europe as a whole and it first nested in Britain in 1955. It is now very widespread in this country and its preferred home is around farm buildings and anywhere else where grain is handled.

Farm buildings provide a home for swallows *(Hirundo rustica)* and house martins *(Delichon urbica)*, though this is little use if the surrounding arable fields are almost devoid of insects. Similarly, the barn owl *(Tyto alba)* has become very dependent on old buildings and haystacks for roost and nest sites; but it needs large areas of rough grassland or unkept hedges to supply sufficient food and is becoming rare in efficiently farmed areas.

Statues and ledges on large buildings provide safe and sheltered perching places for urban pigeons. In many ways, these resemble the cliffs and ledges which are the original home of the rock dove, the ancestor of today's town birds.

Hedgerow birds

Good, mixed farmland may support 30 or more species of birds, but most of these will depend heavily on the hedgerows and marginal land for both food and shelter. The blackbird *(Turdus merula)* is the dominant species, followed by dunnock *(Prunella modularis)*, robin *(Erithacus rubecula)* and chaffinch *(Fringilla coelebs)*. Birds of scrub and rank weed patches, like the whitethroat, are common and hedges are an important home for the linnet *(Acanthis cannabina)*, greenfinch *(Carduelis chloris)*, and yellowhammer *(Emberiza citrinella)*. It is thought that Britain's hedgerows may support about ten million birds.

Hawthorn hedges are particularly good for

The yellowhammer is typical of open farmland, where it nests in hedgerows. As a species it has benefited from the creation of these semi-natural habitats and was probably much less common a thousand years ago.

birds, providing protection from wind and predators as well as food in the form of berries and insects. They also come into leaf earlier in the year, and where there is a choice, birds will prefer the hawthorn sections of a hedge to those parts formed from some other shrub. A good hawthorn hedge may contain 20 species of birds and if other shrub species are present too, there might be 40 pairs of birds nesting in a kilometre of hedge. Both the numbers and diversity of birds depend upon management of the hedge; straggly unkept, overgrown hedges with a broad base support the most. The "short back and sides" treatment meted out by mechanical hedge-cutters will reduce the attractiveness of the hedge, but plenty of birds will still use it.

Urban birds

Pigeons are probably the most abundant urban birds, and certainly the most obvious. The town pigeon is the same species (*Columba livia*) as the rock dove of the coastal cliffs and it is often said that the urban bird has merely exchanged a life on real cliffs for a life on the artificial ledges and precipes of town buildings. In fact this bird has reached the urban environment by way of a period of domestication. In Mediaeval times, large numbers were kept as a readily available source of food. These birds were accustomed to man and many excaped to live as feral ("gone wild") pigeons, enjoying a close association with man whose attitude to the birds is somewhat ambivalent. Feeding the pigeons is a popular pastime, yet 50 tonnes of dung were removed from the Foreign Office roof during a clean-up in Whitehall; and British Rail now threaten to prosecute people for feeding pigeons in certain mainline stations as a means of reducing the nuisance caused there by the birds.

The wood pigeon is a larger bird which has only become a town dweller since the turn of the century. It still prefers to nest in trees, its normal home is in the country, though in the last 20 years or so has begun to nest regularly on man-made structures. Urban wood pigeons seem to be a southern phenomenon, whereas in northern cities magpies are becoming increasingly common as invaders of roadside trees and small town parks. In Manchester they have even taken to breaking into cartons of eggs left on the

The kestrel

The kestrel is Britain's commonest bird of prey, and it is widespread throughout Britain and Ireland. This colourful little falcon is a familiar sight to many road users because of its recently adopted habit of hunting prey over the grass verges, cuttings and embankments of our motorways. It may be seen in considerable numbers during the course of a journey, hovering over the verges quite close to the passing traffic intent on hunting its prey. The bird has also come into close proximity with man in cities where some kestrels nest on buildings and prey on starlings and other urban birds instead of the insects and small mammals that form its staple diet in the country.

Kestrels hover in order to examine the ground below for prey animals, and then move on to another spot to hover again. In this way quite considerable areas can be searched. The prey are caught by a steep swoop to the ground. A more economical method of hunting is sometimes employed when the birds sit on a vantage point such as a bare branch of a tree or a telegraph pole. Occasionally birds are caught in flight, but the kestrel prefers to kill prey on the ground. Kestrels nest in holes in trees, old crow's nests, on cliff ledges and on tall structures such as buildings, chimneys, viaducts and electricity pylons.

Kestrels are birds of open country, but are sufficiently adaptable to take advantage of artificial habitats.

Kestrels normally nest in trees and will do so in urban parks and gardens. However, they will also use roofs, window ledges and gutters and are thus able to breed even in city centres.

Nest boxes

To some extent the bird population of an area is limited by the availability of suitable nesting sites, though there are many other limiting factors too. The provision of artificial nest sites in the form of nest boxes can increase both the numbers of individuals and the number of species that occur in an urban garden.

The nature of the box, the size of the entrance, and the location all affect the types of birds that will use them. The commonest is a wooden box type, which can be purchased from the RSPB or constructed by a handyman. This has a weatherproof roof and an entrance hole, in the front with a hinged door or lid. This basic type of box will attract blue tits if the entrance hole is about 2.5cm in diameter, or great tits if the entrance is about 3cm in diameter, but anything larger than this permits takeover by house sparrow, though the box may be adapted by a nuthatch which will plaster up the hole and any cracks with mud to produce just the size it requires. Large boxes of similar design with a 5cm entrance will be used by starlings if placed well above the ground on walls or in trees.

Curved pieces of bark attached to trees over natural clefts or crevices may attract tree creepers if they are in the vicinity. More specialised nest boxes include artificial house martins' nests which can be fitted under the eaves on a detachable board and concrete boxes for swifts that can be incorporated into the sides of buildings.

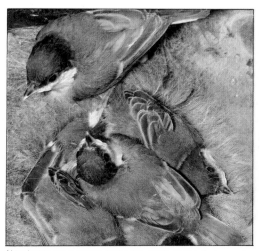

Nest boxes are a secure home for nestlings like these great tits, but mortality is very high when they leave.

Nest boxes with small entrance holes are particularly popular with blue and great tits. Sparrows and starlings prefer larger entrances. This great tit is removing a pack of faeces from the young to avoid fouling the nest.

doorstep by the milkman!

Another recent city arrival is the black redstart. This attractive summer visitor is a bird of stony hillsides and cliffs, reaching the northern limit of its distribution in Britain where it is generally a rare bird. It appears that the rubble of London's war time bomb sites offered a good physical substitute for its natural habitat, in addition to urban warmth – an important advantage for a bird at the northern limit of its range. Within a few years, singing black redstarts became a special feature of urban wasteland and some three-quarters of the British breeding population lived in London. Now that many of the old bomb sites have been tidied up or rebuilt, the birds have mostly moved to power stations and railway yards. In the former, especially, another unexpected advantage of urban life becomes important; it appears that the warm, slightly polluted water from power stations supports high densities of the very midges and flies that the redstarts need for food.

Food is certainly a serious problem for birds in the inner cities, one which the starling has overcome by commuting. Since the turn of the century, starlings have been roosting in cities at night then flying out to the suburbs for the day to feed. At first their roosts were in urban trees, later they took to using buildings, showing a marked preference for Victorian Gothic architecture which offers plenty of sheltered nooks. They also prefer the very centre of the city where it is warmest. Urban roosting began in London, but later spread to Glasgow, Bristol and Manchester; and now most major cities are plagued by flocks of noisy visitors each evening, especially during the winter months. In the summer the flocks tend to disperse and the birds nest in pairs in the country and suburbs.

The starling is a good example of opportunism taking advantage of the benefits offered by town life. Some birds are better at making this sort of adjustment than others. For example, blackbirds seem able to feed on all sorts of things and nest anywhere using whatever materials are available. The song thrush on the other hand is less adaptable in its feeding and nesting habits and is a much less common urban bird, being found only around parks and gardens which provide it with some semblance of its natural habitat.

The tawny owl seems to be another adaptable bird. In the country it feeds on small mammals, but these are scarce in town. Faced with this shortage of prey, even tawny owls have taken to catching birds instead (and even goldfish!) and now live in many city gardens and parks. Similarly, kestrels have adjusted their habits and life style to live on factories and windowsills, whereas their relatives the merlin, peregrine and hobby all struggle to survive in the face of habitat destruction in the countryside. The presence of urban hawks and owls is particularly significant because if they can live and rear their young in towns it shows that there must be large and secure populations of their prey also living there; positive proof that the concrete jungle can support wildlife after all.

By learning to open milk bottles blue tits have gained access to a novel source of food.

A guide to some birds of man-made habitats

Flocks of fieldfare and redwing are frequently seen on farmland, but only in winter and early spring. Waxwings are also winter visitors, often coming to garden shrubberies. Starlings tend to be more numerous in winter, too, because their numbers are swollen by immigrants from the Continent. The jangling song of the corn bunting is a characteristic sound of arable farmland, where the bird likes to perch on wire fences. The yellowhammer is a close relative, but has a preference for hedgerows. Blackbirds and thrushes are common field and garden species. The mistle thrush is larger and greyer than the song thrush; it nests in trees rather than hedgerows and flashes clear white edges to its tail as it flies away, usually making an indignant rattling noise.

Quail are now rather rare but, like the pheasant, partridge and lapwing, typical of farmland. Rooks are usually seen in groups, feeding from the ground. They have a straight beak and bare, grey face. Crows have a more curved beak, feathered face and usually occur in pairs or singly. Jackdaws are smaller with a prominent white eye and grey nape patch. Magpies are scrub and hedgerow birds, but are increasingly seen in suburban areas. Collared doves too are expanding into urban habitats, though are not yet found competing with feral rock doves in the city centres. The black redstart is a bird of rocky hills and cliffs, but has colonised urban wasteland, especially in London. The crescent-winged swift arrives in Britain each summer about a month later than swallows and house martins; and leaves earlier. It nests in holes, particularly in buildings and roofs. House martins stick their mud nests on the outside of buildings, usually under the eaves; swallows nest inside, usually on walls or rafters.

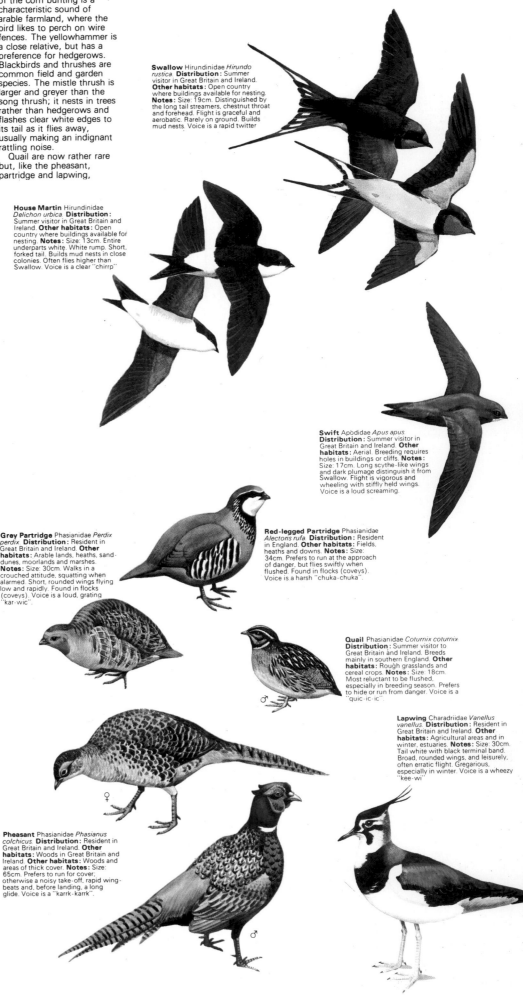

Swallow Hirundinidae *Hirundo rustica.* **Distribution:** Summer visitor in Great Britain and Ireland. **Other habitats:** Open country where buildings available for nesting. **Notes:** Size: 19cm. Distinguished by the long tail streamers, chestnut throat and forehead. Flight is graceful and aerobatic. Rarely on ground. Builds mud nests. Voice is a rapid twitter.

House Martin Hirundinidae *Delichon urbica.* **Distribution:** Summer visitor in Great Britain and Ireland. **Other habitats:** Open country where buildings available for nesting. **Notes:** Size: 13cm. Entire underparts white. White rump. Short, forked tail. Builds mud nests in close colonies. Often flies higher than Swallow. Voice is a clear "chirrp".

Swift Apodidae *Apus apus.* **Distribution:** Summer visitor in Great Britain and Ireland. **Other habitats:** Aerial. Breeding requires holes in buildings or cliffs. **Notes:** Size: 17cm. Long scythe-like wings and dark plumage distinguish it from Swallow. Flight is vigorous and wheeling with stiffly held wings. Voice is a loud screaming.

Grey Partridge Phasianidae *Perdix perdix.* **Distribution:** Resident in Great Britain and Ireland. **Other habitats:** Arable lands, heaths, sand-dunes, moorlands and marshes. **Notes:** Size: 30cm. Walks in a crouched attitude, squatting when alarmed. Short, rounded wings flying low and rapidly. Found in flocks (coveys). Voice is a loud, grating "kar-wic".

Red-legged Partridge Phasianidae *Alectoris rufa.* **Distribution:** Resident in England. **Other habitats:** Fields, heaths and downs. **Notes:** Size: 34cm. Prefers to run at the approach of danger, but flies swiftly when flushed. Found in flocks (coveys). Voice is a harsh "chuka-chuka".

Quail Phasianidae *Coturnix coturnix.* **Distribution:** Summer visitor to Great Britain and Ireland. Breeds mainly in southern England. **Other habitats:** Rough grasslands and cereal crops. **Notes:** Size: 18cm. Most reluctant to be flushed, especially in breeding season. Prefers to hide or run from danger. Voice is a "quic-ic-ic".

Lapwing Charadriidae *Vanellus vanellus.* **Distribution:** Resident in Great Britain and Ireland. **Other habitats:** Agricultural areas and in winter, estuaries. **Notes:** Size: 30cm. Tail white with black terminal band. Broad, rounded wings, and leisurely, often erratic flight. Gregarious, especially in winter. Voice is a wheezy "kee-wi".

Pheasant Phasianidae *Phasianus colchicus.* **Distribution:** Resident in Great Britain and Ireland. **Other habitats:** Woods in Great Britain and Ireland. **Other habitats:** Woods and areas of thick cover. **Notes:** Size: 65cm. Prefers to run for cover, otherwise a noisy take-off, rapid wing-beats and, before landing, a long glide. Voice is a "karrk-karrk".

Mistle Thrush Turdidae *Turdus viscivorus*. **Distribution:** Resident in Great Britain and Ireland. **Other habitats:** Woods, farmland, parks and gardens. **Notes:** Size: 27cm. Distinguished from Song Thrush by large, brown spots on breast, and white underwings. Flight is strong and level despite frequent closures of wings. Voice is a harsh "churring".

Fieldfare Turdidae *Turdus pilaris*. **Distribution:** Winter visitor in Great Britain and Ireland. **Other habitats:** Open country with hedges and copses. **Notes:** Size: 26cm. Grey head and neck. In flight grey rump and white beneath wings is distinctive. Gregarious. Voice is a harsh repeated "chack-chack".

Waxwing Bombycillidae *Bombycilla garrulus*. **Distribution:** Winter visitor to eastern counties. Occasional westward invasions. **Other habitats:** Berry bearing trees of gardens, parks etc. **Notes:** Size: 18cm. Grey rump and lower back.

Redwing Turdidae *Turdus iliacus*. **Distribution:** Winter visitor to Great Britain and Ireland. **Other habitats:** Woodland and open-wooded country. **Notes:** Size: 21cm. Pale eye-stripe and reddish flanks. Streaked breast. Reddish wing linings. Gregarious. Voice is a thin "seeip".

Song Thrush Turdidae *Turdus philomelos*. **Distribution:** Resident in Great Britain and Ireland. **Other habitats:** Woods, orchards, gardens. **Notes:** Size: 23cm. Small spots on buff breast. Buff underwings. Uniform brown upper-parts. Flight is fast and direct. Voice is a thin "sipp" and repeated musical phrases.

Starling Sturnidae *Sturnus vulgaris*. **Distribution:** Ubiquitous resident. **Other habitats:** Everywhere. **Notes:** Size: 21.5cm. In summer has no speckled underneath. Very, very common.

Blackbird Turdidae *Turdus merula*. **Distribution:** Resident in Great Britain and Ireland. **Other habitats:** Woodlands, hedges, gardens. **Notes:** Size: 25cm. Male all black with yellow bill. Female brown. Flight is direct. Tail raised and fanned when landing. Screeching chatter when flushed. Voice is an anxious "tchook".

Common Crow Corvidae *Corvus corone*. **Distribution:** Resident in Great Britain and Ireland. **Other habitats:** Ubiquitous. **Notes:** Size: 45cm. Heavy, black bill. Flight is direct, slow and regular. Rarely soars. Solitary except when roosting. Square tail. Voice is a croaking "kraak".

Corn Bunting Emberizidae *Emberiza calandra*. **Distribution:** Resident mainly in eastern areas. Local in west and Ireland. **Other habitats:** Open farmland, commons, wasteland. **Notes:** Size: 18cm. Voice is an abrupt "quit". Song ends with sound like jangling keys.

Rook Corvidae *Corvus frugilegus*. **Distribution:** Resident in Great Britain and Ireland. **Other habitats:** Agricultural areas with trees for nesting. **Notes:** Size: 46cm. Distinguished from Common Crow by grey bill with bare white patch at base. Has faster wing-beats and baggy thigh feathers. Gregarious. Voice is a harsh "caw".

Yellowhammer Emberizidae *Emberiza citrinella*. **Distribution:** Resident throughout British Isles. **Other habitats:** Farmland, hedgerows, heath, scrub, young plantations. **Notes:** Size: 16.5cm. Female and juvenile browner than male. Call is a metallic "twink". Characteristic high-pitched song.

Jackdaw Corvidae *Corvus monedula*. **Distribution:** Resident in Great Britain and Ireland. **Other habitats:** Open country with ruins, cliffs and old timber for nesting. **Notes:** Size: 33cm. Distinguished from other crows by grey nape, ear coverts and faster wingbeats. Gregarious. Jaunty actions in flight. Voice is a high pitched "chak".

Magpie Corvidae *Pica pica*. **Distribution:** Resident in Great Britain and Ireland, except northern Scotland. **Other habitats:** Farmland, suburban. **Notes:** Size: 46cm. Pied plumage and long tail. Flight rather slow with rapid wingbeats. Often in small parties. Larger gatherings in winter. Voice is a harsh "chak-chak-chak".

Cirl Bunting Emberizidae *Emberiza cirlus*. **Distribution:** Resident in south and south-west England. **Other habitats:** Open areas with scrub, hedges and trees. **Notes:** Size: 16.5cm. Call is a thin "zit". Song is a metallic rattle. Female resembles female Yellowhammer but has chestnut rump.

House Sparrow Emberizidae *Passer domesticus*. **Distribution:** Resident in all areas. **Other habitats:** Varied, usually near habitation. **Notes:** Size: 14.5cm. Voice is a loud "cheep" and various chirps and twitters.

Black Redstart Turdidae *Phoenicurus ochruros*. **Distribution:** Breeds S.E. England. Passage migrant, E. and S. coasts. **Other habitats:** Buildings, cliffs and quarries. **Notes:** Size: 14cm. Black or grey upper parts distinguish from redstart.

Collared Dove Columbidae *Streptopelia decaocto*. **Distribution:** Resident in Great Britain and Ireland. **Other habitats:** Tall trees, close to human habitation. **Notes:** Size: 32cm. Distinguished from Turtle Dove by impression of longer tail. From below, the white terminal half of black tail is diagnostic. Voice is a noisy "coo-cooooo-coo".

Rock Dove Columbidae *Columba livia*. **Distribution:** Resident in isolated western and northern areas. **Other habitats:** Rocky coasts with caves. **Notes:** Size: 33cm. Distinguished from Stock Dove by white rump, two broad black bands across wings. White beneath wings. Voice is a "oo-roo-oo".

Mammals of Man-made Habitats

There are some mammals, like the rats and the house mouse, which are specifically associated with man-made environments. There are also many others which, though not totally dependent upon artificial habitats, are nevertheless strongly associated with them. Hedgehogs for example are widespread in Britain and thrive in many different habitats, but do especially well in parks and gardens.

Many other species, especially small mammals (like the wood mouse and bank vole) are primarily woodland animals, but also do particularly well in man-made hedgerows, gardens and waste land. Bank voles are especially common in suburban gardens where they (and the rather locally distributed yellow necked mouse) are frequent winter inhabitants of garden sheds.

The rabbit's fortunes too have been very much tied up with human activities. It owes its introduction to Britain to human agency and for several centuries its colonies were carefully managed to provide meat and skins. Then, with the great increase in hedgerow planting, mnch new habitat became available; along with extra food in the form of arable crops. Its numbert increased enormously till the introduction (probably by man) of myxomatosis which killed over 90 per cent of the animals.

Before this catastrophe, the rabbit had been a major agricultural pest and yet had sustained an important rural industry. The animals were trapped and shot for meat and fur worth many millions of pounds annually. An important weapon in the fight against rabbits was the ferret. This is an albino, domesticated form of the polecat which used to be put into a warren to flush out the rabbits. Often the ferret would escape or not be recovered, leading to feral populations of ferrets becoming established in many farmland areas. At the same time, the true polecat had declined markedly, due to persecution by gamekeepers. By the 1960's polecats had disappeared from most of England and only retained a stronghold in central and western Wales. However, gamekeepers now seem to adopt a more tolerant attitude and the polecat is extending its range to be paradoxically threatened by the success of its domestic relative the ferret. Feral ferrets interbreed with polecats, raising the prospect of "diluting" the wild polecat blood and producing a population of polecat-ferret hybrids.

The fox is another carnivore closely associated with man. Its recent colonisation of urban habitats has gained considerable publicity and it is easy to forget the past significance of the fox in the countryside. The fox caused a nuisance by raiding chicken runs, but more important it provided sport for the gentry. Foxhunting was an important social activity, especially in the nineteenth century and large areas of countryside owe their present appearance to the planting of copses and other "cover" for the hunted fox. The peculiar paradox of protecting the fox and its habitat to enhance the hunting incidentally benefitted many other creatures and plants found in the same habitat.

Mammals, bottles and litter

Millions of bottles are discarded in Britain every year. Many of them are tossed away carelessly at roadside laybys, picnic spots, in gardens, parks, farmyards and hedgerows. They are a prominent man-made feature of most man-made habitats and each one is a potentially deadly trap for small mammals.

A bottle neck is about the same size as a mouse burrow and inquisitive mammals push their way in and cannot get out again. Even bottles lying flat are difficult to get out of, but those resting at an angle in a bush or hedge or propped up on a roadside bank are like glass pitfall traps from which escape is impossible. Once inside a mammal has only a few hours to live before dying of starvation or cold. A single

The urban fox

The fox is a very adaptable opportunist hunter and scavenger and is successful in a wide variety of habitats from hills and mountains to coastal areas, woodland and farmland. In the past 20 years or so foxes have ventured into provincial towns and even the centre of cities like London. At first sight it is surprising that an animal which is shy and secretive in the country should choose to live in close proximity to man. There are however many areas where the fox can live on railway banks or in field drains, or hiding under potting sheds or on building sites and in cemeteries. It is thought that the loss of rabbits due myxomatosis in the 1950's deprived the foxes of their major food in the country and caused them to penetrate the new habitat offered by suburbia. There they found rich pickings and have established large and permanent populations. Urban foxes are remarkably bold, patrolling well lit streets; one was even seen recently in Trafalgar Square in central London.

The fox is largely nocturnal or crepuscular in habit being active from dusk onwards. They feed on small mammals and invertebrates like slugs and beetles in summer, the fruit and berries of ornamental shrubs and garden plants in autumn and in the winter months they turn their attention to scavenging. Urban dustbins, rubbish tips and garden compost heaps all offer plentiful food, and they may also steal from bird tables. Some people even put out food for the foxes themselves. When surplus food is available the fox will hide a cache. Under urban conditions foxes are believed to reach quite high densities, though their physical condition and health is inferior to that of their country cousins.

milk bottle may trap and kill two dozen animals, though usually only one or two victims are claimed before the bottle gets broken or permanently buried by falling leaves.

The common shrew is the species most often killed, perhaps because it is both abundant and very active in poking about in the very habitats where bottles get thrown away. Wood mice and bank voles are also frequent victims, together with at least 10 other species. including relative rarities like the dormouse and water shrew. Sometimes a dead animal will serve as "bait" to a shrew, or to flies and carrion beetles; which are trapped in their turn often drowned in the milk or rain water at the bottom of the bottle.

Bottles are not the only traps we leave about the countryside. Cattle grids claim a toll of small mammals and so do drink cans. Those cans which are opened by removal of a triangular tab are a particular threat to shrews, though they are generally less lethal traps than most bottles. Other tins may become decayed by rust then, when a deer or sheep treads in it, the hoof perforates the rusty bottom and the animal is left wearing a painful bracelet which may cause a septic wound. Cans of fruit, beans and other food are often opened with a tin opener, leaving the lid as a hinged flap. If a bird or mammal treads on this, the foot enters the tin and the hinged lid digs into the leg and prevents the

The ferret is a domesticated albino form of the polecat. Escaped ferrets are found in many areas.

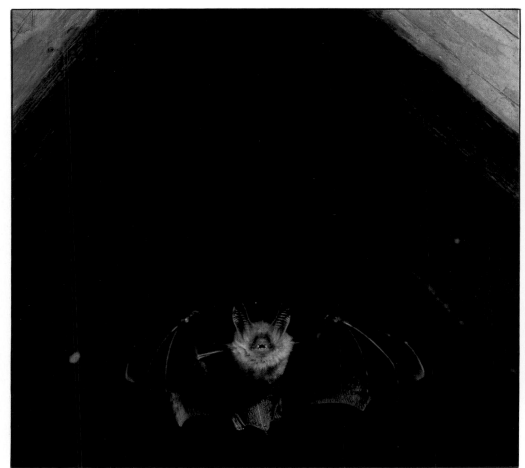

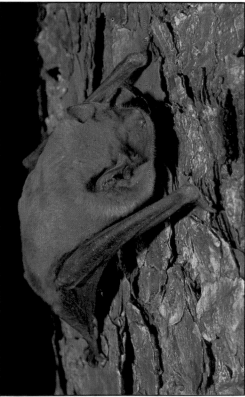

The noctule bat (above), a common British species, is not found in Ireland. Large and long-winged, it probably hibernates in hollow trees and house roofs.

Bats often inhabit house roofs. They are harmless and may even benefit man by eating wood-boring beetles and other pests.

foot being withdrawn. Sometimes part of the leg is actually cut off by the jagged edges, a particular hazard for birds (especially gulls) and mammals which frequent rubbish tips.

Bottles and tins form unsightly litter, but they are also a painful, even lethal, hazard to wild animals. Great suffering can result from thoughtless human untidiness.

Bats

Bats are strongly associated with man and artificial habitats. Like the birds, bats are able to fly freely into different places; but unlike the birds they seem to have very ill-defined habitat preferences. All of them appear to be diminishing in numbers, probably through shortage of food caused by pesticides and habitat

change; and many are rather sensitive to disturbance. Yet certain species, particularly the pipistrelle (the commonest and most widespread British bat) quickly adopt man-made habitats and readily use house roofs for roosting and rearing their young. Perhaps our confusion about bat habits stems from inadequate knowledge, because bats are small, nocturnal and very poorly studied.

About half the British bats are very rare, indeed most of Britain's rarest mammals are bats. Ten species regularly hibernate in caves, mines, grottos and other underground spaces; three species (pipistrelle, noctule and Leisler's) never do, and probably spend the winter in hollow trees or house roofs. In summer practically all the species have been recorded from houses

and buildings; though in only two (pipistrelle and serotine) can it be said that houses represent their main breeding site.

Generally, and without justification, bats are treated with abhorrence; but recently a more tolerant and enlightened attitude has begin to prevail. Recognising the scarcity of many species and the benefit bats may do in controlling insect pests, attempts have been made to help increase bat populations. Bat boxes (like bird boxes, but with a slit in the base instead of a hole in the front) have been put up in many forestry plantations. In these man-made woodlands, hollow trees are scarce and the boxes are a welcome substitute, especially for the attractive long eared bat which readily adopts the boxes as a home for its young.

A noctule bat shows the wing membrane stretching between the elongated digits which correspond to the fingers of the human hand. The tail membrane helps in flight and is also used like a net to catch flying insects.

Index

PICTURE CREDITS

Page 8: HA. 10: HA. 12: PM 13: Aero. 14: HA; HA; HA; HA; HA. 15: HA; HA; HA; HA; HA; HA. 16: PM; HA; HA. 17: HA; HA; HA. 18: HA; HA; HA. 20: HA; HA. 21: HA; HA; HA. 22: HA; HA; HA. 24: HA; HA; HA. 25: HA; HA. 26: HA; PM; HA. 27: HA. 28: HA; HA. 30: HA; HA. 31: HA; HA; HA. 32: PM; PM. 33: HA. 34: PM; HA; HA. PM. 35: HA; PM; HA; HA. 37: PM. 38: HA; Gordon Williamson (BC). 39: PM. 40: Aero. 42: Aero. 44: Aero; BV; PM; HA. 45: HA. 46: Aero; HA. 47: PM; HA. 48: Aero; PM; PM. 49: JM; HA; HA; HA; PM. 50: PM; HA. 51: HA; Aero. 52: HA. 53: HA; HA. 54: JM. 56: HA; HA. 57: JM. 58: RR; HA. 59: RR. 60: RR. 61: HA; HA; HA; HA. 62: HA; IB. 63: HA; IB. 67: HA; PM; RSPB. 68: HA; IB; HA. 71: PM; HA; HA. 72: HA; BV. 73: BV. 74: HA. 76: HA; HA. 80: HA; HA. 81: HA; HA; HA. 82: HA; MC; HA; HA. 83: HA; HA; HA. 84: HA; HA. 86: HA; HA. 88: HA; HA. 89: HA. 90: JM; HA; Aero. 92: HA; NSP; HA. 93: PM. 95: HA. 96: JM; HA; HA. 97: HA; HA. 98: HA; HA. 100: HA; HA; HA. 101: PM. 102: HA. 103: PM. 104: HA. 105: HA; HA. 106: HA; HA; HA. 107: HA; HA. 108: HA; HA; HA. 109: HA; HA; HA. 110: PM. 111: HA; HA; HA. 112: HA; HA; HA. 113: HA; HA. 114: HA; HA; HA; HA. 115: HA; HA. 116: HA; HA. 117: MC; HA. 118: HA. 119: HA. 120: MC; MC; HA. 121: OSF; PM; PM. 122: HA; HA; MC; HA. 124: RR. 125: Robert Smith (Ardea). 126: DS; J. A. Bailey (Ardea). 127: Robert Smith (Ardea). 128: J. A. Bailey (Ardea). 129: RSPB. 130: J. A. Bailey (Ardea); Stephen Bisserot (BC). 133: IB; HA; PM. 134: Hans Reinhard (BC). 135: PM; PM. 136: Aero. 138: Aero; JM. 140: HA; HA; HA. 141: HA; JM; Aero. HA. 144: HA; HA. 145: HA; HA; HA. 146: HA; HA. 147: JM. 149: HA. 150: HA; HA. 151: HA. 152: HA. 153: HA; JM. 154: HA; HA; Jane Burton (BC). 155: MC. 156: PM; PM. 157: HA; HA. 158: NSP. HA. 159: HA. 160: RR; RR; HA; HA. 161: RR; RR; HA. 162: HA; HA. 163: HA. 164: OS. OS. 165: HA. 166: HA; HA; OS. 167: JM; HA; OS. 168: HA; HA. 170: JM; HA. 172: HA. 173: JM; JM. 175: HA. 176: HA. 177: HA. 178: HA. 179: HA. 180: D. Middleton (BC); Udo Hirsch (BC). 182: Stephen Dalton (BC). 183: DS; HA; HA. 184: PM; Andre Fatras (Ardea). 186: PM; PM; PM. 188: Aero. 190: Aero; HA. 192: HA. 193: Aero; BTA. 194: HA; HA; HA; HA. 195: HA; BTA. 196: HA. 197: PM. 198: HA. 201: HA; HA. 204: Tom Willock (Ardea). 205: PM; PM; Aero. 207: JM. 208: Aero. 210: HA; IB; HA. 212: JM; PM. 213: Aero. 215: HA. 216: HA; JM. 217: RR; JM. 218: HA. 219: HA. 220: HA. 221: HA. 222: PM; HA. 223: HA; HA. 224: HA. 225: HA. 226: HA. 227: HA. 228: HA; HA. 229: HA; HA. 230: HA; HA; HA. 231: HA; HA; HA. 232: HA; HA. 234: HA. 235: HA; HA; PM. 236: HA; HA; PM. 237: RR; RR; RR. 238: HA. 239: HA; HA; PM. 240: HA. 241: PM. 242: HA. 243: HA. 244: HA; HA. 245: HA. 246: IB; RSPB. 247: HA. 249: IB. 251: J. A. Bailey (Ardea). 252: IB. 253: RSPB; DS; IB; IB. 254: Jane Burton (BC) G. Kinns (NSP). 255: PM. 257: Aero; JM. 259: JM. 260: Aero. 261: HA. 262: Aero: PM. 263: IB; PM. 264: HA. 265: HA. 266: HA. 268: HA. 269: HA. Stephen Dalton (BC). 272: RR. 274: HA. 275: HA; HA; OS. 276: HA; HA. 277: OS; HA. 279: JM; HA. 280: PM; DS. 281: RSPB; DS; IB; IB. 282: IB. 284: IB; PM. 285: Hans Reinhard (BC); HA; Stephen Bisserot (BC).

Photographs have been credited for each page, from left to right and from top to bottom. Some abbreviations have been made as follows:

Heather Angel: HA. Pat Morris: PM. Aerofilms: Aero. Bruce Coleman Ltd: BC. Richard Reveles: RR. John Mason: JM. Bill Vaughan: BV. Ian Beames: IB. Royal Society for the Protection of Birds: RSPB Michael Chinery: MC. Natural Science Photos: NSP. Oxford Scientific Films: OSF. British Tourist Authority: BTA. David Sewell: DS.